THEORY AND PRACTICE OF
COUNSELLING AND THERAPY

17.

THEORY AND PRACTICE OF COUNSELLING AND THERAPY

FOURTH EDITION

RICHARD NELSON-JONES

SAGE Publications

London ● Thousand Oaks ● New Delhi

First edition published by Holt, Rinehart and
Winston Ltd
Second edition published by Cassell
Third edition published 2001 by Cassell, reprinted by
SAGE Publications 2003, 2004
This fourth edition published by SAGE Publications 2006

SAGE Publications Ltd
1 Oliver's Yard
55 City Road
London EC1Y 1SP

SAGE Publications Inc.
2455 Teller Road
Thousand Oaks, California 91320

SAGE Publications India Pvt Ltd
B-42, Panchsheel Enclave
Post Box 4109
New Delhi 110 017

British Library Cataloguing in Publication data

A catalogue record for this book is available from the British Library

ISBN 1-4129-1977-0
ISBN 1-4129-1978-9 (pbk)

Library of Congress Control Number: 2005926188

Typeset by C&M Digitals (P) Ltd, Chennai, India
Printed on paper from sustainable resources
Printed and bound in Great Britain by Athenaeum Press, Gateshead

contents

Welcome to the fourth edition of *Theory and Practice of Counselling and Therapy*. In this introductory textbook I aim to provide you with clear, concise, easily accessible presentations of the major concepts and practices of many of the main therapeutic approaches used in the helping professions. The focus of this book is on individual therapy. Its purpose is to help you become more aware of both *how* you might counsel or conduct therapy and also of the underlying reasons *why* you might choose to work that way. Furthermore, the relevance of the theoretical positions extends beyond assisting clients in therapy to become happier and more fulfilled to the personal agenda of helping you too.

Intended readership

This is a basic introductory textbook for undergraduate and postgraduate counselling and psychotherapy courses in counsellor education, psychology, social work, nursing, personnel and human resources management, career development, pastoral care, welfare, teacher training and other areas of helping professions education. Another important readership consists of participants in counselling and therapy courses run by voluntary agencies. In addition, this book can be used as a user-friendly introduction to the theory and practice of counselling and therapy for undergraduate students in the behavioural and social sciences.

Contents

The first chapter discusses the structure and functions of theoretical statements, explores the creation of therapeutic approaches, and then looks at how you can develop your own ideas. In the subsequent chapters I review therapeutic approaches selected from each of the three main schools influencing contemporary therapy practice. From the psychodynamic school, I present Freud's psychoanalysis and Jung's analytical therapy. From the humanistic-existential school, I present person-centred therapy, gestalt therapy, transactional analysis, reality therapy, existential therapy and logotherapy. From the cognitive-behavioural school, I present behaviour therapy, rational emotive behaviour therapy, cognitive therapy and multimodal therapy.

In instances where the originators have died – for instance, Freud, Jung, Perls and Rogers – the chapters focus mainly on their presentation of their positions, though mention is also made of further developments since their death. A major reason for this focus is that I think students should start knowing about the original positions and then learn about variations to them.

The next two chapters on multicultural therapy and gender therapy cover topics relevant to all therapeutic approaches. In the book's final chapter I review issues in assessing the quality of the different therapeutic approaches as well as the topics of eclecticism and integration. In addition, the book contains a glossary. Appendices on training information and on professional associations can be accessed at www.sagepub.co.uk/resources/tpct_appendices.pdf.

For those of you familiar with the third edition of this text, the main changes in the fourth edition are a revision and update of all existing chapters and the expansion of the further developments section of chapters, especially where the original theorists have died, to indicate contemporary approaches of their positions.

Features

I draw your attention to the following features of the book, which I hope will make it attractive for you.

- *Authoritative* – This book, which is written from primary sources, provides accurate presentations of the foundations of each counselling and therapy approach. For instance, when preparing the book, I contacted living theorists for their most recent material. In addition, I gave either the theorists themselves or prominent adherents of the approach the opportunity to preview chapters and to suggest alterations.
- *Thorough and clear presentation* – Each of the therapeutic approaches is in a standard chapter format that helps to ensure that the approach is thoroughly and clearly presented. Though you may not understand the meaning of some of the following headings now, once you start working with the book you should experience no difficulty in so doing:

  (a) Introduction
  (b) Originator's biography
  (c) Theory
        Basic concepts
        Acquisition
        Maintenance
  (d) Therapy
        Therapeutic goals
        Process of therapy

The therapeutic relationship
Therapeutic interventions
(e) Case material
(f) Further developments
(g) Annotated bibliography
(h) References and further reading

- *Focus on fundamentals* – The chapters emphasize presenting the theory and practice of the originator of each approach. Some contributions by other adherents of the approach are mentioned in the 'Further developments' section of chapters. However, the chapters emphasize the basic or classical version of each approach. Getting down to basics is important, since introducing developments from the original approach too soon can be confusing. In all of the chapters I review the originator's case material and in most chapters I give directions about accessing audio-visual resources. If available and where budgets permit, I encourage lecturers to use relevant audio-cassettes and videotapes as an accompaniment to using this book.
- *Personal focus* – Originating counselling and therapy approaches is a personal journey. A distinctive feature of this book is the degree to which the lives of the originators are seen as important in understanding the development of their therapeutic approaches. Learning about counselling and therapy approaches is also a personal journey. Each chapter ends not only with review questions, but with personal questions as well that encourage you to relate the material to your own life.
- *Aids to comprehension and revision* – Boxes are used throughout the book to highlight concepts and provide examples of specific interventions. Towards the end of each chapter, I provide a summary and review questions designed to help you learn and revise material for assignments and course requirements.
- *Help with further reading* – I encourage you to use the chapters in this book as stepping stones to reading primary sources. Each chapter ends with an annotated bibliography and with a listing of references. I also encourage you to read further about recent developments in the theoretical positions that interest you.
- *Simple English* – I have tried to use simple, accessible English, while remaining sensitive to the distinctive therapeutic languages used by the different theorists.

Acknowledgments

I acknowledge with gratitude the distinctive contributions of all the originators of counselling and therapy approaches presented in this book. While accepting full responsibility for any shortcomings, I am extremely grateful to the following people for contributing to the preparation of and for previewing chapters: Dr Judith Beck, Dr Alexander Batthyany, Dr Ann Casement, Dr Albert Ellis, Dr Arnold Lazarus, Dr Ian Stewart, Professor Brian Thorne and Dr Irvin Yalom.

I also thank the numerous individuals who provided information for the 'Training information' appendix (www.sagepub.co.uk/resources/tpct_appendices.pdf) and helped me in other ways. In addition, I thank Alison Poyner of SAGE Publications for commissioning the book and, last but not least, I thank the production staff at the publisher's for their work in copy-editing and bringing this book to life.

Since each of the approaches is presented as a self-contained unit, lecturers and readers can choose which parts to study in the order that best suits their purposes. I hope that you enjoy reading and interacting with this book and share my enthusiasm for studying and learning more about counselling and therapy approaches.

Richard Nelson-Jones

Theoretical approaches to counselling and therapy do not spring fully formed out of the heads of their originators. Rather their creation is a process in which many personal, academic and professional factors interact. Furthermore, the theorists covered in this book tended to refine and rework their ideas. In addition other people have contributed to the development of their theoretical positions. Thus theory creation and development is an intensely human and ongoing process combining both subjective experiencing and objective information.

As a counselling and therapy student, you too are engaging in a process of trying to make sense of numerous personal, academic and professional factors to create and develop a way of seeing the therapeutic world that has validity for you and gets results for your clients. Just like the major theorists, you are likely to find yourself continually refining and reworking your ideas. Working with a theoretical approaches text, such as this one, is an early step in the exciting and life-long endeavour of creating, developing and refining your theory and practice.

Counselling and psychotherapy

The word therapy is derived from the Greek word *therapeia* meaning healing. Literally psychotherapy means healing the mind or the soul. Nowadays, most commonly the meaning of psychotherapy is broadened to become healing the mind by psychological methods that are applied by suitably trained and qualified practitioners. However, as illustrated in this book, there are different approaches to therapy and, consequently, it is more accurate to speak of the psychotherapies than of a uniform method of psychotherapy. Moreover, there are different goals for therapy including dealing with severe mental disorder, addressing specific anxieties and phobias, and helping people find meaning and purpose in their lives. Each of the different therapeutic approaches may be more suitable for attaining some goals than others.

Does counselling differ from psychotherapy? Attempts to differentiate between counselling and psychotherapy are never wholly successful. Both counselling and psychotherapy represent diverse rather than uniform knowledge and activities and both use the same theoretical models. In 2000, the British Association for Counselling (BAC) acknowledged the similarity between counselling and psychotherapy by becoming the British Association for Counselling and Psychotherapy (BACP). In Australia, the Psychotherapy & Counselling Federation of Australia exists.

Nevertheless, some people such as Corsini (2005) try to distinguish counselling from psychotherapy. For instance, psychotherapists may be more thoroughly trained; psychotherapy may focus more deeply on uncovering unconscious influences and be longer term; and psychotherapy may be more a medical term that characterizes the work of psychiatrists and clinical psychiatrists, whereas counselling relates more to activities in non-medical settings, such as those of college counselling centres. All of these distinctions can be refuted: for example, there are psychodynamic counsellors; both counselling and therapy can be either brief, medium-term or long-term; and much counselling is performed both by medically and non-medically qualified people inside and outside of medical settings.

Though some perceive different shadings of meaning between counselling and psychotherapy, when it comes to the offering of professional as con- trasted with voluntary services, similarities outweigh differences. Frequently the terms are used interchangeably and most theorists view their work as applicable to both counselling and psychotherapy – Carl Rogers and Albert Ellis being prime examples.

Defining terms

Throughout this book, for the sake of consistency, for the most part I use the terms therapy, therapist and client. Therapy refers both to the theoreti- cal approach and to the process of helping clients. It is notable that the originators of most therapeutic approaches include the word therapy in their approach's title: for instance, person-centred therapy, gestalt therapy, rational emotive behaviour therapy and cognitive therapy. Therapist refers to the providers of therapy services to clients, be they psychoanalysts, psy- chiatrists, clinical psychologists, counselling psychologists, counsellors, social workers or other suitably trained and qualified persons. Client refers to the recipient of therapeutic services whether inside or outside of medical settings.

Overview of counselling and therapy approaches

A useful distinction exists between *schools* of counselling and therapy and *the- oretical approaches* to counselling and therapy. A theoretical approach presents a single position regarding the theory and practice of counselling and ther- apy. A school of counselling and therapy is a grouping of different theoretical approaches that are similar to one another in terms of certain important characteristics that distinguish them from theoretical approaches in other counselling and therapy schools.

Probably the three main schools that influence contemporary individual counselling and psychotherapy practice are the psychodynamic school, the humanistic school and the cognitive-behavioural school. Sometimes the humanistic school incorporates existential therapeutic approaches and then can get the broader title of being the humanistic-existential school. Be careful not to exaggerate the differences between counselling and therapy schools, since there are similarities as well differences among them. Box 1.1 briefly describes some distinguishing features of the psychodynamic, humanistic-existential and cognitive-behavioural schools.

Box 1.1   Three counselling and therapy schools

The psychodynamic school
The term psychodynamic refers to the transfer of *psychic or mental energy* between the different structures and levels of consciousness within people's minds. Psychodynamic approaches emphasize the importance of *unconscious influences* on how people function. Therapy aims to increase clients' abilities to exercise *greater conscious control* over their lives. *Analysis or interpretation of dreams* can be a central part of therapy.

The humanistic-existential school
The humanistic school is based on humanism, a system of values and beliefs that emphasizes the better qualities of humankind and people's abilities to develop their *human potential*. Humanistic therapists emphasize enhancing clients' abilities to *experience their feelings* and think and act in harmony with their underlying tendencies to *actualize themselves* as unique individuals. Existential approaches to therapy stress people's capacity to *choose* how they create their existences.

The cognitive-behavioural school
Traditional behaviour therapy focuses mainly on changing *observable behaviours* by means of providing different or rewarding consequences. The cognitive-behavioural school broadens behaviour therapy to incorporate the contribution of how people *think* to creating, sustaining and changing their problems. In cognitive-behavioural approaches, therapists assess clients and then intervene to help them to *change specific ways of thinking and behaving* that sustain their problems.

Box 1.2 introduces the theoretical approaches, grouped as closely as feasible according to counselling and therapy school, included in this book. So that readers can obtain a sense of the history of the development of ideas within counselling and therapy, I have included the dates of the originators of each approach. The descriptions provided in Box 1.2 reflect the position of the originators of the different positions, rather than developments within a theoretical approach stimulated by others.

Box 1.2   Overview of counselling and therapy approaches

Psychodynamic school

Classical psychoanalysis   *Originator: Sigmund Freud (1856–1939)*
Pays great attention to unconscious factors related to infantile sexuality in the development of neurosis. Psychoanalysis, which may last for many years, emphasizes working through the transference, in which clients perceive their therapists as reincarnations of important figures from their childhoods, and the interpretation of dreams.

Analytical therapy   *Originator: Carl Jung (1875–1961)*
Divides the unconscious into the personal unconscious and the collective unconscious, the latter being a storehouse of universal archetypes and primordial images. Therapy includes analysis of the transference, active imagination and dream analysis. Jung was particularly interested in working with clients in the second half of life.

Humanistic-existential school

Person-centred therapy   *Originator: Carl Rogers (1902–87)*
Lays great stress on the primacy of subjective experience and how clients can become out of touch with their organismic experiencing through introjecting others' evaluations and treating them as if their own. Therapy emphasizes a relationship characterized by accurate empathy, respect and non-possessive warmth.

Gestalt therapy   *Originator: Fritz Perls (1893–1970)*
Individuals become neurotic by losing touch with their senses and interfering with their capacity to make strong contact with their environments. Therapy emphasizes increasing clients' awareness and vitality through awareness techniques, experiments, sympathy and frustration, and dream work.

Transactional analysis   *Originator: Eric Berne (1910–70)*
Transactions between people take place between their Parent, Adult and Child ego states. Therapy includes structural analysis of ego states, analysis of specific transactions, analysis of games – series of transactions having ulterior motivations – and analysis of clients' life scripts.

Reality therapy   *Originator: William Glasser (1925–)*
Clients choose to maintain their misery through choosing inappropriate ways to control the world to satisfy their needs. Therapy includes identifying clients' wants and needs, teaching choice theory, planning and, where appropriate, training clients in the behaviours they need to succeed.

Box 1.2   (Continued)

Existential therapy   *Originators: Irvin Yalom (1931–) and Rollo May (1909–94)*
Draws on the work of existential philosophers and focuses on helping clients deal
with anxieties connected with four main ultimate concerns of human existence:
death, freedom, isolation and meaninglessness. Therapy focuses on clients' current
situations, with different interventions used according to the nature of clients'
enveloping fears.

Logotherapy   *Originator: Viktor Frankl (1905–97)*
Clients can become neurotic because they face an existential vacuum in which they
are unable to find meaning in their lives. Logotherapists use methods such as
teaching the importance of assuming responsibility for finding meaning, Socratic
questioning, offering meanings and analysing dreams.

Cognitive-behavioural school

Behaviour therapy   *Important figures: theory, Ivan Pavlov (1849–1936) and
B.F. Skinner (1904–90); practice, Joseph Wolpe (1915–97)*
Emphasizes the learning of behaviour through classical conditioning, operant
conditioning and modelling. Therapy consists of learning adaptive behaviours by
methods such as systematic desensitization, reinforcement programmes and
behaviour rehearsal.

Rational emotive behaviour therapy   *Originator: Albert Ellis (1913–)*
Emphasizes clients reindoctrinating themselves with irrational beliefs that contribute to
unwanted feelings and self-defeating actions. Therapy involves disputing clients'
irrational beliefs and replacing them with more rational beliefs. Elegant or profound
therapy entails changing clients' philosophies of life.

Cognitive therapy   *Originator: Aaron Beck (1921–)*
Clients become distressed because they are faulty processors of information with a
tendency to jump to unwarranted conclusions. Therapy consists of educating clients
in how to test the reality of their thinking by interventions such as Socratic
questioning and conducting real-life experiments.

Multimodal therapy   *Originator: Arnold Lazarus (1932–)*
Clients respond to situations according to their predominant modalities: behaviour,
affect, sensation, imagery, cognition, interpersonal and drugs/biology. Based on a
multimodal assessment, therapists are technically eclectic, using a range of
techniques selected on the basis of empirical evidence and client need.

So far I have presented the different schools and theoretical approaches as
though they are separate. In reality, many counsellors and therapists regard
themselves as working in either eclectic or integrative ways. A detailed discussion of eclecticism and integration is beyond the scope of this book.

Suffice it for now to say that eclecticism is the practice of drawing from different counselling and therapy schools in formulating client problems and implementing treatment interventions. Integration refers to attempting to blend together theoretical concepts and/or practical interventions drawn from different counselling and therapy approaches into coherent and integrated wholes.

What is a counselling and therapy theory?

A theory is a formulation of the underlying principles of certain observed phenomena that have been verified to some extent. A criterion of the power of a theory is the extent to which it generates predictions that are confirmed when relevant empirical data are collected. The more a theory receives confirmation or verification, the more accurate it is. Facts strengthen rather than replace theories.

Functions of counselling and therapy theories

What do counselling and therapy theories do? Why are they useful? Therapists cannot avoid being counselling and therapy theorists. All make assumptions about how clients become and stay the way they are and about change. Three of the main functions of counselling and therapy theories are: providing conceptual frameworks, providing languages and generating research.

Theories as conceptual frameworks

Therapists are decision makers. They continually make choices about how to think about clients' behaviour, how to treat them, and how to respond on a moment-by-moment basis during therapy sessions. Theories provide therapists with concepts that allow them to think systematically about human development and the therapeutic process.

Counselling and therapy theoretical approaches may be viewed as possessing four main dimensions if they are to be stated adequately. In this context behaviour incorporates both observable behaviour and internal behaviour or thinking. The dimensions are:

1.   a statement of the *basic concepts* or assumptions underlying the theory;
2.   an explanation of the *acquisition* of helpful and unhelpful behaviour;
3.   an explanation of the *maintenance* of helpful and unhelpful behaviour; and
4.   an explanation of how to help clients *change* their behaviour and *consolidate* their gains when therapy ends.

When reading about the different counselling and therapy approaches, you may observe that many if not most have significant gaps in their conceptual frameworks. They are partial rather than complete or comprehensive theoretical statements. Arguably, some of the missing concepts in the theories are implicit rather than explicit. Theorists select for more thorough treatment those dimensions of a theory that they consider important. For instance, Ellis's rational emotive behaviour theory has a wider variety of explanatory concepts concerning how behaviour is maintained than how it is initially acquired.

Theories as languages

Swiss psychiatrist Carl Jung (1961) used to stress that, since all clients are different individuals, therapists require a different language for each client. Another function of theories is similar to that provided by languages. Languages are vocabularies and linguistic symbols that allow communication about phenomena. Like the major spoken languages of English, Spanish and Mandarin Chinese, the different theorists develop languages for the phenomena they wish to describe: for instance, cognitive, psychoanalytic or person-centred languages. Language can both unite and divide. It can encourage communication between people who speak the same language, but discourage communication if they do not. Each theoretical position has concepts described in unique language. However, the uniqueness of the language may mask common elements among theories: for example, the meaning of conditions of worth in person-centred therapy overlaps with that of super-ego in Freud's psychoanalytic therapy, though you would not know this from the language!

The therapy process is a series of conversations requiring languages. In any therapeutic relationship there are at least four kinds of conversations going on: namely, therapist and client inner and outer speech. All therapists who operate out of explicit theoretical frameworks are likely to talk to themselves about clients in the language of that framework. In varying degrees their therapeutic practice will match their language. Therapists do not always act according to how they think. Furthermore, in varying degrees therapists share their theoretical language with clients. For example, unlike in rational emotive behaviour therapy, the language in which person-centred theory is expressed tends not to be shared with clients. Instead, person-centred therapists try to reflect and match clients' outer speech.

Clients are also theorists, though usually without the sophistication of their therapists. Approaches like rational emotive behaviour therapy and cognitive therapy actively try to influence the language in which clients talk to themselves so that it becomes helpful rather than harmful. In a sense the therapist's language is being exported to and imported by clients so that they can better assist themselves once therapy ends.

Theories as sets of research hypotheses

Theories can be both based on research and stimulate research. For example, cognitive-behaviour therapy is based on research into how people think and into how both people and animals behave. Furthermore, cognitive-behaviour approaches, such as rational emotive behaviour therapy and cognitive therapy, have stimulated research into their processes and outcomes.

Theories also provide therapists with frameworks within which to make predictive hypotheses during their practice of therapy. Whether acknowledging it or not, all therapists are practitioner-researchers. Therapists make hypotheses every time they decide how to work with specific clients and how to respond to single or series of client utterances.

Clients are also practitioner-researchers who make predictions about how best to lead their lives. If valid theories of counselling and therapy are transmitted to clients, they may increase the accuracy with which clients can predict the consequences of their behaviours and, hence, gain more control over their lives.

Limitations of counselling and therapy theories

All counselling and therapy theories should carry the psychological equivalent of health warnings. They can be used for ill as well as for good. A criticism of many theories is that they present partial truths as whole truths. For instance, Rogers (1951, 1959) posits a unitary diagnosis of all clients' problems, namely that there is incongruence between self-structure and experience, and sees six relationship conditions as necessary and sufficient in all instances. Ellis focuses on irrational beliefs at risk of paying insufficient attention to other aspects of thinking, for instance perceiving accurately or using coping self-talk. Freud emphasizes uncovering unconscious material through the analysis of dreams, but says little about developing specific effective behaviours to deal with everyday problems.

Some theories may lead to focusing more on what is wrong rather than on what is right with clients. They can make clients' problems out to be more severe than they are. For instance, psychoanalysts can view learned ineffective behaviour as symptomatic of deeper underlying conflicts.

The different languages of theoretical approaches can disguise similarities between them. Theoretical rigidity is also fostered when language differences lead therapists mainly to talk with those speaking the same language rather than to a broader sharing of knowledge and experience. The language of theories can also create a power imbalance between therapists and clients. Therapists who think in a special theoretical language that they do not share can put themselves in superior–inferior relationships with clients. Furthermore, the language of some theories does little to empower clients once they end therapy. Ideally, the language of therapy is that of self-helping. Clients unable to articulate what to think and do when faced with problems after therapy are less likely to maintain gains than clients who can instruct themselves appropriately.

Possibly all the theorists in this book insufficiently take into account cultural differences. In addition, theorists can either ignore or underestimate how socio-environmental conditions like poverty, poor housing and racial discrimination may contribute to explaining ineffective behaviour. Though feminist and gender-aware theorizing is attempting to redress the balance, most theorists insufficiently take into account the influence of sex-role conditioning. In addition, theorists tend to assume heterosexuality and insufficiently take into account the needs of gay, lesbian and bisexual clients.

Origins of counselling and therapy approaches

Theoretical approaches to counselling and therapy are created by human beings. To a large extent these theories reflect the historical context and personal and intellectual life histories of their founders. All theorists are influenced by their families of origin and by previous writers and thinkers. The following section suggests some important factors that have influenced the creation and development of counselling and therapy theory and practice.

Historical and cultural contexts

Theoretical approaches do not incubate and emerge in vacuums. Theorists are influenced by the historical and cultural contexts in which they live. For example, the prevalence of sexual repression in turn-of-the-century Austria influenced Freud to develop a theoretical position in which unacknowledged sexuality plays a large part. Another example is that, during the first half of the twentieth century, parents tended to dominate their families more than they do now. Carl Rogers (1961, 1980) was brought up in the first quarter of the century. His person-centred therapy reflects the need for individuals to have nurturing and accepting relationships within which to work through the effects of judgmental family upbringings so that they can 'become persons'. While Rogers reacted against certainty, the popularity of existential therapy partly represents a reaction to the lack of structure of much of modern society (Yalom, 1980). Old certainties provided by institutions like family and church no longer exist to the same extent and many people are faced with a more obvious need to create their own meaning.

Culture also influences how theoretical approaches develop. For example, ideas of desirable behaviour differ greatly between western and eastern cultures. Western therapies contain a high value on individualism that people from eastern cultures, with their greater emphasis on group harmony, may find uncongenial (Laungani, 1999). The topic of cultural considerations in therapy theory and practice is developed in greater detail later in this book.

Wounded theorists

The origins of behaviour therapy are more in the animal laboratory than in the personal experiences of behavioural theorists. However, without exception, all the other theorists whose work is described in this book encountered periods of significant psychological suffering in their lives. Box 1.3 illustrates this point. Jung's observation that 'Only the wounded physician heals' might be amended to become: 'Only the wounded healer creates a counselling and therapy approach'.

Box 1.3   Wounded theorists

Sigmund Freud *(Psychoanalysis)* suffered for many years from periodic depressions, mood variations and anxiety attacks. He also had occasional attacks of dread of dying, some psychologically induced fainting spells, and became very frightened about train travel.

Carl Jung *(Analytical therapy)* was a solitary child who, at one stage, used fainting spells to get out of going to secondary school. In his late 30s and early 40s Jung experienced schizophrenic-like symptoms.

Carl Rogers *(Person-centred therapy)* was an extremely shy and solitary child who grew up considering his parents as masters of subtle emotional manipulation. Rogers felt it unsafe to share much of his personal feelings at home for fear of being judged negatively.

Fritz Perls *(Gestalt therapy)* grew up in a distressed family where his parents had many bitter verbal and physical fights. Perls's mother beat him with carpet-beating rods and he hated his father's pompous righteousness.

Eric Berne *(Transactional analysis)*, when 11, experienced the death from tuberculosis of his beloved physician father, leaving his mother to support him and his sister.

William Glasser *(Reality therapy)* by age four realized his parents were highly incompatible. His father was gentle and non-possessive. If there was an Olympic event in being controlling, his energetic mother could have gone for the gold medal. Glasser was very shy when an undergraduate and, probably, at an earlier age too.

Box 1.3   (Continued)

Irvin Yalom and Rollo May *(Existential therapy)* Yalom grew up spending many hours hating his mother's vicious tongue. May grew up in a discordant and unhappy family atmosphere. He described his mother as a 'bitch-kitty on wheels'.

Viktor Frankl *(Logotherapy)* as a young man went through a period of hellish despair about the total meaninglessness of life. Later he suffered the horrors of Nazi concentration camps and the extermination of family members.

Albert Ellis *(Rational emotive behaviour therapy)* was a sickly child who was unusually shy and introverted during his childhood and adolescence. Ellis's mother was self-involved and neglectful and his father was often physically absent. Aged 12, Ellis discovered his parents had divorced.

Aaron Beck's *(Cognitive therapy)* mother was periodically deeply depressed. She could also be moody, inconsistent and excitable. While growing up Beck developed many anxieties, including fears related to abandonment, surgery, suffocation, public speaking and heights.

Arnold Lazarus *(Multimodal therapy)* was the youngest of four children and grew up feeling ignored and unimportant at home, which contributed to his feeling shy, inadequate and hypersensitive. Lazarus was also a skinny kid who was bullied a lot.

If one accepts that many originators of counselling and therapy theories experienced more than their share of psychological suffering, the question still remains how this affected their theorizing. For some leading theorists, shyness with people may have stimulated a desire to communicate through words. In addition, early feelings of inferiority may have fuelled their ambition to make their mark. Furthermore, having suffered themselves, theorists may be motivated to develop theories that can alleviate the suffering of others.

Some theorists seem to have been motivated to develop theoretical positions that would help not just clients, but themselves. Freud's self-analysis helped him address his personal suffering at the same time as providing important insights for his main work, *The Interpretation of Dreams* (Freud, 1900/1976; Jones, 1963). Jung's (1961) confrontation with his own unconscious archetypes and primordial images provided a rich source of ideas for helping both himself and others. Frankl's (1988) logotherapy stems from his youthful despair over the apparent meaninglessness of life. Rogers's person-centred therapist has the attributes of empathy, respect and non-possessive warmth that Rogers found missing in his parents and required for his own growth.

Albert Ellis, in his late teens, regularly went to the Bronx Botanic Gardens in New York and forced himself to sit next to women on park benches and strike up conversations with them so that he could learn to control his shyness and build his relating skills. Here, early in life, Ellis was trying to think and behave more rationally in one of his problem areas.

Interest in writing and communicating ideas

As well as a talent for theorizing, theorists need the ability to write passably well in order to get published. When researching the theorists' biographical sketches for this book, I was struck by how many early in life showed an interest in writing. Furthermore, some theorists, for instance Jung and Yalom, were avid readers right from their early years.

In his teens, Lazarus helped edit a body-building magazine and then entered university with a view to becoming a journalist and a writer. Beck was editor of his high school newspaper and an undergraduate English major. Skinner majored in English and planned to become a writer. Ellis too envisaged a writing career and wrote reams in his quest to become the Great American Novelist. May's main interest at college was English literature. Berne studied English along with psychology and pre-medicine as an undergraduate and his mother was a journalist. Later in life at least two theorists – Skinner and Yalom – branched out to write novels (see Skinner, 1948; Yalom, 1992, 1996, 2005).

An ambition to communicate distinctive ideas, become known and, possibly, reap the financial rewards of successful authorship may also fuel theorists' productivity. However, readers should be circumspect about attributing commercial motives to theorists. For example, for over 40 years, Ellis has donated all his royalty, client and workshop income to the Albert Ellis Institute. Furthermore, when theorists start writing books they have no guarantee that their time and effort will be remunerative.

All theorists think they have something of value to offer and want to share it. For instance, throughout his professional life Rogers was very concerned with making an impact on others. Though motivation is complex, probably altruism, social interest and enjoyment are primary factors shaping theorists' willingness to generate and share ideas.

Professional experiences and frustrations

Though behaviour therapy owes much to experimental psychology, for the most part major counselling and therapy theories emanate from people who were practitioners as well as scholars. Frustration, creative insights, clinical experimentation and careful observation can each contribute to developing a theory. Beck, Berne, Ellis and Perls were trained in psychoanalysis. Their negative experiences practising psychoanalysis challenged them to develop their own positions. Each used their work with clients to develop and experiment with different ways of helping them. In addition, Glasser's reality therapy stems from his disillusionment with the psychoanalytic psychology to which he was exposed during his training and from observing many analytic teachers not practising what they taught. Lying can take place behind as well as on the couch.

Lazarus was stimulated to develop his multimodal therapy approach as a reaction to the restrictiveness of traditional behaviour therapy. Rogers developed his person-centred approach from discovering the limitations of existing ways of working. He recalls that, when in the 1930s he worked at the Rochester Child Study Department (later renamed the Child Guidance Centre), he obtained far better results with clients from listening to them than from diagnostic understanding and advice (Rogers, 1980).

Research findings

Research can influence both the initial development of theory and test its usefulness. Behaviour therapy theory is based on the findings of experimental research: for instance, Pavlov's classical conditioning is based on experiments with dogs; Skinner's operant conditioning on experiments with pigeons and rats; and Wolpe's counter-conditioning by reciprocal inhibition on experiments with cats.

Theory can also be developed and validated from researching the processes and outcomes of psychotherapy. Theorists are practitioner-researchers generating and testing hypotheses in their therapy practice. Thus professional experience can act both as informal psychotherapy process and outcome research. Theorists and their adherents differ in the extent to which they either engage in or generate more formal therapy research. On the one hand, the processes and outcomes of approaches like cognitive therapy, rational emotive behaviour therapy, person-centred therapy and behaviour therapy are heavily researched. On the other hand, there is a paucity of research into approaches like transactional analysis, gestalt therapy, existential therapy and reality therapy.

Professional affiliation

Most theorists whose work is presented in this book were or are psychiatrists: for example, Beck, Berne, Frankl, Freud, Glasser, Jung and Yalom. The remainder trained as clinical psychologists: for instance, Ellis, Lazarus, May and Rogers. None of the major theorists are counselling psychologists, counsellors or social workers. Of the clinical psychologists, only Lazarus was primarily affiliated with an academic psychology department.

Access to money

Creating a counselling and therapy approach and getting it published takes time and money. A possible reason why more psychiatrists than psychologists have developed original theories is that they generally get paid more. Hence psychiatrists, who are budding theorists, can afford to schedule more writing time than psychologists. Jung, especially, also married into considerable wealth. In academic life, despite creativity being the seed corn of important research, grants are more likely to be awarded for researching existing approaches to counselling and therapy than for creating new ones. In addition, appointments, promotions and higher salaries go to those with strong research records.

Sex and sexual orientation

Probably most readers have noticed that all of the major theorists presented in this book are men. However, women have been prominent in psychodynamic approaches to therapy: for instance, Anna Freud, Karen Horney and Melanie Klein. In addition, Perls's wife Laura is considered by some to be the cofounder of gestalt therapy (Yontef and Jacobs, 2005). Furthermore, women have contributed to the development of other approaches presented in this book as well as being the driving force behind feminist therapy. All the major theorists appear to have been heterosexual, at least as far as their public personas.

Country of origin and race

The countries of birth of the theorists are as follows: America – Beck, Ellis, Glasser, May, Rogers and Yalom; Austria – Frankl and Freud; South Africa – Lazarus and Wolpe; Switzerland – Jung; Germany – Perls; and Canada – Berne. Of the non-American-born theorists, Berne, Lazarus, Perls and Wolpe spent the bulk of their professional lives in the United States. A high proportion of the theorists in this book are Jewish: for example, Beck, Berne, Frankl, Freud and Yalom. In addition, Ellis had a Jewish mother.

Longevity

If you are going to be a major counselling and therapy theorist, it helps to have good genes. Longevity helps major theorists to develop, refine, proselytize and defend their work. Freud, Jung, May and Rogers lived into their 80s, and Perls lived to over 75. Probably Berne's premature death at aged 60 robbed transactional analysis of the many useful developments and insights. Of the living theorists Ellis (b. 1913) is now over 90 years old, Beck (b. 1921) is 85, Glasser (b. 1925) is over 80, and Yalom (b. 1931) and Lazarus (b. 1932) are around 75. Another aspect of longevity is that many, if not most, major theorists did not publish original work until they were over 40. Dying young may not be a good career move for the budding theorist.

Recency of theory creation

One of the most worrying aspects of analysing the creation of counselling and therapy theories is that so little original work of high quality appears to be recent. None of the major theorists selected for this book were born in the second half of the twentieth century!

Creating your own theoretical approach

Each of you reading this book is engaging in the process of creating your own theoretical approach. Theory creation is both a subjective process of making sense of material as well as an external process of reading, learning, researching and practising therapeutic skills. How can you make yourself a better theorist and hence a more effective therapist? The following are some suggestions.

Work with this book

Though largely based on the writings of the original theorists, this book is a secondary source. Nevertheless, it should provide you with a faithful overview of some of the main counselling and therapy theories. To understand any theory you need to master its basic concepts. It is insufficient just to read about them. You will need actively to work on understanding and memorizing them. At the end of each theory chapter I provide review questions that test your knowledge of basic concepts.

Get personal

Jung (1961: 17) observed: 'My life is a story of the realization of the unconscious'. What about your life's story and what are you trying to realize through your interest in counselling and therapy? Applying the different theories to your own life is one way to make learning more personal, involving and interesting. What do the theories say that seems applicable to you and why? Another way to understand the theories is to think how applicable they are to past, present or future clients. What in different theories might prove useful in your practical work and why? You can also compare and contrast different theories in an attempt to critically evaluate their strengths and weaknesses for you as a person and as a therapist. At the end of each chapter I provide personal questions so that you may apply your learnings and insights to yourself.

Another way to learn about the theories is to try to develop a theoretical approach of your own. For over 20 years I asked counselling and counselling psychology students taking my theories classes to write a paper presenting their current theoretical approach.

Read primary sources

Primary sources are books and articles written by the theorists themselves. Ultimately, there is no substitute for reading primary sources. You will get a much broader and deeper impression of the different theories if you read widely the works of their originators. You can also learn about how the originators applied their counselling and therapy theories by reading case studies of their work. I include a section on case material towards the end of each chapter on the different therapies. In addition, after describing the work of each theorist, I provide a brief annotated bibliography plus other primary source references.

Read secondary sources

You can read secondary sources other than this book. Some secondary sources are counselling and therapy textbooks and here you should always look out for the most recent editions. *Current Psychotherapies* is a widely respected edited therapy textbook containing a mixture of primary and secondary sources (Corsini and Wedding, 2005). All major therapy approaches beget many secondary source books: for instance, Mearns and Thorne's (1999) *Person-Centred Counselling in Action* and Clarkson's (2004) *Gestalt Counselling in Action*.

Here is a warning about reading secondary sources. Choose carefully because some secondary source writers do not really understand the theoretical positions they present. Following are three more traps into which secondary source textbook writers can fall. One trap is to mix the writings of the original theorist together with recent developments in theory, so the student has difficulty in knowing which is which. A second trap is to merge the writings of different theorists into the same chapter: for example, to have a chapter combining either psychodynamic theories or humanistic theories. A problem with this approach is that no theory gets presented thoroughly. If you doubt this point, look at the next two chapters on Freudian Psychoanalysis and Jung's Analytical Therapy and see how well-nigh impossible it would be to combine them so that readers obtain a good introduction to both Freudian and Jungian theory and practice. A third trap is for the secondary source writer only to present case examples of their own work. A risk here is that this secondary source case material does not truly reflect how the originator practised or practises therapy.

Watch and listen to audio-visual material

You can obtain a further insight into the different theorists by watching films and videotapes and listening to cassettes of them discussing their theories and working with clients. For instance, audio-visual material is available for theorists like Beck, Ellis, Perls and Rogers.

Attend training courses and workshops

You may expand your knowledge and skills in the different theories by attending training courses and workshops run by competent adherents of the different approaches. Introductory theories of counselling and therapy courses are likely to be limited in presenting different approaches both by time constraints and by lecturer preferences. You may get a much more thorough introduction to any single approach if you attend workshops and courses run by specialists in it. However, when considering training courses and workshops, be careful about spreading yourself too thinly.

Undergo supervision

A good way to learn about the theory and practice of a counselling approach is to be supervised by a practitioner skilled in it. For instance, you can learn the theory and practice of one therapeutic approach more thoroughly by being supervised by someone knowledgeable and competent in that approach. Then you can broaden how you work by obtaining supervision from practitioners of one or more different approaches. For those practising counselling and psychotherapy, many consider that clinical supervision is essential throughout their careers.

Undergo personal therapy

If a counselling and therapy approach particularly appeals to you, one way to learn about its theory and practice is to become a client of a skilled practitioner in the approach. For some approaches, for example psychoanalysis and analytical therapy, a training analysis is an integral part of learning the approach. Where personal therapy is not a requirement of a particular approach, the need to develop self-awareness and reflective skills about your practice is important.

Evaluate theoretical approaches

In creating your own theoretical approach you will undoubtedly undergo a process of evaluating the existing theoretical approaches. Many considerations go into evaluating theoretical approaches: for instance, how well you understand the theoretical approaches you are trying to evaluate, how thoroughly each approach is researched, and how their goals differ. I leave a more detailed discussion about evaluating counselling and therapy approaches to this book's final chapter.

Review and personal questions

Review questions

1. How would you define the terms counselling and therapy?
2. To what extent do you consider the terms counselling and therapy describe different activities and why?
3. What is a theory?
4. What are the functions of counselling and therapy theories?
5. What are some potential limitations or disadvantages of counselling and therapy theories?
6. What factors are influential in creating counselling and therapy theoretical approaches?

Personal questions

1. Do you consider yourself a prospective counsellor and/or a prospective therapist and why?
2. Describe your present preferences regarding counselling and therapy theoretical approaches.
3. How can you best learn about counselling and therapy approaches?
4. How can you best develop a theoretical position to guide your counselling and therapy practice?

Annotated bibliography

Corsini, R.J. and Wedding, D. (eds) (2005) *Current Psychotherapies* (7th edn). Belmont, CA: Thomson Brooks/Cole.
This book is a mixture of primary and secondary sources. Chapters on cognitive, existential, multimodal, person-centred and rational emotive behaviour therapies are written by their originators, sometimes with coauthors. Secondary source chapters review psychoanalytic, analytical, Adlerian, gestalt, behaviour, experiential and family therapy as well as psychodrama.

References and further reading

Clarkson, P. (2004) *Gestalt Counselling in Action* (3rd edn). London: Sage.

Corsini, R.J. (2005) 'Introduction', in R. Corsini and D. Wedding (eds), *Current Psychotherapies* (7th edn). Belmont, CA: Thomson Brooks/Cole. pp. 1–14.

Corsini, R.J. and Wedding, D. (eds) (2005) *Current Psychotherapies* (7th edn). Belmont, CA: Thomson Brooks/Cole.

Frankl, V.E. (1988) *The Will to Meaning: Foundations and Applications of Logotherapy*. New York: Meridian.

Freud, S. (1900/1976) *The Interpretation of Dreams*. Harmondsworth: Penguin Books.

Jones, E. (1963) *The Life and Work of Sigmund Freud*. New York: Anchor Books.

Jung, C.G. (1961) *Memories, Dreams, Reflections*. London: Fontana Press.

Laungani, P. (1999) 'Culture and identify: implications for counselling', in S. Palmer and P. Laungani (eds), *Counselling in a Multicultural Society*. London: Sage. pp. 35–70.

Mearns, D. and Thorne, B. (1999) *Person-Centred Counselling in Action* (2nd edn). London: Sage.

Rogers, C.R. (1951) *Client-Centered Therapy*. Boston: Houghton Mifflin.

Rogers, C.R. (1959) 'A theory of therapy, personality, and interpersonal relationships, as developed in the client-centered framework', in S. Koch (ed.), *Psychology: A Study of Science* (Study 1, Volume 3). New York: McGraw-Hill. pp. 184–256.

Rogers, C.R. (1961) *On Becoming a Person*. Boston: Houghton Mifflin.

Rogers, C.R. (1980) *A Way of Being*. Boston: Houghton Mifflin.

Skinner, B.F. (1948) *Walden Two*. New York: Macmillan.

Yalom, I.D. (1980) *Existential Psychotherapy*. New York: Basic Books.

Yalom, I.D. (1992) *When Nietzsche Wept*. New York: Basic Books.

Yalom, I.D. (1996) *Lying on the Couch*. New York: Harper Perennial.

Yalom, I.D. (2005) *The Schopenhauer Cure: A Novel*. New York: HarperCollins.

Yontef, G. and Jacobs, L. (2005) 'Gestalt therapy', in R. Corsini and D. Wedding (eds), *Current Psychotherapies* (7th edn). Belmont, CA: Thomson Brooks/Cole. pp. 299–336.

freud's psychoanalysis　2

Introduction

Sigmund Freud, the originator of psychoanalysis, is the best known of the theorists whose work is described in this book. Freud lived in a time of conflict, a major theme of his work. One area of conflict was that between the strait-laced 'Victorian' public morality of late nineteenth-century Austria and human sexuality. To a large extent public acknowledgment of sexuality was frowned upon which fostered widespread ignorance of healthy sexual functioning. Another area of conflict was that caused by human aggression. The nineteenth century had started with the Napoleonic wars, in the second half of the century the Franco-Prussian war took place and, in the second decade of the twentieth century, matters were to get worse with the horrors of the First World War. Though Freud died within a month of the start of the Second World War, he was very conscious of the factors leading up to it, not least because all his professional life, as a Jew, he had been acutely aware of the anti-Semitism in his homeland, and he was to die in exile in Britain, a refugee from Nazism.

Freud's psychoanalysis has been developed by others since his death. There is a section on contemporary psychoanalysis towards the end of the chapter.

Sigmund Freud (1856–1939)

Sigmund Freud was born at Freiberg, a small town in what is now the Czech Republic. He was the eldest son of his father's second wife, who subsequently bore five daughters and two other sons. Jones (1963) writes of Freud's mother's pride in and love for her first-born and also mentions that between the ages of two and two and a half Freud's libido had been aroused towards his mother on seeing her naked. Freud (1935: 12) writes: 'My parents were Jews, and I have remained a Jew myself'. His father, Jakob, was a wool merchant who, when Freud was four, moved his family to Vienna. Freud's early years in Vienna were hard and, throughout his upbringing, his family appears to have been short of money.

When he was nine Freud went to high school (Sperl Gymnasium), where he was at the top of his class for seven years, enjoyed special privileges, and was required to pass few examinations. Freud was a hard worker who enjoyed reading and studying. On leaving school with distinction at 17 he faced the choice of a career, which for a Viennese Jew had to be in industry, business, law or medicine. He recalls not feeling any particular predilection for medicine, since his interests were directed more towards human concerns than natural objects. Freud writes: '... and it was hearing Goethe's beautiful essay on Nature read aloud by Professor Carl Bruhl just before I left school that decided me to become a medical student' (1935: 14).

In 1873 Freud enrolled at the University of Vienna to study medicine, though when he was there his academic interests were more wide-ranging. In 1876 he began the first of his researches, a study of the gonadic structure of eels. Soon afterwards he entered Ernst Brucke's physiological laboratory, where he worked, with short interruptions, from 1876 to 1882. During this period Freud focused chiefly on work connected with the histology of nerve cells. He found 'rest and satisfaction' in Brucke's laboratory as well as scientists 'whom I could respect and take as my models' (p. 15). He thought especially highly of Brucke himself. Freud recalls being decidedly negligent in pursuing his medical studies. Nevertheless, in 1881 he passed his final examinations to become a Doctor of Medicine with the grade of 'excellent'.

In 1882 Freud left Brucke's laboratory, where the year before he had been appointed a demonstrator. For financial reasons, probably influenced by falling in love, Freud decided to earn his living as a physician. He entered the General Hospital of Vienna, where he gained experience in various departments and became an active researcher in the Institute of Cerebral Anatomy. During this period 'with an eye to material considerations, I began to study nervous diseases' (p. 18). Because of inadequate opportunities for learning this subject, Freud was forced to be his own teacher. He published a number of clinical observations on organic diseases of the nervous systems and, in 1885, was appointed lecturer in neuropathology. Around this period Freud both took cocaine and conducted research into its use. Jones observes: 'For many years he suffered from periodic depressions and fatigue or apathy, neurotic symptoms which later took the form of anxiety attacks before being dispelled by his own analysis' (1963: 54–5). Cocaine apparently calmed the agitation and eased the depression. Jones also mentions that all his life Freud was subject to severe bouts of migraine that were refractory to any treatment.

On the award of a travelling fellowship Freud went to Paris where, from October 1885 to February 1886, he studied at the Salpetrière (hospital for nervous diseases) under Charcot. He was very impressed with Charcot's investigations into hysteria, confirming the genuineness of hysterical phenomena, including hysterical paralyses and contractures by hypnotic suggestion. In 1886 Freud returned to Vienna to marry Martha Bernays and to set up a private practice as a specialist in nervous diseases. His 'therapeutic arsenal contained only two weapons, electrotherapy and hypnotism' (Freud, 1935: 26). He soon dropped electrotherapy and increasingly realized the limitations of hypnotic suggestion. During the period 1886 to 1891 he did little scientific work, though in 1891 he jointly published the first of his studies on the cerebral paralyses of children.

In the early 1880s Freud had developed a close friendship with Joseph Breuer, a prominent Viennese physician, who told him how, between 1880 and 1882, he had successfully treated a young girl with hysterical symptoms. His method was to hypnotize her deeply and then encourage her to express in words her memories of earlier emotional situations which were oppressing her. In the late 1880s Freud began repeating Breuer's technique with his own patients, being aware 'of the possibility that there could be powerful mental processes which nevertheless remained hidden from the consciousness of man' (p. 29). In 1893 Freud and Breuer wrote a preliminary paper on the cathartic method and, in 1895, published their book *Studies on Hysteria*.

During the 1890s the transition from catharsis to psychoanalysis took place. Jones writes: 'there is ample evidence that for ten years or so – roughly comprising the nineties – he suffered from a very considerable psychoneurosis ... yet it was just in the years when the neurosis was at its height, 1897–1900, that Freud did his most original work' (1905/1963: 194). Although he showed no conversion symptoms, he had extreme alterations of mood between elation and self-confidence, and depression and inhibition. In the latter moods Freud could neither write nor concentrate, apart from his professional work. Additionally, he had occasional attacks of dread of dying and also became very anxious about travelling by rail.

During the period 1887 to 1900 Freud had an intense friendship with Wilhelm Fleiss, a nose and throat specialist two years younger than him. Fleiss saw sexual problems as central to his own work, encouraged Freud and gave him permission to develop his theories. Jones notes Freud's dependency on Fleiss's good opinion and calls him Freud's 'sole public' during this period. Jones rated Fleiss as intellectually far inferior to Freud.

Against this background, Freud started developing his ideas on the sexual bases of neuroses, abandoned hypnotism yet retained his practice of requiring the patient to lie on a sofa while he sat behind. During 1897 to 1899, he wrote his major work, *The Interpretation of Dreams*. In the summer of 1897 Freud undertook a psychoanalysis of his own unconscious, and this self-analysis generated material for the book. Freud discovered his childhood passion for his mother and jealousy for his father, which he considered a pervasive human characteristic which he termed the Oedipus complex. It took eight years to sell the first edition of 600 copies of *The Interpretation of Dreams*. Jones observes of Freud's self-analysis: 'The end of all that labor and suffering was the last and final phase in the evolution of Freud's personality. There emerged the serene and benign Freud, henceforth free to pursue his work in imperturbable composure' (1963: 205). Fromm's (1959) biography is less kind, suggesting that Freud continued to exhibit some insecurity and egotism in areas of both his professional and his personal life. In 1905 Freud published what is perhaps his other major work, *Three Contributions to the Theory of Sex*, which traces the development of sexuality from its earliest childhood beginnings.

In his autobiographical study Freud observed that, after the preliminary cathartic period, the history of psychoanalysis falls into two phases. From around 1895 until 1906 or 1907 he worked in isolation, but thereafter the contributions of his pupils and collaborators increasingly grew in importance. The historical development of Freud's ideas will be left at this stage. Suffice it to say that for the remainder of his life he published numerous books and articles not only on psychoanalysis as a method of treating the disturbed, but also on the relevance of his theories to everyday life. In 1910, at a congress held at Nuremberg, the analysts formed themselves into an International Psychoanalytical Association divided into a number of local societies, but under a common president. By 1935 the number of the Association's supporters had increased considerably. The growth of psychoanalysis, however, was not smooth and aroused considerable antipathy.

Freud was in the habit of smoking an average of 20 cigars a day and, in 1923, learned that he had cancer of the jaw. He lived the last 16 years of his life in pain that was often extreme, and a total of 33 operations were performed on his jaw. In 1938 Nazism caused Freud to leave Austria with his family and settle in his admired England, which he had first visited when he was 19. He died in London a year later.

Freud had observed that he was by temperament a conquistador or adventurer, with the accompanying traits of curiosity, boldness and tenacity. A modern term for Freud might be an 'ideas person'.

Theory

Basic concepts

Although many of Freud's basic concepts are to be found in *The Interpretation of Dreams* (1900/1976), he was developing and refining his ideas continuously. Thus the same concept may appear in different sources, only some of which will be mentioned here. In general, this chapter represents Freud's later presentation of his work.

The pleasure principle

Originally presented as the unpleasure principle, the pleasure principle follows from the constancy hypothesis that 'the mental apparatus endeavours to keep the quantity of excitation in it as low as possible or at least to keep it constant' (Freud, 1920/1961: 3). Thus everything which increases the quantity of excitation will be felt as unpleasurable and anything which diminishes it will be experienced as pleasurable. Freud qualified the idea of the dominance of the pleasure principle by observing that, although in the mind there exists a strong tendency towards the pleasure principle, there are also other forces opposing it, with the final outcome not always fulfilling the tendency towards pleasure.

The instincts

Instincts represent somatic or biological demands upon the mind. While acknowledging the possibility of distinguishing many instincts, Freud assumed that these could be grouped into two basic instincts, *Eros* and the *destructive instinct*. The erotic instincts 'seek to combine more and more living substance into even greater unities', while the death instincts 'oppose this effort and lead what is living back to an inorganic state' (Freud, 1932/1973: 140). Eros includes the instincts of self-preservation, the preservation of the species, ego-love and object-love, and its energy is called *libido*. Throughout life the basic instincts may either work together (for instance the sexual act is also an act of aggression) or oppose each other.

Freud (1920/1961: 30) saw instincts as historically acquired and conservative and stated: 'It seems, then, that an instinct is an urge inherent in life to restore an earlier state of things'. Given the assumption that living things appeared later than inanimate ones and arose out of them, the death instinct may be viewed as a compulsion to repeat this earlier inorganic state. Consequently, the aim of all life is death. Eros, however, does not follow the same formula. Freud considered that sexual instincts were the single exception among the instincts in not seeking to restore an earlier state of things.

Freud viewed the inclination to aggression as an original instinctual disposition in humans. He quoted Plautus: *'Homo homini lupus'*, a translation of which is 'Man is a wolf to man'. The aggressive instinct is the derivative and main representative of the death instinct. The evolution of civilization represents the struggle between the life-and-death instincts in the human species. The fateful question that Freud posed at the end of *Civilization and its Discontents* was whether Eros would assert itself: 'But who can foresee with what success and what results?' (1930/1962: 92).

The unconscious and consciousness

Heavily influenced by his study of dreams, Freud made a distinction between the unconscious and consciousness. From the very beginning, he stated that there were two kinds of unconscious and, hence, three levels of consciousness.

- *The unconscious*: The unconscious (Ucs), or unconscious proper, is material that is inadmissible to consciousness through repression. In other words, with the unconscious the censorship on material coming into awareness is very strong indeed. The object of psychoanalysis is to help make some of this material accessible to awareness, though during the process strong resistances may be aroused, not least because of the forbidden sexual connotations of much of what is being repressed.

- *The preconscious*: The preconscious (Pcs) consists of everything that can easily exchange the unconscious state for the conscious one. Thus the preconscious is latent and capable of becoming conscious, while the unconscious is repressed and unlikely to become conscious without great difficulty. Material may remain in the preconscious, though usually it finds its way into consciousness without any need for psychoanalytic intervention. The preconscious may be viewed as a screen between the unconscious and consciousness, with, as in the case of dreams, modifications being made in unconscious material through censorship.

- *Consciousness*: Consciousness (Cs or Pcpt Cs) has the function of a sense organ for the perception of psychical qualities. Unlike the two kinds of unconscious, consciousness has no memory and a state of consciousness is usually very transitory. Material becomes conscious, or flows into the consciousness sense organ, from two directions: the external world and inner excitations. Furthermore, the function of speech enables internal events such as sequences of ideas and intellectual processes to become conscious.

Structure of the mental apparatus

Freud structured the mental apparatus into three systems or agencies: the id, the ego and the super-ego. Psychological wellbeing depends on whether these three systems are interrelating effectively. Figure 2.1 shows Freud's own sketch of the structural relations of the mental apparatus, though he acknowledges that the space occupied by the unconscious id ought to have been much greater (Freud, 1932/1973: 111).

The id

The id or 'it' is the oldest of these systems and contains everything that is inherited and fixed in the constitution. The instincts, which originate in the somatic organization, find their mental expression in the id. The id, filled with energy from the instincts, strives to bring about the satisfaction of instinctual needs on the basis of the pleasure principle. Thus the activity of the id is directed towards securing the free discharge of quantities of excitation. The psychical processes of the id are known as primary processes because they are present in the mental apparatus from the first. Furthermore, no alteration in the id's mental processes is produced by the passage of time. Freud (1932/1973: 106–7) viewed the id as 'a chaos, a cauldron full of seething emotions', which 'knows no judgments of values: no good and evil, no morality'. The id consists of wishful impulses. It is not governed by logic, and this applies especially to the law of contradiction, since it contains contrary impulses side by side. In short, the id is the individual's primary subjective reality at the unconscious level.

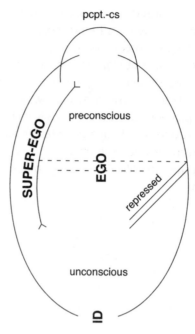

Figure 2.1   Structural relations of the mental apparatus

The ego

The ego or 'I' is first and foremost a bodily ego ultimately derived from bodily sensations, in particular those coming from its surface. The ego is a portion of the id that has undergone a special development or modification through the influence of the external world. The ego acts as an intermediary between the id and the external world and ideally represents reason and common sense, whereas the id contains instinctual passions and would destroy itself without the intervention of the ego. The ego strives to bring the reality principle to bear upon the id in substitution for the pleasure principle. The processes of the ego, which include perception, problem solving and repression, are later devel-opments or secondary processes, in contrast to the original or primary processes of the id. Nevertheless, the ego seeks pleasure and the avoidance of unpleasure, differing from the id only in the means of attaining common ends. A foreseen increase in unpleasure is met by a signal of anxiety. As Figure 2.1 shows, the perceptual-conscious system is the outer layer of the ego, which also includes much preconscious and unconscious material.

The ego is in control of voluntary movement, but interposes thought between experiencing a need and acting on it. The ego deals with external events through perception, memory, avoiding excessive stimuli, adapting to moderate stimuli, and engaging in activities designed to modify the external world to its advantage. Regarding internal events in relation to the id, the ego attempts to control instinctual demands by deciding the timing and manner of their gratification or by suppressing their excitations. Freud makes the analogy of the id being the horse, while the ego is the rider. He observes that often, however, the ego is weak in relation to the id and so is in the habit of transforming the id's will into action as if it were its own.

The super-ego

The super-ego is a residue formed within the ego in which parental influence is prolonged. Parental influence may be defined broadly as including cultural, racial and family influences. As the person grows up, the nature of the 'parental' influence may vary, partly because parents may behave differently. Teachers, admired figures in public life and many others may also contribute to the development of an individual's super-ego, which normally departs more and more from original parental influences.

The function of the super-ego, which engages in self-observation, is to contain the demands of the id through moral influence on the ego. Originally the child engages in instinctual renunciation through fear of loss of love or through fear of aggression from an *external* or parental authority. Subsequently a secondary situation develops in which the external restraint is internalized and thus instinctual renunciation comes about through fear of an *internal* authority, or super-ego.

A characteristic of the super-ego is the ego-ideal, based on the admiration which the child felt for the perfection it saw in its parents and which it strives to emulate. In fact the terms 'super-ego' and 'ego-ideal' are virtually synonymous. The ego-ideal consists of both precepts – 'You ought to be like this' – and prohibitions – 'You ought not to be like that'. These precepts and prohibitions are based in part on the identifications and repressions resulting from the resolution of the Oedipus complex. They represent the individual's conscience, transgressions of which are likely to result in a sense of inferiority and guilt and also possibly in a need for punishment. Freud observed: 'The super-ego is the representative for us of every moral restriction, the advocate of a striving towards perfection – it is, in short, as much as we have been able to grasp psychologically of what is described as the higher side of human life' (1932/1973: 98).

In addition to the demands of the instincts and of the external world, the ego has to take into account the demands of the super-ego. Individuals vary in the severity of their super-egos, which may be benign or punitively harsh and restricting. Conflicts can arise between ego and super-ego, with large portions of both agencies remaining unconscious.

Anxiety

Freud defined anxiety as a specific state of unpleasure accompanied by motor discharge along definite pathways. He saw anxiety as the universal reaction to the situation of danger and the ego as the sole seat of anxiety. In later life, a source of anxiety that is involuntary occurs whenever a dangerous situation arises. Another source is anxiety generated by the ego when danger is merely threatened and the ego feels weak in relation to it. Hence there are three kinds of anxiety, one for each of the ego's three 'taskmasters':

- *realistic* anxiety regarding the dangers of the external world;
- *moral* anxiety regarding conflict with the super-ego; and
- *neurotic* anxiety regarding conflict with the strength of the id's instinctual impulses.

Thus anxiety is either a reaction to actual danger or a signal involving the perception of impending danger.

Psychical energy, cathexis and anti-cathexis

Psychoanalysis is often referred to as having a dynamic view of psychology. What this means is that the concept of psychical or mental energy and its distribution among the id, ego and super-ego is central to psychoanalysis. The id is the source of this somatically based psychical energy, being filled with energy reaching it from the instincts. Sexual excitation is an example of instinctual psychical energy. As the ego and the super-ego are formed they also become charged with energy.

The words 'cathexis' and to 'cathect' describe the idea of psychical energy being drawn to mental agencies and processes, somewhat analogous to an electric charge. Cathexes are the charges of instinctual energy seeking discharge, whereas anti-cathexes are charges of energy that block and inhibit such discharge. The id has only primary-process instinctual cathexes seeking discharge. However, the ego and the super-ego have both urging cathexes and restraining anti-cathexes. Throughout life the ego is the avenue by which libidinal cathexes are transferred to objects and into which they may also be withdrawn again. Two characteristics of libidinal cathexes are mobility, the ease with which they pass from one object to another, and, in contrast, fixation, or being bound to particular objects.

Bisexuality

Freud observed that it was a long-known anatomical fact that in every normally formed male or female there are traces of the apparatus of the other sex, though in atrophied form. Anatomically there may have been an original predisposition to bisexuality, which in the course of the development of the human species has largely been altered to monosexuality.

Psychologically Freud considered that the sexual impulse is probably entirely independent of its object and therefore is not originated by chemical attraction. Another way of stating this is that there is only one libido and it cannot be assigned a sex. Therefore the direction of both heterosexual and homosexual object selection requires further explanation. By studying covert sexual excitations, psychoanalytic research discovered that all men are capable of homosexual object selection and actually accomplish this in the unconscious.

Furthermore, homosexual libidinous feelings 'play no small role as factors in normal psychic life' and an even greater role as 'causative factors of disease' (Freud, 1905/1962: 10).

Freud considered that the same free attachment to male and female objects as observed in childhood and primitive and prehistoric states forms the basis on which both normal and homosexual or inverted sexual development takes place. A degree of homosexuality is congenital in everyone, with the final determination of sexual behaviour being the result of the intensity of constitutional predisposition as well as of life experiences and restrictions in one or the other direction. Both the woman and the man develop out of a child with a bisexual disposition.

Acquisition

Infantile sexuality and amnesia

Freud distinguished between the sexual impulse, the sexual object and the sexual aim. The sexual impulse is the sexual aspect of libido, the sexual object is the person in whom sexual attraction is lodged, and the sexual aim refers to the action, such as touch or intercourse, towards which the sexual impulse strives. Freud further made a sharp distinction between 'sexual' and 'genital', considering that sexual life consists of gaining pleasure from zones of the body sensitive to sexual stimulation and that this is not necessarily in the service of reproduction. Additionally, sexual life includes affectionate and friendly impulses often called 'love'. In a sense, all adult sexual behaviour whose goal is not reproduction, a heterosexual object and intercourse may be considered perverse. Adult sexual behaviour does not suddenly emerge at puberty but develops out of prior sexual dispositions and experiences.

Sexual life starts soon after birth. Infantile sexuality, in the absence of genital maturation and of ego and super-ego development, lacks a central coordinating focus. Instead the component sexual instincts seek their own pleasure. Infantile sexuality is fundamentally autoerotic in that the infant finds pleasure in the object of its own body. Freud considered that the infantile sexual disposition contained great tendencies to perversion and that normal sexual behaviour develops partly in response to organic changes and partly as a result of psychic inhibitions and repressions.

The years of childhood are when the individual is most impressionable. Nevertheless, people are largely unaware of the beginnings of their sexual life and tend to view their childhood as if it were a prehistoric time. However, infantile and childhood sexual experiences leave deep traces in the individual's psychical life, acting as significant determinants for future development. Freud used the term 'infantile amnesia' to refer to the phenomenon by which a veil is drawn over early sexual experiences.

Sexual development

The onset of sexual life takes place in two stages. The first or pre-genital stage of sexual development is a steady process that reaches a climax towards the end of a child's fifth year. After this there is a lull or period of latency. The second or genital stage starts with the re-emergence of the sexual impulse at menarche or puberty. The pre-genital and genital stages of sexual organization are distinguished by whether or not the genital zones have assumed a dominating role.

- The pre-genital stage (birth to about age six)

    The pre-genital stage itself consists of three separate phases of sexual organization through which individuals normally pass smoothly, though fixations or arrested development may occur at each phase. Both sexes seem to pass through the early stages of sexual development in the same manner.

    (a) Oral phase (first 18 months)
    The first organ to be an erogenous zone is the mouth, and hence sexual development starts with the *oral* phase. The infant's act of sucking goes beyond that needed for the taking of nourishment to what may be viewed as the seeking of sexual organ-pleasure independent of nourishment. The oral phase can be further subdivided. The first sub-stage is where there is a focus only on oral incorporation, whereas the second sub-stage is 'oral-sadistic', with the emergence of biting activity. These two sub-stages of the oral phase are the first manifestation of the phenomenon of ambivalence.

    (b) Anal phase (18 months to three years of age)
    The second organ to become an erogenous zone is the anus, and normal sexual development proceeds from the oral to the *sadistic-anal* phase. The active aspect of this phase is the impulse for mastery (sadism), with the strengthening of the musculature of the body and control of sphincter functions. The erogenous mucous membrane of the anus also manifests itself as an organ with a passive sexual aim. Character traits associated with this phase are orderliness, parsimony and obstinacy, which together define the so-called 'anal character'.

    (c) Phallic phase (from about age three to five or six)
    The third organ to become an erogenous zone is the genital apparatus. The period of sexual development in which the male sexual organ (the phallus) and the female clitoris become important is known as the *phallic* phase, which starts in about the child's third year. Here pleasure is obtained from masturbation. During the phallic phase the sexuality of early childhood reaches its greatest intensity and it is during this phase that male and female sexual development become different. The *Oedipus* phase is part of the phallic phase for both sexes (see Box 2.1).

Box 2.1   The Oedipus complex

For boys

At an early age the little boy develops an object-cathexis for his mother and identifies with his father. During the phallic phase the body's libidinal object-cathexis of his mother intensifies and he wishes to get rid of his father and to take his father's place with his mother. The threat of castration causes the boy to abandon and repress his incestuous wishes. The resolution of the boy's Oedipus complex involves renouncing his object-cathexis of his mother, which may lead to an identification with his mother or, more normally, to an intensification of his identification with his father, consolidating the masculinity in his character. The Oedipus situation is often more complex because of the child's bisexual disposition. Thus, instead of affection for his mother and ambivalence towards his father, he may have a mixture of affection for and ambivalence towards each parent. Freud observes that 'in both sexes the relative strength of the masculine and feminine sexual dispositions is what determines whether the outcome of the Oedipus situation shall be an identification with the father or with the mother' (1923/1962: 23). Perhaps it is more accurate to consider the outcome as a predominant rather than an exclusive identification with one or the other parent. Freud further asserts that, especially with neurotics, a bisexual Oedipus complex should be assumed.

For girls

As with the boy, the girl's mother is the first object of her love. During the phallic phase the clitoris is her predominant erogenous zone. Freud considered that during the girl's development to femininity she should change both her predominant erogenous zone (to the vagina) and also the sex of her love object. The powerful attachment of the girl to her mother is ended when the girl, discovering the inferiority of her clitoris and the fact that she does not have a penis, holds her mother responsible. Penis envy or the wish for a penis is a very important feminine trait. The wish for a penis-baby from the father replaces the wish for a penis, and it is at this stage that the girl has entered her Oedipus situation, desiring her father and wishing to be rid of her mother. Again the situation may be complicated by her bisexual disposition. Girls remain in their Oedipus situation for an indeterminate length of time and resolve it late and often incompletely. While the boy is encouraged to surmount the Oedipus complex through fear of castration, the girl has no such motivation. As time goes by, the female Oedipus complex weakens, partly as a result of inevitable disappointments from her father.

- The latency period (about age six to 12)

   The period from around the beginning of the child's sixth year, probably later for girls, to menarche and puberty constitutes the sexual latency period. Latency may be total or partial and, during this period, sexual inhibitions develop. One of the mechanisms by which sexual energy is diverted is called sublimation or the displacement of libido to new aims and cultural pursuits. Furthermore, as the individual develops, libidinous impulses may call forth contrary anti-cathexes or reactions (reaction formations) such as disgust, shame and morality.

- The genital stage (age about 12 and then onwards)

The genital stage, which starts at menarche or puberty, involves the sub-ordination of all sources of sexual feeling to the primacy of the genital zones. Earlier libidinal cathexes may be retained, included in sexual activ-ity or preliminary or auxiliary acts, or in some way repressed or diverted. Puberty brings a greater increase of libido in boys, but in girls there is an increase in repression, especially regarding clitoral sexuality. At menarche and puberty, along with the overcoming of incestuous object-choices, comes the breaking away from parental authority. Given a reasonably adequate prior sexual development, the individual is now ready to engage in a heterosexual genital relationship.

Identification

Identification is an important concept for understanding ego and super-ego development. Identification may be viewed in three ways:

1. as the original form of emotional tie with an object;
2. as a regressive substitute for a libidinal object-tie by means of introjection of the object with the ego, so that the ego assumes the characteristics of the object (for example, a female patient imitating her father's cough); and
3. as a feeling generated by the perception of a common quality with another person who is not libidinally cathected.

The development of the super-ego may be seen in terms of identification with the parental agency, by which young people, wishing to be like their parents, mould their egos after the fashion of those taken as their models. Identification is part of the normal process of development. However, the ego may be restricted, as well as enhanced, depending on the nature of the identification.

Defence mechanisms

During the child's early years its ego is relatively feeble, yet it has to deal with strong instinctual sexual impulses. At this stage anxiety may be generated by loss of an object or loss of love, which may persist into later life. Later sources of anxiety include fear of castration during the phallic phase, and fear of the super-ego during and after the latency period.

In order to cope with the sources of anxiety the ego uses defence mechan-isms. Freud doubted that the ego could do without them during normal development. In many instances, however, the ego pays a high price for employing these mechanisms, since they restrict its functioning, also using in their anti-cathexes psychical energy which might better be expended elsewhere. Defence mechanisms are infantilisms that operate unconsciously and may impede realistic behaviour long after they have outlived their usefulness. Individuals do not make use of all the possible mechanisms of defence, but select some, which become fixated in their egos. The establishment of defensive mechanisms is largely a feature of the child's struggle against its sexuality during the first five years of life. Box 2.2 describes the five main defensive ways in which the ego strives to contain the threatening instinctual cathexis when the ego observes that an emerging instinctual demand may place it in danger.

Box 2.2   The ego's main mechanisms of defence

Repression: Purposely forgetting something and remaining unaware of having done this. The process of repression is of two kinds:

1. material which is in the preconscious and hence admissible to consciousness is pushed back into the unconscious; and
2. unconscious material may be forbidden by censorship to enter the preconscious and hence has to remain unconscious.

For example, either kind of repression might apply to an individual's latent sexually perverted impulses. Repression is the central underlying defensive mechanism of the ego, the basis of all other defences.

Reaction-formation: Adopting thoughts, feelings and behaviours that are the opposite to one's true thoughts and feelings. The ego acknowledges impulses contrary to the ones by which it is threatened. For instance, sexual impulses may be warded off by excessive shame, disgust and loathing of sexuality.

Projection: The ego deals with the threat of an unacceptable instinctual impulse by externalizing it. Thus individuals, instead of acknowledging the extent of their own libidinal and aggressive impulses, may become very aware of such characteristics in others and actually attribute them incorrectly.

Fixation: Where people get highly anxious about moving on to the next phase of their sexual development, they may lag behind or become fixated in varying degrees to an earlier stage in terms of satisfaction of their instincts. For instance, children may cling dependently to their mothers' love rather than make new object-cathexes.

Regression: Resuming behaviours appropriate to an earlier stage of sexual development. Under threat, an individual returns to an earlier phase at which she or he may previously have been fixated. In fact, regressions may be of two kinds: a return to the incestuous objects first cathected by the libido and a return of the sexual organization as a whole to an earlier phase.

Normal development

To summarize, the Freudian view of the normal development of personality may be seen in terms of three interrelated strands.

1. The individual's libidinal development, which starts with a mixture of constitutional and infantile predispositions which mature into genital sexuality in successive but overlapping phases, interrupted by the latency period;
2. The development of both the ego, as it gains in ability to mediate between instinctual demands and the reality of the external world, and the super-ego, based on identifications with parental influences;
3. The establishment of favoured defensive mechanisms on the part of the ego to ward off the anxiety caused by the strength and persistence of the id's libidinal impulses.

Thus normal development may be viewed as passing through successive stages of sexual maturation without major fixations and regressions, developing an ego which copes reasonably effectively with the external world, developing a super-ego based on identifications which are constructive and not punitively moralistic, and evolving defensive mechanisms which drain off some of the energy of the id without serious restriction of ego functioning. Normal development is a dynamic process entailing a continuing distribution and redistribution of psychical energy among id, ego and super-ego, the three systems of the mental apparatus.

Development and activation of neurosis

Freud saw biological, phylogenetic and psychological factors as each contributing to neurosis.

The *biological factor* is that the human animal is born relatively unfinished and thus has to undergo a protracted period of helplessness and dependence. This helplessness creates the initial situation of danger regarding fear of object loss, which in turn creates the human's need to be loved, which it never renounces.

The *phylogenetic factor* is inferred from the interruption in human sexual development of the latency period, whereas the sexual maturation of related animals proceeds uninterrupted. Freud believed that something momentous must have taken place in the history of the human species to bring about this situation and that its pathogenic importance is that most of the instinctual demands of infantile sexuality are treated as dangers to be guarded against by the ego. Furthermore, there is the danger that the sexual impulses of puberty will follow their infantile prototypes into repression.

The *psychological factor* involves three elements that together make for a pathogenic neurotic conflict:

1. *Frustration of sexual impulses* or the damming up of the sexual instinct by the ego. Repressions are especially likely to take place in infancy and early childhood, when the ego is underdeveloped and feeble in relation to the strength of the sexual impulses. Freud (1949: 113) observed: 'We recognize the essential precondition of neuroses in this lagging of ego development behind libidinal development'. The process of repression takes place under the influence of anxiety, in that the ego anticipates that satisfaction of the emerging sexual cathexis will lead to danger. In fact the ego allows an initial reproduction of the feared unpleasure. This feeling of anxiety brings the unpleasure–pleasure mechanism into operation and so causes the ego to repress the dangerous instinctual impulse. By the act of repression, however, the ego has renounced a portion of its organization and the repressed instinctual impulse remains inaccessible to its influence.

2. *Transformation of frustrated sexual impulses into neurotic symptoms.* Frustrated sexual impulses may not disappear, instead getting transformed into neurotic symptoms. Freud saw symptoms such as hysterical or conversion symptoms as the substitute satisfactions for the frustrated sexual instincts. Repression, however, does not always result in symptom formation. For instance, in a successful dissolution of the Oedipus complex the repressed sexual impulses may be destroyed, with their libido being put permanently to other uses.

3. *Inadequacy of previously used repressions.* While repressions may be effective during early childhood and the latency period, they may turn out to be inadequate with the reawakening and intensification of the sexual instincts at menarche and puberty. When this occurs the individual may experience an intense neurotic conflict with all its suffering. Without assistance in undoing its repressions, the ego will have little or no influence over the transformed instincts of the repressed id. Furthermore, the conflict is often heightened through an alliance of the id and super-ego against the ego.

Box 2.3   Examples of normal and neurotic development

Freud (1932/1973) gives as an example of normal and neurotic development the story of the caretaker's and the landlord's little daughters. When young, the two girls played games that took on a sexual character, including exciting each other's genitals. These experiences awakened sexual impulses that afterwards found expression in masturbation.

Normal development
The caretaker's daughter, unscarred by her early sexual activity which she regarded as natural and harmless, took a lover and became a mother.

(Continued)

Box 2.3 (Continued)

Neurotic development
While still a child the landlord's daughter, as a result of education, got the idea that she had done something wrong. She turned into an intelligent and high-minded girl who renounced her sexuality and whose subsequent neurosis precluded her from marrying. While consciously unaware of her sexual impulses, unconsciously these impulses were still attached to her experiences with the caretaker's daughter. Freud observes that, owing to the higher moral and intellectual development of her ego, she came into conflict with the demands of her sexuality.

Maintenance

Freud considered that neuroses are acquired only during early childhood, up to the age of six, even though the symptoms of the neurotic conflict may not appear until much later. He acknowledged the truth of the common assertion that the child is psychologically father of the man or woman. Neurotic people, despite their suffering, are unable to heal their disordered egos and thus their misery is maintained. The reason for this is that, by definition, the significant repressions made by their weak childhood egos are unconscious. Thus their egos pay the price of their defensive operations by not having conscious access to the material through which the neurotic conflict might be resolved. Neurotic people's egos are weakened by their repressions and their personality functioning is impaired by psychical energy being used in harmful defensive anti-cathexes. As long as the repressions continue, so do the conditions for the formation of neurotic symptoms through the rechannelling of frustrated libidinous impulses.

Freud (1936) also saw neurotic disturbances as being perpetuated by the primary and secondary gains that they provide. Primary gain is intrapsychic and is the main means of reinforcing or perpetuating psychological symptoms. Acknowledging the anxiety and distress caused by the symptom is more bearable than recognizing one's own forbidden wishes. Secondary gain refers to gaining the advantages of having an established symptom, for instance getting extra attention because of it.

In a broader sense, maintenance of neurosis results from the unsatisfactory way in which society tries to regulate sexual matters. Freud considered that what is described as morality, or the group super-ego, requires a bigger sacrifice of libidinal impulses than is necessary or desirable. He found it impossible to side with conventional sexual morality and considered that anyone with real self-knowledge would be protected against the dangers of morality, while possibly adopting a lifestyle different from the conventions of their society.

Therapy

Therapeutic goals

The goals of psychoanalysis are threefold:

1. *a less constricted id* – the freeing of impulse;
2. *a stronger ego* – the strengthening of reality-based ego functioning, including widening its perceptions so that it appropriates more of the id; and
3. *a more humane super-ego* – the alteration of the contents of the super-ego so that it represents humane rather than punitive moral standards.

A definition of a neurotic is someone who is incapable of enjoyment and efficiency. To be capable of enjoyment neurotics require the ability to deploy their libido onto real objects instead of transforming it into symptoms. To live efficiently the ego needs to have the energy of the libido at its disposal rather than wasting energy in warding off libidinous impulses through repression. Furthermore, people's super-egos need to be such as to allow them libidinal expression and the efficient use of their egos.

Freud considered psychoanalytic treatment effective for a number of nervous diseases, such as hysteria, anxiety states and obsessional neurosis. Since the alliance between the analyst and the client's ego is a mutual one, the client's ego needs to have retained a minimum degree of coherence or reality orientation. This is not to be expected with psychotics, with whom, therefore, psychoanalysis is contraindicated.

Process of therapy

Freud saw the practice of psychoanalysis as having three main parts:

1. Inducing clients' weakened egos to participate in the intellectual work of interpretation to fill in the gaps of their mental resources and transfer to their analysts the authority of their super-egos;
2. Stimulating clients' egos to struggle against each of the id's demands and to defeat the resistances arising in connection with them; and
3. Restoring order to clients' egos 'by detecting material and impulses which have forced their way in from the unconscious' (Freud, 1949: 77). Such material is both traced back to its origin and exposed to criticism.

Psychoanalysis is a process of re-educating the ego. Repressions were instituted when clients' egos were weak. However, now not only have clients' egos grown stronger, but they possess allies in analysts. Methods by which analysts help weakened egos to lift their repressions, gain insight and make realistic decisions are discussed below. The pathogenic conflicts of neurotics are different from normal mental conflicts because of the ego's weakness relative to the other mental agencies.

Classical psychoanalytic therapy often involves at least four sessions a week with each session lasting for a minimum of 45 minutes. A course of psychoanalytic therapy may last for several years (Arlow, 2005). Freud considered that ultimately the success of psychoanalysis depended upon the quantitative relationship between the amount of energy analysts can mobilize in clients to their advantage in comparison with the amount of energy of the forces working against them.

The therapeutic relationship

As I write this section, I am looking at pictures of Freud's consulting rooms in Vienna and Hampstead. In each, there is a couch that has no back, but one end is raised so that the client's head may comfortably rest there. Cushions are placed at back of the couch against the wall. A middle-eastern rug hangs on the wall just above the couch, which itself has a thick middle-eastern cover. Freud's tub chair facing into the room is placed against the wall behind the raised part of the couch. The nature and positioning of the furniture in psychoanalysis indicates that this is going to be a relationship far removed from normal social interaction: for example, the client cannot see the therapist who, in turn, cannot directly see the client's face.

Seated behind the couch and thus physically keeping out of the way, the analyst encourages the client to say whatever comes into her or his mind without censorship. A major feature of the therapeutic relationship is the development of transference, which is discussed later.

As well as the positioning of client and therapist, a number of other features of the therapist–client relationship aim to encourage clients to reveal the intimate secrets of their minds. Therapists remain anonymous in terms of their own personal life and views. Furthermore, any form of immature personal gratification from the therapeutic relationship is forbidden; for instance, meeting the therapist's own needs for friendship and affection. In addition, confidentiality is strictly observed.

Analysts keep their relationships with clients formal. At the same time they are intensely involved with helping clients gain insight, compassionate, yet emotionally detached. As they spend long periods quietly listening, they attempt to ensure that the patient's thoughts and associations do not represent responses to external stimulation or manipulation. Much power resides with analysts who, like Freud, decide which interpretations are valid and when and how their clients are resisting the therapeutic process.

The practical aspects of the therapeutic contract are strictly regulated. For example, clients are expected to adhere to a fixed schedule of appointments and fees. However, even Freud had problems with bad debts, one of which contributed to the following slip of the tongue and possibly reveals the unconscious fulfilment of a wish. Freud (1901/1960) reported repeatedly addressing a patient Mrs James, who was refusing to pay for her treatment, as Mrs Smith, who paid her fees promptly.

Therapeutic interventions

Free association

A basic pact lies at the heart of analytic relationships. Freud stated: 'The patient's sick ego promises us the most complete candor ... we, on the other hand, assure him of the strictest discretion and put at his service our experience in interpreting material that has been influenced by the unconscious' (1949: 63). The fundamental rule for clients is that of free association. Clients must tell their analysts everything that occurs to them, even if it is disagreeable or if it seems meaningless. As far as possible, clients are encouraged to put their self-criticism out of action and share all their thoughts, feelings, ideas, memories and their associations. The object of free association is to help lift repressions by making unconscious material conscious.

Resistance

Free association is not really free, in that clients associate within the context of the analytic situation. Thus everything that occurs to them has some reference to that situation and they are likely to resist reproducing the repressed material. At its simplest level, resistance involves intentionally not adhering to the fundamental rule. Even if this level of resistance is overcome, resistance will find less obvious means of expression. The client's ego is fearful of potential unpleasure caused by exploring material that it has repressed in the unconscious. The ego protects itself from the repressed id by means of anti-cathexes. The more threatening the repressed material is, the more tenaciously the ego clings to its anti-cathexes, and the more remote are clients' associations from the unconscious material that their analysts seek.

Freud described all the forces that oppose the work of recovery as clients' resistances. He outlined five kinds of resistance.

1. The repression resistance described above;
2. The transference resistance mentioned next;
3. The resistance to foregoing the gain from illness;

4. The resistance of the id, which may resist a change in the direction of its satisfaction and need to 'work through' to a new mode of satisfaction;
5. The resistance, emanating from the super-ego, of the unconscious sense of guilt or need for punishment which resists any success through analysis. Clients must remain ill for they deserve no better. This is the most powerful kind of resistance and the one analysts most dread.

The struggle to overcome resistances is the main work of psychoanalysis and this part of analytic treatment cannot easily be hurried. Forces helping analysts to overcome resistances are clients' needs for recovery, any intellectual interest they may have in the analytic process and, most important, their positive transferences with their analysts.

Transference

From early in his career Freud attached great importance to his relationships with clients. He discovered that clients perceive their analysts as reincarnations of important figures from their childhoods and transfer onto them moderate to intense feelings and emotions appropriate to these earlier models. Freud speaks of transference-love and observes that this love is ambivalent, being a mixture of affection with a reverse side of hostility, exclusiveness and jealousy. The transference represents a development of the original neurosis into a transference neurosis in relation to the analyst.

The transference has at least three advantages.

1. It may start by being positive, which helps analysts, since their clients work to please them. The weak ego can become stronger and the client achieves gains out of love for the analyst;
2. When clients put analysts in the places of their fathers or mothers, they give them access to the power their super-egos have over their egos. Analysts as new super-egos can use their power for 'a sort of *after-education* of the neurotic' (Freud, 1949: 67). They can remedy earlier errors in parental education. However, analysts need always respect their clients' need for independence;
3. In the transference clients reproduce, rather than just remember, important parts of their life history. They act out, in front of their analysts, mental attitudes and defensive reactions connected with their neuroses.

Almost invariably the transference becomes negative and hostile, thus turning into a resistance. The onset of the negative transference is connected with analysts frustrating their clients by being unwilling to satisfy their erotic demands towards them. The revival of pathogenic conflicts gives analysts access to much repressed material, insight into which helps to strengthen their clients' egos. Analysis of the transference has to be continued many times and in many different ways. Working through is a process that consists of repetition, elaboration and amplification. Often the experience of successful analysis of transference stimulates recall of some important event or fantasy that in turn illuminates the nature of the transference.

Handling the transference is a critical skill of analysts, who must again and again show clients the prototype of their feelings in their childhoods. Analysts need to take care that transferences do not get out of hand. They can forewarn clients of this possibility and be alert to early signs of this happening. They can encourage clients not to act out their transferences outside of the analytic setting.

Interpretation

Interpretations are constructions or explanations. They can focus both on what has happened to clients and been forgotten and on what is now happening to clients without their understanding it. Interpretation is the means by which material that is repressed and unconscious is transformed into preconscious material and consciousness.

Analysts employ interpretation not only to understand the impulses of the id, but also to help clients to gain insight into the defensive mechanisms and resistances that their egos use both to cope with the repressed material and to thwart the analytic endeavour. Part of the work of interpretation consists of filling in memory gaps. Analysts interpret the impulses that have become subject to repression and the objects to which they have become attached with the aim of helping clients to replace these repressions by acts of judgment appropriate to their present-day rather than to their childhood situations. The analyst works with the client's ego, encouraging it to overcome resistances and to take control of hitherto repressed libidinal energy. Unconscious impulses are exposed to criticism by being traced back to their origin.

The material for interpretation is obtained from a number of sources. These include the clients' free associations, parapraxes or slips of the tongue, dreams and their transference relationships with their analysts. Analysts need to clearly distinguish between their own and their clients' knowledge. Appropriate timing of interpretations is very important, since if attempted at the wrong time, they meet with resistance. Therefore clients need to be very near to the moment of insight before analysts make interpretations. The closer interpretations are to the details of what has been forgotten, the easier it is for clients to accept them. The later stages of psychoanalysis involve a working through by repeated interpretations, and this is often the most difficult and frequently an incomplete part of analysis.

Interpretation of dreams

Interpreting dreams represents an important – sometimes the most important – part of the analyst's work. When Freud's clients were told to communicate to him every idea or thought that occurred in relation to a particular topic, among other things they told him their dreams. This taught Freud that 'a dream can be inserted into the psychical chain that has to be traced backwards in the memory from a pathological idea' (Freud, 1900/1976: 175). During sleep the ego reduces its repression and thus unconscious material becomes conscious in the shape of dreams. Freud saw dreams as wish fulfilments, the disguised fulfilment of repressed wishes. However, even in sleep the ego still retains some censorship over repressed material and the latent dream thoughts are distorted so as to make the manifest dream content less threatening. Dreams, in fact, are compromises between repressed id impulses and the defensive operation of the ego.

The interpretation of a dream involves understanding the latent dream thoughts that are disguised by the process of dream work. Elements of dream work involve condensing the latent dream thoughts into much smaller dream content, displacing the psychical intensity between elements, and using symbolism. Frequently, symbols in dreams represent sexual material. For instance, all elongated objects, such as sticks, tree trunks, knives, daggers and umbrellas may stand for the penis. The opening of an umbrella may symbolize an erection. Boxes, cases, chests, cupboards and ovens represent the uterus. A dream of going through a suite of rooms is a brothel or harem dream. Not all dream symbols are sexual: for instance, emperors or empresses may represent parents.

Freud prepared clients in two ways for working with their dreams. First, he asked them to increase the attention that they paid to their psychical perceptions. To enhance this, it was advantageous that they 'lie in a restful attitude' (1900/1976: 175). However, he soon abandoned also stressing that they need to shut their eyes. Second, he explicitly insisted that clients abandon all criticism of the thoughts that they perceived (a feature of free association). Clients differed in the ease with which they could adopt the required mental attitude and abandon their critical functions.

Box 2.4 provides a brief illustration, taken from *The Interpretation of Dreams,* of Freud interpreting one of his own dreams (Freud, 1900/1976: 180–99). Dream interpretation can be a complex, multi-layered and lengthy process. For example, Freud took about 20 pages to describe the interpretation of the dream illustrated in Box 2.4. Also, in his famous study of Dora, a case of hysteria, Freud's (1905/1963) descriptions of his interpretations of her first and second dreams take up about 30 and 20 pages respectively.

Box 2.4   An example of dream interpretation

The context
Freud had been giving psychoanalytic treatment to Irma, a good friend of his and his family's. The treatment was partially successful in that Irma was relieved of her hysterical anxiety, but without losing all somatic symptoms. One day Freud received a visit from a junior colleague called Otto, who had been staying with Irma and her family at a country resort. Otto answered Freud's enquiry about Irma with:

Box 2.4 (Continued)

'She's better, but not quite well'. Freud was annoyed with Otto's words, detecting reproof in them. That evening he wrote out Irma's case history with the idea of giving it to Dr M, a common friend.

The dream
The following night or morning, Freud had a dream, which he noted down as soon as he awoke. The dream involved Irma, Otto, Dr M, and a friend called Leopold. Without going into great detail, in the dream Otto was implicated in infecting Irma by giving her an injection with a syringe that was probably unclean.

The interpretation of the dream
The conclusion of Freud's interpretation of his dream was that, in it, he was not responsible for the persistence of Irma's present pains, rather Otto was. Freud observed of his dream: 'Thus its content was the fulfillment of a wish and its motive was a wish' (1900/1976: 196).

Case material

Accounts of analyses by other therapists lose the flavour of how Freud actually worked. Freud published few case studies, possibly because he feared breaking confidentiality. Those wishing to become familiar with how Freud worked are encouraged to read one of more of the following case studies:

- *Dora* was an 18-year-old woman. Freud's analysis revealed her hysterical symptoms as manifestations of repressed sexual impulses that included her homosexual love for an older admirer's wife (Freud, 1905/1963);
- *Little Hans,* five years old, feared a horse would bite him if he went out into the street. Freud helped Hans's doctor father treat him and his analysis demonstrated that Hans's fear expressed phallic phase dynamics, including the Oedipus complex and castration anxiety (Freud, 1909/1955);
- *Schreber* was an appeals court judge who wrote an account of his illness that was diagnosed as paranoia. Based only on Schreber's written account, Freud's analysis demonstrated how Schreber's paranoid delusions were related to his latent homosexuality (Freud, 1911/1958);
- *Wolf Man,* in his 20s, had contracted gonorrhoea, which in turn triggered castration anxiety. Freud's analysis established the relationship between the castration anxiety and a frightening childhood dream involving wolves that followed real or imagined observation of parental sexual intercourse (Freud, 1918/1955).

Further developments

Contemporary psychoanalysis

In 1913, the British Psychoanalytic Society was founded under the leadership of Ernest Jones. The Society has three distinct groups: the Contemporary Freudians, the Kleinians and the Independents. The term Contemporary Freudians was adopted some 20 years ago to reflect developments in psychoanalysis that have transpired since Freud's death. There are, however, still some psychoanalysts who practise in a more traditional Freudian style.

What are some features of a contemporary approach based on Freud? Freud's approach to how the mind works was deterministic in that all events were determined by a sequence of cause, nothing was accidental and links could be traced to early experiences. Contemporary Freudians, such as the Sandlers (Sandler and Sandler, 1984), distinguish between the past unconscious, which stores non-conscious knowledge of formative interpersonal relationships and is not directly accessible in the form of autobiographical memories, and the present unconscious. The present unconscious refers to here-and-now unconscious strivings and responses and, though they are frequently subject to censorship before becoming conscious, its contents may become so. The actual experiences that contribute to the templates of our behaviour were set down very early in our lives and thought to be irretrievable.

Freud stressed psychic determinism, a 'one-person psychology' that stressed that clients' functioning was exclusively based on intra-psychic factors contributed to by early childhood experiences. Contemporary Freudians regard a client's functioning as not completely determined by early experiences. They regard it as difficult to be very specific about the long-term consequences of childhood events. Instead, they espouse what is termed a 'two-person psychology' that reflects the importance of the attachment developed throughout life and how these contribute to changes in how clients relate based on initial family experiences.

Freud's idea of transference was that clients transfer onto the analyst feelings and attitudes that represent a repetition and displacement of feelings and reactions that related to significant figures in early childhood. Thus the transference is a repetition of earlier relationships. Contemporary Freudians acknowledge that the intensity of the therapist–client relationship arouses latent emotional experiences. However, what transpires between clients and their therapists is regarded as a new experience that has been influenced by past rather than just a repetition of old experience. There has also been a shift in the way countertransference, involving the therapist's feelings about and reactions to the client, is regarded. Instead of the Freudian view that countertransference is something that interferes with analysis, countertransference feelings and responses by therapists can be constructively used to understand a client's unconscious communications. Thus, they can act as direct guides for analytic interpretations of current material (Lemma, 2002).

Freud (1905/1962) viewed dream interpretation as the royal road to the unconscious. Freudian psychoanalysts now stress the importance of dreams less. When working with dreams, psychoanalysts ask clients to associate hidden or latent elements of dreams so that their latent meaning can be accessed. Interpretations of dreams are based on an understanding of the meaning of clients' personal associations to them.

Contemporary Freudians believe that understanding how clients construe their early experiences, the meaning they attach to them, is more important than finding out what actually happened in the past. This is in line with contemporary research suggesting that autobiographical memory is unreliable. Thus change no longer stems from accessing repressed memories. Lemma writes: 'Rather change occurs through understanding the vicissitudes of the new relationship created between the patient and the therapist, which is informed by the past and thus gives some clues as to the model that the patient operates from' (2002: 37). Especially important in the practice of contemporary Freudian psychoanalysis is the interpretation of transference. Though there is some variation in emphasis, contemporary Freudians tend to view therapy's outcome as being related to the successful re-evaluation of patterns of relating which become accessible through the analysis and interpretation of transference phenomena.

Freud as a stimulus to others

Arlow (2005) observes that it is almost impossible to grasp the extent to which psychoanalysis has changed since Freud's death in 1939. Even within Freud's lifetime, Jung had broken away from psychoanalysis to develop analytical therapy and Adler was developing a form of analysis based on his individual psychology. The Austrian-born Melanie Klein, who was to spend most of her professional life in Britain, developed the so-called English school of psychoanalysis. Klein's position emphasized the importance of primitive fantasies of loss (the depressive position) and persecution (the paranoid position) in the pathogenesis of mental illness (Klein, 1932, 1960). Anna Freud conducted long-term studies of childhood development and wrote *The Ego and the Mechanisms of Defence* (1936), an outstanding contribution to the psychoanalytic literature.

British psychiatrists Winnicott (1953) and Bowlby (1958) also made significant contributions underlining the importance of the child's early attachment to the mother and the emergence of a sense of self. Winnicott emphasized the continuing influence of the psychological experience of the young child at the stage where the distinction between self and object is not clearly defined and where representations of the external world for a period constitute a stage that he termed the stage of the *transitional object*. Winnicott stressed how subsequent psychological experience demonstrated the role of the transitional object.

Other psychoanalytic approaches influenced by and, in some ways stemming from Freud's work, include Sullivan's (1953) interpersonal theory of psychiatry and Fromm's socially oriented work on both psychoanalysis and on understanding society (Fromm, 1955, 1995; Funk, 2000). More recently, a separate school of analysis known as *self psychology* owes much to the work of Kohut (1971) and Goldberg (1998). The above are just some of the many people who have developed psychoanalysis.

In varying degrees Freud has influenced humanistic and existential psychologists and psychiatrists. For example, points of contact with transactional analysis include the tripartite structure of personality and the importance of early experience. Furthermore, Rogers's concept of levels of awareness resembles Freud's idea of levels of consciousness. In addition, May and Yalom's version of existential dynamics, motivated by underlying death anxiety, also originates in psychoanalysis.

Psychoanalysis, based on the Freudian model, continues to develop and evolve. One stimulus for change is that problems tend to alter with the times: for instance, hysteria and conversion symptoms are less frequent now, but there is an increase in clients suffering from masochistic character disorders and from narcissistic neuroses (Arlow, 2005). Often clients complain of inner emptiness, lack of goals and of an inability to make lasting love relationships.

Some analysts have developed forms of brief psychoanalytic therapy. Reasons for brief psychoanalysis include hoped-for cost-effectiveness; the fact that governments, health insurers and most private individuals cannot afford long-term therapy; and to meet the pressing need to treat more people. However, brief psychoanalytic therapy is essentially different from Freud's version of psychoanalysis described in this chapter. Group psychoanalytic therapy is also offered. However, group psychoanalysis also does not strictly follow from Freud's approach, but reflects an integration of different strands of psychoanalytic thought.

Those readers wanting contemporary information are referred to the British Psychoanalytic Society's *International Journal of Psycho-Analysis*, the American Psychoanalytic Association's *Journal of the American Psychoanalytic Association*, the British-published *Psychodynamic Counselling* and the American-published *Psychoanalytic Quarterly*.

Review and personal questions

Review questions

1. How did Freud view the instincts?
2. Describe each of Freud's three levels of consciousness.
3. How did Freud describe the id, the ego and the super-ego and their functions?

4. Why is psychoanalysis often referred to as presenting a dynamic view of psychology?
5. Describe each stage and phase of a person's sexual development.
6. What is the function of defence mechanisms? Illustrate with specific examples.
7. Describe Freud's views on the development and maintenance of neurosis.
8. In psychoanalysis, what is meant by the term resistance and why is it so important?
9. In psychoanalysis, what is meant by the term transference and why is it so important?
10. Describe as best as you can how Freud approached the interpretation of a dream.
11. What are some developments in psychoanalysis since Freud's death that go under the heading of Contemporary Psychoanalysis?

Personal questions

1. Can you think of material or events in your life that you might view as evidence for unconscious mental processes? If so, provide examples (e.g. dreams).
2. What are some of the significant influences that contributed to the formation of your super-ego? With what moral guidelines, if any, do you consider that your super-ego restricts you from the realistic pursuit of pleasure?
3. Are you aware that your ego uses defence mechanisms to ward off anxiety? If so, what are they? Do you consider that your use of defence mechanisms is normal or neurotic?
4. What do you consider the relevance of Freud's ideas on the interpretation of dreams to interpreting your own dreams?
5. What is the relevance of Freud's and contemporary Freudian's work to understanding your life?
6. How have Freud and contemporary Freudians influenced the way you think about and practise counselling and therapy?

Annotated bibliography

Freud, S. (1900/1976) *The Interpretation of Dreams*. Harmondsworth: Penguin.
This book is Freud's major work. In it he reviews the scientific literature about dreams, demonstrates his method of interpreting dreams, and discusses dreams as fulfilments of wishes, distortion in dreams, the material and sources of dreams, dreamwork, and the psychology of the dream process. The present translation is based on the reprint of the eighth edition (1930), the last published during Freud's life.

Freud, S. (1905/1962) *Three Contributions to the Theory of Sex*. New York: E.P. Dutton.
This book is Freud's major statement on the nature and development of human sexuality.
The three contributions are entitled: the sexual aberrations, infantile sexuality and the
transformations of puberty. Apart from *The Interpretation of Dreams*, this was the only other
book that Freud kept more or less systematically up to date.

Freud, S. (1949) *An Outline of Psychoanalysis*. New York: W.W. Norton.
Written just before Freud's death, this book provides an excellent concise introduction to
psychoanalysis. The book consists of three parts: the mind and its workings; the practical
task; and the theoretical yield.

Jones, E. (1963) *The Life and Work of Sigmund Freud*. Edited and abridged in one volume by
    Lionel Trilling and Steven Marcus. New York: Anchor Books. Also available in a Penguin
    edition.
Written in three volumes by a close associate, this book is the definitive biography of Freud.
It records the main facts of Freud's life and relates his personality and life experiences to the
development of his ideas. In addition, the book traces the history of the psychoanalytic
movement during Freud's lifetime.

References and further reading

Arlow, J.A. (2005) 'Psychoanalysis', in R.J. Corsini and D. Wedding (eds), *Current Psycho-
    therapies* (7th edn). Belmont, CA: Thomson Brooks/Cole. pp. 15–51.
Bowlby, J. (1958) 'The nature of the child's ties to the mother', *International Journal of
    Psychoanalysis, 52*: 137–44.
Freud, A. (1936) *The Ego and the Mechanisms of Defence*. London: Karnac.
Freud, S. (1900/1976) *The Interpretation of Dreams*. Harmondsworth: Penguin.
Freud, S. (1901/1960) *Psychopathology of Everyday Life*. London: Hogarth Press.
Freud, S. (1905/1962) *Three Contributions to the Theory of Sex*. New York: E.P. Dutton.
Freud, S. (1905/1963) *Dora: An Analysis of a Case of Hysteria*. New York: Collier Books.
Freud, S. (1909/1955) 'Analysis of a phobia in a five-year-old boy', in S. Freud, *Standard
    Edition of the Complete Works of Sigmund Freud* (Vol. 10). London: Hogarth Press.
Freud, S. (1911/1958) 'Psycho-analytic notes on an autobiographical account of a case of
    paranoia (dementia paranoides)', in S. Freud, *Standard Edition of the Complete Works of
    Sigmund Freud* (Vol. 12). London: Hogarth Press.
Freud, S. (1918/1955) 'From the history of an infantile neurosis', in S. Freud, *Standard Edition
    of the Complete Works of Sigmund Freud* (Vol. 17). London: Hogarth Press.
Freud, S. (1920/1961) *Beyond the Pleasure Principle*. London: Hogarth Press.
Freud, S. (1921/1959) *Group Psychology and the Analysis of the Ego*. London: Hogarth Press.
Freud, S. (1923/1962) *The Ego and the Id*. London: Hogarth Press.
Freud, S. (1926/1964) *The Question of Lay Analysis*. New York: Anchor Books.
Freud, S. (1930/1962) *Civilization and Its Discontents*. New York: W.W. Norton.
Freud, S. (1932/1973) *New Introductory Lectures on Psychoanalysis*. Harmondsworth: Penguin.
Freud, S. (1935) *An Autobiographical Study*. London: Hogarth Press.
Freud, S. (1936) *The Problem of Anxiety*. New York: W.W. Norton. Originally published in
    1926 under the title *Inhibitions, Symptoms and Anxiety*.
Freud, S. (1937/1950) 'Analysis terminable and interminable', in S. Freud, *Collected Papers*
    (Vol. 5). London: Hogarth Press.

Freud, S. (1949) *An Outline of Psychoanalysis*. New York: W.W. Norton. Originally published posthumously in 1940.

Freud, S. (1953/73) *Standard Edition of the Complete Works of Sigmund Freud*. London: Hogarth Press.

Freud, S. and Breuer, J. (1895/1956) *Studies on Hysteria*. London: Hogarth Press.

Fromm, E. (1955) *The Sane Society*. New York: Holt, Rinehart & Winston.

Fromm, E. (1959) *Sigmund Freud's Mission*. London: George Allen & Unwin.

Fromm, E. (1995) *The Essential Fromm: Life Between Having and Being*. London: Constable.

Funk, R. (2000) *Erich Fromm: His Life and Ideas*. London: Continuum.

Goldberg, A. (1998) 'Self-psychology since Kohut', *Psychoanalytic Quarterly, 67*: 240–55.

Hall, C.S. (1954) *A Primer of Freudian Psychology*. New York: Mentor Books.

Jacobs, M. (1999) *Psychoanalytic Counselling in Action* (2nd edn). London: Sage.

Jones, E. (1963) *The Life and Work of Sigmund Freud*. Edited and abridged in one volume by Lionel Trilling and Steven Marcus. New York: Anchor Books. Also available in a Penguin edition.

Klein, M. (1932) *The Psychoanalysis of Children*. London: Hogarth Press.

Klein, M. (1960) *Our Adult World and Its Roots in Infancy*. London: Tavistock.

Kohut, H. (1971) *The Analysis of the Self. Monograph Series of the Psychoanalytic Study of the Child (No. 4)*. New York: International Universities Press.

Lemma, A. (2002) 'Psychodynamic therapy: the Freudian approach', in W. Dryden (ed.), *Handbook of Individual Therapy* (4th edn). London: Sage. pp. 16–46.

Sandler, J. and Sandler, A.M. (1984) 'The past unconscious, the present unconscious: an interpretation of the transference', *Psychonalytic Enquiry, 4*: 367–99.

Sullivan, H.S. (1953) *The Interpersonal Theory of Psychiatry*. New York: W.W. Norton.

Winnicott, D.W. (1953) 'Transitional objects and transitional phenomena: a study of the first not-me possession', *International Journal of Psychoanalysis, 34*: 89–97.

jung's analytical therapy | 3

Introduction

Sigmund Freud and Carl Jung's lives overlapped, for a time they were close associates, and what Jung called his 'analytical psychology' has some of its roots in Freudian psychoanalysis. Nevertheless, Jung developed a very different psychodynamic theory and practice to that of Freud. In particular, Jung and Freud diverged in their views of the unconscious. While Freud emphasized sexual repression, Jung considered that, at its deepest level, the unconscious consisted of archetypes, or inborn possibilities for psychological apprehension and representation, which may then be expressed in universal myths and symbols.

In 1906, Jung and Freud became friends and intellectual companions. Freud admired Jung's brilliance and regarded him as his crown prince and heir. In addition, Freud thought that, by having Jung prominent in the movement, he might avoid the risk of psychoanalysis being viewed as a mainly Jewish activity. Jung had gone through a troubled relationship with his own father and was fiercely intellectually independent. It was an error of judgment on both men's part to think that any 'father–son' relationship could be maintained. In 1913, Jung and Freud split bitterly never to meet again in the remaining 26 years of Freud's life.

Carl Gustav Jung (1875–1961)

In July 1875, Carl Gustav Jung was born in Kesswil, a small village by Lake Constance in north-east Switzerland, the only surviving son of his parents who had lost two previous boys in infancy. Jung was named after his paternal grandfather who, in 1822, had moved from Germany to become professor of surgery at the University of Basel. Jung's father was a Swiss Reform Church pastor and his mother was the daughter of a well-established Basel family. When Jung was nine, the family was completed by the birth of his sister.

Jung was an introverted, sensitive, solitary and lonely child. His parents, Paul and Emilie, had a troubled marriage and, in 1878, they separated temporarily and his mother spent some time in a mental hospital. During his childhood Jung suffered from his mother's depressive invalidism and critical tongue.

However, he also admired his mother and could enjoy her companionship and cooking. Jung had to contend with his father's irritability, partly connected with his agonizing over his religious faith. Nevertheless in the autobiography compiled at the end of his life, Jung (1961) refers to his 'dear and generous father', who never tyrannized over him.

The earliest dream Jung remembered was when he was between three and four. He had a rich inner life of dreams, fantasies and thoughts about the world. Aged 10, at the end of a ruler Jung carved a manikin about two inches long with frock coat, top hat and shiny black boots. He placed the manikin and an oblong blackish stone from the Rhine in a case and took it to the attic. Whenever Jung felt hurt or stressed he would think of the manikin and, from time to time, visit it in the forbidden attic. Jung regarded this manikin episode, which lasted about a year, as the conclusion of his childhood.

In 1879, the Jungs had moved to Klein Hünigen, near Basel. Aged six Jung went to the local school and, at age 11, he was uprooted from his rustic schoolmates and sent to the Gymnasium at Basel. Jung hated mathematics, was exempted from drawing on the grounds of incapacity, and also loathed gymnastics. Regarding mathematics he writes: 'But my fear of failure and sense of smallness in face of the vast world around me created in me not only a dislike, but a kind of silent despair which completely ruined school for me' (1961: 45). For a time Jung suffered from fainting spells connected with school. He also saw himself as being two persons: a schoolboy who was less intelligent, hard-working and decent than many other boys, and an old man mistrustful of humans but close to nature, to dreams and to whatever God worked through him.

In reality, Jung was a highly intelligent student who, in 1895, passed his final examinations at the Gymnasium and entered the University of Basel Medical School. During medical school Jung suffered from financial worries, partly stemming from the death of his father in 1896. In 1900, he graduated equal first in his medical school class. His medical school thesis was on the psychological foundations of the occult. Jung chose to specialize in psychiatry, which provided a bridge between his scientific, humanities and psychological interests.

Shortly after graduation, he accepted a post at the Burgholzli Mental Hospital in Zurich. The Burgholzli's director was Eugen Bleuler, an expert on schizophrenia, whose influence Jung valued. In 1902, he spent several months studying at the Salpetrière Hospital in Paris with the famous psychiatrist, Pierre Janet. In 1905, in addition to his work at the Burgholzi, he became Lecturer in psychiatry at the University of Zurich and Senior Physician at the psychiatric clinic. He continued to lecture there until 1913. At the Burgholzli, as well as working with patients, Jung conducted research on word associations and the underlying psychological complexes indicated by how people responded. He also had a private practice which became so successful that, in 1909, he resigned from the Burgholzli. As mentioned, Jung also developed a relationship with Freud and became prominent in the psychoanalytic movement.

After his break with Freud, Jung went through a profound mid-life crisis which lasted from 1913 to 1918, and which took him to the edge of insanity. During much of this period of inner uncertainty and disorientation he continued seeing patients. He developed his ideas of the collective unconscious during this period of confrontation with his own unconscious. He writes:

> The years when I was pursuing my inner images were the most important in my life – in them everything essential was decided. It all began then; the later details are only supplements and clarifications of the material that burst forth from the unconscious, and at first swamped me. It was the *prima materia* for a lifetime's work. (1961: 225)

Jung was fond of women, who played a crucial role throughout his life. In 1903 he had married the extremely wealthy Emma Rauschenbach. Under Swiss law at the time Emma married Jung, husbands had complete access to their wives' money and could spend it as they wished without consent. In short, though Jung was always a hard worker, he was financially set up for life independent of his own endeavours.

Despite his wife's disapproval of his behaviour and his growing family, Jung was sexually attracted to other women, allegedly extending to intimate relationships with one or more of his patients, like Sabina Spielrein, though this has never been evidentially corroborated. An ex-patient, Toni Wolff, was able to be of special comfort to him during his near-psychotic period so much so that, in 1916, Jung persuaded Emma to accept her as part of a permanent domestic threesome. Probably Jung abandoned his philandering at this stage. He encouraged Emma to become a Jungian therapist and, eventually, Toni became one too.

After Jung returned to feeling more normal, there were a number of on-going and interweaving strands in his life. At his beautiful home by Lake Zurich, though not the warmest and most present of fathers, Jung engaged in family activities with his wife, four daughters and a son. In 1922 he bought some land at Bollingen, at the upper end of Lake Zurich, and, over the next 30 or so years, developed the 'Tower', a house he built for himself as a retreat from his family. While the family home was the territory of his wife, the only person Jung allowed to stay at Bollingen was Toni Wolff and, in later years, a companion-housekeeper.

Jung continued his large private practice, which he regarded as a valuable source of information for understanding the psyche. Most of Jung's clients were women, almost all were reasonably well off, and a minority were fabulously wealthy Americans, for instance one of John D. Rockefeller's daughters and a member of the Mellon banking family. Jung also continued his own inner journey, analysing his dreams, fantasies and visions.

Jung engaged in wide-ranging scholarly activities. In 1921 he published a large work on psychological types. As well as reading widely in philosophy, world literature, mythology, and astrology, he became increasingly interested in alchemy. He also conducted what might be called fieldwork, by visiting North Africa, Kenya and Uganda, the Pueblo Indians in North America, and India. Jung was immensely interested in the presence and universality of myths and symbols across cultures and in primitive as well as civilized cultures. Based on his scholarly researches, field trips, wide reading and professional and personal experiences, right up to his death Jung was a prolific author across a range of subjects including psychiatry and psychology, parapsychology, alchemy and religion.

Jung lectured extensively not only in the Germanic-, but in the English-speaking world. In 1909 he had gone with Freud to Clark University in Massachusetts, where both men received honorary doctorates, and he was to return to America repeatedly in the following 30 years. Jung was also an Anglophile and visited England many times, for example giving a notable series of lectures at the Tavistock Clinic in 1935. His honorary doctorates included those from Harvard and Oxford Universities. In addition, from the early 1930s, Jung regularly attended the annual Eranos conferences on Jungian studies. At these conferences, held on the estate at the northern end of Lake Maggiore of a wealthy woman who had built a conference hall especially for them, Jung tended to be lionized by the mostly female participants.

Intimations of Jung's mortality included a severe heart attack in 1944, the death of Toni Wolff in 1953, and his wife's death in 1955. Jung's companion-housekeeper during his final years was Ruth Bailey, an Englishwoman. On 6 June 1961 Jung died after a brief illness.

It is tempting when looking at pictures of Jung to view him as a gentle, spiritual, scholarly sage full of the milk of human kindness. Undoubtedly, Jung had many attractive features as well as a charismatic personality, especially for women. However, he was not without his shadow aspects. He held extreme right-wing Social Darwinist political views and strongly believed that different rules applied to 'beasts' and 'supermen' (McLynn, 1996). For various reasons, he strongly favoured the death penalty. Possibly somewhat anti-Semitic, Jung has been criticized for not speaking out loudly enough against the rise of Nazism. He could be domineering and hectoring at professional meetings and a domestic tyrant at home. Jung could also be a bile-laden person and his relationship with Freud became particularly bitter. In addition, he had been a philandering husband, conceivably including some clients among his lovers, though there is no real proof of this.

Like Freud, Jung was an ideas man with an amazing breadth of vision. Some of his ideas have stood the test of time in terms of becoming part of western psychological consciousness, for example the concepts of the collective unconscious and extraversion/introversion. In addition, Jung was the founder of an analytical approach to therapy that still claims many adherents.

Theory

Basic concepts

Psychology is first the science of consciousness and then the science of the products of the unconscious psyche. Jung used the term psyche to refer to the mind or soul. He distinguished between three psychic levels of consciousness. In addition, his was a dynamic psychology that paid attention to the distribution of psychic energy between the different psychic levels. Furthermore, Jung presented a typology of different personality types.

Structure of the psyche

Jung goes beyond distinguishing consciousness from unconsciousness to divide the latter into its personal and collective elements. Thus, the psyche's three levels are: (1) consciousness; (2) the personal unconscious; and (3) the collective unconscious. Though Jung did not wish to push the analogy too far, he saw consciousness like an island arising out of a vast sea of unconsciousness.

Consciousness

Jung observes: 'the child develops out of an originally unconscious, animal condition into consciousness, primitive at first, and then slowly becoming more civilized' (1981: 53). Consciousness is an intermittent phenomenon since people enter the unconscious every time they go to sleep. The conscious mind is narrow since it can only hold a few simultaneous contents at a given moment. Furthermore, consciousness is transitory and people can only get an awareness of the external world through a succession of conscious moments.

The *ego* is the indispensable centre of a person's consciousness. Sometimes Jung refers to it as the ego-complex. The ego gives a person a sense of identity and continuity and it has both external and internal tasks. Its external task is to provide a system of relationship between consciousness and the facts and data coming from the environment. Sensation, thinking, feeling and intuition are four functions by means of which it performs its ecto-psychic task. The ego's internal task is to provide a system of relationship between the contents of consciousness and the processes of the unconscious. Jung states: 'The ego is only a bit of consciousness that floats on an ocean of dark things. The dark things are the inner things' (1968: 21).

The personal unconscious

The contents of the personal unconscious are definitely of a personal origin. These contents fall into two main categories. First, there is material that lost its intensity because it was either forgotten or repressed. Second, there is material that never possessed sufficient intensity to reach consciousness but has somehow entered the psyche, for instance, some sense-impressions. There is nothing peculiar about the contents of the personal unconscious and its contents might just as well be conscious. People differ in regard to the contents of their personal unconscious – some are conscious of things that others are not.

Complexes are an important feature of the personal unconscious. Jung discovered the complex through his research on word associations, finding that complexes disturbed memory and produced blockages in the flow of associations. Complexes are accumulations of associations, sometimes of a traumatic nature, that possess strong emotional content. They are energy-filled constellations of psychic elements that have an archetypal core and erupt into consciousness, often in an autonomous way (Douglas, 2005).

The mother complex is an example of a complex. Jung considered that 'the mother always plays an active part in the origin of the disturbance, especially in infantile neuroses or in neuroses whose aetiology undoubtedly dates back to early childhood' (1982: 113). Typical effects of the mother complex on the son are homosexuality, Don Juanism and, sometimes, impotence. In daughters the mother complex can lead to an exaggeration of the feminine side of personality or its neglect. Other examples of complexes include those connected with inferiority, sex, aesthetic beauty and money.

The collective unconscious

Unlike Freud, who saw the unconscious as a receptacle for things that were repressed, Jung considered the deeper layers of the unconscious lose their uniqueness as they retreat further and further from consciousness. At its deepest levels the unconscious is a vast collective and universal historical storehouse whose contents belong to mankind in general. While the contents of the personal unconscious owe their existence to personal experience, the contents of the collective unconscious have never been in consciousness, but owe their existence to heredity.

Archetypes are inborn possibilities or patterns for representation. Jung borrowed the term archetype from St Augustine. He observes: 'Whereas the personal unconscious consists for the most part of *complexes*, the content of the collective unconscious is made up essentially of *archetypes*' (1976a: 60). Similar to instinctive patterns for action, archetypes provide instinctive patterns for mental activity. Archetypes are 'primordial images' and 'primordial thoughts' rather than the representations of the images or thoughts themselves. For example, well-known motifs appear in myths, fairy tales, legends and folklore across a range of cultures and historical periods. Such motifs include the hero, the redeemer, the dragon, the mother, the wise old man and the descent into the cave. Archetypes are evolutionary predispositions or potentials for such motifs rather than the forms in which the contents become expressed.

Symbols are the images by means of which archetypes are expressed. Jung distinguished between a sign and a symbol. If the image denotes a known thing it is a sign. A symbol is an intuitive way of knowing the not fully knowable. Symbolic images express the best possible formulation of a relatively unknown thing, which for that reason cannot be more clearly or characteristically represented. For example, a triangle with a bare eye enclosed in it is so meaningless that it conjures up a symbolic interpretation.

Archetypes important in shaping the development of personality include the persona, the anima and animus, the shadow and the self.

The persona   The persona is a concept derived from the mask worn by actors in antiquity. At one level, the persona is the individual's system of adaptation or way of coping with the world. At a different level, the persona is not just an individual mask, but a mask of the collective psyche, 'a mask that *feigns individuality*, making others and oneself believe that one is an individual, whereas one is simply acting out a role through which the collective psyche speaks' (Jung, 1976b: 105).

The persona exists for reasons of personal convenience, but should not be confused with genuine individuality. The persona is exclusively concerned with relation to outer objects, an outer attitude. This outer attitude must be distinguished from an inner attitude, which is the relation to the subject or 'inner object' that is the unconscious.

In reality, individuals may have more than one persona, for example wearing different masks at work and home. Furthermore, each profession has its own characteristic persona. However, there is a danger that people become identified with their personas, for instance the professor with his textbook. Too rigid adherence to a persona can lead people to become alienated from the 'subject', the stirrings, feelings, thoughts and sensations that well up from their unconscious. Identifications with social roles are often fruitful sources of neuroses. Jung regarded it as essential for individuals to be able to distinguish themselves from their personas.

The anima and the animus   People are psychologically bisexual. In individuals, the smaller number of opposite sex genes appears to produce a corresponding opposite-sex character, which usually remains unconscious. The anima is the personification of the feminine nature in a man's unconscious, whereas the animus is the personification of the masculine nature in a woman's unconscious. Every man or woman carries within themselves an imprint or archetype of all the ancestral experiences of the opposite sex.

Jung thought that in its primary form the animus is composed of spontaneous, unpremeditated opinions that exercise a powerful influence on the woman's emotional life. Similarly, the anima is composed of feelings that thereafter distort and influence a man's understanding. He wrote: 'as the anima produces *moods*, so the animus produces *opinions*; and as the moods of a man issue from a shadowy background, so the opinions of a woman rest on equally unconscious prior assumptions' (1982: 95–6). Jung stressed the importance of people acknowledging their distinction, not only from their persona but from their anima or animus as well. The animus and anima should function as a bridge leading to the images of the collective unconscious. Both men and women should learn to acknowledge and appropriately express the opposite-sex characteristics of their personalities and avoid falsely projecting them onto others.

The shadow   The shadow archetype reflects the realm of humans' animal ancestors and, as such, comprises the whole historical aspect of the unconscious. For the most part, the shadow consists of inferior traits of personality that individuals refuse to acknowledge. Though Jung emphasized the darker aspects of the shadow, he acknowledged that it also displayed some good qualities, such as normal instincts, appropriate reactions, realistic insights and creative impulses. The shadow is compensatory to consciousness and its effects can be positive as well as negative.

In general, people do not like looking at the shadow side of themselves. However, with insight and goodwill, much of the shadow can be assimilated into the conscious personality without too much difficulty. Nevertheless, there are some unconscious projections from the shadow whose recognition meets the most obstinate resistance and thus prove almost impossible to influence. As a result, the shadow is not, with time, fully assimilated.

The self   The self is the central archetype, the archetype of order. The self, expressing the unity of personality as a whole, encompasses both conscious and unconscious components. The self is a super-ordinate construct to the ego that is restricted to being the focal point of the conscious mind. The ego is related to the self like a part to the whole. Jung considered that there was little hope of ever being able to reach even approximate consciousness of the self, given the huge and indeterminate amount of unconscious material that belongs to it.

The main symbol for the unity of the self archetype is the mandala. The word mandala (Sanskrit for 'circle') is a circular form that often contains a quaternity, symmetrical arrangements of the number four and its multiples. The self also appears in dreams, myths and fairytales in the figure of a super-ordinate personality, such as a king, hero, prophet or saviour.

Dynamics of the psyche

Psychodynamics refers to the activity and interrelation of the various parts of an individual's personality or psyche. More specifically, psychodynamics entails the generation and transfer of energy within the structure of the psyche. Jung's ideas on psychodynamics were influenced by his interest in and knowledge of physics, the branch of science dealing with the properties and interactions of matter and energy.

Psychic energy

Jung emphasized the concept of psychic energy, sometimes referred to as libido, as the psychic analogue of physical energy. All the instincts, including hunger, sex and aggression, are expressions of psychic energy. In physics there are different manifestations of energy, such as electricity, heat and light. The same situation occurs in psychology where energy can appear in various guises. Psychic energy is also provided from the external environment by way of one's senses and feelings. The psyche is a relatively closed energy system. Psychic energy derived from both internal and external sources is continually being shifted and redistributed among the structures of the psyche.

A psychic value is the amount of energy invested in a particular psychic element. When a person places a high value on something, such as an idea or feeling, this means that the idea or feeling exerts a particularly strong influence on them. Complexes, which by definition are strongly emotionally toned, are examples of mental elements with high psychic value.

Opposition

Jung observed: 'Among other things, the psyche appears as a dynamic process which rests on a foundation of antithesis, on a flow of energy between two poles' (1961: 383). Just as in physics all energy proceeds from opposition, so the psyche possesses an inner polarity that is an essential prerequisite for its aliveness. Tension and conflict arising from the clash of opposites are central to Jungian personality dynamics. Consciousness opposes unconsciousness, feminine opposes masculine, ego opposes shadow, and positive aspects of archetypal images oppose their negative elements.

Compensation

The function of compensation is to balance or adjust the energy distributed throughout the psyche. Compensation, for the most part, is an unconscious process that entails an inherent self-regulation of the psychic apparatus. The activity of the unconscious balances the one-sidedness produced by consciousness. Consciousness, because of its selectiveness and need for focus, is bound to become one-sided. As consciousness becomes more and more one-sided, the more antagonistic are the contents arising from the unconscious, so that there is a real opposition between the two. For the most part, unconscious compensation balances rather than opposes consciousness. For example, in dreams the unconscious supplies 'all those contents that are constellated by conscious situation but are inhibited by conscious selection, although a knowledge of them would be indispensable for complete adaptation' (Jung, 1971: 420).

Breakthrough of unconscious content

The energy of all unconscious contents, once they are activated, is normally insufficient to propel their content into consciousness. A lowering of energy in the conscious mind that allows unconscious material to break through into consciousness may come about in two ways. First, there may be a malfunctioning of the conscious mind. Just as primitive people can suffer from 'loss of soul', so can civilized people suffer from loss of initiative for no apparent reason. Carelessness, neglected duties, wilful outbursts of defiance can dam up energy so that certain quanta of it, no longer finding a conscious outlet, stream off into the unconscious. Here they activate other compensating contents, which can in turn start exerting a compulsive influence on the conscious mind. Jung (1966) illustrates this point with the common example of extreme neglect of duty combined with a compulsion neurosis.

The second way in which a loss of energy to the conscious mind may come about is through a 'spontaneous' activation of unconscious contents, which then react upon consciousness. During the incubation period of changes in personality, the new development draws off the loss of energy it needs from consciousness. For example, lowering of energy from the conscious mind takes place before the onset of psychosis and a fallow and quiet period precedes creative work. Jung observed: 'The remarkable potency of unconscious contents, therefore, always indicates a corresponding weakness in the conscious mind and its functions' (1966: 181). In the near-psychotic period of his life, Jung himself had to struggle with the heightened energy of his unconscious contents in relation to his conscious ego.

The transcendent function

The transcendent function is a psychological function similar to a mathematical function of the same name, which is made up of real and imaginary numbers. In face of the disturbing energy of the unconscious, Jung postulates a synthesizing process – the transcendent function – which can get rid of some of the separation between consciousness and unconsciousness.

The transcendent function is both a process and a method. Jung (1971) postulated that there are certain spontaneous *processes* in the unconscious that, by virtue of their symbolism, can compensate the defects in the conscious mind. In turn these reactions, usually manifested in dreams, are brought to conscious realization through the analytical *method*.

The confrontation of two opposed positions can generate a tension charged with energy which creates a living, third thing. Jung talked about the transcendent function manifesting itself as 'a movement out of the suspension between opposites, a living birth that leads to a new level of being, a new situation. The transcendent function manifests itself as a quality of conjoined opposites' (1976c: 298). By means of the transcendent function, consciousness is widened through the confrontation with previously unconscious contents.

The transcendent function is the means by which progress is made towards realizing the unfolding of the individual's original potential for wholeness. However, attaining integration at a new level of consciousness by means of the transcendent function does not always take place. Apart from insufficient skills on the part of therapists, there are many reasons why the synthesizing of opposites to create a new way of being may not take place. These reasons include people having insufficient intelligence to understand the procedure, lacking self-confidence, and being mentally and morally too lazy.

Psychological types

In 1921 Jung published his famous work entitled *Psychological Types*. Here he distinguished between attitude types, based on the habitual direction of an individual's interests, and function types, based on the individual's most differentiated function of psychological adaptation. For simplicity, here these are called attitudes and functions.

Attitudes: introversion and extraversion

The *introvert's* predominant, but not exclusive, conscious attitude is one in which the main interest is the withdrawal of psychic energy from the object as though to prevent the object from gaining power over her or him. The introvert thinks, feels and acts as though the subjective is what is most important and the object is of secondary importance. The introverted attitude type is characterized by an orientation in life that particularly values subjective psychic contents. Introverts tend to be reserved, inscrutable and rather shy people.

The *extravert's* predominant, but not exclusive, conscious attitude is characterized by concentration of interest on the external object. The extravert thinks, feels and acts as though the object were of most importance. This is done so directly and clearly that no doubt can remain about his or her dependence on the object. Extraverts tend to be open, friendly and sociable or they may quarrel with everybody. Nevertheless extraverts always relate to people in some way and in turn are affected by them.

In sum, introversion is characterized by interest in one's internal world and extraversion is characterized by interest in the external world. However, matters are not that simple, since a conscious extraverted attitude is compensated by an unconscious introverted attitude and a conscious introverted attitude is compensated by an extraverted unconscious attitude.

Functions: thinking, feeling, sensation and intuition

The four psychological functions are thinking, feeling, sensation and intuition. As a rule one function predominates.

The *thinking* individual is mainly governed by reflective thinking so that important actions proceed, or are intended to proceed, from intellectually considered motives. The *feeling* individual is mainly governed by values placed on things arising from feelings. Here Jung is regarding feeling as an evaluative function. Thinking and feeling individuals are *rational* types because they are characterized by the primacy of the reasoning and judging functions.

The *sensation* individual is mainly governed by their awareness of external facts provided through the function of the senses: seeing, hearing, touching, tasting and smelling. The *intuition* individual is mainly governed by hunches and insights. Intuition is a predominantly unconscious process. The conscious aspect of intuition is to transmit images or perceptions of relations between things that could not be transmitted by the other functions. Sensation and intuition individuals are *irrational* types because their actions are based on the sheer intensity of perception rather than on any rational judgment.

Combining attitudes and functions to form psychological types

Jung combined attitudes and functions to provide eight main psychological types (see Box 3.1). Though one main attitude and one main function combine in each individual, people categorized within the eight psychological types vary. Furthermore, the other attitude and functions are always part of someone's personality.

Box 3.1   Jung's psychological types

Following are brief descriptions of each of the eight main psychological types:

- *Extraverted-thinking type*: This type makes all activities dependent on intellectual functioning oriented to objective data in the form of external facts or generally accepted ideas. Jung cites the scientist Charles Darwin as an example;
- *Introverted-thinking type*: This type makes all activities dependent on intellectual functioning oriented to subjective data. Jung cites the philosopher Immanuel Kant as an example;
- *Extraverted-feeling type*: This type consists almost exclusively of women who are guided by feelings that appear adjusted to harmonize with objective situations and general values, for instance, the love choice of a 'suitable' man;
- *Introverted-feeling type*: This type is predominantly guided by subjective feelings and their true motives generally remain hidden. This type mainly consists of women of whom it may be said 'still waters run deep';
- *Extraverted-sensation type*: This type consists mainly of men for whom anything new that comes within their range of interest is acquired by way of sensations received from the outside. Guided by the intensity of objective influences, this type encompasses the grossly sensual and those whose sensations are aesthetically highly developed;

(Continued)

Box 3.1   (Continued)

- *Introverted-sensation type*: This type is guided by the intensity of the subjective sensation. No proportional relationship exists between object and sensation, but one that is unpredictable and arbitrary;
- *Extraverted-intuition type*: For this type intuition as the function of unconscious perception is directed wholly to external objects. This type uses intuition to apprehend the widest range of possibilities in objective situations and to discover what they hold in store;
- *Introverted-intuition type*: The peculiar intuition of this type produces mystical dreamers, seers, artists and cranks. The intensification of intuition may lead this type to be out of touch with tangible reality and to experience difficulty in communicating to others.

Acquisition

Jung never developed a rigorous elaboration of the development of the psyche and of human behaviour. A possible reason for this is that he was more interested in researching and understanding the collective unconscious, which he perceived as the inherited foundation of psychological life.

Stages of life

To Jung (1989) the arc of life has four stages: childhood, youth, middle age and extreme old age. He was particularly interested in the problems of middle age.

Childhood (birth to puberty)

Jung likened children, during the first two or three years of life when they are unconscious of themselves, to being in an animal state. In early infancy the psyche is to a large extent the maternal psyche and soon comprises the paternal psyche as well. Gradually the ego develops as the organizing centre for the child's psychic processes and only when children begin to say 'I' is there any perceptible continuity of consciousness. The conscious mind progressively arises out of the unconscious as fragments of the unconscious are added to consciousness and separated from their previous source in the unconscious (Jung, 1981).

Jung saw the origins of childhood neuroses mainly as symptoms of the mental conditions of parents. He wrote:

> The child is hopelessly exposed to the psychic influence of the parents and is bound to copy their self-deception, their insincerity, their hypocrisy, cowardice, self-righteousness, and selfish regard for their own comfort, just as wax takes up the imprint of the seal. (1981: 79)

Jung did not expect parents to commit no faults, but to recognize them for what they were, thus creating a more honest psychological atmosphere for their children.

Youth (puberty to 35–40 years)

The human mind's growth keeps pace with a widening range of consciousness and each step forward can be an extremely painful and laborious achievement. During youth the demands of life put an end to childhood, for example the transitions to marriage and a career. In addition, young people may experience inner psychic difficulties concerned with the sexual instinct or feelings of inferiority. The essential feature of the problems of youth is a clinging to the childhood level of consciousness. Achievement, usefulness and getting established are ways of proceeding out from the problems of the period of youth. People can adapt what they have been given from the past to the possibilities and demands of the future.

Middle age (35–40 to extreme old age)

Jung used the analogy of the sun that rises to a peak in the first part of the day and then descends and in the process illuminates itself. Likewise human life does not inexorably expand, but there is an inevitable and deep-seated shift in the psyche towards contraction with the possibility of self-illumination. While the tasks of the first half of life concern the individual's development and entrenchment in the outer world, the tasks of the second half of life are for people to devote serious attention to understanding and developing themselves more fully. Just as neurotic problems in youth sprang from people not escaping from their childhood, so neurotic problems in middle age can spring from people not escaping from their youth. Jung did not regard this psychological shrinking from approaching old age to be caused by fear of death, rather than from a basic change in the human psyche that takes place around that time. Middle age is a time for contemplation, self-realization and learning to live more in harmony with primordial images and symbols.

Extreme old age

Though childhood and extreme old age are utterly different, Jung regarded them as having one thing in common: submersion into unconscious psychic happenings. The child's mind and ego grow out of unconsciousness. The very old person sinks again into unconsciousness and progressively vanishes within it. Jung viewed childhood and extreme old age as being stages of life without any conscious problems and, hence, they were not his major focus.

Progression and regression

Life requires an ongoing process of psychological adaptation to the reality of the environment. Progression and regression are two important uses of psychic energy. *Progression* is 'the daily advance of the process of psychological adaptation ... a continual satisfaction of the demands of environmental conditions' (Jung, 1983: 59). In progression, the psychic value of conscious and unconscious opposites become balanced through regular interaction and mutual influence.

Regression is the backward movement of psychic energy when a frustrating situation dams the energy of the libido: for instance, a thinking attitude may attempt to deal with a situation that can only be solved by feeling. Regression confronts the individual with the problem of the inner psyche as contrasted with outward adaptation to reality. The struggle between opposites would persist, but for regression which raises the psychic value of material of which the individual was only dimly conscious or totally unconscious. Regression can be positive as well as negative with its unconscious contents containing not only psychological slime, but the seeds of new possibilities. For example, if thinking fails as the adapted function, the unconscious material activated by regression will contain the missing feeling function, although still in embryonic, archaic and undeveloped form. Regression occurs regularly in dreams that can reveal important unconscious material.

Individuation

The central concept of Jung's psychology is the process of individuation. Individuation is the process by which the person becomes differentiated as a separate psychological individual, a separate whole as distinct from the collective psychology. However, the process of individuation also raises a person's consciousness of the human community since it makes people aware of the unconscious, which unites all mankind.

The goal of psychic development is the self, which as shown previously differs from the ego. Individuation may be viewed as coming to self-hood or self-realization. The transcendent function is the means by which individuals are able to bridge some of the gap between consciousness and unconsciousness and live more in harmony with their unconscious processes.

Individuation involves a process of assimilating unconscious content into consciousness. There is a shift of the centre of personality from the ego, which is the centre of consciousness, to the self that moves from being located in the centre of unconsciousness to being at the central point between consciousness and unconsciousness. Creating this new balance between consciousness and unconscious allows the personality to rest on a new and more solid foundation.

Although the self archetype is present from birth, its influence does not become significant until middle age. Individuation proceeds in life's morning through education and appropriate life experiences. However, a major emphasis on realizing the self through the process of individuation might be viewed more as a task of the afternoon of human life.

Maintenance

Jung never systematically identified the factors that contribute to individuals maintaining lower levels of psychic development and individuation than desirable. He differentiated between the tasks of the first part of life, which entailed practical adaptations concerning such matters as relationships and occupation, and the second part of life, which concerned realizing the underlying self. The concept of maintenance should ideally take into account the different factors contributing to problems connected to addressing the tasks of each life stage. To avoid repetition and for the sake of simplicity, the following discussion is restricted to some central, sometimes overlapping, factors.

- *Rigid personas*: people who develop rigid personas develop in a very one-sided fashion and become out of touch with the subjective and unconscious side of themselves. This one-sidedness seeks social adaptation at the expense of inner alienation;
- *Mass collective consciousness*: the collective consciousness in a group, for instance the Swiss nation, may be one that encourages people to avoid examining themselves and dealing more deeply with problems in life. Allied to this, the collective consciousness may be conducive to people reinforcing one another's rigid personas;
- *Complexes*: complexes, such as the mother complex, form part of the personal unconscious. Individuals who remain unaware of their complexes are likely to maintain them;
- *Fear of the shadow*: individuals tend not to like examining what they perceive as undesirable and inferior traits in themselves. People who possess rigid personas may be particularly prone to avoid looking at their shadow sides;
- *Fear of the contents of the unconscious*: fear of the shadow is just one aspect of fear of the unconscious. At varying levels of awareness, individuals may fear that their conscious functioning may be overwhelmed by the strength of their unconscious, with its archetypes and symbolic messages. People may possess insufficient courage to face their inner selves. For example, men and women may be reluctant to admit and explore their feminine (anima) and masculine (animus) aspects, respectively;
- *Projection*: projection means the expulsion of a subjective content into an object. By means of projections, which are unintentional and purely automatic occurrences, individuals get rid of incompatible aspects of themselves by projecting them onto others. Most often these subjective contents are painful, for instance aspects of one's shadow. However, sometimes projections are positive, but for reasons of self-depreciation are inaccessible to individuals;
- *Regression*: earlier, it was mentioned that regression involves the backward flow of psychic energy. Regression only becomes negative, when the

individual becomes stuck in the unconscious activity and material generated by it, rather than being able to use it for regeneration;

- *Inability to understand the language of dreams*: the issue of understanding dreams is covered in the following section on therapy. Suffice it for now to say that the inability to attend to dreams and understand their language and meaning is likely to contribute to maintaining pathology. The corollary of this is that heeding and understanding the language of dreams can foster the process of individuation;

- *Problems using the transcendent function*: the transcendent function is the synthesizing or integrating process whereby unconscious material opposes conscious material to provide a third living thing resembling the conjunction of opposites. Reasons why this synthesizing of opposites to create something new may not take place include ignorance, laziness, and insufficient intelligence and courage.

Therapy

Therapeutic goals

In his paper entitled 'The aims of psychotherapy', Jung (1966) talks about the psychology of life's morning and the psychology of its afternoon. The main therapeutic goal for youth is normal adaptation to overcome neuroses connected with shrinking back from the concrete life tasks. Therapy is mainly focused on attaining specific goals, dealing with complexes, and strengthening consciousness and ego functioning. Jung emphasized the importance for young people, who were still unadapted and yet to achieve anything, to educate their conscious will.

People in the second half of life no longer need to educate their conscious will but to understand their own inner being and the meaning of their lives. Two-thirds of Jung's clients were in the second half of life and about one-third of his clients were not suffering from any clinically definable neuroses, but from the senselessness and aimlessness of their lives. Most of these patients were socially well-adapted individuals to whom normalization meant nothing. For such people, the major therapeutic goal was self-realization involving a deeper comprehension of their psyche and incorporating more unconscious material so that a new balance was created between consciousness and unconsciousness.

Jung did not believe in the concept of cure, rather in being better able to engage in the processes of attaining life's tasks and of synthesizing conscious and unconscious material. Until his death, Jung continued his quest for individuation and self-realization by understanding the meaning of the dreams and symbols from his own unconscious.

Process of therapy

Jungian analysis definitely does not follow the medical model of diagnosis, prognosis and treatment. Jung thought that clinical diagnosis was all but meaningless and that the true nature of a neurosis only reveals itself during the course of therapy.

Jung postulated four stages in analytic psychotherapy: confession, elucidation, education and transformation (see Box 3.2). Though each of the stages has a curious sense of finality about it, normal adaptation will usually only be achieved by proceeding through the first three stages. The fourth stage – transformation – fulfils a further need beyond the scope of the other stages, but is not a final truth.

Jungian analysis is very much tailored to each individual. The process of therapy varies depending on such factors as: the client's stage of life, their personality characteristics, and the nature of their problems. The four stages of therapy are indicative rather than prescriptive. For instance, clients vary in how much work is required in dealing with the transference and its projections. Furthermore, the fourth stage of transformation is more appropriate to those facing problems of self-realization in the afternoon of their lives.

Box 3.2   The four stages of analytical therapy

Stage one: Confession
The prototype of analytical therapy is confession. The first step in the therapeutic process is to share secrets and reveal inhibited emotions. Cathartic confession restores to the ego contents which should normally be part of it and which are capable of becoming conscious. However, confession should not be regarded as a panacea.

Stage two: Elucidation
Elucidation is a process of throwing light upon and clearing up the contents elicited by the transference. Partly by analysing clients' dreams, therapists interpret and explain what clients project on to them. The effects of elucidation are that clients gain insight into their personal unconscious and the infantile origins of their projections and, thus, become more accepting of their shortcomings.

Stage three: Education
Elucidation can leave clients intelligent but still incapable children. Education entails helping clients draw out new and adaptive habits to replace the self-defeating habits of their neurosis. In this stage, therapy moves beyond insight to training clients in responsible actions.

(Continued)

Box 3.2   (Continued)

Stage 4: Transformation

For many people completion of the first three stages may be sufficient. However, some people wish to move beyond being normal and adapted persons because their deepest needs are to be healthy in leading 'abnormal' lives. In the transformation stage with such clients, the therapist as well as the client is 'in the analysis'. In the personal relationship between them there are imponderable factors that bring about a mutual transformation, with the stronger and more stable personality deciding the final issue. The personality of the therapist is the curative or harmful factor and the educator must now become the self-educator going through the stages of confession, elucidation and education so that her or his personality does not react unfavourably on the client.

With difficult cases, Jung would start with three or four sessions a week. He would commence seeing most clients twice weekly, but once analytic therapy was under way, sessions would be reduced to once a week. Jung would also encourage clients to perform between-session activities, for instance recording dreams and painting, which would enable them to make a contribution to their common work. Approximately once every 10 weeks Jung would break off treatment both to stop clients from becoming too dependent and to allow time to be a healing factor. A thorough course of analytic therapy could last for some years. Jung thought that, in most instances, very frequent sessions did not shorten the length of treatment. With clients of limited means, Jung would space sessions out and get clients to work on their own in the interim.

The therapeutic relationship

Jung wrote: 'Analysis is a dialogue involving two partners. Analyst and patient sit facing one another, eye to eye; the doctor has something to say, but so does the patient' (1961: 153). Therapy is different in every case with each client requiring individual understanding. Furthermore, clients needed to reach their own view of things without therapist compulsion or attempts at conversion.

Jung was very aware that within and between therapists and clients relationships take place on conscious and unconscious levels. Since treatment is a dialectical process in which the therapist participates just as much as the client, the personalities of therapists and clients may be more important to treatment outcomes than what the therapist says or does. Therapists should not hide behind professional façades, but be human enough to allow themselves to be influenced by their clients. Nevertheless, boundaries must be observed, including therapists monitoring themselves and questioning how their unconscious experiences situations.

As an example of unconscious contamination, the transference can evoke a countertransference. Just as patients project unconscious material on to therapists, the reverse might be the case to the detriment of therapeutic outcomes. Jung strongly favoured training analyses so that therapists would be better able to protect clients from their own infections as well as to resist being infected by their clients' problems. Furthermore, Jung favoured ongoing contact with a third person, who could monitor the therapists' functioning, and observed that even the Pope had a confessor.

The relationship in analytic therapy differs according to the stage of therapy. For example, the relationship established during the confession stage can lay the foundation for the development of a transference relationship. Furthermore, the deeper levels of therapists' personalities are likely to be more involved in the transformation stage than in the earlier stages, which is why Jung stressed the self-education aspects of this stage.

The therapeutic relationship takes place not only face-to-face, but also in both therapist and client dreams and fantasies. Therapists need be sensitive to the meaning of any dreams involving their clients. Once when analysing his dreams, Jung (1968) understood the message that he was putting a woman, whom he recognized to be a patient, so high that his neck hurt to see her as a compensation for the fact that he was looking down on her in therapy. After disclosing the dream and sharing his analysis of it with her, treatment proceeded much better.

Jung could also confront clients if he thought it necessary. When one imperious aristocratic lady client threatened to slap him after he had to say something unpleasant to her, Jung jumped up and said to her: 'Very well, you are the lady. You hit first – ladies first! But then I hit back!' (1961: 165). The client then slumped back into her chair, observed that no one had ever talked to her like that before, and proceeded to work better in therapy.

Therapeutic interventions

Jung advocated flexibility in adapting the therapy to the client. With people in the morning of life, Jung (1966) generally went along with Freudian and Adlerian approaches since these seemed to bring clients to appropriate levels of adaptation without leaving disturbing after-effects. He also observed: 'We need a different language for every patient. In one analysis I can be heard talking the Adlerian dialect, in another the Freudian' (1961: 153). Jungian language and dialect appears most appropriate for those in the second half of life.

Analysis of the transference

Transferences are emotionally toned unconscious projections that occur from client to therapist. Projections take place because an activated unconscious content seeks expression. The intensity of the transference is related to the importance of the emotional content to the client. Because they are emotionally toned, transference projections arouse emotions in therapists. Countertransference takes place when the unconscious contents of a client's projections are identical with the therapist's own unconscious processes. If therapist and client are bound together by mutual unconsciousness the result can be highly counterproductive for analytical therapy.

Any highly emotional contents of the unconscious can be a matter for projection, including erotic material and activated archetypes. Thus transference projections can come from the personal and the collective unconscious. Though transference can be a spontaneous reaction, usually it occurs during analysis. Very often transference compensates for lack of genuine rapport between therapist and client. Therapists should not actively seek to promote transference projections. Transferences are not necessary for effective analysis, because therapists can obtain all the material they need from dreams anyway.

Transferences take up clients' psychic energy. Once the transference projections are extracted and consciously understood, a corresponding amount of energy will fall back into the client's possession, instead of being wasted.

Jung (1968) described four stages of analysis or therapy of the transference. However, it is possible to condense these four stages into two main stages: handling transference projections from the personal unconscious and handling transference projections from the collective unconscious.

The first main stage involves working through transference projections that are repetitions based on clients' former personal experiences with authority figures. There are basically two tasks. The first task is for clients to realize that they are projecting past negative and positive experiences, with their associated emotions, on to their therapists. The second task is for clients to withdraw the projections from their therapists and assimilate them into their own personalities. Clients need to learn how to assume responsibility for being whole persons, including their good and bad sides. For example, clients who project negative qualities can realize that these qualities represent their shadow side that they find difficulty in acknowledging because they would rather possess a more positive image of themselves. Clients who project positive qualities can realize that perhaps they should develop these qualities in themselves.

The second main stage of transference analysis comes after the projection of personal images has been worked through and dissolved through conscious realization. A transference may still remain based on impersonal and collective rather than on personal unconscious contents. Clients need to learn to discriminate between the personal and the impersonal contents that they project on to their therapists. Jung advocated great sensitivity in handling impersonal projections and taking them seriously rather than trying to dissolve their contents. He provides the example of it being a great mistake to say to a client: 'You see, you simply project the saviour image into me. What nonsense to expect a saviour and to make me responsible' (1968: 180–1). The saviour archetypal image is everywhere and clients need to keep in touch with their impersonal images.

As part of the second stage of transference analysis, clients can learn to differentiate their personal relationship to the therapist from impersonal archetypal images. Clients can have normal human reactions to their therapists for helping them, but such reactions are human and decent only when not sullied by impersonal factors. Clients need also to realize the importance of their archetypal images, many of which have a religious nature. For some clients, the recognition of impersonal values may mean that they join a church or religious creed.

Therapy of the transference is complete when clients learn to objectify their impersonal images. Detaching consciousness from the object, a major aim of eastern religious practices is an essential part of the process of individuation. Clients learn to assume responsibility for their lives and no longer place the guarantees of their happiness on factors outside of themselves. They attain a condition of detachment in which their centre of gravity becomes themselves rather than external objects on which they depend.

Active imagination

Active imagination is a technique devised by Jung to help people get in touch with unconscious material. Clients begin by concentrating on a starting point. Then they allow their unconscious to produce a series of images, which may make a complete story. Box 3.3 provides two examples of active imagination, the second in abbreviated form (Jung, 1968: 190–3).

Though not the only starting point, clients can use a dream as a stimulus for active imagination. If clients do not allow conscious reason to interfere, the images can have a life of their own, which is the origin of the term active imagination. After the active imagination process stops, some clients proceed to develop their unconscious images through painting, drawing, sculpting, weaving, dancing or writing.

Jung stressed that active imagination is not a panacea and that he only used it with some clients. He advised against forcing active imagination upon clients. Sometimes he found using active imagination particularly valuable in the later stages of therapy.

Box 3.3   Examples of active imagination

Example 1: Jung as a child
As a little boy, Jung would go to a spinster aunt's house. The house was full of beautiful old coloured engravings. One of these was a picture of his grandfather on his mother's side, a sort of bishop represented as coming out of the house and standing at the top of a little terrace. There were some stairs coming down from the terrace and a footpath leading to the cathedral. Jung would kneel and look at the picture until he 'actively imagined' his grandfather coming down the steps.

(Continued)

Box 3.3   (Continued)

Example 2: The young artist
A young artist client of Jung's looked at a railway station poster about a place in the Bernese Alps and imagined himself in the poster. He walked up the hill and among the cows depicted in the poster and then imagined himself coming to the top and looking down the other side. He walked down the meadow on the other side, over a stile, and then down a footpath that ran round a ravine, and a rock, and then he came to a small chapel with the door ajar. He pushed open the door and saw an altar with flowers and a wooden Mother of God. At the exact moment he looked up at her face, something with pointed ears disappeared behind the altar.

Dream analysis

Dreams are utterances or statements from the unconscious. They are the doors to the innermost secrets of the psyche. Jung thought that the idea that dreams were merely wish fulfilments as hopelessly out of date. As well as wishes and fears, dreams 'may contain ineluctable truths, philosophical pronouncements, illusions, wild fantasies, memories, plans, anticipations, irrational experiences, even telepathic visions, and heaven knows what else besides' (Jung, 1968: 147). Dreams may also point to solutions to issues and problems and be prescient about future events.

Jung regarded dreams as containing their whole meaning and not having false fronts. Dreams are comparable to texts that appear unintelligible, but the therapist has to discover how to read them. Dreams do not conceal; rather, therapists need to discover their language. An understanding of myths and symbols is central to being able to read the language of dreams.

Jung distinguished between various kinds of dreams. Initial dreams are those that occur at the start of analysis and may deal with the client's attitude towards the therapist. For instance, a client predicted a brief and unsuccessful therapeutic contact with the dream 'I have to cross the frontier into another country, but cannot find the frontier and nobody can tell me where it is' (Jung, 1968: 144). Another distinction is between little dreams, which are concerned with relatively unimportant matters, and big dreams. Big dreams are numinous, a favourite Jung term for inexpressible, mysterious, terrifying and intensely mysterious experiences. Big dreams are of particular importance. Another distinction is that between single dreams and a series of dreams, with Jung's strong preference being to work with series of dreams.

Tasks of dream analysis

The first task in analysing a dream is to establish its context. Here Jung used a technique he called amplification. Amplification involves the elaboration and clarification of dream images by way of directed association. Rather than encourage free association, therapists must encourage clients' associations that stick as close as possible to the dream images. For example, the dream image of a simple peasant's house may mean different things to different clients. To establish the context of the simple peasant's house, Jung would ask: 'So how does that appear to you?' or 'What are your associations to a simple peasant's house?' In this instance, the client replied: 'It is the lazar-house of St Jacob near Basel' (Jung, 1968: 97). From this association, Jung was able to make many connections: for example, the client feeling himself an outcast and being in great danger.

Another example of clarifying context is that of a client, whose writing desk is different, dreaming of 'deal table'. Jung would keep returning to the image and say: 'Suppose I had no idea what the words "deal table" mean, describe this object and give me its history in such a way that I cannot fail to understand what sort of thing it is' (Jung, 1966: 149–50). Therapist and client need to work on establishing the context for all the images in the dream.

Interpretation is the second task of dream analysis. Since basic ideas and themes can be much more clearly recognized in a dream series than in single dreams, clients should keep a careful record of their dreams and of the interpretations made. Jung would also train clients in how to work on their dreams between sessions so that they could come prepared to the next consultation with the dream and its context written out. When interpreting dreams, a basic question for the therapist to address is 'What conscious attitude does it compensate?'

Related to the interpretation of dreams is the third task of dream analysis: assimilation. Jung valued unconscious contents and sought to bring about change in and through the unconscious as well. Assimilation 'means mutual penetration of conscious and unconscious, and not – as is commonly thought and practiced – a one-sided evaluation, interpretation, and deformation of unconscious contents by the conscious mind' (Jung, 1966: 152). Unconscious contents lose their danger the moment clients begin to assimilate contents that were previously repressed.

Assimilation requires the assent of the client to the therapist's interpretations. The values of the client's conscious personality must be respected and left intact, because unconscious compensation requires cooperation with an 'integral consciousness'. Box 3.4 provides an abbreviated version of Jung's analysis of a young man's dream (Jung, 1966: 154–5).

Box 3.4   Example of dream analysis

The young man's dream
My father is driving away from the house in his new car. He drives very clumsily, and I get very annoyed over his apparent stupidity. He goes this way and that, forwards and backwards, and manoeuvres the car into a dangerous position. Finally he runs into a wall and damages the car badly. I shout out at him in a perfect fury that he ought to behave himself. My father only laughs and then I see that he is dead drunk.

(Continued)

Box 3.4 (Continued)

Context of the dream
The young man has a genuinely positive and admiring relationship with an unusually successful father. There was nothing neurotically ambivalent about the relationship.

Jung's interpretation of the dream
The client's relationship to his father is too good and his father is still doing too much for him, so that the client's unconscious is compensating by trying to take the father down a peg. The son's danger is that he cannot see his own reality. The dream forces the son to contrast himself with his father and so that he can become conscious of himself.

The client's assimilation of the dream
Jung's interpretation struck home with the client and received his immediate assent. Jung points out that the interpretation damaged no real conscious values for either father or son.

Dream symbols are expressions of content not yet consciously recognized or consciously formulated. Box 3.5 illustrates Jung's interpretation of the symbol in one of the dreams of a 17-year-old female client (Jung, 1966: 158–60). This dream was taken from long-term analytical therapy where the goal is the client's progressive individuation. In such therapy, over a period of months and years there are successive assimilations of unconscious dream material. This process realizes more of the client's self in the interests becoming a whole human being.

Box 3.5 Example of interpreting a dream symbol

The young woman's dream
I was coming home at night. Everything is quiet as death. The door to the living room is half open, and I see my mother hanging from the chandelier, swinging to and fro in the cold wind that blows through the open windows.

Part of the dream's context
Jung was called in after two specialists had made contrary diagnoses of this 17-year-old woman. One specialist thought she might be in the first stages of progressive muscular atrophy. The other specialist thought that she was a case of hysteria.

Box 3.5   (Continued)

Jung's interpretation of the dream
The mother symbol refers to the archetype of the place of origin, to nature. The symbol also stands for the instinctive and unconscious life and the body. Jung's interpretation was that the unconscious life is destroying itself or that the dream pointed to a grave organic disease that would have a fatal outcome. This prognosis was soon confirmed.

Case material

Perhaps some indication of Jung's attitude to case material can be gleaned from the following quotation: 'Each individual analysis by itself shows only one part of one aspect of the deeper process, and for this reason nothing but hopeless confusion can result from comparative case histories' (Jung, 1966: 161). Case material that illustrates analytic therapy comes from both primary and secondary sources. In his autobiographical *Memories, Dreams, Reflections*, Jung (1961) provides case material, including many dreams, from his own explorations and confrontations with his unconscious. In his 1935 Tavistock Lectures, published as *Analytical Psychology* (1968), Jung provides case examples illustrating active imagination and dream analysis. Numerous further examples of how Jung worked are to be found in the various papers that comprise *The Practice of Psychotherapy* (Jung, 1966). In addition, *Symbols of Transformation* (Jung, 1967) provides lengthy analyses of symbolic material contained in the fantasies of a young American lady, Miss Miller.

Jung was a very original and individualistic therapist with a vast range of scholarship to draw upon. Secondary source case material, such as that provided by Douglas (2005) and Casement (2002) towards the end of their textbook chapters, can only go part way to catching the real essence of how Jung himself worked. In addition, neither of these case studies addresses the transformation stage.

Further developments

In treatment

Samuels (1985) divided the development of analytical psychology into three schools: classical, developmental and archetypal. The classical school is that most closely based on Jung's original theory and practice, the topic of this chapter. Douglas (2005) says that there is a backlash among conservative Jungians who consider that Jung's original words, however socioculturally suspect they may be by today's standards, should be taught as Jung originally presented them. The developmental school incorporates psychoanalytic ways of thinking and working. The archetypal school focuses on the development of symbols and images in the psyche.

The rise of feminism is leading to a reappraisal of Jung's ideas about masculine and feminine characteristics and influences how analysts work with members of each sex. Not surprisingly, Jung's views on women and on his anima–animus concepts have been open to discussion and revision. Douglas (2005) observes that since so much about gender and gender roles is in flux today, current images no longer match those of Jung's time and are changing as culture and experience change. She also considers that contemporary re-evaluation of these concepts holds much promise for the possibility of reappraising homosexuality as a natural occurrence.

Michael Fordham, who tirelessly tried to repair the split between the work of Jung and Freud, is prominent in the developmental school. Fordham extended Jungian theory by stating that a primary self operates in infants from the beginning. Based on his work with infants and children, Fordham considered that this primary self 'de-integrates' from a state of inner wholeness to bring the infant into relation with the environment. In this way the infant's expectation of feeding evokes the appropriate response from the mother's breast in the external world. By postulating that a primary self exists from the beginning of life, Fordham fills a gap in classical psychoanalytic and analytic psychology theory (Casement, 2002; Fordham, 1993).

Fordham's view is that individuation does not have to wait until middle age. Jung thought that individuation was equated with achieving consciousness through differentiation of subject from object. Fordham showed that the child's gradual separation from the mother during its first two years of life is also a process of individuation. He demonstrates how, after birth, the infant's primary self de-integrates and, through increasing identification with the mother, begins to move towards early object-relating. There are other early developments, not mentioned here, which are prerequisites for the goal of individuation, which is a natural part of maturing (Casement, 2002; Fordham, 1976).

Jung was more flexible than Freud about the positive as well as negative effects of countertransference. Fordham (1957) developed a position in which there are two kinds of countertransference: syntonic and illusory. Syntonic countertransference occurs when analysts may be so in tune with clients' inner worlds that they feel or behave in ways that they come to realize that there are aspects of their clients' inner worlds projected into them. Thus clients receive the benefit of parts of their analysts that are spontaneously responding to them in ways that are needed.

Illusory countertransference is when situations from analysts' pasts replace or interfere with their relationships to their patients. Fordham listened to a recording he made of an analytic session he conducted with an 11-year-old boy who had problems with aggression. He discovered that his own aggression had been present, which was due to reactivating a past event from his own childhood. During this time, analysis of his client was impossible (Casement, 2002).

Another development in the work of Jungians is to question the value of verbal interpretation as the main mode of analysis. Instead, clients' affect, feelings and body awareness are emphasized, and analysts are more likely to use the traditionally feminine realm of subjective and shared experience (Douglas, 2005).

Different ways of working

Individual therapy is the main way of conducting analytical therapy. In the United States, the impact of managed care has led to some analysts experimenting with brief therapy. Douglas (2005) talks about developments in Jung's work extending into many different areas, only some of which are mentioned here.

Group therapy

Groups, which are of approximately 6 to 10 members, are often an adjunct to individual therapy and participants are usually clients of the analyst, though some analysts accept referrals. Meetings tend to be weekly and run for about 90 minutes. Douglas sees group therapy as particularly suitable for introverts who have been drawn to Jungian psychology. In group therapy, members tend to project their shadow onto the group and the group inevitably picks up on parts of the personality that an individual conceals. Resistances are more obvious and can be dealt with more easily than in individual therapy.

Family and marital therapy

Contemporary Jungian analysts also often use or refer their patients to analytical marital or family therapy. Analysts often administer a typology test to the couple or family members and differences can often be worked with more easily when they are interpreted as a clash of typologies. People often choose partners whose typology is the opposite to their own. Analysts working with families and couples also emphasize family dynamics caused by members' shadow and anima–animus projections onto other family members.

Body/movement therapy

Jung would have his clients engage in active imagination through body movement and dance. He believed that the body stores, experiences and communicates emotional experience as much, if not more, than words.

Art therapy

Jung felt that drawing an image from a dream or from active imagination was especially valuable for people out of touch with their feelings and who try to deal with their experience solely through logic. Art therapy is a conscious way to express elements of the unconscious. It is not the quality of the finished product that is valuable, but the fact that art therapy allows an active dialogue with the unconscious.

Sand tray therapy

Jung constructed stone 'villages' during his self-analysis. Dora Kalff developed Jung's ideas by filling a rectangular box approximately $30 \times 20 \times 3$ inches with sand to become a miniature world that can be shaped by arranging any of the hundreds of figurines provided by the analyst. Use of the sand tray, like other forms of active imagination, provides a bridge to the unconscious.

Child analysis

Analysts not only treat the child, but intervene when needed to improve the child's family and life situation. Child analysis is similar to adult analysis, but uses a wide variety of touch and non-verbal methods more. Children are encouraged to express dreams, fears and fantasies through sand tray therapy, arts and crafts, modelling clay, playing musical instruments, and body movement. In addition stories and myths are used for illustrating feelings and working out problems.

Societies and journals

In 1922 a Jung club was established in London and, in 1946, a Society of Analytical Psychology (SAP) was founded in Britain. There is an International Association of Analytical Psychology that, as of 2004, had over 2500 certified analyst members in 28 countries (Douglas, 2005).

Professional journals include the *British Journal of Analytical Psychology*; the *San Francisco Jung Institute Library Journal*, the Los Angeles Institute's *Psychological Perspectives* and the New York Institute's *Journal of Jungian Theory and Practice;* the French *Cahier de Psychologie Jungienne;* the German *Zeitschrift für Analytische Psychologie;* and the Italian *La Rivista di Psicologia Analitica.*

Particularly in the western world, interest in Jungian psychology remains strong. Jung has been called a 'homo religiosus' by Gerhard Adler, the founder of the Association of Jungian Analysts (Casement, 2002), and a 'theologian manqué' (McLynn, 1996). His work has continuing appeal to many of those who are dissatisfied with the narrowness of scientific psychology and who seek to understand human beings in their wholeness.

Review and personal questions

Review questions

1. Describe consciousness and the ego.
2. Describe the personal unconscious and its complexes.
3. Describe the collective unconscious and its archetypes.
4. What are Jungian psychodynamics and how do they differ from Freudian psychodynamics?
5. What are Jung's views on psychological types?
6. What are the four stages of life and how do the tasks of life's morning differ and afternoon differ?
7. How do people maintain levels of adaptation lower than desirable?
8. Describe the goals and process of analytic therapy.
9. Describe Jung's ideas on the analysis of the transference.
10. Describe as best as you can how Jung approached the task of dream analysis.
11. Describe some ideas of the developmental school of analytical therapy.

Personal questions

1. Do Jung's ideas of the personal unconscious and the collective unconscious resonate in terms of your own life? If so, please elaborate.
2. What are some aspects of your shadow and what do you intend doing about them?
3. What do you consider is your personality type and why?
4. Try using Jung's method of active imagination.
5. Take one of your dreams and, to the best of your ability, apply Jung's methods of dream analysis to it.
6. What goals would you set for yourself if you were to be a client in either classical or developmental Jungian analysis?

Annotated bibliography

Jung, C.G. (1968) *Analytical Psychology: Its Theory and Practice.* New York: Vintage Books. This book presents the five lectures, plus discussion, that Jung gave at the Tavistock Clinic in London in 1935. Topics covered include the structure of the mind, word association and psychological types, and the methods of active imagination, dream analysis and the analysis of the transference. The book provides an excellent concise introduction to analytical psychology.

Jung, C.G. (1966) *The Practice of Psychotherapy* (2nd edn). London: Routledge.
This book is divided into two parts. Part one, entitled 'General problems of psychotherapy', contains nine papers, including one on the aims of psychotherapy. Part two, entitled 'Specific problems of psychotherapy', contains Jung's ideas on the therapeutic value of abreaction, the practical use of dream analysis, and the psychology of the transference. Some useful case study material is included in an appendix, entitled 'The realities of practical psychotherapy'.

Jung, C.G. (1961) *Memories, Dreams, Reflections*. London: Fontana Press.
Jung regarded his life as a story of the realization of the unconscious. In this book compiled at the end of his life Jung tells his personal myth, an inner journey structured around the following chapter headings: first years, school years, student years, psychiatric activities, Sigmund Freud, confrontation with the unconscious, the work, the tower, travels, visions, on life after death, and late thoughts. Some controversy exists over the extent of Jung's secretary's contribution to this book rather than it being solely a primary source.

Jung, C.G. (1971) *Psychological Types*. London: Routledge.
This book was originally published in 1921 after Jung's fallow period. It starts with a scholarly discussion of the notion of psychological types drawing on material from literature, aesthetics, religion and philosophy as well as from psychology. Jung then presents his ideas on attitudes, functions and psychological types. The book ends with an appendix containing four papers on psychological typology.

References and further reading

Casement, A. (2001) *Carl Gustav Jung*. London: Sage.
Casement, A. (2002) 'Psychodynamic therapy: the Jungian approach', in W. Dryden (ed.), *Handbook of Individual Therapy* (4th edn). London: Sage. pp. 84–111.
Douglas, C. (2005) 'Analytical psychotherapy', in R. Corsini and D. Wedding (eds), *Current Psychotherapies* (7th edn). Belmont, CA: Thomson Brooks/Cole. pp. 96–129.
Fordham, M. (1957) *New Developments in Analytical Psychology*. London: Routledge & Kegan Paul.
Fordham, M. (1976) *The Self and Autism*. London: Heinemann.
Fordham, M. (1993) *The Making of an Analyst*. London: Free Association Books.
Hall, C.S. and Nordby, B.J. (1973) *A Primer of Jungian Psychology*. New York: New American Library.
Jung, C.G (1961) *Memories, Dreams, Reflections*. London: Fontana Press.
Jung, C.G. (1966) *The Practice of Psychotherapy* (2nd edn). London: Routledge.
Jung, C.G. (1967) *Symbols of Transformation* (2nd edn). Princeton, NJ: Princeton University Press.
Jung, C.G. (1968) *Analytical Psychology: Its Theory and Practice*. New York: Vintage Books.
Jung, C.G. (1971) *Psychological Types*. London: Routledge.
Jung, C.G. (1976a) 'The concept of the collective unconscious', in J. Campbell (ed.), *The Portable Jung*. London: Penguin. pp. 59–70.
Jung, C.G. (1976b) 'The relations between the ego and the unconscious', in J. Campbell (ed.), *The Portable Jung*. London: Penguin. pp. 70–138.

Jung, C.G. (1976c) 'The transcendent function', in J. Campbell (ed.), *The Portable Jung*. London: Penguin. pp. 273–300.

Jung, C.G. (1981) *The Development of Personality: Papers on Child Psychology, Education and Related Subjects*. London: Routledge.

Jung, C.G. (1982) *Aspects of the Feminine*. London: Ark Paperbacks.

Jung, C.G. (1983) 'Fundamental concepts of libido theory', in A. Storr (ed.), *The Essential Jung*. Princeton, NJ: Princeton University Press. pp. 59–64.

Jung, C.G. (1989) *Aspects of the Masculine*. Princeton, NJ: Princeton University Press.

McLynn, F. (1996) *Carl Gustav Jung: A Biography*. London: Bantam Press.

Samuels, A. (1985) *Jung and the Post-Jungians*. London: Routledge & Kegan Paul.

Samuels, A. (2001) *Politics on the Couch: Citizenship and the Internal Life*. New York: Karnac Books.

person-centred therapy 4

Introduction

Carl Rogers was the originator of an approach to counselling and therapy that aims to help clients fulfil their unique potential and become their own persons. His approach was partly an attempt to get away from the interpretive psychodynamic therapies described in the previous two chapters. In addition, Rogers was trying to emancipate people from the overbearing influence that parents of his time often had on the thoughts, feelings and actions of their offspring. In the early part of the twentieth century when Rogers was growing up, parents exercised much more power in the home than they do now. Rogers's person-centred therapy challenged authoritarian tendencies in both therapy and parenting and championed the rights of clients to discover their own directions.

On 11 December 1940, Rogers gave a presentation at the University of Minnesota entitled 'Some newer concepts in psychotherapy' which is the single event most often identified with the birth of client-centred therapy (Raskin and Rogers, 2005). In 1974, Rogers and his colleagues changed its name from 'client-centred' to 'person-centred'. They believed that the new name would more adequately describe the human values and the mutuality underlying their approach and would apply to contexts other than counselling and psychotherapy. However, Thorne observes: 'Rogers never completely jettisoned the term client-centred therapy. He uses client-centred and person-centred interchangeably when talking about counselling and psychotherapy but *always* employs the term "the person-centred approach", when referring to activities outside the one-to-one therapy situation' (Thorne, 1994, personal communication).

This chapter is drawn mainly from Rogers's writings. However, he encouraged colleagues and associates to develop it and, consequently, regarded his theory as a group enterprise (Rogers, 1959). Rogers was influenced by psychologists like Combs, Snygg and Maslow. I incorporate the ideas of Rogers's collaborators when they help to add to or clarify his position. In addition, the chapter ends with some recent contributions to person-centred therapy.

Carl Rogers (1902–87)

Carl Ransom Rogers was born in Illinois, America, the fourth of six children. His father was a civil engineer and contractor who had a successful construction business. A rather sickly boy, Rogers lived his childhood in a close-knit family in which hard work and a highly conservative, almost fundamentalist, Protestant Christianity were almost equally revered. Rogers was a shy boy who was teased a lot at home. Included among reasons for the teasing were that he was rather a bookworm and extremely absent-minded; in fact, his family called him 'Professor Moony' after a famous comic-strip character (Cohen, 1997).

When Rogers was 12 his parents bought a farm and this became the family home. Rogers regarded his parents as masters of the art of subtle, loving control. He shared little of his private thoughts and feelings with them because he knew these would have been judged and found wanting. Until Rogers went to college he was a loner who read incessantly and who adopted his parents' attitude towards the outside world, summed up in the statement: 'Other persons behave in dubious ways which we do not approve in our family' (Rogers, 1980: 28). Such dubious ways included playing cards, going to the cinema, smoking, dancing, drinking and engaging in other even less mentionable activities. He was socially incompetent in other than superficial contacts and, while at high school, had only two dates with girls. He relates that his fantasies during this period were bizarre and would probably have been classified as schizoid by a psychological diagnostician.

Rogers entered the University of Wisconsin to study agriculture, but later changed to history, feeling that this would be a better preparation for his emerging professional goal of becoming a minister of religion. His first real experience of fellowship was in a group there who met in a YMCA class. When he was 20, Rogers went to China for an international World Student Christian Federation Conference and, for the first time, emancipated himself from the religious thinking of his parents, a fundamental step towards becoming an independent person. Also, at about this time he fell in love, and, on completing college, married Helen Elliott, who was an artist. This marriage lasted until she died in 1979.

In 1924, Rogers went to Union Theological Seminary, but after two years moved to Teachers College, Columbia University, where he was exposed to the instrumentalist philosophy of John Dewey, the highly statistical and Thorndikean behavioural approaches of Teachers College, and the Freudian orientation of the Institute for Child Guidance where he had an internship. Along with his formal learning, he was starting to understand relationships with others better, and was beginning to realize that, in close relationships, the elements that 'cannot' be shared are those that are the most important and rewarding to share.

Rogers received his MA from Columbia University in 1928 and then spent 12 years in a community child guidance clinic in Rochester, New York. In 1931, he received his PhD from Columbia University and in 1939 published his first book, entitled *The Clinical Treatment of the Problem Child*. During this period Rogers felt that he was becoming more competent as a therapist, not least because his experience with clients was providing him with valuable learning and insights which contributed to a shift from diagnosis to listening.

Furthermore, such a relationship approach met his own needs, since, stemming from his early loneliness, the therapy interview was a socially approved way of getting really close to people without the pains and longer time-span of the friendship process outside therapy.

In 1940, Rogers accepted a position as a professor of psychology at Ohio State University and two years later published *Counseling and Psychotherapy* (1942), the contents of which were derived primarily from his work as a counsellor rather than as an academic psychologist. After initial poor sales, the book became well known because it offered a way to work with veterans returning from the Second World War. From 1942, Rogers had undertaken consultancies relating to the war effort, including training counsellors. After leaving Ohio State University, he spent a very brief spell as director of counselling for the United Services Organization, a serviceman's welfare organization. From 1945 to 1957 Rogers was professor of psychology and executive secretary of the counselling centre at the University of Chicago, where non-directive, or client-centred therapy, as it came to be called, was further developed and researched. In 1951 Rogers published *Client-Centered Therapy*, which contained a theoretical statement as well as a series of chapters related to client-centred practice.

In 1957 Rogers was appointed professor of psychology and psychiatry at the University of Wisconsin, where he examined the impact of the client-centred approach on hospitalized schizophrenics. In 1959 he produced by far the most thorough statement of his theoretical position (Rogers, 1959) and in 1961, *On Becoming a Person*, his most commercially successful book was published. From 1962 to 1963 Rogers was a fellow at the Center for Advanced Study in the Behavioral Sciences at Stanford University. In 1964 he went to the Western Behavioral Sciences Institute at La Jolla, California, as a resident fellow. Then, in 1968, with some colleagues, Rogers formed the Center for Studies of the Person at La Jolla, where he was a resident fellow until his death. During the latter part of his career Rogers developed a great interest in the application of person-centred ideas to group work, community change and preventing 'nuclear, planetary suicide', and ran many large-scale workshops around the world (Kirschenbaum and Henderson, 1990). In addition, as he grew older, having earlier firmly rejected his Christian past, he realized he had underestimated the mystical or spiritual dimension in life.

From the age of 13 Rogers had viewed himself as a scientist. He was a committed researcher and pioneered the use of tape-recorders to study counselling and therapy processes. In 1956 he received the American Psychological Association's Award for Distinguished Scientific Contributions. Rogers was also an author with a deep commitment to clear and cogent communication. When he was 75, he observed: 'Yet there is, I believe, a much more important reason for my writing. It seems to me that I am still – inside – the shy boy who found communication very difficult in interpersonal situations ...' (Rogers, 1980: 80). As well as those already mentioned, his books include *Freedom to Learn* (1969), *Encounter Groups* (1970), *Becoming Partners* (1973), *Carl Rogers on*

Personal Power (1977) and *A Way of Being* (1980). A chronological bibliography of Rogers's books and articles published in the period 1930–80 is printed at the end of *A Way of Being*.

Although the years since 1940 were very successful for Rogers and his ideas, they also contained professional and personal struggles. Two professional struggles were those with psychiatry and with behavioural psychology. Rogers fought for psychologists, as contrasted with psychiatrists, to be allowed to practise psychotherapy and to have administrative responsibility over 'mental health' work. He also constantly highlighted the philosophical and practical issues involved in a humanistic or person-centred as against a behavioural view of human beings.

On a more personal level, Rogers continued striving to become a more real, open and growing person. He struggled, with varying degrees of success, with some personal crises and difficulties. During his Chicago period, with counselling help, he worked through a crisis arising from a 'badly bungled therapeutic relationship' (Rogers, 1980: 39) with a particularly demanding and highly disturbed female client (Thorne, 2003). In the 1970s, Rogers faced the strains of his wife's long illness: from 1972 she was intermittently in a wheelchair and in 1979 she died. In the last years of her life there was much pain in his relationship with Helen. Nevertheless Rogers (1980) movingly talks of how he was able to express his appreciation and love for her two days before she died. Towards the end of his life Rogers was increasingly aware of his 'capacity for love, my sensuality, my sexuality' (1980: 96) and wished to have loving relationships outside of marriage. In August 1975 Rogers met and fell in love with a much younger divorcee called Bernice Todres, but the relationship was never sexually consummated. In December 1979 this only intermittently satisfactory and episodic relationship finally ended.

Rogers was a complex mixture of high intelligence, high energy, ambition, competitiveness, Protestant work ethic, strength, vulnerability, charisma, idealism, altruism, self-centredness, caring, shyness, sensitivity, warmth and ability to touch others deeply. Arguably, as his career developed, he allowed the need to become and maintain the professional persona of Carl Rogers to get in the way of his becoming a more highly developed person. Clearly very conscious of his place in the history of American counselling and therapy, Rogers left the United States Library of Congress 140 boxes of his papers as well as tapes and films of his work.

Even as an old man Rogers was still prone to blame his parents for making him feel that he did not deserve to be loved (Cohen, 1997). A wounded theorist, he was influenced by his own early emotional deprivations to design a counselling approach to overcome their effects and hence to meet his own companionship and growth needs. Other sources of learning included his clients and the stimulus provided by younger colleagues. Rogers claimed that serendipity or 'the faculty of making fortunate and unexpected discoveries by accident' had also been important (1980: 64).

Theory

Basic concepts

In 1951 Rogers presented his theory of personality and behaviour as the final chapter of *Client-Centered Therapy*. Eight years later, in an edited publication entitled *Psychology: A Study of Science*, Rogers presented an updated version that he regarded as his major and most rigorous theoretical statement and 'the most thoroughly ignored of anything I have written' (1980: 60). Later, with collaborators, he restated his theory, but did not alter it (see, for instance, Raskin and Rogers, 2005). Rogers thought that this and any theory should be a stimulus for further creative thinking rather than a dogma of truth.

Perceptual or subjective frame of reference

Combs and Snygg (1959) state that, broadly speaking, behaviour may be observed from either the point of view of outsiders or the point of view of the behavers themselves. It is sometimes stated that the former is viewing behaviour from the external frame of reference while the latter is viewing behaviour from the internal, subjective or perceptual frame of reference. Rogers writes of his fundamental belief in the subjective, observing that 'Man lives essentially in his own personal and subjective world, and even his most objective functioning, in science, mathematics, and the like, is the result of subjective purpose and subjective choice' (1959: 191). It is this emphasis on the subjective, perceptual view of clients that led to the term 'client-centred'. The perceptions of clients are viewed as their versions of reality.

Later, Rogers was again to stress that the only reality people can possibly know is the world that they individually perceive and experience at this moment. The notion that there is a 'real world', the definition of which can be agreed upon by everyone, is a luxury that the human race cannot afford, since it leads to false beliefs, like faith in technology, which have brought our species to the brink of annihilation. His alternative hypothesis is that there are as many realities as there are people. Furthermore, people are increasingly 'inwardly and organismically rejecting the view of one single, culture-approved reality' (Rogers, 1980: 26).

Actualizing tendency

The actualizing tendency is the single basic motivating drive. It is an active process representing the inherent tendency of the organism to develop its capacities in the direction of maintaining, enhancing and reproducing itself. The actualizing tendency is operative at all times in all organisms and is the distinguishing feature of whether a given organism is alive or dead. The organism is always up to something. In addition, the actualizing tendency involves a development towards the differentiation of organs and functions.

Rogers observes, from his experiences with individual and group counselling and from his attempts to provide students in classes with 'freedom to learn', that 'the most impressive fact about the individual human being seems to be the directional tendency toward wholeness, toward actualization of potentialities' (1977: 240). Furthermore, he cited support for the actualizing tendency both in his observations of the natural world, for instance the behaviour of seaweed and of children learning to walk, and in empirical research, be it on sea urchins, rats, human infants and brain-damaged war veterans. The cornerstone of both Rogers's therapeutic work and his political thinking was that, because of their actualizing tendency, people move towards self-regulation and their own enhancement and away from control by external forces. The actualizing tendency is basically positive. It represents Rogers's trust in the wisdom of the organism and its constructive directional flow towards the realization of each individual's full potential.

Maslow (1970) reiterates this assessment of people's basic nature when he writes that the human being does seem to have instinct remnants and that clinical and other evidence suggests that those weak instinctoid tendencies are good, desirable and worth saving. Often, however, people appear to have two motivational systems: their organismic actualizing tendency and their conscious self. Maslow (1962) writes of the basic conflict in humans between defensive forces and growth trends and observes that the actualizing tendency may involve both deficiency and growth motivations. However, given a certain emotional environment, growth motivations will become increasingly strong.

Organismic valuing process

The concept of an organismic valuing process is central to the idea of a real or true and unique self. A person's organismic valuing process relates to the continuous weighing of experience and the placing of values on that experience in terms of their ability to satisfy the organism. For instance, the behaviour of infants indicates that they prefer those experiences – such as curiosity and security – which maintain and enhance their organism, and reject those – such as pain and hunger – which do not. This weighing of experience is an organismic rather than a conscious symbolic process. The source of the valuing process or values placed on the various experiences seems clearly to be in the infants, who react to their own sensory and visceral evidence. As people grow older, their valuing process is effective in helping them to achieve self-actualizing to the degree that they are able to be aware of and perceive the experiencing which is going on within themselves.

Experience and experiencing

Rogers uses the term 'sensory and visceral experience' in a psychological rather than a physiological sense. Perhaps another way of stating sensory and visceral experience is the undergoing of facts and events, which are potentially available to conscious awareness, by the organism's sensory and visceral equipment. People may be unaware of much of their experiencing. For instance, when sitting, you may not be aware of the sensation on your buttocks until your attention is drawn to it. Another example is that you may not be aware of the physiological aspects of hunger because you are so fascinated by work or play. However, this experience is potentially available to conscious awareness. The total range of experience at any given moment may be called the 'experiential', 'perceptual' or 'phenomenal' field. Rogers stressed that physiological events such as neuron discharges or changes in blood sugar are not included in his psychological definition of experience.

The verb *experiencing* means that the organism is receiving the impact of any sensory or visceral experiences that happen at the moment. Experiencing a feeling includes receiving both the emotional content and the personal meaning or cognitive content 'as they are experienced inseparably in the moment' (Rogers, 1959: 198). Experiencing a feeling fully means that experiencing, awareness and expression of the feeling are all congruent.

Perception and awareness

Perception and awareness are virtually synonymous in person-centred theory. When an experience is perceived, this means that it is in conscious awareness, however dimly, though it need not be expressed in verbal symbols. Another way of stating this is that 'perceiving' is 'becoming aware of stimuli or experiences'. Rogers viewed all perception and awareness as transactional in nature, being a construction from past experience and a hypothesis or prediction of the future. Perception or awareness may or may not correspond with experience or 'reality'. When an experience is symbolized accurately in awareness, this means that the hypothesis implicit in the awareness will be borne out if tested by acting on it. Many experiences may not be symbolized accurately in awareness because of defensive denials and distortions. Other experiences, such as buttocks sitting on a chair, may not be perceived, since they may be unimportant to the organism.

Awareness, or conscious attention, is one of the latest evolutionary developments of the human species. One way in which Rogers regarded it was as 'a tiny peak of awareness, of symbolizing capacity, topping a vast pyramid of non-conscious organismic functioning' (1977: 244). Figure 4.1 attempts to illustrate this. When a person is functioning well, awareness is a reflection of part of the flow of the organism at that moment. However, all too often people are not functioning well, and organismically they are moving in one direction while their aware or conscious lives are struggling in another.

Acquisition

Person-centred theory may become clearer to the reader by maintaining a distinction between self and self-concept. The self may be viewed as the real,

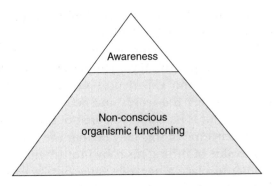

Figure 4.1   Pyramidal view of awareness and non-conscious organismic functioning

underlying, organismic self expressed in popular sayings such as 'To thine own self be true' and 'To be that self which one truly is'. People's self-concepts are their perceptions of themselves, which do not always correspond with their own experiencing or organismic selves. Thus, ideally the actualizing tendency refers to self-actualizing where aspects of self and of self-concept are synonymous or congruent. However, where self and self-concept are incongruent, the desire to actualize the self-concept may work against the deeper need to actualize the organismic self. In Rogers's writings, the above distinction is always implicit, if not always explicit.

Early development of self-concept

The self-concept is the self as perceived and the values attached to these perceptions, or what a person refers to as 'I' or 'me'. Initially, the self-concept may be made up largely of self-experiences, events in the phenomenal field discriminated by the individual as 'I', 'me' or 'self', albeit in a preverbal way. For instance, infants who discover their toes may incorporate the fact that they have toes into their self-concept. Also, infants who are hungry may incorporate into their self-concepts the fact that they value hunger negatively. As young people interact with the environment, more and more experiences may become symbolized in awareness as self-experience. Not least through interaction with significant others who treat them as a separate self, they develop a self-concept which includes both their perceptions about themselves and the varying positive and negative values attached to these self-perceptions.

Conditions of worth

A need for positive regard from others is a learned need developed in early infancy. Positive regard means here the perception of experiencing oneself as making a positive difference in the experiential field of another. It is likely that, on many occasions, young people's behaviour and experiencing of their behaviour will coincide with positive regard from others and hence meet their need for positive regard. For instance, smiling at parents may reflect a pleasurable experience as well as generating positive regard.

However, on other occasions, young people may feel that their experiencing conflicts with their need for positive regard from significant others. Rogers gives the example of the child who experiences satisfaction at hitting his baby brother, but who experiences the words and actions of his parents as saying 'You are bad, the behaviour is bad, and you are not loved or lovable when you behave this way'. An outcome of this may be that the child does not acknowledge the pleasurable value of hitting his baby brother emanating from his own experience, but comes to place a negative value on the experience because of the attitudes held by his parents and his need for positive regard. Thus, instead of an accurate symbolization of the experience, such as 'While I experience the behaviour as satisfying, my parents experience it as unsatisfying', there may come a distorted symbolization, such as 'I perceive this behaviour as unsatisfying' (Rogers, 1951: 500). Such values, which are based on others' evaluations rather than on the individual's own organismic valuing process, are called conditions of worth. Conditions of worth are prevalent because all too often 'individuals are culturally conditioned, rewarded, reinforced, for behaviors that are in fact perversions of the natural directions of the unitary actualizing tendency' (Rogers, 1977: 247).

The concept of conditions of worth is important because it means that people develop a second valuing process. The first is the organismic valuing process that truly reflects the actualizing tendency. The second is a conditions of worth process, based on the internalization or 'introjection' of others' evaluations, which does not truly reflect the actualizing tendency but may serve to impede it. However, people possess a false awareness in regard to this second valuing process, since they feel that decisions based on it are in fact based on their organismic valuing process. Thus experiences may be sought or avoided to meet false rather than real needs.

Family life

The adequacy of the self-concepts of parents affects the ways in which they relate to their children. Thomas Gordon, a contributor to Rogers's 1951 book *Client-Centered Therapy*, has emphasized that the level of self-acceptance or self-regard of parents may be related to their degree of acceptance of the behaviour of their children, though this is not something which is static. Rogers observed that parents are able to feel unconditional positive regard for a child only to the extent that they experience unconditional self-regard. By 'unconditional positive regard' Rogers meant prizing a child even though the parent may not value equally all of his or her behaviours. The greater the degree of unconditional positive regard that parents experience towards the child, the fewer the conditions of worth in the child and the higher the level of its psychological adjustment. Put simply, high-functioning parents create the conditions for the development of high-functioning children. In 1970

Gordon published *Parent Effectiveness Training* based on person-centred principles. This book attempts to teach parents how to listen to and talk with their children, thus helping the attitude of prizing to be communicated to them.

The effect of conditions of worth on self-concept

People differ in the degree to which they internalize conditions of worth, depending not only on the degree of unconditional positive regard they are offered by significant others, but also on the degree of empathic understanding and congruence shown to them. In addition the extent of their need for positive regard influences their vulnerability to introjecting conditions of worth. For some, their self-concepts will develop so as to allow much of their experience to be accurately perceived. However, even the most fortunate are likely to internalize some conditions of worth, and the less fortunate are fated to internalize many.

Examples of conditions of worth are: 'Achievement is very important and I am less of a person if I do not achieve' and 'Making money is very important and if I do not make much money then I am a failure'. Thus conditions of worth entail not only internalized evaluations of how people should be, but also internalized evaluations about how they should feel about themselves if they perceive that they are not the way they should be. Rogers believed that it is common for most people to have their values largely introjected, held as fixed concepts and rarely examined or tested. Thus, not only are these people estranged from their experiencing, but their level of self-regard is lowered and they are unable to prize themselves fully. Furthermore, by internalizing conditions of worth, they have internalized a process by which they come to be the agents of lowering their own level of self-regard or, more colloquially, of 'self-oppression'.

Marriage and education

The person-centred view is that the conditions for the development of adequate self-concepts and those for remedying inadequate self-concepts are essentially the same. Both contain the characteristics of good and loving interpersonal relationships. Implicit in this is the notion that significant experiences for the development of adequate and, regrettably, also of inadequate self-concepts are neither restricted to childhood and adolescence nor to family life.

Rogers saw contributions to the development of adequate self-concepts as potentially available in many other human situations. Most people are less self-actualizing than desirable because they are cluttered up with conditions of worth. Rogers increasingly turned his attentions to the problems of the less disturbed. Relationships between partners, whether marital or otherwise, can have growth-inducing properties in which conditions of worth dissolve and the level of self-regard increases. In *Becoming Partners*, Rogers (1973) gave a moving case study involving Joe's steady and healing concern for and trust in Irene's potential, despite her initial self-conception that 'I don't let you see this little, black, rotten, ugly ball I have buried down inside that's really me, that's unlovable and unacceptable' (1973: 100).

Rogers also turned his attention to the under-realized potential of educational institutions for creating emotional climates for the development of healthy self-concepts. He particularly favoured significant experiential learning that was self-initiated and reflected the concerns of students rather than those of teachers or administrators (Rogers, 1969). In addition, he focused on the politics of interpersonal and intergroup relationships and saw his faith in the actualizing tendency as indicating a more democratic sharing of power and control (Rogers, 1977).

Maintenance

For practising counsellors and therapists the question is not so much how clients become the way they are, as what currently causes them to maintain behaviour that does not meet their current needs. The concept of maintenance, or of how maladjusted behaviour and perceptions are perpetuated, often in the face of conflicting evidence, is critical to a full understanding of person-centred theory and practice. Person-centred theory may be viewed as a theory of human information processing or of the processing of experiences into perceptions. This is a process in which, especially for those who are disturbed, conditions of worth play a large part.

Processing of experience

Rogers observed that when experiences occur in people's lives there are four possible outcomes. First, like the sensation of sitting, they may be ignored. Second, they may be accurately perceived and organized into some relationship with the self-concept either because they meet a need of the self or because they are consistent with the self-concept and thus reinforce it. Third, their perception may be distorted in such a way as to resolve the conflict between self-concept and experiencing. For instance, students with low academic self-concepts may receive some positive feedback about their essays and perceive: 'The teacher did not read it properly' or 'The teacher must have low standards'. Fourth, the experiences may be denied or not perceived at all. For example, people may have had their self-concepts deeply influenced by strict moral upbringings and thus be unable to perceive their cravings for sexual satisfaction.

Figure 4.2 represents the processing of experience by low-functioning and high-functioning people. Previously I mentioned that people have two valuing processes: their own organismic valuing process and an internalized process based on conditions of worth. Low-functioning people are out of touch with their own valuing process for large areas of their experiencing. In these areas their self-concepts are based on conditions of worth that cause

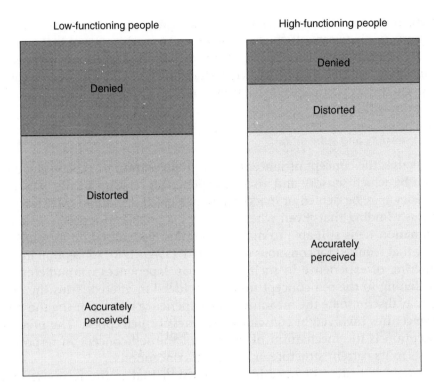

Figure 4.2   Processing of experience by low-functioning and high-functioning people

them to distort and deny much of their experiencing. On the other hand, high-functioning people have fewer conditions of worth and thus are able to perceive most of their experiences accurately.

Both high-functioning and low-functioning people are motivated by the actualizing tendency. The self-concepts of high-functioning people allow them to perceive most significant sensory and visceral experiences and thus their self-actualizing entails no significant blockages to their actualizing tendency. However, with low-functioning people a split occurs and 'the general tendency to actualize the organism may work at cross purposes with the subsystem of that motive, the tendency to actualize the self' (Rogers, 1959: 197). Low-functioning people engage in a process of actualizing insufficiently based on their organism's own valuing process. Consequently, while high-functioning people are able to interact with others and their environments on the basis of largely realistic information, low-functioning people do not have that capacity to any great extent.

Incongruence between self-concept and experience

When experiences are accurately symbolized and included in the self-concept, there is a state of congruence between self-concept and experience or, stated another way, between the self-concept and the organismic valuing process.

When, however, experience is denied and distorted, there exists a state of incongruence between self-concept and experience. This state of incongruence may exist where experiences are positive as well as where they are negative. Counselling and therapy clients tend to have low self-concepts and frequently deny and distort positive feedback from outside as well as inhibit positive feelings from within.

Threat, anxiety and subception

Rogers uses the concept of subception or preperception to explain the mechanism by which sensory and visceral experiences relevant to the actualizing tendency may be denied or inaccurately perceived. He quotes McCleary and Lazarus's finding that 'Even when a subject is unable to report a visual discrimination he is still able to make a stimulus discrimination at some level below that required for conscious recognition' (1949: 178). Subception involves a filtering of experience in such a way that experiences contradictory and threatening to the self-concept may be excluded or altered. Thus the organism may discriminate the meaning of an experience without using the higher nerve centres involved in conscious awareness or perception. The process of subception is the mechanism of defence of the self-concept in response to threats to its current structure or set of self-conceptions.

Anxiety is a state of uneasiness or tension that is the response of the organism to the 'subception' that a discrepancy or incongruence between self-concept and experience may enter perception or awareness, thus forcing a change in the currently prevailing self-concept. The term 'intensionality' is used to describe characteristics of the individual who is in a defensive state. Intensional reactions include seeing experience in absolute and rigid terms, overgeneralization, confusing facts and evaluation, and relying on abstractions rather than on reality testing.

Breakdown and disorganization

This section relates to serious disturbance. The self-concepts of very low-functioning people block their accurate perception of large areas of their significant sensory and visceral experience. If, however, a situation develops in which a significant experience occurs suddenly, or very obviously, in an area of high incongruence, the process of defence may be unable to operate successfully. Thus, not only may anxiety be experienced to the extent to which the self-concept is threatened, but, with the process of defence being unsuccessful, the experience may be accurately symbolized in awareness. People are brought face to face with more of their denied experiences than they can handle, with an ensuing state of disorganization and the possibility of a psychotic breakdown. Rogers mentioned that he had known psychotic breakdowns to occur when people sought 'therapy' from many different sources simultaneously and also when clients were prematurely faced with material revealed under the influence of sodium pentathol. Once acute psychotic behaviours have been exhibited, the defensive processes may work to protect people against the pain and anxiety generated by the perception of the incongruence.

Importance of self-concept

A person's self-concept, especially certain self-perceptions that are viewed as central, has been demonstrated to be fundamental to understanding how psychological maladjustment is maintained. The self-concept is so important to people because it is the constellation of their perceptions about themselves and, as such, the means by which they interact with life in such a way as to meet their needs. Effective self-concepts allow people to perceive their experiences realistically, whether they originate within their organisms or in their environments; in other words, such self-concepts allow them open access to their experiences.

Ineffective self-concepts may be maintained tenaciously for a number of reasons. First, as with the effective self-concepts, ineffective self-concepts are perceived as the means of need gratification and the source of personal adequacy. Second, ineffective self-concepts contain within them many conditions of worth which may have been functional at one stage of people's lives, but which have outgrown any usefulness they once possessed. Nevertheless, because they originate from people's need for positive regard, they may be deeply embedded in the structure of their self-concepts as a kind of 'emotional baggage'. Third, the more deeply embedded such conditions of worth have become the more tenaciously they are maintained, since to alter them would involve the anxiety of perceiving the incongruence between these self-perceptions and experiencing. Fourth, the conditions of worth have the effect of lowering people's sense of worth and thus making it less likely that they will have the confidence to acknowledge and face their areas of incongruence. There is a threshold area for both high-functioning and low-functioning people in which they may be able to assimilate incongruent perceptions into their self-concepts. This threshold area appears to be narrower and more tightly defined for low-functioning people.

Characteristics of self-concept

Since the idea of self-concept, sometimes expressed as 'self-structure', 'perceived self', 'phenomenal self', or just 'self', is so fundamental to person-centred theory, I will briefly review some of its characteristics:

- *Content areas* People's self-concepts are unique complexes of many different self-conceptions that constitute their way of describing and distinguishing themselves. Some content areas of people's self-concepts include bodily, social, sexual, feelings and emotions, tastes and preferences, work, recreation, intellectual activity, and philosophy and values. People vary in the importance they attach to these various areas and also in the kinds of self-conceptions they have in them. For instance, one person may feel the shape of their nose as important while another may be scarcely aware of it. The self-concept may be described in self-referent statements such as 'I am a good carpenter', 'I like ice cream' and 'Meeting new people makes me nervous'.

- *Structure or process*   The self-concept may be viewed as a structure made up of different self-conceptions related to each other in *various* ways. The self-concept is also the means or process by which people interact with the environment and by which they ignore, deny, distort or accurately perceive experience.
- *Central–peripheral*   Combs and Snygg (1959) distinguish between the phenomenal self, the organization or pattern of all those aspects which people refer to as 'I' or 'me', and the self-concept, those perceptions about self which are most vital to people themselves and may be regarded as their very essence. For all people, some self-conceptions are much more central than others, and everyone has their unique way of ordering self-conceptions as central or peripheral, even though this is often more implicit than explicit.
- *Congruence–incongruence*   Many self-conceptions may match the reality of people's experiencing, in which case there is congruence between self-conception and experience. Other self-conceptions may be different in varying degrees from the reality of their experiencing, in which case a state of incongruence exists.
- *Conditions of worth*   Incongruence implies that a self-conception is based on a condition of worth rather than on the organism's own valuing process. For example, an incongruent self-conception for a person may be 'I want to be a doctor', whereas a congruent self-conception may be 'I want to be an artist'. Being a doctor may be based on values internalized from parents, whereas being an artist represents the organism's own valuing process.
- *Subception and defence*   This is an area of self-concept as a process. Experiences may be denied or distorted by the process of subception. This process defends existing self-conceptions by preventing the person from perceiving incongruence and hence possibly changing both self-conceptions and behaviour.
- *Intensionality–extensionality*   Intensionality describes characteristics of a self-concept in a defensive state, for example rigidity and the absence of adequate reality testing. Extensionality describes characteristics of a mature self-concept, such as seeing experience in limited, differentiated terms and testing inferences and abstractions against reality.
- *Levels of self-regard*   Another way of expressing levels of self-regard is the degree to which individuals prize themselves. Rogers stated that when people's self-concepts were such that no self-experience could be discriminated as more or less worthy of positive regard than any other, then they

were experiencing unconditional positive self-regard. Level of self-acceptance is another way of stating level of self-regard.

- *Real–ideal*   While real self-conceptions represent my perceptions of how I am, ideal self-conceptions represent my conceptions of how I would most like to be. Both real and ideal self-conceptions form parts of people's self-concept complex.

Therapy

Therapeutic goals

The question of goals in the person-centred framework can be addressed in two ways: first, the goals of individual clients in therapy and, second, overall goals reflecting the human potential for growth. Clients in person-centred therapy are responsible for having their own purposes and goals. Therapists do not tell clients where they should be going or how to get there. At the start of therapy there is no process of assessment and goal setting. Rather clients may come with some goals and then, within the context of a safe therapeutic relationship, may choose to reveal further goals and, as therapy progresses, still different goals may emerge. Much of person-centred therapy focuses on helping clients become more in touch with their feelings and organismic valuing process. During this process clients may evolve a greater sense of what truly are their goals. For some clients, working through to what are personal goals, as contrasted with goals that are 'hand me downs' from significant others, may take many therapy sessions.

Much of the time Rogers (1959, 1961) saw overall goals in terms of characteristics of the fully functioning person. However, he also wrote a later statement on the qualities of the person of tomorrow who can live in a vastly changed world (Rogers, 1980). He considered that a paradigm shift was taking place from old to new ways of conceptualizing the person. Table 4.1 presents characteristics, albeit overlapping, of the fully functioning person and the person of tomorrow.

Here I identify six main dimensions or themes concerning goals in Rogers's writings, including the scale he developed with some colleagues to measure process changes in psychotherapy (Walker et al., 1960). Clients might come into therapy at differing levels on these dimensions and then, during the course of successful therapy, move forward to higher levels of functioning.

Openness to experience

A self-concept that allows all significant sensory and visceral experiences to be perceived is the basis for effective functioning. Rogers frequently used the

Table 4.1   Characteristics of the fully functioning person and the person of tomorrow

The fully functioning person	The person of tomorrow
• Open to experience and able to perceive realistically • Desire for authenticity • Rational and not defensive • Engaged in existential process of living • Trusts in organismic valuing process • Construes experience in extensional manner • Accepts responsibility for being different • Accepts responsibility for own behaviour • Relates creatively to the environment • Accepts others as unique individuals • Prizes himself or herself • Prizes others • Relates openly and freely on the basis of immediate experiencing • Communicates rich self-awareness when desired	• Openness to the world, both inner and outer • Scepticism regarding science and technology • Has a desire for wholeness as a human being • Has the wish for intimacy • Process persons • Cares for others • Has an attitude of closeness towards nature • Is anti-institutional • Trusts the authority within • Considers material things unimportant • Has a yearning for the spiritual

term 'openness to experience' to describe the capacity for realistic perception and observed that 'There is no need for the mechanism of "subception" whereby the organism is forewarned of experiences threatening to the self' (1959: 206). Openness to experience makes for more efficient behaviour in that people have a wider perceptual field and are able to behave more often from choice than from necessity. Openness to experience may also increase the possibility of spontaneity and creativity, since people are less bound by the straitjacket of conditions of worth. In other words, openness to experience enables people to engage in an existential process of living where they are alive, able to handle change, and alert to the range of their choices for creating their lives.

Rationality

A feature of openness to experience is that it allows for rationality. When people are in touch with their organismic experiencing their behaviour is likely to be rational in terms of maintaining and enhancing their organism. Rogers thought it tragic that the defences of most people kept them out of touch with how rational they could be. What was earlier described as extensionality rather than intensionality is a characteristic of this rationality.

Personal responsibility

The term personal responsibility refers to people's taking responsibility *for* their own personal development and not just feeling responsible to others. This covers Rogers's ideas of individuals' trust in their organismic valuing process, trust of the authority within, acceptance of responsibility for their own behaviour, and also acceptance of responsibility for being different from others. Personally responsible people, within the existential parameters of death and destiny, are capable of taking control of their lives. The person-centred philosophy in many aspects is one of self-control, self-help and personal power, hopefully within the context of caring relationships. Acknowledgment of personal responsibility is a central part of the self-concepts of effective people.

Self-regard

Self-regard is another important part of the self-concepts of effective people. One way of expressing this is that a person possesses a high degree of unconditional self-regard, or self-acceptance. This is a self-regard based on their organismic valuing process rather than on the praise and needs of others. People with a high degree of unconditional self-regard will prize themselves, even though they may not prize all their behaviours and attributes.

Capacity for good personal relationships

Self-acceptance means that people are less likely to be defensive and hence more likely to accept others. The capacity for good personal relationships incorporates Rogers's notions of accepting others as unique individuals, prizing others, relating openly and freely to them on the basis of immediate experiencing, and having the capacity, when appropriate, to communicate a rich self-awareness. These relationships are characterized by mutual concern for both persons' development. Rogers considered congruence, genuineness or 'realness' to be probably the most important element in the ordinary interactions of life, while empathy has the highest priority where the other person is anxious and vulnerable.

Ethical living

Person-centred theory is based on a view that people, at their core, are trustworthy organisms. This shows itself in the social relations of well-functioning people in at least two ways. First, they are capable of a wide identification with other human beings, so they are likely to seek others' development along with their own. Consequently, they are careful not to infringe on the rights of others while pursuing their own ends. Second, they appear to be able to distinguish sharply between ends and means and between good and evil. Qualities which are likely to contribute to such people's ethical living are trust in internal rather than in external authority; an indifference to material things, such as money and status symbols; an attitude of closeness to and reverence for nature; and a yearning and seeking for spiritual values that are greater than the individual.

Process of therapy

The process of person-centred therapy is built on a basic trust of the client's ability, within a growth-promoting climate, to actualize her or his human potential. Right from the beginning Rogers would encourage clients to assume responsibility for the contents of the therapy sessions. Therapy starts with an invitation indicating that the therapist will be an interested listener to whatever the client wants to share. Following is Rogers's opening statement from a demonstration interview conducted in his later years:

> I don't know what you might want to talk about, but I'm very ready to hear. We have half an hour, and I hope that in that half an hour we can get to know each other as deeply as possible, but we don't need to strive for anything, I guess that's my feeling. Do you want to tell me whatever is on your mind? (Raskin and Rogers, 2005: 147)

There is no formal assessment in person-centred therapy since all clients are viewed as being out of touch with their experience on account of their conditions of worth. If therapists were, from their own external frames of reference, to assess clients they would risk replicating the circumstances that had led the latter to acquire and maintain their conditions of worth. In addition, therapists avoid any interpretations or placing external constructions on what the client reveals. Rather they act as companions as clients share whatever seems important at the time. In particular, Rogers would assist clients to express, experience and explore feelings – be they positive, negative, ambivalent or confused – at a rate comfortable for them.

Rogers would define his and the client's role not only by his opening remarks but also by how he listened carefully to what clients communicated without trying to judge or influence their stream of talk in any direction other than their own. Furthermore, Rogers would refuse to allow clients to place him in roles that allowed him to assume responsibility for directing and leading them. For example, if a client said: 'What do you think I should do?' Rogers would show acceptance and understanding of the client's feeling of really wanting an answer about what to do without usurping the client's authority and supplying the answer. In such situations, Rogers might indicate that, without having the answers himself, he hoped he could assist the client to find an answer that was right for her or him. The initial session would end without any attempt to summarize the session or tie up loose ends before closing. Therapist and client would respectfully take their leave of one another.

Person-centred therapy is a process that goes on between as well as within sessions. Though no formal homework is set, most often clients continue the process of therapy by means of their thoughts, feelings and actions between sessions. Subsequent sessions start with clients being allowed to assume responsibility about where to begin, for instance with an opening remark such as 'Where would you like to start today?' Again, Rogers would attempt to provide a growth-promoting climate as clients attempted to get in touch with and experience their own feelings, explore the circumstances of their lives, and settle upon goals and directions that seemed appropriate for them. The same growth-promoting climate allows clients, when ready, to address the issue of terminating therapy and how best to lead their lives afterwards.

A more poetic impression of the process of person-centred therapy can be gathered from one of Rogers's favourite sayings from Lao-Tse.

It is as though he listened
and such listening as his enfolds us in a silence
in which at last we begin to hear
what we are meant to be.

The therapeutic relationship

How is a growth-promoting relationship achieved? Person-centred therapy does not rely on techniques or on doing things to clients. Rogers believed that in therapy 'it is the *quality* of the interpersonal encounter with the client which is the most significant element in determining effectiveness' (1962: 416). Person-centred therapy is a process that can intensely involve the thoughts and feelings of clients and therapists. There is a coherence between how person-centred therapists see the origins of clients' self-alienation and inner schisms and how they can assist them to grow and become healed. Person-centred therapists try to provide the attitudinal conditions that are the antidote to the emotional deprivations that their clients have experienced.

What are the conditions for client growth and reintegration? In 1957, Rogers presented his six necessary and sufficient conditions for therapeutic personality change. He stated that the following conditions had to exist and continue over a period of time for constructive personality change to occur. Also, that 'No other conditions are necessary' (Rogers, 1957: 96). First, two people need to be in psychological contact. Second, the client is in a state of incongruence and is vulnerable or anxious. Third, the therapist 'is congruent or integrated in the relationship'. Fourth and fifth, the therapist experiences 'unconditional positive regard for the client', and 'an empathic understanding of the client's internal frame of reference and endeavours to communicate this to the client' (p. 96). Sixth, the therapist is minimally successful in communicating empathic understanding and unconditional positive regard to the client. Rogers regarded congruence, unconditional positive regard and empathy as 'the attitudinal conditions that foster therapeutic growth' (Rogers and Sanford, 1985: 1379). He stressed that they were not all or none conditions, but exist on continua.

Congruence

Other words for congruence are genuineness, realness, openness, transparency and presence. Congruence is the most basic of the attitudinal conditions. Therapists need to be in touch with the feelings that they experience, have them available to awareness, and 'to live these feelings, be them in the relationship, and ... communicate them if appropriate' (Rogers, 1962: 417). Therapists should encounter their clients in direct person-to-person contact. They should avoid an intellectual approach in which clients get treated as objects. Congruent therapists are not playing roles, being polite or putting on professional façades.

Rogers acknowledged that no one fully achieves congruence all the time. Imperfect human beings can be of assistance to clients. It is enough for therapists, in particular moments in immediate relationships with specific persons, to be completely and fully themselves with their experiences accurately symbolized into their self-concepts.

Congruence does not mean that therapists 'blurt out impulsively every passing feeling' (Rogers, 1962: 418). Nor does it mean that they allow their sessions to become therapist-centred rather than client-centred. However, it can mean that they take the risk of sharing a feeling or giving feedback that might improve the relationship because it is expressed genuinely. An example is that of therapists sharing their experience of fatigue rather than trying to cover it up. Such openness may restore the therapist's energy level and allow the client to see that they are dealing with a real person. Another example is that Rogers thought that, if he felt persistently bored with a client, he owed it to the client and their relationship to share the feeling. He would own the bored feeling as located in himself rather than make it into an accusatory statement. He would share his discomfort at sharing the feeling and communicate that he would like to be more in touch with the client. Rogers strove to overcome the barrier between them by being real, imperfect and sharing his genuine feeling. He would hope that the client could use this as a stepping stone to speak more genuinely.

Another insight into congruence may be obtained from what Rogers says about the concept of presence. In therapy, both therapists and clients can attain altered states of consciousness in which they feel they are in touch with and grasp the meaning of the underlying evolutionary flow. There can be a mystical and spiritual dimension in counselling and therapy. Rogers considered that he was at his best as a therapist when he was closest to his inner intuitive self and 'when perhaps I am in a slightly altered state of consciousness. Then simply my *presence* is releasing and helpful to the other' (1980: 129). In such a state, behaviours that may be strange, impulsive and hard to justify rationally turn out to be right. Rogers wrote: 'It seems that my inner spirit has reached out and touched the inner spirit of the other. Our relationship transcends itself and becomes a part of something larger. Profound growth and healing and energy are present' (1980: 129).

Unconditional positive regard

Other terms used to describe this condition include non-possessive warmth, caring, prizing, acceptance and respect. Unconditional positive regard relates to Rogers's deep trust in his clients' capacity for constructive change if provided with the right nurturing conditions. Rogers stressed the importance of the therapist's attitude towards the worth and significance of each person. The therapist's own struggles for personal integration are relevant to unconditional positive regard since they can be only respectful of clients' capacities to achieve constructive self-direction if that respect is an integral part of their own personality make-ups.

Unconditional positive regard involves the therapist's willingness for clients 'to *be* whatever immediate feeling is going on – confusion, resentment, fear, anger, courage, love, or pride' (Rogers, 1986a: 198). This respect is equivalent to the love expressed by the Christian concept of *agape*, without any romantic or possessive connotations. Rogers makes the analogy between the kind of love parents can feel for their children, prizing them as people regardless of their particular behaviours at any moment. Therapists do not show positive regard for their clients – *if*. *If* they are smarter, less defensive, less vulnerable and so on. Person-centred theory explains the need for clients to seek therapy because in their pasts they were shown positive regard – *if*.

There are boundaries to showing unconditional positive regard, for instance where a client were to physically threaten a therapist. Unconditional positive regard does not mean that therapists need, from their frames of reference, to approve of all their clients' behaviours. Rather, unconditional positive regard is an attitude and philosophical orientation, reflected in therapist behaviour, that clients are more likely to move forward if they feel prized for their humanity and they experience an emotional climate of safety and freedom in which, without losing their therapist's acceptance, they can show feelings and relate events.

Empathy

Other terms for empathy include accurate empathy, empathic understanding, empathic responsiveness, an empathic way of being, an empathic stance and an empathic attitude. Rogers wrote: 'To sense the client's private world as if it were your own, but without ever losing the "as if" quality – this is empathy' (1957: 99). There are various facets to an empathic way of being with clients. Therapists need to 'get into the shoes of' and 'get under the skin of' their clients to understand their private subjective worlds. They need to be sensitive to the moment-by-moment flow of experiencing that goes on both in clients and themselves. They need the capacity to pick up nuances and sense meanings of which clients are scarcely aware. With tact, sensitivity and awareness of what clients can handle, they need to communicate their understandings of their sensings of clients' worlds and personal meanings.

Therapists should communicate their commitment to understanding their clients' worlds by frequently checking the accuracy of their understandings and showing their willingness to be corrected. Empathy is an active process in which therapists desire to know and reach out to receive clients' communications and meanings (Barrett-Lennard, 1998). An empathic attitude creates an emotional climate in which clients can assist their therapists to understand them more accurately.

Responding to individual client statements is a process of listening and observing, resonating, discriminating, communicating and checking your understanding. Needless to say, the final dimension is that the client has, to some extent, perceived the therapist's empathy. Even better is that the therapist's empathy has enabled the client to get more in touch with the flow of her or his experiencing. Box 4.1, taken from a demonstration film with Rogers as the therapist (Rogers, 1965), illustrates this process. The client, Gloria, is talking about how her father could never show he cared for her the way she would have liked.

Box 4.1   Dimensions of the empathy process

Gloria's statement: 'I don't know what it is. You know when I talk about it feels more flip. If I just sit still a minute, it feels like a great big hurt down there. Instead, I feel cheated'.

Rogers's responding processes

Observing and listening: Observes and listens to the client's verbal, vocal and bodily communication;

Resonating: Feels some of the emotion the client experiences;

Discriminating: Discriminates what is really important to the client and formulates this into a response;

Communicating: 'It's much easier to be a little flip because then you don't feel that big lump inside of hurt';
Communicates a response that attempts to show understanding of the client's thoughts, feelings and personal meanings;
Accompanies verbal with good vocal and bodily communication;

Checking: In this instance, Gloria quickly made her next statement that followed the train of her experiencing and thought. However, Rogers could either have waited and allowed Gloria space to respond or could have enquired if his response was accurate.

Gloria's perception of Rogers's responding

How Gloria reacted indicated she perceived that Rogers showed excellent empathy and that she was able to continue getting more in touch with her experiencing.

Though the next example of empathy comes from an encounter group (Rogers, 1975: 3), the empathic process it demonstrates holds true for working with individual clients. A man has been making vaguely negative statements about his father. First, the facilitator enquires whether he might be angry with his father. When the man says he doesn't think so, the facilitator says: 'Possibly dissatisfied with him?', to which the man rather doubtfully responds: 'Well, yes, perhaps'. Then the facilitator enquires whether the man is disappointed in his father, to which he quickly responds: 'That's it! I *am* disappointed that he's not a strong person. I think I've always been disappointed in him ever since I was a boy'.

In the above example, the facilitator is not interpreting the client, nor would Rogers. Rather the facilitator progressively checks out his understanding to grasp exactly what the man wishes to say. Gendlin mentions how Rogers would take in each correction until the client indicated 'Yes, that's how it is. That's what I feel' (1988: 127). Characteristically this statement would be followed by a silence in which the client fully received the empathic understanding. Very often during these silences clients would get in touch with something deeper.

A word now about what empathy is not. True empathy does not have any judgmental or diagnostic quality about it. Empathy is most definitely not a 'wooden technique of pseudo-understanding in which the counselor "reflects back what the client has just said"' (Rogers, 1962: 420). In his 1975 article on empathy, Rogers observed how at first he found it helpful to think that the best response was to 'reflect' feelings back to clients, but that later on in his career the word 'reflect' made him cringe. Still unhappy with the term 'reflection of feelings', Rogers (1986b) later suggested that therapists' mirroring responses be better labelled as 'testing understanding' or 'checking perceptions'. To Rogers, empathy was an attitude, a very special form of companionship, a gentle and sensitive way of being with clients. However well intended, mechanical reflections form no part of offering empathy.

Therapeutic interventions

Person-centred therapy is unique among the therapies covered in this book in that Rogers considered a growth-promoting relationship characterized by the attitudinal conditions necessary and sufficient for client change to occur. The same attitudinal conditions are relevant when dealing with clients' feelings towards therapists. Rogers considered that some client feelings towards their therapists were understandable responses to therapist behaviour, whereas other feelings were projections 'transferred' from previous relationships. Even in dealing with clients' transference feelings, there was no call for special interventions, such as interpreting the transference. Rogers observed, whether the feelings be therapist-caused or transference reactions: 'If the therapist is sensitively understanding and genuinely acceptant and non-judgmental, then therapy will move forward through these feelings' (1990: 130).

Case material

Rogers was very diligent in providing case material and researching the processes and outcomes of person-centred therapy. Readers are encouraged to explore primary sources to get a feel of how Rogers worked. Following are some suggestions about where to look. In *Counseling and Psychotherapy*, Rogers (1942) provides a transcript plus some commentary for each of his eight sessions with Herbert Bryan, a young man in his late 20s whom he regarded as definitely neurotic. In *On Becoming a Person*, Rogers (1961) provides two excerpts from the case of Mrs Oak, a housewife in her late 30s who was experiencing difficulties in marital and family relationships. This case study is also available in *Case Studies in Psychotherapy* (Rogers, 2005). Rogers's work with Gloria is both on film (Rogers, 1965) and part of it is written up as a case example (Raskin and Rogers, 2005). Raskin and Rogers (2005) also provide an example of the first and final thirds of a demonstration interview conducted by Rogers in 1983 illustrating the process of therapy, followed by a brief commentary. Elsewhere Rogers (1986a) presented excerpts and a commentary from another demonstration interview with a woman called Jan, conducted before a workshop of 600 participants in Johannesburg, South Africa.

Thorne (2002) provides a person-centred case study in which he works with Jeremy, a man in his early 30s. This case study demonstrates the strength of the therapeutic relationship and the therapist's commitment to his client who at one stage, without getting in touch, did not appear for a session.

Further developments

Person-centred therapy has been presented here in relation to individual work. However, Rogers's interests and influence were much more extensive. Rogers championed the use of person-centred principles in encounter groups, classroom teaching, management, and peace and conflict resolution.

Rogers has also influenced other people to develop his ideas. For example, in Britain, Mearns and Thorne (2000) have expanded Rogers's notion of self into configurations of self. Their initial working definition is: 'A configuration is a hypothetical construct denoting a coherent pattern of feelings, thoughts and referred behavioural responses symbolized or pre-symbolized by the person as reflective of a dimension of existence within the Self' (2000: 102). Though it is the experience of some clients, Mearns and Thorne have not yet found the need to hypothesize a 'governing' configuration. Configurations of self can be growthful, but sometimes are 'not for growth'. For example, a client repeatedly abused by her partner says: 'I know I should leave him, but a big part of me does not want to do that'. Some configurations may well be inconsistent with other parts of the self and carry restricted access to being 'owned' by the individual. Therapists must maintain a therapeutic relationship with both the 'growth' and 'not for growth' configurations in the 'family of selves'. Therapists should remember that some clients symbolize themselves in pluralist terms and others do not. Consequently, they should not insert pluralist conceptions that have not come from clients.

Mearns and Thorne (2000) also advocate an *actualizing process* which is described by a psychological homeostasis where the balance is under 'dual control', with the drive of the actualizing tendency and the restraint of social mediation both able to exercise power. Though not relevant for the majority of clients, therapists should avoid differentially reinforcing the prompting of the actualizing tendency against the forces of social mediation. Therapists need to beware of being partial to some configurations of self and not to others and need to attend equally to those parts of the client which might be expressing a 'not for growth' imperative.

Regarding the therapeutic relationship, Mearns and Thorne (1999) see its development as containing three elements: trust, intimacy and mutuality. Developing trust is important not only at the start of therapy relationships, but as they continue. Intimacy can contribute to developing therapeutic relationships. Many moments of intimacy correspond to times when the client experiences the therapist as demonstrating complete understanding and valuing. As the relationship develops, mutuality may become established with both therapist and client regarding their work as truly shared. Intimacy comes easily and there is an absence of defensiveness. Therapists can release their empathic sensitivity in whatever ways are most congruent to them. Establishing mutuality is likely to be a time when clients increasingly trust their inner locus of evaluation.

The mutuality element echoes Mearns's (1997, 2003) idea of meeting the client at relational depth. Therapists who are willing to work with clients at relational depth try to leave aside conventional ways of responding and project themselves fully into the clients' experiencing. Clients, too, may make suggestions as to how therapy may proceed. If and when clients feel convinced of their therapists' ability to meet them at relational depth, they may feel the safety and companionship that allows them to share their very existence as they are experiencing it. Mearns writes of the client experiencing relational depth: 'In this territory he does not talk *about* his experiencing – he *is* his experiencing ... In this existential process he cannot lie – lying belongs to a much more superficial level of relating' (2003: 5). In meeting clients at relational depth, the maxim of person-centred counselling that it is more about *being* than about *doing* holds true.

The Canadian psychologist David Rennie (1998) has developed what he terms an experiential approach to person-centred therapy. Rennie's approach revolves around clients' and therapists' *reflexivity*, which he defines as self-awareness and agency within that self-awareness. Rennie's approach goes beyond empathic responding to focus on both client and therapist processes.

Two elements of process work are process *identification* – 'I notice that you seem to have come to a halt' – and process *direction* – 'I don't know if it would be useful or not, but one thing you could try would be to see if you can make contact with the feeling of *being* stuck' (Rennie, 1998: 119).

Rogers's influence pervades the work of therapists of other theoretical orientations: for example, now all competent cognitive and cognitive-behaviour therapists heavily emphasize the quality of the relationship when assessing clients and delivering interventions. Rogers has also influenced many therapists who describe themselves as eclectic. For example, some eclectic therapists might use a person-centred approach as the treatment of choice for some clients either at the start of therapy or throughout therapy. Furthermore, eclectic therapists can also integrate a more client-focused approach into how they apply interventions derived from many other theoretical positions. However, for many person-centred therapists such eclecticism or integration of person-centred ideas and practices constitutes a violation of the person-centred approach as a coherent functional philosophy.

The development of person-centred therapy and therapists proceeds by means of journals and training centres. Journals devoted to Rogers's approach include *The Person-Centered Journal* and *Person-Centred & Experiential Psychotherapies*.

In 2000, at a conference in Chicago, the constitution of a World Association for Person-Centered and Experiential Counseling and Psychotherapy was formally approved. In 1989 the British Association for the Person-Centred Approach (BAPCA) was founded and there is also the Association for Person-Centred Therapy in Scotland. Training opportunities for developing person-centred counselling and therapy skills are provided in numerous countries throughout the world. The centre of gravity for person-centred work appears to be moving from the United States – where since Rogers's death its influence has rapidly declined (Thorne, 2002) – to Europe. The person-centred approach is firmly established in professional and institutional therapy domains in Holland, Germany, Belgium and Britain (Mearns and Thorne, 2000). There is also continuing interest in the approach in South America and the Far East.

Review and personal questions

Review questions

1. Critically review Rogers's concept of the actualizing tendency. What evidence might support or negate Rogers's views about the concept?
2. What does Rogers mean by organismic valuing process?
3. What does Rogers mean by the terms experience, experiencing and awareness?
4. What are conditions of worth and how do they develop?

5. Specify how low-functioning people process their experiences differently from high-functioning people.
6. With reference to a person's self-concept and experience, what does Rogers mean by the term incongruence? Provide an example.
7. Why does Rogers present how to conduct therapy in terms of growth-promoting attitudinal conditions rather than techniques?
8. Describe each of the three therapist-offered, growth-promoting attitudinal conditions.
9. In what ways do clients change both during and at the end of successful person-centred therapy?
10. What do you consider the strengths and weaknesses of Rogers's model of the person?
11. What do you consider the strengths and weaknesses of Rogers's model of therapy?

Personal questions

1. Are you aware of any of your conditions of worth? If so, what are they and how did you acquire each of them?
2. Examine a past or current relationship that you think has helped or is helping you to attain a more adequate self-concept. What characteristics of the other person were or are helpful?
3. Examine a past or current relationship that you think has hindered you from attaining a more adequate self-concept. What characteristics of the other person were or are harmful?
4. Assess yourself on each of the following attributes of fully functioning or self-actualizing people: openness to experience, rationality, personal responsibility, self-regard, capacity for good personal relationships and ethical living.
5. If you conduct therapy, how congruent are you and how do you know?
6. If you conduct therapy, how well do you offer unconditional positive regard and how do you know?
7. If you conduct therapy, how empathic are you and how do you know?
8. What relevance, if any, has the theory and practice of person-centred therapy for how you conduct therapy?
9. What relevance, if any, has the theory and practice of person-centred therapy for how you live?

Annotated bibliography

Rogers, C.R. (1959) 'A theory of therapy, personality, and interpersonal relationships, as developed in the client-centered framework', in S. Koch (ed.), Psychology: A Study of Science (Study 1, Volume 3). New York: McGraw-Hill. pp. 184–256.

Rogers regarded this chapter as one of his most significant publications. He worked for three or four years on it and was proud of its thoroughness and rigour. He endeavoured to make every major statement in it something that could be tested by research. This chapter is the major reference for readers wishing to understand Rogerian theory.

Rogers, C.R. (1951) *Client-Centered Therapy.* Boston: Houghton Mifflin.
This book describes the attitudinal orientation of the counsellor, the therapeutic relationship experienced by the client, the process of counselling, and various issues and applications of the client-centred approach. The book concludes with an important 19-proposition statement of Rogers's theory of personality and behaviour.

Rogers, C.R. (1957) 'The necessary and sufficient conditions of therapeutic personality change', *Journal of Consulting Psychology, 21*: 95–103.
Regarded also by Rogers as one of his most significant publications, this article presents and discusses six conditions for effective counselling practice. The article elaborates on the counsellor conditions of congruence, unconditional positive regard and empathic understanding.

Rogers, C.R. (1961) *On Becoming a Person.* Boston: Houghton Mifflin.
Another publication regarded by the author as one of his most significant. Rogers acknowledged the book as certainly his most popular and thought it had spoken to people all over the world. The book comprises seven parts: speaking personally; how can I be of help?; the process of becoming a person; a philosophy of persons; the place of research in psychotherapy; what are the implications for living?; and the behavioural sciences and the person.

Rogers, C.R. (1975) 'Empathic: an unappreciated way of being', *The Counseling Psychologist, 5*: 2–10.
This article, reprinted in *A Way of Being*, is Rogers's re-evaluation of the attitudinal condition of empathy. It is his major statement on the subject.

Rogers, C.R. (1980) *A Way of Being.* Boston: Houghton Mifflin.
A collection of 15 papers written between 1960 and 1980, this book is divided into four parts: personal experiences and perspectives; aspects of a person-centred approach; the process of education and its future; and looking ahead: a person-centred scenario. This book is written in the same reader-friendly style as *On Becoming a Person*.

Raskin, N.J. and Rogers, C.R. (2005) 'Person-centered therapy', in R.J. Corsini and D. Wedding (eds), *Current Psychotherapies* (7th edn). Belmont, CA: Thomson Brooks/Cole. pp. 130–65.
An authoritative overview of the theory and practice of person-centred therapy based on a chapter originally written by Rogers.

Mearns, D. and Thorne, B. (1999) *Person-Centred Counselling in Action* (2nd edn). London: Sage.
Engagingly written, this best-selling text introduces person-centred theory and practice in a way that clearly and sensitively brings to life the processes going on within and between counsellors and clients. The book's eight chapters are: the person-centred approach; the counsellor's use of the self; empathy; unconditonal positive regard; congruence and 'beginnings', 'middles' and 'endings'.

References and further reading

Barrett-Lennard, G.T. (1998) *Carl Rogers' Helping System: Journey and Substance*. London: Sage.

Cohen, D. (1997) *Carl Rogers: A Critical Biography*. London: Constable.

Combs, A.W. and Snygg, D. (1959) *Individual Behavior*. New York: Harper & Row.

Gendlin, E.T. (1988) 'Carl Rogers (1902–1987)', *American Psychologist*, 43: 127–8.

Gordon, T. (1970) *Parent Effectiveness Training: The Tested New Way to Raise Responsible Children*. New York: Wyden.

Kirschenbaum, H. and Henderson, V.L. (eds) (1990) *The Carl Rogers Reader*. London: Constable.

Maslow, A.H. (1962) *Toward a Psychology of Being*. Princeton, NJ: Van Nostrand.

Maslow, A.H. (1970) *Motivation and Personality* (2nd edn). New York: Harper & Row.

McCleary, R.A. and Lazarus, R.S. (1949) 'Autonomic discrimination without awareness', *Journal of Personality*, 18: 171–9.

Mearns, D. (1997) *Person-Centred Counselling Training*. London: Sage.

Mearns, D. (2003) *Developing Person-Centred Counselling*. London: Sage.

Mearns, D. and Thorne, B. (1999) *Person-Centred Counselling in Action* (2nd edn). London: Sage.

Mearns, D. and Thorne, B. (2000) *Person-Centred Therapy Today: New Frontiers in Theory and Practice*. London: Sage.

Raskin, N.J. and Rogers, C.R. (2005) 'Person-centered therapy', in R.J. Corsini and D. Wedding (eds), *Current Psychotherapies* (7th edn). Belmont, CA: Thomson Brooks/Cole. pp. 130–65.

Rennie, D.L. (1998) *Person-Centred Counselling: An Experiential Approach*. London: Sage.

Rogers, C.R. (1939) *The Clinical Treatment of the Problem Child*. Boston: Houghton Mifflin.

Rogers, C.R. (1942) *Counseling and Psychotherapy*. Boston: Houghton Mifflin.

Rogers, C.R. (1951) *Client-Centered Therapy*. Boston: Houghton Mifflin.

Rogers, C.R. (1957) 'The necessary and sufficient conditions of therapeutic personality change', *Journal of Consulting Psychology*, 21: 95–103.

Rogers, C.R. (1959) 'A theory of therapy, personality, and interpersonal relationships, as developed in the client-centered framework', in S. Koch (ed.), *Psychology: A Study of Science* (Study 1, Volume 3). New York: McGraw-Hill. pp. 184–256.

Rogers C.R. (1961) *On Becoming a Person*. Boston: Houghton Mifflin.

Rogers, C.R. (1962) 'The interpersonal relationship: the core of guidance', *Harvard Educational Review*, 32: 416–29.

Rogers, C.R. (1969) *Freedom to Learn*. Columbus, OH: Charles E. Merrill.

Rogers, C.R. (1970) *Encounter Groups*. London: Penguin.

Rogers, C.R. (1973) *Becoming Partners: Marriage and Its Alternatives*. London: Constable.

Rogers, C.R. (1974) 'In retrospect: forty-six years', *American Psychologist*, 29: 115–23.

Rogers, C.R. (1975) 'Empathic: an unappreciated way of being', *The Counseling Psychologist*, 5: 2–10.

Rogers, C.R. (1977) *Carl Rogers on Personal Power*. London: Constable.

Rogers, C.R. (1980) *A Way of Being*. Boston: Houghton Mifflin.

Rogers, C.R. (1986a) 'A client-centered/person-centered approach to therapy', in I. Kutash and A. Wolf (eds), *Psychotherapist's Casebook: Theory and Technique in the Practice of Modern Therapies*. San Francisco: Jossey Bass. pp. 197–208.

Rogers, C.R. (1986b) 'Reflection of feelings', *Person-Centred Review*, 1: 375–7.

Rogers, C.R. (1990) 'Reflection of feelings and transference', in H. Kirschenbaum and V. Henderson (eds), *The Carl Rogers Reader*. London: Constable. pp. 127–34.

Rogers, C.R. (2005) 'The case of Mrs Oak', in D. Wedding and R. Corsini (eds), *Case Studies in Psychotherapy* (4th edn). Belmont, CA: Thomson Brooks/Cole. pp. 55–76.

Rogers, C.R. and Sanford, R.A. (1985) 'Client-centered psychotherapy', in H.I. Kaplan, B.J. Sadock and A.M. Friedman (eds), *Comprehensive Textbook of Psychiatry* (4th edn). Baltimore, MD: William & Wilkins. pp. 1374–88.

Thorne, B. (2002) 'Person-centered therapy', in W. Dryden (ed.), *Handbook of Individual Therapy* (4th edn). London: Sage. pp. 131–57.

Thorne, B. (2003) *Carl Rogers* (2nd edn). London: Sage.

Walker, A.M., Rablen, R.A. and Rogers, C.R. (1960) 'Development of a scale to measure process changes in psychotherapy', *Journal of Clinical Psychology,* 16: 79–85.

On film

Rogers, C.R. (1965) 'Client-centered therapy', in E. Shostrom (ed.), *Three Approaches to Psychotherapy.* Santa Ana, CA: Psychological Films.

5

Introduction

Gestalt therapy, according to Perls, its main originator, is an existential approach 'not just occupied with dealing with symptoms or character structure, but with the total existence of a person' (1969a: 71). Toward the end of his life Perls (1969a) wrote that he considered gestalt therapy one of the three then-existing types of existential therapy, the two others being Frankl's logotherapy and Binswanger's daseins therapy. Clients who come for gestalt therapy are in states of existential crisis and need to learn to take responsibility for their existences. Perls considered all other existential philosophies borrowed concepts from other sources: for example, Binswanger from psychoanalysis, Tillich from Protestantism, and Sartre from Communism. Gestalt therapy is the only existential approach that has support in its own formation since gestalt formation – the emergence of needs – is a primary biological phenomenon. Perls observed: 'Gestalt therapy is a philosophy that tries to be in harmony, in alignment with everything else, with medicine, with science, with the universe, with what *is*' (1969a: 17). This chapter ends with some more recent developments in gestalt therapy.

Fritz Perls (1893–1970)

Friederich (Frederick or Fritz) Soloman Perls was born in Berlin, the son of a Jewish travelling salesman of Palestinian wines. He grew up with his two sisters in a disturbed family in which his parents had many bitter fights, both verbal and physical. Perls's mother used carpet-beating rods on him but he claims she did not break his spirit, rather he broke the carpet-beaters. He saw his father as a hypocrite who preached one thing and lived another and who progressively isolated himself from his family. Perls wrote: 'Basically I hated him and his pompous righteousness, but he could also be loving and warm. How much my attitude was influenced by my mother's hatred of him, how much she poisoned us children with it, I could not say' (1969b: 250–1). During his puberty years, a period during which he was initiated into both sex and acting, Perls was the black sheep of his family. Throughout his life Perls was a rebel rather than a complier, a man with a very quick eye for others' phoniness and pseudo-authenticity, and somewhat of an exhibitionist himself. His early experiences of rejection and insecurity may have deeply influenced his later life.

Perls's ideas were largely formed in the Austro-Germanic world. On leaving high school, he enrolled as a medical student at Berlin University. At the start of the First World War, Perls had been declared physically unfit for active service. However, by 1916 fitness requirements were much lower and Perls interrupted his medical studies to serve as a medical officer, including a spell in the trenches from 1916–17. In 1918 Perls returned to being a student at the universities of Freiburg and Berlin and in 1920 he received his MD from the latter institution.

In 1926 Perls moved to Frankfurt where he accepted a post as assistant to the gestalt psychologist Kurt Goldstein at the Frankfurt Neurological Institute. Also in 1926, Perls met Laura Posner, whom he was to marry in 1929. Together they shared a strong interest in gestalt psychology. Perls considered he had a peculiar relationship with the gestalt psychologists, admiring much of their work, but unable to go along with them when they became logical positivists. He did not read any of their textbooks, but had read some papers by Lewin, Wertheimer and Kohler. He observed: 'Most important for me was the idea of the unfinished situation, the incomplete gestalt' (1969b: 62). The academic gestaltists never accepted Perls and he did not regard himself as a pure gestaltist.

For some years, Perls had been undergoing training as a Freudian psychoanalyst. He moved to Vienna in 1927 and a year later completed his analytical training. On returning to Germany, from 1928 to 1933 Perls worked as a certified Freudian psychoanalyst mainly in Berlin.

In addition to gestalt psychology and Freudian psychoanalysis there were numerous other influences on Perls. He had a love of acting and, early in life, studied under Max Reinhardt, the noted director of the Deutsche Theater. Reinhardt insisted that his students observe very closely how people express emotions through their voice and gestures (Clarkson and Mackewn, 1993). Perls was also interested in Reich's idea of character armour, whereby repressions and resistances became total organismic functions. Later influences were to include Moreno, with his ideas on therapy by means of psychodrama, American humanistic psychology and eastern religion, especially Zen Buddhism.

In 1933, with the rise of Hitler, Perls fled from Germany to Holland. Apart from being Jews, Fritz and Laura Perls had to leave quickly to avoid being rounded up by the Nazis because of their left-wing political activism. At the time of his departure Perls's analyst was Wilhelm Reich and his supervisors were Otto Fenichel and Karen Horney. Perls wrote: 'From Fenichel I got confusion; from Reich, brazenness; from Horney, human involvement without terminology' (1969b: 39). In 1934, on the recommendation of Ernest Jones, Freud's friend and biographer, accompanied by wife and young daughter, Renate, Perls moved to Johannesburg as a training analyst. In 1935, despite Fritz wanting her to abort her pregnancy, Laura gave birth to their son Stephen, who came to regard him as a distant and disengaged father very much wrapped up in his own world (Perls, 1993).

Fritz and Laura Perls soon had successful private practices and, in 1935, they established the South African Institute for Psychoanalysis. From 1942 to 1945, Perls worked as a South African army medical officer and psychiatrist near Pretoria in the war against the Nazis. During his South African years Perls was influenced by the holism of Jan Smuts, the South African general, prime minister and philosopher. Smuts (1926/1987) wrote about the way individuals and the universe are actively 'whole-making' and introduced the idea from physics that everything has a field and that things and organisms must be considered in relation to their fields. In 1942 Perls's first book *Ego, Hunger and Aggression* was published in South Africa, with the British edition being published in 1947, with the sub-title *A Revision of Freud's Theory and Method*. Perls's wife Laura authored several chapters in this book and she was an important collaborator in the founding of gestalt therapy (Yontef and Jacobs, 2005).

Fritz and Laura Perls became increasingly concerned at the beginning of apartheid policies in South Africa. In 1946 Perls emigrated to the United States and established a private practice in New York City. Laura and their two children joined him in the autumn of 1947. In 1951 Perls published *Gestalt Therapy: Excitement and Growth in the Human Personality*, a book coauthored by Ralph Hefferline, Professor of Psychology at Columbia University, and Paul Goodman, a social philosopher and writer. Some view Goodman, an uninhibited and radical bisexual, as the third cofounder of gestalt therapy (Clarkson and Mackewn, 1993).

In 1952 Perls established the New York Institute of Gestalt Therapy and, in 1954, the Cleveland Institute for Gestalt Psychotherapy. Between 1952 and 1956, Perls had increasing differences of opinion with Laura Perls and Paul Goodman about directions for gestalt therapy. In 1957, partly for health reasons due to a recently diagnosed heart condition, Perls moved to the milder climate of Miami and was never again to live with Laura for any length of time. In Miami Perls became friends and lovers with Marty Fromm, even as she continued to be in therapy with him (Clarkson and Mackewn, 1993).

In 1960 Perls moved to the West Coast of the United States and, in 1964, joined the staff of the Esalen Institute at Big Sur, California, as resident associate psychiatrist. During this period, he began doing gestalt demonstrations on stage in front of increasingly large groups, including illustrating his hot seat technique. However, Perls realized that large group gestalt demonstrations were not gestalt therapy proper. In May 1969, Perls moved to Cowichan on Vancouver Island in British Columbia where he was establishing a gestalt community. Here he was very happy and finally at peace with the world. In

December 1969 Perls left Cowichan for what was to be the last time, went to Europe, but was clearly unwell on his return. After a brief illness Perls died in a Chicago hospital of a heart attack on 14 March 1970, at the age of 76. During his last illness, Laura had flown to join him only to find Perls sometimes confiding in her and sometimes shouting at and ignoring her.

In 1969 Perls had published *Gestalt Therapy Verbatim* and the autobiographical pot-pourri of prose, poetry and psychology entitled *In and Out of the Garbage Pail*. At the time of his death Perls was working on two books, *The Gestalt Approach* and *Eye Witness to Therapy*, and these were published posthumously in 1973 as a single book entitled *The Gestalt Approach & Eye Witness to Therapy*.

Theory

Basic concepts

Perls (1973) wrote in his introduction to *The Gestalt Approach & Eyewitness to Therapy* that gestalt theory was grounded in experience and observation, had changed with years of practice and application and was still growing. The following presentation is almost exclusively based on Perls's own writings, some in conjunction with collaborators. Although, as shown later, others have developed gestalt therapy after Perls's death, no other really major figure has emerged since then.

Gestalt

The German noun *gestalt* means form or shape, and among the meanings of the verb *gestalten* are to shape, to form, to fashion, to organize and to structure. Other terms for gestalt include pattern, configuration or organized whole. The major thrust of the experimental work of the gestalt psychologists was to show that humans do not perceive things in isolation but organize them through their perceptual processes into meaningful wholes (for example, a row of dots may be perceived as a straight line).

People's visual fields are structured in terms of 'figure' and 'background' or 'ground'. While 'figure' is the focus of interest (an object or pattern, for example), 'ground' is the setting or context. Perls and his colleagues (Perls et al., 1951) noted that the interplay between figure and ground was dynamic. For instance, the same ground may, with differing interests and shifts of attention, give rise to different figures. A given figure may itself become ground in the event that some detail of its own becomes figure. The relation between that which stands out (figure) and the context (ground) is meaning, which in a good gestalt is clear (Yontef and Jacobs, 2005).

The holistic doctrine

The human organism is a unified whole. In particular Perls objected to the old mind–body split. The emergence of psychosomatic medicine made the close relationship of mental and physical activity increasingly apparent. In fact mental activity seemed to be an activity of the whole person carried out at a lower energy level than those activities called physical. Human beings are wholes engaging in fantasizing, play-acting and doing. For instance, people's actions provide clues as to their thoughts and their thoughts provide clues concerning what they would like to do. In short, people do not have organisms but *are* organisms engaged in activities of the same order that are often wrongly dichotomized into mental and physical activities.

Another erroneous dichotomy is that between self and external world. Individuals are not self-sufficient but can only exist in an environmental field. Environments do not create individuals nor do individuals create environments. Rather each is what it is because of its relationship to the other and the whole. For instance, in the example of a person seeing a tree, there is no sight without something to be seen nor is anything seen if there is no eye to see it.

There are numerous other false dichotomies such as those between emotional (subjective) and real (objective), infantile and mature, biological and cultural, love and aggression, and conscious and unconscious. For instance, regarding the split between infantile and mature, it is often lack of certain childhood traits that devitalizes adults while other traits called infantile may be the introjections of adult neuroses. A consistent theme of the gestalt approach is to search for the overall pattern rather than for false dichotomies.

Contact boundary and contact

Earlier I mentioned that Perls disdained the split between self and the external world considering that the organism and the environment stood in a relationship of mutuality to one another. The contact boundary is the boundary between organism and environment and it is at this boundary that psychological events take place. Perls and colleagues (1951: 229) considered that 'psychology studies the operation of the contact-boundary in the organism/environment field'. Such 'contact' or 'being in touch with' involves both sensory awareness and motor behaviour. The organism's sensory system provides it with a means of orientation, with the motor system providing a means of manipulation. Both orientation and manipulation take place at the contact boundary. In healthy functioning, once the system of orientation has performed its function, the organism manipulates itself and the environment in such a way that organismic balance is restored and the gestalt is closed.

All thoughts, feelings and actions take place at the contact boundary. In healthy functioning, people have an effective contact-withdrawal rhythm or means of meeting psychological events at the contact boundary. Contacting the environment represents forming a gestalt, whereas withdrawal is either closing a gestalt completely or mobilizing resources to make closure possible. More simply contact and withdrawal may respectively be viewed as acceptance and rejection of the environment. The components of contact and withdrawal are almost invariably present, but the neurotic person has a reduced capacity to discriminate between the appropriateness of these dialectical elements and consequently behaves with reduced effectiveness as will be seen in the later section on interruptions of contact.

Homeostasis and balance

The basic tendency of every organism is to strive for balance. The organism is continuously faced with an imbalance that is disturbing through either external (demands from the environment) or internal (needs) factors. Life is characterized by a continuous interplay of balance and imbalance in the organism. Homeostasis or organismic self-regulation is the process by which the organism satisfies its needs by restoring balance when faced with a demand or need that upsets its equilibrium. Health constitutes the appropriate operation of the homeostatic process, whereas sickness means that for too long a time the organism has remained in a state of disequilibrium, of being unable to satisfy its needs. Death constitutes a total breakdown of the homeostatic process.

Though psychological and physiological are interrelated, the organism may be perceived as having psychological as well as physiological contact needs. A simple example of a physiological need is that, for the organism to be in good health, the water content of the blood must be kept at a certain level, neither too low nor excessive. If, for instance, the water content of the blood falls too low the individual feels thirst, with its symptoms of dry mouth and restlessness and the wish to restore the imbalance by drinking. A possible example of a more psychological need is that of mothers to keep their children happy and contented. Consequently, even when sleeping, they may be very sensitive to the cries and whimpers of their offspring.

The homeostatic process also operates where several needs are experienced simultaneously. However, here a selective process takes place based on the organism's need for survival and for self-actualization; with the simultaneous experiencing of many needs, the individual attends to the dominant survival and self-actualization need before attending to the others. Put another way, the dominant need or the need that presses most sharply for satisfaction becomes the foreground figure while the other needs recede, at least momentarily, into the background. Perls (1969a) wrote about doing away with the whole of instinct theory and simply considering the organism as a system that needs balance if it is to function properly. Though practically people have hundreds of unfinished situations in them, the most urgent situation always emerges. Individuals, to be able to satisfy their needs (to complete or to close incomplete *gestalten*) must be able both to sense what they need and to manipulate themselves and their environments to obtain what is necessary.

Life is basically an infinite number of unfinished situations or incomplete gestalts, with no sooner than one gestalt being completed than another comes up. The homeostatic process is the means by which the organism maintains itself 'and the only law which is constant is the forming of gestalts – wholes, completeness. A gestalt is an organic function. A gestalt is an ultimate experiential unit' (Perls, 1969a: 16). With the introduction of the concept of the homeostatic process, it was possible to see gestalt formation as a primary biological drive, with the gestalt being the basic experiential unit having such properties as figure and ground and completeness or incompleteness.

The self and self-actualization

The self is the system of contacts at the contact boundary at any moment. The self exists where there are boundaries of contact and its activity is that of forming figures and grounds. The self always integrates the senses, motor coordination and organic needs. It is the integrator or artist of life and though it 'is only a small factor in the total organism/environment interaction ... it plays the crucial role of finding and making the meanings that we grow by' (Perls et al., 1951: 235).

The self consists of the identifications and alienations at the contact boundary. For instance, individuals may identify with their families, but feel alien to people from different countries. Inside the boundary tends to be perceived as good and outside as bad. Self-actualization may be viewed as the expression of appropriate identifications and alienations. Healthy functioning involves identifying with one's forming organismic self, not inhibiting one's creative excitement, yet alienating what is not organismically one's own. Sickness involves restricting one's areas of contact through alienating parts of one's forming organismic self by means of false identifications.

Perhaps a more accessible way of stating this is to make a distinction between self-actualizing based on the existential principle that 'a rose is a rose is a rose' and self-image actualizing in which people live for their image of how they should be rather than how they are. Perls considered that 'Every external control, even *internalized* external control – "you should" – interferes with the healthy working of the organism. There is only one thing that should control: the *situation*' (1969a: 20). If people understand the situations they are in, and let these situations control their actions, then they learn how to cope with life. An even more simple view of Perls's ideas on self-actualization may be gained from his dictum: 'So lose your mind and come to your senses' (Perls, 1970a: 38).

Excitement

Humans secure their energy from the food and air they take in. Perls emphasized vitality and the need to integrate the social being and the animal being.
Perls used the word excitement to describe the energy we create, because it
coincides with the physiological function of excitation. This life force or *élan
vital* is at the heart of the gestalt approach. Perls observed: 'Now normally the
élan vital, the life force, energizes by sensing, by listening, by scouting, by
describing the world – how is the world there. Now this life force first mobilizes
the center – *if* you have a center. And the center of the personality is what used
to be called the soul: the emotions, the feelings, the spirit' (1969a: 68).

Excitement varies according to the task on the basis of hormonal differentiation: for instance, it gets tinged with some other substance, for example
adrenalin for anger or sexual hormones for erotic contact. Much of our excitement goes into energizing the motor system because the muscles link people
with the environment. Even for most emotional events, emotion is transferred into movement. However, some excitement goes into energizing the
senses. Healthy people allow their excitement to get to their senses and muscles, but unfortunately many people allow much of their excitement to be
drained off into their fantasy life, into their computer (unproductive thinking), and into self-image actualization. Perls (1969a) believed that modern
humans live in a state of low-grade vitality in which the average person at
most lives only 5 to 15 per cent of their potential and the person who has
even 25 per cent of their potential available is considered a genius.

Emotion

Emotion, which is the organism's direct evaluative experience of the organism/
environment field, is immediate rather than being regulated by thoughts
and verbal judgments. Emotion is a continuous process since all instances in
people's lives carry some feeling tone of pleasantness or unpleasantness.
Excitement is modified into specific emotions according to the situation that
has to be met and the emotions mobilize the sensory and motor system so
that needs may be satisfied. Gestalt therapy attaches great importance to the
emotions which are not only essential as energy or excitement regulators but
are also 'unique deliveries of experience which have no substitute – they are
the way we become aware of our concerns, and, therefore, of what we are and
what the world is' (Perls et al., 1951: 96).

Acquisition

Aggression, assimilation and introjection

An aggressive attitude towards experience is necessary if it is really to be
assimilated or made the organism's own. An analogy may be made between

the aggression required for eating and that required for assimilating experience. Food needs to be destroyed or destructured before that which is valuable to the organism can be retained and undesirable substances can be eliminated. Undesirable substances that are not eliminated may be poisonous and detrimental to the organism. Every organism in an environmental field grows by incorporating, digesting or destructuring, and assimilating or absorbing selectively new matter whether it is food, lectures or parental influence. Loving parents are likely to provide their children with experiences which they will assimilate since they are relevant to their own needs as they grow from environmental support to self-support.

Not all experience, however, goes through the destructuring and assimilation process required for healthy functioning. Introjections are experiences that are swallowed as wholes rather than being properly digested. The outcome of introjection is that undesirable as well as desirable substances have been retained, thus weakening the organism. Hateful parents are likely to provide their children with experiences that have to be introjected or taken in whole even though they are contrary to the needs of the organism.

Frustration and manipulation

The young baby is virtually totally dependent on its mother, but as time goes by the child learns to communicate, to crawl and walk, to bite and chew, and to accept and reject. In short the child learns to realize some part of its potential for existence. Growth comes about through learning to overcome frustrations by mobilizing one's innate resources to manipulate the environment to satisfy needs. The term manipulation refers to a person's ways of mobilizing and using the environment to satisfy needs. Both healthy and unhealthy organisms manipulate the environment, with healthy organisms manipulating it on an underlying basis of self-support, whereas unhealthy organisms are seeking environmental rather than self-support.

Perls wrote: 'Without frustration there is no need, no reason to mobilize your resources, to discover that you might be able to do something on your own, and in order not to be frustrated, which is a pretty painful experience, the child learns to manipulate the environment' (1969a: 35). Perhaps it would be more accurate to say that with the right kind of frustrations the child learns to manipulate the environment in such a way as to meet its needs and restore effective organismic balance. However, with lack of frustration (the spoiled child) or with frustrations which block or are beyond the child's coping capacity, the outcome is likely to be that the child starts to mobilize the environment by playing phony roles and games: for instance playing stupid, playing helpless, playing weak and flattering. These false manipulations cause individuals to alienate parts of themselves, be it their eyes, ears or genitals.

Interruptions of contact

Humans are forced to learn much more through education than by using their biologically based instincts. Consequently much of the animal's intuition as to what is the 'right' procedure is either missing or blocked. Instead there is a whole range of composite fantasies, handed down and modified through the generations, as to what constitutes the 'right' procedures. These procedures perform mostly support functions for social contacts (manners and ethics) and have the disadvantage of not necessarily being biologically based. Consequently there are frequently interruptions in the contact provided by ongoing organismic processes that, if left alone, would be conducive to self-support. Examples of such interruptions are 'Don't touch that' or 'Don't do this'. Even withdrawals may be interrupted as in the example 'You stay here now, keep your mind on your homework and don't dream'. People often incorporate their parents' interruptions as introjections in their own lives, for example 'Grown men don't cry'. Unhealthy organisms or neurotics are self-interrupters who need to become aware both of the fact that they are interrupting themselves and also of what they are interrupting.

Suppression of emotion

Suppression of emotion is a major way in which adults interrupt the contact of their children. Such adults, who frequently have been brought up in environments in which 'the authorities' were afraid of emotion, tend to squelch the emotions of their children and thus prevent their emotions from undergoing natural development and differentiation. This is mainly achieved through an overemphasis of the 'external world' and the demands of 'reality' and a belittling of organismic needs and emotions. The outcome of this is that children 'adjust' to such unremitting pressure by dulling their body-sense and losing some of their vitality. However, because emotions are inherent to the organism, this suppression of emotions does not eliminate 'undesirable' emotions, rather it disturbs 'the intricate organism/environment field by setting up a great number of situations which, *unless avoided, are immensely emotion-arousing!*' (Perls et al., 1951: 97, emphasis in original).

Maintenance

Though Perls often used the terms neurosis and neurotic, he considered that problems of poor gestalt formation and closure were extremely widespread. In this section I examine the gestalt view of how people maintain their contact deficiencies. Needless to say, people's difficulties are compounded because they live in cultures or environments where self-image actualizing rather than self-actualizing is common.

Zones of awareness

There are three zones or layers of awareness: outer, self and intermediate (see Box 5.1). Perls sometimes used the Indian word *maya* to describe the intermediate zone or DMZ. *Maya* means illusion or fantasy and is a kind of dream or trance. More colloquial and crude is Perls's use of the term 'mind f**king' to describe the activity of the DMZ which hinders people from coming to their senses.

Box 5.1   The three zones of awareness

The outer zone (OZ)
This zone consists of awareness of the world, of those things, facts and processes that are available to everyone.

The self zone (SZ)
This zone is the place within the skin, our authentic organismic selves.

The intermediate zone (DMZ)
This zone, which is located within the self zone, is often called 'mind' or consciousness which prevents people from good contact or being 'in touch' with themselves or the world. The DMZ is a zone of fantasy activity that consumes excitement and leaves little energy over for being in touch with reality.

Anxiety and stage fright

Gestalt theory has both a physiological and psychological definition of anxiety. The physiological definition is: 'Anxiety is the experience of breathing difficulty during any blocked excitement' (Perls et al., 1951: 128). The idea underlying this definition is that heightened energy mobilization, with the need for more air (an increase in the rate and amplitude of breathing), occurs whenever there is strong concern and contact. As such it is a healthy way of being in erotic, aggressive, creative and other sorts of exciting or energy-mobilizing situations. A less healthy response is to control, interfere with and interrupt the excitement by trying to continue breathing at the rate that was adequate prior to it. This leads to a narrowing of the chest to force exhalation in order to create a vacuum into which fresh air can rush. Anxiety, derived from the Latin word *angustia*, meaning narrowness, is the product of an emergency measure caused by the conflict between excitement and control.

The psychological definition of anxiety is that it is 'the gap between the now and the later' or 'stage fright' (Perls, 1969a: 32–3). As such it is the result of the fantasy activity of the DMZ. This fantasy activity is rehearsing for a future that people do not really want to have because they are afraid of it. Perls wrote: 'We fill in the gap where there should be a future with insurance policies, status quo, sameness, *anything* so as not to experience the possibility of openness towards the future' (Perls, 1969a: 48–9, emphasis in original). People who are in the now and have access to their senses are unlikely to be anxious because their excitement can flow immediately into the kind of spontaneous, creative and inventive activity which achieves solutions to unfinished situations. They are not blocked from good contact with themselves and the environment by *maya* or fantasies, prejudices, apprehensions and so on. They are prepared to take reasonable risks in living. Perls distinguished between catastrophic fantasies, which entail too much precaution, and anastrophic fantasies that entail too little. He thought some people managed a balance between catastrophic and anastrophic fantasies, thus having both perspective and rational daring.

Neurosis

Neurotic individuals allow society to impinge too heavily on them. They cannot clearly distinguish their own needs and see society as larger than life and themselves as smaller. Society can consist of any one of a number of groups, for example, the family, the state, the social circle and coworkers. When the neurotic and one or more of these groups simultaneously experience different needs, the neurotic is incapable of distinguishing which need is dominant and thus can make neither a good contact nor a good withdrawal. Consequently one or more of the contact boundary disturbances of neurosis seem the most effective way to maintain balance and a sense of self-regulation in situations where the odds appear to be overwhelmingly adverse.

Perls distinguished between health, psychosis and neurosis. In health, people are in touch with the realities both of themselves and the world. In psychosis, people are out of touch with reality and in touch with *maya*, especially fantasies about megalomania and worthlessness. In neurosis a continual fight is taking place between *maya* and reality.

Contact boundary disturbances

The neuroses, which entail significant contact boundary disturbances, operate primarily through four mechanisms, albeit interrelated. These neurotic boundary disturbances are 'nagging, chronic, daily interferences with the processes of growth and self-recognition' (Perls, 1973: 32). Introjection, projection, confluence and retroflection are the four mechanisms of contact boundary disturbance. However, these mechanisms are only neurotic when used chronically and inappropriately. They are useful and healthy when authentically chosen and used temporarily in particular circumstances not by compulsion, but by choice (Clarkson, 2004).

Introjection

I have already mentioned *introjection* as the process by which material from outside is swallowed whole rather than digested properly, with the valuable elements being assimilated and the undesirable or toxic elements discarded. Introjects, or undigested thoughts, feelings and behaviour, are the results of the process of introjection. Introjection may be viewed as the tendency to 'own' as part of the self what actually is part of the environment. Two outcomes of introjection are, first, that the introjects prevent individuals from getting in touch with their own reality because all the time they are having to contend with these foreign bodies and, second, that the introjects may be incompatible with one another and thus contribute to personality disintegration.

Projection

Projection is the reverse of introjection in that it is the tendency to 'own' as part of the environment what actually is part of the self. Projection can take place on two levels: in relation to the outer environment and in relation to the self. Perhaps most commonly, projection involves shifting those parts of ourselves that we dislike and devalue onto others rather than recognizing and dealing with the tendencies in ourselves. Projections are associated with introjects because people usually devalue themselves in relation to introjected self-standards, whose unacceptable derivatives in terms of self-evaluations are then projected onto the environment.

Projection in relation to the self takes place when people disown as part of themselves either areas in which or certain impulses that arise. For instance, people may say of their anger 'It took control of me' whereby the anger is given an objective existence outside of themselves so that they can make it responsible for their troubles and avoid full recognition of the fact that *it* is part of *her* or *him*.

Confluence

With *confluence*, the individual lacks any distinction or experiences no boundary at all between self and environment. People who are unaware of the contact boundaries between themselves and others are neither able to make good contact with them nor, where appropriate, to withdraw. A feature of confluence is demanding likeness and refusal to tolerate differences. Two examples of confluence are marital partners and parents who, respectively, refuse to see their spouses and children as different from themselves.

Retroflection

In *retroflection*, the individual fails to discriminate between self and others accurately and treats themselves the way they originally wanted to treat other people or objects. For instance, the harassed mother at the end of a long day in which everything has gone wrong may turn her destructive impulses against herself. Retroflection means literally 'to turn sharply back against'.

When people retroflect they redirect their activity inward and substitute themselves instead of the environment as the targets of their behaviour. Retroflection is not necessarily neurotic. In certain situations it may be to the individual's advantage to suppress particular responses. However, retroflection is pathological when it is chronic, habitual and out of control.

Perls was sensitive to the use of language both in representing and helping to sustain contact boundary disturbances. For example, in introjection the personal pronoun 'I' is used when the real meaning is 'they', in projection the pronouns 'they' or 'it' are used when the real meaning is 'I', in confluence the pronoun 'we' is used when there may really be differentness, and retroflection uses the reflexive 'myself' as in the statement 'I am ashamed of myself'.

The following is Perls's succinct summary of the lacks of discrimination, interferences and interruptions entailed in the four main contact boundary disturbances:

> The introjector does as others would like him to do, the projector does unto others what he accuses them of doing to him, the man in pathological confluence doesn't know who is doing what to whom, and the retroflector does to himself what he would like to do to others. (1973: 40)

Layers of neurosis

Perls (1969a, 1970a) came to see the structure of neurosis as consisting of five layers, each of which is described in Box 5.2. A major feature in the maintenance of neuroses is that people are not willing to undergo the pain of the impasse, the feeling of being stuck and lost. An example involving the later layers of neurosis is that of a young woman who had recently lost her child and who needed to be able to face her nothingness and her grief to be able to come back to life and make real contact with the world.

Box 5.2   The five layers of neurosis

The cliché layer
For example, the meaningless tokens of meeting, such as a handshake or 'Good morning'.

The Eric Berne or Sigmund Freud layer
The layer in which people engage in the counterproductive manipulations of phony roles and games (for example, the bully, the very important person, the cry baby, the nice little girl, the good boy and so on).

Box 5.2   (Continued)

The impasse
When the role-playing layer is worked through, then therapist and client come to the third layer called the impasse or sometimes the sick-point. This layer is characterized by a phobic attitude manifested in avoidance and flight from authentic living. In particular suffering is avoided, especially the suffering of frustration.

The death or implosive layer
Behind the impasse is the death or implosive layer, which appears either as fear of death or a feeling of not being alive. Here people implode by contracting and compressing themselves.

The explosion
The explosion is the final neurotic layer. There are four basic kinds of explosions from the death layer: into grief, if a person works through a loss that has not been assimilated; into orgasm, for sexually blocked people; into anger; and into joy. The explosions, which may be mild depending on the amount of energy invested in the implosive layer, connect with the authentic, organismic person.

Therapy

Therapeutic goals

Clients come to gestalt therapy because they are in existential crises. Perls had a rather cynical view of their motivation stating: 'Anybody who goes to a therapist has something up his sleeve. I would say roughly 90% don't go to a therapist to be cured, but to be more adequate in their neuroses' (1969a: 79). Gestalt therapy goals revolve around the client's movement from environmental support to self-support. Beginning clients are mainly concerned with solving problems. Gestalt therapists assist clients to support themselves not only in solving current problems, but in living more authentically. In order to be self-supporting clients need to be in touch with their organismic existential centres ('I am what I am'). People who are in touch with their organismic selves or with their senses are self-actualizing or self-supporting.

The process of self-actualizing involves an effective balance of contact and withdrawal at the contact boundary and the ability to use energy or excitement to meet real rather than phony needs. Furthermore, self-actualizing involves being able to withstand frustration until a solution emerges. Self-supporting people take responsibility for their existences and possess *response-ability* or freedom of choice. They are able appropriately to use aggression to assimilate their experiences and are largely free from the neurotic contact boundary disturbances of introjection, projection, retroflection and confluence. They possess relatively little self-destructive unfinished business since they are good at forming and closing strong gestalts.

Yontef and Jacobs (2005) observe that the only goal of gestalt therapy is awareness. Clients require awareness both in particular areas, awareness of content, and also of the processes or automatic habits by which they block awareness, awareness of process. This latter self-reflective kind of awareness, sometimes called 'awareness of awareness', enables clients to use their skills in awareness to rectify disturbances in the awareness process.

Process of therapy

It is important to distinguish how Perls worked in groups towards the end of his life and the practice of ongoing individual gestalt therapy, which is its most common form today. Perls was a showman who conducted gestalt therapy in workshops at Esalen that included communal baths as an adjunct. He required six elements for his performance: '(1) My skill; (2) Kleenex; (3) The hot seat; (4) The empty chair; (5) Cigarettes; and (6) An ashtray' (Perls, 1969b: 227). Perls viewed all therapy interviews as experimental. Therapists need to try things out to help clients become aware of how they are now functioning as persons and organisms. Sometimes he would do mass experiments or exercises, but mostly he worked with a series of single people, or sometimes couples, in front of the group.

In ongoing individual gestalt therapy assessment can be done as part of the therapeutic process rather than as an initial diagnostic procedure, though some therapists also undertake initial assessments. Clients need to be willing to work within the gestalt therapy framework and feel that their therapist is someone whom they can trust. In the initial session therapists are likely to discuss details of fees, cancellation of sessions policy and other pertinent practical matters.

Gestalt therapists' offices are designed to be friendly and comfortable and avoid having desks or tables between therapists and clients. Where possible, space is available for movement and experimentation. In addition, every effort is make to ensure privacy both in terms of soundproofing and safeguarding of records.

Sessions are usually once weekly which gives clients time to digest what happened in the previous session. Though more frequent sessions are possible, gestalt therapists take care to encourage self-support rather than dependency by not becoming too available. Often individual therapy is combined with group therapy, couples therapy, family therapy, workshops, and with meditation or biofeedback training.

Evaluation of therapeutic process and outcomes occurs as part of therapy and both therapists and clients participate. Beginning clients may be most concerned with solving problems and relief of psychological discomfort. Therapists encourage their clients to assume responsibility for self-support in addressing their problems and resultant discomfort. Initially clients may talk about problems but show little insight into the how of their behaviour. As therapy progresses, clients become more aware both of how they behave and of how unaware they have hitherto been. As therapy continues, client and therapist may pay more attention to general personality issues and the general patterns and conditions that contribute to clients' insufficient awareness. The idea is that clients increasingly carry their higher levels of awareness into their everyday lives and maintain and build upon them after therapy ends.

The therapeutic relationship

There are at least two ways of looking at the therapist–client relationship in gestalt therapy: that of Perls in his demonstrations and workshops and that of other important practitioners, for instance Laura Perls, Gary Yontef and Lynne Jacobs. The relationship and style of Perls's Esalen workshops is often called 'Perlsism' or 'Perlsian Gestalt' to differentiate it from the relationship and style of therapy practised by those other leading gestalt therapists.

Perls was a charismatic and dominating personality who, once he became well known, may have attracted clients who felt they might benefit from his confronting approach. Though ostensibly he advocated a democratic dialogue between therapist and client, the reality was that much of the time he was controlling the therapeutic process. Perls's son Stephen was to observe that his father did not know how to relate to another person on an equal basis (Perls, 1993). Perls's relationships with clients contained the paradox of advocating personal responsibility at the same time as assuming the major responsibility for the therapeutic process himself.

At his best Perls was so concerned with helping clients that he would not allow them to sabotage their growth by being phony, an important word in his vocabulary. A contemporary phrase for Perls's relationships with clients is 'tough love'. Other leading practitioners have conducted gestalt therapy within the context of more equal or horizontal therapist–client relationships.

In gestalt therapy relationships, therapists concentrate on what clients do moment to moment and on what is happening between therapist and client. Therapists attend closely to what clients experience because they believe that the client's subjective experience is as real and valid as the therapist's 'reality' (Yontef and Jacobs, 2005).

All gestalt therapists regard the therapeutic relationship as a 'working' rather than a 'talking' relationship. In this working relationship, both therapists and clients are self-responsible: therapists for the quality of their presence and self-awareness, their knowledge and skills in relating to the client, and for maintaining an open and non-defensive stance; and clients for their commitment to working to become more in charge of their lives through developing greater self-awareness. Furthermore, therapists are responsible for not colluding in clients' manipulations to get them to do what clients fear they cannot do for themselves. Instead, therapists should relate to clients in a warm, respectful, direct and honest manner.

Therapeutic interventions

The use of gestalt therapy interventions 'hinges on questions of *when, with whom,* and *in what situation*' (Shepherd, 1970: 234, emphasis in original). In 'Perlsian' therapy, he would be likely to intervene without much, if any, consultation. With most gestalt therapists, appropriate interventions are decided upon in an ongoing dialogue between therapist and client. Such interventions are considered as experiments. A major purpose of encouraging clients to experiment with different ways of thinking and acting is to collect information to achieve genuine understanding rather than mere changes in behaviour. Repeatedly clients are encouraged to 'Try this and see what you experience' (Yontef and Jacobs, 2005). Creativity from therapists and clients in setting up and carrying out appropriate experiments is highly valued. Parlett and Hemming observe that, within the gestalt therapy approach, 'each therapist applies Gestalt principles in individual ways and uses different methods according to her/his professional background and personal style' (2002: 224). The following are some interventions and experiments used by Perls.

Awareness technique

Gestalt therapy is an experiential rather than a verbal or interpretive approach. Assessment data about how clients interrupt their contact with life are collected as therapists and clients work together. Gestalt therapy demands that clients experience themselves as fully as possible in the here and now both to understand their present manipulations and contact boundary disturbances and also to re-experience the unfinished business of past problems and traumas.

Perls (1973) regarded the simple phrase 'Now I am aware' as the foundation of the gestalt approach. The 'now' because it keeps therapists and clients in the present and reinforces the fact that experience can only take place in the present. The 'aware' because it gives both therapists and clients the best picture of the latter's present resources. Awareness always takes place in the present and opens up possibilities for action.

Clients are asked to become aware of their body language, their breathing, their voice quality and their emotions as much as of any pressing thoughts. Below are some examples of Perls directing Gloria's attention to her non-verbal behaviour taken from the *Three Approaches to Psychotherapy* film series (Dolliver, 1991: 299; Perls, 1965):

'What are you doing with your feet now?'
'Are you aware of your smile?'
'You didn't squirm for the last minute.'
'Are you aware that your eyes are moist?'
'Are you aware of your facial expression?'

One way of following up a client's awareness report is for the therapist to say: 'Stay with it' or 'Feel it out'. Such instructions can encourage clients to more fully experience and work through feelings to completion. For example, staying with moist eyes may lead to further experiencing and then identifying the reasons for feeling sad and to crying.

Exaggeration, which may focus on either movement and gesture or on verbal statements, is another way of heightening clients' awareness of how they communicate. In each instance, clients are asked progressively and repeatedly to exaggerate the behaviour. Examples of exaggeration requests from Perls's interview with Gloria are as follows (Dolliver, 1991: 300; Perls, 1965):

'Can you develop this movement?'
'Develop it as if you were dancing.'
'Now exaggerate this.'
'What you just said, talk to me like this.'
'Do this more.'

Yet another way of heightening clients' awareness of their here-and-now communication is to ask them to use the phrase *'I take responsibility for it'*. For instance, 'I am aware that I am moving my leg and I take responsibility for it'.

When using awareness techniques, therapists may self-disclose and provide here-and-now feedback about how they see clients communicating. Furthermore, therapists can judiciously share how they are affected.

Since clients are self-interrupters they often find it difficult to remain in the here and now. The awareness technique is really a concentration technique, sometimes called *focal awareness*, by which clients learn to experience each now and each need and also how their feelings and behaviour in one area are related to feelings and behaviour in other areas. Thus they come to an awareness not only of the fact that they are interrupting their contact with themselves and the world, but also of what they are interrupting and how they are doing it through the neurotic mechanisms of introjection, projection and so on. Clients are also asked to do some homework that consists of reviewing the session in terms of a systematic application of the awareness technique.

Sympathy and frustration

Empathizing with clients is insufficient since the therapists are withholding themselves and at worst allowing confluence. Sympathy alone spoils clients. What is needed is a combination of sympathy and of frustration. Clients must be frustrated in their efforts to control the therapist by neurotic manipulations and instead learn to use their powers of manipulation to meet their real needs. The therapist focuses on getting clients to become more aware and not to become phobic when they start feeling uncomfortable.

Perls provided situations in which his clients experienced being stuck in frustration and then frustrated their avoidances still further until they were willing to mobilize their *own* resources. He repeatedly frustrated clients until they were face to face with their blocks, inhibitions, and ways of avoiding having eyes, ears, muscles, authority and security in themselves. Frustration often leads to the discovery that the phobic impasse does not exist in reality but in fantasy, in that clients have been preventing themselves from using their own available resources through catastrophic expectations. Furthermore frustration helps clients to express their needs and requests directly rather than to cover them over with neurotic manipulations. The imperative is the primary form of communication and clients who can actually state what they need and mean what they state have made the most important step in their therapy.

Eliciting fantasies

A limitation of the awareness technique is its slowness. In order to speed up therapy Perls made considerable use of fantasizing, be it verbal, written down or acted out as a drama. Below is an example taken from the *Three Approaches to Psychotherapy* film series in which Perls encourages Gloria to describe a fantasy (Dolliver, 1991: 300; Perls, 1965):

'Can you describe the corner you'd like to go to?'
'Imagine you are in this corner and you are perfectly safe. Now what would you do in that corner?'
'What should I do when you are in that corner?'

During the interview, Perls also asked Gloria to describe her fantasies about him (Dolliver, 1991: 301):

'Now what can I do to you?'
'How old must I be?' (for Gloria to scold him)
'How should I be? Give me a fantasy. How could I show my concern for you?'
'What would I do? How would I conceal my feelings?'

Dolliver observes that whenever Gloria offered Perls's feedback about her experience of him, Perls always regarded it as a transference fantasy representing her projected attributes.

Drama techniques

'Monotherapy', perhaps better termed monodrama, is a form of psychodrama with a difference. In monotherapy, instead of having other people as well as the client involved in the drama, the client creates his own stage and plays all the roles under his or her own direction and expression.

In the *shuttle* technique clients are asked to shuttle their attention from one area to another. For instance, a client can shuttle between the visualization of a memory and the organismic reliving of it in the here and now. Another example involves getting clients to shuttle between their feelings in and about an incident and their projections in the incident. For example, a client who feels angry with a colleague for 'apple-polishing' his boss may shuttle to experiencing his own needs and desires for approval from the boss. A further example is that of getting clients to shuttle between talking and listening to themselves. After each sentence, clients are asked: 'Are you aware of this sentence?'. The purpose here is to help clients stop compulsive talking which interrupts their experiencing of themselves and listening to others.

Drama and fantasy work can involve both the *hot seat* and the *empty chair*. The individual with whom the counsellor works in front of the group occupies the hot seat. The empty chair is a second chair which is a 'projection-identification gimmick ... waiting to be filled with fantasized people and things' (Perls, 1969b: 224). Essentially it is a method of highlighting the shuttling process by getting clients to change chairs as they shuttle between parts of themselves or between different people in a drama.

Topdog–underdog dialogues are one of the main examples of the use of the shuttle technique involving both fantasy work and the empty chair. Perls considered that in their fantasies many people played self-torture games in which they were fragmented into an inner conflict between controller (topdog) and controlled (underdog). The topdog (or superego) is righteous, authoritarian, full of 'shoulds' and 'should nots', perfectionistic and manipulates with threats of catastrophe if his demands are not carried out. The underdog (or intraego) is cunning and manipulates with being wheedling, defensive, apologetic, playing the crybaby and so on. Typical underdog statements are 'I try my best' and 'I have such good intentions'. Through shuttling between these polarities, clients are helped to understand the structure of their behaviour and also to reconcile these two fighting clowns by becoming more in touch with their organismic selves.

Dreamwork

Perls (1970b) regarded dreams as the royal road to integration. Dreams are existential messages, not just unfinished situations, current problems or symptoms. Especially if the dreams are repetitive, a very important existential issue for the client is likely to be involved. There are four stages to dreamwork (see Box 5.3).

Box 5.3   The four stages of dreamwork

- **Stage 1   Sharing the dream:** The client relates the dream.
- **Stage 2   Retelling the dream in the present tense:** The client retells the dream or a section of it as a drama by changing the past tense into the present tense, for example 'I was climbing a mountain' becomes 'I am climbing a mountain'. Perls would ask clients to say their dreams, or parts of their dreams, again 'in the *present tense*: as if you were dreaming it *now*?' (1970b: 205, emphasis in original).
- **Stage 3   Talking to the different actors in the dream:** The client becomes the stage director and sets the scene and talks to the different actors in the dream or section of it. For example, when working with Mary Anne's dream, Perls introduced the action element with the statement: 'Now let's start acting it out. Tell this to the man. Talk to the man – express your resentment' (1970b: 206). The client is encouraged to become the different actors, the props and all that is there. Clients do not have to work with a whole dream, for even if they reidentify with just one or a few items in the dream the exercise is valuable.
- **Stage 4   Conducting a dialogue between different elements in the dream:** The fourth stage of dreamwork may be facilitated by the empty chair technique to allow for dialogues between the different people, objects or parts of the self that are encountering each other. These dreamwork encounters provide opportunity for two things: the integration of conflicts and reidentification with those parts of the self that are alienated, especially the assimilation of projections. Dreamwork is an excellent way of finding the holes in a client's personality. These tend to be manifested as voids and blank spaces that are accompanied by nervousness and confusion.

Responsibility language

Perls was interested in semantics and he was conscious of how clients could interfere with self-support through poor use of language (Levitsky and Perls, 1970; Perls, 1970a). Using verbs that acknowledge choice and personal agency is one example of using responsibility language: for example, rephrasing 'I can't do that' to 'I *won't* do that'. In addition, clients can be alerted to use the personal pronoun 'I' rather than 'It' or 'They' and send messages directly to their therapists and to others. Furthermore, if clients ask the kind of questions that manipulate the environment for support, therapists can encourage them to change those passive questions into more active and self-supporting statements.

Case material

Since gestalt therapists both differ in how they work and also work with many different here-and-now techniques, it is hard to get an overall feel for the approach from reading case material. Perls's book *Gestalt Therapy Verbatim* (1969a) is primarily made up of verbatim transcripts from his large-scale weekend dreamwork seminars between 1966 and 1968 and from an intensive four-week gestalt therapy workshop in 1968, all of which were held at Esalen. Perls presents his therapy with a number of different clients from the seminars and the workshop, including working with dreams in the case of Jane (Perls, 2005). In addition, the *Eyewitness* part of *The Gestalt Approach & Eyewitness to Therapy* (1973) contains transcripts that Perls considered had great teaching potential, taken from his conducting therapy films. In the 'Gestalt Therapy' film in the earlier *Three Approaches to Psychotherapy* series, Perls (1965) introduces his approach, conducts a brief interview with Gloria and then summarizes his impressions of the session.

Another example of gestalt therapy is that of Laura Perls (1968) working first with a 25-year-old black woman and then with a 47-year-old central European Jewish refugee. Joen Fagan (1974) presents transcripts with commentary for three sessions with Iris, who had agreed to be videotaped and had no previous experience with gestalt therapy. Clarkson (2004) illustrates the various stages of long-term gestalt therapy with a progressive case example, contributed by Sue Fish, where the client is Gary, a university lecturer. As therapy progressed, Gary left a relationship that had become unsatisfactory. He became more able to mobilize and use his own resources, including supporting himself in an interdependent relationship with another woman.

Yontef and Jacobs (2005) present a case example in the form of an excerpt taken from the fourth year of therapy with Miriam, whose world was characterized by extreme isolation due to terrifying and degrading childhood abuse. In this session, the therapist gently and gradually accedes to the client's wish for touch by touching her fingertips at the same time as helping her talk about the experience.

Further developments

I have already mentioned that many other leading gestalt therapists developed more horizontal relationships with clients than did Perls. Since Perls's death, the practice of gestalt therapy has altered in many other ways and continues to develop (Clarkson, 2004; Mackewn, 1994; Parlett and Hemming, 2002; Yontef and Jacobs, 2005). Contemporary gestalt therapists are more supportive, compassionate and kind. There is less emphasis on frustration and abrasively confronting those clients perceived as manipulative. When using confrontation, gestalt therapists take great care not to humiliate or retraumatize clients by triggering unnecessary shame in them.

Therapists are less likely to pose as experts and more likely to reveal their humanity, including their fears, defensiveness and confusions. Gestalt therapists are encouraged to make 'I' statements to enhance their contact with clients and clients' focusing. In describing how she works, Laura Perls (1970) provides examples of disclosing her awareness and feelings, sharing personal problems and life experiences, and using physical contact. Her guiding principle is to use such disclosures only if they might help clients take their next steps.

Many contemporary gestalt therapists attempt to exemplify Buber's (1937/1958) concept of the 'I–Thou' relationship in which two unique people encounter and openly respect one another's essential humanity. 'I–Thou' relationships are here-and-now person-to-person existential encounters in which therapist and client are open to being changed by the other (Clarkson, 1997). Such relationships may be contrasted with 'I–It' relationships in which others are treated as objects to be used and manipulated.

Contemporary gestalt therapy tends to be highly individual with a different therapy being tailor-made for each client. Therapists and clients creatively generate and carry out appropriate experiments as therapy progresses. Clarkson (2004) provides a good example of how one leading gestalt therapist works. She presents a seven-stage cycle of gestalt formation and production: sensation, awareness, mobilization, action, final contact, satisfaction and withdrawal. The cycle's last six stages are then used as a framework for illustrating the gestalt therapy process. Clarkson suggests some appropriate experiments for each stage.

Another development is that, drawing on gestalt therapy's empty chair technique, Greenberg and colleagues (1993) have devised an empty chair dialogue intervention geared to the resolution of 'unfinished business' with significant others. Such unresolved negative feelings can contribute to anxiety and depression as well as be transferred into other relationships where they are inappropriate. This intervention 'in which the client engages in an imaginary dialogue with the significant other, is designed to access restricted feelings allowing them to run their course and be restructured in the safety of the therapy environment' (Pavio and Greenberg, 1995: 419).

Some gestalt therapists may openly use psychoanalytic formulations to describe character structure (Yontef, 1988). When conducting groups, though a minority mainly still follow Perls's working with individuals in front of the group style, the trend is for gestalt therapists to make greater use of the interactions between and contributions from group members than Perls did. This can be done either by getting participants to talk to each other with an emphasis on direct here-and-now communication or by mixing Perls's style with direct here-and-now communication between participants (Yontef and Jacobs, 2005). A further development is that gestalt therapy techniques have been integrated into other approaches. For example, gestalt techniques and experiments are commonly used in conjunction with transactional analysis (Dusay and Dusay, 1989; James and Jongeward, 1971).

Gestalt therapy has training institutes in every major city of the United States and in most countries of Europe and South America as well as in Australia. Training standards for gestalt therapists in Britain are among the most stringent in the United Kingdom Council for Psychotherapy (UKCP). In Britain there are several hundred psychotherapists who primarily identify themselves as gestalt therapists (Clarkson, 2004). However, in Britain and elsewhere, there are also many people who call themselves gestalt therapists after attending a few workshops and without adequate academic preparation (Yontef and Jacobs, 2005).

There are national gestalt therapy associations in many countries and The International Gestalt Therapy Association is a new group attempting to form a more international governing structure. There are now four English-language gestalt journals: the *International Gestalt Journal*, the *Gestalt Review*, the *British Gestalt Journal* and the *Australian Gestalt Journal*. In addition, gestalt therapy literature is prominent in much of the world.

Review and personal questions

Review questions

1. What did Perls mean by gestalt formation?
2. Why did Perls consider it important for people to take an aggressive attitude to experience?
3. In growing up what is the role of frustration?
4. Describe each of Perls's three layers of awareness.
5. Describe each of the following mechanisms of contact boundary disturbance: introjection, projection, retroflection and confluence.
6. What are the goals of gestalt therapy?
7. How and why do gestalt therapists use awareness techniques?
8. How and why do gestalt therapists use sympathy and frustration?
9. How and why do gestalt therapists use drama techniques?
10. What is the purpose of dreamwork and what are its four stages?
11. What is 'Perlsian' gestalt therapy and how does it differ from the way some of Perls's collaborators and many contemporary therapists practise gestalt therapy?

Personal questions

1. What specific events in your life may have influenced you to come to your mind and lose your senses?
2. Assess how you relate to your environment in terms of each of Perls's mechanisms of contact boundary disturbance: introjection, projection, confluence and retroflection.
3. What are the phony roles and games that you use to obtain environmental support rather than rely on self-support?

4. Sit in a comfortable chair and, for the next three minutes, say to yourself: 'Now I am aware ...' each time you become aware of your body language, your breathing, your emotions and any pressing thoughts. For example, 'Now I am aware I'm uncrossing my legs'.

5. Spend the next three minutes focusing on your response-ability for your life by staying in the now and saying to yourself about all your current behaviour: '... and I take responsibility for it'.

6. Use the shuttle technique and change chairs as you shuttle between different parts of yourself or between yourself and another person.

7. What is your fantasy of how it would be like for you to be in the hot seat being in therapy with a gestalt therapist like Perls?

8. What relevance, if any, has the theory and practice of gestalt therapy for how you conduct therapy?

9. What relevance, if any, has the theory and practice of gestalt therapy for how you live?

Annotated bibliography

Perls, F.S., Hefferline, R.F. and Goodman, P. (1951) *Gestalt Therapy: Excitement and Growth in the Human Personality*. London: Souvenir Press.
This book contains an introduction and two volumes. Volume 1 is a series of 18 experiments: experiments 1 to 11 focus on contacting the environment, technique of awareness and directed awareness; experiments 12 to 18 focus on retroflection, introjection and projections. Volume 2 is a major statement of gestalt theory consisting of three parts: introduction; reality, human nature and society; and theory of the self. This detailed book is for serious students and therapists.

Perls, F.S. (1969a) *Gestalt Therapy Verbatim*. New York: Bantam Books.
This book consists of three parts: talk; dreamwork seminar; and intensive workshop. The talk and dreamwork seminar parts are selected and edited material from audiotapes made at weekend dreamwork seminars conducted by Perls at the Esalen Institute, Big Sur, California, between 1966 and 1968. The intensive workshop part is taken from audiotapes of a four-week intensive workshop conducted in 1968. The talk part of the book provides an easily readable introduction to gestalt theory.

Perls, F.S. (1969b) *In and Out of the Garbage Pail*. New York: Bantam Books.
As the book's cover says, 'Joy. Sorrow. Chaos. Wisdom. The free-floating autobiography of the man who developed Gestalt Therapy'. A pot-pourri of self-disclosure by means of prose and poetry. This book is a good way to meet Perls, the man.

Perls, F.S. (1973) *The Gestalt Approach & Eyewitness to Therapy*. New York: Bantam Books.
This book is a combination of two projects that Perls was working on at the time of his death. *The Gestalt Approach* is his final statement of his theory and was written because he regarded his two previous theoretical works *Ego, Hunger and Aggression* and *Gestalt Therapy* as too outdated and difficult to read. *Eyewitness to Therapy* provides descriptions of gestalt therapy in action.

Clarkson, P. (2004) *Gestalt Counselling in Action* (3rd edn). London: Sage.
This book starts by introducing gestalt theory and the fundamentals of gestalt practice. A seven-stage cycle of gestalt formation and production is presented and, using the cycle as a framework, the practice of gestalt counselling is reviewed. This engaging and well-written book is a rich source of ideas about how to integrate experiments into gestalt practice.

Yontef, G. and Jacobs, L. (2005) 'Gestalt therapy', in R.J. Corsini and D. Wedding (eds), *Current Psychotherapies* (7th edn). Belmont, CA: Thomson Brooks/Cole. pp. 299–336.
This chapter provides a good overview of a contemporary approach to gestalt therapy. However, the annotated bibliography at the end of the chapter does not contain a single book written by Perls.

References and further reading

Buber, M. (1937/1958) *I and Thou* (2nd edn). Edinburgh: T. & T. Clark.

Clarkson, P. (1997) 'Variations on I and thou', *Gestalt Review*, 1(1): 56–70.

Clarkson, P. (2004) *Gestalt Counselling in Action* (3rd edn). London: Sage.

Clarkson, P. and Mackewn, J. (1993) *Fritz Perls*. London: Sage.

Dolliver, R.H. (1991) 'Perls with Gloria re-viewed: Gestalt techniques and Perls' practices', *Journal of Counseling and Development*, 69: 299–304.

Dusay, J.M. and Dusay, K.M. (1989) 'Transactional analysis', in R.J. Corsini and D. Wedding (eds), *Current Psychotherapies* (4th edn). Itasca, IL: Peacock. pp. 405–53.

Fagan, J. (1974) 'Three sessions with Iris', *The Counseling Psychologist*, 4(4): 42–60.

Fagan, J. and Shepherd, I.L. (eds) (1970) *Gestalt Therapy Now: Theory, Techniques, Applications*. Palo Alto, CA: Science & Behavior Books.

Greenberg, L.S., Rice, L.N. and Elliott, R. (1993) *Facilitating Emotional Change: The Moment by Moment Process*. New York: Guilford Press.

James, M. and Jongeward, D. (1971) *Born to Win: Transactional Analysis with Gestalt Experiments*. Reading, MA: Addison-Wesley.

Levitsky, A. and Perls, F.S. (1970) 'The rules and games of gestalt therapy', in J. Fagan and I.L. Shepherd (eds), *Gestalt Therapy Now: Theory, Techniques, Applications*. Palo Alto, CA: Science & Behavior Books. pp. 140–9.

Mackewn, J. (1994) 'Modern gestalt – an integrative and ethical approach to counselling and psychotherapy', *Counselling*, 5(2): 105–8.

Parlett, M. and Hemming, J. (2002) 'Gestalt therapy', in W. Dryden (ed.), *Handbook of Individual Therapy* (4th edn). London: Sage. pp. 209–38.

Pavio, S.C. and Greenberg, L.S. (1995) 'Resolving "unfinished business": efficacy of experimental therapy using empty-chair dialogue', *Journal of Consulting and Clinical Psychology*, 63: 419–25.

Perls, F.S. (1947) *Ego, Hunger and Aggression: A Revision of Freud's Theory and Method*. London: Allen & Unwin.

Perls, F.S. (1969a) *Gestalt Therapy Verbatim*. New York: Bantam Books.

Perls, F.S. (1969b) *In and Out of the Garbage Pail*. New York: Bantam Books.

Perls, F.S. (1970a) 'Four lectures', in J. Fagan and I.L. Shepherd (eds), *Gestalt Therapy Now: Theory, Techniques, Applications*. Palo Alto, CA: Science & Behavior Books. pp. 14–38.

Perls, F.S. (1970b) 'Dream seminars', in J. Fagan and I.L. Shepherd (eds), *Gestalt Therapy Now: Theory, Techniques and Applications*. Palo Alto, CA: Science & Behavior Books. pp. 204–33.

Perls, F.S. (1973) *The Gestalt Approach & Eyewitness to Therapy*. New York: Bantam Books.

Perls, F.S. (2005) 'The case of Jane', in D. Wedding and R.J. Corsini (eds), *Case Studies in Psychotherapy* (4th edn). Belmont, CA: Thomson Brooks/Cole. pp. 157–75.

Perls, F.S., Hefferline, R.F. and Goodman, P. (1951) *Gestalt Therapy: Excitement and Growth in the Human Personality*. London: Souvenir Press.

Perls, L.P. (1968) 'Two instances of gestalt therapy', in P.D. Pursglove (ed.), *Recognition in Gestalt Therapy*. New York: Funk & Wagnalls. pp. 42–68.

Perls, L.P. (1970) 'One gestalt therapist's approach', in J. Fagan and I.L. Shepherd (eds), *Gestalt Therapy Now: Theory, Techniques, Applications*. Palo Alto, CA: Science & Behavior Books. pp. 125–9.

Perls, S. (1993) 'Frederick Perls: a son's reflections', talk given by Stephen Perls on 23 April at the Fifteenth Annual Conference on the Theory and Practice of Gestalt Therapy, Hotel du Parc, Montreal, Canada (the text of this talk is available at www.gestalt.org).

Shepherd, I.L. (1970) 'Limitations and cautions in the gestalt approach', in J. Fagan and I.L. Shepherd (eds), *Gestalt Therapy Now: Theory, Techniques, Applications*. Palo Alto, CA: Science & Behavior Books. pp. 234–8.

Smuts, J. (1926/1987) *Holism and Evolution*. Cape Town: N & S Press.

Yontef, G.M. (1988) 'Assimilating diagnostic and psychoanalytic perspectives into gestalt therapy', *Gestalt Journal, 11*(1): 5–32.

Yontef, G.M. and Jacobs, L. (2005) 'Gestalt therapy', in R.J. Corsini and D. Wedding (eds), *Current Psychotherapies* (7th edn). Belmont, CA: Thomson Brooks/Cole. pp. 299–336.

Perls on film, videotape and cassette

Perls, F. (1965) 'Gestalt therapy', in E. Shostrom (ed.), *Three Approaches to Psychotherapy*. Santa Ana, CA: Psychological Films.

The Gestalt Journal Press lists a comprehensive bibliography of gestalt books, articles, videotapes and cassettes (go to www.gestalt.org for more information).

transactional analysis   6

Introduction

Eric Berne, the originator of transactional analysis (TA), stated that the criterion distinguishing his approach from other approaches was that it was based on the personality theory of Child, Parent and Adult ego states. Throughout this chapter Parent, Adult and Child start with a capital letter when describing ego states. The dividing line between what was and what was not transactional analysis rested on whether or not human behaviour was explained in terms of such ego states. Although Berne was strongly influenced by Freud, the theory and practice of transactional analysis are very different from those of psychoanalysis. Berne saw an element of his approach, called script analysis, as being 'para-Freudian' rather than anti-Freudian (1970: 400), and conceivably the same might be said for the whole of transactional analysis.

Berne differed from other humanistic theorists and from Freud in his greater emphasis on social psychiatry, which he defined as 'the study of the psychiatric aspects of specific transactions or sets of transactions which take place between two or more particular individuals at a given time and place' (1961: 12). Berne analysed what was going on in people's internal worlds when they came into contact with, influenced and were influenced by others in their external worlds.

In Chapter 1, I mentioned that one of the functions of counselling and therapy theories is to provide languages for conducting the therapeutic conversation. Berne was a leader in realizing the importance of therapists and clients using the same language. Transactional analysis provides an easily understood language that therapists and clients can use together to analyse and work on problems and transactions in the interests of clients' achieving greater autonomy and intimacy. This chapter mainly focuses on traditional or classical Bernian transactional analysis. However, at the end of the chapter, I present some recent TA developments.

Eric Berne (1910–70)

In 1910, Eric Berne was born Eric Lennard Bernstein in Montreal, Canada, and he grew up in a poor Jewish section of the city. His father appears to have been a dedicated general practitioner who often took Berne on his rounds. His mother, Sara, was a professional writer and editor who, after her husband died in 1921, supported Berne and his sister by her writing. Berne dedicated his first book to his mother who was probably influential in developing his writing interest and skills.

Berne's interest in medicine stemmed more from his father's example. James (1977) considers that the little Child in Berne was traumatized by his father's death. Certainly his father appears to have had a strong influence on Berne, whose goal was always to cure patients. This influence is reflected in the Latin dedication in Berne's seminal book *Transactional Analysis in Psychotherapy* (1961), a translation of which is 'In Memory of My Father David, Doctor of Medicine, Master of Surgery, and Doctor to the Poor'.

Berne studied English, psychology and pre-medicine at McGill University in Montreal and received his BA in 1931. In 1935 he obtained his MD and Master of Surgery degree from the same institution. Berne then went to the United States, where he became an American citizen. After an internship at Englewood Hospital in New Jersey, he became a psychiatric resident at Yale University School of Medicine. Reacting to the anti-Semitism of this period, he changed his name to Berne and began a private psychiatric practice in Norwalk, Connecticut. He also contracted the first of three marriages, each of which ended in divorce. Berne became Clinical Assistant at Mt Zion Hospital in New York and, in 1941, began training at the New York Psychoanalytic Institute, being analysed by Paul Federn, a former colleague of Freud.

In 1943 Berne entered the Army Medical Corps as a psychiatrist and it was during the war period that he started working with groups. On his discharge in 1946 he moved to Carmel, California, and finished *The Mind in Action,* since extensively revised and now published as *A Layman's Guide to Psychiatry and Psychoanalysis.* He also resumed his psychoanalytic education at the San Francisco Psychoanalytic Institute and underwent a training analysis with Erik Erikson. In 1950 he took a position at Mt Zion Hospital, San Francisco, and restarted private practice. For the remainder of his life he worked both in San Francisco and in Carmel, 125 miles away.

From his days in the army, Berne developed a research interest in intuition and developed the concept of ego image, which is a therapist's intuitive image of a person that in some ways describes his ego. Ego images are largely based on observation and listening to what patients say about themselves. During the period 1954 to 1958 Berne developed his ideas on the diagnosis of ego states or structural analysis; the analysis of individual transactions; the analysis of a series of transactions with covert as well as overt content, otherwise known as game analysis; and the longitudinal view of a patient's whole life from which it was possible to extrapolate her or his future, now called script analysis. In September 1954 Berne started his first transactional analysis group. His ideas were developed further in a series of regular seminars in Carmel that, in 1958, were succeeded by the San Francisco Social Psychiatry Seminars, later called the Eric Berne Seminars.

Berne was moving away from orthodox psychoanalysis and, in 1956, his application for membership of the Psychoanalytic Institute of San Francisco was rejected for the third time. Of this event he comments: '... after fifteen years the psychoanalytic movement and the writer officially parted company (on the most friendly terms) ...' (1961: 13). When, some years later, the Psychoanalytic Institute offered him membership, he declined with thanks. Berne had increasingly felt that the effective therapist had to be more active than was allowed in orthodox psychoanalysis and had to practise transactionally rather than from the head of a couch.

At the November 1957 Western Regional Meeting of the American Group Psychotherapy Association in Los Angeles Berne presented a paper entitled 'Transactional analysis: a new and effective method of group therapy', which was published in 1958. During three successive summers he broadened his experience by going to the South Pacific to study socialization and mental illness in various island cultures. By 1961 he had visited mental hospitals in about 30 different countries in Europe, Asia, Africa and the islands of the Atlantic and Pacific to test his ideas in various racial and cultural settings.

In 1961 Berne's most systematic statement *Transactional Analysis in Psychotherapy* was published. In 1963 he published a discussion of the application of transactional analysis to groups in *The Structure and Dynamics of Organizations and Groups*. In 1964 his ideas on analysing psychological games were publicly presented in *Games People Play: The Psychology of Human Relationships*, though these ideas had appeared three years earlier in a private edition of the book. The principles of transactional analysis for therapists were explained in his 1966 book *Principles of Group Treatment*, and his ideas on script analysis were developed in *What Do You Say After You Say Hello?*, published posthumously in 1972. Berne also wrote *The Happy Valley* (1968b) for children and *Sex in Human Loving* (1970) for both non-professionals and professionals.

During the 1960s, along with his writing and private practice, Berne held a number of appointments. These included Consultant in Psychiatry to the Surgeon General, US Army; Attending Psychiatrist to the Veterans Administration Mental Hygiene Clinic; Lecturer in Group Therapy, Langley-Porter Neuropsychiatric Clinic; Visiting Lecturer in Group Therapy, Stanford Psychiatric Clinic; and Adjunct Psychiatrist, Mt Zion Hospital, San Francisco. Early in 1970 Berne and his third wife were divorced. He died of a heart attack on 15 July the same year. Berne's work was continued by a number of his colleagues who attended the San Francisco seminars, including Claude Steiner, who developed script analysis.

It is interesting to speculate on Berne's own life script. The son of a doctor and a writer, he spent his life curing and writing about curing people. Some idea of his professional ideals may be gleaned from the introduction to his *Principles of Group Treatment*, which is written for those who wish to become 'real doctors' as contrasted with the 'non-real' or 'unreal' variety. A 'real doctor'

(a) has the overriding consideration throughout his practice of curing his patients;
(b) plans his treatment so that at each phase he knows what he is doing and why he is doing it;
(c) clearly distinguishes research and experimentation from good medical or surgical care, the former always being subsidiary to the latter; and
(d) takes complete responsibility for the welfare of his patients. (Berne, 1966: xvii)

The development of transactional analysis represents Berne's own commitment to being a 'real doctor'.

Theory

Basic concepts

Berne saw transactional analysis both as a theory of personality and social interaction and as a method of therapy. Some of his assumptions and basic concepts are presented below.

The fundamental OK position

Berne had a positive view of human nature which is stated in the transactional-analytic position 'I am OK; you are OK'. Another way he expressed this is by his statement 'Every human being is born a prince or a princess; early experiences convince some that they are frogs, and the rest of the pathological development follows from this' (Berne, 1966: 289–90).

Related to the basic assumption of human OKness are two further assumptions. First, Berne regarded practically every human being as possessing the complete neurological apparatus for adequate reality-oriented or Adult functioning. The only exceptions were those with the most severe type of organic brain injuries. Thus the therapeutic task is that of how to strengthen this already existing apparatus so that it may take its normal place in the client's psychic organization. Second, Berne believed that people have a built-in drive to both mental and physical health. The transactional analyst's job is to help nature by removing obstructions to patients' emotional and mental development, so letting them grow in their own directions.

Ego states

The fundamental building block of transactional analysis is the concept of ego states. Berne stated: 'An ego state may be described phenomenologically as a coherent system of feelings related to a given subject, and operationally as a set of coherent behavior patterns; or pragmatically as a system of feelings which motivates a related set of behaviour patterns' (1961: 17). Though not always emphasized by Berne, ego states involve thinking as well as feeling and behavior.

Each human being exhibits three kinds of ego states: Parent, Adult and Child. At any given moment any individual in a social grouping will predominantly exhibit one or another of these states. The three ego states, depicted in Figure 6.1, are described as follows:

- *Parent*: The Parent or exteropsychic ego state is a set of feelings, thoughts, attitudes and behaviours that resemble those of parental figures. It is both an accumulation of data and a way of relating to people. The Parent ego state may be seen behaviourally in one of two forms. The *controlling* or prejudicial Parent is manifested as a set of seemingly arbitrary and rigid rules, usually prohibitive, which may either agree or disagree with the rules of a person's culture. The *nurturing* Parent is manifested as sympathy and care for another individual or for oneself. Thus the Parent can be over-controlling and inhibiting or supportive and growth enhancing. The Parent ego state may also influence a person's Adult or Child ego states. The function of the Parent is to conserve energy and to diminish anxiety by making certain decisions automatic.
- *Adult*: In the Adult or neopsychic ego state the person autonomously and objectively appraises reality and makes judgments. Berne likened the neopsyche to a partially self-programming probability computer and stressed that the criterion of its adequacy was the use made of data available to a given individual. Characteristics by which an Adult ego state may be recognized include organization, adaptability and intelligence.
- *Child*: The Child or archaeopsychic ego state is a set of feelings, thoughts, attitudes and behaviour patterns which are archaic relics of an individual's childhood. Berne considered that we all carry within ourselves a little boy or girl who feels, thinks, acts and responds just as we did when we were children of a certain age. The Child ego state is exhibited behaviourally in two major forms. The *adapted* Child is manifested by feelings and behaviour that inferentially are under parental influence, such as sulking, compliance, rebelliousness, withdrawal and inhibition. The *natural* Child is manifested by spontaneous expression such as self-indulgence or creativity. Berne considered the natural Child to be the most valuable part of the personality. The proper function of a 'healthy' Child is to motivate the Adult so as to obtain the greatest amount of gratification for itself. This it does by letting the Adult know what it wants and by consulting the Parent about its appropriateness.

Structural analysis of ego states

Structural analysis consists of diagnosing and separating one feeling-thinking-and-behaviour pattern or ego state from another. Further analysis of ego

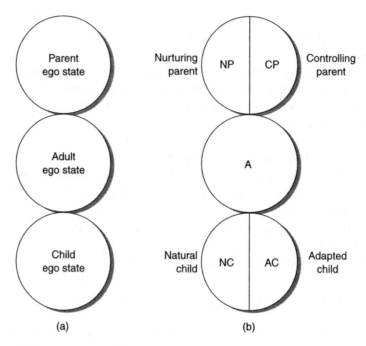

Figure 6.1   (a) Structural and (b) descriptive diagrams of personality

states does not provide new ego states, but rather subdivisions of the existing ones. Such analysis is called second-order structural analysis and can get very detailed. In particular, it focuses on further analysis of the Parent and Child.

In Figure 6.2 the Parent is divided into two components, one derived from the father and one derived from the mother. Children incorporate some characteristics of each parent into their Parent ego state, including the ways in which their parents exhibited thinking and feeling when expressing values. Consequently, second-order structural analysis includes the Parent, Adult and Child ego states of both parents.

Within the Child ego state, Parent, Adult and Child ego states, which were already there when the child made its basic decision concerning its life script, can be observed. Berne (1972) sometimes called the Parent in the Child the 'electrode', and Steiner (1974) described it as the 'Pig Parent'. Berne called the Parent in the Child the electrode because when it 'pushes the button', the person automatically does something negative. Examples of such negative behaviour include excessive alcohol consumption, reckless gambling and getting sexually turned off if coming on too strong.

Berne saw the Adult in the Child as a keen and perceptive student of human nature, which he called the Professor (Berne, 1961). Steiner (1974) calls the Adult in the Child the Little Professor and observes that it is the ego state which Berne himself used in his studies on intuition, when he would

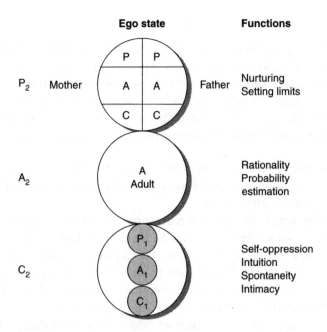

Figure 6.2   Second-order structural diagram of personality

guess the occupations of people using his own intuition. The Adult in the Child is the source both of intuitive and creative thinking and of delusion, since it may not always be right. The Child in the Child ego state is the source of innate wants and feelings. Spontaneity is a central characteristic of the Child in the Child, but sometimes this spontaneity can be self-destructive.

Psychic energy and cathexis

Transactional analysis is a dynamic theory of personality in that it uses the concepts of psychic energy and of cathexis or distribution of energy. At a given moment the ego state that is most strongly cathected will have executive power. Berne wrote of the flow of cathexis which gives rise to shifts in ego states. He considered that the most convenient way of acknowledging the differentiation of ego states was to view each state as having a boundary that separates it from other ego states. Under most conditions ego-state boundaries are semi-permeable. Shifts in ego state depend on three factors:

1. the forces acting on each state;
2. the permeability of the boundaries between ego states; and
3. the cathectic capacity of each ego state.

Berne (1961) observed that it is the quantitative balance between these three factors that determines the clinical condition of the client and thus indicates the therapy procedures.

Stimulus, recognition and structure hunger

The psychobiological basis of social psychiatry is that the ability of human beings to maintain coherent ego states depends on a changing flow of sensory stimuli. Berne cited Spitz's (1945) work, which demonstrated that sensory deprivation in infants resulted not only in psychological changes, but also in organic deterioration. Berne posited that there were three principal forms of drive, hunger or motivation: stimulus, recognition and structure hunger.

- *Stimulus hunger*: The most favoured forms of stimuli are those offered by physical intimacy. Berne acknowledged the dangers of over-stimulation as well as of under-stimulation.
- *Recognition hunger*: Recognition hunger may be viewed as a partial transformation of infantile stimulus hunger. Berne used the term 'stroking' to denote any act implying recognition of another's presence. There are numerous rituals, such as saying 'Hello!', which imply recognition and give gratification. Biologically, even negative recognition has an advantage over no recognition at all. Put colloquially, 'Folks need strokes!'
- *Structure hunger*: Structure hunger addresses the everyday problem of how to structure one's waking hours. Such time structuring is concerned only with social time or the time people spend with others.

Time structuring

Berne observed that if two or more people were in a room together they had six possible kinds of social behaviour or time structuring from which to choose. These are discussed below.

- *Withdrawal*: Here two people do not overtly communicate with one another, for example if they are on a bus or are withdrawn schizophrenics. In withdrawal, people remain wrapped up in their own thoughts.
- *Rituals*: Rituals are stylized signs of mutual recognition dictated by tradition and social custom. At the simplest level, two people saying 'Good morning' engage in a ritual.
- *Activities*: Activities – more commonly called work – are not just concerned with dealing with the material means of survival. They also have a social significance in that they offer a framework for various kinds of recognition and satisfactions. Berne considered that work transactions were typically Adult-to-Adult, oriented mainly towards external reality.
- *Pastimes*: Pastimes are semi-ritualistic, topical conversations that last longer than rituals but are still mainly socially programmed. They might include 'Ain't it Awful' and 'Motor Cars' types of conversations. The focus of pastimes tends to be external to the participants rather than directly self-referent.
- *Games*: Games, in contrast to pastimes, are sequences of transactions which are based more on individual than on social programming. A psychological

game is a set of covert or ulterior as well as overt transactions that lead to a predictable outcome or payoff. Frequently these payoffs involve negative feelings or 'rackets' such as anger and depression. Collecting racket feelings is known as collecting 'trading stamps', which may some day be cashed in for behaviours, such as a good cry or going out and buying some new clothes. More drastically, 'trading stamps' may be cashed in for divorce or attempted suicide. Each game has a motto by which it can be recognized, for example 'Why don't you? Yes but' and 'If it weren't for you' (Berne, 1964).

- *Intimacy*: Berne defined bilateral intimacy as 'a candid, game-free relationship, with mutual free giving and receiving and without exploitation' (1972: 25). Intimacy represents individual and instinctual programming in which social programming and ulterior motivations are largely, if not totally, suspended. Intimacy is the most satisfying solution to stimulus, recognition, and structure hunger, but unfortunately it is not very common for people to live as 'princes' and 'princesses'. Berne's idea of intimacy included, but was not restricted to, sexual intimacy.

Types of transactions

In transactional analysis a stroke or unit of recognition is viewed as the fundamental unit of social interaction. An exchange of strokes constitutes a transaction. Thus rituals, activities, pastimes, games and intimacy may all be viewed as involving transactions. During transactions, at any given time each person is likely to have one of their three ego states predominantly energized or cathected. Thus transactions take place between ego states and, at its simplest level, transactional analysis involves diagnosing the ego states involved in a stimulus and response exchange. In other words, the transactional stimulus may come from the Parent, Adult or Child of one person and the transactional response from the Parent, Adult or Child of the other person.

There are three main types of transactions: complementary, crossed and ulterior.

Complementary transactions

Complementary transactions are ones in which the directions of the stimulus–response transactions are consistent, such as discussing the ills of the world (Parent–Parent), talking about work (Adult–Adult), or having fun together (Child–Child). Another way of stating this is that complementary transactions are ones in which people receive a response from the ego state that they have addressed. An example of a complementary transaction is given in Figure 6.3. There are nine possible types of complementary transactions (PP, PA, PC, AP, AA, AC, CP, CA, CC). Berne's first rule of communication was that communication will proceed smoothly as long as transactions are complementary. In the example in Figure 6.3 Mike responds (a) from the ego state addressed by Bill and (b) to the ego state from which Bill addressed him.

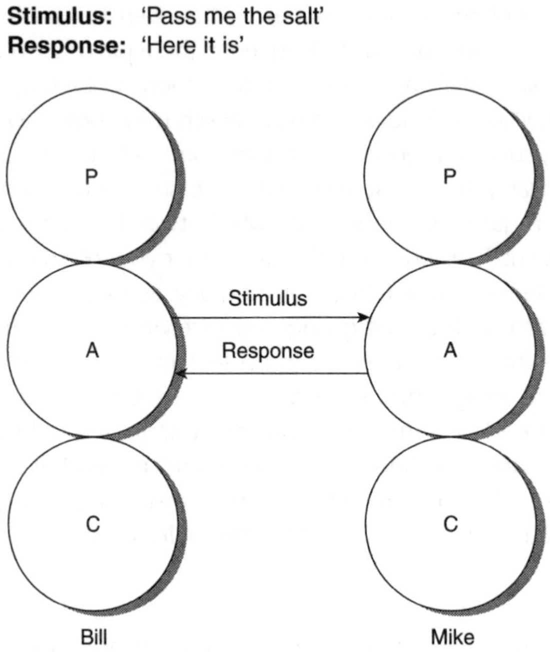

Stimulus: 'Pass me the salt'
Response: 'Here it is'

Figure 6.3   Example of a complementary transaction

Crossed transactions

In a crossed transaction the transactional response (a) comes from an ego state different from the one addressed, and/or (b) may go to an ego state that did not send the original stimulus. Berne's second or converse rule of communication was that communication is broken off when a crossed transaction occurs. In fact, the break may be only slight and momentary. However, at the other extreme, communication may be broken off completely. Figure 6.4 is an example of a crossed transaction. There are 72 possible types of crossed transactions, but only a few occur frequently.

Ulterior transactions

An ulterior communication is where, under the guise of an overt and socially more acceptable communication, an individual engages in an underlying and socially more risky communication. Another way of viewing this is that in much human interaction there is an underlying psychological as well as an overt social agenda. Psychological games, by definition, involve ulterior transactions.

Ulterior transactions may occur in everyday situations such as when a salesman says to a customer: 'Perhaps you shouldn't buy that beautiful and expensive coat', when his psychological message is 'Come on, I want you to buy it'. Potential sexual situations are other everyday situations in which ulterior transactions may occur. Figure 6.5 illustrates such an ulterior transaction.

Stimulus: 'Would you please help with the washing up?'
Response: 'Why do you always keep asking me?'

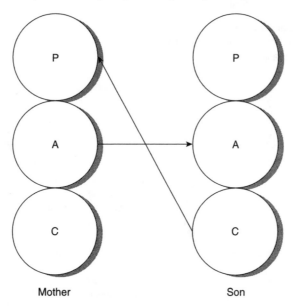

Figure 6.4   Example of a crossed transaction

Acquisition

The script

Berne defined a script as 'A life plan based on a decision made in childhood, reinforced by the parents, justified by subsequent events, and culminating in a chosen alternative' (1972: 445). He regarded scripts as preconscious life plans by which people structure their time. Scripts determine people's destinies, including their approach to relationships and to tasks. He considered that scripts are usually based on child-like illusions that may persist throughout a whole lifetime. People's scripts are the product of parental programming plus the decisions they made in response to that. Children seek out parental programming for three reasons:

1. to give a purpose in life which otherwise might be wanting;
2. to provide a way of structuring their time acceptable to their parents; and
3. since people have to be told how to do things. (Berne, 1972)

Scripts lead people to have an illusion of personal autonomy when in fact they are carrying out, often unthinkingly, the directives of their scripts. At times, however, some people may question their scripts and this may cause

Social level
Bob: 'That was a great film. How about coming back to my place for a drink?'
Sue: 'Yes, I'd like that'

Psychological level
Bob: 'Let's have some fun together'
Sue: 'I'm available'

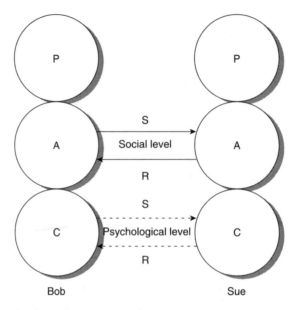

Figure 6.5   Example of an ulterior transaction

identity crises that may or may not be resolved satisfactorily by removal of
some of the blockages to genuine autonomy and a well-functioning Adult.
Berne's view of human life, as contrasted with human nature, was pessimistic,
as he tended to see humans as driven by script directives which led to ways
of time structuring seriously detrimental to attaining autonomy and creative
activity.

The script matrix

The script matrix is a diagram used to help understand the development of
people's scripts. It is helpful to an understanding of the transmission of scripts if
the matrix depicts a second-order structural breakdown of the Child. Figure 6.6
depicts such a script matrix for a hypothetical person, Mary. The diagram aims to
show how script directives are transmitted to her. Although, during her upbringing, it is desirable for Mary to experience much of the nurturing Parent ego state
of her parents and also their reasoning Adult and spontaneous Child, she may
also be experiencing negative directives from the Parent in the Child ego state of
one or both of her parents. As depicted in Figure 6.6, the directives to Mary may
be contradictory.

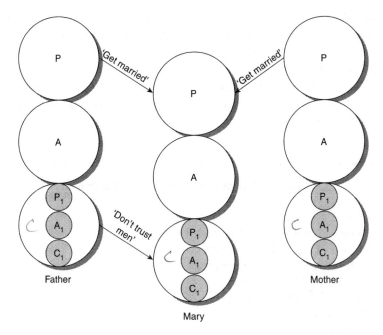

Figure 6.6   Script matrix showing transmission of script directives

Although a chapter in Berne's book *Transactional Analysis in Psychotherapy* (1961) is devoted to analysis of scripts, he acknowledged the valuable work of Steiner in devising the script matrix and in helping to develop script theory. Berne proposed that it was the parent of the opposite sex who usually tells the child what to do and the parent of the same sex who usually demonstrates how to do it. Steiner (1974) added that it was the Child in the Parent who gives the restrictive directives or injunctions and the Adult in the Parent who gives the child the pattern or programme of behaviour.

Injunctions, attributions and discounts

Although directives from parents can be nurturing and conducive to the child's emotional development, they can also be restrictive, reflecting the fears and insecurities of the Child in the parent.

Injunctions

Injunctions are expressed as messages beginning with 'Don't'. They can be relatively mild or highly restrictive. Steiner (1974) gives the following as injunctions by which people learn to block intimacy:

- do not give strokes if you have them to give;
- do not ask for strokes when you need them;
- do not accept strokes if you want them;
- do not reject strokes when you do not want them; and
- do not give yourself strokes.

He considers that the above injunctions are the basis of depression. Other injunctions may stop people from thinking, especially perhaps if they are female. Still others may interfere with the capacity to experience feelings, especially perhaps for males.

Box 6.1 presents 12 injunctions that Mary and Robert Goulding have repeatedly found when analysing scripts (Goulding and Goulding, 1979: 34–9; Stewart, 1996a).

Box 6.1   List of common script injunctions

- 'Don't exist';
- 'Don't be you' (sometimes, 'Don't be the sex you are');
- 'Don't be a child' (or 'Don't enjoy');
- 'Don't grow up' (or 'Don't leave me');
- 'Don't make it' ('Don't succeed');
- 'Don't' (i.e. 'Don't do anything');
- 'Don't be important';
- 'Don't belong';
- 'Don't be close';
- 'Don't be well' (or 'Don't be sane');
- 'Don't think';
- 'Don't feel'.

Attributions

Steiner states that children are also strongly influenced by attributions, or being told what they are and what they must do, and how they are feeling. Family reinforcement schedules tend to reward children who follow attributions and punish children who disobey injunctions.

Discounts

Children are also liable to receive discounts from their parents. Steiner regards a discount as a crossed transaction in which a person says something from an Adult ego state to another person's Adult and the other person responds from his or her Parent or Child. For instance, children's inquisitiveness may be discounted by parental rebuffs. More generally, a discount in TA is the minimization of some aspect of oneself, another person, or a situation.

Decisions

On the basis of early transactions related to feeding, toilet training, weaning and family relationships, the young person starts developing a view of the world. Where children are given unconditional protection they are less likely to develop restrictive scripts. However, when parents make their nurturing conditional on their child's submission to their injunctions and attributions, the child may make a conscious decision to adhere to parental wishes even though this means the sacrifice of autonomy. These decisions tend to be made in the preschool years and are as realistic as the capacity of the Adult in the Child or Little Professor at the time of the decision. As a result of this decision, however, the child tends to take a different and more negative position and also develops a script. Berne acknowledged that some scripts could be winner's scripts.

Life positions

The fundamental assumption of transactional analysis is that of human OKness as expressed in the statement or life position 'I'm OK – You're OK'. By making a decision children move out of this position. Instead, they adopt one of three other life positions, namely: 'I'm not OK – You're OK'; 'I'm OK – You're not OK'; and 'I'm not OK – You're not OK'. Each of these three 'not OK' positions reflects and sustains impaired ego state development. 'Not OK' positions militate against the development of intimacy and are the bases on which individuals play out their games. Just as stimulus, recognition and structure hunger can be viewed as motivators, it is also possible to view the need to justify a basic life position as a motivator. Perhaps, though, it is more accurate to consider position hunger as a refinement of the other motivators, indicating how their fulfilment is to be attained. Box 6.2 is an example of a decision leading to a life position in the case of Rita (Berne, 1966).

Box 6.2   Rita: an example of a decision leading to a life position

When she was a little girl, Rita used to run to greet her father when he came home from work. As time went on her father's behaviour became erratic because of his drinking and he would push Rita away. One day her father had a particularly bad row with her mother. Rita, who was six years, two months and 23 days, was bewildered and frightened and at 5 pm that afternoon she made a decision that she would never again love a man. In order to maintain her decision, Rita took a position regarding her father that, even when amiable and sober, he was fundamentally bad. Over time she generalized her position to most other men, the not OKness of whom she epitomized in the slogan 'All men are beasts'. Her position also became the basis of a game in which her seductive behaviour provoked 'decent' men to make advances, which she then rejected. Berne observed that Rita's seductive manoeuvres were an attempt to establish an intimate relationship that she was unable to carry through.

Development of games

During children's upbringing they are taught the rituals, activities and pastimes appropriate to their situations in life. They also learn games through significant experiences in their family life from their earliest months. Berne (1964) gave as an example of how a game might be learned the case of three-year-old Mike who, when his seven-year-old brother was allowed to leave the dinner table and lie down because of a stomach-ache: said 'I have a stomach-ache too', as though he wanted the same consideration. Mike's parents, however, did not cooperate and thus may have saved him from the game of pleading illness (social transaction) in order to gain some privilege for himself (ulterior or psychological transaction). Berne considered that games are imitative in nature, and also that they are deliberately initiated by the neopsychic Adult or Little Professor in the Child, frequently between the ages of two and eight. As illustrated by Rita, games are often formulated to help justify a life position.

The counterscript

In the development of a script, the person is given not only script injunctions and attributions from their parents' Parent in the Child, but also counterscript messages from their parents' Parent. Berne (1972) used the word 'prescription' for counterscript messages and observed that prescriptions were usually transmitted from grandparents. Examples of prescriptions are 'Be a good boy (or girl)!' and 'Work hard'. Script injunctions and counterscript prescriptions are sometimes contradictory, and life may involve an alternation between compliance first to one and then to the other. The counterscript may lead to a period of time in which an unhappy life plan gives way to a happier period. However, in the end the script injunctions always prevail, though again the possibility of winner's scripts should be acknowledged.

Steiner (1974) indicates that an alcoholic's Parent may give the counterscript 'Be sober' while the parent in the Child is giving the injunction 'Don't think! Drink'. In Figure 6.6 Mary's parents' Parent counterscript prescription was 'Get married' while her father's Parent in the Child injunction was 'Don't trust men'. Frequently injunctions are transmitted non-verbally by approval or disapproval of certain kinds of behaviour, and this may make them harder to bring into awareness than when they are transmitted more openly.

Maintenance

In the preceding section the ways in which people acquire scripts and games were described. The question to be answered in this section is why people persist in acting out scripts and playing games rather than enjoying autonomy and intimacy, or, in other words, why people stay frogs when it might seem more rewarding to revert to being princes or princesses. Part of the answer is that both scripts and games have their rewards or payoffs.

Script payoffs

Berne (1972) defined the script payoff as the ultimate destiny or final display that marks the end of a life plan. He considered that there were four main pay-offs in clinical practice: be a loner, be a bum, go crazy or drop dead. While these ultimate destinies are one way of viewing the concept of script payoff, another way is to look at it in terms of current as contrasted with ultimate rewards. Steiner (1974) observes that when people enter their counterscript phase, despite a superficial sense of wellbeing, they experience a deep visceral discom-fort. However, people experience visceral comfort when reverting to script behaviour. This is because adherence to script injunctions represents acquies-cence to parental wishes, albeit the parental Parent in the Child, and thus is associated with the wellbeing and comfort of parental protection. Steiner also notes that an alcoholic, even in the pain of a hangover, is receiving approval for acquiescing to the parental Child's injunction 'Don't think! Drink'. Steiner is perhaps more pessimistic about scripts than many other TA therapists.

Game payoffs

Games too have their payoffs, which are related to the life positions adopted in their players' scripts. For instance, the payoff in Rita's script was manipulating men to boorish behaviour that confirmed her position that men are not OK. Berne (1964) observed that, beyond their social function of time structuring, games are urgently needed by some people to keep their health. Their life positions are so tenaciously maintained that to interfere with or deprive them of the payoffs from their games may cause disturbance, or even psychosis. Thus game analysis must be approached cautiously.

An example of a game with a payoff is 'If it weren't for you'. A person can complain endlessly that if it were not for a husband, wife, child, boss or some other person, they could engage in an activity from which at present they feel restricted. Sometimes, however, these other people are being used to defend the person against the realization that, if it were not for them, she or he might be unable to perform a difficult or anxiety-evoking task. If the task were per-formed, it would no longer be possible to cause the other person discomfort by saying 'If it weren't for you'. This game validates the life position that others are not OK.

The illusion of autonomy

Berne (1972) considered that only the strongest can live without illusions and that one of the illusions which is the hardest to relinquish is that of autonomy or self-determination. An autonomous person knows what is practical and

Adult, what he accepts that comes from others, and what he does that is determined by early impulses. The illusion of autonomy is where a person does not acknowledge feelings and behaviours coming from his Child and Parent ego states, but instead believes that they come from the Adult ego state.

Berne distinguished between delusions and illusions, both of which are contaminations of the Adult ego state and, as such, prevent it from effectively dealing with here-and-now situations. Delusions are the prejudices and directives from parents that a person treats as though they were his own ideas. Illusions are those wishful ideas, impulses and early tastes coming from the Child which are accepted as Adult and rational. The significance of the illusion of autonomy is that an individual, being unaware of the delusions and illusions that are causing 'frog-like' behaviour, lacks the necessary insight and motivation for change. Thus destructive ways of time structuring are sustained rather than ameliorated. What is needed is a realignment and strengthening of the Adult ego-boundary to allow accurate processing of all relevant information.

Contamination and exclusion

With a truly autonomous person the ego-boundaries are strong, yet appropriately permeable to allow psychic energy to move between Parent, Adult and Child ego states. The illusion of autonomy indicates a structure where ego-boundaries are insufficiently well defined and the Adult ego state is being contaminated by the Parent and/or Child ego states. Exclusion, on the other hand, occurs in situations where psychic energy becomes exclusively cathected in a constant Parent, a constant Adult or a constant Child (Berne, 1961). Thus one ego-state is strongly cathected while the other two are decommissioned.

Berne considered that the excluding Parent is to be found in 'compensated' schizophrenics, where exclusion is the principal defence against confused Child or archaeopsychic activity. He gave as an example of an excluding Adult, Dr Quint, who had a sincere commitment to data processing as a way of life, yet possessed no healthy Child or Parent characteristics. Narcissistic impulsive personalities exhibit the excluding Child, where both rational and nurturing and limit-setting ego states are avoided. The excluding Parent, Adult or Child may defend itself; for instance, by the use of intellectualization in the case of the excluding Adult.

Inadequate information

The last point to be made regarding the maintenance of maladaptive behaviour is that the effectiveness of the Adult is dependent on the adequacy of the information available to it. Furthermore, the Adult may need to develop some skills of effective Adult functioning, including the ability to collect and adequately assess relevant information. James and Jongeward (1971) state that the computer phrase 'Garbage in, garbage out' applies to the Adult or, for that matter, to any other ego state.

Therapy

Therapeutic goals

Four categories of goals

Transactional analysis seeks to help clients obtain an 'I am OK – You are OK' life position. For clients who have been turned by their life's experiences from princes and princesses into frogs, Berne (1961, 1972) saw four possible goals. Stewart (1996a) views these goals as progressive stages in the direction of cure:

1. *Social control*: Though still feeling distress, clients can control their symptoms in their interactions with others;
2. *Symptomatic relief*: Getting better, or 'progress', that Berne regarded as making clients into more comfortable frogs;
3. *Transference cure*: Here clients can stay out of their scripts so long as they can keep their therapists either literally or mentally around;
4. *Autonomy*: Clients cast 'off the frog skin and take up once more the interrupted development of the prince or princess' (Berne, 1966: 290). The client's Adult takes over the role of the therapist as the client attains autonomy. Autonomy refers to the capacity for 'non-script' behaviour 'with no particular time schedule, developed later in life, and not under parental influence' (Berne, 1972: 418).

Autonomous behaviour is the opposite of script behaviour. It involves the total or partial overthrow of (a) the weight of a whole tribal or family historical tradition; (b) the influence of the individual's parental, social and cultural backgrounds; and (c) seeking ulterior payoffs from games. Furthermore, autonomy consists of the active development of personal and social control so that significant behaviour becomes a matter of free choice. Berne summarized the process of the attainment of autonomy as 'obtaining a friendly divorce from one's parents (and from other Parental influences) so that they may be agreeably visited on occasion, but are no longer dominant' (1964: 183).

The attainment of autonomy involves the person's regaining three basic capacities of the fundamental OK position: awareness, spontaneity and intimacy.

- *Awareness*: Awareness means the capacity to see and hear directly and not in the way in which one was brought up. It means living in the here-and-now, open to the sensations coming from the environment in the way a painter, poet or musician might be;

- *Spontaneity*: Spontaneity means the capacity to feel directly and to express feelings directly and not in the way in which one was brought up. The spontaneous person can choose feelings, be they Parent, Adult or Child feelings;
- *Intimacy*: Intimacy means the capacity to relate to another person or persons in an aware, spontaneous, loving and game-free way. Berne regarded intimacy as essentially a function of the natural, uncorrupted Child.

Contractual therapy goals

Transactional analysis takes a contractual approach to therapy. A key question in such an approach is 'How will both you and I know when you get what you came for?' (Dusay and Dusay, 1989: 427). Therapist and client negotiate a contract that defines both treatment goals and mutual responsibilities in achieving the goals. Contract goals can focus on outcomes and actions. Outcome goals include: physiological changes, for instance lowering of diastolic blood pressure; and relief of psychological symptoms, such as impotence or a specific phobia. Action goals specify behaviour changes, for instance not hitting children, refraining from alcohol or drugs, or holding a job for a specified time period. Stewart (1996a: 68) suggests the following principles for establishing contracts:

1. Contracts in TA may be either for outcomes or for actions.
2. However, any contract for an outcome must be supported by at least one contract for a related action.

Contracts are open to amendment as therapy proceeds. Updates and changes of goals are frequent. Furthermore, the therapist's or the client's ultimate goal may differ from the set of operational criteria for improvement stated as initial goals. During therapy, transactional analysts always observe determinants underlying symptoms and responses. Berne (1966) gave the example of the therapist, who wished to investigate a client's archaic attitudes towards parental figures, stating goals in terms of alleviation of symptoms first and later proposing an amendment to the contract that focused on the goal of altering attitudes towards parental figures.

Process of therapy

Settings for transactional analysis range from home-like surroundings to more business-like offices. Since body language clues are important in conducting transactional analysis, in most therapists' offices there are no tables or chairs that block therapist's and client's views of one another. The majority of TA settings include whiteboards, blackboards or giant paper pads that both therapists and clients can use to illustrate transactions and games and other relevant matters. Some therapists employ audio-visual aids to provide feedback and heighten clients' awareness.

In the initial session or sessions, therapists work in a number of ways. They introduce and use a simple common vocabulary. During therapy there is no gossiping or small talk. Ground rules for the therapeutic contact are agreed, such as no violence or threats of violence, and no use of alcohol or mind-altering drugs. Furthermore, an initial fee-for-service business contract may be established. Therapists conduct an initial assessment of clients and work with them to establish contract goals, including a time frame for ending therapy.

The therapeutic relationship

Transactional analysts provide supportive and nurturing relationships conducive to clients assuming greater personal responsibility for their lives. Within the framework of a common and easily understandable language, therapists provide permission for clients to play an active role in therapy. Therapists support clients as they reveal and analyse themselves more fully and try out more Adult patterns of feeling, thinking and behaving.

Transactional analysis, as originally formulated by Berne, is largely an educational process and thus the therapist–client relationship resembles a democratic teacher–learner relationship. Early on in therapy, therapist and clients establish ground rules and define the elements of their working or learning contract. Therapists train clients in the skills of analysing ego states, transactions, games and scripts. Furthermore they encourage and assist clients to identify Adult options for dealing with people, problems and situations in their lives. As indicated earlier, more often than not therapists' offices contain educational aids like whiteboards and large writing pads.

Therapists are sensitive to clues regarding clients' inauthentic ways of relating to others, including their therapists. Where there are problems in the therapeutic relationship, such as non-payment of fees or missed appointments, therapists view these transactions as psychological games and provide therapy accordingly (Dusay and Dusay, 1989).

Therapeutic interventions

Berne regarded transactional analysis as an umbrella term for four different, but interrelated, approaches to treatment. These approaches are structural analysis, transactional analysis, game analysis and script analysis. Berne (1961) saw a progression from structural analysis, through transactional and game analysis, to script analysis, though he realized that the script analysis state was not always attained.

Structural analysis

As mentioned earlier, structural analysis consists of diagnosing and separating one feeling-thinking-and-behaviour pattern or ego state from another. Structural analysis helps clients to identify and become aware of both the existence and the contents of their ego states. Its aim is to free people to have appropriate access to all their ego states without debilitating exclusions and contaminations. A related aim is to help the Adult to remain in control of the personality in stressful situations.

Transactional analysis

Berne (1961) saw one aim of transactional analysis as social control or the ability of the Adult to decide when to release the Parent or Child and when to resume the executive. If a person does not have social control, others can consciously or unconsciously activate that person's Parent or Child ego states in ways that may not be helpful. Transactional analysis proper, as Berne (1972) called it, is the analysis of single transactions by means of transactional diagrams. Clients are helped to understand the ego state transactions involved in situations and relationships in which they are experiencing difficulty as a means towards greater competence in handling them.

Game analysis

Game analysis is another way of attaining social control. Just as an understanding of structural analysis is a prerequisite of transactional analysis, so an understanding of analysis of single transactions is a prerequisite of understanding the more complex series of transactions called games. In game analysis the client is encouraged to learn more satisfying ways of structuring time and acquiring strokes. The methods of game analysis include helping a client to see what game she or he is playing, what the moves are, what the racket or bad feeling payoffs are, and how the games justify a life position. It is also important to help the client to express constructively the natural Child need or feeling that she or he has been discounting.

Script analysis

The script analyst must take care not to behave in ways that promote a client's script. The purpose of script analysis is to help clients to get out of their script and thus to behave autonomously. The therapist needs to listen carefully to and observe the client's verbal and non-verbal behaviour for script signs or signals. Additionally, script analysis may involve the use of a script checklist to help both analyst and client to know the client's script (Berne, 1972). Script analysis aims to help clients to abandon their early decisions, *previously* made in different circumstances and with an incomplete neopsychic or Adult apparatus, by *now* making and enacting redecisions for change.

A script antithesis is a therapeutic intervention that directly contradicts a parental injunction and thus brings temporary or permanent release from a script. Berne (1972) considered that the final common pathway of a patient's behaviour is the preconscious dialogue between Parent, Adult and Child, or voices in the head, which can easily be brought into consciousness. Redecision can be helped by getting into the client's head another voice, that of the therapist. This process involves the three 'Ps' of script antithesis: potency, permission and protection.

Potency is defined by whether the therapist's voice in the client's head has been powerful enough to prevail over the voices or injunctions of the client's Parents in the Child. Permissions can be positive or negative. Positive permissions or licences involve the therapist saying 'Let her/him do it!', whereas with negative permissions or releases the therapist is saying 'Stop pushing her/him into it!'. When clients follow a script antithesis and go against a parental injunction, their Child may get very anxious. Protection means that during the period of change clients can call upon their therapists to exercise their potency again in time of need.

Basic interventions and interpositions

Berne originally designed transactional analysis as a group therapy adjunct to psychoanalysis. Berne (1966: 233–47) identified eight categories of basic therapeutic techniques that have relevance for individual, couples and family work as well as for groups of seven to eight clients. He divided these basic techniques into interventions and interpositions. Dusay and Dusay observe that interpositions go beyond interventions by being 'an attempt by the therapist to interpose something between the patient's Adult and other ego states and to stabilize the Adult and make it more difficult to slide into Parent of Child activity' (1989: 441).

Interventions

1. *Interrogation*: Therapists use interrogation primarily to clarify, pin down and document specific points that might be clinically useful in the future. Examples of interrogation are: 'Did you actually steal the money?' and 'Did you really hit her?' Therapists who ask too many questions may find clients happy to play 'Psychiatric history'.

2. *Specification*: Specification is intended to fix something in both the therapist's and the client's minds so that it can be referred to later in therapy. Examples are: 'So you always wanted to buy more expensive things' and 'I'm hearing that you felt angry'.

3. *Confrontation*: In confrontation therapists use information previously elicited and specified in order to point out an inconsistency and, thereby,

to disconcert a client's Parent, Child or contaminated Adult. Therapists should not use confrontation when genuinely convinced that clients are incapable of seeing the inconsistency.

4. *Explanation*: Therapists use explanation to strengthen, decontaminate or reorient the client's Adult. An example is: 'So you see the Child in you was threatening to become active, and when that happens your Adult fades out and your Parent takes over and that's when you shout at the children'.

Interpositions

1. *Illustration*: Illustrations are anecdotes, similes or comparisons that follow a successful confrontation for the purpose of reinforcing it and softening any undesirable after-effects. Illustrations are attempts by therapists to interpose something between the client's Adult and the other ego states to make it more difficult for her/him to slide into Parent or Child activity.

2. *Confirmation*: When clients provide confirmatory evidence after confrontations, therapists can use confirmation to stabilize the client's Adult. For example, if a client were to say 'I just can't do this – Oops, I mean I won't do it' the therapist will immediately confirm the client's greater self-awareness (Dusay and Dusay, 1989: 441).

3. *Interpretation*: Therapists use the preceding interventions and interpositions with the primary object of cathecting and decontaminating the Adult. Interpretations are not always necessary for treatment to be successful. However, in some cases the therapist may choose to postpone moving on to crystallization until the Child has been deconfused by psychodynamic interpretation. Alternatively, therapists may first use crystallization to establish Adult control and then undertake the analytic deconfusion of the Child.

4. *Crystallization*: Transactional analysis aims to bring clients to the point where crystallizing statements from therapists are effective. A crystallization is a statement of a client's position from the therapist's Adult to the client's Adult. An example of a crystallization is: 'So you are now in a position to stop playing that game if you want to'.

Berne (1966) stressed that therapists using interventions and interpositions should:

- never get ahead of the clinical material offered by clients;
- never miss a legitimate opportunity to forge ahead; and
- never push against resistance except for testing purposes based on well-thought-out concrete hypotheses.

Case material

As an appendix to *Transactional Analysis in Psychotherapy*, Berne (1961) presents 'A terminated case with follow-up'. The client, a 34-year-old woman called

Mrs Enatosky had complained initially of depression, though Berne stated the formal diagnosis was best stated as schizo-hysteria. The client showed a special aptitude for structural and transactional analysis and soon began to exert social control for the games that went on between her, her husband and her 13-year-old son. In *Games People Play*, Berne (1964) illustrated the characteristics of games in general by choosing the most common game between spouses, colloquially called 'If It Weren't for You' (IWFY). Towards the end of *What Do You Say After You Say Hello?*, Berne (1972) presented three brief case histories that illustrate working with scripts.

Those who have developed Berne's work have also presented case material. Dusay's (1978) book *Egograms* illustrates the functional aspects of ego states and presents many examples of how energy imbalance in clients is treated by re-decision and exercises. The case of Judd, who had been diagnosed as a hypochondriac by many physicians, illustrates the use of egograms in TA group work (Dusay and Dusay, 1989). In another example drawn from group therapy, the Gouldings (1978) present the case of Tim, which demonstrates in detail combining transactional analysis and gestalt, a fairly common practice. Based partly on the work of the Gouldings, Stewart (2000) presents an extended case study of John that runs through his book.

Further developments

Dusay and Dusay state that, to date, there have been four transactional analysis phases: the ego state phase (1955–62); the transactions and games phase (1962–6); the script analysis phase (1966–70); and a fourth post-Berne phase 'stimulated by the action techniques of the human-potential movement, Gestalt, psychodrama, encounter, and many of the other explosive, energy-liberating systems' (1989: 448). Stewart (1996b) observes that in the 1970s three main schools emerged in TA: the classical (Bernian) school; the redecision school; and the cathexis (Schiffian) school. Since then further developments have included both a focus on the Process Model and personality and also a renewed interest in the psychodynamic ideas that provided the original base for transactional analysis. Below I selectively overview some developments that have taken place after Berne's untimely early death.

The use of egograms

Ego states may be viewed not only in terms of their content, but also in terms of the degree to which they are cathected both before and after treatment. Dusay (1972; Dusay and Dusay, 1989) devised a diagram called the egogram that graphs the extent to which each of a person's ego states are cathected. An

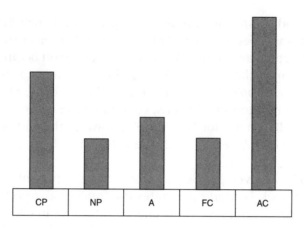

Figure 6.7   Example of an egogram

egogram shows in bar-graph form how much of a person's energy exists in the five functional ego states: Critical Parent (CP); Nurturing Parent (NP); Adult (A); Free Child (FC); and Adapted Child (AC). A bar-graph profile identifies what may be the client's probable types of problems and where their strengths and weaknesses lie. Figure 6.7 is an example of an egogram.

Dusay (1972) suggested a constancy hypothesis, namely, that the amount of psychic energy within a person is constant and that if energy is taken away from one ego state more will be available for other ego states. Thus, as treatment progresses, the AC ego state may be less strongly cathected, while the A and FC ego states may attain stronger cathexes. In terms of the egogram in Figure 6.7, the height of AC would become lower, with the amount taken away distributed between raising the heights of A and FC.

Dusay and Dusay (1989) observe that each person has different ego-state imbalances. They use a variety of techniques and exercises for people needing to raise or lower the energy cathected in specific ego states: for example, assertiveness techniques for those low in Critical Parent; empathy techniques for those low in Nurturing Parent; thinking exercises for those low in Adult; creative and intuitive activities for those low in Free Child; and compromise and getting along with others exercises for those low in Adapted Child.

The cathexis school and reparenting

Stewart and Joines (1987) identified a cathexis school of transactional analysis based on Schiff's reparenting work with schizophrenics (Schiff, 1969, 1970, 1975). Performed in residential treatment centres, severely disturbed clients with a tendency to regress and relive early childhood experiences are 'reparented' by positive parents. This level of intense and continuing therapeutic involvement is not appropriate for non-psychotic clients. Nevertheless, therapists may act as 'replacement parents' for less disturbed clients giving them positive messages and permissions to replace restrictive injunctions received from their natural parents.

The redecision school and incorporation of gestalt methods

Gestalt and psychodrama methods may be used in conjunction with transactional analysis. The Gouldings (Goulding, 1974; Goulding and Goulding, 1976, 1979) have developed an approach called *redecision therapy* that combines TA and gestalt theory and practice. They consider that early decisions are made from a feeling rather than a thinking position. Therefore, to get out of script decisions, people must get in touch with their original feelings at the time of the decisions, deal with unfinished emotional business, and make more appropriate *redecisions* (Stewart and Joines, 1987). The Gouldings see impasses as developing between ego states. They use the gestalt empty chair technique to enable clients to have dialogues between ego states. During this process, clients may connect with and reveal strong feelings suppressed since childhood.

Another example of the incorporation into TA of gestalt techniques are the exercises and experiments in James and Jongeward's (1971) book *Born to Win*. For instance, as part of an exercise on the Adapted Child, readers are asked: 'Can you admit to any top-dog and/or under-dog positions with yourself?' and 'Can you relate these to your Parent and Child ego states?' (1971: 155).

The Process Model and personality adaptations

The Process Model developed by Kahler (1979) rests upon Berne's idea that people might enact their scripts within extremely short time periods. By focusing on the process rather than the content of clients' communication, therapists can identify driver behaviours. In the TA tradition, Kahler has given his five drivers colloquial names: 'Be Perfect', 'Be Strong', 'Try Hard', 'Please You' and 'Hurry Up'. Driver behaviours are so called because they have a 'driven' quality about them. While over time everyone shows all five driver behaviours, most people have a primary driver that they show most often and first in any interaction. Stewart (1996a) regards driver behaviours as the 'gateway to the script'. Drivers are external indicators or early warning signals that the person may be replaying a specific script belief internally. Clients always enact driver behaviours just before they move into their scripts.

Ware (1983) presents six personality adaptations: obsessive-compulsive, paranoid, schizoid, passive-aggressive, hysteric and antisocial. Since each adaptation contains a specific set of script beliefs about the world, correct identification of a client's adaptation assists the therapist to plan the most appropriate treatment. Being able to spot a client's primary driver helps therapists reliably diagnose her or his main personality adaptation. With each of the adaptations, often primary drivers are accompanied by secondary drivers. For example, clients whose primary driver is 'Try Hard' will have the passive-aggressive personality adaptation. Clients who have the driver behaviours 'Be Perfect' and 'Be Strong' shown with approximately equal intensity will have the paranoid adaptation (Stewart, 1996b). Combining the Process Model with personality adaptations provides a powerful means of analysing and treating scripts.

Journal and training

The *Transactional Analysis Bulletin* started in 1962 with Berne as editor. This journal has now become a quarterly *Transactional Analysis Journal*. In 1964 the International Transactional Analysis Association (ITAA) was formed as a training and accreditation body for transactional analysis. Now the European Association for Transactional Analysis also performs training and accreditation functions.

Review and personal questions

Review questions

1. Describe each of the following ego states:

    (a) Parent
    (b) Adult
    (c) Child.

2. Why is transactional analysis a dynamic theory of personality?
3. What are stimulus, recognition and structure hungers?
4. What did Berne mean by time structuring and what are the ways in which people can structure time?
5. Provide an example of and draw a diagram for each of the following types of transactions:

    (a) complementary
    (b) crossed
    (c) ulterior.

6. What did Berne mean by a script?

7. What are games and how do people develop them?
8. What are script payoffs and game payoffs?
9. What are the goals of transactional analysis?
10. Describe briefly each of the following:

   (a) structural analysis
   (b) transactional analysis
   (c) game analysis
   (d) script analysis.

Personal questions

1. Do a first-order PAC structural analysis on yourself (Figure 6.1 (a)) indicating thoughts, feelings and behaviours belonging to your:

   (a) Parent ego state
   (b) Adult ego state
   (c) Child ego state.

2. Assume that you have 100 units of energy to divide among your Critical Parent, Nurturing Parent, Adult, Free Child, and Adapted Child ego states. In terms of the way you usually feel and behave, draw an egogram distributing the 100 units of energy among the five ego states.
3. Provide an example from your own life of each of the following types of transactions:

   (a) complementary
   (b) crossed
   (c) ulterior.

4. Take a relationship with a significant other in your life (parent, spouse, child, colleague, and so on) and analyse one or more of the transactions in it in terms of the Parent, Adult and Child ego state, or states, cathected in each person.
5. Identify some of the games you play, including the moves involved and their negative feeling payoff or your racket. Suggest an easily remembered name for each of your games.
6. Draw a script matrix for yourself as in Figure 6.6 and indicate some of the main script injunctions and counterscript prescriptions you received from your parents.
7. Identify any early decisions you made which are no longer appropriate. Formulate appropriate statements of redecision that will allow you to change the ways in which you are currently scripted to feel and behave.

8. What relevance, if any, has the theory and practice of transactional analysis for how you conduct therapy?
9. What relevance, if any, has the theory and practice of transactional analysis for how you live?

Annotated bibliography

Berne, E. (1961) *Transactional Analysis in Psychotherapy*. New York: Grove Press.
This book is Berne's major statement of structural analysis and transactional analysis. It consists of four parts: psychiatry of the individual and structural analysis; social psychiatry and transactional analysis; psychotherapy; and frontiers of transactional analysis. A case study is provided as an appendix.

Berne, E. (1964) *Games People Play: The Psychology of Human Relationship*. New York: Grove Press.
This book is Berne's international best-seller. It consists of three parts: analysis of games; a thesaurus of games; and beyond games. The chapters in the thesaurus of games cover: life, marital, party, sexual, underworld, consulting room, and good games. Berne gave each game a catchy title.

Berne, E. (1966) *Principles of Group Treatment*. New York: Oxford University Press.
This book is a systematic treatise on the use of transactional analysis in groups. The book's first part describes the basic principles of group treatment. The focus of the book's second part is transactional analysis, its general principles and basic techniques, and the handling of the more common games that occur in the course of group treatment.

Berne, E. (1972) *What Do You Say After You Say Hello?* London: Corgi Books.
Published posthumously, this book elaborates Berne's ideas on scripts. The book is divided into five parts: general considerations; parental programming; the script in action; the script in clinical practice; and scientific approaches to script theory.

Steiner, C.M. (1974) *Scripts People Live*. New York: Grove Press.
A comprehensive discussion of script theory by the creator of the script matrix. There is a special focus on political and social institutions.

Stewart, I. (2000) *Transactional Analysis Counselling in Action* (2nd edn). London: Sage.
This book introduces the core concepts and basic techniques of TA. The systematic process of TA is illustrated by a case study from the client's first contact and intake, through diagnosis and treatment planning, to contract making and the implementation of the planned treatment sequence. Self-assessment questions are incorporated to build readers' TA skills.

Stewart, I. and Joines, V. (1987) *TA Today: A New Introduction to Transactional Analysis*. Nottingham: Lifespace Publishing.
This is a systematic textbook, aimed at the general reader, which explains TA ideas from basic principles upwards. The book's presentation is structured around the syllabus of the internationally recognized basic TA training course and includes numerous examples and exercises.

References and further reading

Berne, E. (1958) 'Transactional analysis: a new and effective method of group therapy', *American Journal of Psychotherapy, 12*: 735–43.

Berne, E. (1961) *Transactional Analysis in Psychotherapy*. New York: Grove Press.

Berne, E. (1963) *The Structure and Dynamics of Organizations and Groups*. Philadelphia: J.B. Lippincott.

Berne, E. (1964) *Games People Play: The Psychology of Human Relationships*. New York: Grove Press.

Berne, E. (1966) *Principles of Group Treatment*. New York: Oxford University Press.

Berne, E. (1968a) *A Layman's Guide to Psychiatry and Psychoanalysis*. Harmondsworth: Penguin.

Berne, E. (1968b) *The Happy Valley*. New York: Grove Press.

Berne, E. (1970) *Sex in Human Loving*. Harmondsworth: Penguin.

Berne, E. (1972) *What Do You Say After You Say Hello?* London: Corgi Books.

Dusay, J.M. (1972) 'Egograms and the "constancy hypothesis"', *Transactional Analysis Journal, 2*: 27–41.

Dusay, J.M. (1978) *Egograms*. New York: Harper & Row.

Dusay, J.M. and Dusay, K.M. (1989) 'Transactional analysis', in R.J. Corsini and D. Wedding (eds), *Current Psychotherapies* (4th edn). Itasca, IL: Peacock. pp. 405–53.

Goulding, M. and Goulding, R.E. (1979) *Changing Lives through Redecision Therapy*. New York: Brunner Mazel.

Goulding, R.E. (1974) 'Thinking and feeling in psychotherapy (three impasses)', *Voices, 10*: 11–13.

Goulding, R.E. and Goulding, M. (1976) 'Injunctions, decisions and redecisions', *Transactional Analysis Journal, 6*: 41–8.

Goulding, R.E. and Goulding, M. (1978) 'The case of Tim', in R.E. Goulding and M. Goulding, *The Power is in the Patient: A Transactional Analysis/Gestalt Approach to Psychotherapy*. San Francisco: TA Press. pp. 43–55.

James, M. and Jongeward, D. (1971) *Born to Win*. Reading, MA: Addison-Wesley.

James, M. et al. (1977) *Techniques in Transactional Analysis: For Psychotherapists and Counselors*. Reading, MA: Addison-Wesley.

Kahler, T. (1979) *Process Therapy in Brief*. Little Rock, AR: Human Development Publications.

Schiff, J. (1969) 'Reparenting schizophrenics', *Transactional Analysis Bulletin, 8*: 158–64.

Schiff, J. (1970) *All My Children*. New York: Evans.

Schiff, J. (1975) *The Cathexis Reader*. New York: Harper & Row.

Spitz, R. (1945) 'Hospitalism, genesis of psychiatric conditions in early childhood'. *Psychoanalytic Study of the Child, 1*: 53–74.

Steiner, C.M. (1974) *Scripts People Live*. New York: Grove Press.

Stewart, I. (1996a) *Developing Transactional Analysis Counselling*. London: Sage.

Stewart, I. (1996b) 'Developments in transactional analysis', in W. Dryden (ed.), *Developments in Psychotherapy: Historical Perspectives*. London: Sage. pp. 62–90.

Stewart, I. (2000) *Transactional Analysis Counselling in Action* (2nd edn). London: Sage.

Stewart, I. and Joines, V. (1987) *TA Today: A New Introduction to Transactional Analysis*. Nottingham: Lifespace Publishing.

Ware, P. (1983) 'Personality adaptations', *Transactional Analysis Journal, 13*(1): 11–19.

reality therapy　7

Introduction

Reality therapy is an approach originally developed in the 1950s and 1960s by William Glasser, a California-based psychiatrist. In the early 1980s, Glasser added control theory as a theoretical base for the practice of reality therapy. In 1996, Glasser changed the name of the theory underlying reality therapy from control theory to choice theory, whose most basic concept is 'We can control only our own behaviour' (Glasser and Glasser, 2000: 40). Glasser strongly emphasizes the distinction between choice theory, which gives people the freedom to sustain healthy relationships and lead productive lives, and relationship-destroying external-control psychology, based on the ancient 'I know what is right for you' tradition.

William Glasser (1925–)

William Glasser grew up in Cleveland, Ohio. By the time he was about four, he realized that his parents were almost totally incompatible. Glasser's parents were living illustrations of the difference between choice theory and external control psychology. His father was a gentle man, with his own business, who gave him the freedom to develop on his own terms. His mother presented much more of a challenge. Glasser writes: 'If the Olympics had an event in controlling, my mother could have gone for the gold medal. My father was totally choice theory. Never in the more than sixty years that I knew him did I ever see him try to control another person except when he was goaded by my mother. And even then his heart was not in it' (1999: 90). Had she been born 50 years later, Glasser thinks his mother could have used her brains and tremendous energy in a job.

Glasser studied chemical engineering at Case Institute of Technology in Cleveland. At 19 he was extremely shy, though this did not prevent him from marrying his first wife Naomi during his undergraduate years. For three years Glasser studied for a PhD in clinical psychology at Western Reserve University, but did not complete the degree, switching to medicine instead. In 1953, Glasser obtained his MD from Western Reserve University. He then commenced psychiatric training at the Veterans Administration Brentwood

Hospital and, in 1957, completed his final year at the University of California at Los Angeles.

Reality therapy stems from Glasser's dissatisfaction with psychoanalytic psychiatry as taught during his training. He thought that there was too much emphasis on clients' feelings and past history and insufficient emphasis on what clients were doing and on 'What are you doing about what you are doing?' (Evans, 1982: 460). Also he noticed that many of his teachers did not practise what they taught and that what seemed to work was not what they said worked.

In 1956, after an attempt at private practice that was hampered by a shortage of referrals, Glasser accepted a position with the California Youth Authority as head psychiatrist at the Ventura School for Girls. Reality therapy evolved in its initial phase from his work with delinquent teenage girls (1956–67), with private outpatients with a variety of problems (1956–82), and with physically injured clients in a rehabilitation centre (1957–66). A further influence was the work of his former residency consultant and mentor G.L. Harrington with severely psychotic patients at a Veterans Administration Hospital (1955–62). In 1961 Glasser's first book, *Mental Health or Mental Illness?* was published, followed in 1965 by *Reality Therapy: A New Approach to Psychiatry.*

In 1965, Glasser began consulting in the California school system, spending much time in elementary schools in the deprived Watts area of Los Angeles. This work led to his focus on applying his ideas to education and institutional change and not just to individuals. In 1968, Glasser opened the Institute for Reality Therapy in Brentwood, a suburb of Los Angeles. That year he also created the Educator Training Center to research and develop programmes for the prevention of school failure. In 1969, Glasser's *Schools Without Failure* was published. In this book he advocated that education was causing students to fail because of non-involvement, non-relevance and limited emphasis on thinking and that schools needed to move towards the opposite philosophy of involvement, relevance and thinking. By 1974, Glasser was saying 'I've all but given up my private practice' (Barr, 1974: 67).

Glasser's interest in control theory was stimulated after his 1976 book *Positive Addiction* in which he discussed how addictions like running and meditation are extremely strengthening. While reading widely on how the brain functions during meditation, he discovered William Powers's 1973 book *Behavior: The Control of Perception.* Powers's theory of how the brain functions as a control system provided a theoretical base both for positive addiction and reality therapy. In 1982, Glasser began teaching control theory to the general public. His 1984 book *Control Theory: A New Explanation of How We Control Our Lives* both describes the theory and then shows how people can apply it to gain greater control over their lives. Glasser's books *The Quality School* (1992) and *The Quality School Teacher* (1993) apply control theory ideas to school management and teaching, respectively. Though much of the content remains the same, since 1996 Glasser uses the term choice theory instead of control theory. In addition to *Choice Theory: A New Psychology of Personal Freedom* (1999), Glasser's recent books include *Reality Therapy in Action* (2000) and *Warning: Psychiatry Can Be Hazardous to Your Mental Health* (2003). He has also collaborated with his second wife Carleen Glasser to produce *The Language of Choice Theory* (Glasser and Glasser, 1999) and *Getting Together and Staying Together: Solving the Mystery of Marriage* (Glasser and Glasser, 2000).

In 1946, Glasser married Naomi Glasser, and together they raised three children. In December 1992, after a brief illness, Naomi died of cancer. Shortly before her death, Naomi said to Glasser: 'You won't do well by yourself; I hope you can find someone with whom you can be happy'. Glasser did not see himself as a good bachelor and his difficult search for a new mate culminated in his meeting, marrying and finding happiness again with his second wife Carleen (Glasser and Glasser, 2000). Carleen Glasser is a senior instructor at the William Glasser Institute.

Glasser continues training and certifying reality therapists through the William Glasser Institute over which he presides. He remains positively addicted to promoting, both in the United States and overseas, his choice theory, reality therapy, quality school and institutional change ideas.

Theory

Basic concepts

Choice theory versus external control psychology

Glasser encourages people to replace external control psychology with choice theory (Glasser, 1999, 2003; Glasser and Glasser, 2000). In the twentieth century, the huge strides in technical progress have not been accompanied by human progress as represented by better relationships. The main reason for this is that many people are still trying to control others and allowing themselves to be controlled by others. External control is doubly dangerous because people's belief in it both creates the problems they are trying to solve and is also used to deal with the problems. For example, when punishment does not work, invariably people punish harder.

To create and maintain the high quality of relationships that people need, they must move from:

- *external control psychology*, whose seven deadly habits are criticizing, blaming, complaining, nagging, threatening, punishing and bribing or rewarding to
- *choice theory*, whose seven caring habits are listening, supporting, encouraging, respecting, trusting, accepting and always negotiating disagreements (Glasser and Glasser, 2000).

Reality therapy is based on choice theory. Box 7.1 presents an abridged version of the ten axioms of choice theory (Glasser, 1999: 332–6).

Box 7.1   The ten axioms of choice theory

1. The only person whose behaviour we can control is our own;
2. All we can give or get from other people is information;
3. All long-lasting psychological problems are relationship problems;
4. The problem relationship is always part of our present lives;
5. Revisiting the painful past can contribute little or nothing to what we need to do now to improve an important, present relationship;
6. We are driven by five genetic needs: survival, love and belonging, power, freedom and fun;
7. We can satisfy these needs only by satisfying a picture or pictures in our quality worlds;
8. All behaviour is total behaviour and is made up of four inseparable components: acting, thinking, feeling and physiology;
9. All total behaviour is designated by verbs named by the component that is most recognizable: for example, 'I am choosing to depress' or 'I am depressing';
10. All total behaviour is chosen, but we have direct control only over the acting and thinking components – we can control our feelings and physiology indirectly through how we choose to act and think.

Basic needs and feelings

Choice theory sees humans as driven by basic needs that are genetic in origin. All human behaviour represents an attempt to control the world to best satisfy these needs. People have no rest from their needs. Once aware of a need they have no choice but to attempt to satisfy the need and, when satisfied, other needs emerge. Human life is a constant struggle to satisfy these different needs and to solve the ever-present conflicts between them. The five basic needs are: survival, love and belonging, power, freedom and fun (Glasser, 1999; Glasser and Glasser, 2000; Wubbolding, 2000).

Glasser distinguishes between the old brain and cerebral cortex or 'new brain' that evolved much later than the old brain. There is much communication between the small unconscious old brain and the huge conscious new brain, which is the source of awareness and of voluntary behaviour. For most people, the old brain with the assistance of the new brain satisfies the survival need reasonably well. However, much of life is concerned with satisfying the more complex and often conflicting needs that arise in the conscious new brain. Glasser calls these 'psychological needs' because people have to satisfy their genetic instructions psychologically rather than physically. He stresses that their source is still biologic and their genetic instructions no less urgent than the genetic instructions for the physical need to survive and reproduce. Following are the five needs, the first one physical and the remaining four psychological.

1. *Survival*: This physical need is located in the old brain which is located in a small group of structures clustered at the top of the spinal cord. People's genes instruct their old brain to carry out all the survival activities that promote health and reproduction.

2. *Love, loving sex and belonging*: People's love and belonging needs demand that they keep love going throughout their lives. This need for love and belonging may be satisfied by marital partners, family, friends, groups, classes and even pets. Love and friendship are two-way streets. Probably failure to meet love and belonging needs is the prime cause of human misery.

3. *Power*: The power need, or the inner control need, may be satisfied by status, recognition and getting others to obey us. Most people's power needs are satisfied if they are listened to and respected. It is also possible to gain power by working for the common good. Power is ultimately a sense of self-worth and can be met by valuing oneself independently of external recognition. Good marriages and friendships are based on equal power.

    The need for power is often in competition with the need to belong. The need to belong propels people into relationships that can then turn into power struggles. In an external control world, the need for power is often at someone else's expense.

4. *Freedom*: People need freedom to choose how they live their lives or at least some aspects of their lives. They need to move around as they like, express themselves freely and associate with whom they choose. The need for freedom can conflict with other needs, for instance the need to belong as either a spouse or parent. Furthermore, it is fundamental that chosen need-satisfying behaviours should not prevent others engaging in need-satisfying behaviours.

5. *Fun*: The need for fun or enjoyment is as fundamental a need as the other needs. Fun is a basic genetic instruction for all higher animals because that is how they learn. Fun removes the drudgery from learning and enhances motivation. Even in old age, learning without play is difficult. Sharing a strong need for fun supports all human relationships and is a vital ingredient in successful marriages. When asked how he knows he is having fun, Glasser says he finds himself laughing a lot. The need for fun and enjoyment also includes being interested and having interests.

It is possible to rate each of the needs on a five-point scale: 1 = very weak; 2 = below average; 3 = average; 4 = above average; and 5 = very strong. By putting their individual need assessments together, people can create a need-strength profile. For example, Glasser rates himself as follows: survival – 3, average; love and belonging – 4, above average; power – 4, above average; freedom – 4, above average; and fun – 5, very strong (Glasser and Glasser, 2000). It is also possible to compare people's need-strength profiles and assess their compatibility.

The quality world

Throughout their lives, people develop personal picture albums consisting of detailed pictures of what they want to satisfy their needs. Glasser (1984) gives the example of the baby who was screaming and then given a chocolate-chip cookie that was much liked. Immediately the baby took a picture of the cookie and stored it away as something to look for when hungry again. Human senses combine into a sensory camera that, among others, can take visual, gustatory and tactile pictures. Glasser prefers the word pictures to perceptions both because it is easier to understand and because about 80 per cent of perceptions stored in personal albums are visual.

Personal picture albums are a small and selective part of total memory. The personal picture album is a special world that Glasser now calls the quality world. It is more than an ideal world of 'What I would like to be' since it contains very specific pictures of what will satisfy my needs for love, worth, success, freedom and fun right now. The pictures in people's quality worlds fall into three categories: (1) the *people* they most want to be with; (2) the *things* they most want to own or experience; and (3) the *ideas or systems of belief* that govern much of their behaviour. Glasser observes: 'Anytime we feel good, we are choosing to behave so that someone, something, or some belief in the real world has come close to matching a person, thing, or belief in our quality worlds' (1999: 45).

All pictures are need-fulfilling. People must have at least one picture in their quality worlds for every need. It is virtually impossible to have a need without quickly finding a picture to satisfy it. However, people commonly have pictures in their albums that cannot be satisfied in the real world. Furthermore, the pictures in their quality worlds may be neither rational nor compatible with each other. In addition, some pictures can be blurred and ill-defined, though individuals may define them more sharply later (Wubbolding, 2000).

People can add pictures to their quality worlds or remove them if they do not satisfy needs. When people change important pictures, they change their lives. The only way pictures can be taken out of quality worlds is to replace them with something that fits the same basic need reasonably well. For example, the picture of a loved one is usually replaceable with someone else. Sometimes people choose a lifetime of misery because they do not replace pictures: for example, battered wives who stay with husbands because they remain the only 'possible' pictures of loving persons.

Changing our own pictures can be difficult. Changing other people's pictures can be even more difficult and can only be achieved through negotiation and compromise. It is the pictures in each person's quality world, and nobody else's, that cause them to do what they do. Box 7.2 illustrates the importance of understanding the individual nature of people's quality worlds (Glasser, 1999).

Box 7.2   Example of harmful and helpful quality worlds in a school

Students' harmful quality worlds
In an inner-city middle school in which he and Carleen Glasser worked the students did not have teachers, each other or schoolwork in their quality worlds. However, in their quality worlds they did have drugs, violent clowning around and non-loving sex. The more teachers used punishment and threats, the more the students resisted and focused on what was in their and not their teachers' quality worlds. The students had no idea that it was possible to be happy at school.

Students' helpful quality worlds
Using choice theory, the Glassers began to build relationships with the students and through these relationships helped them so that they began to picture themselves satisfying their needs in school. They also trained the staff. As the students began to put the staff and each other into their quality worlds, they also became happier.

The pictures in people's quality worlds are central to understanding the choice theory view of motivation. Behaviour always starts with the pictures in people's quality worlds. Behaviour is generated by the difference between the pictures in people's quality worlds, what they want, and what is going on in the real world, what they have. When a difference exists, people behave to reduce this difference. It is a biological fact that people must choose to do something to reduce the difference. However, what they do is almost invariably their choice.

Total behaviour

In choice theory, behaviour is how people choose to attempt to control the world to satisfy needs rather than a response to stimulation. Behaviour is more than conduct or action. Glasser uses the term total behaviour to describe his expanded concept of behaviour. Total behaviour, the whole, 'always consists of the four components: acting, thinking, feeling, and the physiology associated with all our actions, thoughts, and feelings' (Glasser, 1999: 72).

1. *Acting*: The acting component consists of active behaviours, like walking or running, that involve voluntarily moving some part of the body. However, some involuntary actions accompany routine activities, for instance swallowing when eating.

2. *Thinking*: The thinking component consists of voluntarily generating thoughts as well as involuntarily generating them, for instance in dreams.
3. *Feeling*: The feeling component consists of a wide variety of pleasurable and painful feelings that people generate and choose.
4. *Physiology*: The physiological component, for instance sweating, encompasses the voluntary and involuntary body mechanisms that people generate and choose involved in the doing, thinking and feeling components of total behaviour.

Glasser (1989) uses the analogy of total behaviour as a four-wheel drive car, with each component as one wheel of the car. The front wheels are the acting and thinking components and the rear wheels are the feeling and physiology components. The needs are the engine and the driver steers in the direction closest to the picture most wanted from his or her quality world album. As in a car, the person has total voluntary control of where to steer the front wheels of his or her 'car'. Whatever clients' problems are they can choose to steer their life 'cars' in better directions than they do now. However, clients have nowhere near the degree of voluntary control over the rear wheels of feeling and physiology that they have over the front wheels of acting and thinking. Consequently, reality therapy focuses on helping clients change their actions and thoughts (the front wheels) much more than their feelings and physiology (the rear wheels).

While doing and thinking are always expressed as verbs, such as running and meditating, feelings are usually expressed as adjectives, for instance depressed, or nouns, for instance depression. However, people do not only choose how they think and act, they also choose how they feel. A feeling like depression does not happen to people, they choose to depress. Consequently, Glasser (1999) uses verbs rather than nouns and adjectives to refer to feelings. Examples of the use of verbs to denote feelings are depressing or choosing to depress for depression, anxietying or choosing to be anxious for anxiety, and phobicking or choosing to be phobic for phobia. Active language attempts to describe the behaviour that people generate and choose in their attempts to control the world to satisfy their needs.

Glasser (2003) provides the example from a group of Bev, who got angry when Joan and Barry told her that she was choosing to depress. What choice theory would teach Bev is, instead of thinking 'I'm depressed', to think 'I'm choosing to depress', or, even better, 'I'm choosing the total behaviour of depressing'. The four components of Bev's depressing total behaviour are as follows. The *acting* component is to use external control on someone. The *thinking* component is 'This person is not doing what I want her to do'. The *feeling* component is the feelings of both depressing and angering. The *physiology* component is probably a lot of fatigue caused by trying to control someone day after day and failing. The more this depressed client can both realize that the feeling component is just one of the four components of a total behaviour and use a verb like depressing to describe the behaviour, the more the client will be in control of her life. The client who admits to depressing or choosing to depress then has three choices: (1) change what she or he wants; (2) change what she or he is doing; or (3) change both.

Acquisition

Learning about needs

At birth, people do not know what their needs are or how to satisfy them. However, babies do know how they feel. They also know that when their needs are not satisfied they do not feel good. This knowledge enables them to gain some idea of what their needs are. For instance, babies do not have concepts of food, eating or survival. However, they know when they are hungry and, when fed, they usually feel better. As this occurs, babies first begin to know about food and then later about eating and about their survival need. People can also learn about their psychological needs for power, belonging, freedom and fun in that they know that, when these needs are satisfied, they feel better. Even if it is never clear what their needs are, through their efforts to feel good people will still try to satisfy these needs.

Acquisition of quality worlds

Already, the example has been given of the baby who was given a chocolate-chip cookie when screaming, took a picture of it, and stored it in his quality world as something to look for when hungry. As people go through life, they store in their quality worlds anything that they believe will satisfy one or more of their basic needs. Glasser considers it likely that people have hundreds and even thousands of pictures that will satisfy each need. People may acquire pictures in their quality worlds that put them at risk. For example, anorexic people have pictures about the desirability of being excessively thin. Alcoholics have pictures about satisfying their needs through alcohol. Abused and rejected people who have given up on being happy in relationships may replace people pictures in their quality worlds with non-people pictures of violence, drugs and unloving sex.

Acquisition of total behaviours

Babies know that in order to survive they must do all that they can to control the world around them to meet their needs. For the sake of their survival, babies are born with the total behaviour of angering. Angering is the baby's way of signalling to the world that she or he has unmet needs. In order to encourage independence, shortly after birth most mothers stop allowing their babies totally to control them with angering. When babies scream and nothing happens they quickly learn to look for different behaviours, for instance smiling, with which to control their worlds. Humans are creative and, aided by imitating, quickly learn other total behaviours. Children's most effective teachers are people they care for and respect. Other ways of learning new behaviours to control the world include going to school, reading books and watching television.

Glasser (1989) considers that, usually early in life, everyone learns to add misery, craziness, sickness and dysfunctional angering behaviours like fighting to their existing repertoires of total behaviours. It is common for children to depress to control adults or to fight to control other children. Thus children add miserabling and angering as ways to control themselves and others to meet their needs. In these examples, children learn to choose behaviours that may have short-term payoffs. However, as time goes by, the same choices are likely to lessen people's control over their lives because they are more likely to produce negative than positive consequences for self and others.

Raising children

Glasser advises: 'Try as hard as possible to teach, show and help your children to gain effective control over their lives' (1984: 198). Children are going to live according to their own and not their parents' quality worlds. Too often parents try to mould their children to their quality worlds and, by doing so, create power struggles. It is important that parents keep their children's pictures of them as loving people. Around two years old, babies start checking out the extent of their power to control their parents. Then, if parents allow it, children can begin to take advantage of their parents' love to control them. Good parents who make clear what they and others will do and what children have to do for themselves can help the children create sensible quality worlds.

Children are born without knowing how to fulfil their needs. Glasser (1984) distinguishes between doing things *for, to* and *with* children and leaving them alone. Many parents do too much for their children in ways that assist them to have less control over their lives later. Parents also do far too much to their children, for instance yelling at them and punishing them when they do not do as parents want. Most parents do too little with their children, for example playing with them or discussing mutual interests. At all ages, parents do not leave children alone enough, for instance letting them cry out temper tantrums or make their own entertainment on rainy days. Allowing children space to achieve goals on their own can lead to feelings of success that satisfies their power needs. In short, children learn most about how to have healthy quality worlds and make effective choices in their lives from adults who do things with them and encourage them to do things for themselves.

Inevitably children will break rules and challenge parents. Since both parents and children have strong needs for power, negotiation and compromise are the only ways that they can get along with each other. Choice theory distinguishes between discipline and punishment. Discipline always starts with trying to teach children to follow reasonable rules through negotiation. Parents attempt to assist children to see that there are better pictures for their quality worlds and behaviours that would be within the rules. Punishment starts and finishes with trying to force children to follow rules, whether reasonable or not, by trying to inflict pain if they refuse. Parents make no attempt to give them the opportunity to negotiate and review other pictures for their quality worlds and behaviours that fall within the rules. Punished children feel deep losses of power and control.

When negotiating plans with children, parents should try to do as much with and as little to or for them as possible. Where children do not want to change or negotiate, parents can impose sanctions appropriate to the child's age until the problem is worked through: for instance, going to one's room for 10 minutes might be a maximum sanction for a five-year-old and an evening without television appropriate for a 10-year-old. Sanctions should not be so great that children lose their willingness to try to correct the situation. Furthermore, it is preferable that parents do not impose sanctions unless they have previously discussed with the child the consequences of not complying. Parents should always explain to children their element of personal choice regarding the sanction – they can either choose to comply or choose to accept the consequences of not complying.

Maintenance

Glasser (1999) sees all clients at the start of therapy as choosing some form of self-destructive behaviour that represents their misguided attempts to regain control over their poorly controlled and frustrating lives. People who are depressing, guilting, angering and headaching insufficiently realize both what their needs are and that they can make better choices about satisfying them than they currently do.

Reasons for choosing misery

There are three main reasons that people choose the suffering, pain and misery in their lives:

1. *Restraining anger*: By about two years old, most children realize that angering will not get them what they want and look for alternatives. Children unable to go for walks when everyone else is busy may choose to keep angering under control. Instead, they may choose depressing out of their behavioural systems. Depressing, despite its pain, may be a safer and more effective way for children to take control over others. By the time people become adults, they have created and learned from others a wide variety of painful feeling behaviours that they substitute for displaying anger, for instance depressing, anxietying, guilting or headaching.
2. *Attracting help*: Depressing is a very powerful way of getting help without begging and risking damaging one's need for power. Many people

are vulnerable to being controlled by being the targets of depressing behaviour.

3. *Avoidance*: Pain, misery and depressing are commonly used as excuses for either doing nothing, or being frightened of doing something, or a mixture of the two. The choice to stay miserable, despite the pain, protects people from becoming aware of the need to work on problems. Furthermore, depressing can hide their fears of failure which might make their lives even harder to control than they are now. However, depressing can also help people 'buy time' and allow them to recoup before taking more positive action.

Reasons for remaining unaware of choosing misery

A major reason that people maintain their choosing-to-stay-miserable behaviour is that they remain unaware that they are doing so. They do not want to take the responsibility of doing something about it as soon as they accept that their misery is a choice. Following are three important reasons blocking people from becoming aware that negative feelings involve choices:

1. *Mistaking short-term pure feelings for long-term feeling behaviours*: What people feel is divided into two stages. First, there is the immediate experiencing of a feeling, which Glasser (1984) calls 'pure feeling'. These pure feelings are derived from the early evolutionary need to be aware of threats to survival and tell people whether or not they are in control. Such feelings are not chosen and begin to diminish as soon as they occur. Second, people choose a long-term feeling behaviour, for instance depressing or loving, to prolong either the pain or the pleasure initiated by the pure unchosen feeling.

    Glasser (1984) gives the example of Tom who had the pure feeling of a sharp pang of disappointment when he opened his pay packet and saw a dismissal slip. This pain alerted him that he had lost control of an important part of his life. Then Tom chose the long-term pain of depressing that quickly superseded the pure pain of the initial disappointment. However, since it is difficult to tell when the switch occurs, people tend to confuse the pure brief unchosen pain with the chronic chosen pain.

2. *Most painful choices become automatic*: Frustrated children often consciously choose whether to sulk or to anger. However, for adults who have been making such choices over a period of years, the choice process has become automatic and below awareness. Distinctly painful behaviours, such as headaching, are limited to about 20 and most people use only four or five that 'work well' for them. People are more likely to acknowledge in awareness their responsibility for choosing pleasurable total behaviours than for choosing painful ones.

3. *Not wanting to lose self-esteem*: People's need for power and self-esteem is so strong that, if they were to acknowledge that they choose painful

feelings, this knowledge might cause them to experience some loss of control. Consequently, to maintain control of themselves as well as of others, people repress from awareness that they are choosing much of the misery they feel. However, to regain control people need to acknowledge that they choose their misery and can choose other behaviours and, if necessary, change the pictures in their quality worlds to satisfy their needs.

Staying controlled by others' misery

Glasser stated that one of the most important guidelines of control theory was 'Never let anyone control you with the pain and misery he or she chooses' (1984: 202). The same guideline holds true for choice theory. People can give up their freedom of choice about how they lead their lives to others who have their own control agendas. Box 7.3 provides an example of someone choosing to stay controlled by another's misery.

**Box 7.3   Example of choosing to stay controlled
by another's misery**

Physically healthy, Carol chooses to depress for the purpose of controlling her middle-age daughter Phyllis. Phyllis in turn creates her own misery and guilting by allowing her mother to control her with misery. Carol is not going to change on her own accord since choosing misery is her way of keeping control of her life. Phyllis needs to realize that Carol is choosing all the misery about which she complains. Then she needs to regain control by separating herself from her mother's control, for instance, by choosing to set regular times to visit and not going over for 'emergencies'. In addition, she needs to stop choosing to set herself up for letting her mother take control of her by keeping asking: 'How do you feel, Mum?'

Therapy

Therapeutic goals

The main goal of reality therapy is to assist clients to replace external control psychology with choice theory so that they may have healthy life-enhancing relationships. More specifically reality therapy has the following goals. First, reality therapists try to impart to clients the choice theory framework for understanding their behaviour. Second, the approach aims to raise clients' awareness of their choosing behaviours and how they try to control their worlds through them. Third, reality therapy increases clients' sense of their responsibility for making choices that work for them. Clients are taught that they need no longer be victims of a self-defeating past and of current choices. Fourth, clients are assisted to identify and understand their basic needs for survival, belonging, power, freedom and fun. Fifth, reality therapy assists clients to have realistic pictures in their quality worlds to satisfy their basic needs. Sixth, reality therapy teaches clients to evaluate the effectiveness of their total behaviour in light of what they want and choose different behaviours as needed. Seventh, reality therapists assist clients to develop and implement specific behaviours that will help them meet their present and future needs without infringing others' needs. Eighth, reality therapy teaches clients how to avoid allowing themselves to be controlled by others' negative controlling behaviour.

Reality therapy aims to help clients to help themselves. Clients are better prepared not only to deal with current problems, but to prevent or solve future problems.

Process of therapy

Most clients who enter reality therapy voluntarily are seen in individual therapy (Glasser, 1999; Glasser and Wubbolding, 1995). The reality therapist discusses professional details that may encompass the therapist's credentials, informed consent, and confidentiality and its limitations. The therapist also briefly explains the reality therapy approach including the rights and responsibilities of therapist and client. Then the therapist invites clients to tell their stories.

The therapist attempts to use good active listening skills, such as reflection and clarification, to create a safe emotional climate in which clients can share their inner worlds. As clients talk, the therapist listens carefully for the extent to which clients engage in external control rather than choice theory psychology, how much responsibility they have taken for past behaviour and how much responsibility they can be expected to take for immediate future choices. Having gained a sense of their perceived locus of control by patiently listening to clients' perception of their problems, the therapist helps them to set therapeutic goals by asking what they want to get from therapy. In particular, therapists encourage clients to focus on what they want to get out of this session. As part of this process, reality therapists offer encouragement to clients for coming to therapy and being willing to work on their problems. Clients are helped to see such behaviours as strengths.

Glasser (1999) saves time in therapy in three main ways. First, he does not probe at length for the problem, since it is always an unsatisfying present relationship. Second, since the problem is in the present, there is no need to make a long investigation into clients' pasts. Third, he focuses on what clients are choosing to do now since the only persons clients can control are themselves.

Wubbolding (2000; see also Glasser and Wubbolding, 1995) has formulated the process of reality therapy into the following WDEP system with each letter representing a cluster of skills and techniques for assisting clients to make better choices in their lives:

W   Ask clients what they want;
D   Ask clients what they are doing and their overall direction;
E   Ask clients to conduct a searching self-evaluation;
P   Ask clients to make plans to fulfil their needs more effectively.

W: 'What do you want?'

Therapists attempt to discover what in their quality worlds clients want or are 'controlling for' by their current behaviour. When therapists ask clients 'What do you want?', they are asking 'What do you really want right now?' Wubbolding writes: 'The exploration of wants includes but is not limited to the three essential elements in the quality world: relationships, treasured possessions, and core beliefs' (2000: 98). Therapists assist clients in describing what they want from themselves, the world around them, the therapy process, parents, children, spouse, friends, associates, job, religion and from any institution that impinges upon their lives. Clients are assisted to describe both what they are getting and not getting from each of these relationships.

Therapists ask clients: 'How hard do you want to work at solving the problem or gaining a better sense of control for yourself?' (Wubbolding, 2000). Therapists also try to find out how much clients are in touch with what they really want. The less in touch they are, the more difficult it can be to work with them. Clients may answer that they want to obtain another job, have a better relationship with someone, or find someone to love. Then therapists try to get them to describe in some detail the pictures in their quality world of what they want right now.

Reality therapists introduce clients to the choice theory concept of basic needs. Then they can assist clients to explore which of their basic needs they want to satisfy. Brierly mentions the 'needs tray' technique whereby clients are asked 'If I had a tray and you could have one or more of these needs today before you leave, which would you choose: love, personal power, fun or freedom?' (1989: 174). Clients' answers can illuminate where therapy might focus. Clients are in a better position to generate and evaluate pictures in their quality worlds for satisfying needs when clear about the needs they wish to satisfy.

The W refers to perceptions as well as to wants. Therapists discuss with clients their perceived source or locus of control over events in their lives. Reality therapists consider that there is a high correlation between perceived external locus of control and ineffective behaviours. Where clients focus on wanting to change someone else, they are refocused on how they can change themselves, since their behavioural systems cannot control others. Reality therapists help clients to focus on what it is possible for them to achieve and on assuming personal responsibility for achieving their goals.

D: 'What are you doing and in what direction are you going?'

When clients identify what they want and need, the next step is to ask them: 'What are you doing now?' or 'What behaviours are you choosing now?' Frequently clients talk as though they are passive victims of circumstances or of other people. Clients who sit home depressed and yet say they want love choose the action behaviour of sitting at home, the feeling behaviour of depressing, the thinking behaviour that 'I'm too depressed to do anything', and any accompanying physiological symptoms or behaviours, for instance disturbed sleep.

Often reality therapists ask significant others whom clients are trying to control or feel controlled by to join the client in a session. The purpose of this is to help both clients and therapists understand the client's behaviour better. Sometimes these ancillary people benefit too from the session.

In particular, reality therapists focus on the action and thinking components of total behaviour because they are the components most amenable to change. Also therapists look for effective behaviours that clients have in their repertoires and may enquire about times in the past when clients functioned effectively. Therapists look for strengths both to help clients understand their assets and also because often it is easier to develop behaviours that are already in clients' repertoires than those which are not.

Reality therapists also ask clients questions about overall direction, such as:

- 'Where are your current choices taking you?'
- 'Are you headed in a direction where you want to be in a month, a year, two years from now?'
- 'Will you describe the direction you are going without making a judgment about it?'

Such global questions increase clients' awareness of how helpful or harmful their current choices are 'from a distance'. This can have the effect of loosening up clients so that they are more ready to evaluate and change their thinking and behaviour (Glasser and Wubbolding, 1995).

E: 'Conduct a thorough self-evaluation'

Reality therapy emphasizes client inner self-evaluation as a central and necessary step in the process of change. Furthermore, assisting clients to self-evaluate speeds the change process. Wubbolding writes: 'In the counselling technique of self-evaluation, the helper holds a metaphorical mirror before clients' eyes and asks them to evaluate themselves, to examine the effectiveness of their lives. This is done in an explicit and precise manner' (1998: 196). Because they have not conducted a thorough self-evaluation, many people seeking change do not realize how and why their behaviour is ineffective.

Reality therapists assist clients to judge their behaviour in light of their wants and needs. As well as 'Is your behaviour getting you what you want?', other questions that reality therapists use to get clients to evaluate their behaviour include: 'Is what you're doing getting you what you want?', 'How is your behaviour helping you?', and 'Is this what is best for you?' The purpose of such questions is to encourage clients to realize that the behaviours they are choosing are not getting them what they claim they need. For instance, the client who wants love and sits at home and depressed is forced to face that by this behaviour he is choosing not to obtain love. The middle-aged client Phyllis, who wants more independence yet keeps going over whenever her mother Carol complains, is led to realize that her behaviour is not getting her what she wants. Evaluating behaviour questions encourage clients to acknowledge that their current choices are not giving them effective control over their lives.

Box 7.4 provides a range of illustrative questions that reality therapists might ask to help clients to evaluate themselves (Wubbolding, 1998). Such questions would be adapted to the specific situations, age and degree of insight of clients.

Box 7.4   Some illustrative questions that help clients to evaluate themselves

1. 'Is the overall direction of your life a plus or a minus?'
2. 'Are your specific actions effective in getting what you want?'
3. 'Did such and such a behaviour violate the rules?'
4. 'Is what you are doing in line with or against any unwritten rules?'
5. 'Is what you want from others, from yourself, from school, from work, and from society realistically attainable?'
6. 'Is what you want genuinely good for you?'
7. 'Does it help you to view the world – parents, students, friends, employees and so on – in the manner you have chosen?'
8. 'Are the plans you have made for change genuinely satisfying to you, and are they helpful in attaining your wants (goals that have been evaluated previously)?'

P: 'What is your plan?'

Planning and changing total behaviour involves the following components: searching for alternative behaviours, negotiating plans, getting commitment to plans, developing relevant behaviours, and evaluating progress in implementing plans.

- *If your current behaviour is not getting you what you want, then what do think might be better?*

  Once clients realize that their current behaviour is not giving them effective control over their lives, they are ready to look at alternative ways of regaining control. Reality therapists realize that clients are sensitive to being told what to do, so they ask questions that encourage clients to come up with their own better behaviour. Such questions include: 'If your current behaviour is not getting you what you want, then what do you think might be better?', 'What are better choices than those you are currently making?', and 'What can you do to regain more control over your life?'.

- *Tell me your plan*

  Plans are ways that clients can satisfy important pictures in their quality worlds outside of therapy. Reality therapists lead clients to develop their own plans rather than do it for them. This involves therapists working closely with clients, yet encouraging their self-reliance. Plans focus particularly on the doing and thinking components of total behaviour since, to use the earlier analogy, these are the front wheels of the car. Plans can include finding new quality world pictures that are satisfying. Plans should be feasible in terms of clients' abilities and motivation. They should not attempt too much too soon since clients seeking to regain control may need small successes to build up confidence for more difficult tasks.

  Glasser and Wubbolding summarize what makes for an effective plan when they write: 'The plan should have SAMIC characteristics: "Consistent, Attainable, Measurable, Immediate, and Committed to"' (1995: 306). Wubbolding has added a second I – 'Involved or assisted by the helper' – and two Cs – 'Controlled by the client' and 'Consistent or repetitive' (2000: 150). Frequently simple planning sheets are used to help clients make plans that fulfil these characteristics.

  When planning, reality therapists often ask questions that pin clients down to clarifying the specific details of their plans. For instance, when a teenage girl who has never looked for a job says she is going to do so, the therapist might ask: what time and day she is going to start, what she plans to wear, and how she is going to look up what jobs to apply for. In addition, the therapist might pin down the client regarding what she would do if her first three or four attempts at going for a job interview were unsuccessful. In general, the more reality therapists pin down clients with respect to the details of their behaviour change plans, the more chance clients have of successfully implementing them. Box 7.5 presents an example of developing and implementing a plan (Glasser, 1984).

Box 7.5   Example of developing and implementing a plan

The client
Randy was a business school graduate student who was phobicking about going to class because, if he finished business school, he might not obtain the high-level job that he pictured in his quality world.

The plan
Together Glasser and Randy developed a plan focusing on the action component of total behaviour and that had implications for the thinking component. Randy was to disclose his phobia to his instructors and ask them if he could sit at the back of the class near the open door, leave quietly if it became too difficult to stay, pull himself together in the empty hall, and then return to class.

The outcome
By implementing his plan Randy was able to regain some control in a previously out-of-control situation. Partly because his instructors did not reject him when he disclosed his phobia, Randy also altered the self-defeating perfectionist pictures in his quality world. He obtained more realistic pictures both of job requirements and of his resources as a potential employee. Randy implemented his plan with the feelings behaviour outcome that he stopped phobicking almost entirely.

- *Do you commit yourself to making an effort to follow your plan through?*
    It is one thing to make a plan and another to have the commitment to implementing it. Reality therapists seek commitments from clients to implementing plans. If therapists have established themselves as need-fulfilling people in clients' quality worlds, clients will take their commitments to them seriously. In addition, clients are making commitments to themselves. Strong commitments enhance the likelihood of strong follow through. A key to feelings of control is the ability to make and follow through plans.
    Wubbolding (2000) has three suggestions when clients fail to follow through plans. First, he addresses the issue of whether self-evaluation was weak. Therapists and helpers revisit the E of the WDEP system by relentlessly asking: 'If you don't follow through will anything change? Will you feel better? Will you get what you want?' Second, he asks clients to experiment with a plan as though they are simply 'trying' or 'testing' a technique. Often, because they feel that the plan is not permanent, clients paradoxically adopt it. The third suggestion is to ask clients to do something to feel better or get along better for a very short time period, say 30 seconds or a minute. Then they are asked whether they can do it for a longer period of time. Again, the idea is that, by making changes when

they do not need to change their behaviour permanently, clients can then decide whether it is worth the effort to continue.

- *Developing relevant behaviours*

   Where necessary, reality therapists work with clients to develop specific behaviours required to implement plans. For instance, in the above case of the teenage girl who has never looked for a job, a reality therapist might develop her skills by role-playing an employer interviewing her. Brierly (1989) gives the example of practising conversational skills in her office with Susan, a shy, quietly spoken girl of 20, to build her skill level to where she could succeed when trying out her new behaviours.

- *Evaluating progress: no excuses and no punishment*

   Clients are asked to implement plans as homework. Within the context of firm but always friendly relationships, reality therapists check progress by helping clients to self-evaluate their own progress. They assume that commitments to reasonable plans can always be fulfilled. In accepting no excuses therapists might say that they are not interested in why clients cannot do something, but rather in when they can do it and how they can do it. Reality therapists assist clients to keep focusing on what they can do now rather than lose control by looking for reasons to be miserable and ineffective. However, in instances where plans genuinely turn out to be unreasonable, therapists and clients work together to remake better ones.

   Therapists praise clients who succeed in carrying out plans. Any kind of negative statement by therapists is viewed as punishment. Punishment weakens clients' involvement with their therapists and reinforces their failure identities. The negative consequences stemming from not carrying out plans are viewed as quite different from punishment.

   In private therapy, termination decisions are made by both therapists and clients on the basis of whether clients have learned to use choice theory sufficiently well to adopt more effective need-fulfilling behaviours in their relationships and lives.

The therapeutic relationship

The therapeutic relationship is very important. Glasser and Wubbolding write: 'The atmosphere in the counseling relationship is one of firmness and friendliness. The ideal relationship is a partnership in which both client and therapist struggle to find more effective behavioral patterns for the client' (1995: 304). A first step in reality therapy is to 'make friends' with clients. Most clients who come for therapy are lonely. Therapists should be caring and involved human beings to whom clients can relate and by whom they can feel supported. However, being involved also means being honest about the limits of involvement, such as length of sessions and rules about between-session contact. Compassion, acceptance and patience are further desirable therapist attributes. In addition, without trivializing their work together, both therapists and clients are encouraged to use humour.

In reality therapy a tension exists between showing acceptance and communicating to clients that their needs must be met and their problems solved in the present. Reality therapists try to avoid allowing clients to control them with the same inadequate behaviours that they use to control others, such as angering, depressing and anxietying. Usually reality therapists, while showing sympathy for what clients have experienced, do not allow them to dwell on past hurts and sufferings. However, on occasion, clients may be allowed to dwell on their pasts and talk about their feelings to strengthen the relationship for subsequent work on the role of their present choices in sustaining problems.

Reality therapists are strongly committed to their clients. Frequently, reality therapists tell clients: 'Don't give up so easily'. Therapists persevere with clients to the point where clients realize that therapists will neither allow themselves to be controlled nor give up. Good friends do not give up easily.

Therapeutic interventions

The following are two broad categories of interventions – teaching choice theory and questioning within the WDEP system – that characterize all stages of reality therapy. Applying the interventions depends on such factors as the nature of the client, including his or her culture, and how the therapist likes to work.

Teaching choice theory

Reality therapists make an active effort to teach choice theory to any client whom they believe may be receptive to these ideas. Rather than focus on the past, Glasser helps clients make better choices now in their lives. He writes: 'To do so, I begin to teach the clients choice theory, which they can then use to make better choices and learn to handle many problems that might have lengthened therapy. It's a kind of therapeutic stitch in time that saves nine' (1999: 117). Reality therapists approach teaching choice theory in a number of ways:

- *Initial structuring*: Reality therapists try to instil hope in clients early on by letting them know that, during therapy, they will learn to make better choices and, in doing so, gain better control over their lives. Clients are also informed that they will have to work hard to achieve and maintain this control.
- *Using choice theory concepts*: Reality therapists teach choice theory concepts by getting clients to rework the problems within them. For instance, clients learn to use concepts like basic needs, quality world and total behaviour. In addition they learn the basic assumption of choice theory that their behaviour is always their best attempt at controlling the world

and themselves so that they can best satisfy their basic needs for survival, belonging, power, freedom and fun. Furthermore, therapists work with clients on the assumption that the only person whose behaviour they can control is their own.

- *Bibliotherapy*: Assuming they are receptive and capable of understanding the ideas, reality therapists can ask clients to read Glasser's book *Choice Theory: A New Psychology of Personal Freedom* (1999) and together they can discuss its contents. Then therapists and clients can analyse the client's problems according to choice theory. Though not necessary to therapy, much time may be saved by clients reading and using this book. In addition, clients can be helped to become creative in how they use choice theory language – as contrasted with external control language – by reading all or some of the examples in Glasser's and his wife Carleen Glasser's book *The Language of Choice Theory*. Box 7.6 shows two examples in the area of love and marriage from this book (1999: 48–51).

Box 7.6 Examples of the language of choice theory

Example 1

External control
'Why are you so afraid of making a commitment? Our relationship is going nowhere! I'm tired of waiting for you to make up your mind. Marry me or I'm leaving'.
Choice theory alternative
'Since we're spending the weekend together, I want to have a really good time. I've decided not to talk about our future. In fact, I'm not ever going to talk about it again. Ever! It's up to you. And I'm not going to nag or criticize you. I've just given up begging you to marry me. I haven't given up on getting married'.

Example 2

External control
'You said you'd call last night, but you didn't. You'd better have a damn good reason why'.
Choice theory alternative
'It's good to hear from you. What's happening? Any news about that contract you've been working on so hard?'

Questioning within the WDEP system

Reality therapists need to develop and use good questioning skills within the WDEP system. Skilled questioning can accelerate the therapy process more than if the therapist had taken a passive stance. Purposes of questioning include: entering clients' inner worlds, gathering information, giving information, enabling clients to mentally 'stand back' and evaluate their situations or lives with greater perspective, and helping clients take more effective control of their lives by making better choices (Brickell and Wubbolding, 1996; Wubbolding, 2000).

The ability of therapists to ask skilled questions within the WDEP system is not an end in itself. The ultimate purpose of reality therapist questioning is to help clients develop self-questioning and self-evaluation skills for when they are no longer in therapy. Reality therapy is an educational process in which therapists heighten clients' awareness of themselves as persons who can make good or poor choices. Therapists also train clients to engage in a process of questioning the wisdom of their choices. An example is that of a therapist assisting a client to relate better by developing the habit of asking her/himself before raising sensitive issues with a partner: 'How might I phrase that in choice theory rather than in external control language?'

Case material

In *Choice Theory*, Glasser (1999) presents excerpts from a number of different cases illustrating his use of the choice theory framework in reality therapy. He conducts and comments on an imaginary initial interview with Francesca, the leading female character from James Waller's *The Bridges of Madison County*. A brief extramarital romantic interlude has left Francesca feeling that she is dead inside stuck in the confines of her current rural life and marriage. Glasser shows how he instils hope in her that she can start rebuilding her life. Another case excerpt shows Glasser helping Tina move from external control psychology to choice theory in her relationship with Kevin, whom she had been dating for two years and wanted to marry.

A further case example is that of using reality therapy with Terri, who came to see Glasser because she was unable to have satisfying emotional and sexual relationships in that, as soon as she would get close to a man, she chose to behave in ways that destroyed the relationship. Other case material in *Choice Theory* includes Glasser's work with Linda, a divorced woman suffering from tension headaches and a troubled relationship with her 16-year-old daughter Samantha, and Glasser conducting structured marital therapy with Ed and Karen whose quality world pictures of each other as husband and wife were very shaky, but still intact.

Glasser's *Reality Therapy in Action* (Glasser, 2000) takes readers into his consulting room and illustrates through a series of case studies including conversations with his clients how he puts his theory into practice. The examples show how he has incorporated the direct teaching of control theory into the use of reality therapy.

In 1996, Glasser replaced control theory with choice theory, so case material before then must be viewed with that change in mind. Glasser and Wubbolding

(1995) present a typical first session with Louis, unemployed for eight months and unsuccessfully looking for a job at middle management level. Louis also had long-standing tensions with his wife Sally. In the same chapter, Glasser and Wubbolding present the case example of Fay who, when men got too close, turned away from them. Wubbolding (1988) illustrates the use of reality therapy in two cases: Jane, a divorced mother of two, who came to see him having previously been diagnosed as manic-depressive; and Helen and Stephen, who had considerable strengths, yet a number of serious areas of conflict in their marriage. In *Reality Therapy for the 21st Century*, Wubbolding (2000) demonstrates a number of the skills that are involved in various aspects of the WDEP system with case illustrations.

Further developments

Reality therapy based on the choice theory framework is used in marital therapy (Glasser and Glasser, 2000). Early on it is important to clarify whether the partners want to evaluate the advantages and disadvantages of continuing the marriage or whether they have made a definite decision to try to preserve the marriage. Marital therapy focuses on how couples can live together within a choice theory framework without attempting to control one another in ways that they do not want to be controlled.

Reality therapists also work in groups, often as joint leaders. Group members can help each other to evaluate the adequacy of current behaviours in satisfying needs and quality world pictures, planning alternative behaviours, and making commitments. For example, a member's plan can be written down and a public commitment made by having each member of the group read and sign it.

Reality therapy and choice theory principles are widely used in educational settings. Many of Glasser's books (Glasser, 1992, 1993, 2002) have been focused on improving the skills of administrators and teachers in creating environments in which students can learn to take effective control of their lives. Glasser's book *Choice Theory* includes chapters on the application of choice theory in quality schools. Regarding the workplace, Glasser (1999) has written about the difference between boss management, based on external control psychology, and lead management, based on choice theory.

Reality therapy as a system is being developed not only by Glasser, but by prominent adherents such as Robert Wubbolding in the United States and John Brickell in Britain (Wubbolding, 2000; Wubbolding and Brickell, 1999). In 1981, the *Journal of Reality Therapy* was launched, edited by Dr Larry Litvak. This journal, still edited by Litvak, is now called the *International Journal of Reality Therapy*. By 2005, over 7000 people had completed the reality therapy certification process worldwide (Wubbolding, 2005). In addition to the United States, training opportunities in reality therapy exist in Britain and Australia as well as many other countries.

Review and personal questions

Review questions

1. What are the main differences between external control psychology and choice theory?
2. List and define the five basic needs.
3. Define and identify the content of the quality world.
4. What is total behaviour? Provide an example illustrating each element of total behaviour.
5. Why do people choose their misery and how do people remain unaware that they are choosing misery?
6. What are the goals of reality therapy?
7. Define the content of and therapist skills required for each element of the WDEP system outlining the process of reality therapy:

    (a) What do you want?
    (b) What are you doing and what is your overall direction?
    (c) Conduct thorough self-evaluation.
    (d) What is your plan?

8. In reality therapy, what is the nature of the therapeutic relationship?
9. How might reality therapists teach choice theory to clients?
10. Why is it important for reality therapists to become skilled questioners and for clients to become skilled at questioning and evaluating themselves?

Personal questions

1. Do you think Glasser's view of basic needs is accurate in reflecting your basic needs?
2. To what extent do you consider the pictures in your quality world are helpful or harmful to fulfilling your basic needs?
3. In an area where your current total behaviour in a relationship is not getting you what you want, apply the WDEP system to yourself so that you can make better choices in future.
4. What relevance, if any, has reality therapy and its choice theory framework for how you conduct therapy?
5. What relevance, if any, has choice theory for how you live?

Annotated bibliography

Glasser, W. (1999) *Choice Theory: A New Psychology of Personal Freedom.* New York: HarperPerennial.

Glasser makes a passionate plea for a shift from relationship-destroying external control psychology to relationship-enhancing choice theory psychology. There are chapters on the main concepts of choice theory as well as on the practice of reality therapy within a choice theory framework in marital therapy, families, schooling and the workplace. In addition, Glasser presents his ideas on the quality community and on how to redefine your personal freedom.

Glasser, W. (2000) *Reality Therapy in Action*. New York: HarperCollins.
A sequel to his original 1965 book *Reality Therapy*, this book illustrates the practice of choice theory and reality therapy by means of a series of over 12 case studies.

Glasser, W. and Glasser, C. (1999) *The Language of Choice Theory*. New York: HarperPerennial.
This small companion volume to *Choice Theory* contains a brief introduction highlighting the difference between traditional external control language and creative choice theory language. The remainder of the book comprises a series of examples contrasting external control language with its choice theory alternative in four areas: parent to child, love and marriage, teacher to student, and manager to employee.

Glasser, W. and Wubbolding, R. (1995) 'Reality therapy', in R.J. Corsini and D. Weddding (eds), *Current Psychotherapies* (5th edn). Itasca, IL: Peacock. pp. 293–321.
This is an authoritative account of the theory and practice of reality therapy just prior to the change from a control theory to a choice theory framework.

Wubbolding, R. (2000) *Reality Therapy for the 21st Century*. Bristol, PA: Accelerated Development.
This book is Wubbolding's update of reality therapy. Much of the book is taken up with descriptions, often illustrated, of interventions that form parts of the WDEP formulation. The book also includes an interview with William Glasser, a chapter summarizing the multicultural dimensions of reality therapy, and a chapter on research validating reality therapy.

Wubbolding, R. and Brickell, J. (1999) *Counselling with Reality Therapy*. Bicester: Speechmark Press.
This first British-published book on reality therapy provides an introduction to choice theory concepts, creating the counselling environment and the 'Cycle of Counselling' procedures that can be applied to virtually any setting, including coaching and managing. Applications to specific areas include: one-to-one counselling, working with groups, relationship counselling, and working in schools.

References and further reading

Barr, N.I. (1974) 'The responsible world of reality therapy', *Psychology Today, 7*(9): 64–8.
Brickell, J. and Wubbolding, R. (1996) 'Understanding reality therapy', *CMS News, 47*: 5–7.
Brierly, S.A. (1989) 'Breaking away from the family mold and developing a strong comfortable identity', in N. Glasser (ed.), *Control Theory in the Practice of Reality Therapy: Case Studies*. New York: Harper & Row. pp. 163–80.
Evans, D.B. (1982) 'What are you doing? An interview with William Glasser', *Personnel and Guidance Journal, 60*: 460–5.
Glasser, W. (1961) *Mental Health or Mental Illness?* New York: Harper & Row.
Glasser, W. (1965) *Reality Therapy: A New Approach to Psychiatry*. New York: Harper & Row.
Glasser, W. (1969) *Schools Without Failure*. New York: Harper & Row.

Glasser, W. (1976) *Positive Addiction*. New York: Harper & Row.

Glasser, W. (1984) *Control Theory: A New Explanation of How We Control Our Lives*. New York: Harper & Row.

Glasser, W. (1989) 'Control theory', in N. Glasser (ed.), *Control Theory in the Practice of Reality Therapy: Case Studies*. New York: Harper & Row. pp. 1–15.

Glasser, W. (1992) *The Quality School: Managing Students Without Coercion* (2nd edn). New York: Harper & Row.

Glasser, W. (1993) *The Quality School Teacher*. New York: Harper & Row.

Glasser, W. (1999) *Choice Theory: A New Psychology of Personal Freedom*. New York: HarperPerennial.

Glasser, W. (2000) *Reality Therapy in Action*. New York: HarperCollins.

Glasser, W. (2002) *Unhappy Teenagers: A Way for Parents and Teachers to Reach Them*. New York: HarperCollins.

Glasser, W. (2003) *Warning: Psychiatry Can Be Hazardous to Your Mental Health*. New York: Quill.

Glasser, W. and Glasser, C. (1999) *The Language of Choice Theory*. New York: HarperPerennial.

Glasser, W. and Glasser, C. (2000) *Getting Together and Staying Together: Solving the Mystery of Marriage*. New York: Quill.

Glasser, W. and Wubbolding, R. (1995) 'Reality therapy', in R.J. Corsini and D. Wedding (eds), *Current Psychotherapies* (5th edn). Itasca, IL: Peacock. pp. 293–321.

Powers, W.T. (1973) *Behavior: The Control of Perception*. Chicago: Aldine.

Waller, J. (1992) *The Bridges of Madison County*. Secacus, NJ: Warner Books.

Wubbolding, R. (1988) *Using Reality Therapy*. New York: Harper & Row.

Wubbolding, R. (1998) 'Client inner self-evaluation: a necessary prelude to change', in H. Rosenthal (ed.), *Favorite Counseling and Therapy Techniques*. Washington, DC: Accelerated Development. pp. 196–7.

Wubbolding, R. (2000) *Reality Therapy for the 21st Century*. Bristol, PA: Accelerated Development.

Wubbolding, R. (2005) Personal Communication. 20 July.

Wubbolding, R. and Brickell, J. (1999) *Counselling with Reality Therapy*. Bicester: Speechmark Press.

Useful addresses

The William Glasser Institute
22024 Lassen Street, Suite 118
Chatsworth, CA 91311
USA
Website: hhtp://www.wglasser.com

Dr Robert Wubbolding, Director
Center for Reality Therapy
7672 Montgomery Street 383
Cincinnati, Ohio 45236
USA
Email: wubsrt@fuse.net
Website: www.realitytherapywub.com

existential therapy   8

Introduction

Yalom writes: 'Existential psychotherapy is a dynamic therapeutic approach that focuses on concerns rooted in existence' (2001: xvi). The word existence is derived from the Latin word *existere*, literally meaning 'to stand out, to emerge'. Existence is not a static process, but entails coming into being or becoming. Existential approaches to therapy are concerned with the science and processes of being. The science of being is known as *ontology*, from *ontos* the Greek word for being.

Existential approaches to therapy are rooted in existential philosophy. Prominent existential philosophers include Kierkegaard, Nietzsche, Heidegger and Sartre. Kierkegaard's existentialism was within a Christian framework and he described the dread, anxiety and despair – 'the sickness unto death' – of humans estranged from their essential nature (Kierkegaard, 1954). Nietzsche was an atheist existentialist who presented a nihilistic picture of the world in which 'God is dead' as the background for human self-affirmation (Tillich, 1952). Heidegger's (1962) *Being and Time* focused on the quest for being and analysed the concept of *dasien*, being there or existence. Sartre, a Marxist, echoed Nietzsche's thoughts about a godless world. He emphasized human's inescapable need, in their struggle against despair and non-being, to make the choices that make the essence of their existences (Sartre, 1956). So long as they are alive, humans have no exit from the need to define themselves.

Existential approaches to therapy have also been influenced by religious philosophers, for instance Buber, the Jewish theologian, and Tillich, the Protestant Christian theologian. Buber (1965, 1970) thought that humans were not separate entities, but existed as creatures of the in-between. The two special types of in-between relationships were 'I–It' relationships, involving functional relationships in which others were objects, and 'I–Thou' relationships, involving mutual influence and a full experiencing of another. Tillich's (1952) book *The Courage to Be* examines human existence within a religious framework. For Tillich the courage to be is 'the ethical act in which man affirms his own being in spite of those elements which conflict with his essential self-affirmation' (1952: 3).

Existential psychotherapeutic approaches go beyond dealing with surface problems to assist clients to confront the basic issues of their existence: anxiety, despair, death, loneliness, alienation and meaninglessness. All the preceding issues have the potential to generate 'existence pain' (Yalom, 1989). Existential approaches to therapy are also concerned with questions of freedom, responsibility, love and creativity. Now people face far more of a challenge than previously to create and define their own existences.

There are many existential approaches to therapy from many countries. In Britain, van Deurzen (1998, 2002) and Spinelli (1989, 1997; Spinelli and Marshall, 2001) are prominent theorists. However, this chapter describes the theory and practice of the Americans Yalom and May's existential therapy and the next chapter reviews the Austrian's Frankl's logotherapy.

Irvin Yalom and Rollo May

Irvin Yalom (1931–)

Irvin Yalom was born in 1931 in Washington, DC, the son of Russian immigrant parents who, in the 1920s, had arrived penniless in the United States. His parents had virtually no formal education, never read books and struggled to survive economically by running a grocery store. The family lived in a cockroach-infested apartment above the store, in a poor neighbourhood of Washington. Though he admired his father, Yalom stated that he 'spent too many hours in my childhood silently hating my mother's vicious tongue' (1989: 147). For instance, when he was 13, his father suffered a serious coronary in the early hours of the morning. As mother, father and son waited for the family physician to arrive: ' "It's all your fault," she shouted, "you did this – all the aggravation, all the grief you gave him – you did this to him. You. You" ' (Yalom, 1998: 437). When his mother grew old, she lost her fangs and his relationship with her became much closer (Yalom, 2001). Yalom wrote that he grew up in facing two additional existential perils because 'In the streets, the black attacked me for my whiteness, and in school, the white attacked me for my Jewishness' (1989: 88). However, reading – especially reading fiction – provided a refuge from the external harshness and, early in life, Yalom (2005a) developed the notion that writing fiction was the finest thing a person could do.

Facing a choice between medical school and going into business with his father, Yalom opted for the former. In 1952, he received a BA degree from George Washington University and, in 1956, obtained an MD from Boston University. During the next six years, Yalom served as an intern at New York's Mt Sinai Hospital, a psychiatric resident at Baltimore's Johns Hopkins Hospital, a consultant at the Patuxent Institution in Maryland, and as a US Army Captain in Honolulu. In 1962, he was appointed an instructor in psychiatry at Stanford University School of Medicine, a decision partly made to put 3000 miles between his mother and himself (Yalom, 2001). He became an assistant professor, associate professor and professor in 1963, 1968 and 1973, respectively. In

1994, Yalom retired and became an Emeritus Professor of Psychiatry at Stanford. He now devotes much of his time to writing psychotherapy novels and stories. Throughout a 45-year career so far, his extensive personal therapy has included being in 750 hours of five-time-a-week orthodox Freudian analysis, two years of gestalt therapy, three years with Rollo May as well as many brief stints with other approaches.

In 1963 Yalom married his wife Marilyn, who received a PhD in Comparative Literature from Johns Hopkins and went on to become a university professor. The Yaloms have four grown-up children and an increasing number of grandchildren.

Yalom has published numerous scientific papers. In addition, his professional writing includes: *Existential Psychotherapy* (1980), *Inpatient Group Psychotherapy* (1983), *The Theory and Practice of Group Psychotherapy* (1995), and coauthorship of *Encounter Groups: First Facts* (Lieberman et al., 1973), *Every Day Gets a Little Closer* (Yalom and Elkins, 1974) and *Concise Guide to Group Psychotherapy* (Yalom and Vinogradov, 1989). Furthermore, Yalom has collaborated with his former therapist, Rollo May, to write and keep updating a chapter about existential therapy for a current psychotherapies textbook (May and Yalom, 2005).

Yalom's psychological novels and non-fiction stories include: *Love's Executioner and Other Tales of Psychotherapy* (1989), *When Nietzsche Wept* (1991) – which won the Commonwealth Club's Gold Medal for Fiction for the Best Novel of 1992 – *Lying on the Couch* (1996), *Momma and the Meaning of Life* (1999) and *The Schopenhauer Cure* (2005b). Yalom intends these best-selling books both as entertainment and as pedagogical works representing a new genre of teaching psychotherapy novels and stories. A Yalom compilation, entitled *The Yalom Reader* (1998), combines material illustrating his three major interests: group psychotherapy, existential psychotherapy and writing.

Rollo May (1909–94)

Rollo May was born in Ohio in 1909. One of seven children, his father was a YMCA secretary who moved his family quite often. May's parents' relationship was discordant and his family life unhappy, a stimulus for his later interest in therapy. May describes his mother as a 'bitch-kitty on wheels' (Rabinowitz et al., 1989: 437). His only sister, who was older than him, was psychotic and spent some time in a mental hospital. May obtained relief from family misery by sitting and playing on the shores of the St Clair river.

A rebel during high school, May studied liberal arts at Oberlin College, obtaining his BA in 1930. He then went to Greece for three years where he taught boys aged 12–18 in a gymnasium and studied ancient Greek civilization. In addition, one summer vacation he went to Vienna where he studied individual psychology with Alfred Adler. In 1938, May received his BD from Union

Theological Seminary, where he met and developed an ongoing friendship with Paul Tillich, who had recently been expelled from Nazi Germany, and who was a major influence on his thinking. In 1949, May obtained his PhD in clinical psychology from Teachers College of Columbia University.

While pursuing his doctoral degree, May came down with tuberculosis. His recovery involved spending nearly two years bed-ridden in an upstate New York sanatorium where he spent much time reading and thinking about the nature of anxiety. Ultimately, this work led to his writing *The Meaning of Anxiety* (1950). During his New York City years, May conducted a private practice, authored books and articles, was an adjunct professor at the New School of Social Research and New York University, and served as a training analyst and supervisor at the William Alanson White Institute. He then lived in San Franscisco where he wrote, taught and saw clients. May was divorced twice and in 1989 confided: 'I've always had good friends and lovers, but I'm scared to death of marriage' (Rabinowitz et al., 1989: 437). He died on 22 October 1994 at the age of 84.

Reflecting his early interest in English literature, May was a prolific author of books and articles. Over a long period he was at the forefront of applying existential and humanistic ideas to counselling. May's books include *The Art of Counseling* (1939), *The Meaning of Anxiety* (1950), his co-edited book *Existence* (which includes two important chapters by him, 1958), *Psychology and the Human Dilemma* (1967), *Love and Will* (1969), *Power and Innocence: A Search for the Sources of Violence* (1973), *The Courage to Create* (1975), *Freedom and Destiny* (1981) and *My Quest for Beauty* (1985). Though he enjoyed his twilight years, towards the end of his life May observed: 'I wouldn't want to go through this life again. I mean, one time is enough. I don't know that I'd do anything differently, but it would be too boring' (Rabinowitz et al., 1989: 439).

Theory

Basic concepts

Being and non-being

May (May et al., 1958) observed that being as a participle of a verb and implies that someone is in the process of becoming something. He stated that, when used as a noun being means *potentia*, the source of potential. An analogy is that the acorn has the potential to become an oak. This analogy is only partially accurate for humans since they have the capacity for self-consciousness. Humans can choose their own being. The choices that they make about being are not just concerned with whether or not to commit suicide, but are relevant to every instant of their lives.

Because of widespread collectivist and conformist trends in society, modern humans have repressed their sense of being. People's sense of being refers to their whole experience of existence, both conscious and unconscious. They need to experience themselves as beings in the world and have a basic 'I Am' experience, expressed by one of May's clients as 'Since, I Am, I have the right to be' (May et al., 1958: 43). The 'I Am' experience is not the solution, but rather the precondition for the solution to clients' problems.

The opposite of being is non-being or nothingness. Existence implies the possibility of not existing. Death is the most obvious form of non-being. However, there are numerous other threats to being in the form of loss of potentiality through anxiety and conformity and through lack of clear self-awareness. In addition, destructive hostility and physical sickness can pose threats to being. However, people who are able to confront non-being can emerge with a heightened sense of being including a greater awareness not only of themselves, but of others and the world around them.

The three forms of being-in-the-world

Existential therapy distinguishes three modes of world that characterize people's existence as being-in the world. First, there is the *Umwelt*, the 'world around'. The *Umwelt* represents the natural world, the laws of nature and the environment. For animals and human beings alike, the *Umwelt* includes biological needs, drives and instincts. It also includes each organism's daily and life cycles. The natural world is accepted as real.

Second, there is the *Mitwelt*, the 'with-world'. This is the social world of relating to fellow humans singly and in groups. Both in personal and group relationships people influence each other and the structure of meaning that develops. May writes: 'The essence of relationship is that in the encounter both persons are changed' (1958: 63). How people relate in intimate relationships, for instance their degree of commitment, influences the meaning of the relationships for them. Similarly, how much of themselves people put into groups influences the meaning of the groups for them.

Third, there is the *Eigenwelt*, or 'own world'. The *Eigenwelt* is uniquely present in humans and entails self-consciousness and self-awareness. Also, the *Eigenwelt* entails grasping the personal meaning of a thing or person. Individuals need their own relationships to things and people, for instance, 'This flower is beautiful' means 'For me, this flower is beautiful'.

The three modes of being are interrelated. For instance, love entails more than the biological drives of the *Umwelt*. Furthermore, it entails more than the social or interpersonal relationship of the *Mitwelt*. In addition, love requires the *Eigenwelt*, in that, when relating to another, people need to be sufficient to themselves.

Normal and neurotic anxiety

To be human is to be anxious. Anxiety is an unavoidable part of human life. May (1950) distinguishes between normal and neurotic anxiety. He defines anxiety as 'the threat to our existence or to values we identify with our existence' (May, 1977: 205). In the course of normal development everyone experiences various threats to their existence. One source of normal anxiety is human's existential vulnerability to Nature, sickness and death. Another source is the need to progressively become independent from parents with the tensions and crises that this process can create. However, people can use such threats constructively as learning experiences and continue to develop.

The reaction of normal anxiety has three characteristics. First, it is proportionate to the objective threat in the situation being confronted. Second, it does not involve repression. Third, it can be used creatively to identify and confront the conditions bringing it about. Existential therapists view their main function as helping clients come to terms with the normal anxieties that are part of human existence.

Neurotic anxiety possesses the opposite characteristics to normal anxiety. Neurotic anxiety is a disproportionate reaction to an objective threat, involves repression, and is destructive rather than constructive. Another way of viewing neurotic anxiety is that people subjectively react to objective threats in terms of their inner psychological patterns and conflicts. The repression and blocking of awareness involved in neurotic anxiety leaves people more vulnerable to threats since they lose access to important information with which to distinguish and deal with the threats.

Normal, neurotic and existential guilt

Like anxiety, guilt is part of human existence. A distinction may be drawn between normal and neurotic guilt. Neurotic guilt derives from *imagined* transgressions against others, parental injunctions and societal conventions. Normal guilt is a call to conscience and sensitizes people to the ethical aspects of their behaviour.

Existential or ontological guilt represents another form of guilt. May distinguishes between three forms of existential guilt. The first form, which corresponds to *Eigenwelt,* is failure to live up to potential. As such, people can be guilty of transgressions against themselves. The second form, which corresponds to *Mitwelt,* relates to distorting the reality of one's fellow humans. The third form of existential guilt, which involves *Umwelt* as well as the other two modes of being, is 'separation guilt' in relation to nature as a whole.

Existential guilt is universal. It is rooted in self-awareness and does not arise from violation of parental injunctions, 'but arises from the fact that I can see myself as the one who can choose or fail to choose' (May et al., 1958: 55). Thus existential guilt is inexorably linked with the notion of personal responsibility. Existential guilt is not in itself a form of neurotic guilt, though it possesses the potential to turn into neurotic guilt. However, if correctly addressed, existential guilt can have constructive outcomes both in terms of greater humility and sensitivity to others and in increased creativity.

Transcendence

Humans' unique capacity to think and talk in symbols allows them the possibility of transcending time and space. Humans can project themselves into the past and into the future. In addition they can transcend themselves in their social relations and see themselves as others see them and give appropriate weight to others' perceptions. The capacity to transcend immediate concrete situations provides humans with the basis of both their freedom and their responsibility.

Transcendence is derived from the Latin word *transcendere*, meaning 'to climb over and beyond'. The ability to transcend immediate situations is part of the ontological nature of human beings. Existing involves humans in a continuous process of emerging in that they transcend their pasts and presents to create their futures. Unless seriously ill or blocked by anxiety or despair, all humans engage in this process.

Existential ultimate concerns

Yalom (1980) has identified four existential ultimate concerns – death, freedom, isolation and meaninglessness – with considerable relevance for counselling and therapy. Each concern begets a different existential conflict.

1. *Death*: The first existential conflict is that between awareness of the inevitability of death and the wish to continue to live: the conflict between fear of non-being and wishing to be. Life and death, being and non-being, are interdependent rather than concurrent. Death is the fundamental source of anxiety, whether it be neurotic, normal or existential. Perhaps the term 'death terror' denotes the force of death concern better than death anxiety. Death anxiety – the fear of ceasing to be – can be both conscious and unconscious. From early in their lives children are extremely preoccupied with death. Strong death anxiety is likely to be repressed. To cope with the terror of potential non-being, people erect denial-based defences against death anxiety. To a large extent psychopathology has its origins in failed attempts to transcend death.

2. *Freedom*: The second existential conflict is that between people's confrontation with groundlessness and freedom and their wish for ground and structure. Humans are 'condemned to freedom' (Sartre, 1956: 631); they do not live in a well-ordered and structured universe. There is no secure ground undergirding existence. Rather there is lack of structure and groundlessness that generates both anxiety and dread. Because of their freedom, humans are also condemned to responsibility. They are not only responsible for imbuing the world with significance, but entirely responsible for their lives, for their actions and their failures to act.

3. *Isolation*: The third existential conflict is that between people's awareness of their fundamental isolation and their wish for contact, protection and to be a part of a larger whole. There are three forms of isolation:

    (a) *Interpersonal isolation*, often experienced as loneliness, means that people are in varying degrees cut off from others. This may be through deficient social skills, psychopathology or by choice and of necessity;

    (b) *Intrapersonal isolation* means that people are blocked from aware-ness of or dissociated from parts of themselves. While interpersonal isolation may not contain pathology, intrapersonal isolation does so by definition;

    (c) *Existential isolation* is rooted in the human condition in that each person enters, lives in and leaves the world alone. Ultimately there is an unbridgable gap between self and others. Yalom observes that existential isolation refers to an even more fundamental form of isolation, namely 'Separation from the world' (1980: 355).

4. *Meaninglessness*: The fourth existential conflict is that of humans con-fronting their need for meaning in an indifferent world that has no mean-ing. What is the meaning of life? Humans require coherence, purpose and significance. They organize random stimuli into figure and ground. They are neuropsychologically organized to seek patterns and meaning. However, the human paradox is that of existence in an indifferent universe with no predetermined meaning. A distinction may be made between cosmic meaning, whether human life fits into some overall cosmic pattern, and terrestrial meaning, the meaning of my life. With the decline in reli-gious beliefs, modern humans are faced with the need to discover secular personal meaning in the absence of cosmic meaning.

Existential psychodynamics

In personality theory, the term dynamics relates to the concept of energy or force. The notion of psychodynamic conflict relates to the clash between opposing forces. The Freudian model of dynamic conflict was that of the clash between ego and instinctual sexual and aggressive drives. To Freud, the deeper conflicts were associated with the earliest psychosexual conflicts.

Existential psychodynamics differ in two important ways from Freudian psychodynamics. First, existential conflicts and existential anxiety flow from people's inescapable confrontations with the givens of existence: death, free-dom, isolation and meaninglessness. Second, existential dynamics do not assume a developmental or archaeological model where first is synonymous with deep. When existential therapists and clients explore deeply, they do so not by focusing on everyday concerns, but thinking deeply about existential ultimate concerns.

Acquisition

Despite existential anxieties and conflicts being inescapable parts of life, the question still remains of how people develop different modes of dealing with the ultimate concerns of existence.

Death

Young children, even though not intellectually equipped to understand what death means, grasp its essence. Yalom (1980) believes that children then deny their first knowledge of death. Mechanisms of denial include such beliefs as death is temporary, children do not die, I will not die because I am special, and that there is an ultimate rescuer. Coming to terms with the concept of death is a major developmental task which some children handle better than others.

Exposure to death can be for good or ill. Factors likely to be helpful include the presence of already existing ego resources, good genes and supportive adults able to deal with their own death anxieties. However, exposure to death can be traumatic when these factors are insufficiently present. Deaths of siblings and of parents can be especially frightening and exceed children's coping resources. Research indicates that both neurotic and psychotic psychiatric patients have lost a parent more frequently than the general population. The degree of cultural acceptance of death also influences how much anxiety death will generate in both adults and children.

The quality of death education that parents offer to their children affects their awareness and acceptance of death. Children are often shielded from death by misinformation, denial, fairy tales, euphemisms and assurances that children do not die. As with sex, children do not ignore the issue, but turn to other sources of information of varying degrees of reliability. Western cultures offer no real guidelines about how parents should educate their children about death. Many adults, who seek comfort in child-like beliefs, do not help this state of affairs.

Freedom

The modern-day emphasis on freedom and responsibility as existential concerns derives from the breaking down of traditional belief systems, religions, rituals and rules. In the 20th and continuing into the early 21st century, there has been a rapid disintegration of structures and values. Permissive parenting has now left many young people with the need to choose but without clear guidelines as to how or what to choose. Numerous people are unprepared for the freedom they now have. Frequently, when confronted with the existential fact of their responsibility for their lives, they experience difficulty in handling this realization. Now people are less faced with what they 'must' do, instead the emphasis is on what they want to do. In what may be a transitional period between old and new ways of being in the world, many people have failed to learn adequately how to wish, how to will and how to decide and stay committed to their decisions.

Isolation

There are different types of isolation:

- *Interpersonal isolation*: Cultural and technological change plays a large part in the creation of this form of isolation. In the United States and other western cultures there has been a decline in community links: churches, local shops, neighbours who know each other and have local roots, family doctors and so on.
- *Intrapersonal isolation*: This stems from obstructions and frustrations that occur early in life and threaten some vital aspect of the individual's nascent sense of self.
- *Existential isolation*: This is closely interwoven with interpersonal isolation. Many people fail to develop the inner strength, confidence and sense of identity that enable them to face existential isolation. Never having received genuine growth-inducing love, they do not know how to offer it to others. If committed and authentic therapist–client relationships can help clients confront and come to terms with their existential isolation, it can safely be inferred that clients have insufficiently experienced such relationships in their pasts.

Meaninglessness

Many factors in contemporary culture contribute to people having a diminished sense of life's meaning compared to their forebears in the preindustrial agricultural world. First, instead of meaning being supplied by religion, now most people neither believe in religion nor go to church. Second, the spread of urbanization and industrialization has contributed to people losing a sense of meaning through their contact with nature. No longer are most people closely connected with the cycles of the land and of farm animals. Third, most contemporary humans no longer belong to or have roles in rural communities, but instead often live in relatively impersonal urban communities.

Fourth, many contemporary humans are alienated from their work and think that they engage in mechanical and routine tasks of little intrinsic interest. Fifth, contemporary humans are less beset with basic survival needs, such as food, shelter and water. Their greater security and leisure confronts them much more with the abyss of meaninglessness. Time on their hands means time to be haunted by issues of meaning. In addition, in economic recessions, many people are confronted by unemployment with the loss of and need for meaning. Sixth, contemporary humans face the possibility of nuclear annihilation and global environmental destruction. If the world is not going to last, why bother?

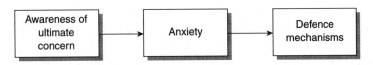

Figure 8.1   Existential model of defence mechanisms

Maintenance

The existential model of defence mechanisms

How do people maintain insufficient awareness and psychopathological behaviour within the existential framework? They evolve both conscious and unconscious psychological operations to deal with the anxiety generated by ultimate existential concerns. These psychological operations or *defence mechanisms* are of two types. First, there are conventional defence mechanisms, such as projection, which defend people against anxiety regardless of its source. Second, there are specific defences for each of the four ultimate concerns that defend people against these fundamental fears. These defence mechanisms may not only be relevant to individual clients, but they may be reinforced by whole cultures colluding in them.

Figure 8.1 depicts the existential model of defence mechanisms in reaction to awareness at some level of an inner conflict raised by an ultimate concern. Such defence mechanisms provide a modicum of psychological safety at the expense of restricting people's potential for growth and of generating existential guilt.

Death anxiety defences

Although the specific defences for each ultimate concern are mentioned separately, they may overlap. Furthermore, they require recombining or merging into an overall existential model of psychopathology. Children's modes of coping with death awareness and death terror involve denial. For children and adults alike, Yalom (1980) has identified two major death anxiety defence mechanisms:

- *Specialness*: While at the conscious level most people accept their lives as finite, deep down they can develop irrational beliefs about their own immortality and inviolability. Where this defence is weak or absent, then people may develop one of a number of clinical syndromes, including compulsive heroism, being a 'workaholic' and turning a deaf ear to time's message, narcissism, and the drive for power and control. Frequently, such people seek therapy when they can no longer ward off their death anxiety through these pretences.
- *Belief in an ultimate rescuer*: This defence represents the belief that, however bad things may get, the individual is not alone in an indifferent

universe and some omnipresent servant will come to the rescue. People using the defence of the ultimate rescuer may restrict their lives by locating and serving a 'dominant other'. Most people do not acknowledge their belief system until it fails to serve its purpose: for instance, if they acquire a fatal illness or their 'dominant other' dies or psychologically withdraws.

Freedom anxiety defences

Freedom anxiety defences protect individuals from awareness of their responsibility for the authorship of their lives. Awareness of responsibility entails being 'aware of creating one's own self, destiny, life predicament, feelings and, if such be the case, one's own suffering' (Yalom, 1980: 218). Compulsivity is one defence against responsibility awareness. Yalom (1980) gives the example of Bernard, a 25-year-old salesman who was compulsively driven in his sex, work and leisure lives. His compulsivity obliterated choice, yet Bernard was responsible for creating as well as maintaining his compulsivity. Other defences against freedom anxiety include: displacing responsibility on to others, including therapists; denying responsibility by posing as the innocent victim or losing control; avoidance of autonomous behaviour; and pathology in wishing, willing and deciding.

Isolation anxiety defences

In isolation anxiety defences people do not relate to others in their own right, but use them for defensive functions. One defence against ultimate aloneness is to exist and seek affirmation in others' eyes. Such people exist so far as they are part of others' consciousness and receive approval from them. Frequently, under the guise of loving, they can hide their inability to love. However, ultimately others are likely to get fed up with meeting their needs for affirmation. Fusion with an individual or group is another isolation anxiety defence. Rather than confront and come to terms with their fundamental isolation, people feel and think they are not alone because they are part of others. In addition, compulsive sexuality is a defence against isolation anxiety. Sexually compulsive people treat their partners as objects rather than persons. They do not take the time to know and be known. Instead, their serial relationships are caricatures of the real thing.

Meaninglessness anxiety defences

People handle meaninglessness anxiety in different ways. Compulsive activity is one way of avoiding a confrontation with meaninglessness. Individuals compulsively engage in any of a range of activities as a reaction to an underlying deep sense of purposelessness. Sooner or later many individuals who have compulsively sought money, pleasure, power, recognition and status start questioning their values. Crusadism is a form of compulsive activity where people seek out issues that they can make into time- and energy-consuming crusades. Nihilism is another defence against meaninglessness anxiety. Here people avoid confronting meaninglessness, by disparaging all sources of meaning that others find in their lives, for instance love or service.

Therapy

Therapeutic goals

Existential therapy is more a mode of viewing human beings than a rigorous system. In the final analysis, existential therapists view clienthood as ubiquitous. However, generally clients are more troubled than their therapists.

The overriding goal of existential therapy is that clients experience their existence as real. The underlying assumption is that the fundamental neurotic process is the repression of the ontological sense, thus involving the loss of a sense of being and the truncation of awareness and potential. Since therapy is primarily concerned with helping clients experience their existence, any symptomatic 'cure' is a by-product or secondary goal. Existential therapists attempt to avoid a technical, mechanical approach to clients that can lead to the latter obtaining a symptomatic 'cure' at the expense of constricting their existence. Great stress is placed in viewing clients in human rather than behavioural terms and on authentic therapist–client relationships.

More specifically, existential therapy entails assisting clients to embark on a journey of self-investigation, whose goals are

- to understand the unconscious conflict;
- to identify the maladaptive defence mechanisms;
- to discover their destructive influence;
- to diminish secondary anxiety by correcting restrictive modes of dealing with self and others; and
- to develop other ways of coping with primary anxiety (May and Yalom, 2005).

Process of therapy

Existential therapists respect the individuality of each client and approach each client with the aim of sharing the story they have to tell. Yalom observes:

> … the therapy process I ultimately developed is closely linked to the creative process, to the reading and writing of fiction: *reading* in that I always listen for the unique fascinating story of each patient's life; *writing* in that I believe, with Jung, that therapy is a creative act and the effective therapist must invent a new therapy for each patient. (1998: 307, emphasis in original)

Clear instances of when to use an existential approach to therapy are when clients face boundary situations associated with ultimate concerns. Such existential crises include death, personal and work transitions, irreversible decisions, and becoming unexpectedly isolated among others. The decision to work on existential conflicts should be a joint therapist–client decision.

Existential therapists seek to assist clients to understand their inner conflicts in relation to the ultimate existential concerns of death, freedom, isolation and meaninglessness. They continually focus on how clients avoid assuming personal responsibility for their distress. They attempt to identify clients' maladaptive defence mechanisms and help raise awareness of their negative consequences. As well as assisting clients to develop other ways of coping with primary or existential anxiety, existential therapists work to lessen secondary anxiety by helping clients alter limiting ways of relating to self and others. For this purpose therapists may use a variety of interventions employed by other therapeutic approaches so long as they are consistent with a basic existential framework.

Long-term therapy is most appropriate for thoroughly addressing existential issues that affect deeper layers of the individual's mode of being in the world. However, aspects of an existential approach, for instance an emphasis on responsibility and authenticity, can still be incorporated into briefer forms of therapy.

The therapeutic relationship

The quality of the therapist–client relationship is central to existential therapy. Yalom writes: 'Therapists must convey to the patient that their paramount task is to build a relationship together that will itself become the agent of change' (2001: 34). The therapy relationship is not viewed in terms of transference and little time is spent trying to dig up clients' pasts. Since existential therapists emphasize the depth of confrontations with ultimate concerns at the given moment, they try to understand their clients' *current* situations and enveloping fears.

Presence, authenticity and commitment are words that describe the quality of relationship that existential therapists strive to offer. Yalom (2001) also uses the terms engagement, openness and egalitarianism. Existential therapy conducted on an individual basis takes place between two real people. The existential therapist is not a shadowy reflector, but a live human who tries to understand and experience the client's being. For the many clients who present with relationship difficulties, Yalom might say:

> ... I've found that I can be more helpful to you by focusing on the one relationship where I have the most accurate information – the relationship between you and me. It is for this reason I shall often ask you to examine what is happening between the two of us. (2001: 86)

Therapists who are present to clients do not impose their own thoughts and feelings on them. Nor do they transfer to clients thoughts and feelings coming from previous relationships, what is sometimes called *countertransference*. Yalom (1989) recalls that he had always been repelled by fat women and had to work through these feelings to be fully present to a grossly overweight client who entered his office. Furthermore, existential therapists are conscious that clients have many ways of inviting involvement with their therapists in order to avoid focusing on personal problems.

Yalom (1980) talks about surreptitious 'throw-ins' making all the difference in therapy. He cites a number of critical incidents in therapy in which therapists showed their commitment and engaged their clients in human rather than stereotyped encounters. An example is that of a therapist seeing an acutely ill client for a long emergency session on a Saturday afternoon. In Yalom's case study *Every Day Gets a Little Closer* (Yalom and Elkins, 1974), written from both therapist's and client's perspectives, he was struck by the importance his client attached to small personal touches such as warm looks and compliments about the way she looked. In addition to presence, characteristics of good therapist–client relationships include caring, extending oneself, touching clients at a profound level and wisdom (Yalom, 1980). Therapists help clients 'by being lovingly present with that person; by being trustworthy, interested; and by believing that their joint activity will ultimately be redemptive and healing' (Yalom, 1989: 227).

Self-disclosure

Therapist self-disclosure is an important issue in existential therapy. The overriding goal is that of an authentic relationship in the client's best interests. Existential therapists can use two kinds of self-disclosure. First, they can disclose about their personal struggles to come to terms with ultimate existential concerns and be human. Yalom regards himself as having erred on the side of too little self-disclosure and writes that 'whenever I have shared a great deal of myself, patients have invariably profited ...' (1989: 164).

Second, existential therapists can have a process as contrasted with a content focus. They can use their thoughts and feelings about what is going on in the here-and-now to try to improve the therapeutic relationship. For instance, Yalom (1989, 2005c) felt bored with his fat lady client, Betty. Initially he tried to sort out how much of his boredom was countertransference. However, he pinpointed two reasons for his boredom, that Betty was always revealing something that occurred elsewhere and that she hid behind a mask of false gaiety. He tactfully confronted Betty by pointing out that he thought she masked her pain by staying jolly and asking her permission to interrupt and point out when she was entertaining him the moment it occurred. This self-disclosure acted as a springboard for deepening their relationship.

Therapeutic interventions

Each of the ultimate concerns has implications for which therapeutic interventions may be appropriate.

Therapy and death

Increased awareness of death can lead to heightened appreciation of life. Terminally ill cancer patients react to the diagnosis in varying ways. Many do not fully hear what their doctors say. Some are flooded with existential terror. Others acknowledge the news briefly, regroup their defences, engage in internal processing, and then are ready for more information. Many cancer patients are able to use their illness as an opportunity for personal growth. They reassess priorities, choose not to do the trivial, gain an enhanced sense of living in the present, become more in touch with nature, communicate more deeply with loved ones, and have fewer interpersonal fears about rejection and taking risks. Mechanisms for change in cancer patients include the beliefs that existence cannot be postponed and the wisdom of counting your blessings. Increased death awareness can also bring about a radical shift in perspective in clients who are not terminally ill.

Yalom states that a good working rule for clinicians is 'death anxiety is inversely proportional to life satisfaction' (1980: 207). Interventions for increasing death awareness may increase clients' anxiety in the short term. The objective is not to anaesthetize the anxiety, but to help clients come to terms with it and use it constructively. Following are some methods that existential therapists use to increase clients' death awareness.

Giving permission
Existential therapists can cue clients that discussion of issues concerning death is valued in therapy. Some of this cueing may be by encouraging and showing interest in clients' disclosures in the area. Yalom (2001) early in therapy makes a point of obtaining a history of the clients' experiences with death. He asks questions such as 'When did you first become aware of death?', 'What deaths have you experienced?' and 'How have your attitudes about death changed during your life?'. Clients raise the topic of death more frequently once therapists demonstrate that they are comfortable with the topic.

Another part of giving permission is that of avoiding colluding in clients' denial of death. Therapists can play active roles in keeping therapy superficial. They require the ability to tolerate their own death anxiety to follow adequately clients' leads. Some therapists may require further personal therapy until they work through personally and professionally debilitating death anxiety blockages.

Identifying defence mechanisms
Two of the main defence mechanisms against death anxiety are the belief in specialness and the belief in the existence of an ultimate rescuer. Existential

therapists collaborate with clients to identify such maladaptive defence mechanisms and their negative consequences. Clients are assisted to acknowledge the reality of their finiteness rather than deny it. Existential therapists require tact, persistence and good timing to help clients to identify and relinquish child-like ways of viewing death.

Working with dreams

Existential therapists encourage clients to share their dreams. In dreams and nightmares unconscious themes can appear without being repressed or heavily edited. Death themes are common in dreams and nightmares. Discussion and analysis of dreams relates to clients' current existential conflicts. However, clients are not always ready to deal with the material revealed in their dreams. Box 8.1 illustrates a nightmare of Marvin, a 64-year-old client of Yalom's, the latter's private reflections about it, and what happened afterwards (Yalom, 1989: 242–6).

Box 8.1   Example of working with a dream

Marvin's nightmare
The two men are tall, pale and very gaunt. In a dark meadow they glide along in silence. They are dressed entirely in black. With tall black stovepipe hats, long-tailed coats, black spats and shoes, they resemble Victorian undertakers or temperance workers. Suddenly they come upon a carriage, ebony black, cradling a baby girl swaddled in black gauze. Wordlessly, one of the men begins to push the carriage. After a short distance he stops, walks around to the front, and, with his black cane, which now has a glowing white tip, he leans over, parts the gauze, and methodically inserts the white tip into the baby's vagina.

Yalom's private reflections about the meaning of Marvin's nightmare
I am old. I am at the end of my life's work. I have no children, and I approach death full of dread. I am choking on darkness. I am choking on the silence of death. I think I know a way. I try to pierce the blackness with my sexual talisman. But it is not enough.

What happened afterwards
When Yalom asked Marvin to associate to his dream he said nothing. When Marvin was then asked what he made of all the death imagery, he preferred to discuss the dream from the perspective of sex rather than of death.

Working with reminders of finiteness

Therapists can assist clients to identify and constructively deal with their death anxiety by being 'tuned into' the signs of mortality that are parts of normal life. The death of loved ones can be a powerful reminder of personal mortality. The death of parents means that ours is the next generation to die. The death of children can invoke a sense of powerlessness in relation to cosmic indifference. Also, where it is an only child who dies, parents realize that they will not be immortal through passing on their seed. In addition, severe illness can confront clients with their finiteness and vulnerability.

Transitions remind clients of their mortality. Such transitions include the passage from adolescence to adulthood, commitment to a permanent relationship, children leaving home, and marital separation and divorce. In middle age many clients become more aware of deaths, realizing that they are no longer growing up, but instead growing old. In addition, retirement or unexpected career threats can powerfully increase death awareness.

In daily life reminders of the passage of time are ever present. Physical signs of ageing – greying, wrinkling, skin plaques, stiffening of the joints, loss of stamina, poorer eyesight – shatter the illusion of permanent youthfulness. Going to reunions shows that everyone else is ageing. Frequently, since they are milestones of the ageing process, birthdays and anniversaries can generate existence pain as well as or instead of joy.

Aids to increasing death awareness

While many existential therapists would not use artificial aids to increase clients' death awareness, some therapists do. Clients can be asked to write their obituaries or fill out death anxiety questionnaires. In addition they can be taken on guided fantasies regarding their deaths, imagining 'where', 'when', 'how', and their funeral. Yalom (1980) describes two different ways of getting clients to interact with the dying: observing a group of terminally ill people, and introducing a person with terminal cancer into an everyday therapy group.

Desensitizing clients to death

Therapists can assist clients to deal with death terror by exposing them over and over to the fear in lessened doses. Yalom (1980) cites that in working with groups of cancer patients, he has seen many times their dread gradually diminish through sheer familiarity.

Understanding anxieties associated with death

Therapists may break down and identify the anxieties associated with death. A distinction needs to be made between the true helplessness arising from the fundamental existential fact of death and the ancillary feelings of helplessness. Clients can be encouraged to regain more of a sense of control over aspects of their lives they can influence. Also, they can be helped to identify and rationally confront their ancillary fears, such as having a painful death, loneliness and concern over loved ones. In the adult's unconscious dwell child-like irrational terrors about death. Such terrors can be brought into the open and assessed realistically.

Therapy and freedom

Therapy in relation to the ultimate concern of freedom focuses on increasing clients' awareness of their responsibility for their lives and on assisting them to assume this responsibility. The therapist has to look at the clients' rather than other people's roles in their lives, because that is where they can be of most help. Yalom writes: 'Responsibility assumption is the essential first step in the therapeutic process' (2001: 141). He reports that all the research data suggest that successful therapy clients become more aware of their personal responsibility for their lives (Yalom, 1980). Therapists can use a wide variety of techniques to assist responsibility awareness and assumption:

- *Identifying defences and methods of responsibility avoidance*: Therapists can help clients to understand the functions of some of their behaviours, for instance compulsiveness, in avoiding responsibility for choices. In addition, therapists can explore with and, if necessary, confront clients with their responsibility for their own distress. For instance, when lonely clients keep belittling others, the therapist can say: 'And you are lonely'. A general guideline is that when clients complain about their situations, therapists enquire about how they created them. In addition, therapists can focus on how clients use responsibility avoidance language: for instance, saying 'I can't' instead of 'I won't'.
- *Identifying responsibility avoidance in the here and now*: Clients' responsibility avoidances can manifest themselves in the therapist–client relationship. Therapists need awareness of their own feelings about clients to identify how they might elicit similar reactions from others. For instance, a woman with a history of relating to abusive men may distort her perception of her male therapist and behave towards him in ways that, in another context, might elicit the abuse she dreaded. Therapists can also confront clients with their here-and-now attempts to transfer responsibility for what happens either inside or outside of therapy on to them. If so, therapists may need to work through clients' resistances such as 'If I knew what to do, I wouldn't need to be here'.
- *Confronting realistic limitations*: All human beings have realistic adverse circumstances with which to deal. Therapy can help clients to change their attitude to or reconstrue external circumstances that they cannot alter. In addition, therapists can assist clients in identifying areas in their lives that they can influence. For instance, therapists dealing with cancer patients can assist them to assume more responsibility for their relationships to their doctors, such as assertively requesting information about their illness.
- *Confronting existential guilt*: Existential therapists view one of the functions of anxiety as a call to conscience. One source of anxiety is guilt about failure to actualize potential. For instance, a client who engaged in compulsive sexual behaviour also had difficulty being assertive in his business life. Identifying how he transgressed his potential as a human being through

limiting his life through compulsive sex was the springboard for his gaining the confidence to become more assertive. No longer was the client inwardly terrified about exposure of all the shameful episodes in his life. As his compulsiveness declined, his sense of being a chooser increased. A distinction exists between guilt for bad choices made in the past and refusal to make new choices. So long as clients continue to behave in the present as they did in the past, then they cannot forgive themselves for their past choices.

- *Freeing-up wishing*: Wishing precedes willing (May, 1969). However, for clients to wish they need to be in touch with how they feel. Working with affect-blocked clients can be a slow and repetitive process. Dramatic breakthrough methods are avoided since their effects tend not to be sustained. Instead, within the context of authentic relationships, existential therapists explore the source and nature of clients' blocks and the underlying feelings they try to express. In addition, therapists repeatedly ask affect-blocked clients questions like 'What do you feel?' and 'What do you want?'.

- *Facilitating deciding*: Existential therapists encourage clients to see that every action is preceded by a decision. Decisions are difficult because alternatives exclude. As such, decisions are boundary situations which people create themselves, despite their fundamental groundlessness. Many clients paralyse their decision-making capacity through 'What ifs': for instance, 'What if I lose my job and can't find another?'. Therapists can assist clients to explore the ramifications of each 'What if' and analyse the feelings they generate. While ensuring that responsibility for decisions remains with clients, therapists can assist them to generate and evaluate decision options. Therapists can encourage clients to make decisions actively in ways that reinforce acceptance of their power and resources.

  Where necessary, existential therapists try to disencumber their clients' wills. Therapist acceptance is crucial for clients learning to trust their wills and gain the belief that they have a right to act. Following are 'insights' that existential therapists commonly offer to will-stifled clients: 'Only I can change the world I have created'; 'There is no danger in change'; 'To get what I really want, I must change'; and 'I have the power to change'. Decisions to change may take place over a considerable period of time.

Therapy and isolation

The following are ways in which existential therapists can assist clients in confronting and dealing better with the ultimate concern of isolation:

- *Confronting isolation*: Therapists can help clients realize that ultimately everyone is alone. Clients can learn both what they can and what they cannot obtain from relationships. Therapists can ask clients to experiment with periods of self-enforced isolation in appropriate doses. Benefits of this experiment can include increased awareness both of the terror of loneliness and of hidden resources and courage.

- *Identifying defence mechanisms*: Clients can be helped to identify the defences they use to cope with the conflict of the need to belong and the fact of existential isolation. Becoming aware that existing in the eyes of others, fusion with others, and compulsive sexuality are defence mechanisms against existential anxiety can act as a springboard for doing something about them.
- *Identifying interpersonal pathology*: Using the ideal of a need-free or 'I–Thou' relationship as a yardstick, clients' ways of avoiding real relationships with others can be identified. To what extent do they relate to others as objects to satisfy their wants and needs? How well can they love others? How good are they at listening and revealing themselves? What are their specific distancing operations? Therapists can instruct clients in 'the ABCs of the language of intimacy' (Yalom, 1989: 43). Such ABCs include how to own and express feelings.
- *Using the therapist–client relationship to illuminate pathology*: Existential therapists have reservations about seeing clients as transferring feelings and attitudes from important past relationships on to them. Instead they prefer to use the therapist–client relationship to illuminate pathology that may interfere with current and future relationships. Frequently clients distort aspects of their relationship with their therapists. Therapists can raise clients' awareness of such distortions, including their consequences for other relationships.
- *The healing relationship*: As mentioned earlier, existential therapists strive to develop real relationships with clients. Even though therapist–client relationships are temporary, the experience of intimacy can be permanent. The relationship can be powerfully affirming for clients because someone whom they respect and who *really* knows them fully accepts them. Therapists who have deep relationships with clients can help them face their existential isolation. Also, they help clients realize that they alone are responsible for their lives.

Therapy and meaninglessness

The following are some ways in which existential therapists can work with clients complaining of lack of meaning in their lives:

- *Redefining the problem*: When clients complain that 'life has no meaning', they appear to assume that life has a meaning that they cannot find. The existential position is that people are meaning giving rather than meaning getting. Existential therapists raise clients' awareness that there is no inherent meaning in life, rather they are responsible for creating their own meaning. Frequently, what is subsumed under meaninglessness, is best pursued under the other ultimate concerns of death, freedom and isolation.

- *Identifying meaninglessness anxiety defences*: Existential therapists can assist clients to become more aware of their meaninglessness anxiety defences. To what extent does their search for money, pleasure, power, recognition and status flow from their failure to confront the existential issue of meaninglessness? Clients can be helped to recognize the consequences and costs of their defences. Their defences against meaninglessness may contribute to their leading superficial lives that create the very problems that consciously or unconsciously they seek to avoid.
- *Assisting engagement in life*: Therapists should approach the problem of meaninglessness by assisting their clients to become more engaged in the stream of life. They should assume that the desire to engage in life is always present in clients. Therapists can offer clients authentic relationships that demonstrate their own engagement in the therapeutic process. They can explore clients' long-range hopes and goals, belief systems, capacity to love and attempts to express themselves creatively. In addition, they can identify and try to remove a block in the clients' progress towards engagement. Clients may find insufficient meaning in their relationships, work, leisure, creative pursuits and religious strivings. Each area can be analysed for obstacles that clients can then work to remove.

Case material

May (1973: 81–9, reproduced in Wedding and Corsini, 1995) gives an example of existential therapy with Mercedes, a black woman who moved during therapy from almost complete impotence to self-esteem and the capacity for aggression. Being black and a woman were two contributing factors in Mercedes's sense of powerlessness. A further case example, that of David, a 50-year-old scientist highly anxious about confronting his wife of 27 years about his decision to separate from her, is provided towards the end of May and Yalom's (2005) summary chapter on existential psychotherapy. Numerous brief case illustrations illuminate Yalom's (1980) *Existential Psychotherapy*. In addition, in *Every Day Gets a Little Closer*, Yalom as therapist and Ginny Elkins as client share their end-of-session thoughts over the course of long-term therapy (Yalom and Elkins, 1974).

Yalom's use of literature as a teaching device also sheds light on the processes of and issues in conducting existential therapy. Yalom is acutely aware that effective therapists need to be humanly involved when relating to clients, a point well illustrated in his books of therapeutic short stories *Love's Executioner* (1989) and *Momma and the Meaning of Life* (1999). In addition, in *Lying on the Couch* (1996), he illustrates issues of therapist and client transparancy, therapeutic boundaries, and the use of dreams in existential therapy.

Further developments

Yalom writes: 'I considered revising *Existential Psychotherapy* but in the end rejected that plan – there was no tradition of an evolving literature, no research to update and review. Besides it seemed silly to update a book that purported to deal with timeless elements of the human condition' (1998: 339). In addition, further developments in May and Yalom's existential therapy have been forestalled somewhat by Rollo May's death in 1994 and Irvin Yalom's journey from conducting psychotherapy to concentrating on writing psychotherapy fiction.

Though primarily an individual approach, existential therapy is sometimes conducted in groups of eight to 10 members (Yalom, 1995). Therapy groups provide here-and-now information on members' ways of avoiding or assuming responsibility. Also, the interactional format of groups gives therapists and members opportunities to observe and work on interpersonal distortions and maladaptive behaviours. Existential group therapists attempt to take group members through the following sequence: learning how their behaviour: (a) is viewed by others; (b) makes others feel; (c) creates the opinions others have of them; and (d) influences their opinions of themselves. In addition, groups can work on issues surrounding the ultimate concerns of death and meaninglessness. For instance, in groups of cancer patients the issue of confronting death is likely to be a major area for work.

Review and personal questions

Review questions

1. What does the word existential mean?
2. What are the characteristics of and inner conflicts associated with each of the four existential ultimate concerns: death, freedom, isolation and meaninglessness?
3. What are existential psychodynamics and what is the existential model of defence mechanisms?
4. What are some defences for anxiety attached to each ultimate concern?
5. What are the goals of existential therapy?
6. What are desirable characteristics in existential therapist–client relationships?
7. Describe some interventions existential therapists can use for working with clients' death anxiety.
8. Describe some interventions existential therapists can use for enhancing clients' responsibility awareness and assumption.

9. Describe some interventions existential therapists can use for working with clients' problems of existential isolation.
10. Describe some interventions existential therapists can use for working with clients' problems of meaninglessness.

Personal questions

1. To what extent do you experience your existence as real? Answer as specifically as possible.
2. To what extent and in what ways do you experience existential anxiety? What are some of your main defences against existential anxiety?
3. Assess the degree to which you currently take personal responsibility for making or creating your existence. In what ways might you engage in less responsibility avoidance and in greater responsibility assumption?
4. Do you consider that meaninglessness is a major problem for people in western society? If so, how does this affect you personally?
5. What relevance, if any, has the theory and practice of Yalom and May's existential therapy for how you conduct therapy?
6. What relevance, if any, has the theory and practice of Yalom and May's existential counselling and therapy for how you live?

Annotated bibliography

Yalom, I.D. (1980) *Existential Psychotherapy*. New York: Basic Books.
This book is a major contribution to the counselling and therapy literature. It develops a psychodynamic theory of existential anxiety centred on humans' confrontations with the ultimate concerns of death, freedom, isolation and meaninglessness. The book suggests ways in which existential therapists can assist clients to confront and come to terms with each of these sources of existential anxiety. Both theory and practice are illuminated by numerous vignettes and case examples.

May, R. and Yalom, I.D. (2005) 'Existential psychotherapy', in R.J. Corsini and D. Wedding (eds), *Current Psychotherapies* (7th edn). Belmont, CA: Thomson Brooks/Cole. pp. 269–98.
This chapter provides an authoritative overview of the theory and practice of May and Yalom's existential therapy.

Yalom, I.D. (2001) *The Gift of Therapy*. London: Piatkus.
A series of 85 brief offerings covering the therapist–client relationship; methods of exploring death, meaning and freedom; a variety of issues in the everyday conduct of therapy; the use of dreams in therapy; and the hazards and privileges of being a therapist.

Yalom, I.D. (1998) *The Yalom Reader: Selections from the Work of a Master Therapist and Story Teller*. New York: Basic Books.

This book charts Yalom's writing career as it has progressed from texts of psychotherapy to novels of psychotherapy. The material selected for the book's three parts address each of Yalom's major interests: group therapy; existential psychotherapy; and writing.

Yalom, I.D. (1989) *Love's Executioner and Other Tales of Psychotherapy.* London: Bloomsbury. The human face of existential therapy. A series of beautifully written case studies in which Yalom works with his clients. Both therapist and clients come alive as real people struggling with the concerns of existence. The book provides Yalom's insights into 'grey areas' regarding their own behaviour existential therapists are likely to face.

Yalom, I.D. (1996) *Lying on the Couch.* New York: HarperPerennial.
This psychological novel is a spoof on contemporary psychotherapy in which all participants interweave with their hidden agendas, duplicity, self-deceptions and potential for unexpected growth and human intimacy. On a more serious note, the book illustrates issues of therapist and client transparency, therapeutic boundaries and working with dreams.

References and further reading

Buber, M. (1965) *Between Man and Man.* New York: Macmillan.
Buber, M. (1970) *I and Thou.* New York: Charles Scribner.
Cohn, H. (1997) *Existential Thought and Therapeutic Practice.* London: Sage.
Cohn, H. (2002) *Heidegger and the Roots of Existential Therapy.* London: Sage.
Heidegger, M. (1962) *Being and Time.* London: SCM Press.
Jaspers, K. (1964) *The Nature of Psychotherapy.* Chicago: University of Chicago Press.
Kierkegaard, S. (1954) *Fear and Trembling and the Sickness unto Death.* Garden City, NY: Doubleday.
Lieberman, M.A., Yalom, I.D. and Miles, M.B. (1973) *Encounter Groups: First Facts.* New York: Basic Books.
May, R. (1939) *The Art of Counseling.* Nashville, TN: Cokesbury.
May, R. (1950) *The Meaning of Anxiety.* New York: Ronald Press.
May, R. (1953) *Man's Search for Himself.* New York: W.W. Norton.
May, R. (1967) *Psychology and the Human Dilemma.* Princeton, NJ: Van Nostrand.
May, R. (1969) *Love and Will.* New York: W.W. Norton.
May, R. (1973) *Power and Innocence: A Search for the Sources of Violence.* New York: W.W. Norton.
May, R. (1975) *The Courage to Create.* New York: W.W. Norton.
May, R. (1977) *The Meaning of Anxiety* (rev. edn). New York: W.W. Norton.
May, R. (1981) *Freedom and Destiny.* New York: W.W. Norton.
May, R. (1985) *My Quest for Beauty.* New York: W.W. Norton.
May, R. and Yalom, I.D. (2005) 'Existential psychotherapy', in R.J. Corsini and D. Wedding (eds), *Current Psychotherapies* (7th edn). Belmont, CA: Thomson Brooks/Cole. pp. 269–98.
May, R., Angel, E. and Ellenberger, H.F. (eds) (1958) *Existence: A New Dimension in Psychiatry and Psychology.* New York: Basic Books.
Rabinowitz, F.E., Good, G. and Cozard, L. (1989) 'Rollo May: a man of myth and meaning', *Journal of Counseling and Development,* 67: 436–41.
Sartre, J.P. (1956) *Being and Nothingness.* New York: Philosophical Library.
Spinelli, E. (1989) *The Interpreted World: An Introduction to Phenomenological Psychology.* London: Sage.

Spinelli, E. (1997) *Tales of Unknowing*. London: Duckworth.
Spinelli, E. and Marshall, S. (2001) *Embodied Theories*. London: Sage.
Tillich, P. (1952) *The Courage to Be*. New Haven, CT: Yale University Press.
van Deurzen, E. (1998) *Paradox and Passion in Psychotherapy*. Chichester: Wiley & Sons.
van Deurzen, E. (2002) *Existential Counselling and Psychotherapy in Practice* (2nd edn). London: Sage.
Wedding, D. and Corsini, R.J. (1995) *Case Studies in Psychotherapy*. Itasca, IL: Peacock.
Yalom, I.D. (1980) *Existential Psychotherapy*. New York: Basic Books.
Yalom, I.D. (1983) *Inpatient Group Psychotherapy*. New York: Basic Books.
Yalom, I.D. (1989) *Love's Executioner and Other Tales of Psychotherapy*. London: Bloomsbury.
Yalom, I.D. (1991) *When Nietzsche Wept*. New York: Basic Books/Harper.
Yalom, I.D. (1995) *The Theory and Practice of Group Psychotherapy* (4th edn). New York: Basic Books.
Yalom, I.D. (1996) *Lying on the Couch*. New York: HarperPerennial.
Yalom, I.D. (1998) *The Yalom Reader: Selections from the Work of a Master Therapist and Story Teller*. New York: Basic Books.
Yalom, I.D. (1999) *Momma and the Meaning of Life*. New York: Basic Books.
Yalom, I.D. (2001) *The Gift of Therapy*. London: Piatkus.
Yalom, I.D. (2005a) 'Autobiographical information', available at: www.yalom.com.
Yalom, I.D. (2005b) *The Schopenhauer Cure: A Novel*. New York: HarperCollins.
Yalom, I.D. (2005c) 'Existential psychotherapy: fat lady', in D. Wedding and R.J. Corsini (eds), *Case Studies in Psychotherapy*. Belmont, CA: Thomson Brooks/Cole. pp. 133–55.
Yalom, I.D. and Elkins, G. (1974) *Every Day Gets a Little Closer*. New York: Basic Books.
Yalom, I.D. and Vinogradov, S. (1989) *Concise Guide to Group Psychotherapy*. Washington, DC: American Psychiatric Press.

Introduction

Logotherapy is sometimes called the third Viennese school of psychotherapy, the other two being Freud's psychoanalysis and Adler's individual psychology. Another way of viewing logotherapy is that it is a supplement rather than a replacement for psychotherapy (Frankl, 1975a). *Logos* is a Greek word that connotes both 'meaning' and 'spirit', the latter word without any primary religious connotation. Humans are meaning-seeking beings and the search for meaning in itself is not pathological. Existence confronts people with the need to find meaning in their lives. The main purpose of logotherapy is to assist clients in their search for meaning.

Viktor Frankl (1905–97)

Viktor E. Frankl, born on 26 March 1905 in Vienna, Austria, was the son of Jewish parents. His mother was descended from an old, established, patrician Prague family. His father, the son of an impecunious master bookbinder, was a public servant who became director of the youth welfare department of the Austrian government. One of three children, Frankl grew up in a secure environment, describing his mother as kind-hearted and deeply pious and his father as spartan, stoic, religious and with a strong sense of duty. Frankl saw himself as possessing a tension between the rationality of his father and the deep emotions of his mother.

Aged three, Frankl decided to become a physician, which probably pleased his father who had given up his medical studies for financial reasons. Frankl's own search for meaning started early in life, and during the years of his youth, as he had breakfast or coffee in bed, he would ponder for a few minutes about the meaning of life, especially the meaning for him in the coming day (Frankl, 1997a). Frankl was an intellectually gifted and precocious schoolboy, who corresponded with Freud. In 1924, the young Frankl had his first article published at Freud's invitation in the *International Journal of Psychoanalysis*.

Frankl was both influenced by and reacted against some of the ideas of Freud and Adler. In addition, he was influenced by existential philosophers such as Heidegger, Jaspers and Scheler. The origins of logotherapy go back to Frankl's early struggles to find meaning in his own existence. Frankl readily confesses that when a young man 'I had to go through the hell of despair over the apparent meaninglessness of life, through total and ultimate nihilism, until I could develop an immunity against nihilism. I developed logotherapy' (1988: 166).

Frankl coined the term logotherapy in the 1920s and in the 1930s used the word *Existenzanalyse*, existential analysis, as an alternative word for logotherapy. To avoid confusion he mostly refrains from using the term existential analysis in his English-speaking publications. In 1928, Frankl founded the Youth Counselling Centres in Vienna, heading them until 1938. In 1930, he received his MD from the University of Vienna. From 1930 to 1938, he was on the staff of the Neuropsychiatric University Clinic. From 1938 to 1942 he was Specialist in Neurology and Psychiatry, and then Head of the Neurological Department, at the Jewish Hospital in Vienna. During this time he wrote the first draft of his first book.

Shortly before America entered the Second World War, Frankl was given the opportunity to immigrate to the United States. He let this opportunity pass because he chose to abide by the commandment 'Honor father and mother and you will dwell in the land' (Frankl, 1988: 59). He thought that, by retaining his hospital position, he might protect his parents from being sent to a concentration camp. Though unable to do so, Frankl was able to administer morphine to his beloved father as he was dying from pulmonary edema in Theresienstadt concentration camp 'and [...] spared him the unnecessary agony of death' (Frankl, 1997a: 26). Frankl's mother, brother and first wife, Tilly, died in concentration camps, but his sister who had emigrated to Australia survived.

From 1942 to 1945 Frankl had the harrowing experience of being imprisoned in four Nazi concentration camps: Theresienstadt, Auschwitz-Birkenau, Kaufering 111 and Turkheim. On arrival at Auschwitz, Frankl was shaved of all his body hair. He was number 119,194. The manuscript of his first book was confiscated. During the next three years, he survived selections of who should live or die, forced labour, brutal Capos (guards), beatings, malnutrition, disease, the vagaries of fate and the existential challenge to find meaning in his suffering. Most of the time his work was digging and laying tracks for railway lines. Only in the last few weeks of his internment did he work as a doctor.

During this period, Frankl had the opportunity to observe human nature under extreme circumstances. Many prisoners gave in and some even made the choice to vegetate. However, other prisoners deepened spiritually and took the camps' difficulties as tests of their inner strength. They rose to the challenge of finding meaning in their lives. Frankl quotes Nietzsche: 'He who has a *why* to live for can bear almost any *how*' (1963: 121, emphasis in original). Despite their adversity, these prisoners retained their freedom to choose both in their inner life and in how they behaved towards others. They turned their tragedies into triumphs. On returning to Vienna after the war, between spells of collapsing into a chair weeping, Frankl dictated the third and last draft of *The Doctor and the Soul* (1955). Afterwards, in nine days he dictated *Man's Search for Meaning* (1963), at that time thinking it would be published anonymously. By 2005 the book had sold close to 10 million copies.

In 1946, Frankl became Head of the Department of Neurology at the Poliklinik Hospital in Vienna where he worked until 1970. In 1946 he also met his second wife, Elly, whom he married the next year. In 1947 he was appointed Assistant Professor of Psychiatry and Neurology at the University of Vienna and then, in 1955, University Professor. Frankl was a past president of the Austrian Medical Society of Psychotherapy. In addition, he had been Distinguished Professor of Logotherapy at the US International University in California and also Visiting Professor at Stanford, Harvard and Duquesne universities, among others. Over 200 universities worldwide invited him to give lectures: as well as in the United States, he lectured widely in Europe, Australia, South America, Asia and Africa.

Frankl was a prolific author writing over 30 books, some of which have been translated into many languages, and numerous articles. In addition to those already mentioned, his books include *Psychotherapy and Existentialism: Selected Papers on Logotherapy* (1967), *The Unconscious God: Psychotherapy and Theology* (1975a), *The Unheard Cry for Meaning: Psychotherapy and Humanism* (1985) and *The Will to Meaning: Foundations and Applications of Logotherapy* (1988).

Until his 80th birthday mountain climbing was Frankl's most passionate hobby. Having experienced the depths of human depravity, Frankl was able to ascend the heights of human achievement by turning his personal tragedy into a triumph of the human sprit. In his autobiographical recollections, Frankl writes: 'As I have said, I know of only a few good qualities in myself, and perhaps only one: I do not forget any good deed done to me, and I carry no grudge for a bad one' (1997a: 35). Frankl died in 1997, but his work and the inspiration of his indomitable spirit live on.

Theory

Basic concepts

Freedom of will

Frankl uses the term existential in three ways. First, the term existential refers to *existence* itself, which is a specifically human mode of being. Second, existential refers to the *meaning* of existence. Third, existential refers to the striving to find meaning in personal existence or, put another way, to the will to meaning. Life is transitory. However, this transitoriness does not make life meaningless. Rather the transitory aspects of life are potentialities. Humans need to realize the transitory possibilities. They are constantly choosing which of the mass of transitory potentialities will be actualized and which condemned to non-being.

Humans possess freedom of will. Alone among animals, they possess the capacity for self-detachment. Humans are capable of reflecting upon and judging their choices. What matters is not the features of people's character or their drives and instincts, but the stand they take towards them. People are free to shape their own characters and are responsible for what they make out of themselves. When people rise above the somatic and psychic dimensions of their existence, they enter a new dimension that Frankl terms the 'noological dimension'. In this noological dimension are located distinctly human functions, for instance reflection, the capacity to make self into an object, humour and conscientiousness.

Will to meaning

The will to meaning is the fundamental motivational force in humans. People are confronted with the need to detect meaning literally to their last breaths. Frankl writes, 'Man's search for meaning is a primary force in his life ... This meaning is unique and specific and can be fulfilled by him alone; only then does it achieve a significance that will satisfy his own will to meaning' (1963: 154). As Frankl observed in his concentration camp experiences, people need something to live for. Humans are beings who encounter other people and reach out for meanings to fulfil. However, meaning does not coincide with being; rather it sets the pace for being. Human existence is at risk unless people live in terms of transcendence towards something beyond themselves.

Logotherapy focuses on the will to meaning whereas psychoanalysis focuses on the will to pleasure and individual psychology focuses on the will to power. Frankl acknowledges that Freud and Adler did not use the terms 'will to pleasure' and 'will to power' as such. However, both pleasure and power are by-products or derivatives of the will to meaning. The will to meaning is not a rationalization of instinctual drives nor concerned with reducing tension and returning to a state of homeostasis. What people need is not a tensionless state, but rather the tension of striving for some meaning that is worthy of them.

The will to meaning also differs as a motivating force from self-actualizing. Frankl views self-actualization as also only a side-effect of the will to meaning. People can only actualize themselves to the extent that they fulfil meaning.

Consciousness and the unconscious

What is the source or referent point against which people can detect meaning in their lives? The search for meaning can involve both conscious activity and getting in touch with unconscious layers of the self.

Consciousness

Humans are spiritual beings and logotherapy focuses on their spiritual existence. In this context, the word spirit has no religious connotations. Spiritual phenomena in humans can be either conscious or unconscious. Consciousness implies awareness. Logotherapy aims to increase clients' consciousness of their spiritual selves. Humans need to be conscious of their responsibility for detecting and acting in terms of the unique meaning of their lives in specific situations in which they are involved.

The spiritual unconscious

Each human has an existential, personal spiritual core. Centred around their spiritual core, people are not only individualized, but integrated in their somatic, psychic and spiritual aspects. Though the border between the conscious and the unconscious is 'fluid', Frankl regards the spiritual basis of human existence as ultimately unconscious. The deep centre of each human is unconscious.

A sharp distinction exists between the instinctual unconscious and the spiritual unconscious. Freud saw the unconscious as a reservoir of repressed sexual and aggressive instincts. For Frankl depth psychology, instead of focusing on repressed instincts, needs to follow humans into the depths of their spirits. However, the self does not yield to total self-reflection and, in a sense, this makes human existence basically unreflectable. Frankl writes: 'Existence exists in action rather than reflection' (1975a: 30).

Conscience

The origins of conscience are located in the spiritual unconscious. *Logos* is deeper than logic. Existentially authentic decisions take place intuitively, unreflectedly and unconsciously. Frankl writes: 'It is the task of conscience to disclose to man the *unum necesse*, the one thing that is required' (1975a: 35). Conscience can intuitively reveal the unique possibilities for meaning to be actualized in specific situations. Conscience, or the 'ethical instinct', is highly individual in contrast to the other instincts that work for the greatest number of the species. In addition to moral conscience, Frankl considers love and art as rooted in the emotional, intuitive, non-rational depths of the spiritual unconscious.

Freedom can be considered in terms of 'from what' and 'to what'. The 'to what' is responsibleness to conscience. Conscience has a transcendent quality. People can only be the servants of their conscience when they can have a dialogue rather than a monologue with it as something other than themselves. Through conscience a trans-human agent 'is sounding through' (Frankl, 1975a: 53). Sounding through is *per-sonare* in Latin that is linked to the concept of the human 'person'. Conscience has a key position in disclosing the essential transcendence of the spiritual unconscious. Conscience is the voice of transcendence and is itself transcendent.

The religious unconscious

The existential analysis of dreams makes obvious the fact of repressed and unconscious religiousness. Not only is *libido* repressed, but *religio* also. Conscience is not the last 'to what' of responsibleness. Though humans are responsible for themselves, they are not responsible before themselves. This 'to what' of responsibleness is prior to responsibleness itself. Unconscious religiousness, or the religious unconscious, exists within the spiritual unconscious. Humans have always stood in an intentional relation to transcendence, even if only on an unconscious level. This 'unconscious God' is hidden in two ways. First, the human relationship to God is hidden. Second, God is hidden. Even in highly irreligious people, religiousness is latent.

The religious unconscious is an existential agent rather than an instinctual factor. Frankl calls it 'a deciding being unconscious rather than a being driven by the unconscious' (1975a: 65). In relation to Jung's ideas, he stresses that unconscious religiousness stems from the personal centre of each individual rather than from an impersonal pool of images shared by mankind.

Repression of the religiousness, as with repression of other aspects of the unconscious, leads to neurosis: '… once the angel in us is repressed, he turns into a demon' (1975a: 70). The existentiality of religiousness needs to be spontaneous. Genuine religiousness must unfold at its own pace. Humans commit themselves to it by choosing to be religious in the broadest sense.

Meaning of life and death

Meaning of life

Frankl writes that 'being human means being responsible for fulfilling the meaning potential inherent in a given life situation' (1975a: 125). Being human means being at the same time different, conscious and responsible. The concept of responsibility is the foundation of human existence. Human freedom as not a 'freedom from', but rather a 'freedom to', namely the freedom to accept responsibility. Freedom is what people 'are': it is not something that they 'have' and can therefore lose. People have many potentialities within them. They are not fully conditioned or determined. Rather, moment by moment, they are free to decide what they will become in the next moment. Their decisions determine which of their potentialities gets actualized. During no stage of their lives can people 'escape the mandate to choose among possibilities' (Frankl, 1955: 85).

All the time people are questioned by life. The way to respond is by being responsible for their lives. Working with the matter that fate has supplied them, people are like sculptors who chisel out and hammer unshaped stone so that it takes more and more form. Though always surrounded by biological, sociological and psychological restrictions, humans can either conquer and shape them or deliberately choose to submit to them.

Meaning of death

Death does not rob life of its meaning. If people were immortal they might put off doing things indefinitely. Death belongs to life and gives it meaning.

People's responsibility springs from their finiteness. Consequently, they need to realize the full gravity of the responsibility that they bear throughout every moment of their lives. Destiny, like death, is essential to the meaning of life. Destiny refers to those factors that are beyond people's power. Freedom can be viewed not only in the contexts of life and death, but also in the context of destiny. The opportunities and tribulations that come people's way are unique. Nevertheless, people still can exercise their inner freedom to take a stand against their destiny.

Self-transcendence

Self-transcendence is an essential characteristic of human existence. Humans are essentially beings who reach out beyond themselves. They become most human when they transcend the boundaries of their selves by either fulfilling a meaning or encountering another person lovingly. Frankl sees the basic human need as a search for meaning rather than a search for the self. Identity is only achievable through being responsible for the fulfilment of meaning. People can become overly focused on themselves. The self-transcendent quality of human life is most apparent when people forget themselves. Frankl believed the main lesson he learned from Nazi concentration camps was that unless life pointed to something beyond itself, survival was pointless, meaningless and impossible.

Suffering from neurotic problems that reflect difficulties in self-transcendence is the converse of people finding meaning by transcending themselves. Hyper-reflection and hyper-intention are two of the main ways in which people choose not to transcend themselves. Hyper-reflection is a tendency to overbearing self-reflection. Hyper-intention is a tendency to pay excessive attention to achieving that which one desires.

Sources of meaning

Frankl (1963) suggests that self-transcendence is achievable by discovering or detecting meaning in three different ways: by doing a deed, by experiencing a value and by suffering. Elsewhere Frankl (1967, 1988) talks of three principal ways in which people can find meaning in life:

1. by what they give to life (*creative values*);
2. by what they take from life (*experiential values*); and
3. through the stand they take towards a fate they can no longer change, for instance an inoperable cancer (*attitudinal values*).

In addition, past experiences and religion are two further areas in which people can discover meaning.

Meaning in work

Work is a major area in which people can reach out beyond themselves. The meaning of work goes beyond a particular occupation to include the manner in which people bring their unique human qualities to their work. For instance, a nurse may go beyond her regimented duties to say a kind word to a critically ill patient. Frankl views all work as allowing such opportunities, though acknowledges that some jobs are very routine. In such instances, much creative meaning may need to be found in leisure pursuits.

Unemployment is an example of how people can be affected by lack of creative meaning. Frankl views unemployment neurosis, characterized by apathy and depression, as an existential position. Some people respond to the existential challenge of unemployment by remaining active and involved and so stay free of unemployment neurosis. Employment can also be for good or ill. Some people run away from the emptiness of their existence by taking refuge in their work or profession. Achieving creative meaning in life is not synonymous with work satisfactions alone.

Meaning in love

Unlike in psychoanalysis, in logotherapy love is not regarded as a secondary phenomenon to sex. While sex can be an expression of mature love, it is not a form of love in itself. Love as a form of self-transcendence has various characteristics. It entails relating to another person as a spiritual being. As such, love involves understanding or grasping the inner core of the personality of another person. People are moved to the depths of their spiritual beings by their partner's spiritual core. Infatuation seldom lasts long. When gratified, the sex drive vanishes promptly. Love, however, has a quality of permanence in that the spiritual core of the other person is unique and irreplaceable. Furthermore, love can outlast death in that the essence of the unique being of the beloved is timeless and imperishable.

Another characteristic of love is that, since it is directed at what the other 'is' rather than at the other as a possession, it leads to a monogamous attitude. A further characteristic is that it involves seeing the potential in the beloved and helping her or him achieve this potential. In addition, in a real love relationship, there is no room for jealousy since the other person is not treated as a possession.

Frankl (1967) is at pains to point out that love is not the only, nor even the best way, to fill life with meaning. Furthermore, he distinguishes between neurotic failure and failure to attain love imposed by destiny.

Meaning in suffering

Human destiny has a twofold meaning: to be shaped where possible and to be endured where necessary. Attitudinal values are inherent in the stand that people take to circumstances that they cannot change, for instance an incurable illness or concentration camp internment. Through attitudinal values even the tragic aspects of human existence – the 'tragic triad' of pain, guilt and death – can be turned into something positive and creative. However, people need be careful not to accept fate too readily. The time to enlist attitudinal values is only when they can be certain that they cannot alter their fates.

Inescapable negative situations give people the opportunity 'to actualize the highest value, to fulfill the deepest meaning, the meaning of suffering' (Frankl, 1963: 178). People have choices in how they respond to suffering. For instance, life can retain meaning up to the last moment for people with terminal illnesses who accept the challenge to suffer bravely. Frankl quotes Goethe: 'There is no predicament that we cannot ennoble either by doing or enduring' (Frankl, 1955: 115). Some people can rise to the challenge of suffering and grow richer and stronger because of it. Though people may be helpless victims of fate, they can still exercise the inner freedom to turn their predicaments into accomplishments at the human level.

Meaning from the past
Though the search for meaning is primarily oriented towards people's futures, the past can still be a source of meaning. Often people discount their past experiences as a source of meaning. At Auschwitz Frankl went through considerable soul searching about the meaning of suffering when the manuscript of his first book was confiscated. However, he came to realize that nothing in his past was lost, but rather it was irrevocably stored. The meaning of his life did not depend on whether a manuscript of his was printed. His experiences in the past constituted a full granary. Often in times of suffering, but not always so, the search for meaning can entail acknowledging and identifying sources of meaning in the past relevant to creating meaning in the present. Also, even short lives can still have pasts full of meaning. Furthermore, even for those who have led sterile lives, their unconditional faith in an unconditional meaning may turn their failure into a triumph (Frankl, 1988).

The supra-meaning
Humans are incapable of understanding the ultimate meaning of human suffering. However, that does not mean that suffering does not have an ultimate meaning. Frankl (1963, 1988) uses the term supra-meaning to denote the ultimate meaning of suffering and life. People cannot break through the dimensional differences between the human world and the divine world. The supra-meaning can only be grasped by faith and not by intellectual means. Unlike in secular existential philosophy, the human task is not to endure life's meaninglessness. Instead, people need to bear their inability to grasp in rational terms life's ultimate meaningfulness. Trust in God precedes people's ability to have faith in life's ultimate meaning. As always, the infinite God is silent rather than dead.

The trend in modern life is not away from religion, but away from an emphasis on differences between individual denominations. Frankl (1988) does not advocate a form of universal religion. Rather he sees a trend towards a profoundly personalized religion in which people address themselves to the ultimate being in their own individual language and words.

The existential vacuum

The existential vacuum describes a state in which people complain of an inner void. They suffer from a sense of meaninglessness, emptiness and futility. The existential vacuum is an 'abyss experience' in contrast to the peak experience described by Maslow.

Frankl suggests three causes of the existential vacuum.

1. Unlike other animals, humans are no longer programmed by drives and instincts in what to do.
2. Humans are no longer told by traditions, conventions and values what they should do. Sometimes they do not know what they wish to do and retreat into conformism, doing what others do, or into totalitarianism, doing what others wish them to do.
3. Especially in America, students are exposed to 'reductionism'. Humans are reduced to drives, instincts, creatures of conditioning, reaction formations and defence mechanisms rather than viewed as deciding agents. Frankl (1975a: 94) cites as an example of reductionism the case of a couple who were told, during their induction into the American Peace Corps, that they were helping the less privileged because of their unconscious need to prove themselves superior.

Existential frustration

Existential frustration results when the will to meaning is frustrated. Apathy and boredom are the main characteristics of existential frustration. Existential frustration is not in itself pathological nor pathogenic. People's concern, even their despair, over the meaning of their lives is a spiritual distress rather than a disease. Frankl regards the existential vacuum, with its attendant frustration, as 'something sociogenic and not at all a neurosis' (1975a: 139). Despair over the meaninglessness of life can be a sign of intellectual sincerity and honesty. In his later writings, Frankl (1988) stated that there was no doubt that the existential vacuum was spreading.

Noogenic neurosis

The existential vacuum can lead to neuroticism. The term noogenic neurosis refers to those cases where the existential vacuum leads to clinical symptomatology. Frankl defines the noogenic neurosis as 'a neurosis which is caused by a spiritual problem, a moral or ethical conflict, as for example, a conflict between the mere superego and the true conscience' (1988: 89). Existential frustration plays a large part in noogenic neuroses. Such neuroses arise from spiritual conflicts to do with people's aspirations for a meaningful existence and the frustration of their will to meaning. Doctors and therapists need to distinguish sharply between the spiritual dimension of problems as against the instinctual.

The mass neurotic triad

Frankl speaks of the neurotization of humanity because of the existential vacuum. The worldwide effects of the existential vacuum go beyond feelings of meaninglessness and noogenic neuroses. Frankl uses the term 'mass neurotic triad' (1975a: 96) for the three main effects: depression, addiction and aggression.

- Regarding *depression*, there is ample evidence that suicide rates are increasing, especially among the young. Frankl sees the cause as the spreading existential frustration;
- Regarding *addiction*, people with low purpose in life are more likely to try to find feelings of meaningfulness in drugs than those with high purpose in life. A frequently cited reason for taking drugs is the desire to find meaning in life. Also, many alcoholics suffer from a sense of meaninglessness in their lives;
- Regarding *aggression*, not only does sexual libido thrive in an existential vacuum, but 'aggressive destrudo'. Frankl considers that statistical evidence favours his hypothesis that people are most likely to become aggressive when they are caught in feelings of emptiness and meaninglessness.

Acquisition

A sense of meaninglessness is not necessarily acquired through learning and indoctrination. It can be part of the human response to life and, if worked through satisfactorily as in Frankl's own case, a growth experience. However, Frankl considers that the existential vacuum and existential frustration are becoming more widespread: furthermore, that there is an increasing neurotization of humanity. If this is the case, individuals are more likely to acquire a sense of meaninglessness because they grow up in cultures and societies in which it is harder to find meaning than in the past. First, the erosion of traditional values and the tendencies to reductionism make it more difficult for many people to find meaning in their lives. Second, because there are fewer people in society who have satisfactorily found meaning, it is more difficult for young people to grow up learning from models who are successful at realizing the spiritual aspects of themselves. Put another way, young people may suffer from a lack of access to meaning educators and exemplars. Despite Frankl's (1975a: 84) belief in people's potential humanness, '*humane* humans are, and probably will always remain a minority' (emphasis in original).

Maintenance

Maintaining the existential vacuum

How do people maintain their sense of meaninglessness? Some suggestions may be inferred from Frankl's writings:

- *Repression*: Logotherapy concerns itself with the frustration and consequent repression of the will to meaning. Frankl observes 'Not eros but logos is the victim of repression' (1975a: 131). People repress their spirituality and religiousness. Thus they remain out of touch with their spiritual centres that are the deepest sources for a sense of meaning. Their repression of the will to meaning blocks their perception of the existence of meaning.

- *Avoiding responsibility*: Among mechanisms mentioned by Frankl for avoiding responsibility for the search for meaning are conformism, totalitarianism, and taking refuge in the neurotic triad of depression, addiction and aggression.
- *Erosion of traditions and values*: The erosion of traditions has a continuing influence on creating and maintaining the existential vacuum.
- *Reductionism*: Reductionist models of psychology and education lead people to believe, and then maintain their beliefs, that they are determined rather than determining.
- *Insufficient emphasis on self-transcendence*: Much of modern psychology focuses on self-actualization and on self-expression. People continue to be insufficiently helped to realize that happiness and fulfilment are by-products of self-transcendence, of forgetting oneself rather than excessively focusing on oneself.
- *Neurotization of humanity*: The fact that problems and symptoms of meaninglessness are widespread makes it harder for individuals to obtain assistance in their personal search for meaning, thus contributing to maintaining their inner void.

Therapy

Therapeutic goals

Frankl divides what he terms mental illness into three categories: noogenic (neurosis), psychogenic (neurosis) and somatogenic (psychosis). The existential vacuum is neither a neurosis nor a psychosis. Therapeutic goals are similar whether the existential vacuum is on its own or a part of a noogenic neurosis.

Logotherapy is the treatment of choice for dealing with the existential vacuum. The meaning of logotherapy is in helping clients find meaning in their lives. Logotherapists seek to confront and reorient clients towards their life's tasks. Logotherapy is an education for responsibility that seeks to unblock clients' will to meaning. With their will to meaning unblocked, clients are more likely to find ways of self-transcendence through creative, experiential and attitudinal values. Clients need to become aware of their existential responsibleness for finding their life's meaning through their conscience. However, making the spiritual unconscious conscious is only a transitory phase in the therapy process. What therapy seeks to achieve is first to convert an unconscious potential into a conscious act and then to allow it to recede back into an unconscious habit. Frankl (1975a) is at pains to stress that a religious therapist may only bring religion into therapy if the patient wants it: otherwise he has to be strictly abstinent on this question.

The overcoming of symptoms of existential frustration, such as apathy and boredom, is a by-product of searching for and discovering meaning. Furthermore, when clients find more meaning in their lives, any symptoms they possess from the mass neurotic triad of depression, addiction and aggression, are likely to get better if not disappear.

The psychogenic neuroses include obsessive-compulsions and phobias where the therapeutic goal is to overcome clients' tendencies to hyper-intention or trying too hard. Also the psychogenic neuroses include sexual and sleep problems where the therapeutic goal is to overcome clients' tendencies to hyper-reflection or excessive self-consciousness.

With the psychoses, such as endogenous depression and schizophrenia, logotherapy may be used in conjunction with medication that addresses the somatic aspect that has become diseased. Logotherapy itself deals with the healthy part of the personality and frequently its goal is to help clients find meaning in their suffering.

A broader goal of Frankl's logotherapy is the rehumanization of psychiatry. Therapists should not view the mind as a mechanism and the treatment of mental illness merely in terms of technique. Within the limits of their environment and endowment, humans are ultimately self-determining. In the concentration camps, some chose to behave like swine and others like saints.

Process of therapy

In diagnosing the existential vacuum, logotherapists are alert to overt signs, for instance saying 'My life lacks meaning' and covert signs, for instance apathy and boredom, which indicate that clients feel an inner void. Issues of meaning are considered legitimate areas in which clients can work, though noogenic neuroses account for 'only about 20 percent of the case material accruing to our clinics and offices' (Frankl, 1988: 68). Often Frankl reassures 'non-patients' that their existential despair is an achievement rather than a neurosis. It is a sign of intellectual depth rather than of superficiality.

Frankl stressed that meaning is an individual matter. Logotherapists must both individualize how they work and improvise. Logotherapy is neither teaching, preaching nor moral exhortation. Frankl (1963) uses the analogy of the ophthalmologist who enables people to see the world as it really is. Similarly, the logotherapist's role is that of widening and broadening clients' visual fields so that the whole spectrum of meaning and values becomes visible to them. For clients facing the existential vacuum, Frankl employed a range of interventions to assist them to find meaning in their lives. For clients with hyper-intention or hyper-reflection, Frankl used paradoxical intention and dereflection, respectively.

The therapeutic relationship

Frankl (1988) observed that therapy usually consists of both strategies and 'I–Thou' relationships. He also stresses that logotherapy cannot become too individualized. Thus, although the logotherapist is a responsibility educator, it is in the context of a committed and caring relationship that respects the uniqueness of each client. Frankl appreciated humane humans and was concerned for the rehumanization of psychiatry. His work shows much compassion and wisdom. By offering humane relationships, logotherapists provide contexts for assisting clients to find their own meanings. If necessary, Frankl assured clients that their wish to search for meaning was an accomplishment rather than a drawback. Furthermore, Frankl could be forthright in sharing his opinions about how to search for meaning.

Therapeutic interventions

Logotherapy for the existential vacuum

How does the logotherapist deal with clients in states of existential vacuum? Though Frankl has not systematically listed his methods, below are some suggestions drawn from his writings. Box 9.1 illustrates ways in which Frankl would increase a client's existential awareness of the finiteness of life and the importance of responsibility.

Box 9.1   Methods of increasing existential awareness

Explaining
Explaining that finiteness gives meaning to human existence rather than robs life of meaning.

Offering maxims
One of Frankl's leading maxims is: 'Live as if you were living for the second time and had acted as wrongly the first time as you are about to act now' (1955: 75).

Using similes
- Clients can imagine their lives as moving pictures that are being 'shot'. However, the irreversibility of life is brought home to them by being told that they cannot 'cut' anything and that nothing can be retrospectively changed.
- Clients can see themselves as sculptors who have a limited time span for completing their works of art, but are not informed of when the deadline will be.

The following are some methods by which Frankl focused on issues of meaning.

- *Teaching the importance of assuming responsibility for meaning*: Frankl viewed his task as helping clients achieve the highest possible activation of their lives. He shared his views that human life never, under any circumstances, ceases to have a meaning. Clients need to learn that they are always responsible for detecting the meaning of specific situations in their unique lives. Logotherapy teaches clients to view their lives as an assignment. For religious logotherapists working with religious clients, this can go one stage further in that they assist clients to see that they are not only responsible *for* fulfilling their life's tasks but they are also responsible *to* the taskmaster.

- *Assisting clients to listen to their consciences*: Frankl often said that meaning must be found and cannot be given. Clients are guided in their search for meaning by their consciences. They require alert consciences if they are 'to listen to and obey the ten thousand demands and commandments hidden in the ten thousand situations with which life is confronting him' (Frankl, 1975a: 120). Though therapists cannot give meanings to clients, they can provide existential examples of their commitment to the search for meaning.

- *Asking clients about meanings*: Therapists can ask clients about creative accomplishments they might bring about and support them as they search for answers. Clients can also explore and identify meanings in their relationships and in their suffering.

- *Broadening horizons about sources of meaning*: Logotherapists can assist clients to obtain broader views of sources for meaning. Frankl (1955) cites a client who declared that her life was meaningless and that she would only get better if she found a job that fulfilled her, such as doctor or nurse. Frankl assisted her to see that it was not only the job that she did, but her attitude towards how she performed her job, that might allow her a unique opportunity for fulfilment. Furthermore, in her private life outside her occupation, she could find meaning as a wife and mother.

- *Eliciting meaning through Socratic questioning*: Frankl (1988) gives the example of the female client who expressed concern with life's transitoriness. He asked her to identify a man whose accomplishments she respected and she named her family doctor. Then by means of a series of questions he led her to acknowledge that, even though the doctor died and even though through lack of gratitude some patients might not remember what they owed him, the meaningfulness of his life remained.

- *Eliciting meaning through logodrama:* Frankl (1963) gives an example of eliciting meaning through a 'logodrama' in a therapy group. A woman, admitted to his clinic after a suicide attempt, had lost a son who died aged 11 and was left alone with an older son who had infantile paralysis. Frankl first asked another woman in the group to imagine she was 80 and to look back on a life that was childless, but full of financial success and prestige.

This woman ended by saying her life had no purpose. Frankl then asked the mother of the handicapped son similarly to look back over her life. During her reply she realized her life was full of meaning because she had made a better and fuller life possible for her crippled son.

- *Offering meanings*: Logotherapists can offer suggestions regarding the meaning of situations. Frankl provides the example of an elderly and severely depressed doctor who could not get over his grief for his beloved wife who had died two years earlier. First, Frankl asked him what would have happened if he had died first. The doctor replied that she would have suffered terribly. Whereupon Frankl replied: 'You see, Doctor, such a suffering has been spared her, and it is you who have spared her this suffering; but now, you have to pay for it by surviving and mourning her' (1963: 178–9).
- *Analysing dreams*: Logotherapists can work with clients' dreams to lift spiritual phenomena into consciousness. Frankl (1975a) gives the example of the woman who dreamed that, along with her dirty washing, she took a dirty cat along to the laundry. On going to pick up her washing, she found the cat dead. Her free associations indicated that 'cat' was the symbol for 'child' and 'dirty' was the 'dirty linen' of gossip surrounding her daughter's love life, about which she had been very critical. Frankl saw the dream as expressing a warning to the mother not to keep tormenting her daughter or else she might lose her. Religious logotherapists may also analyse dreams to bring the religious unconscious into consciousness. Frankl considers that many people conceal and repress their religiousness because of 'the intimate quality inherent in genuine religiousness' (1975a: 48).

Logotherapeutic techniques for psychogenic neurosis

Paradoxical intention and dereflection are the two main logotherapeutic techniques for the psychogenic neuroses (Frankl, 1955, 1975b). Both techniques rest on the essential human qualities of self-transcendence and self-detachment.

Paradoxical intention

Paradoxical intention's use is recommended for the short-term treatment of obsessive-compulsive and phobic clients. With phobias, paradoxical intention targets anticipatory anxiety whereby clients react to events with fearful expectations of their recurrence. These fearful expectations cause excessive attention – or hyper-intention – which prevents clients from accomplishing what they want. In short, anticipatory anxiety brings about the very things that clients fear.

In paradoxical intention, clients are invited to intend precisely that which they fear. Their fear is replaced by a paradoxical wish through which 'the wind is taken out of the sails of the phobia' (Frankl, 1955: 208). In addition, paradoxical intention enlists clients' sense of humour as a means of increasing their sense of detachment towards their neuroses by laughing at them.

While obsessive-compulsive neurotics also display fear, their fear is more fear of themselves than 'fear of fear'. They fear the potential effects of their strange thoughts. However, the more these clients fight their thoughts, the stronger their symptoms become. If therapists succeed in assisting clients through paradoxical intention to stop fighting their obsessions and compulsions, their symptoms soon diminish and may finally disappear. Box 9.2 provides examples of logotherapists helping clients to use paradoxical intention.

Box 9.2   Examples of using paradoxical intention

Example 1: Paradoxical intention for fear of perspiring
A young physician was afraid of perspiring on meeting people. Whenever he met someone who triggered his anticipatory anxiety he was encouraged to say to himself: 'I only sweated out a litre before, but now I am going to pour out at least ten litres!' (Frankl, 1955: 139). After one session of paradoxical intention he freed himself of a phobia that had lasted four years.

Example 2: Paradoxical intention for fear of trembling
A medical student whose fear of trembling led her to begin trembling when the anatomy instructor entered the dissecting room overcame her problem by using the following paradoxical intention technique: whenever the instructor came she said to herself, 'Oh, here is the instructor! Now I'll show him what a good trembler I am – I'll really show him how to tremble!' (Frankl, 1955: 140). However, whenever she tried, she was unable to tremble.

Example 3: Paradoxical intention for counting and checking compulsions
A married woman who had been suffering for 14 years by a counting compulsion and a compulsion to check whether or not her dresser drawers were in order and securely locked (Frankl, 1955: 143) was shown by her doctor how to throw things carelessly into her dresser and to say to herself, 'These drawers should be as messy as possible!' After two days her counting compulsion disappeared and after the fourth day she felt no need to recheck her dresser. She continued her improvement and, whenever occasionally any obsessive-compulsive ideas returned, she was able to ignore them or make them into a joke.

Dereflection

Just as paradoxical intention tries to counteract hyper-intention – excessive intention – dereflection aims to counteract hyper-reflection –

excessive attention. Frankl (1988) considers the compulsive tendency to self-observation particularly a problem in the United States. Paradoxical intention tries to assist clients to ridicule their symptoms, while dereflections assist clients to ignore them. Sexual neuroses, such as frigidity and impotence, are one area for dereflection. Clients must be dereflected from their disturbance to the task at hand. Box 9.3 provides examples of logotherapists helping clients to use dereflection.

Box 9.3   Examples of using dereflection

Example 1: Dereflection to counter excessive self-observation regarding sexual performance

A young woman, who complained of being frigid, had been sexually abused in childhood by her father. However, this event in itself did not cause her frigidity. Because she had read popular psychoanalytic literature, she feared all the time that her traumatic sexual abuse experiences would create sexual difficulties. As a result of excessive intention to confirm her femininity and excessive attention to herself, the orgasm was no longer an unintended effect of her commitment to her partner. When her attention was dereflected from herself and refocused towards her partner, she experienced spontaneous orgasms (Frankl, 1963).

Example 2: Dereflection to counter excessive self-observation regarding swallowing

A woman became very thin because she compulsively observed her swallowing and feared her food would go down the wrong way. The client was dereflected by the formula: 'I don't need to watch my swallowing, because I don't really need to swallow, for actually I don't swallow, but rather *it* does' (Frankl, 1955: 235). She learned to trust the automatically regulated functioning of her organism.

Medical ministry for somatogenic psychoses

Frankl (1988) used the term medical ministry for how the logotherapist works with somatogenic cases where the somatic cause cannot be removed. He regarded it as a responsibility of the medical profession to comfort and console the sick. The medical ministry is not to be confused with the pastoral ministry. Where possible, the logotherapeutic treatment of clients with endogenous depressions and psychoses is aimed at working with the non-diseased part of clients to assist them in finding meaning in the attitude that they take towards their suffering. A residue of freedom is left even to people with psychoses and their innermost core is not touched by their psychosis. It is extremely demoralizing for sick people to believe that their suffering is meaningless. Box 9.4 provides an example of Frankl medically ministering to a psychotic patient.

Box 9.4   Example of medical ministry with a somatogenic case

A 17-year-old schizophrenic Jewish youth, who had been institutionalized in Israel for two and a half years because of the severity of his symptoms, started doubting his Jewish faith and blamed God for having made him different from other people. Frankl suggested to the youth that perhaps God wanted to confront him for a specific period in his life with the task of his confinement. The youth said that it was why he still believed in God and that possibly God wanted him to recover. Frankl responded that what God wanted was not only his recovery but that his spiritual level should be higher than before his illness. Afterwards the youth improved dramatically and Frankl considers that he enabled him to find meaning 'not only despite but because of psychosis' (1988: 131).

Case material

Three sources of case material are available concerning logotherapy:

- *Client case material*: Case vignettes, such as the ones I have used in abbreviated form in this book, are to be found throughout Frankl's writings: for example in *The Doctor and the Soul* (1955). In addition, in *The Will to Meaning* (1988) Frankl provides transcripts of excerpts taken from logotherapy interviews with a 25-year-old man, who for several years had been suffering from states of anxiety, and with an 80-year-old woman, depressed because she was suffering from a cancer that could not be successfully treated.
- *Concentration camp testimony*: In books such as *Man's Search for Meaning* (1963, 2004a) and *Viktor Frankl Recollections* (1997a) Frankl bears witness to the effect that presence or absence of a sense of meaning or purpose in life had on concentration camp inmates.
- *Personal example*: Frankl's own life is a testimony to the strengthening and ennobling effect that meaning can provide to individuals, however harsh and tragic their circumstances.

Further developments

Frankl's legacy continues in terms of institutional structures and how many therapists work. The Viktor Frankl Institute in Vienna, Austria, founded in 1992, is a scientific not-for-profit organization whose primary mission is to promote logotherapy and existential analysis as a comprehensive psychiatric, psychological and philosophical research discipline as well as an applied clinical theory. The Institute hosts the private archives of Frankl and possesses the largest collection of books, articles, audiotapes, videotapes and historical documents on his life and work and on the international history of logotherapy and existential analysis. From 1993 to 1998 the Institute published the *International Journal for Logotherapy and Existential Analysis*.

Together with the City Council of Vienna, the Viktor Frankl Institute cofounded the Viktor Frankl Foundation that was formally constituted in April 2000. It supports the work of senior and young researchers by endowments, which are bestowed annually. In addition, it supports and stimulates relevant scientific and practical projects by the yearly announcement of the Viktor Frankl award. An international list of around 70 affiliated or befriended institutes and societies dedicated to advancing Frankl's work is available on the Institute's website (www.viktorfrankl.org). The website also hosts a comprehensive bibliography of logotherapeutic literature. The address of the Viktor Frankl Institute is Langwiesgasse 6, A-1140 Vienna, Austria.

Last, Batthyany and Guttmann (2005) have published an annotated bibliography of empirical research and validation of logotherapy. This book summarizes and comments on over 600 empirical studies that were published in peer-reviewed psychiatry and psychology journals from 1975 to 2004.

Review and personal questions

Review questions

1. What is the will to meaning?
2. How does Frankl distinguish between consciousness and the unconscious? What are some important characteristics of the unconscious?
3. What does Frankl mean by self-transcendence?
4. Describe each of these sources of meaning: meaning in work; meaning in love; meaning in suffering; meaning from the past; and the supra-meaning.
5. What do the terms existential vacuum and existential frustration mean?
6. What do the following terms mean: noogenic neuroses; psychogenic neuroses; and somatogenic psychoses?
7. What are the goals of logotherapy? Please specify according to category of human distress.
8. Describe how a logotherapist might use each of the following methods to focus clients on finding meaning in their lives:

    (a) teaching the importance of assuming responsibility for meaning;
    (b) assisting clients to listen to their consciences;
    (c) asking clients about meanings;

(d) broadening horizons about sources of meaning;

(e) eliciting meaning through Socratic questioning;

(f) eliciting meaning through logodrama;

(g) offering meanings;

(h) analysing dreams.

9. Describe the technique of paradoxical intention and give an example of its use.
10. Describe the technique of dereflection and indicate its uses.
11. What does Frankl mean by medical ministry?

Personal questions

1. To what extent do you experience the existential vacuum and suffer from existential frustration?
2. Assess the extent to which you find meaning in each of the following sources: work, love, suffering, the past and the supra-meaning.
3. If currently you have insufficient meaning in your life, how might you help yourself to find more meaning?
4. If possible, apply the technique of paradoxical intention to coping with a problem in your life.
5. If possible, apply the technique of dereflection to coping with a problem in your life.
6. What relevance, if any, has the theory and practice of logotherapy for how you conduct therapy?
7. What relevance, if any, has the theory and practice of logotherapy for how you live?

Annotated bibliography

Frankl, V.E. (2004a) *Man's Search for Meaning: An Introduction to Logotherapy.* London: Random House/Rider.
Part one of this small volume, entitled 'Experiences in a concentration camp', provides a highly readable and moving account of Frankl's experiences as a concentration camp inmate. Frankl recounts instances of human brutality, weakness and nobility. He incisively describes qualities making for psychological survival and growth. The second part of the book, entitled 'Basic concepts of logotherapy', was written some years later. It provides a clearly written and concise introduction to logotherapy theory and practice. This book provides an excellent introduction to Frankl, the man and the therapist.

Frankl, V.E. (2004b) *The Doctor and the Soul: From Psychotherapy to Logotherapy.* London: Souvenir Books.
This book traces the development of logotherapy. Frankl next discusses the meanings of life, suffering, work and love. Then he gives his views of the psychology of anxiety

neurosis, obsessional neurosis, melancholia and schizophrenia. Next come descriptions of the logotherapeutic techniques of paradoxical intention and dereflection. Frankl ends the book by presenting logotherapy as a form of medical ministry.

Frankl, V.E. (1988) *The Will to Meaning: Foundations and Applications of Logotherapy.* New York: Meridian.
This book arose from a series of lectures Frankl gave in 1966. Part one of the book, entitled 'Foundations of logotherapy', covers metaclinical implications of psychotherapy, self-transcendence as a human phenomenon, and what is meant by meaning. Part two, entitled 'Applications of logotherapy', discusses the existential vacuum, logotherapeutic techniques and medical ministry. The book concludes with a chapter on dimensions of meaning and then has an afterword on the degurufication of logotherapy.

Frankl, V.E. (1975a) *The Unconscious God: Psychotherapy and Theology.* New York: Simon & Schuster. Extended by a lecture manuscript and published in 1997 under the title *Man's Search for Ultimate Meaning.* New York: Plenum.
The first part of the 1975 book, entitled 'The unconscious god', was originally published in 1948 in Austria. Frankl asserts that there is not only an instinctual unconscious, but a spiritual unconscious as well. Within the spiritual unconscious, there exists unconscious religiousness. Frankl discusses unconscious religiousness as well as the relationship between psychotherapy and theology. The second part of the book, entitled 'Postscript 1975: New research in logotherapy', presents Frankl's ideas interspersed with references to research.

Frankl, V.E. (1967) *Psychotherapy and Existentialism: Selected Papers on Logotherapy.* Harmondsworth: Penguin.
This book is a compilation of many of Frankl's most important articles regarding the theory and practice of logotherapy.

Frankl, V.E. (1997a) *Viktor Frankl Recollections: An Autobiography.* New York: Insight Books.
Frankl discusses his childhood and youth, his experiences as a young doctor of neurology in prewar Vienna, his early disagreements with Sigmund Freud and Alfred Adler, the impact of Nazism on himself and his family, the rebuilding of his life in postwar Vienna, and the development of logotherapy. The book provides numerous personal insights, such as his pleasures and hobbies, and contains some very personal and heart-rending passages.

References and further reading

Batthyany, A. and Guttmann, D. (2005) *Empirical Research in Logotherapy and Existential Analysis.* Phoenix, AZ: Zeig, Tucker, Theisen.
Frankl, V.E. (1955) *The Doctor and the Soul: From Psychotherapy to Logotherapy.* Harmondsworth: Penguin.
Frankl, V.E. (1963) *Man's Search for Meaning: An Introduction to Logotherapy.* New York: Washington Square Press.
Frankl, V.E. (1967) *Psychotherapy and Existentialism: Selected Papers on Logotherapy.* Harmondsworth: Penguin.
Frankl, V.E. (1975a) *The Unconscious God: Psychotherapy and Theology.* New York: Simon & Schuster.
Frankl, V.E. (1975b) 'Paradoxical intention and dereflection', *Psychotherapy: Theory, Research and Practice, 12:* 226–37.

Frankl, V.E. (1985) *The Unheard Cry for Meaning: Psychotherapy and Humanism.* New York: Simon & Schuster.

Frankl, V.E. (1988) *The Will to Meaning: Foundations and Applications of Logotherapy.* New York: Meridian.

Frankl, V.E. (1997a) *Viktor Frankl Recollections: An Autobiography.* New York: Insight Books.

Frankl, V.E. (1997b) *Man's Search for Ultimate Meaning.* New York: Plenum.

Frankl, V.E. (2004a) *Man's Search for Meaning: An Introduction to Logotherapy.* London: Random House/Rider.

Frankl, V.E. (2004b) *The Doctor and the Soul: From Psychotherapy to Logotherapy.* London: Souvenir Books.

Frankl, V.E. (2004c) *On the Theory and Therapy of Mental Disorders: An Introduction to Logotherapy and Existential Analysis.* London: Routledge.

Introduction

Adherents of behaviour therapy view their practice as firmly rooted in experimentally derived principles of learning. However, behavioural theory is an overall theory as well as an experimentally based attempt to describe the specific laws or principles of human behaviour. As an overall theory the distinctive emphasis is on the overwhelming role of environmental contingencies in influencing the acquisition and maintenance of behaviour. In its most radical form the behavioural model sees human actions as derived solely from three sources: biological deprivations, such as hunger and sexual tension; the individual's learning history; and the characteristics of and contingencies provided by environmental contexts. There is no place for concepts such as mind and free will. However, a distinction has emerged in behaviour therapy between approaches based on conditioning, radical behaviour therapy, and those which emphasize cognitive mediating variables – cognitive behaviour therapy. The latter emphasis is less deterministic than the former.

As a set of experimentally derived principles of learning, the behavioural model offers a greater degree of specificity in analysing observable, as contrasted with intrapsychic, human behaviour than that offered by the humanistic, existential or psychoanalytic models. Much of the research on which the behavioural model is based has been performed on animals such as dogs, cats and pigeons. This raises issues of the generalizability of a model derived largely from non-human animals in laboratory settings to humans in natural settings. Nevertheless, the point remains that, at the molecular level or level of observations of specific behaviours, behavioural psychologists and researchers have made a distinctive contribution to developing a theoretical framework for psychotherapy.

This chapter differs from that of the preceding ones. It aims to introduce the reader to some key behavioural concepts through discussing selectively the ideas and experimental work of five leading theorists: Pavlov's classical conditioning; Watson's conditioned behaviourism; Skinner's operant conditioning; Wolpe's reciprocal inhibition; and Bandura's social cognitive theory. Of these theorists, only Wolpe was also a practising therapist. Both in the biographical and theory sections of this chapter, the theorists are presented in roughly historical order, though their working lives overlapped.

Biographical information

Ivan Petrovich Pavlov (1849–1936)

Pavlov was born in 1849, his father a priest in the Russian Orthodox Church known for his erudition and his mother a bright, but illiterate, priest's daughter. After the death of her third child, his mother suffered a 'nervous condition', an experience that may have contributed to Pavlov's lifelong interest in psychiatry (Windholz, 1997). In the 1860s, while studying at the Riazan Ecclesiastic Seminary, Pavlov became interested in the natural sciences and subsequently rejected a career in the church. In 1870 he matriculated at the Faculty of Physical-Mathematical Sciences of the University of St Petersburg. In 1883 he was awarded an MD degree by the Imperial Military-Medical Academy in St Petersburg. In 1890 Pavlov was appointed a professor of pharmacology and then, in 1895, became a professor of physiology at the Imperial Military-Medical Academy.

Beginning in 1891 Pavlov made fundamental discoveries concerning the nature and physiology of digestion and, in 1904, received the Nobel Prize in physiology and medicine for this work. In 1901 Pavlov redirected his research interests from the digestive processes to the functioning of the cerebral hemispheres of dogs by means of the salivary reflex conditioning method. He spent the remainder of his life on this research, eventually with a large staff. His books include *The Work of the Digestive Glands* (1897/1902) and *Conditioned Reflexes: An Investigation of the Physiological Activity of the Cerebral Cortex* (1927).

John Broadus Watson (1878–1958)

Watson, sometimes viewed as the founder of behaviourism, was born in Greenville, South Carolina, to an energetic and religious mother and a philandering father, who left home when Watson was 13 years old. He was educated at Furman University in Greenville and at the University of Chicago, where his doctoral thesis was on animal education. Watson married when he was 25. At 30 he became professor of psychology at Johns Hopkins University in Baltimore and, at 36, he was elected president of the American Psychological Association. During the 1910s, Watson moved his emphasis from animal to human observation and experimentation and from 1913 he worked hard at establishing behaviourism as a method of psychology.

In his personal life Watson had a decided tendency to respond to female stimuli, a characteristic with which his first wife was prepared to live so long as the relationships were not really serious. However, in 1919 Watson, who was then 41, met an overwhelming stimulus in the shape of a 19-year-old graduate student called Rosalie Raynor. In 1920 Watson was forced to resign from Johns

Hopkins University on the grounds of adultery with a student and no other university would employ him. Divorced in late 1920 Watson married Rosalie in January 1921 and lived happily with her until her tragic death from illness in 1936.

After leaving university life Watson became a highly successful advertising executive with J. Walter Thompson's and later with Esty's agencies. In the 1920s he conducted some research on children with Mary Cover Jones and also did some popular psychological writing. His two children by his second marriage, Billy and Jimmy, were brought up by behavioural methods, including an absence of overt shows of parental affection so that they would not become dependent. Billy, who became a psychiatrist interested in Freudian ideas, committed suicide a few years after Watson's death in 1958, and Jimmy underwent psychoanalysis.

Watson's books include *Animal Education* (1903), *Behavior* (1914), *Psychology from the Standpoint of a Behaviorist* (1919), *The Psychological Care of the Infant and Child* (1928) and *Behaviorism* (1931). A bibliography of Watson's work can be found at the end of David Cohen's biography, *J.B. Watson, the Founder of Behaviourism* (1979).

Burrhus Frederick Skinner (1904–90)

Skinner was born in Susquehanna, Pennsylvania. In 1926 he graduated from Hamilton College where, majoring in English, he had planned to become a writer. In 1928, after an unsuccessful trial period at writing, Skinner entered Harvard University as a graduate student in psychology, obtaining his doctorate in 1931. From 1931 to 1936, he worked as a postdoctoral fellow in the laboratory of W.J. Crozier, a distinguished experimental biologist.

Skinner held early academic appointments, from 1936 to 1945, at the University of Minnesota and, from 1945 to 1948, at Indiana University. In 1948 he became professor of psychology at Harvard where he retired from active teaching in 1974. Throughout the remainder of his life Skinner continued writing and lecturing. Among his numerous academic awards, in 1958 Skinner received the American Psychological Association's Award for Distinguished Scientific Contributions.

Skinner's 19 books include his seminal work *The Behavior of Organisms* (1938), *Walden Two* (1948), a novel about a behavioural utopia, *Science and Human Behavior* (1953), *Verbal Behavior* (1957) which he considered his most important book, *Schedules of Reinforcement* (Ferster and Skinner, 1957), *The Analysis of Behavior* (Holland and Skinner, 1961), *Contingencies of Reinforcement* (1969), *Beyond Freedom and Dignity* (1971), *About Behaviorism* (1974) and *Particulars of My Life* (1976). Skinner 'always viewed his own work – as he views science generally – as the product of environmental contingencies and not the result of a creative mind' (Holland, 1992: 667).

Joseph Wolpe (1915–97)

Wolpe was born on 20 April 1915 and educated in Johannesburg, South Africa. Trained as a doctor, during the Second World War he served in the South African Medical Corps, where the failure of conventional treatments to war neuroses stimulated his interest in psychology. From 1948 to 1956 and again from 1957 to 1959 Wolpe was a lecturer in the department of psychiatry at the University of Witwatersrand, Johannesburg, as well as conducting a private psychiatric practice.

In the late 1940s, as a result of laboratory experiments with cats as subjects, he developed a method based on reciprocal inhibition for deconditioning neurotic fear responses. Wolpe then applied his experimental findings in his clinical work, with great success. From 1956 to 1957 Wolpe was a Fellow at the Center for Advanced Study in the Behavioral Sciences at Stanford University in California. As the fruits of his Stanford sabbatical, in 1958 both Wolpe's experimental work and its psychotherapeutic derivatives were published in a book entitled *Psychotherapy by Reciprocal Inhibition*. This publication created a great stir and acted as a major impetus to the burgeoning development of behaviour therapy.

Wolpe later returned to the United States where, from 1960 to 1965, he was professor of psychiatry at the University of Virginia at Charlottesville, from 1965 to 1984 at Temple University in Pennsylvania and, afterwards, at the Medical College of Pennsylvania in Philadelphia. Wolpe's other books include *Theme and Variations: A Behaviour Therapy Casebook* (1976), *The Practice of Behavior Therapy* (1990) and *Life Without Fear: Anxiety and its Cure*, which he coauthored with his son David (Wolpe and Wolpe, 1988). In 1979 Wolpe received the American Psychological Society's Distinguished Scientific Award for his pioneering research that contributed to the establishment of behaviour therapy.

Albert Bandura (1925–)

Bandura was born and raised in Mundare in northern Alberta, Canada. In 1949 he graduated from the University of British Columbia with a psychology major and in 1952 he received a doctorate in clinical psychology from the University of Iowa, followed by a one-year postdoctoral internship at the Witchita Guidance Center. Afterwards he went to Stanford University in California as an instructor and, by 1964, had been appointed a full professor. In 1974 the university awarded him an endowed chair named the David Starr Jordan Professorship of Social Science in Psychology. Also, in 1974 Bandura was President of the American Psychological Association. Among his many honours and awards, in 1980 he received the American Psychological Association's Award for Distinguished Scientific Contributions.

Bandura has published numerous journal articles on his experimental work on such topics as moral development, observational learning, fear acquisition, participant modelling treatment strategies, effects of the media, and the cognitive regulation of behaviour, especially the mechanisms of human agency and people's perceptions of their efficacy to exercise influence over events which affect their lives. His books include: *Social Learning and Personality Development* (Bandura and Walters, 1963), *Principles of Behavior Modification* (1969), *Aggression: A Social Learning Analysis* (1973), *Social Learning Theory* (1977), *Social Foundations of Thought and Action: A Social Cognitive Theory* (1986), *Self-Efficacy in Changing Societies* (1995) and *Self-Efficacy: The Exercise of Control* (1997).

Pavlov's classical conditioning

Pavlov considered that both instincts and reflexes were alike in being inevitable responses of the organism to internal and external stimuli. 'Reflex' was the preferred term since it had been used from the beginning with a scientific connotation. The whole nervous activity of animals is based on inborn reflexes, which may be either excitatory or inhibitory. Such reflexes 'are regular causal connections between certain definite external stimuli acting on the organism and its necessary reflex reaction' (Pavlov, 1927: 16). The inborn reflexes alone are inadequate to ensure the continued existence of the organism, with the more specialized interaction between the animal and the environment provided through the medium of the cerebral hemispheres. The 'most general function of the hemispheres is that of reacting to signals presented by innumerable stimuli of interchangeable signification' (1927: 16).

In his book *Conditioned Reflexes,* subtitled 'An investigation of the physiological activity of the cerebral cortex', Pavlov (1927) describes the precautions taken to build a laboratory so as to eliminate, as far as possible, any stimuli outside his control. In order to register the intensity of the salivary reflex, all the dogs used in his experiments were subjected to a minor operation that consisted of transferring the opening of the salivary duct from the mucous membrane of the mouth to the outside skin. In the experimental laboratory a dog would be harnessed to a stand in one section of a double chamber, while the experimenter was in the other section.

In the following experiment a conditioned reflex was obtained by pairing or linking up the action of a new stimulus with an unconditioned reflex. An experimental dog was introduced to a routine in which stimulation by a metronome was linked with feeding. If the dog was then placed in the experimental condition its salivary glands remained inactive as long as no special stimulus was introduced. However, when it was allowed to hear the sounds of a beating metronome, salivary secretion began after nine seconds, and in the course of 45 seconds 11 drops were secreted. Furthermore, in this experiment the dog turned in the direction from which it had customarily received food and began to lick its lips vigorously.

In another experiment food was shown to the animal. After five seconds salivary secretion began, and in the course of 15 seconds six drops were collected. In yet another experiment food was introduced into the dog's mouth and secretion began in one to two seconds.

Food in the dog's mouth, as contrasted with the sight of food or the association of food with the beating of a metronome, produces an inborn reflex. This reflex is brought about by the physical and chemical properties of the food acting upon the mucous membrane of the mouth and tongue. However, even salivation at the sight of food is a learned reflex, as is salivation at the beating of the metronome. Both the sight of food and the beating of the metronome are signals, and the reaction to them involves signalization through the activity of the cerebral hemispheres. Thus inborn reflexes do not involve learning or signalization, while conditioned reflexes are learned and involve signalization. The definition of reflexes as causal connections between definite external stimuli and their necessary reflex reactions still holds true when signalization is involved. The difference is that the reflex reaction to signals depends on more variables than those entailed in unconditioned reflexes.

In a further experiment on the same dog, contrary to the usual routine, stimulation by the metronome was not followed by feeding. The stimulus of the metronome was repeated for periods of 30 seconds at intervals of two minutes. Pavlov gives details indicating a lengthening of the latency period prior to secretion and a diminution of drops of saliva over successive trials. He writes that the phenomenon of the weakening of a reflex to a conditioned stimulus that is repeated a number of times without reinforcement might appropriately be termed extinction of conditioned reflexes. Indeed, if the above experiment had been continued, the conditioned reflex would have disappeared entirely.

Box 10.1 diagrammatically depicts the metronome experiments, with the term 'response' substituted for 'reflex'. Food in the mouth is an unconditioned stimulus (UCS), which automatically elicits the inborn response of salivation (UCR). Through repeated reinforcement consisting of stimulation by the metronome followed by feeding, the metronome becomes a conditioned stimulus (CS), thus becoming a signal for food and eliciting the conditioned response of salivation (CR). However, if the metronome (CS) is no longer reinforced by feeding, then the conditioned response (CR) undergoes extinction and diminishes, or even disappears (ECR).

Learning a conditioned response in the above manner has come to be termed classical or respondent conditioning. Pavlov and his colleagues explored many other areas, such as conditioned inhibition and the generalization of stimuli, but these researches are not described here. Pavlov's researches into the conditioned reflex were essential to the founding of behaviour therapy.

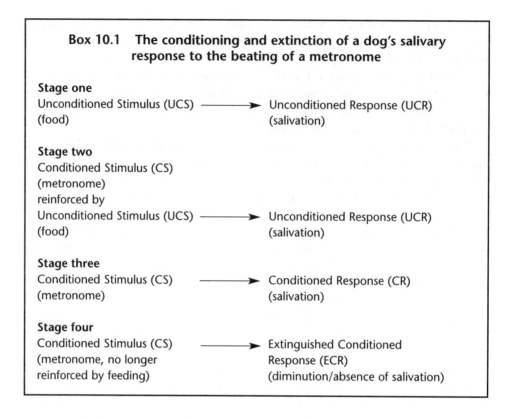

Box 10.1   The conditioning and extinction of a dog's salivary response to the beating of a metronome

Stage one
Unconditioned Stimulus (UCS) ⟶ Unconditioned Response (UCR)
(food)   (salivation)

Stage two
Conditioned Stimulus (CS)
(metronome)
reinforced by
Unconditioned Stimulus (UCS) ⟶ Unconditioned Response (UCR)
(food)   (salivation)

Stage three
Conditioned Stimulus (CS) ⟶ Conditioned Response (CR)
(metronome)   (salivation)

Stage four
Conditioned Stimulus (CS) ⟶ Extinguished Conditioned
(metronome, no longer   Response (ECR)
reinforced by feeding)   (diminution/absence of salivation)

Watson's conditioned behaviourism

To the behaviourist 'the subject matter of human psychology is *the behaviour of the human being*' (Watson, 1931: 2, emphasis in original). Furthermore, the behaviourist views psychology as a purely objective experimental branch of natural science, with its theoretical goal being the prediction and control of behaviour. In his paper 'Psychology as the behaviorist views it', Watson (1913) observed that he had devoted nearly 12 years to experimentation on animals and that it was natural that he should drift to a theoretical position in harmony with his experimental work. What is observable is the real field of psychology and what can be observed is what the organism does or says, that is to say its behaviour.

Watson considered that there were two points of view dominant in the American psychological thinking of his time: introspective or subjective psychology, which he termed the old psychology, and the new and objective psychology of behaviourism. Concepts such as consciousness and introspection, the subject matter of the old psychology, were magic.

Psychology, being an objective and experimental branch of the natural sciences, needs such concepts as little as do the sciences of chemistry and physics. As the behaviour of animals can be investigated without referring to consciousness, so can the behaviour of man. In fact 'the behaviour of man and the behaviour of animals must be considered on the same plane; as being equally essential to a general understanding of behaviour' (Watson, 1913: 176).

Stimulus, response and conditioning

Both humans and animals adjust themselves to their environments by means of hereditary and habit equipments. Through the process of evolution humans have developed sense organs, such as the eye, skin and viscera, which are most sensitive to differing kinds of stimuli. A stimulus, or thing that evokes a reaction, may come from objects in the external environment. Also, humans are affected constantly by stimuli in their internal environment arising from tissue changes in their bodies. By means of conditioning there is an ever-increasing range of stimuli to which people respond.

Stimuli evoke responses that usually involve the organism moving or altering in such a way that the stimulus no longer arouses reaction. One classification of responses is that between overt and implicit. Another general classification is that between learned and unlearned responses. Unlearned responses include all the things people do from earliest infancy, such as perspiration and breathing, prior to the processes of conditioning and habit formation that produce learned responses.

The Watsonian behaviourist sees all psychological problems and their solutions as being schematized in *stimulus* (or the more complex *situation*) and *response* terms, often abbreviated to S–R terms. In the ideal behaviourist world, given the response the stimuli can be predicted and given the stimuli the response can be predicted. Box 10.2 illustrates this view of psychological problems.

Stimuli may be unconditioned in that from birth they call forth definite responses, such as the responses of turning the eyes away from or closing the eyes to light. On the other hand, most stimuli to which humans respond are conditioned or learned, for example all the printed words to which humans respond. Similarly, responses may be unconditioned, as in the above light example, but very frequently they are conditioned, as in the case of a two-year-old child who has learned to substitute screaming for laughter at the sight of a dog. Watson observed that the whole body of man is built around the keynote 'rapid, and when needed, complicated reactions to simple and complex stimuli' (1931: 91).

Box 10.2   Schematization of unsolved and solved psychological problems

Unsolved

S..R
Given   ? (to be determined)

S..R
? (to be determined)   Given

Solved

S..R
has been determined   has been determined

Hereditary equipment

Watson viewed humans as animals born with certain types of structure, subject to individual variations, which force them to respond to stimuli in certain ways. For instance, at birth the human responds with breathing, beating heart, sneezing and so on. These kinds of reactions are the human's unlearned behaviour. Some unlearned behaviours, such as suckling and unlearned grasping, are short lived. Others, such as blinking, menstruation and ejaculation, begin later in life and last much longer. Unlearned behaviours form a relatively simple list of human responses, each of which, including our respiration and circulation, becomes conditioned shortly after birth. The concept of instinct is redundant in psychology, since observation of children indicates that everything which people tend to call 'instinct' is largely the result of training or conditioning and, as such, is part of the human's learned behaviour.

Watson developed the idea of the activity stream, a 'ceaseless stream of activity beginning when the egg is fertilized and becoming more complex as age increases' (1931: 139). Each human action system starts with an unlearned beginning and is then made more complex by conditioning. For instance, vocal responses constitute unlearned behaviour while talking represents a conditioned action system.

Determinism and habit formation

The Watsonian behaviourist is a strict determinist. Watson considered that, given total control over a dozen healthy infants from birth, he could take any one at random and train this person to become any type of specialist he might select, including doctor, lawyer, artist, beggar and thief. Inheritance of capacity, talent, temperament, mental constitution and characteristics does not really exist, since these things depend on training.

Habit formation probably starts in embryonic life and is very rapid after birth. Though very helpless at birth, greater development of three habit systems differentiates the human from other animals. These habit systems are:

1. visceral or emotional;
2. manual; and
3. laryngeal or verbal.

The development of emotional habits will be used to illustrate the importance of conditioning.

Conditioning of emotions

Watson states that there are three types of unlearned beginnings of emotional reactions, or unlearned emotional responses, to stimuli. These responses are fear, rage and love. These emotional reactions might be viewed as unconditioned reflexes or responses. For instance, a loud sound is a fundamental stimulus for eliciting the fear response.

Watson and Raynor (1920) did a series of experiments on an 11-month-old boy called Albert. The first experiment involved the establishment of a conditioned emotional response of fear to a white rat. This was achieved by linking on some trials the loud sound of the striking of a bar with Albert's touching the white rat. When later the white rat was presented alone, Albert exhibited fear responses of crying, falling over and crawling away.

A second experiment showed that there was a transfer of the conditioned fear response, though less strong, from the white rat to other furry animals (rabbit, dog) and objects (fur coat, cotton wool) when five days later they were presented to him. The above tests were carried out on a table covered with a mattress in a small, well-lit room.

A further experiment indicated, after 31 days, the persistence in a less intense form of both the conditioned fear response to the rat and the transferred fear responses to the fur coat and the rabbit. Watson and Raynor concluded that it was probable that many of the phobias in psychopathology are conditioned emotional reactions of either the direct or the transferred type. Emotional disturbances can be retraced to conditioned and transferred responses set up in infancy and childhood to all three of the fundamental human emotions.

Watson and Raynor did not remove Albert's conditioned emotional responses prior to his discharge from hospital to be adopted by a family that lived outside Baltimore. However, Mary Cover Jones (1924), an associate of Watson's, conducted an experiment in which Peter, a boy of about three years, was unconditioned or reconditioned of his 'home grown' fears of a rabbit, a white rat and related stimuli.

The experimenters were given permission to give Peter his lunch of crackers and a glass of milk. Just as he began to eat his lunch, the rabbit was displayed in a cage of wire mesh just far enough away not to disturb his eating. Gradually the rabbit was brought closer and closer and finally Peter would eat with one hand and play with the rabbit with the other. There was a transfer of unconditioning of fear responses to other furry objects, with degrees of success varying from total to greatly improved.

Watson contended that human emotional life is the result of the wear and tear of environmental forces. Through experiments such as those described above, an initial understanding was developing of how emotional reactions could be conditioned and unconditioned. Watson was excited and cautiously optimistic about the place of his natural science approach in the treatment of the emotionally disturbed.

Thinking and memory

Watson argued that 'thinking' referred to all subvocal word behaviour. In other words, thinking is the same as talking to oneself. Furthermore, language development represents the conditioning of verbal responses on unlearned vocal sounds. Sometimes the subvocal use of words has become an automatic habit. On other occasions, for example in reacting to a new situation, human thinking is similar to the trial-and-error behaviour of a rat in a maze. When subjects are asked to think aloud it is easy to see how they worked out their problem by word behaviour. New verbal creations, such as a poem, are arrived at by manipulating words and shifting them about until a new pattern is arrived at. There is no such thing as personal meaning in the behaviourist's theory.

Memory is viewed as the retention of verbal habits. If people meet a stimulus again after a period of time they do the habitual thing they learned to do when the stimulus was first present. For instance, a person who meets a friend after an absence will say the old words and exhibit the old visceral reactions.

Watson considered that there is no need to introduce the concept of mind into the so-called mental diseases. Diagnosis should involve an analysis of behaviour alone. Personality problems are behaviour disturbances and habit conflicts that need to be cured by unconditioning and conditioning.

Skinner's operant behaviourism

Like Watson, Skinner was dedicated to a science of behaviour that deals with facts and searches for lawful relations among the events in nature. Skinner's distinctive contribution to psychology has been to elaborate the importance of the after-effects or consequences of behaviour. He was assiduous in conducting experiments with pigeons and rats to map out the details of this principle. He considered that he had gone beyond stimulus and response to take into account the action of the environment upon the organism *after* the response has been made.

Operant behaviour

Skinner observed that a response that has occurred cannot be predicted or controlled, but all that can be predicted is the probability of a similar response occurring in the future. The unit of a predictive science of behaviour is an operant. The term 'operant' emphasizes the fact that behaviour *operates* on the environment to generate consequences. Thus the consequences define the properties with respect to which responses are viewed as similar. Skinner used the term 'operant' both as an adjective, as in operant behaviour, and as a noun, which indicates the behaviour defined by a given consequence. He acknowledged that Pavlov called all events that strengthened behaviour in his dogs 'reinforcement' and the resulting changes in their voluntary and involuntary behaviour 'conditioning'. However, the critical difference is that in Pavlov's work the reinforcer is paired with the *stimulus*, whereas in operant behaviour it is contingent upon a *response*. Classical and operant conditioning are the only two possible kinds of conditioning.

Contingencies of reinforcement

Skinner stressed the role of the environment in shaping and maintaining behaviour. Behaviour both operates on the environment to produce consequences and also is controlled or contingent upon the consequences produced by that environment. Any adequate description of the interaction between an organism and its environment must specify three elements:

1. the occasion on which a response occurs;
2. the response itself; and
3. the reinforcing consequences.

The interrelationship of these three elements constitutes the contingencies of reinforcement. For example, in an experiment with pigeons, any stimuli deriving from the experimental space, such as sound or light, and from the operanda of the experiment, such as a translucent disc on the wall that may be pecked, and from any special stimulating devices prior to the response, are the 'occasion' of the response. The response itself might be pecking the disc and the reinforcing consequence might be food provided at a time when the pigeon is hungry.

Positive and negative reinforcement

The probability of a response is increased after both positive and negative reinforcement. Positive reinforcements consist of presenting something, such as food, water or sexual contact, in a situation. Negative reinforcements consist of removing something, such as a bright light or an electric shock, from the situation. Thus the difference between positive and negative reinforcement hinges on whether it is the presence or absence of a given reinforcer that increases the probability of a response. The withdrawal of a positive reinforcer has the same effect as the presentation of a negative reinforcer.

Primary and conditioned reinforcers

Skinner considered that all reinforcers eventually derive their power from evolutionary selection and that it is part of 'human nature' to be reinforced in particular ways by particular things. For instance, both the positive reinforcer of food and the negative reinforcer of escape from a dangerous situation have obvious survival value. Only a small part of behaviour is immediately reinforced by food, water, sexual contact or other reinforcers of evident biological significance. Such reinforcers are the primary or unconditioned ones.

Most behaviour is emitted in response to reinforcers that have become associated with or conditioned to primary reinforcers. For instance, if each time food is given to a hungry pigeon a light is turned on, the light eventually becomes a conditioned reinforcer. The light may then be used to condition an operant in the same way as food. A conditioned reinforcer is generalized when it is paired with more than one primary reinforcer. The importance of this is that a generalized conditioned reinforcer, such as money, is useful because it is not attached to just one state of deprivation, such as hunger, but to many. Therefore, under this kind of reinforcement, a response is more likely to occur. Other generalized conditioned reinforcers are attention, approval and affection.

Schedules of reinforcement

Ferster and Skinner (1957) observed that many significant features of the shaping and maintenance of behaviour can be explained only by reference to the properties of schedules of reinforcement, and also that intermittent reinforcement can be a very important source of reinforcement in its own right and not just the poor relation of inevitable or continuous reinforcement. Box 10.3 depicts non-intermittent and intermittent reinforcement schedules.

Box 10.3   Schedules of reinforcement

Non-intermittent schedules of reinforcement

- *Continuous reinforcement*, where every response emitted is reinforced;
- *Extinction*, where no responses are reinforced.

Intermittent schedules of reinforcement

- *Fixed interval*, in which the first response occurring after a given period of time (for example, five minutes) is reinforced, with another period beginning immediately after the reinforcement;
- *Fixed ratio*, in which every *n*th response is reinforced (the word 'ratio' refers to the ratio between responses and reinforcements);
- *Variable interval*, in which reinforcements are scheduled according to a random series of intervals having a given mean and lying between arbitrary values;
- *Variable ratio*, in which reinforcements are scheduled according to a random series of ratios having a given mean and lying between arbitrary values;
- *Multiple*, in which one schedule of reinforcement is in force in the presence of one stimulus and a different schedule in the presence of another stimulus. For instance, there is a fixed interval when the key in the pigeon's experimental box is red, and a variable interval when the key is green;
- *Differential reinforcement of rate of response*, in which a response is reinforced only if it follows the preceding response after a specified interval of time (for example, three minutes) or before the end of a given interval (for example, half a second).

Maintenance and extinction

Skinner did not consider the term 'learning' to be equivalent to 'operant conditioning'. Learning emphasizes acquisition of behaviour, whereas operant conditioning focuses on both acquisition and maintenance of behaviour. Thus behaviour continues to have consequences, and if these consequences or reinforcements are not forthcoming then extinction occurs. For instance, when a pigeon's behaviour, such as the lifting of its head, which has been reinforced by the consequence of food, no longer continues to receive this reinforcement, the head lifting tends to occur with a reduced frequency. Similarly, when people engage in behaviour that no longer has rewarding consequences, they find themselves less inclined to behave that way.

Schedules of reinforcement are relevant to extinction. For example, the resistance to extinction generated by intermittent reinforcement may be much greater than that under continuous reinforcement. The task of a science of behaviour is to account for the probability of a response in terms of its history of reinforcement and extinction. Skinner used the term 'operant strength' to indicate the probability of a given response and observes that with humans the condition of low operant strength resulting from extinction often requires treatment. For instance, psychotherapy might sometimes be viewed as a system of reinforcement designed to reinstate extinguished behaviour.

Shaping and successive approximation

Behaviour may be shaped by reinforcing successive approximations to the desired response. Skinner gives the example of teaching a pigeon to bowl by swiping, with a sharp sideward movement of its beak, a wooden ball down a miniature alley towards a set of toy pins. When he and his colleagues waited for the complete response, which was to be reinforced by food, nothing happened. Then they decided to reinforce any response that had the slightest resemblance to a swipe and, afterwards, to select responses which more closely approximated the final form. This was a highly successful procedure and within minutes the pigeon was striking the ball as if it had been a champion squash player. In another experiment, by reinforcing successive approximations, a rat was conditioned to pull a string to get a marble from a rack, pick up the marble with its forepaws, carry it across the cage to a vertical tube rising two inches above the floor, lift the marble, and drop it into the tube.

Stimulus discrimination and control

Operant behaviour is emitted through important connections with the environment. For instance, in a pigeon experiment, neck stretching is reinforced when a signal light is on and allowed to extinguish when a signal light is off. The contingencies of reinforcement are that a stimulus (the light) is the occasion, the response is stretching the neck, and the reinforcement is food. The process through which the response is eventually more likely to occur when the light is on is called discrimination. Another way of viewing discrimination is to say that a response has come under the control of a discriminative stimulus or, more briefly, under stimulus control. Once an operant discrimination has been conditioned, the probability of the response occurring may be increased or decreased by presenting or removing the discriminative stimulus. An example of the effect of stimulus control on humans is the increased probability of purchasing behaviour through the effective display of merchandise in a shop.

Stimulus generalization

When the reinforcing effect of one stimulus spreads to other stimuli, the effect is that of generalization or induction. For instance, if a response to a round, red spot one square inch in area is reinforced, a yellow spot of the same size and shape may also be reinforcing through the common properties of size and shape. However, by reinforcing only responses to the red spot with the above dimensions, and by extinguishing the response to the yellow spot, the red spot may be given exclusive discriminative control. An example of stimulus generalization in everyday life is reacting to people in a similar way because they resemble someone we know.

The self

Skinner regarded a self as a repertoire of behaviours appropriate to a given set of reinforcement contingencies. The traditional view of the causation of behaviour regards people as autonomous agents responsible for their own lives. The scientific view is that people are members of a species shaped by evolutionary contingencies of survival whose behaviour is under the control of the environment in which they live. Although Skinner acknowledged the nomad on horseback in Outer Mongolia and the astronaut in outer space as being different people, he considered that if they had been exchanged at birth they would have taken each other's place (though this might be interfered with by genetic factors which set limits on learning). The ways in which people perceive and know are determined by environmental contingencies. Also, consciousness or awareness is a social product shaped by the environment. Furthermore, the complex activity called thinking is explicable in terms of contingencies of reinforcement. Thus the self is a repertoire of behaviours acquired through an environmental history of reinforcement and maintained or extinguished through current contingencies of reinforcement.

Self-control

A functional analysis of behaviour implies discovering the independent variables that, once they are controlled, in turn control behaviour. In self-control, people manipulate events in their environments to control their behaviour. Self-control involves two interrelated responses. First, there is the controlling response that acts on the environment to alter the probability of the second or the controlled response. For instance, an adult may engage in the controlling response of walking away so that he is able to control his response of anger. Similarly, removal of discriminative stimuli, such as food, may help to avoid over-eating. On the other hand, presence of certain discriminative stimuli may make desirable behaviours more probable. For instance, a certain desk may act as a stimulus to study behaviour and a knot in a handkerchief may reinforce acting at a later date.

Environmental design

A technology of behaviour that will help humans to design better environments is available. Although such environments will exercise control over behaviour, their task is to release people for more reinforcing activities, consequently also reducing the need for corrective psychotherapy. The basic premise for the design of a culture is that behaviour can be changed by changing the conditions of which it is a function. Humans are the products of both biological and cultural evolutions. Though humans are controlled by a culture, it is largely of their own making. The task of evolving a more effective culture may be seen as a gigantic exercise in self-control. Skinner affirmed his belief in operant behaviourism by concluding *Beyond Freedom and Dignity* with the following statement: 'A scientific view of man offers exciting possibilities. We have not yet seen what man can make of man' (1971: 210).

Wolpe's reciprocal inhibition

Wolpe acknowledged his debt to other learning theorists, especially Pavlov and Hull, in developing his approach to the learning and unlearning of neurotic behaviour. Wolpe considered that Pavlov's major legacy to behaviour therapy was his discovery of 'experimental neuroses', which his students Erofeeva and Shenger-Krestovnikova demonstrated could be produced and eliminated through conditioning and counter-conditioning (Wolpe and Plaud, 1997).

Reciprocal inhibition

Wolpe, in a discussion of the extinctive or unlearning processes, observed that a partial recovery of the response, known as spontaneous recovery, takes place if the stimulus is not applied for some time. The partial nature of spontaneous recovery indicates that two elements are involved in the inhibition of a response during extinction: reactive inhibition, which describes an inhibitory state dissipating with time, and negative conditioning, which leads to a permanent decrease in response probability. The Miller–Mowrer explanation of the extinctive process posits that every time an organism makes a response to a stimulus, there follows a fatigue effect which has an inhibitory effect on a closely following repeat of the same response. Stimuli present at the time are in closest contiguity with the drive reduction associated with cessation of the activity and, in some measure, become conditioned to an inhibition of a response to which previously they were positively joined. The result of this is that, at the next presentation of these stimuli, the strength of the response decreases, even after a time interval long enough to eliminate all reactive inhibition effects. However, when the response is a reinforced one, the positive effects override the development of conditioned inhibition. In other words, in this explanation of conditioned inhibition, the inhibition is built up during extinction through traces of the conditioned stimuli being simultaneous with reactive inhibition of the conditioned response.

Wolpe offered a further explanation of conditioned inhibition. He noted that old habits are often eliminated by allowing new habits to develop in the same situation. The term *reciprocal inhibition* encompasses all situations in which the elicitation of one response appears to bring about a decrement in the strength of evocation of a simultaneous response. He hypothesized that if an incompatible response were to inhibit the conditioned response and lead to much drive reduction, then a significant degree of conditioned inhibition of the original response would be developed. Eventually, his work led to his framing the following general reciprocal inhibition principle:

> If a response antagonistic to anxiety can be made to occur in the presence of anxiety-evoking stimuli so that it is accompanied by a complete or partial suppression of the anxiety responses, the bond between these stimuli and the anxiety responses will be weakened. (Wolpe, 1958: 71)

In a later work, Wolpe suggests that the term mutual inhibition might be more comprehensible than reciprocal inhibition (Wolpe and Wolpe, 1988).

The learning and unlearning of neurotic fears and habits in cats

Wolpe (1958) conducted fundamental laboratory research on the learning and unlearning of neurotic fears. The subjects were 12 domestic cats between the ages of six months and three years. Lasting neurotic effects were induced in all the cats by the administration of several electric shocks in a small experimental cage. Six of the cats were subject to a procedure by which, after control observations, the cat was given five to 10 grid shocks preceded by a 'hoot' lasting two to three seconds. The other six cats were subject to a different procedure in which they were first conditioned to perform food-approach responses to a buzzer. This response was strongly reinforced over eight to 16 experimental sessions. The next stage of the procedure involved sounding the buzzer and shocking the cat when it made its food-approach response until it ceased to do so. The mean number of shocks required was four.

The immediate responses of the cats to the shocks included combinations of the following: rushing hither and thither, clawing at the cage, getting up on hind legs, crouching, trembling, howling, pilo-erection and rapid respiration. Persistent responses displayed by all animals were: (a) resistance to being put into the experimental cage; (b) signs of anxiety when inside the cage; and (c) refusal to eat meat pellets anywhere in the cage even after one, two or three days' starvation. The above symptoms were invariably intensified by presentation of the original auditory stimuli. Furthermore, all cats showed some of these symptoms outside the experimental cage.

The learned neurotic reactions of six of the cats were associated with inhibition of feeding. This suggested to Wolpe that under different conditions feeding might inhibit the neurotic reactions. The neurotic anxiety reactions were subsequently removed, or unlearned, in all cats by getting them to eat in the presence of successively larger doses of anxiety-evoking stimuli. The cats were subject to a number of procedures. One procedure was to place the cat in the experimental cage and move pellets of meat towards its mouth on the flat end of a four-inch rod held in the experimenter's hand, in the hope that the human hand would act as a stimulus to overcome the inhibition to eating. After some persistence, four out of the nine cats undergoing this procedure were induced to eat. However, only one of the three cats whose food-approach responses had been shocked was induced to eat in this way. The three cats not subject to the human-hand procedure were induced to eat by Masserman's 'forced solution' procedure. This involved repetitions of a procedure, in the experimental cage, of gradually pushing a hungry, neurotic cat by means of a movable barrier towards an open food box containing appetizing food.

The five cats which remained unaffected by the human-hand method were eventually induced to eat in the experimental cage by a procedure which involved a hierarchy of anxiety-evoking rooms ranging from the most anxiety-evoking, the experimental room or Room A, to the least anxiety-evoking, which turned out to be the passage outside Room D. The five cats initially ate at different points in the hierarchy, but by a method of gradual ascent all cats were eventually induced to eat in Room A and then in the experimental cage. By similar methods the cats' neurotic responses to the conditioned auditory stimuli were inhibited.

Wolpe explained the success of his experiments by stating that, when stimuli to incompatible responses are present simultaneously, the occurrence of the response that is dominant in the circumstances involves the reciprocal inhibition of the other. Thus, as the number of feedings increased, the anxiety responses gradually became weaker, so that to stimuli to which there was initially an anxiety response there was ultimately a feeding response with inhibition of anxiety.

Reciprocal inhibition in therapy

Wolpe states that: 'The behavior therapist deliberately uses competing responses to overcome useless fears' (Wolpe and Wolpe, 1988: 27). In overcoming the neurotic reactions of clients or patients, Wolpe considers it vital to conduct a thorough behaviour analysis to determine which stimuli actually or potentially evoke them currently. Suffice it for now to say that Wolpe's method involves deciding which of a number of incompatible or competing responses can most appropriately be used to obtain reciprocal inhibition of neurotic anxiety responses. Wolpe (1958) listed eight incompatible responses at the disposal of therapists through which deliberate intervention for change may be made. These are: assertive responses; sexual responses; relaxation responses; respiratory responses; 'anxiety-relief' responses; competitively conditioned motor responses; 'pleasant' responses in the life situation (with drug enhancement); and (a) interview-induced emotional responses and (b) abreaction.

Relaxation, as part of systematic desensitization, is probably the main incompatible response used in Wolpe's approach to behaviour therapy. Desensitization means that clients become less and less sensitive to whatever has been triggering their fears. Systematic means that only after therapists have accomplished the desensitization at one level of anxiety before they move on to deal with the next level. The purpose of relaxation, achieved through the tensing and relaxing of various muscles, is to bring about a state of emotional calmness. Systematic desensitization is discussed in much more detail in the next chapter.

Bandura's social cognitive theory

All the theorists presented so far in this chapter focused mainly on conditioning. Although Bandura is often listed among the major behavioural theorists (see for instance, Wilson, 2005), he differs from the other theorists reviewed here in attributing much more influence to human agency, observational learning and perceived self-efficacy. Bandura's labelling of his theoretical position as 'social cognitive' acknowledges both the social contribution to how people think and act and the importance of cognitive processes to motivation, emotions and actions. For many academics and practitioners Bandura's theoretical and research input has helped broaden behaviour therapy into cognitive-behaviour therapy. Bandura's writing is voluminous and is treated very selectively here.

Human nature and personal agency

Except for elementary reflexes, people are not equipped with inborn repertoires of behaviour and hence must learn them. Biological factors, however, set limits to the learning process. For instance, genes and hormones affect physical development that, in turn, influences behavioural potentialities. Nevertheless, within biological limits, human nature possesses a vast potential to be fashioned by direct and vicarious experience into a variety of forms.

Thoughts are psychoneural processes. However, it is important to distinguish between psychological laws and biological laws. A simplistic reductionism is to be avoided in which psychology is reduced to biology, which is reduced to chemistry, which is reduced to physics and then to atomic particles. Focusing on psychological knowledge can address questions like how best to create belief systems and personal competencies. Such understanding cannot be derived just by studying the neurophysical mechanisms that

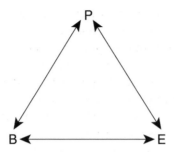

Figure 10.1   Representation of reciprocal determinism

subserve such activities. An interesting question is how people activate the cerebral processes that go beyond existing cognitive structures to generate new cognitive events and which characterize the exercise of personal agency.

Human agency is the capacity to exercise self-direction through control over one's own thought processes, motivation and action. Human agency has been conceptualized in three main ways: autonomous agency, in which people are totally independent agents of their actions; mechanical agency, where agency rests in environmental determinants; and emergent interactive agency, which is the model of social cognitive theory.

Emergent interactive agency is based on a model of triadic reciprocality. Reciprocal refers to mutual causation between the three factors. Behaviour (B), cognitive and personal factors (P), and environmental influences (E) each operate independently as determinants on one another. Figure 10.1 depicts this reciprocal determinism position. The 'influences vary in their selective strength and they do not occur simultaneously' (Bandura, personal communication, 1 February 1994).

Although environmental control has been minutely researched, personal control tends to have been neglected. Nevertheless, the fact remains that environments have causes as well as consequences. Environmental determinists, such as Skinner, are inconsistent when they assert that people are controlled by external events and, at the same time, advocate that they apply a technology of behaviour to obtain intentional control over their environments. Furthermore, psychological perspectives on determinism influence behaviour. For instance, personal determinists may be more likely to develop self-directed personalities. In the final analysis, human behaviour is the result of reciprocal interaction of external events and personal determinants such as genetic endowment, acquired competencies, reflective thought and self-initiative. People are free to the extent that they are able to exercise self-influence and determine their actions.

Social cognitive theory identifies four core features of human agency: intentionality; forethought; self-reactiveness; and self-reflectiveness (Bandura, 2004). Intentionality means that people form intentions that include action plans and strategies for attaining them. Forethought involves people setting themselves goals and anticipating the likely outcomes of prospective actions for guiding and motivating their efforts. Self-reactiveness means that people are self-regulators who adopt personal standards and monitor and regulate their actions by self-reactive influence: doing things that provide satisfaction and a sense of worth and avoiding actions that bring self-reproach. Self-reflectiveness means that people reflect on their efficacy, the soundness of their thoughts and actions, and adjust or change them, if necessary. The capacity for human agency enables humans to participate, individually and collectively, in shaping their lives and social systems.

Observational learning

Functions

The two main modes of learning are observational learning – learning by watching – and enactive learning – learning by doing. Most human behaviour and cognitive skills are learned from observing models. Functions that observational learning can perform include the following: *Modelling* can instruct observers in the skills and rules of behaviour. Also, modelling can inhibit and disinhibit behaviour already in people's repertoires. Yet another function is that of *response facilitation*. Modelled behaviour can serve as prompts and cues for people to perform behaviour already in their repertoires, yet is not inhibited. A further function of modelling is that of eliciting emotional arousal. People can perceive and behave differently in states of heightened arousal. In addition, symbolic modelling shapes people's images of social realities by the way in which it portrays human relations and the activities they pursue.

Processes

Learning involves processing information. The power of modelling is derived from its ability to influence this. Observational learning entails four main processes:

1. *Attentional processes*: If people are to learn from modelling it is important that they pay attention to and accurately perceive the modelled behaviour. One set of attentional variables concerns characteristics of the modelling stimuli, such as availability, distinctiveness, personal attractiveness and the functional value of the modelled behaviour. Another set of attentional variables revolves around observer characteristics, such as sensory capacities, arousal level, perceptual habits and past reinforcements.
2. *Retention processes*: To be effective modelling must be remembered. This involves either imaginal storing of information or, more frequently, coding of modelled events into readily usable verbal symbols. Material that

is meaningful to observers and builds on their prior experience is more likely to be remembered. Further aids to retention include either imaginal rehearsal of the modelled behaviour or actually carrying it out. Observers' cognitive skills and structures can enhance retention. Motivation to learn also plays a part in retention, though incentives are facilitative rather than necessary.

3. *Production processes*: At some stage, symbolic representations of modelled behaviour will probably need to be translated into effective action. Observers require accurate cognitive representations of modelled behaviours against which to compare sensory feedback from their enactments. Corrective modelling is an effective way of providing feedback when observers exhibit performance deficits. Observer variables influencing reproduction of behaviour include their physical capacities, whether their response repertoire already includes the necessary component responses, and their ability to make corrective adjustments when trying out the new behaviour.

4. *Motivational processes*: The distinction between learning and performance is highlighted by the fact that people are not motivated to enact everything they learn. The observer is more likely to adopt the modelled behaviour, if it (a) brings external rewards; (b) is internally positively valued; and (c) has been observed to bring rewards to the model. Anticipation of positive and negative outcomes affects which aspects of modelled behaviour are observed or ignored.

Modelling thought processes

People can learn thinking skills from observing models. However, often covert thought process are inadequately conveyed by modelled actions. For instance, a model may solve a problem cognitively, but the observer only sees the resulting actions without gaining insight into the thought processes leading up to them. An approach to learning cognitive skills is to have models verbalize aloud how they think as they engage in problem-solving activities. Advantages of combining non-verbal with verbal modelling include the ability of non-verbal modelling to gain and hold attention and the chance of overt behaviour conferring added meaning to cognitive processes. Observers' cognitive skills are likely to improve more with models who demonstrate actions and thought processes rather than demonstrate actions alone.

Role of reinforcement

The social cognitive view is that observational learning does not necessarily require extrinsic reward. Such learning occurs through cognitive processing during modelling and before observers perform any responses. With Skinner's operant conditioning model, seemingly observational learning gets achieved when responses corresponding to the model's actions are reinforced, divergent responses are either unrewarded or punished, and others' behaviour becomes a stimulus for matching responses. However, this explanation of observational learning has shortcomings. Observers may not perform modelled behaviour in the same setting in which it was modelled. Neither the model nor the observer may be reinforced. The modelled behaviour may take place days or weeks later. Thus the operant model fails to explain how new response structures are acquired through observation.

The main role of incentives in observational learning is before rather than after modelling. For instance, observers' attention can be increased by anticipation of rewards from using modelled behaviours. Furthermore, anticipated rewards can motivate them to symbolize and rehearse modelled activities. Incentives are facilitative rather than necessary.

Self-efficacy and goals

Defining self-efficacy

Conceptions of personal efficacy are the foundation of human agency. It is not simply a matter of knowing what to do. To enact skilled performance people need both to possess the requisite skills and the self-beliefs of efficacy to use them. Bandura writes: 'Unless people believe they can produce desired effect by their actions they have little incentive to act or to persevere in face of difficulties' (2004: 621–2).

Judgments of personal efficacy are different from response outcome expectations. Perceived self-efficacy refers to beliefs in one's capabilities to organize and execute the courses of action required to manage prospective situations (Bandura, 1995). Outcome expectations are judgments about the likely consequences such behaviour will produce. The judgment that one can jump six feet is an efficacy judgment. However, the anticipated social recognition from jumping six feet is an outcome expectation. Outcomes are consequences of acts not the acts themselves.

Magnitude, generality and strength are three important dimensions of efficacy expectations (Bandura, 1977). Efficacy expectations can vary according to the magnitude or level of difficulty of tasks: for instance, being confident about performing well in easy rather than in difficult tasks. Generality refers the degree of generalization of mastery expectations beyond the specific treatment situation. Strength refers to the persistence of personal mastery expectations despite disconfirming experiences.

Function and effects of self-efficacy

Self-efficacy beliefs determine goals and outcomes and determine how environmental facilitators and impediments are viewed (Bandura, 2004). People of high self-efficacy view impediments as surmountable by persevering through effort and by improving their self-management skills. People of low self-efficacy are easily put off from trying in the face of impediments.

Efficacy beliefs contribute to how people operate in diverse ways. Conceptions of personal efficacy affect choice behaviour: for instance what to do. Perceived efficacy can foster engagement in activities, whereas perceived inefficacy can lead people to avoid potentially enriching experiences. Extreme misjudgments of efficacy are dysfunctional. However, the efficacy judgments that possibly are most functional are those that slightly exceed what one can do at any given moment.

Efficacy beliefs also influence how much effort to expend and how long to persist in face of setbacks and difficulties. Unlike self-doubt, strong self-efficacy beliefs strengthen people's resilience when engaging in difficult tasks. In addition, efficacy beliefs influence how people think and feel. Those judging themselves inefficacious in dealing with environmental demands tend to exaggerate their personal deficiencies, become disheartened more easily and give up in face of difficulties. Those with a strong sense of efficacy, though they may be temporarily demoralized by setbacks, are more likely to stay task-oriented and to intensify their efforts when their performances fall short of their goals. In endeavours where staying power is needed, it is resiliency of perceived self-efficacy that counts. Traditional behaviourist theory has to answer the question of how organisms capable of forecasting the future have no capacity for self-influence. People can produce their own futures rather than simply foretell it.

Perceived efficacy can influence the development of sub-skills necessary for complex tasks, whereas perceived inefficacy may retard their development. Perceived efficacy is subject to disincentives and performance constraints. People may possess the requisite subskills and self-efficacy, but have no incentives to use them. Also, efficacious people may lack adequate material and financial resources. Possessing accurate efficacy beliefs can be particularly difficult for cognitive skills, since frequently what is required is not readily apparent from what is easily observable. Sometimes people's efficacy beliefs are inaccurate because of faulty cognitive activities: for instance deficits in perceiving feedback and in memory.

Sources of self-efficacy information

There are four major ways of developing a strong sense of efficacy (Bandura, 1997, 2004). Any method of treatment may work with one or more of these sources.

1. *Mastery experiences*: Personal experiences of success provide the most fundamental source of efficacy expectations. Success raises efficacy expectations, whereas repeated failure lowers them. Once established, enhanced efficacy beliefs tend to be generalized, especially to situations similar to those in which the beliefs were enhanced.

2. *Social modelling*: Efficacy expectations may be altered by observing others and noting the positive and negative consequences of behaviour for them. Efficacy expectations induced by modelling are generally weaker than those induced by successful task performance. Modelling affects efficacy beliefs in two ways (Bandura, personal communication, 1 February 1994). First, observers make inferences from modelled successes and failures. Seeing people similar to themselves succeed by sustained effort raises observers' beliefs in their capabilities. However, seeing others fail despite high effort lowers observers' judgments of their own efficacy and undermines their motivation. Second, competent models transmit knowledge and teach observers effective skills and strategies for managing environmental demands. Acquisition of better skills raises perceived self-efficacy.

3. *Social persuasion*: Verbal persuasion, such as suggestion and exhortation, may also influence self-efficacy. Persuasion may be most useful where it persuades people to try hard enough to succeed which in turn enhances their efficacy beliefs. However, the raising of unrealistic efficacy beliefs that are not corroborated by successful enactment may do more harm than good.

4. *Physical and emotional state*: Physical and emotional states affect efficacy beliefs in three ways. First, when people are tense and anxious, their physical state or level of emotional arousal can negatively influence their efficacy expectations. High arousal usually debilitates performance and thus lowered expectations of efficacy then become, in part, based on lowered performance. Approaches that lessen debilitating emotional arousal to subjective threats can enhance both efficacy beliefs and performance. Perceived self-efficacy to control thoughts beneficially influences cognitively generated arousal. When the extent of aversive cognitions is controlled, perceived efficacy or inefficacy to control one's thoughts are strongly related to anxiety level. Second, mood states affect people's judgment of their personal efficacy: positive moods enhance perceived efficacy and depressed moods diminish it. Third, in activities involving strength and stamina, people judge their fatigue, aches and pain as signs of weak physical efficacy.

Efficacy information from enactive, vicarious, persuasive and physical sources is cognitively processed. Regarding vicarious efficacy information, observers may consider that models similar or slightly higher in ability provide the most valid comparative information. Regarding persuasive efficacy information, its effect is related to how confident recipients are in the judgment of their persuaders. Physical efficacy information is also cognitively processed. Salient considerations here include the sources and level of arousal, and past experiences of how arousal affects performance.

Functions of goals

Personal agency or intentional regulation of behaviour operates through two cognitively based sources of motivation: first, forethought and, second, goalsetting with self-evaluative reactions to one's behaviour. Bandura observes: 'Human motivation relies on *discrepancy production* as well as *discrepancy reduction*. It requires both *proactive control* and *reactive or feedback control*' (1989: 1179–80, emphasis in original). Initially people motivate themselves through setting standards or levels of performance that create a state of disequilibrium and then they strive to attain them. Feedback control involves subsequent adjustments of effort to achieve desired results. Goals act as motivators by specifying the conditions for self-satisfaction with performance.

In addition, goals are important for the development of self-efficacy. They provide people with standards by which to judge their capabilities. Particularly useful are progressively difficult short-term subgoals. Such subgoals provide both incentives for action and, when attained, produce efficacy information and confidence to persist. Perceived inefficacy can cause people to lower their goals and thus decrease their dissatisfaction with substandard performances.

Review and personal questions

Review questions

1. What does Pavlov mean by inborn reflex?
2. What is the function of the cerebral hemisphere in the organism's survival?
3. What is meant by classical conditioning?
4. How does Watson view the connection between stimulus and response?
5 How did Watson and his associates condition and uncondition emotional responses?
6. What does Skinner mean by each of the following terms?

    (a) operant conditioning;
    (b) contingencies of reinforcement;
    (c) positive reinforcement;
    (d) negative reinforcement;
    (e) primary reinforcers;
    (f) conditioned reinforcers;
    (g) non-intermittent schedules of reinforcement;
    (h) intermittent schedules of reinforcement;
    (i) extinction;
    (j) shaping and successive approximation;
    (k) stimulus discrimination and stimulus control;
    (l) stimulus generalization;
    (m) self-control.

7. Express in simple English what Wolpe means by the term reciprocal inhibition.

8. Why does Bandura use the term social cognitive theory to designate his theoretical framework?
9. Describe each of the processes of observational learning.
10. What does the term perceived self-efficacy mean and why is it important?
11. How does goal setting influence behaviour and self-efficacy?

Personal questions

1. Do you think you have acquired any of your behaviours through classical conditioning? If, so please illustrate.
2. Give some examples from your own life of:

    (a) behaviours acquired and maintained through operant conditioning;
    (b) behaviours extinguished by lack of reinforcement.

3. If possible, give examples from your own life of engaging in a competing response to inhibit the anxiety you experienced with an existing response.
4. Identify a significant activity or cognitive skill that you have learned by observing one or more models. Describe the processes by which observational learning became an effective way of acquiring it.
5. Provide one or more examples from your own life of the distinction between an efficacy expectation and an outcome expectation.
6. For a significant area in your life, describe what have been the effects and consequences of your efficacy beliefs.
7. What is the relevance of behavioural theory for understanding your own life?
8. What is the relevance of behavioural theory for how you conduct therapy?

Annotated bibliography

Pavlov, I.P. (1927) *Conditioned Reflexes: An Investigation of the Physiological Activity of the Cerebral Cortex*. Oxford: Oxford University Press.
In this book Pavlov defines terms such as reflex, describes his experimental laboratory and gives details of some of his path-finding experiments into the functioning of the cerebral hemisphere of dogs.

Watson, J.B. (1931) *Behaviorism*. London: Kegan Paul, Trench & Traubner.
This book presents Watson's answer to the question 'What is behaviorism?' and includes his views on conditioning, instincts, thinking, memory, personality and ethics.

Skinner, B.F. (1938) *The Behavior of Organisms*. New York: Appleton-Century-Crofts.
In this book Skinner describes his seminal experiments in conditioning rats using a 'box' containing a food or water dispenser operated by a lever that could be depressed by a rat. His independent variables included deprivation and satiation, various categories of reinforcement, and aversive consequences.

Skinner, B.F. (1953) *Science and Human Behavior.* New York: Macmillan.
This book presents Skinner's ideas on applying the science of behaviour to individuals and groups. In addition, Skinner examines controlling agencies such as government and law, religion, psychotherapy, economic control and education.

Skinner, B.F. (1957) *Verbal Behavior.* New York: Appleton-Century-Crofts.
This book presents Skinner's interpretation of language and the uses of language. Verbal behaviour results from the same principles of operant learning as found in other species. Skinner analyses the various controlling relationships in verbal behaviour.

Wolpe, J. (1958) *Psychotherapy by Reciprocal Inhibition.* Stanford, CA: Stanford University Press.
This is Wolpe's seminal book in which he describes his fundamental animal research and its therapeutic applications. The book is a classic in the behaviour therapy literature.

Bandura, A. (1986) *Social Foundations of Thought and Action: A Social Cognitive Theory.* Englewood Cliffs, NJ: Prentice-Hall.
This huge volume is the definitive statement of Bandura's position. In it he presents a theoretical framework for analysing human motivation, thought and action from a social cognitive perspective.

References and further reading

Bandura, A. (1969) *Principles of Behavior Modification.* New York: Holt, Rinehart & Winston.
Bandura, A. (1973) *Aggression: A Social Learning Analysis.* Englewood Cliffs, NJ: Prentice-Hall.
Bandura, A. (1977) *Social Learning Theory.* Englewood Cliffs, NJ: Prentice-Hall.
Bandura, A. (1986) *Social Foundations of Thought and Action: A Social Cognitive Theory.* Englewood Cliffs, NJ: Prentice-Hall.
Bandura, A. (1989) 'Human agency in social cognitive theory', *American Psychologist, 44*: 1175–84.
Bandura, A. (ed.) (1995) *Self-Efficacy in Changing Societies.* New York: Cambridge University Press.
Bandura, A. (1997) *Self-Efficacy: The Exercise of Control.* New York: Freeman.
Bandura, A. (2004) 'Swimming against the mainstream: the early years from chilly tributary to transformative mainstream', *Behaviour Research and Therapy, 42*: 613–30.
Bandura, A. and Walters, R. (1963) *Social Learning and Personality Development.* New York: Holt, Rinehart & Winston.
Cohen, D. (1979) *J.B. Watson, the Founder of Behaviourism.* London: Routledge & Kegan Paul.
Ferster, C.B. and Skinner, B.F. (1957) *Schedules of Reinforcement.* New York: Appleton-Century-Crofts.
Holland, J.G. (1992) 'B.F. Skinner (1904–1990)', *American Psychologist, 47*: 665–7.
Holland, J.G. and Skinner, B.F. (1961) *The Analysis of Behavior.* New York: McGraw-Hill.
Jones, M.C. (1924) 'A laboratory study of fear: the case of Peter', *Pedagogical Seminary, 31*: 308–15.
Pavlov, I.P. (1897/1902) *The Work of the Digestive Glands.* London: Griffin.
Pavlov, I.P. (1927) *Conditioned Reflexes: An Investigation of the Physiological Activity of the Cerebral Cortex.* Oxford: Oxford University Press.
Skinner, B.F. (1938) *The Behavior of Organisms.* New York: Appleton-Century-Crofts.

Skinner, B.F. (1948) *Walden Two*. New York: Macmillan.

Skinner, B.F. (1953) *Science and Human Behavior*. New York: Macmillan.

Skinner, B.F. (1957) *Verbal Behavior*. New York: Appleton-Century-Crofts.

Skinner, B.F. (1958) 'Reinforcement today', *American Psychologist, 13*: 94–9.

Skinner, B.F. (1969) *Contingencies of Reinforcement*. New York: Appleton-Century-Crofts.

Skinner, B.F. (1971) *Beyond Freedom and Dignity*. Harmondsworth: Penguin.

Skinner, B.F. (1974) *About Behaviorism*. New York: Alfred A. Knopf.

Skinner, B.F. (1976) *Particulars of My Life*. London: Jonathan Cape.

Watson, J.B. (1903) *Animal Education*. Chicago: University of Chicago Press.

Watson, J.B. (1913) 'Psychology as the behaviorist views it', *Psychological Review, 20*: 158–77.

Watson, J.B. (1914) *Behavior*. New York: Holt.

Watson, J.B. (1919) *Psychology from the Standpoint of a Behaviorist*. Philadelphia: Lippincott.

Watson, J.B. (1928) *The Psychological Care of the Infant and Child*. New York: W.W. Norton.

Watson, J.B. (1931) *Behaviorism*. London: Kegan Paul, Trench & Traubner.

Watson, J.B. and Raynor, R.R. (1920) 'Conditioned emotional reactions', *Journal of Experimental Psychology, 3*: 1–14.

Wilson, G.T. (2005) 'Behavior therapy', in R.J. Corsini and D. Wedding (eds), *Current Psychotherapies* (7th edn). Belmont, CA: Thomson Brooks/Cole. pp. 202–37.

Windholz, G. (1997) 'Ivan P. Pavlov: an overview of his life and psychological work', *American Psychologist, 52*: 941–6.

Wolpe, J. (1958) *Psychotherapy by Reciprocal Inhibition*. Stanford, CA: Stanford University Press.

Wolpe, J. (1976) *Theme and Variations: A Behaviour Therapy Casebook*. Oxford: Pergamon Press.

Wolpe, J. (1990) *The Practice of Behavior Therapy* (4th edn). Oxford: Pergamon Press.

Wolpe, J. and Plaud, J.J. (1997) 'Pavlov's contribution to behavior therapy', *American Psychologist, 52*: 966–72.

Wolpe, J. and Wolpe, D. (1988) *Life Without Fear: Anxiety and its Cure*. Oakland, CA: New Harbinger Publications.

behaviour therapy: practice 11

Introduction

This chapter provides an introduction to some basic methods of behaviour therapy. The term behaviour therapy was originally used to describe a series of therapeutic interventions based mainly on the principles of learning described in Chapter 10. However, Wolpe (1973) observes that the behaviour therapist need not be confined to methods derived from principles, but may also employ methods that have been empirically shown to be effective.

Nowadays definitions of behaviour therapy differ according to whether the therapist mainly emphasizes learning principles based on classical and operant conditioning, or emphasizes personal agency and cognitive intervening variables as well. For instance, Wolpe defined behaviour therapy as a conditioning therapy involving 'the use of experimentally established principles of learning for the purpose of changing maladaptive behavior. Unadaptive habits are weakened and eliminated; adaptive habits are initiated and strengthened' (1973: lx). Wolpe's (1958, 1990; Wolpe and Wolpe, 1988) approach to behaviour therapy is based largely on classical conditioning. However, traditional behaviour therapy also incorporates operant conditioning assumptions and practices.

Wolpe and Skinner stressed that behaviourism takes into account thinking and feelings. Skinner especially viewed thinking as having the dimensions of behaviour and not as a process involving personal agency. For Skinner, mind was a myth, with all the power of myths (Bjork, 1993). Radical or traditional behaviourists stress the relation between the behaviour, including thinking behaviour, and the context in which it occurs. Reitman and Drabman observe: 'radical behaviorists study thinking and other private events from within a contextual scientific framework that places, a priori, all causal events outside the organism itself' (1997: 421). In cognitive behaviourism it is the individual's inner cognitions that cause much of their behaviour. Because of this fundamental difference between radical and cognitive behaviourists in explaining the causes of behaviour, the designation cognitive-behaviour is something of a contradiction in terms.

This chapter focuses predominantly on conditioning methods for altering observable behaviour, traditional behaviour therapy, rather than on approaches to altering behaviour by means of altering cognitions, cognitive-behaviour therapy. Practitioners of traditional behaviour therapy are a declining breed. Galassi and Perot observe that: 'Undoubtedly, the single most important change is the cognitive revolution that has swept through behaviour therapy in the last dozen years or so' (1992: 627). The cognitive revolution gained its momentum in the early 1970s. By 1990, 69 per cent and 27 per cent of American Association of Behavior Therapy members identified themselves as cognitive-behavioural and behavioural, respectively (Craighead, 1990). Now most therapists using the methods described in this chapter, especially the younger ones, are more likely to view themselves as cognitive-behavioural therapists rather than behaviour therapists.

Both Skinner and Wolpe were concerned about how cognitive behaviourism deviated from the basic scientific research base on which behaviour therapy rests. Wolpe regarded much of the current practice of behaviour therapy as a retreat from principles. Towards the end of his life Wolpe wrote: '*behavior therapy* was a poor choice of label; *conditioning therapy* would have been both more distinctive and more informative' (1990: 4, emphasis in original).

Nevertheless, both traditional behaviour therapy and cognitive-behaviour therapy share a commitment to empirically supported treatment interventions. In addition, both of these approaches to therapy focus on the necessity of changing observable behaviours. Furthermore, debates exist over the exact mechanisms of change in both traditional behaviour therapy and in cognitive-behaviour therapy and over the extent to which the approaches overlap, are suitable for different problems, and might be used to enhance one another.

Therapy

Therapeutic goals

At the risk of introducing a level of generality which behaviour therapists, with their emphasis on specific goals for individual clients, might find uncongenial, the following is a list of behaviour therapy goals derived from the writings of the five theorists reviewed in the preceding chapter:

- overcoming deficits in behavioural repertoires;
- strengthening adaptive behaviours;
- weakening or eliminating maladaptive behaviours;
- absence of debilitating anxiety reactions;
- the capacity to relax;
- the ability to assert oneself;
- effective social skills;
- adequacy at sexual functioning; and
- capacity for self-control.

The above goals are for individuals. Of the behavioural theorists, Skinner in particular focused on the need for groups to design environments in which humans can behave in more reinforcing ways. Thus, further behavioural goals might focus on groups and include the capacity for group self-control, both by shaping environmental consequences and also by cognitive self-regulation.

Specifying goals in therapy

In behaviour therapy, therapists need to conduct and formulate a behavioural assessment so that treatment goals can be selected and specified. Such an assessment entails descriptions of what the problems are, how they appear to have arisen, and what maintains them. These descriptions are in the form of hypotheses to be tested in therapy. The end product of the behavioural assessment is an exact specification of what variables are in need of modification be they situational antecedents, components of the problem behaviour itself, and/or consequent reinforcers. Frequently, the main goal or goals of treatment are called target behaviours (Kazdin, 1994). However, many behaviour therapists go beyond stating goals in terms of observable behaviours to specifying anxiety-reduction goals as well.

Selecting goals in turn leads to decisions about how to define them so that therapists and clients can assess whether or not clients change. Clearly defined goals assist therapists to select appropriate interventions to attain them. It is fundamental that behaviour therapists allow clients a major say in establishing treatment goals (Wilson, 2005). Clients tend to have more than one area of concern and, though it may be possible to deal with those simultaneously, sometimes an ordering of priorities is necessary. Here a prime consideration is the extent to which the problem behaviours interfere with clients' abilities to lead satisfactory lives. In most instances, client and therapist will agree on goals and treatment interventions. Where disagreement exists, further discussion may be all that is necessary to resolve the issue. Referral to another therapist may be indicated if the disagreement persists.

Process of therapy

Assessment

Early on the behaviour therapist invariably conducts a behavioural assessment, sometimes known as a functional analysis, to identify and understand clients' problem areas (Cormier and Nurius, 2002; Wolpe, 1990). Adequate behavioural assessments allow therapists to identify the context, antecedents and consequences of the responses they wish to treat, while inadequate behavioural assessments may lead to the wrong methods being applied to the wrong problems. After initial sessions, behavioural assessment aims to assist both in evaluating treatment effectiveness and in deciding whether to continue, discontinue and alter treatment.

When clients make statements like 'I seem to be very depressed these days', 'I don't seem to have many friends' or 'I get very tense at work', behaviour therapists attempt an analysis based on an *SRC* assessment, where *S* refers to the *stimulus* or *situational antecedents*, *R* to the *response variables* and *C* to the consequences or *consequent variables*. The purpose of the *SRC* analysis is to search for the key variables that control clients' behaviour. Sometimes these may be masked: for instance, aggression at work may reflect a poor marital relationship. Behavioural assessment aims for a high degree of specificity. For instance, in analysing a response, information on duration, frequency, generality and strength of the response should be collected. Therapists seldom ask 'why' questions, since those starting with how, when, where and what are more useful (Wilson, 2005).

Behaviour therapists differ in the extent to which they gather historical material concerning how the presenting concerns were learned, though this may be important in obtaining an accurate picture. Wolpe (1990), for instance, gathered historical material on his clients' presenting concerns, family life, educational and occupational development, and sexual development. He also explored his clients' current social relationships.

Other possible elements of initial assessments include observations about clients' verbal and non-verbal behaviour. Socially awkward people may demonstrate at least part of their problems during the interview. Therapists note clients' personal assets and ways of either coping with or avoiding coping with problems. In addition, they assess clients' motivation for change, any influences in their environments that are likely to hinder or help change, and their expectations regarding the possibility of change. Therapists also notice the kinds of things which clients find reinforcing, such as personal attention or praise, since these may be useful for eliciting behavioural change.

There are a number of additional sources of assessment data, one or more of which therapists may find useful both for generating more accurate hypotheses about treatment goals and for collecting baseline information against which to assess therapeutic progress and outcomes.

Behavioural observation

Sometimes therapists collect behavioural information by asking clients to role-play situations in which they experience difficulty, with the therapists playing the other person. On other occasions therapists go with clients into real-life settings to observe how they behave. An example of this might be going into pubs or restaurants with clients who experience difficulty drinking or eating in public, then observing and discussing their behaviour and emotions as they happen or shortly afterwards. However, when therapists are present, clients may behave differently from usual.

Another form of observation in real-life settings is to collect information from significant people who interact with clients in their everyday lives, such as teachers or parents in the case of children, or spouses in the case of married people. Therapists need to bear in mind both the degree to which the reported behaviours may be representative of their clients' behaviours in particular situations and also potential contamination by observer bias. Again, if clients know they are being observed they may behave differently. However, there are ethical problems in observing and reporting on clients without their knowledge or consent. Sometimes valid indirect observations in natural settings may be made by making frequency counts of various carefully defined categories of behaviour.

Self-monitoring

Clients may be asked to collect baseline data by monitoring their current behaviour. One way to go about this is to ask clients to fill in three-column daily diary sheets investigating the *SRC* elements of a specific behaviour being monitored – one column heading each for situation, response and consequences. Such behavioural monitoring diaries might be kept for a week or however long it takes to obtain the relevant information.

Questionnaires

Therapists may ask clients to complete self-report questionnaires. Such measures may focus on overt *behaviour* – how the client acts – on *emotions* – how the client feels – and on clients' perceptions of their environments. Perhaps the most commonly used type of questionnaire is the sort that asks clients to indicate the kinds of situations that cause them anxiety. One such questionnaire is Wolpe and Lang's *Fear Survey Schedule* (1969) in which clients are provided with five categories, ranging from 'Not at all' to 'Very much', for rating how disturbed they currently feel in 87 situations, such as 'People in authority', 'Angry people', 'Darkness' and 'Airplanes' (see also Wolpe, 1990). A questionnaire focused on self-report of behaviour is Alberti and Emmons's *Assertiveness Inventory* (2001), with such items as 'Do you speak out or protest when someone takes your place in line?'. Another kind of questionnaire, which focuses on activities, events and experiences which clients find rewarding, is MacPhillamy and Lewinsohn's *Pleasant Events Schedule* (Lewinsohn et al., 1986). Such a questionnaire is useful in identifying actual and potential reinforcers that may be used in conjunction with treatment.

Additional sources of assessment data are: medical information, including obtaining a medical assessment if there is any suspicion of a physiologically based problem or one with medical implications; and records of previous psychological or psychiatric treatment. An insight into how behaviour therapists assess in practice is Kazdin's conclusion, based on studying the research evidence, that 'the accumulating verdict regarding judgmental biases in decision making in general and, more specifically, within the context of clinical work has not been kind ... The collection of systematic information in the context of treatment does not eliminate bias' (1993: 13). However, Kazdin also argues that systematic information improves client care more than impressionistic evaluation of treatment progress.

Treatment

Depending on the specification of goals at the end of the behavioural assessment, behaviour therapy offers a range of treatment interventions, including reinforcement procedures, systematic desensitization, exposure and assertive training. Homework assignments are a regular part of behaviour therapy.

Behavioural assessment and monitoring take place throughout the course of behaviour therapy and not just at the beginning. One function of such monitoring is to see whether treatment goals are being achieved. Another function is to see whether therapists or clients think it advisable to alter or revise their goals. Perhaps some new situation, such as getting married or acquiring a more responsible position at work, may precipitate changing goals. If goals are altered, treatment interventions have to be amended accordingly.

Often behaviour therapy treatment is short term. For instance, a therapist might contract with a client to pursue a treatment plan for two to three months (approximately eight to 12 sessions) and re-evaluate progress at the end of this period (Wilson, 2005). Therapy lasting from 25 to 50 sessions is also moderately common, though any contact over 100 sessions is rare. Richards (2002) gives an even briefer time frame for behaviour therapy: traditionally, eight to 10 weeks and, in practice, often much less. Behaviour therapy sessions vary in length, from the traditional therapeutic hour to 30 minutes or even 15 minutes when specific interventions are in use.

Since therapeutic goals have often been stated clearly at the start of therapy, therapist and client can monitor progress in attaining goals and make termination of therapy decisions accordingly. Many behaviour therapists avoid ending abruptly by lengthening the time between successive therapy sessions, from weekly to fortnightly to monthly and so on. Follow-up telephone contact can also help therapists and clients monitor progress and deal with any issues connected with maintaining gains.

The therapeutic relationship

Behaviour therapists realize that the quality of the therapeutic relationship can significantly influence the success of therapy. Behaviour therapy is not a mechanistic procedure, rather therapists attempt to form good working relationships with clients in the interests of accurate behavioural assessment and effective treatment. Wolpe observes that: 'Objectivity, empathy, and sensitivity to suffering are intrinsic to the behavior therapist's approach to his patients' (1990: 59). Behaviour therapists are highly accepting of clients since they view their behaviour as a combination of physical endowment and the effects of experience and of current environmental contexts. Clients are not judged as good or bad; instead therapists work with them to discover and modify the controlling variables that interfere with attaining specific goals.

Frequently, early on in initial sessions, therapists offer clients a rationale for their problems: since psychological distress results from learning faulty habits, it makes sense to treat it by using scientific knowledge of how habits are made and broken (Wolpe, 1990). Then therapists invite clients to help them to identify and understand the stimuli that trigger maladaptive thoughts, feelings and behaviour.

Behaviour therapy is basically an educational process. To a large extent, therapists are teachers and clients are learners. However, unless therapists can use good relationship skills with clients, they will inadequately discover what they need to teach and then teach it with more difficulty than necessary. Some characteristics of skilled behaviour therapists are that they are concerned, sensitive, warm, sincere, task-oriented, thorough, systematic, flexible and appropriately directive.

Therapeutic interventions

Behaviour therapists have a repertoire of interventions that they tailor to assist clients to attain their goals. Where possible, they rely heavily on research findings concerning the effectiveness of an intervention when applied to a particular problem. In those cases where the empirical evidence is insufficiently clear or non-existent, therapists use clinical acumen and judgment within the framework of behavioural principles.

Systematic desensitization

Where behavioural assessments indicate that clients have certain specific anxiety or phobic areas, rather than just general tension, systematic desensitization may be the preferred intervention. However, adequate behavioural assessments are essential. For instance, anxiety about tests or about occupational decisions may be the consequence of inadequate revision or poor decision-making skills. In such instances the anxiety is likely to be more effectively diminished by skills training rather than by systematic desensitization.

Wolpe (1958, 1990; Wolpe and Wolpe, 1988) was the originator of systematic desensitization, a treatment he considered to be based on the reciprocal inhibition principle described in Chapter 10. He acknowledges that systematic desensitization may be conducted concurrently with other behavioural interventions. Systematic desensitization involves three elements: (a) training in deep muscular relaxation; (b) the construction of hierarchies of anxiety-evoking stimuli; and (c) asking the client, when relaxed, to imagine items from the anxiety-evoking hierarchies.

Training in relaxation

Clients may be taught to relax in recliner chairs, or on mattresses or, at the very least, in comfortable upright chairs with headrests. From the start therapists can endeavour to see that clients view relaxation training as learning a coping skill that can be used in daily life rather than just treating them as passive persons. Furthermore, clients should understand that success at learning relaxation, just like success at learning any other skill, requires practice and that relaxation homework will be required. Before starting relaxation, therapists can suggest that clients wear loose-fitting, comfortable clothing both during interviews and when doing relaxation homework, and that it is helpful to remove items such as glasses and shoes.

Bernstein and Borkovec (1973) observe that in teaching muscular relaxation there is a succession of events that must be observed with each muscle group. This tension–relax cycle has five elements: (a) *focus,* focusing attention on a specific muscle group; (b) *tense,* tensing the muscle group; (c) *hold,* maintaining the tension for five to seven seconds; (d) *release,* releasing the tension in the muscle group; and (e) *relax,* focusing attention on the letting go of tension and further relaxation of the muscle group. Clients need to learn this *focus–tense–hold–release–relax* cycle so that they may apply it in their homework. Having explained the basic tension–relax cycle, therapists may then demonstrate it by going through the cycle in relation to their own right hand and forearm and at each stage asking their clients to do the same.

Therapists are then likely to take clients through the other muscle groups, demonstrating them as necessary. The 16 muscle groups often used are right hand and forearm; right biceps; left hand and forearm; left biceps; forehead; eyes, nose and upper cheeks; jaw and lower cheeks; neck and throat; chest and shoulders; stomach; right thigh; right calf; right foot; left thigh; left calf; and left foot. The arms tend to come at the beginning, since they are easy to demonstrate. For most clients relaxing parts of the face is particularly important because the most marked anxiety-inhibiting effects are usually obtained there. With left-handed people, tensing instructions for the left side of the body should come before those for the right.

Once clients have learned how to tense the various muscle groups, they are instructed to keep their eyes closed during relaxation training and practice. Towards the end of relaxation sessions, therapists may ask clients for a summary of their relaxation, along the lines of 'Well, how was your relaxation today?' and discuss any issues that arise. Terminating relaxation sessions may be achieved by therapists counting from five to one and when they get to one asking their clients to wake up pleasantly relaxed as though from a peaceful sleep.

The importance of practising muscular relaxation may be further stressed at the end of the initial relaxation session. Clients are likely to be given the homework assignment of practising muscular relaxation for one or two 15-minute periods a day. Therapists should ask clients whether they anticipate any obstacles to practising, such as finding a quiet place, and help them to devise strategies for ensuring good homework. There is some evidence that clients who monitor their relaxation practices are much more likely to continue doing it (Tasto and Hinkle, 1973). Consequently, it is helpful for therapists to give clients logs for monitoring their relaxation homework.

- *Brief muscular relaxation procedures*: When the full muscular relaxation procedures have been learned and clients are able to attain deep relaxation, briefer muscular relaxation procedures may be introduced. Bernstein and Borkovec (1973) provide examples of sequential brief muscular relaxation procedures. One variation is to tense seven muscle groups: the right arm muscles, the left arm muscles and the facial muscles are each tensed as single groups; the neck and throat muscles are tensed as previously; and the chest, shoulder and stomach muscles, the right leg and foot muscles and the left leg and foot muscles are each tensed as single groups. A four-muscle group variation, even more than the seven-muscle group variation, involves simultaneous as well as sequential relaxation groups: arm muscles; face, neck and throat muscles; chest, shoulder and stomach muscles; and leg and foot muscles.

Simultaneous muscular relaxation involves tensing virtually all muscles at once. An introductory therapist statement might be: 'When I give the signal, I would like you to close your eyes tightly, take a deep breath and simultaneously clench your fists and flex your biceps, frown very deeply, pull your shoulder blades together and tense your legs and feet. Now take a deep breath and tense everything … hold for five seconds … now release and relax as quickly and deeply as you can'. When ready, brief muscular relaxation procedures should be incorporated into clients' relaxation homework.

- *Mental relaxation*: Often as part of systematic desensitization, clients are encouraged to engage in mental relaxation. Such relaxation usually involves imagining a peaceful scene, such as 'lying in a meadow on a nice warm summer's day, feeling a gentle breeze, watching the clouds'. Therapists can discover which particular scenes clients find most conducive to relaxation. Frequently, mental relaxation is used after going through a muscular relaxation procedure.
- *Relaxation training considerations*: Behaviour therapists differ in the number of sessions they take for relaxation training. Furthermore, clients differ in the speed with which they attain a capacity to relax. Wolpe (1990) taught progressive muscular relaxation in about six lessons and asked his patients to practise at home for two 15-minute sessions per day. Bernstein and Borkovec (1973) suggest a 10-session relaxation training timetable, with the first three sessions devoted to training in relaxing all muscle groups, the next four sessions to brief muscular relaxation, and the final three sessions to verbal relaxation procedures. Again, daily homework practice is assigned. Therapists may vary their relaxation training timetable according to their clients' needs and their own workload. Nevertheless, it is important that subjects have sufficient sessions to learn relaxation adequately.

Constructing hierarchies

Wolpe writes: 'An anxiety hierarchy is a thematically related list of anxiety-evoking stimuli, ranked according to the amount of anxiety they evoke' (1990: 160). There are a number of considerations in constructing desensitization hierarchies. First, suitable themes have to be identified around which anxiety-evoking stimuli can be clustered. Second, clients can be introduced to the notion of a subjective scale of anxiety or fear. A common way of checking on the anxiety-evoking potential of hierarchy items is to say that zero is a feeling of no anxiety at all, and 100 is the maximum anxiety possible in relation to a particular theme. Thus individual items can be rated according to their positions on this subjective units of disturbance (SUDS) scale.

Third, appropriate hierarchy items need to be generated around each theme. Since clients are going to be asked to imagine the items, the situations require being specifically and graphically described. Fourth, the items generated around a particular theme need to be ordered into a hierarchy. This involves rating the items on a SUDS scale and ordering them accordingly. In general, gaps of over 10 units on the subjective anxiety scale are to be avoided. Where such gaps occur, therapists and clients can generate one or more intervening items. For instance, the hierarchy for a client with a fear of examinations may have 15 items ranging from item 1, rated 5 – 'Thinking about exams while revising at my desk three months before the exam' – to item 15, rated 100 – 'Having to leave the exam room due to panic'. During treatment, hierarchy items may need to be reordered or reworded, or additional items introduced.

Presenting hierarchy items

A desensitization session may start with therapists verbally relaxing clients. When therapists are assured that clients have attained states of deep relaxation, they may start presenting scenes along the lines of 'Now I want you to imagine that you are thinking about exams while revising at your desk three months before exams …'. Therapists start with the least anxiety-evoking scene on hierarchies. Wolpe (1990) used to ask clients to raise their index finger when the scene was clear. Then he would let the scene remain for five to seven seconds and terminate by saying: 'Stop the scene'. Next, clients would report their SUDS level. After 20 to 30 seconds, clients could be asked to imagine the same scene again. If this caused no anxiety the therapist could withdraw the scene, possibly spend time further relaxing the client, and move on to the next hierarchy item.

In instances where the anxiety created by the presentation is no more than moderate, the therapist can repeat the presentation of the scene, possibly encouraging clients to relax more deeply before further presentations. If a scene repeatedly causes anxiety, therapists can consult with clients about presenting less anxiety-evoking hierarchy items. An important assumption underlying systematic desensitization is that once a low anxiety-evoking item, for example 10 units, has ceased to cause anxiety, all the other items in the hierarchy become less anxiety-evoking by 10 units. Thus the 100-unit item becomes a 90-unit item, and so on. In general, only weak anxiety-evoking stimuli are presented to clients during desensitization sessions.

Therapists may work from more than one hierarchy during desensitization sessions. Indeed, time spent on desensitization may form only part of longer interviews in which therapists focus on other problems using other methods. A record is kept of all scene presentations and their outcomes. Wolpe's (1990) desensitization sessions lasted 15 to 30 minutes and he observed that 'whereas at an early stage eight or ten presentations may be the total at a session, at an advanced stage the number may be 30 or even 50'.

Exposure

Systematic desensitization is a complex treatment presently less used than in the past. Direct exposure methods are now increasingly used. In exposure, confrontation with the feared stimulus continues until the unwanted responses to the stimulus have become reduced. However, therapists and clients need to observe certain key principles (Richards, 2002). Since fear does not lessen until it is confronted for a sufficient length of time, exposure to the feared stimulus must be for a long time. Prolonged exposure to the feared stimulus will lead to a gradual reduction in fear over time. Furthermore, the prolonged exposure to the feared stimulus must be repeated. Subsequent confrontations with feared stimuli can lead to a decrease in the initial fear as well as to a more rapid reduction of the fear response. Clients can have further sessions until the reduction in their fear levels both within and between sessions becomes sufficiently reduced and habituated.

In exposure, clients face real-life stimuli that are graded to make up a hierarchy. As they habituate to lower items by means of prolonged and repeated exposures, they work up the hierarchy towards more difficult situations. In those instances, where it is not possible to use real-life feared stimuli, imaginal exposure may be used.

Systematically graduated real-life exposure can form a central part of the behaviour therapy treatment of agoraphobia (Wilson, 2005). Therapists can accompany clients during the exposure sessions and supply support, encouragement and positive reinforcement. Furthermore, therapists ensure that clients understand the importance of staying in the feared situations until their anxiety decreases. Afterwards, therapists debrief clients about what happened.

Assertive training

Often behavioural assessments highlight clients' deficits in the area of assertion. Wolpe wrote: 'Assertive behavior is the socially appropriate verbal and motor expression of any emotion other than anxiety' (1990: 135). An early trend in assertive training was that of standing up for one's rights or what might be termed *oppositional* behaviour. For some time now, assertive training has been extended to include the expression and accurate communication of *affectionate* behaviour, where appropriate. Thus assertive behaviour now encompasses the expression of positive as well as of negative thoughts and feelings (Alberti and Emmons, 2001).

Wolpe regarded virtually all clients as inhibited from normal behaviours because of their neurotic fears. Assertive training deconditions unadaptive habits of responding with anxiety to other people's behaviour in two ways: by weakening clients' fears and by changing how they speak and act. Clients require encouragement to express legitimate emotions that are already present in problem situations. Legitimate expression of emotions 'can then successfully compete with the fear that has been inhibiting just this expression, and each time it does so, it weakens to some extent the fear habit' (Wolpe and Wolpe, 1988: 54).

Therapists and clients work together to define what may be appropriate behaviours in specific situations: for instance, asking a boss for a pay rise or a girl for a date. This stage involves the generation and consideration of alternative responses. Additionally, clients may be encouraged to observe effective models. Assertiveness must take into account the styles of individual clients, and appropriate assertive behaviour should be as 'natural' for them as possible. Responses that might seem appropriate for therapists may not be appropriate for particular clients. Timing is also important, in that clients should not be encouraged to engage in assertiveness tasks for which they are not ready. Consequently, it may be necessary to construct a hierarchy of progressively more difficult assertion tasks.

Once appropriate responses have been formulated, therapists train clients in assertiveness by means of behaviour rehearsal. Alberti and Emmons (2001) stress that assertive training should not focus only on verbal behaviour, but also on other components such as eye contact, body posture, gestures, facial expression, voice tone, inflection and volume, and fluency and timing of assertion. Therapists need to rehearse and coach their clients in these non-verbal and para-verbal aspects of assertiveness. Behaviour rehearsals can also include rehearsing clients in handling the negative and positive consequences of their assertion as well as in how to handle a variety of situations. Cassettes and video-recorders are used by some therapists to provide feedback to clients about their assertive behaviours.

Enactment in real life follows behaviour rehearsal. Clients should be set appropriately difficult assertiveness homework assignments. Monitoring between-session assertive behaviour attempts is likely to help them. Feedback from real-life attempts at assertive behaviour indicates the adequacy of the behaviour and where, if necessary, it might be improved. Furthermore, therapists can draw clients' attention to any positively reinforcing consequences of their assertive behaviour. If the consequences were negative, therapists and clients can review the appropriateness of the targeted behaviours. Even when properly enacted assertiveness may lead to conflict, and so therapists and clients may need to focus on managing conflict as well as on assertion.

Reinforcement interventions

Reinforcement interventions aim to modify behaviour by altering its consequences and, as such, reflect operant rather than classical conditioning principles. To recapitulate, both positive and negative reinforcement strengthen the probability of a response. Positive reinforcers involve presenting and negative reinforcers removing something in a situation. Punishment, or the presentation of a negative state of affairs, aims to weaken the probability of a response without necessarily increasing the frequency of other behaviours. Extinction also aims to weaken the probability of a response by withdrawal of customary reinforcers. Readers are referred to the section on Skinner in Chapter 10 for further discussion of reinforcement concepts, such as schedules of reinforcement.

Identifying reinforcers

Many reinforcers, such as praise, affection and attention, are given out relatively unthinkingly during the course of everyday life. Reinforcement interventions, however, involve the systematic application of reinforcement to initiate and strengthen adaptive behaviours and to weaken and eliminate maladaptive behaviours. In order to use reinforcement systematically, it is necessary to discover what is reinforcing for individual clients. Ways in which therapists can find out what their clients consider reinforcing include asking them, asking others about them, observing what they say and do in the interview setting, and getting them to observe and monitor themselves outside interviews.

Some self-report questionnaires exist for assessing reinforcers. Cautela (1967a) has devised a *Reinforcement Survey Schedule* to identify possible reinforcing stimuli together with their relative reinforcing values. Another self-report questionnaire is MacPhillamy and Lewinsohn's *Pleasant Events Schedule* (Lewinsohn et al., 1986; MacPhillamy and Lewinsohn, 1971). This instrument consists of 320 events and activities generated after an extensive search of possible 'pleasant events'. Subjects rate each item in the schedule on a five-point scale of pleasantness. A shortened version of the *Pleasant Events Schedule* can be derived from those items associated with improved mood for a substantial proportion of people. Lewinsohn and Graf (1973) list 49 such items and suggest that they fall into three categories: social interactional, effects incompatible with depression, and ego supportive, or activities leading to feelings such as adequacy and competence.

When working with children, pictures may be used instead of words to portray reinforcers. An example of this is the 'reinforcement menu' devised by Daley (1969) for finding effective reinforcers for eight-year-old to 11-year-old mentally retarded children. Twenty-two high-probability activities, such as talking, writing and colouring, were drawn in colour by an artist and enclosed in a single book or 'menu' with one activity per page. Children were encouraged to identify the activities in which they wanted to engage.

Reinforcement programmes and token economies

Positive reinforcement is the major method for changing behaviour in applied settings. Positive reinforcement programmes can be used both to increase desirable behaviours and to decrease undesirable behaviours. The second goal can be accomplished by positively reinforcing alternative or incompatible behaviours (Kazdin, 1994).

In designing reinforcement programmes it is particularly important that, when a behaviour is initiated, the reinforcement contingent upon that behaviour is immediate, otherwise its differential effect may be lost. Acquisition of desired behaviours may initially involve reinforcement either of component behaviours or related behaviours and build up to the desired behaviours by successive approximation. Therapists can use continuous reinforcement to establish behaviours initially. Afterwards, they can use intermittent reinforcement, since resistance to extinction is greater if fewer responses are reinforced.

Reinforcement may either be administered directly, by provision of actual reinforcers, or indirectly, by means of tokens which may later be exchanged for reinforcers. Furthermore, clients may be reinforced vicariously by observing models to obtain rewards for desired behaviours (Bandura, 1986). An example of direct reinforcement is Sanborn and Schuster's (1969) use of sweets to reinforce desired behaviours in a remedial reading class. For instance, the first boy to sit down was rewarded with a sweet and the contingency for the reward was verbally transmitted: 'This is for taking your seat'. As the class progressed pupils were rewarded for other specific behaviours.

Sometimes positive reinforcement can reward the wrong behaviours. For instance, institutionalized elderly people can receive the social reward of attention for dependency and helplessness behaviours whereas independence behaviours go unrewarded (Baltes, 1988). For such institutionalized elderly people, a positive reinforcement programme should target increasing the likelihood of appropriate independence responses.

Tokens are tangible conditioned reinforcers that may be exchanged for back-up reinforcers such as prizes, opportunities to engage in special activities, food or other purchases. Token reinforcement programmes need to establish clearly the rules of exchange that specify the number of tokens required to obtain back-up reinforcers (Wilson, 2005). Token economies or token reinforcement programmes have been used with school children, delinquents and hospital patients. Applications of token economies in elementary and secondary school settings have improved students' classroom performance in reading, writing and arithmetic (Kazdin, 1994). In one American programme, first-grade students received points at various intervals depending on how well they were working that they could exchange for prizes ranging in value from $0.05 to $1.50 at a 'good study store' in class (Breyer and Allen, 1975: 385).

Kazdin and Bootzin (1972) suggest that extinction of the desired behaviours generally follows removal of token reinforcement. They state that generalization should be planned rather than depended on as an inadvertent consequence of the token economy. One method of enhancing resistance to extinction is to focus on teaching those behaviours that will continue to be reinforced after training. Another method involves gradually removing or fading the token reinforcement, possibly offering substitute kinds of reinforcement such as praise as the fading takes place. Yet another method for maintaining the behavioural gains is to encourage clients to use self-reinforcement by giving themselves reinforcers contingent upon the performance of desired behaviours.

Reinforcement programmes and token economies may involve the cooperation and training of significant others in the clients' environments. For instance, therapists may need to work with teachers or parents in devising reinforcement procedures for individuals or groups of children. Furthermore, both teachers and parents may need to become aware of how they may inadvertently be reinforcing some of the behaviours they say they are trying to stop. Teaching the skills of effective reinforcement involves both theoretical learning and relevant practice. Furthermore, therapists may need to support and guide teachers and parents as they apply their new skills in real-life settings.

Time out and response costs

Time out is a procedure frequently recommended by behaviour therapists for use with disruptive children. It involves removal of clients from situations in which they might otherwise be receiving reinforcement. For instance, a child's attention-seeking behaviour in a classroom may be being reinforced by teacher attention and peer approval, neither of which is available when the child is made to leave the classroom for a set period of time. Time-out procedures involve a clear instruction, adequate warning that the time-out procedure is contingent upon the undesired behaviour and, if this goes unheeded, application of time out in a systematic and unemotional way. Nemeroff and Karoly observe: 'Most successful programmes with children employ TO durations of between 5 and 20 minutes, and for very young children, periods as short as 1 to 5 minutes may be effective' (1991: 150).

Response costs involve deductions of certain amounts from clients' collections of reinforcers if they perform undesired behaviours. For instance, participants in a token economy may lose some of their tokens. Where possible, response costs should be used in conjunction with positive reinforcement of desirable or alternative behaviours.

Helping clients to obtain reinforcement

A very important aspect of behavioural treatment may be that of helping clients to increase the number and scope of reinforcers available to them (Cormier and Nurius, 2002). Another way of saying this is that, instead of passively relying on others, clients can be helped to identify and actively seek out people, activities and situations that provide the desired reinforcements. Lewinsohn and Libet (1972) assert that a low rate of positive reinforcement is a critical antecedent of depressive behaviours and that improvement is likely to be accompanied by an increase of positive reinforcement. They report the findings of a study in which the 160 items from the *Pleasant Events Schedule* that a subject judged to be most pleasant were made into an activity schedule for that subject, who, for 30 consecutive days, was asked to indicate at the end of each day the activities in which he or she engaged. They found a significant association between mood and pleasant activities over their 30 subjects, though there were large individual differences. They see the clinical utility of activity schedules as including: (a) assessing which activities are potentially reinforcing; (b) illustrating to clients their low rates of emitting behaviours which bring positive reinforcement; (c) goal setting; and (d) monitoring behaviour change.

Another study by Turner and his colleagues (1979) in which the subjects were moderately depressed college students confirmed the effectiveness of using activity schedules and also instructing the subjects to increase their pleasant activities over their usual level. A further study by Zeiss and colleagues (1979) indicated that, with depressed outpatients, treatments focusing on interpersonal skills, or cognitions, or activity schedules (with increasing frequency of target activities) all significantly alleviated depression.

Training clients to use self-reinforcement

Training clients to use self-reinforcement is often termed a self-control or self-management strategy. It can involve assisting clients to observe their behaviour, set goals for themselves, identify suitable reinforcers, plan graded steps to attain their goals and specify when to administer consequences (Cormier and Nurius, 2002; Watson and Tharp, 2001). In helping clients to design self-reinforcement programmes, it is important that they perceive both that they have chosen their goals or target behaviours and also that they have the confidence to complete tasks that will bring desired outcomes. Consequently, frequently therapists design self-reinforcement programmes with graded steps to ensure that clients build up their confidence with success experiences. This enhances motivation both initially and later. Some clients may have to build up component skills prior to initiating self-management programmes.

Self-reinforcers can be external or internal. External reinforcers include: (a) self-administration of new reinforcers that are outside clients' everyday lives, such as a new item of clothing or a special event; and (b) initial denial of some pleasant everyday experience and later administration of it contingent upon some desired action. Internal reinforcers include self-talk statements like 'That's great', or 'Well done', or 'I'm glad I made it' that clearly indicate the client's satisfaction with achieving target actions.

When collaborating with clients to design self-reinforcement programmes, behaviour therapists are mindful of external resources that clients can use. For instance, participating in activities of a social, educational, recreational or religious nature may provide opportunities for gaining confidence and skills. In addition, reading appropriate self-help books and manuals can be incorporated into a programme. Such material should be easily comprehensible to clients, but this is often not the case.

Stimulus control

Thoresen and Mahoney (1974) indicate that there are two general self-control strategies that clients can use to influence their actions. First, they can try modifying their environments to control target actions *prior to* their execution. Second, they can self-administer a reward *following* or *contingent upon* an action or series of actions that achieves either a goal or a subgoal.

Behaviour therapists assist clients to use stimulus control as one form of environmental modification. Stimulus control entails either modifying in advance the stimuli or cues associated with maladaptive responses and/or establishing cues associated with adaptive responses. For example, ways in which behaviour therapists might suggest that people on weight reduction programmes modify their environments to control their food intake include: ensuring that food is placed out of sight and of easy reach; equipping their refrigerators with time locks; only keeping as much food in the house as can be consumed in a short period of time; and, where appropriate, avoiding contact with people associated with excessive eating.

Stimulus control can also be used to enhance adaptive behaviours. For example, students can learn to associate their desks with work if they use them only for that purpose. Some behaviour therapists use stimulus control in treating sleep disorders by having insomniac clients only associate their beds with sleep (Morawetz, 1989).

Self-punishment

Thus far I have mainly emphasized positive self-reinforcement and stimulus control. However, though less frequently used, behaviour therapists can encourage clients to self-administer aversive consequences. For example, weight loss programme clients can give to charity a specified sum of money for every 100 calories in excess of a daily intake limit or they can present themselves with a noxious odour after each extra snack (Thoresen and Mahoney, 1974).

Covert sensitization

Often clients who engage in negative communications/actions deny or rationalize the negative consequences of their behaviour. Therapists can assist clients in gaining greater awareness of the consequences of their negative communications/actions. Covert sensitization, sometimes known as covert conditioning, is an intervention for stopping or lessening clients' unwanted behaviours (Cautela, 1967b). Here therapists administer and assist clients to self-administer aversive consequences in their imaginations: for instance imagining the sight and smell of puking all over themselves if they eat a piece of chocolate cake. The following is a synopsis of a case study using covert sensitization:

> Barlow (2005) used covert sensitization to stop the paedophilic sexual arousal and actions of Reverend X, a minister who for over 20 years had been touching and caressing probably over 50 girls between the ages of 10 and 16. Most

typically Reverend X's behaviour consisted of hugging or caressing their breasts, but on occasion he would also touch their genitals.

The aversive images used were of Reverend X being caught in the act by his absolutely disgusted wife and two daughters, feeling nauseous and vomiting over himself and the young girl to the point where the girl's flesh would actually begin to rot before his eyes and worms and maggots would begin crawling round in it.

The scenes, which were both therapist-administered and self-administered, were presented in two formats: 'punishment', in which the client stayed in the scene, and 'escape' in which the client would begin imagining the sexually arousing scene, contemplate the negative consequences and then flee the scene feeling greatly relieved and relaxed as he got further from the situation.

At a follow-up consultation two years after treatment ended, Reverend X, who was now second in command of a small chain of hardware stores, confirmed that there had been no return of his paedophilic sexual arousal patterns whatsoever.

Participant modelling

Perhaps Bandura's most distinctive contribution to behaviour therapy has been his participant modelling approach (Bandura et al., 1974, 1975; Cormier and Nurius, 2002). This approach emphasizes *in vivo* performance of feared tasks, with the consequences generated by successful performance being viewed as the primary vehicle for psychological change. Participant modelling involves a number of stages. First, therapists repeatedly model feared activities, for instance handling snakes or dogs, to show clients both how they can be successfully performed and that the feared consequences do not occur. Second, joint performance with their therapists may enable clients to start engaging in activities that would be too threatening to engage in on their own. Therapists, who function as guides and anxiety inhibitors, use hierarchies of increasingly difficult subtasks.

Third, therapists may introduce response-induction aids or protective conditions to reduce expectations of feared consequences and thus help clients to perform the desired tasks. For instance, when treating snake phobias, response-induction aids might include the model holding the snake securely by the head and tail, the use of protective gloves and presenting a smaller snake. Fourth, therapists gradually withdraw performance supports to ensure that clients can function effectively without assistance. Fifth, clients may have a period of self-directed performance in which they spend time interacting with the feared object on their own. During the initial period of self-directed performance, therapists may stay in the room with clients, but later withdraw possibly to observe clients behind one-way mirrors. The idea is that clients' confidence is best strengthened by independent achievements in which it is clear that successful consequences are due to their ability to master feared situations on their own.

Preventing relapses

Behaviour therapists should arrange for clients to be practised in skills and have plans so that they may maintain their targeted behaviours. It can be useful for clients to distinguish between 'lapse' and 'relapse', so that they use lapses as cues to get back on track rather than to give up. Marlatt and Gordon (1985) developed relapse prevention plans for clients with alcohol problems and drug abuse problems. These plans helped clients to recognize triggers indicating that their problems may be relapsing. Clients could then immediately use a series of exercises to prevent them from engaging in self-destructive activities. Similar homework plans can be developed to help clients to sustain other targeted behaviours. Then many clients can get to the stage where they find not engaging in troublesome behaviours sufficiently rewarding on its own.

Case material

With the rise of cognitive-behaviourism, it is increasingly difficult to find case material based solely on conditioning assumptions. Case illustrations liberally illustrate Wolpe's (1990) *The Practice of Behavior Therapy.* Wolpe presented vignettes, interview transcripts and also discussed four instructive complex cases: social anxiety; multidimensional automobile phobia; washing compulsion; and reversal of sexual preference.

In *Life Without Fear: Anxiety and its Cure*, Wolpe wrote: 'Complex cases are not at all exceptional; rather, they are the rule' (Wolpe and Wolpe, 1988: 95). In this book Wolpe presented some complex cases including: a case of anxiety and depression; fear of marriage; a multifaceted case of depression; fear of being alone based on fear of losing control; an unusual case of male sexual failure; and a many-sided phobia.

Richards (2002) provides a case study whereby he successfully used exposure treatment, with Ellen, a 27-year old who had been excessively concerned about cleanliness since her late teens. Wilson (2005) provides a case study using many interventions to treat successfully Mr B, a 35-year-old married man with two sons aged eight and five, who for the past 20 years had been a persistent exhibitionist exposing his genitals to unsuspecting adult women as often as five or six times a week. The interventions included relaxation to reduce tension, assertion training and aversion conditioning to decrease the positive appeal of exposure. Towards the end of treatment, Mr B's wife participated in several joint sessions to improve their marital communication. Throughout, homework was part of the overall treatment.

Further developments

Traditional or radical behaviour therapy, based on conditioning principles, possibly had its heyday in the 1960s and 1970s. For around 30 years, it has been increasingly challenged by cognitive-behaviour therapy with its internal cognitive rather than external contextual view of the causation of behaviour. Reitman and Drabman (1997) argue for the value of behaviour therapists valuing the differences between the contextual and the cognitive traditions within their fold. They assert that radical behaviour therapy interventions may turn out to be the treatment of choice for some problems. Indeed, some therapists use either behaviour therapy or cognitive-behaviour therapy depending on the client's problem(s).

Behaviour therapy is well represented by associations. In the United States there is the Association for the Advancement of Behavior Therapy (AABT), in Europe, the European Association of Behaviour Therapy; in Britain, the British Association for Behavioural and Cognitive Psychotherapies (BABCP); and in Australia, the Australian Association for Cognitive and Behaviour Therapy (AACBT). In addition, there are active behaviour therapy organizations in many countries of Latin America. Though training in behaviour therapy is widely available, frequently it is more cognitive-behavioural rather than behavioural in orientation.

Numerous journals are devoted to behaviour therapy, with two of the most prominent being *Behavior Therapy*, published by the AABT, and *Behaviour Research and Therapy*. Nowadays, many if not most of the articles in these journals are cognitive-behavioural rather than behavioural.

Review and personal questions

Review questions

1. How do traditional behaviour therapists and cognitive behaviour therapists differ in how they explain the causes of behaviour?
2. What might behaviour therapists view as appropriate goals for clients?
3. What are the functions of behavioural assessment and how do behaviour therapists collect assessment information?
4. Describe the goals and methods of systematic desensitization.
5. Describe the treatment involving exposure.
6. Describe the goals and methods of assertive training.
7. How can behaviour therapists assist clients to identify what they find reinforcing?

8. Describe and illustrate what behaviour therapists mean by the terms:

    (a) reinforcement programmes; and
    (b) token economies.

9. How can behaviour therapists assist clients in obtaining reinforcement in their daily lives?
10. What are the goals of stimulus control? Provide an example of stimulus control.
11. Describe and illustrate what is meant by participant modelling.

Personal questions

1. Identify an area of your own behaviour that you wish to change and formulate your goal(s) in behavioural terms.
2. For the behaviour that you wished to change above, for one week keep a behaviour monitoring diary collecting material in an *SRC* format.
3. Practise relaxing yourself for 15 to 20 minutes a day over a period of at least a week. Keep a monitoring log of your relaxation homework. During your relaxation homework cover:

    (a) progressive muscular relaxation;
    (b) brief muscular relaxation;
    (c) mental relaxation.

4. Identify themes in your own life that are appropriate for hierarchy construction and then construct one or more hierarchies around them. Then, for one or more of the above hierarchies, apply systematic desensitization to yourself.
5. If relevant, apply exposure methods to help you manage a feared situation.
6. Pick a specific situation in your life where you consider you could be more assertive. Set yourself verbal and non-verbal behavioural goals for change and self-administer assertiveness training, including rehearsing targeted behaviours, to attain your goals.
7. Make a list of at least 25 items that you personally find reinforcing. Rate each item using the following scale: 1, slightly reinforcing; 2, moderately reinforcing; 3, strongly reinforcing; 4, very strongly reinforcing.
8. Design a positive self-reinforcement programme. Specify:

    (a) your goal in behavioural terms;
    (b) how you intend to observe your behaviour, establish a baseline and monitor progress;
    (c) the positive reinforcer(s) you intend using;
    (d) the precise conditions for self-administering the positive reinforcer(s);

(e) whether and how you intend using graded steps and subgoals to attain your goal; and

(f) a time schedule for your programme.

9. What is the relevance of the practice of behaviour therapy to how you conduct therapy?

10. What is the relevance of the practice of behaviour therapy to how you lead your life?

Annotated bibliography

Wolpe, J. (1990) *The Practice of Behavior Therapy* (4th edn). Oxford: Pergamon Press.
This book describes in detail the author's views on the causes of neurosis, behaviour analysis, and a range of treatment methods including assertiveness training, systematic desensitization and its variations, and operant conditioning. In addition, Wolpe presents some complex cases and provides an evaluation of behaviour therapy.

Kazdin, A.E. (1994) *Behavior Modification in Applied Settings* (5th edn). Pacific Grove, CA: Brooks/Cole.
This book takes a scholarly, yet practical, approach to behavioural assessment and the design and evaluation of behaviour modification programmes. Chapters are included on positive and negative reinforcement, punishment, extinction, self-control techniques, and response maintenance and transfer of training.

Wolpe, J. and Wolpe, D. (1988) *Life Without Fear: Anxiety and its Cure*. Oakland, CA: New Harbinger Publications.
This short book is designed to provide an authoritative account of the essential features of behaviour therapy for professionals in the mental health field and for the educated public. It explores the processes of generating, maintaining and changing useless fears. Then the authors describe the practice of behaviour analysis and therapy. The book contains many case examples.

Wilson, G.T. (2005) 'Behavior therapy', in R.J. Corsini and D. Wedding (eds), *Current Psychotherapies* (7th edn). Belmont, CA: Thomson Brooks/Cole. pp. 202–37.
A chapter by a prominent cognitive-behaviour therapist that overviews the theory, practice, development and current status of behaviour therapy.

Cormier, S. and Nurius, P.S. (2002) *Interviewing and Change Strategies for Helpers: Fundamental Skills and Cognitive-Behavioral Interventions* (5th edn). Belmont, CA: Wadsworth Publishing.
This huge and extremely detailed book presents skills and strategies for four major stages of the helping process: relationship; assessment and goal setting; strategy selection and implementation; and evaluation and termination.

Reitman, D. and Drabman, R.S. (1997) 'The value of recognizing our differences and promoting healthy competition: the cognitive behavioral debate', *Behavior Therapy*, 28: 419–29.
This article intelligently explores differences between the radical and cognitive-behavioural therapists regarding the causal state of cognitions. They assert that the cause of developing empirically supported treatments for clients' problems is best served by encouraging variation to ensure that better therapies emerge.

References and further reading

Alberti, R.E. and Emmons, M.L. (2001) *Your Perfect Right: A Guide to Assertive Living* (8th edn). Atascadero, CA: Impact Publishers.

Baltes, M.M. (1988) 'The etiology and maintenance of dependency in the elderly: three phases of operant research', *Behavior Therapy, 19*: 301–19.

Bandura, A. (1986) *Social Foundations of Thought and Action: A Social Cognitive Theory.* Englewood Cliffs, NJ: Prentice-Hall.

Bandura, A., Jeffery, R.W. and Wright, C.L. (1974) 'Efficacy of participant modeling as a function of response induction aids', *Journal of Abnormal Psychology, 83*: 56–64.

Bandura, A., Jeffery, R.W. and Gadjos, E. (1975) 'Generalizing change through participant modeling with self-directed mastery', *Behaviour Research and Therapy, 13*: 141–52.

Barlow, D.H. (2005) 'Covert sensitization for paraphilia', in D. Wedding and R.J. Corsini (eds), *Case Studies in Psychotherapy* (4th edn). Belmont, CA: Thomson Brooks/Cole. pp. 105–13.

Bernstein, D.A. and Borkovec, T.D. (1973) *Progressive Relaxation Training: A Manual for the Helping Professions.* Champaign, IL: Research Press.

Bjork, D.W. (1993) *B.F. Skinner: A Life.* New York: Basic Books.

Breyer, N.L. and Allen, G.L. (1975) 'Effects of implementing a token economy on teacher attending behavior', *Journal of Applied Behavior Analysis, 8*: 373–80.

Cautela, J. (1967a) 'A Reinforcement Survey Schedule for use in therapy, training and research', *Psychological Reports, 20*: 1115–30.

Cautela, J. (1967b) 'Covert sensitization', *Psychological Reports, 20*: 459–68.

Cormier, S. and Nurius, P.S. (2002) *Interviewing and Change Strategies for Helpers: Fundamental Skills and Cognitive-Behavioral Interventions* (5th edn). Belmont, CA: Wadsworth Publishing.

Craighead, W.E. (1990) 'There's a place for us: all of us', *Behavior Therapy, 21*: 3–23.

Daley, M.F. (1969) 'The "reinforcement menu": finding effective reinforcers', in J.D. Krumboltz and C.E. Thoresen (eds), *Behavioral Counseling: Cases and Techniques.* New York: Holt, Rinehart & Winston. pp. 42–5.

Galassi, J.P. and Perot, A.R. (1992) 'What you should know about behavioral assessment', *Journal of Counseling and Development, 70*: 624–31.

Jacobson, E. (1938) *Progressive Relaxation* (2nd edn). Chicago: University of Chicago Press.

Kazdin, A.E. (1993) 'Evaluation in clinical practice: clinically sensitive and systematic methods of treatment delivery', *Behavior Therapy, 24*: 11–45.

Kazdin, A.E. (1994) *Behavior Modification in Applied Settings* (5th edn). Pacific Grove, CA: Brooks/Cole.

Kazdin, A.E. and Bootzin, R.E. (1972) 'The token economy: an evaluative review', *Journal of Applied Behavior Analysis, 5*: 343–72.

Lewinsohn, P.M. and Graf, M. (1973) 'Pleasant activities and depression', *Journal of Consulting and Clinical Psychology, 41*: 261–8.

Lewinsohn, P.M. and Libet, J. (1972) 'Pleasant events, activity schedules and depression', *Journal of Abnormal Psychology, 79*: 291–5.

Lewinsohn, P.M., Munoz, R.F., Youngren, M.A. and Zeiss, A.M. (1986) *Control Your Depression* (rev. edn). New York: Prentice-Hall.

MacPhillamy, D.J. and Lewinsohn, P.M. (1971) *Pleasant Events Schedule.* Mimeograph, University of Oregon.

Marlatt, G.D. and Gordon, J.R. (1985) *Relapse Prevention: Maintenance Strategies in Addictive Behavior Change.* New York: Guilford.

Morawetz, D. (1989) 'Behavioral self-help treatment for insomnia: a controlled evaluation', *Behavior Therapy, 20*: 365–79.

Nemeroff, C.J. and Karoly, P. (1991) 'Operant methods', in F.H. Kanfer and A.P. Goldstein (eds), *Helping People Change: A Textbook of Methods* (4th edn). New York: Pergamon Press. pp. 122–60.

Reitman, D. and Drabman, R.S. (1997) 'The value of recognizing our differences and promoting healthy competition: the cognitive behavioral debate', *Behavior Therapy, 28*: 419–29.

Richards, D. (2002) 'Behaviour therapy', in W. Dryden (ed.), *Handbook of Individual Therapy* (4th edn). London: Sage. pp. 324–46.

Sanborn, B. and Schuster, W. (1969) 'Establishing reinforcement techniques in the classroom', in J.D. Krumboltz and C.E. Thoresen (eds), *Behavioral Counseling: Cases and Techniques*. New York: Holt, Rinehart & Winston. pp. 131–52.

Tasto, D.L. and Hinkle, J.E. (1973) 'Muscle relaxation treatment for tension headaches', *Behaviour Research and Therapy, 11*: 347–9.

Thoresen, C.E. and Mahoney, M.J. (1974) *Behavioral Self-Control*. New York: Holt, Rinehart & Winston.

Turner, R.W., Ward, M.F. and Turner, J. (1979) 'Behavioral treatment for depression: an evaluation of therapeutic components', *Journal of Clinical Psychology, 35*: 166–75.

Watson, D. and Tharp, R. (2001) *Self-Directed Behavior: Self-Modification for Personal Adjustment* (8th edn). Belmont, CA: Wadsworth Publishing.

Wilson, G.T. (2005) 'Behavior therapy', in R.J. Corsini and D. Wedding (eds), *Current Psychotherapies* (7th edn). Belmont, CA: Thomson Brooks/Cole. pp. 202–37.

Wolpe, J. (1958) *Psychotherapy by Reciprocal Inhibition*. Stanford, CA: Stanford University Press.

Wolpe, J. (1973) *The Practice of Behavior Therapy* (2nd edn). Oxford: Pergamon Press.

Wolpe, J. (1990) *The Practice of Behavior Therapy* (4th edn). Oxford: Pergamon Press.

Wolpe, J. and Lang, P.J. (1969) *Fear Survey Schedule*. San Diego, CA: Educational & Industrial Testing Service.

Wolpe, J. and Wolpe, D. (1988) *Life Without Fear: Anxiety and its Cure*. Oakland, CA: New Harbinger Publications.

Zeiss, A.M., Lewinsohn, P.M. and Munoz, R.F. (1979) 'Nonspecific improvement effects in depression using interpersonal skills training, pleasant activity schedules, or cognitive training', *Journal of Consulting and Clinical Psychology, 47*: 427–39.

rational emotive behaviour therapy 12

Introduction

When it was first developed in 1955, Albert Ellis termed his approach rational therapy (RT). In 1961 he changed its name to rational emotive therapy (RET). In 1993, Ellis (1993a) further changed its name to rational emotive behaviour therapy (REBT). What Ellis means by 'rational' is cognition that is effective in self-helping rather than cognition merely empirically and logically valid. He wishes that he had used the word cognitive from the start since many people narrowly restrict the word rational to mean intellectual or logico-empirical. People's rationality rests on judging soundly which of their desires or preferences to follow and, therefore, is based on thoughts, emotions and feelings (Ellis, 1990).

Ellis introduced 'behaviour' into his approach's name for the sake of accuracy. From its start, the approach has strongly emphasized behaviour along with cognition and emotion. Ellis writes: 'So, to correct my previous errors and to set the record straight, I shall from now on call it what it has really always been – rational emotive behavior therapy (REBT)' (1993a: 258).

Ellis (2005) distinguishes between general REBT and preferential REBT. General REBT is virtually the same as cognitive-behaviour therapy and aims to teach clients rational or appropriate behaviours. Preferential REBT emphasizes a profound philosophic change. At the same time as including general REBT, it also teaches clients how to dispute irrational ideas and self-defeating behaviours and how to use powerful cognitive-emotive-behavioural methods as self-helping skills. This chapter focuses on preferential REBT, which from now on will be referred to as rational emotive behaviour therapy (REBT).

Albert Ellis (1913–)

Albert Ellis was born in 1913 in Pittsburgh, Pennsylvania, and grew up in New York City. He had a brother and sister who were 19 months and four years younger than him, respectively. His travelling salesman father was physically absent much of the time. His Jewish mother was benignly neglectful and 'was much more immersed in her own pleasures and ego-aggrandizing activities than she was in understanding and taking care of her children' (Ellis, 1991a: 3).

Aged 12, he discovered that his parents had divorced. Afterwards, although living fairly close, his father came round to visit less than once a year.

Another childhood misfortune was that, aged four and a half, Ellis almost died of nephritis and, until the age of nine, was hospitalized eight times, once for a period of 10 months. When young Ellis also had psychological as well as physical problems. He writes: 'It took me almost two decades to talk myself out of that crap of being ingratiating. I was born and reared to be shy and scared. Throughout my childhood and teens I had a real social phobia. I viewed public speaking as a fate worse than public masturbation' (Ellis, 1997a: 69). Nevertheless, he did very well at school. However, his difficult childhood helped him to 'become a stubborn and pronounced problem solver' (Ellis, 2004a: 63). For instance, aged 19, he overcame his terror of public speaking by persisting in giving political talks over a period of three months. Furthermore, to overcome his shyness with women, he forced himself to talk to a 100 girls in a row in the Bronx Botanical Gardens (Ellis, 1997a). As with public speaking he was able to make a 180-degree change in how he performed. These experiences were important precursors to REBT because Ellis discovered the great value of reasoning and self-persuasion in changing his dysfunctional feelings and actions.

Beginning his writing career at the age of 12, Ellis turned out a large number of stories, essays and comic poems and received as many rejection slips too. In 1934, despite his early ambition to become the Great American Novelist, Ellis received a bachelor's degree in business administration from the City University of New York. Early occupations included a business matching trousers to still suitable jackets and being personnel manager of a gift and novelty firm. Ellis devoted much of his spare time to writing fiction. Partly because of difficulties getting his fiction published, he turned exclusively to writing non-fiction, especially focusing on the 'sex–family revolution'.

Discovering that he liked therapy as well as writing, in 1942 Ellis entered the clinical psychology programme at Columbia University, receiving a master's degree in 1943. Soon after obtaining this, he began a small private practice in psychotherapy and marital and sex therapy. In 1947 Ellis received his doctorate from Columbia University with a thesis on personality questionnaires, an earlier thesis on love having been censored before it got off the ground. After his doctorate, Ellis's ambition was to become an outstanding psychoanalyst and so he completed a training analysis with an analyst from the Karen Horney group and began to practise psychoanalysis under his teacher's direction. From 1948 to 1952 Ellis worked for the New Jersey Department of Institutions and Agencies, mainly as Chief Psychologist of the New Jersey State Diagnostic Center and then as Chief Psychologist of the entire state of New Jersey. He also continued his private practice in New York.

For some time, Ellis had employed active-directive methods in his psychotherapy, marital and sex therapy. Also, before undergoing analysis, Ellis had worked through many of his own problems by reading and practising the philosophies of Epictetus, Marcus Aurelius, Spinoza and Bertrand Russell, and so he started teaching clients the philosophic principles that had helped him. Between 1953 and 1955 Ellis increasingly rebelled against psychoanalysis and began calling himself a 'psychotherapist' rather than a 'psychoanalyst'. He writes: 'I finally wound up, at the beginning of 1955, with RET' (1991a: 15). He gave his first paper on it at the American Psychological Association's annual meeting in Chicago on 31 August 1956.

In 1959 he founded the Institute for Rational Living, Inc., now called the Albert Ellis Institute, as a non-profit-making scientific and educational organization to teach the principles of rational living. Since then, Ellis has donated all his royalties and income from clients and workshops to the Institute. In 1964 the Institute bought a large New York townhouse, where it is still headquartered.

Ellis is a man of boundless energy, probably a genetic inheritance from his 'two highly energetic parents who both lived reasonably long lives and were active until the last day of their lives' (Dryden, 1989: 545). He spends most of his time working. When he was over 83, in a week where he was mainly in New York 'I usually see individual and group clients from 9:30 am to 11 pm – with a couple of half hour breaks for meals, and mostly for half hour sessions with individual clients. So during each week I may see over 80 individual clients and over 40 more group clients' (Ellis, 1997b: 17). In addition, Ellis holds his 7.30–9.00 Friday night workshop where he interviews people in public. On Saturday night and Sunday he works on books, writing, researching, attending to correspondence and various other things. Until recently, Ellis gave numerous workshops and seminars in America and overseas and used the travel time to write and read.

Ellis's work is his main priority. However, he has 'had two marriages, two living together arrangements (LTAs), many passionate love experiences, and scores of (relatively brief) sexual affairs from my twenty-fourth to my ninetieth year' (Ellis, 2004a: 216). In 1964, he met 24-year-old Janet Wolfe and lived with her in an open relationship from 1965 to 2002. During this period he commented that his life 'would be greatly bereft of laughter, warmth, and intimacy without her' (Dryden, 1989: 541). Ellis and Janet had no children, since they regarded it as unfair that, due to his work, he would not have much time to spend with them.

Ellis (1997b) has had to work around physical disabilities to attain and maintain his phenomenal productivity level. From the age of 19 he has been hampered by chronically fatigable eyes. The upshot of this is that he rarely reads for more than 20 minutes and often keeps his eyes shut during therapy sessions. Aged 40 Ellis was diagnosed as having full-blown diabetes and has had to find ways of minimizing the inconvenience attached to this condition: for instance eating small meals about ten times a day – even three or four times in the middle of the night. In his late 60s his hearing began to deteriorate and by his mid-70s he had two hearing aids that, even when in good working order, had their limitations. More recently, Ellis has also had to suffer from a bladder that is easily filled but slow to empty, so that peeing has become a more lengthy process. However, efficient as ever, he has found ways of combining peeing with other activities. In June 2003, Ellis had a colonectomy, and since then has had nursing care around the clock. He is 'also greatly helped by my assistant and dearest friend, Debbie Joffe, with whom I enjoy an extremely close and loving connection' (Ellis, 2004a).

Ellis's work has been controversial. His REBT ideas challenged psychoanalytic and Rogerian orthodoxies. His ideas on sex challenged conventional morality. In addition, Ellis has not been afraid to speak his mind. However, over the past 40 years or so, cognitive-behavioural ideas have become increasingly fashionable and Ellis now regards himself as the father of REBT and the grandfather of cognitive-behaviour therapy. Ellis has received numerous honours and awards, including the American Psychological Association's major award for Distinguished Professional Contributions to Knowledge, the American Counselling Association's major Professional Development Award, and the American Humanist Association's Humanist of the Year Award.

Ellis has always been a prolific writer, even before publishing in the area of psychology. He has published over 800 papers in psychological, psychiatric and sociological journals and anthologies. In addition, he has authored or edited over 75 books and monographs including: *Reason and Emotion in Psychotherapy* (1962), *A Guide to Rational Living* (Ellis and Harper, 1997), *The Practice of Rational Emotive Behaviour Therapy* (Ellis and Dryden, 1997), *Rational Emotive Behaviour Therapy: A Therapist's Guide* (Ellis and MacLaren, 2004), *The Albert Ellis Reader* (Ellis and Blau, 1998), *Ask Albert Ellis?: Straight Answers and Sound Advice from America's Best-Known Psychologist* (2003b) and *Rational Emotive Behaviour Therapy: It Works for Me – It Can Work for You* (2004a). Ellis is also well known for his rational-humorous songs: for example, Beautiful Hangup to the tune of Stephen Foster's Beautiful Dreamer, the first two lines of which are:

'Beautiful hangup, why should we part
When we have shared our whole lives from the start?'.

Apart from humour, the guiding principles of Ellis's (1991a: 30) work have been 'Science, efficiency, honesty, revolutionism, and passionate skepticism'.

Theory

Basic concepts

Fundamental and primary goals

Virtually all humans have three fundamental goals (FG): to survive, be relatively free from pain, and to be reasonably satisfied or content. As subgoals or primary goals (PG), humans want to be happy: when by themselves; gregariously with other humans; intimately, with a few selected others; informationally and educationally; vocationally and economically; and recreationally (Ellis, 1991b). Furthermore, people live in a social world and self-interest requires putting others a close second (Ellis and Dryden, 1997).

REBT sees humans' basic goals as preferences or desires rather than needs or necessities. Rational living consists of thinking, feeling and behaving in ways which contribute to the attainment of the chosen goals, whereas irrationality consists of thinking, feeling and behaving in ways which block or interfere with their attainment. Living rationally consists of striking a sensible balance between short-range and long-range hedonism, or between the pleasures of the here-and-now and the longer-range pleasures gained through present discipline. Thus rationality may be defined as the use of reason in pursuit of chosen short-range and long-range hedonism.

Emotion, cognition and behaviour

In an early paper on 'Rational psychotherapy' Ellis (1958) proposed three fundamental hypotheses. First, thinking and emoting are closely related. Second, thinking and emoting are so closely related that they usually accompany each other, act in a circular cause-and-effect relationship, and in certain (though hardly all) respects are essentially the same thing, so that one's thinking becomes one's emotion and emoting becomes one's thought. Third, both thinking and emoting tend to take the form of self-talk or internalized sentences and, for all practical purposes, the sentences that people keep saying to themselves are or become their thoughts and emotions. Thus people's internal self-statements are capable of both generating and modifying their emotions. In addition, Ellis stresses that thinking and emotion interact with behaviour. For instance, people usually act on the basis of thoughts and emotions and their actions influence how they think and feel.

Healthy and unhealthy emotions

REBT is not an approach of no emotions; rather it emphasizes healthy or appropriate emotions. Negative emotions may be either healthy, unhealthy or mixed (Ellis and MacLaren, 2004). Unhealthy emotions are those which interfere with achieving a sensible balance between short-range and long-range hedonism. For instance, it may be appropriate for people in an alien and difficult world to be fearful, cautious or vigilant so that they may take any necessary steps for realistic protection. However, anxiety and overconcern are unhealthy emotions, since they are based on irrational thinking or unsane beliefs and, in fact, may interfere with or block attaining goals. Similarly, hostility may have a healthy and an unhealthy part. The healthy part of hostility involves acknowledging discomfort or annoyance as a basis for action designed to overcome or minimize the irritation. The unhealthy part of hostility may involve blaming others and the world in such a way as to block effective action and possibly generate even more unhappiness for oneself and further hostility from others.

Pleasurable and enjoyable emotions can also be healthy or unhealthy. For example, people may feel excessive pride when praised by others because they possess an unsane belief about the necessity of others' approval. A sensible balance between achieving short-range and long-range hedonistic goals involves a balance between achieving short-range and long-range appropriate pleasurable emotions.

Two biological tendencies

In all people a tension exists between two opposing biological creative tendencies (Ellis, 2005). On the one hand, people have innate tendencies to create, develop and actualize themselves as healthy goal-attaining human beings. They have a great potential to be rational and pleasure producing. On the other hand, they have innate tendencies to create, develop and implement irrational cognitions, unhealthy emotions and dysfunctional behaviours. REBT theorizes that often people are 'biologically predisposed to strongly, passionately, and rigidly construct and hold on to their disturbance-creating musts and other irrational beliefs' (Ellis, 1993b: 199). Thus, they possess a huge potential to be destructive of themselves and of others, to be illogical and continually to repeat the same mistakes.

Ellis believes that all the major human irrationalities exist in virtually all humans regardless of culture and educational level. Human fallibility has an inherent source. The fact that people seem so easily conditioned into dysfunctional thinking and behaviour and that these are so hard to modify are both viewed as evidence for an innate tendency to irrationality (Ellis, 1980). People's failure to accept reality almost always causes them to manifest the characteristics of emotional disturbance. However, differences exist in genetic predisposition to irrationality.

People are not only born and raised to be irrational, they also have some degree of free choice in how much they make themselves emotionally disturbed. For example, when growing up, Ellis's younger sister chose to make the worst of her childhood conditions (Ellis, 1991a, 2004a). However, people can use their biological tendency to have some degree of free choice to help as well as to damage themselves. First, they can choose to think differently and act more effectively about what is going on. Second, because they possess the capacity to think about how they think, people can choose to acquire and maintain the cognitive skills for containing and counteracting their tendencies to irrationality.

ABC theory of personality

Ellis has an ABC theory of personality to which he has added D and E to cover change and the desirable result of change. In addition, the letter G can be placed first to provide a context for people's ABCs:

G Goals, both fundamental and primary;
A Adversities or activating events in a person's life;
B Beliefs, both rational and irrational;
C Consequences, both emotional and behavioural;
D Disputing irrational beliefs;
E Effective new philosophy of life.

Just as cognitions, emotions and behaviours interact with each other and are virtually never entirely pure, so do the ABCs of REBT. Goals (G), activating events (A), beliefs (B) and consequences (C) 'all seem to be part of a collaboration with one another' (Ellis, 1991b: 145).

Rational and irrational beliefs

Ellis (2005; Ellis and MacLaren, 2004) divides belief systems into two basic categories: rational beliefs and irrational beliefs:

- *Rational beliefs (rBs)* are healthy, productive, adaptive, consistent with social reality, and generally consist of preferences, desires and wants. When thinking rationally about adversities (As) that either block or sabotage their goals (G), people engage in preferential thinking. Preferential as contrasted with demanding thinking involves either explicitly and/or tacitly reacting with their belief systems (Bs) in realistic ways and experiencing appropriate emotional and enacting goal-oriented behavioural consequences (Cs).
- *Irrational beliefs (iBs)* are rigid, dogmatic, unhealthy, maladaptive, mostly get in the way of people's efforts to achieve their goals, and are comprised of demands, musts and shoulds. When thinking irrationally about adversities (As) that either block or sabotage their goals (Gs), people engage in demanding thinking.

In reality, people's responses to adversities (As) mainly result from a combination of rational and irrational beliefs, though often one becomes in the 'winning' mode. Ellis (2005) observes that a person's self-defeating behaviour usually follows from the interaction of A (Adversity) and B (Belief about A) and that C (disturbed Consequences) generally follows the formula $A \times B = C$. Box 12.1 contrasts ABCs for preferential and demanding thinking.

Box 12.1   ABCs of preferential and demanding thinking

Preferential thinking
A Adversity or activating event perceived as blocking or sabotaging goals.
B Belief system involving preferential thinking: 'I prefer to have my important Goals unblocked and fulfilled!'
C Consequences: emotional – frustration and unhappiness; behavioural – avoiding or trying to eliminate the adversity.

Box 12.1   (Continued)

Demanding thinking

A   Adversity or activating event perceived as blocking or sabotaging goals.

B   Belief system involving demanding thinking: 'I absolutely must have my important Goals unblocked and fulfilled!'

C   Consequences: emotional – anxiety and/or excessive hostility; behavioural – self-defeating overreaction or underreaction to the adversity.

Demanding beliefs and their derivatives

Irrational belief systems often operate on at least four levels: primary demanding belief(s), derivatives of the primary demanding belief(s), secondary demanding belief(s), and derivatives of the secondary demanding belief(s).

1. *Primary demanding belief(s)*: The primary demanding belief or beliefs involves people's main demands and commands in relation to the adversity. Ellis (1980) has coined the term 'musturbation' to indicate that these beliefs are usually expressed as musts, shoulds, ought-tos, have-tos and got-tos. He has identified three major clusters of irrational beliefs that create inappropriate emotional and behavioural consequences:

    (a)   I *must* do well and win approval for all my performances;

    (b)   Others *must* treat me considerately and kindly;

    (c)   Conditions under which I live *must* be arranged so that I get practically everything I want comfortably, quickly and easily.

2. *Derivatives of the primary demanding belief(s)*: People usually create highly unrealistic and overgeneralized inferences and attributions as derivatives of their musturbatory and absolutistic demands. Three common irrational derivatives that often accompany their musturbatory beliefs (Ellis, 1991b; Ellis and MacLaren, 2004) are:

    (a)   *Awfulizing* – 'If I don't have my important Goals unblocked and fulfilled as I must, it's awful!' In this context, 'awful' means totally bad or more than bad;

    (b)   *I can't-stand-it-itis* – 'If I don't have my important Goals unblocked and fulfilled as I must, I can't stand it!'

    (c)   *Damning oneself and others*: 'If I don't have my important Goals unblocked and fulfilled as I must, I'm a stupid, worthless person'; 'Others are bad people for blocking my important goals'.

3. *Secondary demanding belief(s)*: Once people make themselves miserable at C, they tend to exacerbate their misery by making themselves miserable about being miserable. In other words, they transform the negative consequence (C) of the primary demanding belief ABC into an adversity or activating

event (A) for a secondary-level demanding belief ABC. Box 12.2 provides an example of such chaining. Frequently, people make themselves anxious about being anxious, depressed about being depressed, guilty about feeling guilty and so on.

4. *Derivatives of secondary demanding belief(s)*: People can now choose to create and derive awfulizing, I can't-stand-it-itis, and damning oneself and others from their secondary as well as their primary musturbatory beliefs. They now have two negative consequences and their derivatives for the price of one. Also, in an ever-spiralling cycle, they can intensify the unhappiness they create with their beautiful hang-ups.

Box 12.2   ABCs for primary and secondary demanding beliefs

Primary ABC
A1   'I did poorly on my job today'
B1   'Since I must do well, isn't that horrible!'
C1   'I feel anxious, depressed and worthless'

Secondary ABC
A2 (C1) 'I feel anxious, depressed and worthless'
B2   'Since I must not feel anxious, depressed and worthless, isn't that horrible!'
C2   'I feel even more anxious, depressed and worthless'

Ego disturbance and low frustration tolerance

Ellis (1988) proposes that neurotic problems can be grouped in two main headings according to the three main musturbatory beliefs and their derivatives: (a) ego disturbance (self-damning) and (b) low frustration tolerance (LFT) or discomfort disturbance. *Ego disturbance* arises from the belief that 'I *must* do well and win approval for all my performances' because it leads to people thinking and feeling that they are inadequate and undeserving persons when they do not do as well as they must. He regards this as god-like grandiosity since people demand that they be special, perfect, outstanding and superhuman.

Low frustration tolerance arises from the grandiose belief that people think they are so special that conditions must be easy and satisfying for them. They then progress to holding either or both the irrational beliefs that 'Others must treat me considerately and kindly' and 'Conditions under which I live *must* be arranged so that I get practically everything I want comfortably, quickly and easily'. Awfulizing and I can't-stand-it-itis are derivatives of such beliefs. Basically in ego disturbance and low frustration tolerance what people are insisting on is that 'I must have an easy life, I must be perfect, and people and conditions should always cater to *me, me, me, me!*' (Ellis, 1988: 119).

Acquisition

How do people acquire rational and irrational beliefs? Ellis's emphasis is much more on how people sustain their irrationality than on how they initially acquire it. The past cannot be undone and it is counterproductive to excessively focus on how people feel about the past. Ellis advises people to 'Forget your "Godawful" past' (1988: 69). He considers that psychology has focused on how people originally become illogical and that this by no means indicates how people maintain or perpetuate their illogical behaviour, or what they should do to change it. Consequently, Ellis's treatment of the development of irrational cognitions and musturbatory beliefs is cursory. However, three main strands may be identified: biology, social learning and choosing irrational cognitions. Since biological or innate tendencies to irrationality have been previously discussed, the main focus here is on social learning and choosing.

Social learning

Given that human beings are born with a distinct proneness to irrationality, this tendency is frequently exacerbated by their environment, especially early in life, when people are most vulnerable to outside influences. Ellis sees humans as basically highly suggestible, but acknowledges innate differences. Irrational ideas, which once might have been appropriate in view of the helpless state of the child, are acquired for a number of reasons (Ellis, 1991b, 2005; Ellis and Harper, 1997). First, young children are unable to think clearly, in particular insisting on immediate rather than on future gratification and being unable accurately to distinguish real from imagined fears. However, as they grow older, normal children become less insistent on having their desires and demands immediately gratified. Second, frequently childish demands can be assuaged by magic, for instance parents saying that a fairy godmother will satisfy them. Third, children are dependent on the planning and thinking of others and their suggestibility or conditionability is greatest when they are very young. Fourth, parents and members of the family group themselves have irrational tendencies, prejudices and superstitions which they inculcate into their children. Fifth, this process is exacerbated by the indoctrinations of the mass media. Lastly, cultures and religions can impart irrational, self-defeating and society-defeating views.

Choosing irrational cognitions

The process of acquiring irrationality is not simply a matter of reacting to how others behave. Humans largely create their own emotional disturbances through not developing and exercising their capacity for rational choice. Negative social learning experiences do not in themselves lead to people acquiring irrational cognitions. Many people who have had negative upbringings choose not to disturb themselves unduly. Still others, with or without support, work through their problems. The reverse is also true. Favourable social learning experiences do not in themselves lead to rational cognitions. Many people who have had favourable upbringings develop significant irrational beliefs. While social learning experiences influence people for good or ill, they still have the capacity to choose how they react to them. Ellis and Dryden conclude: 'Thus, the REBT theory of acquisition can be summed up by the view that as humans we are not disturbed simply by our experiences; rather we bring our ability to disturb ourselves to our experiences' (1997: 21).

Maintenance

Why do people persist in holding their irrational beliefs and their derivatives? People not only become irrational, they stay irrational. In fact, often they become even more irrational. Staying rational in an irrational world is a struggle. Once acquired, people tend to repeat their irrational beliefs again and again and again. Ellis continually stresses that people have strong tendencies to reindoctrinate themselves with their self-defeating ideas. People's irrational beliefs do not continue because they were once 'conditioned' and so now hold them 'automatically'. Instead, people still, here and now, actively reinforce them, and their present active self-propagandizations and constructions keep these beliefs alive (Ellis, 2005).

Reasons contributing to humans staying irrational

Following are some reasons that contribute to humans staying irrational, often at great personal cost to themselves, others and to society.

Biological tendencies

Humans' biological tendencies to irrationality do not go away with maturation, but are part of their life-long genetic inheritance. Ellis stresses that humans: 'are powerfully predisposed to unconsciously and habitually prolong their mental dysfunctioning and to fight like hell to give it up' (1987: 365). Rather than strike a realistic balance between short-range and long-range hedonism, humans mostly embrace short-range hedonism. This preference for the pleasures of the moment is a main source of resistance to change.

Emotional contributions

Absolutistic musts are often 'hot' cognitions that have a strong evaluative feeling component in them. Such cognitions are held strongly and powerfully and, as such, can be difficult to change. In addition, people then not only develop derivatives of their primary irrational beliefs, but also secondary irrational beliefs and their derivatives. As a result they raise the level of their emotionality and then may think even more irrationally. They may fail to see how upset they are. Furthermore, they are now so upset that they fail to test reality and dispute their irrational beliefs in ways that they might otherwise do. Instead of making people better, the consequences of irrational beliefs make them worse.

Insufficient scientific thinking

People continue to disturb themselves because they fail to think scientifically about what is going on in the world. To think scientifically people need constantly to observe and check the 'facts' so see the extent to which they are 'true' and whether or not they have changed. Scientific thinking is flexible and requires evidence to uphold or negate viewpoints. Also, the scientific method is sceptical that the universe has any absolute standards of 'good' and 'bad'. Science does not have absolute rules in regard to human behaviour.

Reinforcing consequences

People can emotionally, cognitively and behaviourally reinforce their irrational beliefs. Emotionally, absolutistic musturbatory beliefs lead to strong negative feelings – such as severe anger and depression – that make them seem true. Cognitively and behaviourally, people reinforce their beliefs in different ways according to the belief. For instance, people who must be socially approved avoid taking social risks, and by doing so, convince themselves that it is too difficult and dangerous to do otherwise. Furthermore, when avoiding social situations, they may feel a sense of emotional relief. The combination of their emotional, cognitive and behavioural reactions makes them more rather than less socially anxious.

Emphasizing one's 'Godawful' past

Ellis states as an REBT insight: 'Your early childhood experiences and your past conditioning did not originally make you disturbed. You did' (1988: 70). People maintain their emotional disturbance by looking for causes in their pasts. Focusing on the past interferes with people focusing on the present in which they still may be upsetting themselves with the same irrational beliefs with which they upset themselves in their pasts. People cannot undo their pasts, but they can change their presents and futures. Furthermore, often focusing on the past leads to an overemphasis not only on the past relative to the present, but also to an overemphasis on other people's behaviour relative to one's own.

Unrealistic beliefs about change

People's low frustration tolerance can be both cause and consequence of unrealistic beliefs about working to change, with or without professional assistance, their thoughts, feelings and actions. Irrational beliefs about change include (Ellis, 1987, 1993b):

- 'I must be able to change with little discomfort, work and practice on my part';
- 'Changing how I think, feel and behave shouldn't be so hard';
- 'I must change quickly and profoundly';
- 'When changing, I must not have any setbacks';
- 'Since I tried to change and failed to do so, I will settle for how I function now'.

Other cognitive factors
The following are some other factors and processes whereby people maintain and worsen their irrational beliefs and emotional disturbances (Ellis, 1987; Ellis and Dryden, 1997):

- *Naïvety*: People can have and hang on to hugely naïve personal theories about the nature of their psychological problems and how they are maintained.
- *Ignorance*: People, including therapists, can consider that it is statistically normal and healthy for them to be unnecessarily upset. They fail to distinguish between healthy and unhealthy thoughts, feelings and behaviours.
- *Stupidity*: Many people are too unintelligent to work effectively on their emotional problems. They fail to gain sufficient insight into the fact that they create their own disturbances.
- *Unperceptiveness*: Without therapy, many disturbed people rarely look at their irrational beliefs and ideas and how these create and drive their upset-ness. Even when pointed out to them in therapy, many disturbed people are still incapable of grasping how they upset themselves.
- *Rigidity*: Even when they acknowledge their self-defeating irrational beliefs, many people rigidly stick to their musturbatory beliefs and their derivatives, for instance awfulizing and I can't-stand-it-itis. Some such people may be psychotic or have borderline personality disorders, whereas others are simply rigid thinkers.
- *Defensiveness*: Humans are prone to avoid facing and dealing directly with their problems. They use various methods of distorting and denying problems, for instance rationalization and avoidance.
- *Pollyannaism and indifference*: Some people who are prone to extreme anxiety and suffer from a serious illness, such as heart disease or cancer, may deal with it by denying its seriousness. Sometimes, such defensive manoeuvres may help people to cope. However, on many occasions, such thinking may block efforts to attain physical health and psychological change.
- *Changing the situation*: For many, the easy way out is to change the situation, for instance, obtain a divorce, rather than try to change themselves and then consider whether or not to change the situation. For every neurotic who really tries to have a fundamental shift in the way they think, there are

probably ten times as many trying to *feel* better by changing the situations in which they behave self-defeatingly rather than to *get* better. This ratio holds true whether or not people come for therapy.

- *Other palliative means*: People and their would-be helpers resort to many palliative means to dealing with emotional disturbances rather than get to the root of them. Many clients and potential clients use distraction techniques such as progressive relaxation, biofeedback, meditation and yoga. Some try superficial positive thinking. Many people lose themselves in political, religious and mystical cults. Short-term feel-good remedies like alcohol and drugs are very common. In brief, many disturbed people seek low-level and palliative remedies rather than more rigorous and long-lasting solutions.

Insufficiently challenging beliefs through action

People may reinforce their beliefs through unwillingness to change their actions. Their 'tried and true' self-defeating ways may bring short-term relief at the expense of long-term gain. An Ellis insight is: 'You can change irrational beliefs (iB's) by acting against them: by performing behaviours that contradict them' (Ellis, 1988: 109). Why then don't people change their actions to challenge their beliefs? One reason is that they may not have insight into their irrational beliefs, their derivatives, and their emotional and behavioural consequences. Another reason is that people resist the risk and effort involved in taking action. Some people may not be clear on what to do. Still others may know what to do, but lack the skills, confidence and support to do it. Another category is people who change their actions, but lack the staying power to maintain them, especially when faced with difficulties and setbacks. Such people suffer from low frustration tolerance.

Therapy

Therapeutic goals

Earlier in this chapter, I presented Ellis's GABCDE outline. There are two meanings to E depending on whether the change goals of REBT are inelegant or elegant.

Inelegant change goals

Ellis writes: 'Inelegant change largely consists of some kind of symptom removal' (1980: 13). Here, at D, REBT targets the cognitions, emotions and behaviours that accompany self-defeating feelings, like anxiety and depression, and dysfunctional behaviours, like avoiding social and public speaking situations. The goal of focused or inelegant REBT is that of focused or inelegant change. Here the letter E stands for an effective new philosophy focused on one or more specific symptoms or problems. Effectiveness in relation to these symptoms can be cognitive (similar to rational beliefs), emotional (healthy feelings) and behavioural (desirable behaviours).

Elegant change goals

In contrast to inelegant change, elegant change involves clients with disturbances making 'a profound ideational and philosophic change – which means that it tries to help them acquire several core attitudes that they can use to undisturb themselves in a large variety of situations, and not merely with the emotional-behavioral problem with which they mainly came to psychotherapy' (Ellis, 2003a: 233). In elegant change, E goes further than an effective new philosophy that supports the removal of specific symptoms to assisting clients to develop and implement an effective philosophy of life. Ellis writes: 'To do this, clients need to acknowledge how often and how strongly they escalate their healthy goals, desires, and preferences into arrogant and grandiose *must*-urbation – and apply themselves to anti-*must*urbatory thinking' (1997c: 337, emphasis in original). Thus E stands for the goal of effective new philosophies for specific symptoms in inelegant REBT and for the goal of an effective philosophy of life (which includes effective new philosophies for specific symptoms) in elegant REBT.

As part of teaching anti-musturbatory thinking, Ellis (1999a, 2003a) actively encourages practically all his clients to achieve three highly important cognitive-emotional-behavioural states or goals:

- *Unconditional self-acceptance (USA)*: Clients can always choose to accept themselves just because they are alive and human, whether or not they perform well or are approved of by others.
- *Unconditional other acceptance (UOA)*: Whatever other people do and however abominably they act, clients can choose to accept the sinner, though not their sins, to try to help them behave better, and to refuse to damn them as people.
- *Unconditional life acceptance (ULA)*: Otherwise known as high-frustration tolerance (HFT), unconditional life acceptance means that clients can choose to acknowledge that their desires are not needs, adversities are not awful but can be highly inconvenient, they can stand what they do not like, and 'long-range hedonism, or striving for today's pleasures, without neglecting tomorrow's, will often get them more of what they want and less of what they dislike' (Ellis, 1999a: 39).

Process of therapy

Right from the start, therapists show clients that REBT is an active-directive structured therapy focusing on helping clients not only to feel better, but by changing their thinking and behaviour, to get better. Orientation or induction can be by way of pre-therapy demonstrations, brief explanatory lectures at the start of therapy, and using clients' problem material to illustrate the application of REBT (Ellis and Dryden, 1997).

Before commencing therapy some REBT therapists like clients to fill out a basic biographical information form that also elicits information about their presenting problems (Ellis and Dryden, 1997: 88–95). In addition, therapists may ask clients to fill out a personality data form which asks clients questions about their feelings in the following areas: acceptance, frustration, injustice, achievement, worth, control, certainty and catastrophizing (1997: 36–9).

Clients are encouraged to focus on specific problems right from the start. Early in therapy Ellis frequently reads out the client's answer to item 23 in the biographical information questionnaire which asks: 'Briefly list (PRINT) your present main complaints, symptoms and problems'. Then clients are asked to discuss what problem is most bothersome. Probably the main form of assessment in REBT is that which comes from having a number of sessions with clients and working with the material that they share. Towards the end of the initial phase of REBT, both therapist and client should have an understanding of the client's main emotional and behavioural problems and have started to prioritize these to provide a structure for their future work together.

The middle phase of REBT is focused on therapists adopting an educational approach to teaching clients how to strengthen their rational beliefs and weaken the irrational ones. This phase of REBT has two main agendas: helping clients solve their particular emotional and behavioural problems and teaching them the skills of identifying and solving problems. In general, in addition to focusing on what clients have been most bothered about during the previous week, therapists encourage them to work through a consistent problem before moving on to the next. Homework tasks are assigned and particular attention is paid to what the client has learned or failed to learn between sessions so that blocks to the learning process can be addressed. Frequently, clients are asked to fill out REBT self-help forms as part of homework assignments. Hard and persistent challenging of irrational beliefs tends to be a prominent feature of the middle phase. REBT 'realistically and unromantically now says: Yes, strongly persuade and push your clients to strongly persuade themselves in the direction of their main goals and preferences and against sabotaging their own purposes' (Ellis, 2003a: 238).

The main object of the end phase of REBT is to help clients become their own therapists. Termination may take place not when clients have worked through all their problems using REBT skills, but when they feel confident that they can use these skills to address the remaining problems on their own. Therapists work towards termination either by decreasing the frequency of sessions or by negotiating a specific termination date. During the end phase, therapists can work with clients to anticipate problems and difficulties and articulate how they might use their REBT skills to deal with these problems. Most REBT therapists schedule follow-up sessions to monitor client progress.

REBT is committed to assisting clients to maintain their changes. However, Ellis (1988) acknowledges the likelihood of backsliding. Right from the start, clients are taught that they can only change and maintain change with work and practice. Throughout therapy, homework assignments are used to help clients build skills for both outside and after therapy. When clients find themselves backsliding, they are told to go back to the ABCs and see what they did to fall back into their old patterns. Then they are encouraged to forcefully dispute (D) these irrational beliefs. They are advised to try again and again until they genuinely replace their irrational beliefs with their effective new philosophies (E).

Most often therapists see clients for weekly individual sessions. Ellis's own therapy sessions often last for 30 minutes. Clients normally have five to 50 sessions. Brief therapy of one to 10 sessions is used for clients who have specific problems or for those only prepared to stay in therapy for a short time (Ellis, 1996). Individuals who are not too generally disturbed can usually attain the inelegant change of symptom removal in brief therapy. Preferably, individuals with severe problems should come for individual and/or group therapy for at least six months so that they can practise what they learn.

REBT can be used with most kinds of clients, ranging from those who are mildly disturbed to juvenile delinquents, borderline personality disorders, psychotics when they have some contact with reality and individuals with higher-grade mental deficiency. Normally, Ellis does not consider REBT suitable for clients who are out of contact with reality, in a highly manic state, seriously autistic or brain injured, and in the lower ranges of mental deficiency. Seriously disturbed clients are often referred for medication in addition to REBT.

REBT is significantly more effective with mildly disturbed clients and with those who have a single major symptom, say sexual inadequacy, than with strongly disturbed clients. Therapists find it much more difficult to assist the latter to change since REBT theory hypothesizes that the causes of musturbatory thinking and emotional disturbance are largely innate.

The therapeutic relationship

In REBT, the main role of the therapist is that of an authoritative, but not authoritarian, teacher who strives to impart to clients self-helping skills conducive to thinking rationally, feeling appropriately and behaving effectively so that they can attain their goals. REBT practitioners often employ a fairly rapid-fire active-directive-persuasive-philosophic methodology. In most instances, they quickly pin clients down to a few basic dysfunctional beliefs (Ellis, 2005).

What kind of a therapeutic relationship best supports this active-directive teaching role? Therapists try to build rapport with clients by using empathic listening, including reflecting feelings. Ellis and Dryden (1997) distinguish between *affective* empathy – understanding how clients feel – and *philosophic* empathy – understanding the philosophies or thinking underlying these feelings. Therapists attempt to offer both kinds of empathy. In addition, therapists offer clients unconditional other acceptance (UOA), accepting them as fallible human beings and not judging the goodness or badness of their personhood against predetermined moral standards. However, frequently, if appropriate, therapists will share their reactions to clients' negative behaviours.

REBT therapists do not show undue warmth to most of their clients. They are wary of colluding in clients' dire needs for approval. They try to encourage clients to confront their own problems and assume responsibility for finding their own warmth and happiness rather than seeking it from therapists. Often clients perceive REBT therapists as warm and caring because of their commitment to their welfare and tolerance for all individuals.

Particularly during early sessions, therapists do most of the talking. They do not hesitate to confront clients with how they contribute to their own distress. They forcefully dispute and debate their clients' illogical thinking as well as helping clients to do this for themselves. They freely share their opinions and self-disclose, so long as this is not detrimental to clients. Furthermore they use humour, but never at their clients' expense, since they consider that many of them take themselves and their problems far too seriously. Therapists also use humour to attack disturbance-producing ideas.

A distinction exists between REBT content and the therapist's style of working with clients. Ellis's therapeutic style, like that of many of his followers, is hard-hitting and forceful. However, Ellis may well go more slowly and gently before doing any vigorous disputing when working with clients who have suffered from extreme traumas, such as rape or child abuse. Other REBT practitioners, either with specific clients or with all of their clients, choose varying degrees of passive and gentle styles.

Therapeutic interventions

Detecting irrational beliefs and their derivatives

Therapists as teachers detect clients' irrational beliefs, their musturbations, and their derivatives, for instance awfulizing. Furthermore, they teach clients how to do this for themselves. In order to relinquish demandingness, it helps if clients can acknowledge that they may possess this characteristic. Ellis teaches them his ABC system. Within the ABC system, irrational beliefs can be traced cognitively, emotionally and behaviourally. Cognitively, irrational beliefs can be detected through overt or implicit signs of demandingness. In particular, Ellis looks for 'musts', 'shoulds', 'oughts', 'have tos' and 'got tos' that signal clients' musturbatory absolutistic beliefs. In addition, he looks for explicit and implicit phrases such as 'That is horrible!' and 'I can't stand it' that indicate derivatives of possessing primary and secondary irrational beliefs.

Emotionally, irrational beliefs are signalled by unhealthy feelings, such as panic and depression. Behaviourally, self-defeating actions offer clues to irrational beliefs. Sometimes the cognitive, emotional and behavioural clues are obvious to both therapists and clients. On other occasions, though obvious to therapists, clients may resist acknowledging the evidence. In still other instances clients may hold irrational beliefs in subtle and tricky ways that make them seem natural (Ellis, 1987). Such beliefs can challenge therapists' powers of detection.

Disputing irrational beliefs and their derivatives

It is insufficient for musts and their derivatives to disappear just to acknowledge them. Instead, therapists and clients combine to fight them by disputing them. The technique of disputing is the most typical and perhaps the most often used method of REBT. Disputing involves challenging and questioning unsubstantiated hypotheses that clients hold about themselves, others and the world. In most instances, REBT therapists quickly pin clients down to a few central irrational ideas and their derivatives that they then challenge and dispute. In addition, they teach clients how to dispute their own beliefs. Cognitions, feelings and behaviours interact in how people create and maintain irrational beliefs. Therefore, when disputing irrational beliefs and their derivatives, therapists are likely to be more effective if they work in all three of the cognitive, emotional/experiential and behavioural modalities rather than in one or two. However, no modality is entirely pure or free from the others.

Cognitive interventions

Scientific questioning

Disputing may be approached using either a didactic or a Socratic style. In a didactic or lecturing style, therapists can provide explanations and illustrations. In a Socratic or scientific questioning approach, through a series of leading questions therapists attempt to pinpoint where clients' thinking, feeling and behaving is becoming problematic. Such questions are not only for therapists to ask clients, but for clients to learn to ask themselves. When practising disputing, it is very important that clients do so outside of stressful situations to give them the chance to build up and fine-tune their skills for the actual situations.

Box 12.3 illustrates four areas of cognitive disputing (Ellis and MacLaren, 2004).

Box 12.3   Four areas of cognitive disputing

Functional disputes
Functional disputing aims to point out to clients that their beliefs may be interfering with their attaining their goals. Typical questions are:

- 'Is it helping you?'
- 'How is continuing to think this way (or behave, or feel this way) affecting your life?'

Box 12.3   (Continued)

Empirical disputes
Empirical disputing aims to help clients evaluate the factual components of their beliefs. Typical questions are:

- 'Where is the evidence that you must succeed at all important tasks?'
- 'Where is the proof that it is accurate?'
- 'Where is it written?'

Logical disputes
Logical disputing aims to highlight illogical leaps that clients make from desires and preferences to demands when thinking irrationally. Typical questions are:

- 'How does it follow that just because you'd like this thing to be true and it would be very convenient, it *should* be?'
- 'How is it logical that because you sometimes *act* badly that makes you a *bad person*?'

Philosophical disputes
Philosophical disputing aims to address the meaning of and satisfaction in life issues. Often clients get so focused on identified problems that they lose perspective on other areas of life. A typical question might be:

- 'Despite the fact that things will probably not go the way you want some/most of the time in this area, can you still derive some satisfaction from your life?'

The desired cognitive outcome of disputing specific irrational beliefs and their derivatives is a sound set of preferential beliefs or effective new philosophies (E) related to each belief. Desirable emotional and behavioural effects should stem from and interact with the effective new philosophies. For clients seeking elegant change, the desirable effect of learning how to dispute irrational beliefs is an Effective New Philosophy that can be applied both now and in the future. Box 12.4 provides an ABCDE example, which includes disputing and its effects (Ellis, 1988).

Box 12.4   An ABCDE example of cognitive disputing

A   • I go for an interview and fail to get the job.
iB • 'I must never get rejected'
     • 'How awful to get rejected!'
     • 'I can't stand the rejection!'

(Continued)

Box 12.4   (Continued)

- 'This rejection makes me a rotten person'
- 'I'll always do poorly in job interviews'

C
- Undesirable emotional consequences: depression, worthlessness, anxiety, anger.
- Undesirable behavioural consequences: Refusing to go for other job interviews. Functioning poorly on job interviews through anxiety.

D
- 'Why must I never get rejected?'
- 'Why is it awful to get rejected for a job?'
- 'Why can't I stand this rejection?'
- 'How does this rejection make me a rotten person?'
- 'Why must I always do poorly on job interviews?'

E
- 'I'd prefer to have got this job, but there is no evidence that I absolutely must have it.'
- 'Nothing makes it awful to get rejected, though I find it highly inconvenient'
- 'I can stand rejection, though I'll never like it'
- 'Rejection never makes me a rotten person, but a person with some unfortunate traits'
- 'I don't always have to do poorly on job interviews, especially if I try to learn from my errors'
- Illustrative emotional effect: feeling sorrowful, but not depressed.
- Illustrative behavioural effect: I went for some more job interviews.

Rational coping statements

Therapist and client can formulate rational coping statements. This step is usually taken after forceful disputing of irrational beliefs, but sometimes it can accompany such disputing. Some coping statements can be simple encouragements: for instance, 'I can accomplish this task' or 'I don't have to get upset in these situations'. Rational coping statements can also address areas of irrational thinking: for example, statements such as 'I'd prefer to have got this job, but there is no evidence that I absolutely must have it' and 'Nothing makes it awful to get rejected, though I find it highly inconvenient' illustrated in area E of Box 12.4.

Discussion

Therapists can discuss with clients various aspects of their irrational thinking. For instance, with Roger, a 24-year-old computer programmer afraid of public speaking, Ellis (1991e) discussed the harm of self-rating and how he could choose to unconditionally accept himself whether or not he failed at speaking and whether or not he was anxious about failing and showed his anxiety to others.

Cognitive homework

Clients need repeatedly to challenge their irrational beliefs and to practise their disputing skills both to learn them and also to reinforce their new rational philosophies. REBT uses various homework techniques to develop disputing skills:

- *Cassettes of sessions*: Therapists encourage clients to record sessions and listen to each one several times.
- *Self-help forms*: Clients are encouraged to fill out self-help forms. Therapists check the forms to see how accurately clients dispute their irrational beliefs. For instance in Sichel and Ellis's (1984) form, clients identify an activating event (A) and the consequences or conditions (C) they would like to change. Then the form consists of three columns. In the first column, clients circle which of 13 irrational beliefs (B) – for instance 'I MUST do well or very well!' and 'People MUST live up to my expectations or it is TERRIBLE!' – lead to their consequences (C). In addition, they can add other relevant irrational beliefs. In the second column, there is space for them to dispute (D) each circled irrational belief. In the third column, they write in effective rational beliefs (E) to replace their irrational beliefs. After the columns there is a space (F) where they can write in the feelings and behaviours experienced after arriving at their effective rational beliefs. The form ends with the following self-statement about the necessity of work and practice: 'I WILL WORK HARD TO REPEAT MY EFFECTIVE RATIONAL BELIEFS FORCEFULLY TO MYSELF ON MANY OCCASIONS SO THAT I CAN MAKE MYSELF LESS DISTURBED NOW AND ACT LESS SELF-DEFEATINGLY IN THE FUTURE' (Sichel and Ellis, 1984: 2).

  Another self-help form is known as DIBS (Disputing Irrational Beliefs). DIBS consists of six questions about: the belief I want to dispute; whether the belief can be rationally supported; existing evidence for the belief; existing evidence against the belief; the worst that could happen to me if I never achieved what I wanted in respect to the belief; and good things that might happen if I never achieved what I wanted (Dryden and Ellis, 1986). A further self-help form is Dryden and colleagues' written self-help form that takes clients through the ABCDE sequence (Dryden et al., 1992; Ellis and Dryden, 1997).
- *Reminder cards*: Clients can write out rational coping statements on 3" × 5" cards and repeat them at various times between sessions.
- *Referenting*: Referenting is a term for asking clients to do a cost–benefit analysis in which they list the real advantages and disadvantages of changing their irrational thoughts and behaviours.
- *Practising REBT on others*: Encouraging clients to practise talking their friends and relatives out of their disturbances.
- *Visualizing*: Clients can be shown how to visualize themselves competently performing situations that they currently fear.

- *Bibliotherapy*: Assigning clients self-help books to read, for instance Ellis (1999b, 2003b), Ellis and Crawford (2000) and Ellis and Harper (1997). Ellis (1993d) is keenly aware of the advantages and disadvantages of self-help materials.
- *Self-help cassettes*: Ellis has made innumerable audio-cassettes, including *Solving Emotional Problems* (1982), *How to be Happy Though Human* (1984) and *How to Stop Worrying and Start Living* (1987). In addition, clients can watch videotapes of therapists working with clients in areas such as coping with anger and overcoming low frustration tolerance. Many clients find listening to cassettes and observing videotapes to be helpful.

Problem solving

Clients bring their goals (G) to the activating events and adversities (A) in their lives. These goals present many practical or reality problems for them to try to solve: for instance, obtaining a good education, finding a mate, getting a job and succeeding at work. Clients have a choice about whether they solve these reality problems or choose to upset themselves about them. If clients upset themselves, then they have an emotional problem about their reality problem. In such cases, therapists can assist them to detect and actively dispute the relevant irrational beliefs. Sometimes it is better that clients do not address practical difficulties until they have worked through related emotional difficulties. For instance, an individual or couple might defer a decision to divorce until they have given themselves sufficient chance to see whether or not, with a lessening of their irrational beliefs, they might happily live together.

Therapists willingly assist clients to solve reality problems. However, where necessary, they also insist on vigorously detecting and disputing accompanying irrational beliefs. In assisting problem solving, therapists help clients to state problems and goals clearly, generate and evaluate alternative strategies, outline the steps to attain goals, identify resources and supports, and develop the requisite practical skills for success.

Emotive/experiential interventions

REBT therapists use emotional/experiential interventions to supplement and reinforce cognitive interventions (Ellis and MacLaren, 2004). Such interventions include the following:

- *Rational emotive imagery*: In rational emotive imagery (REI), clients are encouraged to imagine one of the worst activating event or adversity (A) that could happen to them, for instance, rejection by someone whose approval they really want (Ellis, 1993f; Ellis and MacLaren, 2004). They vividly imagine this adversity occurring and bringing a host of problems into their life.

  Then they are encouraged to get in touch with the undesirable negative emotional consequence triggered by this adversity (A) – for instance, anxiety, depression, rage, self-hatred or self-pity – and really, really feel it (C1). They should spontaneously feel what they feel and not what they are supposed to feel. Once they feel unhealthily upset at C1, they should hold on to this feeling for a minute or two. Then, keeping the same adversity (A) in their imagination, they should work on changing their disturbed negative feeling to a prescribed healthy negative feeling consequence (C2), such as sorrow, disappointment, regret, frustration, irritation or displeasure. The way to do this is by telling themselves strongly and repetitively sensible rational beliefs or coping statements, for example, 'Yes, they really did treat me shabbily and unfairly, which I wish they wouldn't have done. But there is no reason why they must treat me fairly, however *preferable* that would be' (Ellis, 1993f: 9). Clients should persist with their imagery and rational statements until they change their unhealthy feeling (C1) to a healthy negative feeling (C2) – it usually takes only a few minutes. They should have the homework assignment of carrying out this imagery procedure daily for about 30 days for each disturbed feeling they are trying to change.

- *Forceful disputing*: Forceful disputing may be performed both by therapists on clients and by clients on themselves (Ellis, 1993e). Since many irrational beliefs involve hot cognitions that possess a large emotional component, they require forceful and vigorous disputing. Often therapists need to strongly argue, persuade and point out the shaky logic of their clients' beliefs. Weak or moderately strong disputing may be insufficient. Ellis showed Roger, the computer programmer, how to create strong anti-worrying statements about public speaking and say them to himself forcefully, for example, 'I NEVER, NEVER, NEVER have to speak well or unnervously in public, though it would be nice if I did!' (Ellis, 1991e: 454). In addition, Ellis worked out with Roger a dialogue with himself in which he cassette-recorded some of his potent irrational beliefs, such as 'I'm a nervous slob who deserves to be mute rather than risk making a fool of myself in public!' and in which he vigorously, forcefully and heatedly disputed them. Clients can make, and remake more powerfully, such recordings for themselves as homework. Then they can play them back to themselves, their therapists and, if in therapy groups, to the other group members.

- *Role playing*: Ellis uses role playing as a way of showing clients what their false ideas are and how they affect relating to others. In role playing, therapists place clients in simulated situations and offer assistance in thinking more effectively in them. For instance, Roger role played giving a difficult talk in front of Ellis and the therapy group he had joined as an adjunct to individual sessions. When Roger appeared anxious during the role play, Ellis stopped the performance to let Roger ask himself: 'What am I telling myself right now to *make* myself anxious? And what can I do right now to think and feel away this anxiety?' (Ellis, 1991e: 454).

- *Reverse role playing*: Reverse role playing is another REBT forceful disputing technique. Client and therapist switch roles, so clients are now in a position to dispute actively their own irrational beliefs, which the therapist holds on to as strongly as the client did in earlier sessions. For example, Ellis (1993e) role-played Roger tenaciously holding on to some of his irrational beliefs so that Roger could practise forcefully attacking them.

- *Unconditional acceptance*: The therapist's basic acceptance of them as people helps clients feel and think that they are acceptable, despite any negative characteristics.
- *Humour*: The judicious use of humour can help reduce clients' irrational beliefs and self-defeating behaviours to absurdity. Therapists frequently exaggerate clients' nutty ideas and use 'various kinds of puns, witticisms, irony, whimsy, evocative language, slang, and deliberate use of sprightly obscenity' (Ellis, 1980: 26). For example, Ellis said to Roger, his public-speaking phobic client: 'You really should feel ashamed of avoiding making speeches. Every other person your age speaks fluently and has no anxiety. What a unique jerk you are!' (Ellis, 1991e: 454). Encouraging clients to sing to themselves rational humorous songs and telling amusing anecdotes are further methods to counteract clients' tendencies to take themselves, others and the world too seriously.

Behavioural interventions

As with emotional/experiential interventions, REBT therapists use behavioural interventions to supplement and reinforce cognitive interventions. Ellis doubts whether people ever truly change their irrational beliefs until they act many times against them. When young, Ellis suffered from severe fears of public speaking and meeting new women. He forced himself to repetitively engage in activities, giving political talks and talking to women on a park bench in the Bronx Botanical Garden, that challenged his fears. In both instances his actions helped rid him of his irrational fears (Ellis, 1997a, 2004a). Following are some REBT behavioural interventions.

- *Assignments that challenge demandingness*: Clients who have musturbatory beliefs about approval and derivatives of these beliefs about the awfulness of rejection may be encouraged to ask someone for a date or force themselves to socialize. Simultaneously they convince themselves that it is not awful, but only inconvenient to get rejected. Clients who have perfectionist beliefs may have the assignment of deliberately making a real attempt to speak badly in public.

  Clients are encouraged to do their assignments *repetitively*. For instance, Roger, the speech-anxious client, was asked to speak in public as often as he could, once or twice a week (Ellis, 1991e). Often clients are asked to do their assignments *floodingly*, staying in situations they perceive as highly dangerous until they see that their 'danger' is largely imagined. For instance, clients afraid of riding on buses or underground trains are urged to do this immediately, many times a day in rush hours, if that is what they most fear. Concurrently, in all instances where clients dispute their musturbatory beliefs behaviourally, they can dispute them cognitively too.

- *Shame-attacking exercises*: Ellis hypothesizes that ego anxiety is highly related to feelings of shame, guilt, embarrassment and humiliation. Consequently, the more people confront the irrational beliefs behind these feelings, the less they are likely to disturb themselves. Clients are encouraged to do things in public that they regard as particularly shameful or embarrassing. Examples are yelling out the stops on elevators, buses or underground trains or asking for sex-related items in loud voices in chemist shops.

  After explaining the principle of shame-attacking exercises, REBT therapists can negotiate exercises with clients. The purpose of these exercises is to prove that these behaviours in themselves are really not shameful and that they can be done with relative comfort and self-acceptance. In addition, clients are urged to disclose more about what they perceive, or what they perceive others perceive, as shameful. Box 12.5 provides an example of a shame-attacking exercise (Ellis, 1996: 91–4).

- *Skill training*: The distinction between behavioural skills and cognitive skills is imprecise. Always, when therapists assist clients with behavioural skills – for instance assertion and communication skills – they train clients cognitively in disputing the accompanying irrational beliefs and derivative self-statements. Sometimes clients are asked to seek additional training experiences to acquire relevant skills. For instance, Ellis thought that speech-anxious Roger showed insufficient assertion skills at work, for instance not refusing to do presentations when genuinely unprepared. Ellis (1991e) encouraged Roger to attend a six-week assertion course at his Institute as well as take a five-month public speaking course at a local college.

- *Use of rewards and penalties*: REBT therapists use rewards and penalties to encourage clients to do homework and implement self-change programmes (Ellis, 1980; Ellis and Dryden, 1997). For instance, every time Roger filled out an RET Self-Help Report or gave a public speech, he would reward himself by listening to one of his favourite CDs. Whenever he failed to carry out an assignment he would talk to his boring aunt for 30 minutes. Two doses of this excruciating penalty cured Roger of not doing assignments (Ellis, 1991e)!

Box 12.5   Example of a shame-attacking exercise

The therapist
Albert Ellis

The client
Chana, who was anxious about test-taking, kept procrastinating on her studies and refused to take some important subjects at school because she knew that taking them would entail several tests during the term. Chana was afraid of people finding out how poorly she did on tests.

(Continued)

Box 12.5   (Continued)

The shame-attacking exercise
Chana chose the exercise of asking strangers for a dollar bill. Ellis instructed Chana, when asking strangers for dollar bills, to work on possible feelings of humiliation and embarrassment and then choose not to make herself feel unashamed and unembarrassed.

During the exercise
At first Chana felt very nervous and tongue-tied about going up to a stranger. However, she reminded herself that she did not need the stranger's approval and, by the third time she tried it, she really began to feel shameless and, by the fifth time, started enjoying the exercise.

After the exercise
As a result of the exercise Chana saw that she could do shame-attacking exercises with people who knew her in which she talked about her test-taking problems. As part of this process, Chana developed the Effective New Philosophy: 'I don't need their goddamned approval. Let them think what they think!'

Overcoming resistance

When clients resist following therapy procedures and doing homework assignments, they mainly do so because of the following irrational beliefs (Ellis, 1986a): (a) 'I *must* do well at changing myself'; (b) 'You (the therapist and others) *must* help me change'; and (c) 'Changing myself *must* occur quickly and easily'. Stemming from such beliefs (iB), resisters have negative feelings consequences, for instance depression self-pity, and behavioural consequences, such as procrastination and withdrawal. In addition, they employ derivatives of irrational beliefs, such as awfulizing. The main REBT approach to resistant clients is to teach them to find and forcefully dispute the main irrational beliefs contributing to their resistance.

Therapists can encourage resistant clients to use rational coping statements, for instance 'Therapy doesn't have to be easy. I can, in fact, enjoy its difficulty and its challenge' (Ellis, 1986a: 262). In addition, therapists can ask clients to list the disadvantages of resisting and the advantages of working at therapy and then regularly reviewing and thinking about these lists. Furthermore, some resistant clients can be helped by proselytizing REBT and using it on friends and relatives.

Case material

Ellis has been conscientious about providing case demonstrations of REBT in action, only some of which are mentioned here. Ellis (1971) presents a case example containing verbatim transcripts of the first, second and fourth sessions with a woman who comes to therapy because she is self-punishing, impulsive and compulsive, afraid of males, has no goals in life, and is guilty about her relationship with her parents (see also Wedding and Corsini, 2005).

Ellis (1996) provides verbatim transcript, plus commentary, of his conducting a first session of REBT brief therapy with Ted, a 38-year-old African-American, married 20 years, with two children who became panicked whenever he took the train to work or back to his office and whenever he thought about having intercourse with his wife. Another verbatim transcript case example is that of the first 15 minutes of an initial interview Ellis (2005) conducted with a 25-year-old single woman, Sara, who worked as the head of a computer programming section in her firm and who, without any traumatic or violent history, was very insecure and self-denigrating. Ellis also discusses Sara's overall treatment of a further six sessions of individual work, followed by 24 weeks of REBT group therapy and one weekend of a rational encounter marathon group.

A further verbatim transcript case example is that of Ellis working with a woman therapist who volunteers to bring up problems of feeling inadequate as a therapist and as a person. Ellis and Dryden (1997) then review the transcript and analyse its REBT aspects. In yet another case example of REBT, though this time without transcripts, Ellis illustrates the cognitive, emotive and behavioural methods he used during therapy with Jane, a 27-year-old woman afflicted with severe social and work anxiety (Ellis and Dryden, 1997).

Ellis may also be seen conducting therapy. An early example is his work with Gloria in the *Three Approaches to Psychotherapy* film series (Ellis, 1965). In addition, videos of Ellis and other prominent REBT therapists conducting sessions are available from the Albert Ellis Institute (address and website at end of chapter). For example, Ellis has made a videotape in which he conducts therapy with a woman dealing with guilt over her husband's suicide. In another videotape, entitled *Dealing with Addictions*, Ellis interviews a 32-year-old man with low frustration tolerance, short-term hedonism and polyabuse.

Further developments

Other applications of REBT include group therapy and marathons either along with individual counselling or instead of it (Ellis, 1992; Ellis and Dryden, 1997). In group REBT, members are taught to apply detecting and disputing irrational beliefs on one another (Ellis, 2005). They also get practice at attacking their ego disturbance irrational beliefs through disclosing material that they perceive as risky. In addition clients in groups, while working on assertion and other communication skills, can partake in role plays.

Ellis (1986b, 1991c, 1991d, 1993c, 2005; Ellis and Crawford, 2000; Ellis and Dryden, 1997) has a major interest in the application of REBT to marital, couples and family relationship problems. Therapists usually see marital or love partners together, listen to their complaints, and then teach them that even though their complaints may accurately describe behaviour at A, their upset-ness at C is not justified. In particular, work focuses on musturbatory beliefs generating hostility. Also, frequently, therapists teach partners compromising and relationship skills. In family REBT, tolerance for oneself and others, inde-pendent of how obnoxious specific behaviours may be, is repeatedly taught to both parents and children.

Ellis is possibly the most influential English-speaking psychological educa-tor of the 20th and early 21st century in terms of helping ordinary people learn how to overcome their emotional disturbances and become more self-actualizing. Through his books and cassettes, he has made a major contribu-tion to educating the public in America and elsewhere on how to live more effectively. Also, he has influenced numerous other writers of self-help books. A fairly recent public education application of REBT has been the develop-ment of nine-hour intensive workshops (Ellis and Dryden, 1997).

REBT is practised widely throughout the world, with institutes or centres established in Britain, Australia, the United States, France, Germany, Holland, Italy, India, Israel and Mexico. Ellis (2005) concludes that REBT is what its name implies: rational and emotive, realistic and visionary, empirical and humanistic. Such an approach befits humans in all their complexity.

Review and personal questions

Review questions

1. Why does Ellis now call his approach rational emotive behaviour therapy?
2. Describe the differences between healthy or appropriate and unhealthy or inappropriate emotions.
3. What does Ellis consider to be the biological basis of personality?
4. Give an example of Ellis's ABC theory where B represents

   (a) demanding musturbatory thinking;
   (b) preferential thinking.

5. Critically discuss Ellis's ideas about the derivatives of irrational beliefs.
6. Discuss the roles of social learning and free choice in acquiring irrational beliefs.
7. Describe the contribution of each of the following factors to maintaining, and possibly strengthening, irrational beliefs:

   (a) biological tendencies;
   (b) emotional contributions;
   (c) insufficient scientific thinking;

    (d)   reinforcing consequences;

    (e)   emphasizing one's 'Godawful' past;

    (f)   unrealistic beliefs about change;

    (g)   insufficiently challenging beliefs through action.

8. What are the differences between inelegant and elegant therapy goals?

9. Outline the process of REBT individual therapy.

10. What is the nature of the therapist–client relationship in REBT?

11. Give at least one example of each of the following ways of disputing irrational beliefs: functional, empirical, logical and philosophical. Apart from scientific questioning, what other cognitive interventions do REBT therapists use?

12. Describe emotional/experiential interventions used in REBT.

13. Describe behavioural interventions used in REBT.

14. Critically discuss the issue of overcoming resistance in REBT.

Personal questions

1. Identify at least two of your irrational beliefs based on absolutistic demanding thinking in relation to each of the following:

    (a)   yourself;

    (b)   others;

    (c)   the conditions under which you live.

2. For one of the irrational beliefs you identified above state:

    (a)   how you acquired it;

    (b)   how you maintain it.

3. From your own life, give an example of each of the following:

    (a)   the ABCs of rational thinking;

    (b)   the ABCs of irrational thinking.

4. Choose one of your irrational beliefs (B) that you wish to change. How could you dispute (D) it by:

    (a)   cognitive methods;

    (b)   emotive/experiential methods;

    (c)   behavioural methods.

What new effective new philosophy (E) would you arrive at?

5. What relevance, if any, has the theory and practice of rational emotive behaviour therapy for how you conduct therapy?

6. What relevance, if any, has the theory and practice of rational emotive behaviour therapy for how you live?

Annotated bibliography

Ellis, A. and Dryden, W. (1997) *The Practice of Rational Emotive Behaviour Therapy*. London: Free Association Books and New York: Springer.
This book presents the general theory and basic practice of rational emotive behaviour therapy (REBT), with special chapters on how it is used in individual, couples, family, group, marathon, and sex therapy. This book gives details of many REBT procedures.

Ellis, A. and MacLaren, C. (2004) *Rational Emotive Behavior Therapy: A Therapist's Guide* (rev. edn). Atascadero, CA: Impact.
Practical and accessible, this REBT therapist guide includes chapters on the philosophical and personality theory foundations of REBT, its theory of personality disturbance and change, assessment, cognitive techniques, emotive/experiential techniques, behavioural techniques and the integration of REBT with other systems of therapy.

Ellis, A. (2005) 'Rational emotive behavior therapy', in R.J. Corsini and D. Wedding (eds), *Current Psychotherapies* (7th edn). Belmont, CA: Thomson Brooks/Cole. pp. 166–201.
An authoritative overview of the theory and practice of rational emotive behaviour therapy written by its originator.

Ellis, A. and Harper, R.A. (1997) *A Guide to Rational Living*. North Hollywood, CA: Wilshire Books.
This is a completely revised and rewritten version of the REBT self-help classic that is often recommended by cognitive-behaviour therapists to clients. The book is a succinct, straight-forward approach to REBT based on self-questioning and homework and shows how readers can help themselves with various emotional problems.

Ellis, A. (1999b) *How to Make Yourself Happy and Remarkably Less Disturbable*. Atascadero, CA: Impact.
Every therapist is at risk of crooked thinking. An excellent way to learn about REBT is to apply it to yourself. This entertaining self-help book presents Ellis's views on emotional disturbance and on the importance of scientific thinking. Readers are then presented with a series of chapters showing them in simple language 'how to' take and maintain more control of their thoughts, feelings and actions.

Dryden, W. (1999) *Rational Emotive Behaviour Counselling in Action* (2nd edn). London: Sage.
This introductory book succinctly and systematically presents the theory and practice of REBT. The book's three parts are: (a) the basic principles of rational emotive behavioural counselling; (b) the rational emotive behavioural counselling sequence; and (c) the rational emotive behavioural counselling process.

References and further reading

Dryden, W. (1989) 'Albert Ellis: an efficient and passionate life', *Journal of Counseling and Development*, 67: 539–46.
Dryden, W. (1999) *Rational Emotive Behaviour Counselling in Action* (2nd edn). London: Sage.

Dryden, W. and Ellis, A. (1986) 'Rational-emotive therapy (RET)', in W. Dryden and W. Golden (eds), *Cognitive-Behavioural Approaches to Psychotherapy*. London: Harper & Row. pp. 129–68.

Dryden, W., Walker, J. and Ellis, A. (1992) *REBT Self-Help Form*. New York: Albert Ellis Institute for Rational Emotive Behavior Therapy.

Ellis, A. (1958) 'Rational psychotherapy', *Journal of General Psychology, 59*: 35–49.

Ellis, A. (1962) *Reason and Emotion in Psychotherapy*. Secaucus, NJ: Citadel.

Ellis, A. (1971) 'A twenty-three-year-old woman, guilty about not following her parents' rules', in A. Ellis, *Growth Through Reason: Verbatim Cases in Rational-Emotive Therapy*. North Hollywood, CA: Wilshire Books. pp. 223–86.

Ellis, A. (1977) *Anger: How to Live With and Without It*. Sydney: Macmillan Sun Books.

Ellis, A. (1980) 'Overview of the clinical theory of rational-emotive therapy', in R. Grieger and J. Boyd (eds), *Rational-Emotive Therapy: A Skills-Based Approach*. New York: Van Nostrand Reinhold. pp. 1–31.

Ellis, A. (1986a) 'Rational-emotive therapy approaches to overcoming resistance', in A. Ellis and R.M. Grieger (eds), *Handbook of Rational-Emotive Therapy* (Vol. 2). New York: Springer. pp. 246–74.

Ellis, A. (1986b) 'Application of rational-emotive therapy to love problems', in A. Ellis and R.M. Grieger (eds), *Handbook of Rational-Emotive Therapy* (Vol. 2). New York: Springer. pp. 162–82.

Ellis, A. (1987) 'The impossibility of achieving consistently good mental health', *American Psychologist, 42*: 364–75.

Ellis, A. (1988) *How to Stubbornly Refuse to Make Yourself Miserable about Anything, Yes Anything!* Sydney: Pan Macmillan.

Ellis, A. (1990) 'Is rational-emotive therapy (RET) "rationalist" or "constructivist"?', in A. Ellis and W. Dryden, *The Essential Albert Ellis*. New York: Springer. pp. 114–41.

Ellis, A. (1991a) 'My life in clinical psychology', in C.E. Walker (ed.), *The History of Clinical Psychology in Autobiography* (Vol. 1). Pacific Grove, CA: Brooks/Cole. pp. 1–37.

Ellis, A. (1991b) 'The revised ABC's of rational-emotive therapy (RET)', *Journal of Rational-Emotive and Cognitive Behavior Therapy, 9*: 139–72.

Ellis, A. (1991c) 'Using RET effectively: reflections and interview', in M.E. Bernard (ed.), *Using Rational-Emotive Therapy Effectively*. New York: Plenum. pp. 1–33.

Ellis, A. (1991d) 'Rational-emotive behavior marriage and family therapy', in A.M. Horne (ed.), *Family Counseling and Therapy* (3rd edn). Itasca, IL: Peacock. pp. 489–513.

Ellis, A. (1991e) 'Rational-emotive treatment of simple phobias', *Psychotherapy, 28*: 452–6.

Ellis, A. (1992) 'Group rational-emotive and cognitive-behavioral therapy', *International Journal of Group Psychotherapy, 42*: 63–80.

Ellis, A. (1993a) 'Changing rational-emotive therapy (RET) to rational emotive behavior therapy (REBT)', *The Behavior Therapist, 16*: 257–8.

Ellis, A. (1993b) 'Reflections on rational-emotive therapy', *Journal of Consulting and Clinical Psychology, 61*: 199–201.

Ellis, A. (1993c) 'The rational-emotive therapy (RET) approach to marital and family therapy', *The Family Journal: Counselling and Therapy for Couples and Families, 1*: 292–307.

Ellis, A. (1993d) 'The advantages and disadvantages of self-help therapy materials', *Professional Psychology: Research and Practice, 24*: 335–9.

Ellis, A. (1993e) 'Vigorous RET disputing', in M.E. Bernard and J.L. Wolfe (eds), *The RET Resource Book for Practitioners*. New York: Institute for Rational-Emotive Therapy. p. 7.

Ellis, A. (1993f) 'Rational-emotive imagery: RET version', in M.E. Bernard and J.L. Wolfe (eds), *The RET Resource Book for Practitioners*. New York: Institute for Rational-Emotive Therapy. pp. 8–10.

Ellis, A. (1994) *Reason and Emotion in Psychotherapy* (rev. edn). Secaucus, NJ: Citadel.

Ellis, A. (1996) *Better, Deeper and More Enduring Brief Therapy: The Rational Emotive Behavior Approach*. New York: Brunner/Mazel.

Ellis, A. (1997a) 'The evolution of Albert Ellis and rational emotive behavior therapy', in J.K. Zeig (ed.), *The Evolution of Psychotherapy: The Third Conference*. New York: Brunner/ Mazel. pp. 69–82.

Ellis, A. (1997b) 'Using rational emotive behavior therapy techniques to cope with disability', *Professional Psychology Research and Practice, 28*: 17–22.

Ellis, A. (1997c) 'Extending the goals of behavior therapy and of cognitive behavior therapy', *Behavior Therapy, 28*: 333–9.

Ellis, A. (1999a) 'Three methods of rational emotive behavior therapy that make my psychotherapy effective', *Psychotherapy Bulletin, 34*: 38–9.

Ellis, A. (1999b) *How to Make Yourself Happy and Remarkably Less Disturbable*. Atascadero, CA: Impact.

Ellis, A. (2001) *Feeling Better, Getting Better, Staying Better: Profound Self-Help for Your Emotions*. Atascadero, CA: Impact.

Ellis, A. (2003a) 'Similarities and differences between rational emotive behavior therapy and cognitive therapy', *Journal of Cognitive Therapy: An International Quarterly, 17*: 225–40.

Ellis, A. (2003b) *Ask Albert Ellis?: Straight Answers and Sound Advice from America's Best-Known Psychologist*. Atascadero, CA: Impact.

Ellis, A. (2003c) *Overcoming Resistance: A Rational Emotive Behavior Therapy Integrated Approach*. New York: Springer.

Ellis, A. (2004a) *Rational Emotive Behavior Therapy: It Works for Me – It Can Work for You*. Amherst, NY: Prometheus Books.

Ellis, A. (2004b) *Sex Without Guilt in the Twenty-First Century*. New York: Barricade Books.

Ellis, A. (2005) 'Rational emotive behavior therapy', in R.J. Corsini and D. Wedding (eds), *Current Psychotherapies* (7th edn). Belmont, CA: Thomson Brooks/Cole. pp. 166–201.

Ellis, A. (in press) *Discussion of Christine A. Padesky and Aaron T. Beck, Science and Philosophy: Comparison of Cognitive Therapy and Rational Emotive Behavior Therapy*.

Ellis, A. and Blau, S. (eds) (1998) *The Albert Ellis Reader*. Secaucus, NJ: Carol Publishing Group.

Ellis, A. and Crawford, T. (2000) *Making Intimate Connections: 7 Guidelines for Great Relationships and Better Communication*. Atascadero, CA: Impact.

Ellis, A. and Dryden, W. (1997) *The Practice of Rational Emotive Behaviour Therapy*. London: Free Association Books and New York: Springer.

Ellis, A. and Harper, R.A. (1997) *A Guide to Rational Living*. North Hollywood, CA: Wilshire Books.

Ellis, A. and MacLaren, C. (2004) *Rational Emotive Behavior Therapy: A Therapist's Guide* (rev. edn). Atascadero, CA: Impact.

Sichel, J. and Ellis, A. (1984) *RET Self-Help Form*. New York: Institute for Rational-Emotive Therapy.

Wedding, D. and Corsini, R.J. (2005) *Case Studies in Psychotherapy* (4th edn). Belmont, CA: Thomson Brooks/Cole.

Ellis on cassette (illustrative)

Ellis, A. (1977) *A Garland of Rational Songs* (with songbook). New York: Institute for Rational-Emotive Behavior Therapy.

Ellis, A. (1982) *Solving Emotional Problems*. New York: Institute for Rational-Emotive Behavior Therapy.

Ellis, A. (1984) *How to Be Happy Though Human*. New York: Institute for Rational-Emotive Behavior Therapy.

Ellis, A. (1987) *How to Stop Worrying and Start Living*. Washington, DC: Psychology Today Tapes.

Ellis on film

Ellis, A. (1965) 'Rational-emotive therapy', in E. Shostrom (ed.), *Three Approaches to Psychotherapy*. Santa Ana, CA: Psychological Films.

Ellis on videotape (illustrative)

Coping with the Suicide of a Loved One (49 mins)
Dealing with Addictions (55 mins)

Useful addresses

For further details of REBT publications, cassettes and videotapes, contact:
Albert Ellis Institute
45 East 65th Street
New York, NY 10021-6593
USA
Website: www.rebt.org
Email: info@rebt.org

cognitive therapy

Introduction

Cognitive therapy was initially developed in the early 1960s by Dr Aaron Beck of the University of Pennsylvania. The theory postulates that during clients' cognitive development they learn incorrect habits of processing and interpreting information. Cognitive therapists attempt to unravel clients' distortions and help them to learn different and more realistic ways of processing and reality-testing information.

Cognitive therapy's theoretical underpinnings come from three main sources (Beck and Weishaar, 2005). First, the phenomenological approach to psychology, which posits that the individual's view of self and personal world are central to how they behave. Second, structural theory and depth psychology, in particular Freud's theory, contributed to Beck's structuring cognition into primary and secondary processes. Third, the work of early cognitive psychologists like Allport, Piaget and George Kelly in particular influenced Beck (Padesky and Beck, 2003). For example, Kelly's concept of personal constructs is similar to Beck's idea of schemas.

Influences on the practice of cognitive therapy include Rogers, Ellis and the behaviour therapists. The gentle style of questioning and emphasis on unconditional acceptance owes much to person-centred therapy. The emphasis on finding solutions to conscious problems resembles rational emotive behaviour therapy. Setting goals and session agendas, testing hypotheses, using specific behaviour change procedures and assigning homework are among the contributions from behaviour therapy.

Aaron Beck (1921–)

Aaron Temkin 'Tim' Beck was born on 18 July 1921, in Providence, Rhode Island, the fourth, but third surviving, son of Russian Jewish immigrant parents. In 1919 Beck's parents lost their only daughter in an influenza epidemic, an event that precipitated a deep depression in his mother that lasted off and on the rest of her life. Aged seven, Beck had a near fatal illness that reinforced his mother's overprotectiveness. While his father was tranquil, Beck did not like his mother's moody, inconsistent and excitable behaviour. Beck's father, who ran a printing business, encouraged his interest in science and nature. At high school Beck edited the school paper and graduated first in his class. When growing up he developed many anxieties and phobias, including fears of abandonment, surgery, suffocation, public speaking and heights (Weishaar, 1993).

In 1942 Beck graduated from Brown University, having majored in English and political science. Beck took premedical courses both before and after graduating and, in 1946, received his MD from Yale University School of Medicine. From 1946 to 1948 he served a rotating internship and a residency in pathology at the Rhode Island Hospital and from 1950 he started a neurology residency at the Cushing Veterans Administration Hospital in Framingham, Massachusetts. Due to a shortage of psychiatry residents, against his wishes Beck was forced to complete a six-month rotation in psychiatry. Deciding to remain in psychiatry, from 1950 to 1952, he was a Fellow in psychiatry at the Austen Riggs Center in Stockbridge, Massachusetts. In 1953 the American Board of Psychiatry and Neurology certified Beck in psychiatry and, in 1958, Beck graduated from the Philadelphia Psychoanalytic Institute. Since 1954, Beck has been a faculty member in the University of Pennsylvania's Department of Psychiatry. Currently he is University Professor Emeritus of Psychiatry and President of the independent Beck Institute for Cognitive Therapy and Research, where staff are affiliated with the University Psychiatry Department.

In the late 1950s, Beck began research on the dreams of depressed patients to test the psychoanalytic theory that depression was anger turned inwards. The data did not support psychoanalytic theory, so Beck continued to collect data to construct a more empirically derived model of depression (Padesky and Beck, 2003). The period from 1960 to 1963 saw the development of cognitive therapy. Beck observes: 'There's nothing that I've been associated with since 1963 the seeds of which were not in the 1962 to 1964 articles. That was the critical period: changing from psychoanalysis to developing a new theory of therapy' (Weishaar, 1993: 21).

Beck's process of developing theory is that he first observes patients, then develops ways of measuring these observations, then formulates a theory if the observations are validated by a number of cases, then designs interventions congruent with the theory, then over time and through further experimentation continues to assess whether the theory is confirmed or negated and to refine it. When developing theory Beck also uses self-observation. Finally, treatment protocols are tested via outcome studies, including examination of relapse and post-treatment course (Padesky and Beck, 2003). Beck and others continue to evolve cognitive therapy based on new research.

Beck has authored or coauthored over 375 articles in professional and scientific journals. His books include *Cognitive Therapy and the Emotional Disorders* (1976), *Cognitive Therapy of Depression* (Beck et al., 1979b), *Anxiety Disorders and Phobias* (Beck and Emery, 1985), *Love is Never Enough* (1988), *Cognitive Therapy of Personality Disorders* (Beck et al., 2003), *The Integrative Power of Cognitive Therapy* (Alford and Beck, 1997), *Scientific Foundations of Cognitive Theory and*

Therapy of Depression (Clark et al., 1999) and *Prisoners of Hate: The Cognitive Basis of Anger, Hostility and Violence* (1999). Tests and measures that Beck has developed with colleagues include the *Beck Depression Inventory*, the *Beck Hopelessness Scale*, the *Suicide Intent Scale*, the *Suicide Ideation Scale*, the *Beck Self-Concept Test*, the *Beck Youth Inventories*, and the *Clark–Beck Obsessive-Compulsive Inventory*.

Beck's awards and honours include being awarded, in 1979 the American Psychiatric Association's Foundation Fund Prize for Research in Psychiatry for his research in depression and the development of cognitive therapy; in 1989 the American Psychological Association's Distinguished Scientific Award for Applications of Psychology; in 1997 the Cummings PSYCHE Award for Lifetime Achievement; and, in 1998, the Lifetime Achievement Award of the Association for the Advancement of Behavior Therapy. In addition, in 1987, Beck was elected a Fellow of Britain's Royal College of Psychiatrists.

Beck continues to be active in writing, research and training. In 1950 he married his wife Phyllis, a continuing source of strength and support, who developed her own career by becoming a Pennsylvania Superior Court Judge. The Becks have four children and many grandchildren.

Theory

Basic concepts

Cognition is the key to understanding and treating psychological disorders. Alford and Beck write: 'Cognition is defined as that function that involves inferences about one's experiences and about the occurrence and control of future events' (1997: 14). Humans need to adapt to changing environmental circumstances. Cognition includes the processes involved in identifying and predicting complex relations among events for the purposes of adaptation. Humans have the capacity both for primal/primitive and for higher level cognitive processing.

Schemas

Schemas are structures that consist of people's fundamental beliefs and assumptions. Schemas are meaning-making cognitive structures. There are two categories of meaning: first, the objective or public meaning of an event, which may have few significant implications for the individual; and second, its personal or private meaning. Meaning assignment controls the psychological systems, such as behavioural, emotional, attentional and memory, so that the individual can activate strategies for adaptation.

Schemas are relatively stable cognitive patterns that influence, through their beliefs, how people select and synthesize incoming information. They are developed early in life from personal experiences and identifications with significant others and reinforced by further learning experiences. Schemas are not pathological by definition – they may be adaptive or maladaptive. They are analogous to George Kelly's (1955) formulation of personal constructs. People categorize and evaluate their experiences through a matrix of schemas.

Schemas possess structural qualities such as degree of breadth, flexibility and their relative prominence in a person's cognitive organization. In addition, according to the degree of energy invested in them at any time, schemas can range from latent to predominant. When schemas are hypervalent, they are pre-potent and easily triggered. Psychopathology is characterized not only by the activation of inappropriate schemas but, in all probability, by their crowding out or inhibiting more adaptive schemas.

Modes

Contemporary cognitive theory stresses the concept of modes. Modes are net-works of cognitive, affective, motivational and behavioural schemas. Modes are fundamental to personality since they interpret and adapt to emerging and ongoing situations (Beck and Weishaar, 2005). In earlier writings, cogni-tions were viewed as the mediating variable that triggered people's affective, motivational and behavioural systems. Now, instead of a linear relationship, all aspects of human functioning are viewed as acting together as a mode. Alford and Beck observe: 'The operation of a mode (e.g., anger, attack) across diverse psychological systems (emotion, motivation) is determined by the idiosyncratic schematic processing derived from an individual's genetic pro-gramming and internalised cultural/social beliefs' (1997: 10).

Modes can be primal, which means that they are universal and linked to survival. Anxiety is an example of a primal mode. Examples of modes under conscious control include conversing and studying. Primal modes include pri-mary process thinking that is primitive and that conceptualizes situations in global, rigid, biased and relatively crude ways. Primal modes of thinking may originally have been adaptive in an evolutionary sense, yet they can become maladaptive in everyday life when triggered by systematically biased thinking and misinterpretations.

In addition, humans are capable of higher levels of cognitive processing that test reality and correct primal, global conceptualizations. However, in psychopathology, these corrective functions become impaired and primary responses can escalate into full-blown psychiatric disorders. Nevertheless, conscious or higher-level thinking can override primal thinking and make it more flexible and realistic. Cognitive therapy approaches dysfunctional modes by deactivating them, modifying their content and structure, and by constructing adaptive modes to neutralize them.

Cognitive vulnerability

The term *cognitive vulnerability* refers to humans' cognitive frailty. Because of their schemas, each person has a set of unique vulnerabilities and sensitivities that predispose them to psychological distress. People's schemas and beliefs influence the way they process data about themselves. When they exhibit psychological problems, their dysfunctional schemas and beliefs lead them systematically to bias information in unhelpful ways.

Beck and colleagues (2003) give the example of Sue, who heard noises coming from the next room where her boyfriend Tom was working on some chores. Sue's first thought was that 'Tom is making a lot of noise'. However Sue's information processing continued and she made the following interpretation of her experience: 'Tom is making a lot of noise *because he's angry at me*'. Her attribution of causality was produced by a conditional schema or belief that 'If an intimate of mine is noisy, it means he is angry at me'. Further down her hierarchy were the beliefs that 'If people reject me, I will be all alone' and 'Being alone will be devastating'. At the most basic level Sue had the belief or schema that 'I am unlovable'. When activated, Sue's basic belief (or schema) 'I am unlovable' acted as a 'feed-forward' mechanism moulding the information about Tom's behaviour in a way to fit the schema. Beck provides an alternative explanation that might have better fitted the information available to Sue, namely that 'Loud hammering is a sound of exuberance'.

Automatic thoughts

Automatic thoughts are less accessible to awareness than voluntary thoughts, but not so deeply buried as beliefs and schemas. These thoughts are similar to what Freud termed 'preconscious' thinking and what Ellis terms 'self-statements'. People's self-evaluations and self-instructions appear to be derived from deeper structures – their self-schemas. Automatic thoughts reflect schema content – deeper beliefs and assumptions. In normal functioning self-appraisals and self-evaluations operate more or less automatically to help people stay on course. However, in psychopathology certain automatic thoughts operate to help people stay off course. Most psychological disorders are characterized by specific systematic biases in processing information. For example, depressive disorders are characterized by a negative view of self, experience and the future, and anxiety disorders by fear of physical or psychological danger.

The following are some salient characteristics of automatic thoughts. Automatic thoughts:

- are part of people's internal monologue: what and how they talk to themselves;
- can take the form of words, images, or both;
- occur very rapidly and usually at the fringe of awareness;
- can precede and accompany emotions, including feelings and inhibitions – for instance, people's emotional responses to each other's actions follow from their interpretations rather than from the actions themselves;
- are generally plausible to people who assume that they are accurate;

- have a recurring quality, despite people trying to block them out;
- affect tone of voice, facial expression and gestures, even though they may not be expressed verbally;
- can be linked together with more subtle thoughts underlying more obvious thoughts – for instance, when a husband boasts about his wife's cooking, his wife's secondary obvious automatic thought is 'He's fishing for a compliment', while her primary subtle automatic thought is 'They'll think that's all I'm good for' (Beck, 1988); and
- though often hard to identify, therapists can train clients to pinpoint these thoughts with great accuracy.

Cognitive distortions

Dysfunctional beliefs embedded in cognitive schemas contribute to systematic cognitive distortions, more accessible in automatic thoughts, that both characterize and maintain psychological distress. Box 13.1 includes some of the main cognitive distortions (Beck and Weishaar, 2005).

Box 13.1   Cognitive distortions

Arbitrary inference
The process of drawing specific conclusions without supporting evidence and sometimes in the face of contradictory evidence. An example of arbitrary inference is that of the working mother who after a busy day concludes: 'I am a terrible mother'.

Selective abstraction
Selectively attending to a detail taken out of context at the same time as ignoring other more salient information. An example of selective abstraction is that of the boyfriend who becomes jealous at seeing his girlfriend tilt her head towards a man at a noisy party in order to hear him better.

Overgeneralization
Drawing a general rule or conclusion from one or a few isolated incidents and then applying the rule too broadly to unrelated situations. An example of overgeneralization is the woman who concludes after a disappointing date: 'All men are alike. I'll always be rejected'.

Magnification and minimization
Evaluating particular events as far more or far less important than they really are. An example of magnification is the student who catastrophizes: 'If I appear the least bit nervous in class it will mean disaster'. An example of minimization is that of a man describing his terminally ill mother as having a 'cold'.

(Continued)

Box 13.1   (Continued)

Personalization
Having a tendency without adequate evidence to relate external events to oneself. For instance concluding, when an acquaintance walking down the opposite side of a busy street does not acknowledge a wave of greeting: 'I must have done something to offend him/her'.

Dichotomous thinking
Black-and-white, either-or, and polarized thinking are other terms for dichotomous thinking. Thinking in extreme terms, for instance 'Unless I do extremely well on this exam, I am a total failure'.

Evolutionary and genetic factors

The cognitive structures and schemas relevant to depression, anxiety disorders and personality disorders reflect our evolutionary history (Beck, 1991; Beck et al., 2003). It is reasonable to consider that the notion of long-standing cognitive-affective motivational processes influence people's automatic processes: the way we construe events, what we feel, and how we are disposed to act. Much animal behaviour is regarded as programmed, with underlying processes reflected in overt behaviour. Though there are risks in extrapolating from animal to human ethology, similar developmental processes may be operative in humans. Animal analogies may clarify many aspects of normal and abnormal human behaviour. For instance, observations of primate behaviour seem highly relevant to depressed behaviour in humans.

'Strategies' are forms of programmed behaviour designed to serve biological goals. Regarding anxiety and anger, Beck (Beck and Emery, 1985) suggests four 'primal' survival strategies – fight, flight, freeze and faint – to perceptions of threat. Also, he proposes that strategies associated with traditional personality disorders may have possible antecedents in our evolutionary past (Beck et al., 2003). The dramatic strategy of the histrionic personality may have roots in the display rituals of non-human animals. The attack strategy of the antisocial personality may have roots in predatory behaviour.

Human strategies may be adaptive or maladaptive depending on their circumstances. The strategies adopted by people with personality disorders are maladaptive exaggerations of normal strategies. For instance, with the dependent personality disorder the cognitive substrate or basic belief is 'I am helpless' which leads to a strategy of attachment based on fear of abandonment. With the avoidant personality disorder, the basic belief is 'I may get hurt' which leads to a strategy of avoidance.

Genetic factors

Mention has already been made of the role of evolution in laying the foundation for cognitive schemas and behavioural strategies. In addition, biological factors, such as variations in the gene pool, differentiate individuals in terms of their vulnerability to different kinds of distress. For instance, predisposing factors in depression are hereditary susceptibility and diseases that cause persistent neurochemical abnormalities.

Beck and colleagues (2003) regard the evidence as strong for relatively stable temperamental and behavioural differences being present at birth. These innate 'tendencies' can be strengthened or weakened by experience. For instance, because of the quality of their interpersonal interactions and learning experiences, not all shy children become shy adults. Furthermore, mutually reinforcing cycles can be established between people's innate tendencies and others' reactions to them. For instance, individuals with innate care-eliciting tendencies can elicit care-producing behaviour in others, even beyond the age when such behaviour is adaptive.

Acquisition

This section on acquisition seeks to answer two main, yet interrelated, questions. First, how are cognitive schemas, automatic thoughts and cognitive distortions initially acquired? Second, how are symptoms of psychiatric and other disorders activated? Here my focus is on dysfunctional cognitions and behaviour, though much of what follows is relevant to acquiring adaptive cognitions and behaviour.

Acquisition of vulnerability

Cognitive therapy views the acquisition of the potential for psychological distress as the result of many interacting factors: evolutionary, biological, developmental and environmental. Though many of the factors are common across individuals, each individual has their unique variations and way of attaching personal meaning to events. Below are some ways in which people acquire vulnerabilities.

Childhood traumas

Specific affect-laden incidents in childhood may create the potential for later distress by generating dysfunctional underlying beliefs (Beck and Emery, 1985). One example is the client who suffered a sense of doom and dread every Christmas season. His earliest memory of this feeling was when, aged seven, he saw his mother taken away to a tuberculosis sanatorium. His underlying belief became 'Something bad is going to happen over the Christmas holidays'. Another example is the five-year-old, who went away on a trip and returned to find the family dog dead, developing the belief that 'When I'm not physically close to others, something bad will happen to them'. A further example is that of the seven-year-old whose father left the family permanently after a marital fight developing the underlying belief that 'If I make others angry they will leave me'.

Negative treatment in childhood

Children can be subject to ongoing negative treatment that affects their self-esteem and later makes them vulnerable to psychological distress. Furthermore, parents and significant others can model abusive behaviour which their children later use against others. Box 13.2 provides examples of acquiring cognitive vulnerability in childhood (Beck, 1988; Beck et al., 2003).

Box 13.2   Childhood abuse and later cognitive vulnerability

Example 1   Dysfunctional belief: 'I am a wimp'
Gary had periodic violent outbursts against Beverley, whom he perceived as needling him all the time for not doing chores. Gary had suffered from being brought up in a household where people controlled each other through power and might. His father and older brother intimidated him and Gary developed a core schema 'I am a wimp'. To compensate for this belief Gary adopted an interpersonal strategy of intimidation to control other people's inclination to dominate him like his family had earlier done.

Example 2   Dysfunctional belief: 'I am a bad kid'
In her childhood, a 28-year-old single woman who now suffered from panic disorder, had come home from school early one day and her mother screamed at her for waking her up saying, 'How dare you interrupt my sleep!' Despite the fact that her mother drank a lot and was irritable and unpredictable, the woman developed the beliefs 'I am a bad kid' and 'I am wrong because I upset my mother'.

Example 3   Dysfunctional tendency to self-criticism
A female client kept criticizing herself unnecessarily. She lessened her self-criticism when she re-experienced childhood scenes of criticism and obtained the insight 'I criticize myself now not because it's right to do so, but because my mother always criticized me and I took this over from her'.

Social learning

Beck endorses social learning theory. However, he also stresses that individuals have unique learning histories and idiosyncratic ways of attaching meanings to earlier events. Many reasons exist for personality disorders – for example obsessive-compulsive and paranoid behaviour may develop either as a compensation for or from fear. However, the reinforcement of relevant strategies by parents and significant others is among the reasons for specific personality disorders. For instance, the dependent personality's help-seeking and clinging strategies may have been rewarded and attempts at self-sufficiency and mobility discouraged. Identification with other family members can be important in what personality disorder strategies get developed. In addition, negative life experiences may worsen an initial predisposition so that, for instance, the shy child turns into an avoidant personality.

Modelling is a key process in social learning theory. For example, marital partners have memories about how their parents behaved. Parental modelling provides a basis for rules, shoulds and should nots, that they bring into their own marriages. Beck (1988) provides the example of Wendy and Hal who married very young and had trouble freeing themselves from parental modelling and reinforcement. Wendy had absorbed her mother's traditional rule that 'The role of a wife is to take care of her husband'. When Wendy failed to live up to the rule she disparaged herself. Hal's father had stressed and rewarded perfectionism so much that Hal had developed the belief 'I can never do anything right'. His mother reinforced his self-doubts because she had a negative attitude towards men: 'Men can't do anything. They're weak and helpless'. Hal's rules and beliefs made him vulnerable both to creating and dealing with difficulties in his marriage.

Inadequate experiences for learning coping skills

People may have been inadequately provided with personal experiences to learn coping skills. For example, an element in the anxious person's assessment of a threat is their ability to cope with the threat. A boy who has developed the coping skills of dealing with a bully is likely to feel less anxious about the bully because of this. People who fail to develop adequate assertion skills may be more prone to depression: first they may lose self-esteem through others' actions and, second, they may then disparage themselves for lack of assertion. Most couples have learned insufficient skills in marital communication 'and so unwittingly produce continual abrasions, misunderstandings, and frustrations' (Beck, 1988: 275).

Activation of vulnerability

The term *cognitive shift* describes the shift of energy away from normal or higher-level cognitive processing to a predominance of processing by pathological primal schemas. According to the disorder, energy is used to activate and inhibit unconscious patterns. For instance, in depression, generalized anxiety disorders and panic attacks, the depressive, danger and panic modes are energized, respectively. The concept of mode reflects the manner in which a schema is expressed. For example, a schema such as 'I'm inadequate' may lead to a predominance of catastrophizing cognitions when the anxiety mode is activated and to a predominance of self-blame and hopelessness cognitions when the depressed mode is activated.

Thinking and behaving in ways that indicate vulnerability is a matter of degree. The *continuity hypothesis* suggests that anxiety, depression and personality disorders are exaggerated mechanisms of normal functioning. People can acquire dysfunctional schemas, rules, automatic thoughts and behaviours and not have them activated so that they become full-blown disorders or highly damaging factors in marital relationships.

The *cognitive shift* gets triggered when people perceive that their vital interests are at stake or have been affected. Often, initially, the shift into psychopathology is activated in response to major life stressors. Later the shift may be activated by less severe stressors (A. Butler, personal communication, 8 April 1994). With repeated activations over the life span, people become increasingly sensitive to triggers so that it takes objectively less severe or salient stressors to precipitate a shift.

In non-endogenous unipolar depression, people have a cognitive vulnerability that is triggered by stressful life events or a series of traumatic experiences. An example of the development of vulnerability to activation of the cognitive shift is that of a person with recurrent depression whose first episode may have been precipitated by a severe life stressor (e.g. losing a job). Later episodes may be precipitated by relatively minor and less directly relevant stressors (e.g. hearing of a friend in another field being fired) that take on inordinate meaning due to prior experiences.

Three activating or precipitating factors are proposed for generalized anxiety disorders (Beck and Emery, 1985). First, people may face increased demands, for instance after the birth of a child or a job promotion. Second, there may be increased threat in an area of a person's life, for example, a new mother having a baby susceptible to infections, or an employee getting a hostile new boss. Third, stressful events and reversals may undermine confidence. An example is that of a young lawyer who failed his bar examination and, at about the same time, was told by his girlfriend that she did not love him. Fearing for his future as a lawyer and family man, he became chronically anxious.

Maintenance

When people's cognitive vulnerabilities get activated and their cognitive processes go awry, why do they stay that way? Many people cope with the activation of their cognitive vulnerabilities by instigating adaptive cognitive and behavioural strategies. However, those with psychopathological disorders and those with deeply distressed marriages may remain stuck in faulty patterns of information processing and behaviour, to their own and other people's great disadvantage. There is no single cause why people continue to process information inefficiently. The evolutionary history of the species and genetic influences play a part. Also, the extent and depth of people's experiences of childhood traumas, negative treatment in childhood, faulty social learning and inadequate experiences of learning coping skills play their parts too.

Failure to turn off predominant modes

The type of schema that is evoked may be determined by the mode that is active at any given time. Normally there is a balance between modes so that when one predominates or is hypervalent for a long time, an opposing mode is activated. For instance, during a period of elation a person may become aware of negative feedback, or hostility may be counterbalanced by anxiety. In psychopathological disorders there seems to be an interference in the turn-off of the dominant mode. This results in systematically biased interpretations of negative events in depression, of positive events in mania and of dangerous events in anxiety disorders. Beck considers the reasons to be obscure as to why the opponent mode remains relatively inactive, thus failing to contribute to a more balanced view of reality. One possibility is that neurochemical disturbances either stimulate a prolonged overactivity of the dominant mode or fail to stimulate sufficient activity in the opposing mode.

Inability to reality-test dysfunctional interpretations

Since clients accept their dysfunctional beliefs so readily during anxiety and depression, Beck believes that they have temporarily lost their ability to reality-test their interpretations. Their information processing, based on dysfunctional schemas and beliefs, is permeated with automatic thoughts containing cognitive distortions. Cognitive distortions are not only manifestations of psychopathology, they serve to maintain it by interfering with clients' ability to test the reality of their thinking. Clients think in rigid, stereotypical terms. They fail to distinguish adequately between fact and inference. Instead of viewing the content of their thoughts as testable hypotheses, they jump to conclusions on inadequate evidence and then view their conclusions as facts. They insufficiently take into account any feedback that might modify or negate their thoughts and perceptions. Thus information processing systems become closed, instead of remaining open to assessing new data as they become available.

Resistances to change

Many reasons exist for why clients resist changing. For instance, clients may be fearful of the negative effects of their changing on others. Marta was a 42-year-old woman living with her mother and diagnosed as having a dependent personality disorder. Whenever she thought of moving she feared that this would kill her mother and her mother reinforced this thinking (Beck et al., 2003). Many highly anxious, depressed and suicidal clients fear change as an unknown. Sometimes clients fear the positive as well as the negative consequences of change, for instance having to deal with the added responsibility of a promotion or marriage.

Beck (1988) considers that partners in distressed relationships may need to confront many beliefs, possibly expressed in the form of automatic thoughts, which weaken their motivation for change. Such thoughts include: 'My partner is incapable of change' and 'She/he hurt me. She/he deserves to be hurt'.

Cognitive models

A systematic bias in information processing characterizes most psychological disorders. Overviews of Beck's cognitive models of depression, anxiety disorders, anger and distressed couple relationships are now presented.

The cognitive model of depression

Beck views *depression* not just as a mood state, but a cognitive state as well (Beck, 1999; Beck et al., 1979b). Depression entails clients activating three major cognitive patterns known as *the cognitive triad*, involving negative views of:

- *themselves* as unlovable, worthless, helpless and lacking in the ability to attain happiness;
- *their past and present experiencing of the world* – their personal world is extremely demanding and presents huge obstacles to achieving goals;
- *the future* which is viewed as hopeless and unlikely to improve – this hopelessness may bring about ideas of suicide.

These cognitive patterns lead to the motivational, behavioural and physical symptoms of depression. An illustrative motivational symptom is *paralysis of will* created by the belief that one lacks the ability to cope or control an event's outcome. Inertia and fatigue are illustrative behavioural and physical symptoms, respectively.

Depressive schemas are formed early in life. Situations of loss similar to those originally embedding the schema may trigger a depression. Series of traumatic events may also activate depressions. As the depression worsens, depressive schemas become hypervalent to the point where clients may become unable to view their negative thoughts objectively and find themselves completely preoccupied with repetitive negative thoughts. As dysfunctional schemas become more activated, so does the incidence of systematic cognitive distortions.

The cognitive model of anxiety disorders

The main cognitive theme in anxiety disorders is *danger*. Anxiety is a strategy in response to threat. In anxiety disorders the normal evolutionary survival mechanism of anxiety becomes exaggerated and malfunctioning. Beck and Emery (1985) adopt Lazarus's (1966) distinction between primary and secondary appraisal. Primary appraisal is the first impression of a situation that suggests the situation is noxious. Then successive reappraisals are made concerning the nature and relevance of the threat to a person's vital interests, including physical and psychological injury. Secondary appraisal involves the person assessing his or her resources for dealing with the threat. This process takes place at the same time as evaluating the nature of the threat. As with depression a person's underlying dysfunctional schemas and beliefs may predispose them to anxiety. Their dysfunctional beliefs may be activated by increased demands, threats and stresses that may interact with previous problems. Cognitive distortions reflecting dysfunctional schema include overestimating the probability and severity of the threat, magnification of the negative consequences (catastrophizing), underestimating one's resources for dealing with the threat, and insufficiently taking into account support factors, for instance the presence of others who might help. In brief, anxious individuals maximize the likelihood of harm and minimize their ability to cope.

The cognitive model of anger

The evoking of *anger* depends upon the inference that a person has been wronged in some way (Beck, 1999). Many reasons may contribute to this perception. People may insufficiently apply the rules of evidence by looking at all the pros and cons relevant to their interpretation of a situation. They may inadequately consider alternative explanations. Instead of problem solving, people attend to their own subjective meaning of an event. In addition they may possess beliefs that lead to distress: for instance, 'If a person criticizes me, it means she or he doesn't respect me' and 'If I don't receive respect, then I am open to further assaults'. In addition people may have unrealistic rules and imperatives, for instance, the desire 'I wish my wife was more respectful' can get transferred into an absolute rule: 'My wife *should* be more respectful'.

People may gloss over unpleasant feelings immediately following the negative interpretation of an experience and be more aware of their subsequent angry feelings. For instance, they may feel sad or anxious and such feelings may need to be acknowledged and understood. In addition anger-prone people place an excessive emphasis on protection of their rights. They can remain unaware that other people may have a different view of their entitlements and that the rigid assertion of their rights leads to distress and non-productive anger. Though a degree of anger has information value, the powerful nature of some people's angry feelings can draw their attention away from the specific nature of their problems and thus interfere with solving them. Frequently, angry people need to be trained in communication skills. They also may need training in how to deal with violent impulses. A man who acquires insight into the labile nature of his self-esteem, can then work to substitute more realistic beliefs that leave his self-esteem less vulnerable. For instance, instead of 'A man does not take any crap' he can think 'A man can take the crap without allowing it to get to him'. In addition, the permissions that violent people give themselves can be elicited, challenged and changed.

The cognitive model of distressed couples relationships

Beck observes 'what attracts partners to each other is rarely enough to sustain a relationship' (1988: 46). Poor communication skills are one reason for marital difficulties. In addition partners bring much personal baggage into the relationship in terms of hidden expectations of each other and the relationship. The expectations in marriage are less flexible than in uncommitted relationships. Furthermore, much behaviour in marriage has idiosyncratic symbolic meanings attached to it revolving around symbols of love or rejection, security or insecurity.

When disappointment in a relationship sets in and emotions run high, partners lose some or virtually all of their ability to reality-test their interpretations of their own and each other's thoughts, feelings and actions. Instead they react to their 'invisible reality' that is likely to be based more on their internal states, fears and expectations than on what actually happens. Dysfunctional schemas and beliefs can be triggered leading to a negative cognitive set about the other person. A distressed couple's voluntary and automatic thinking contains numerous cognitive distortions. Partners tend to fixate on what is wrong in their relationship rather than on what is right. They misperceive and misinterpret what the other says or does, engage in mind reading and attribute undesirable and malicious motives to each other, and fail to check out the accuracy of their negative explanations and illogical conclusions.

In addition, partners send each other barbed messages that trigger hurt and anger. They perceive they have been wronged, get angry, and feel impelled to attack and attack. Hostility is part of a primitive fight–flight survival mechanism. However, acting on the primitive urge to attack is often destructive to the relationship. It increases the level of threat in the relationship and hence partners' tendencies to think in rigid and erroneous ways. Furthermore, hostility can increase partners' resistances to working on their relationship.

Therapy

Therapeutic goals

Cognitive therapy aims explicitly to re-energize the reality-testing system. In varying degrees, clients with psychopathological disorders and couples in distressed relationships have lost the ability to reality-test dysfunctional interpretations. Cognitive therapy teaches clients adaptive meta-cognition – how to think about their thinking – so that they can correct faulty cognitive processing and develop assumptions that allow them to cope. While cognitive therapy may initially address symptom relief, its ultimate goal is to remove systematic biases in how clients think. In addition, cognitive therapy aims to impart behavioural skills relevant to clients' problems, for instance, listening and communication skills for distressed couples or assertion skills for shy people.

Clients are told that a goal of cognitive therapy is for them to learn to become their own therapists (Beck and Weishaar, 2005). When working with clients' cognitions, goals include teaching them to:

1. monitor their negative automatic thoughts;
2. recognize the connections between cognition, affect and behaviour;
3. examine and reality-test the evidence for and against distorted automatic thoughts;
4. substitute more realistic interpretations for biased cognitions; and
5. learn to identify and alter the beliefs that predispose them to distort their experiences (Beck et al., 1979b).

Clients need not be highly intelligent to gain from cognitive therapy – in fact Beck's researches show no relationship between intelligence and cognitive therapy outcomes.

Cognitive therapy works best with clients who can focus on their automatic thoughts and take some responsibility for self-help. It is not recommended for clients with impaired reality-testing, such as hallucinations and delusions, or for clients with impaired memory and reasoning abilities, such as with organic brain syndromes. For some disorders, such as recurrent major depressive episodes, a combination of cognitive therapy and medication is recommended.

Process of therapy

At the Beck Institute for Cognitive Therapy and Research in suburban Philadelphia, clients undergo a three-hour intake protocol consisting of a clinical interview and psychological tests. The clinical interview provides a thorough history of the background factors contributing to the client's distress. The interview also assesses current levels of functioning, prominent symptoms and expectations for therapy. The *Beck Depression Inventory* (Beck et al., 1961), the *Anxiety Checklist* (Beck, 1978) and the *Dysfunctional Attitudes Scale* (Weissman, 1979) are prominent among the psychological tests used during the intake protocol.

The initial interview has many purposes: initiating a relationship; providing a rationale for cognitive therapy; producing symptom relief; and eliciting important information. Right from the start therapists impart to clients the expectation that cognitive therapy will be time-limited. During the initial interview, therapists start to define problems. Definitions of problems entail both functional and cognitive analyses.

The *functional* analysis seeks to answer questions such as: 'What are the component parts of the problem?'; 'How is it manifested?'; 'In what situations does it occur?'; 'What is its frequency, intensity and duration?'; and 'What are its consequences?'.

The *cognitive* analysis identifies the client's thoughts and images when an emotion is triggered, the extent to which the client feels in control of thoughts and images, and predictions about the likelihood of the problem occurring and what will happen. From the beginning, therapists train clients to monitor their feelings, thoughts and behaviour and to recognize the connections between them. *Homework* is a feature throughout cognitive therapy. An example of an early homework assignment might be asking clients to record their automatic thoughts when distressed.

During initial sessions, therapists and clients draw up *problem lists*. Problem lists can consist of specific symptoms, behaviours or pervasive problems. Their function is to assign treatment priorities. Considerations in prioritizing treatment include magnitude of distress, symptom severity and pervasiveness of theme. Therapists approach each problem by choosing the appropriate cognitive and behavioural techniques to apply. Therapists always offer a rationale for each technique. In addition, both when suggesting and implementing techniques, therapists elicit feedback from clients.

While the early stages of therapy may focus on symptom removal, middle and later stages are more likely to emphasize changing clients' patterns of thinking. Clients are helped to understand the interrelationships between their thoughts, feelings and behaviours. Once they can evaluate automatic thoughts that interfere with effective functioning, then they can identify and examine the underlying assumptions or beliefs generating such thoughts. Assumptions may be revealed as themes in automatic thoughts across time and across situations. Once assumptions and core beliefs have been identified and their disruptive power understood, then cognitive therapy aims to assist clients to examine their validity and current usefulness and then discard or amend them, as appropriate.

As cognitive therapy progresses, clients develop their skills of being their own therapists and assume more responsibility for identifying problems, analysing their thinking and creating suitable homework assignments. The role of the therapist shifts from being fairly didactic to facilitating clients as they develop their cognitive self-helping skills. The frequency of sessions decreases as clients become more proficient.

Being mainly a short-term structured approach, cognitive therapy tends to have its ending built into its beginning. Therapy ends when goals are reached and clients feel confident about implementing their new skills. From the outset therapists discuss with clients criteria and expectations for termination. There are a number of ways of assessing progress including: relief from symptoms, changes in reported and observed behaviour, and changes in thinking both inside and outside therapy. Performance in homework assignments, such as filling in the *Daily Record of Automatic Thoughts* and carrying out specific tasks and experiments, also assists in assessing progress. In particular, therapists look out for clients' ability to reality-test and, if necessary, modify or discard distorted interpretations. Termination is often gradual, say from weekly to biweekly sessions, followed by booster sessions one and two months after termination. The purpose of such sessions is to consolidate gains and assist clients to keep employing their new skills (Beck and Weishaar, 2005).

Cognitive therapy sessions generally last for 45 minutes. The standard treatment length for unipolar depression is eight to 16 sessions at weekly intervals. Moderately to severely depressed clients may be seen twice a week for the first two or three weeks. Clients with anxiety disorders generally receive from five to 15 sessions (Clark and Beck, 1988). The treatment of personality disorders generally takes longer and may last for a year or more.

The therapeutic relationship

Cognitive therapy is an educational process in which therapists are active in developing relationships with clients and using their expertise in helping clients examine and modify beliefs and behaviour. The quality of the therapist–client relationship is an important medium for improvement. Cognitive therapy is not an impersonal approach, but one in which therapists seek to understand their clients as individuals. Beck regards his therapeutic style as somewhat Rogerian. Therapists strive to create an emotional climate of genuine warmth and non-judgmental acceptance. Furthermore, cognitive therapists give clients their phone numbers in case of emergency.

Cognitive therapists attempt to demystify counselling by using a language that clients can understand. They treat clients with respect by offering rationales both for their overall approach and for each technique that they propose. In addition, they share responsibility for what happens in therapy by discussing case conceptualizations and involving clients in setting goals and session agendas. Cognitive therapists also elicit feedback from clients about both their suggestions and their behaviour. Therapists are sensitive to signs of transference and allow clients' reactions to them to be aired. Therapists can use these transference reactions to identify and work with clients' automatic thoughts and interpersonal distortions.

With most personality-disordered clients, cognitive therapists offer a closer and warmer relationship than in acute disorders, such as anxiety and depression. Therapists can face problems of non-collaboration from clients, especially those with personality disorders (Beck et al., 2003).

Serving as coinvestigator – collaborative empiricism

In addition to offering accepting and warm relationships, cognitive therapists play an active role in the therapy process and encourage clients to play an active role too. All of the client's cognitions are viewed as testable hypotheses. Therapists and clients collaborate together in the scientific endeavour of examining the evidence to confirm or negate the client's cognitions. Based on what clients say and how they say it, therapists develop hypotheses that can identify cognitive errors as well as underlying assumptions and beliefs. Therapists then ask clients to comment on whether their hypotheses fit the facts. By this means, clients are encouraged both to view their thoughts as personal views of reality and to build their skills of evaluating their validity. Throughout the process of identifying and exploring the evidence for biased thinking, as appropriate either the therapist or the client takes the more active role.

Serving as a guide – guided discovery

There are a number of different facets to guided discovery. Therapists can operate as guides to assist clients to discover the themes that run through their present automatic thoughts and beliefs. This can be taken one stage further where therapists and clients link the beliefs to analogous experiences in the past and collaboratively piece together the developmental history of the beliefs. Another use of guided discovery is that therapists act as guides in assisting clients to reality-test their possible errors in logic by designing new experiences that involve the client experimenting with different behaviour. Therapists do not use cajoling, disputation and indoctrination to assist clients to reality-test their thinking and adopt new beliefs. Rather they encourage clients to develop their own skills of using and assessing information, facts and probabilities in order to obtain more realistic perspectives than sometimes offered by their initial thoughts.

Therapeutic interventions

Both cognitive and behavioural interventions are used in cognitive therapy. The interventions selected depend on such factors as the nature of the client's problems, the therapeutic goals and how well they are functioning.

Cognitive interventions

The following are some of the main cognitive interventions used by cognitive therapists to assist clients to replace their distorted automatic thoughts and beliefs with more realistic ways of processing information.

Eliciting and identifying automatic thoughts

In order to change their thinking, clients need first become aware of their thought processes. Included below are some specific interventions for eliciting and identifying automatic thoughts.

1. *Providing reasons*: Therapists can provide reasons for the importance of examining the connections between how clients think, feel and act. Furthermore, they can introduce the concept of automatic thoughts and provide an example of how underlying perceptions influence feelings. In addition, therapists can communicate that a major assumption of cognitive therapy is that clients are experiencing difficulties in reality-testing the validity of their interpretations. Box 13.3 provides an example of a cognitive therapist showing the relationship between cognition, affect and behaviour (Beck et al., 1979b: 147–8).
2. *Questioning*: Clients may be questioned about automatic thoughts that occur during upsetting situations. Where clients experience difficulty recalling thoughts, imagery or role playing may be used. When questioning, therapists observe clients carefully for signs of affect that may offer leads for further questioning.
3. *Using a whiteboard*: When clients see their initial thoughts written up on the board, this may trigger them to reveal less obvious and more frightening thoughts.

4. *Encouraging clients to engage in feared activities*: Frequently, during sessions, clients are encouraged to engage in anxiety-evoking activities: for instance, making phone calls or writing letters they had been putting off. As they perform the activity, therapists can ask the question: 'What is going through your mind right now?' Therapists can also go with clients into real-life situations where they experience difficulty, for instance crowded places, and get them to verbalize what they think.

5. *Focusing on imagery*: Gathering information about imagery can be an important way of accessing automatic thoughts. Though individual differences exist, clinical observations suggest that many people visualizing scenes react to them as though they were real.

6. *Self-monitoring of thoughts*: Clients may be set homework in which they record their thoughts. They may complete a *Daily Record of Automatic Thoughts* log in which they record in their respective columns:

    (a) *date*;
    (b) *situation* leading to negative emotion(s);
    (c) *emotion(s)* felt and their degree on a 0–100 per cent scale;
    (d) *automatic thought(s)* and a rating of how strongly they believed the automatic thought(s) on a 0–100 per cent scale.

Therapists may encourage some clients to use wrist counters to help them learn to recognize automatic thoughts as they occur.

Box 13.3   Example of showing the influence of cognitions on affect and behaviour

The client
A 43-year-old depressed male patient.

The scene
The therapist instructed the client to imagine a person was home alone one night and heard a crash in another room.

Interpretation 1
This person thinks 'There's a burglar in the room'.

Possible consequences of Interpretation 1
The therapist then asked the client:

- 'How do you think this person would feel?', to which the client answered 'Very anxious, terrified';
- 'And how might he behave?', to which the client replied that he might hide or phone the police.

(Continued)

Box 13.3   (Continued)

Interpretation 2
The therapist then instructed the client to imagine that the person heard the same noise and thought: 'The windows have been left open and the wind has caused something to fall over'.

Possible consequences of Interpretation 2
The therapist then asked the client:

- 'How would he feel?', to which the client replied the person wouldn't be afraid, though he might be sad if he thought something valuable had been broken;
- 'And would his behaviour be different following this thought?', to which the client replied it would be different in that he would probably go and see what the problem was and certainly wouldn't phone the police.

Main teaching points
The therapist emphasized that this example showed:

- that usually there were a number of ways the client could interpret a situation; and
- the way he interpreted a situation would affect how he felt and behaved.

Reality-testing and correcting automatic thoughts

Interventions for assisting clients to treat their thoughts as hypotheses that require testing against reality and, if necessary, discarding, modifying or replacing include the following:

1. *Conducting Socratic dialogues*: Questions comprise the largest category of verbal statements in cognitive therapy. Questions reflect the basic empirical orientation of the approach and have the immediate goal of converting clients' closed belief systems into open systems. More specifically, questions seek to help clients: become aware of what their thoughts are; examine them for cognitive distortions; substitute more balanced thoughts; and make plans to develop new thought patterns. A basic raising awareness question is to ask clients: 'What is going through your mind right now?'

    Therapists use questioning rather than indoctrination and disputation. Conducted in an emotional climate of warmth and acceptance, the Socratic style of questioning assists clients to expand and evaluate how they think. Typical questions are:

    (a) 'Where is the evidence?'
    (b) 'Where is the logic?'
    (c) 'Are there other ways of perceiving the situation?'

(d) 'What do I have to lose?'
(e) 'What do I have to gain?'
(f) 'What would be the worst thing that could happen?', and
(g) 'What can I learn from this experience?' (Beck and Emery, 1985).

Clients learn to ask themselves the same questions that their therapists have asked. For instance, however plausible their automatic thoughts may 'feel', clients in distressed relationships can question their validity by asking themselves the following series of questions:

(a) 'What is the evidence in *favour* of my interpretation?'
(b) 'What evidence is *contrary* to my interpretation?'
(c) 'Does it *logically follow* from my spouse's actions that my spouse has the motive that I assign to him or her?', and
(d) 'Is there an *alternative* explanation for his or her behaviour?' (Beck, 1988).

Box 13.4 provides an example of some of Beck's questions to evaluate a client's thinking (Beck, 1976: 249–52).

2. *Identifying cognitive distortions*: Therapists can teach clients what the common cognitive distortions are, for instance arbitrary inference and magnification. Both during therapy and as homework clients can be asked to identify the distortions in how they think. Clients may use the three-column technique for this:

(a) column one – describe a situation that elicits negative emotions;
(b) column two – identify their automatic thoughts in the situation;
(c) column three – list the types of distortions in these thoughts.

3. *Decatastrophizing*: In decatastrophizing, the basic question is 'So what if it happens?' Areas covered in this technique include: the event's probability and severity, the client's coping capacity and support factors, and the client's ability to accept and deal with the worst possible outcomes.

4. *Reattribution*: Reattribution techniques test automatic thoughts and underlying beliefs by considering alternative ways of assigning responsibility and cause. Clients can be encouraged to rate on a 0–100 scale the degree of responsibility they feel for negative events and feared outcomes. By means of questioning, the therapist attempts to loosen them up by generating and evaluating alternative explanations.

5. *Redefining*: Redefining problems entails making them more concrete and stating them in terms of what the client might do. For example, a lonely person who feels uncared for may redefine his or her problem as 'I need to reach out to other people and be caring'.

6. *Decentring*: Decentring involves assisting clients to evaluate their belief that everyone is focusing on them. Clients can be encouraged to assess more closely what others are doing: for instance, other students may be

daydreaming, looking at their lecturer, or taking notes. In addition, clients can be asked to closely observe how frequently they attend to others. This may help them realize how limited their observations are and thus infer that other people's observations are the same.

7. *Forming rational responses*: Cognitive therapists train clients in how to form more rational responses to their automatic thoughts. Again, questioning is an important way to assist clients in learning to use their inner monologue for rather than against themselves. Box 13.5 provides an example of a client providing a counteracting rational response to herself (Beck, 1988: 264). Finding a rational response can help clients see their automatic thoughts as an interpretation rather than as 'the truth'.

8. *Daily recording of rational responses*: When ready, clients can be encouraged to fill out rational response and outcome columns on their *Daily Record of Automatic Thoughts*. In the outcome column, clients:

    (a) rerate their beliefs in their automatic thought(s) on a 0–100 per cent scale; and

    (b) specify what their subsequent emotions are and rate them on a 0–100 per cent scale.

9. *Imagery techniques*: Numerous imagery techniques are discussed by Beck and Emery (1985). Among these techniques are assisting clients to gain more realistic perspectives through repeated visualizations of fantasies, through projecting themselves into the future and looking back on their present situations, and by getting them to exaggerate images, for instance of harming others.

Box 13.4   Case example: Evaluating the thought that 'Failure is a catastrophe'

The client
A medical student inhibited in numerous situations where assertion was essential. Here the therapist focuses on the client's fears of giving a talk in front of his class tomorrow.

The therapist's questions
-   'What are you afraid of?'
-   'Suppose you do make a fool of yourself, why is that so bad?'
-   'Now look here, suppose they ridicule you, can you die from it?'
-   'Suppose they decide that you are the worst public speaker that ever lived, will this ruin your career?'
-   'But if you flubbed it would your wife or parents disown you?'
-   'Well, what would be so awful about it?'

Box 13.4   (Continued)

When the client answers that he would feel pretty bad, the therapist asks:
'For how long?' and the client replies 'For about a day or two' and the therapist then
says: 'And then what?', to which the client replies, 'Then I'd be OK'.

The therapist's summary
The therapist pointed out to the client that, somewhere along the line his thinking
got fouled up, and that he tended to regard failure as a catastrophe. The client
needed to start challenging his wrong premises and to label failures accurately
as failures to attain goals and not as disasters.

Subsequent therapy sessions
As therapy proceeded the therapist coached the client in changing his notion that
failure was a catastrophe as well as challenged maladaptive attitudes producing
psychological distress in other social situations.

Box 13.5   Example of forming a rational response

The situation
Wendy was phoned by her husband Hal to say he was tied up at the office.

- *Emotional reaction*:   Anger.
- *Automatic thought*:   'Its not fair. I have to work too. If he wanted to, he could be
                          home on time'.
- *Rational response*:   'His job is different. Many of his customers come in after
                          work'.

Identifying and modifying underlying beliefs

Underlying beliefs may be harder for therapists and clients to access than
automatic thoughts. Often they fall into one of three main belief clusters cen-
tring on issues of:

- *acceptance* – for instance, 'I'm flawed and therefore unacceptable';
- *competence* – for instance, 'I'm inferior'; and
- *control* – for instance, 'I have no control'.

Underlying beliefs are signposted by the themes in clients' automatic thoughts.
Clients' behaviour, coping strategies and personal histories are additional sources

for therapists to form belief hypotheses. Most clients find it difficult to articulate their beliefs without assistance. Generally therapists present hypotheses to clients for verification. Where clients disagree, therapists can work with them to form more accurate statements of their beliefs.

The following are some cognitive interventions for modifying beliefs:

1. *Socratic questioning*: Therapists can use questions that encourage clients to examine their beliefs: for instance'; 'Does the belief seem reasonable?'; 'Can you review the evidence for it?'; and 'What are the advantages and disadvantages of maintaining the belief?'

2. *Hypothesis testing*: Together therapists and clients can set up experiments that encourage clients to test the reality of their beliefs. Box 13.6 provides an example of such an experiment (Beck, 1988: 224).

3. *Using imagery*: Imagery can be used to assist clients to 'relive' past traumatic events and so restructure their experiences and the beliefs derived from them.

4. *Reliving childhood memories*: Beck and colleagues (2003) consider that with chronic personality disorders it is crucial to use childhood material to assist clients in reviewing and loosening their underlying beliefs. By recreating 'pathogenic' developmental situations through role playing and role reversal, clients have an opportunity to restructure or modify beliefs formed during this period.

5. *Refashioning beliefs*: Therapists can assist clients to refashion their beliefs. Beck gives the example of M.K., a director of a research institute at a major university who suffered from a major depressive disorder and generalized anxiety disorder. The client had strong beliefs of inadequacy and rejection which he crystallized as 'I must be *the best* at everything I do'. One of M.K.'s beliefs was refashioned thus: 'It is rewarding to succeed highly, but lesser success is rewarding also and has no bearing on my adequacy or inadequacy. I am adequate no matter what' (Beck and Rush, in press: 48).

Box 13.6   Example of hypothesis testing concerning a belief

The client
Marjorie, who was afraid to make a mental commitment to her spouse, Ken, because she was afraid she might find out that she could not trust him.

Marjorie's underlying belief
'I must never allow myself to be vulnerable'.

Consequence of Marjorie's distorted thinking
Her aloof behaviour and fault finding created distance in their relationship.

Box 13.6   (Continued)

The experiment
Beck and Marjorie set up a three-month experiment for her to test the hypothesis 'If I totally commit myself to the relationship, look for the positive instead of the negative, I will feel more secure'. During the experiment, Marjorie was to change how she thought and acted.

Result of the experiment
Marjorie discovered that she was more secure and had fewer thoughts about leaving Ken.

Behavioural interventions

Behavioural interventions have many purposes in cognitive therapy. First, behavioural interventions can lay the foundation for later cognitive work. An issue arises whether to focus on behaviour first, cognition first, or both concurrently. Behavioural interventions may sometimes be used before cognitive interventions to promote symptom relief and enhance motivation. For instance, severely depressed clients may be encouraged to perform small tasks to counteract their withdrawal, get them involved in constructive activities, and open their minds to the possibility of gaining satisfaction from previously pleasurable activities. However, in contrast to normal people, depressed clients can change their behaviour markedly, but do not necessarily change their negative hypervalent cognitions (Beck et al., 1979b). In working with couples, Beck (1988) concentrates on changing behaviour first since he regards it as easier to change actions than thinking patterns. In addition, spouses may immediately reward each other's changes in behaviour.

Second, behavioural interventions can be used to assist clients in reality-testing their automatic thoughts and beliefs. A third use of behavioural interventions is, along with cognitive interventions, to assist clients to engage in feared activities. A fourth use is to train clients in specific behavioural skills. Since the uses of behavioural interventions overlap, below they are not categorized according to purpose.

The following are some of the main behavioural interventions used by cognitive therapists:

1. *Activity scheduling*: Activity scheduling is a form of timetabling. Planning specific activities with clients can be important in helping clients to realize that they can control their time. A principle of activity scheduling is to state what activity the client agrees to engage in rather than how much they will accomplish. Clients can set aside time each evening to plan their activities for the next day.

2. *Rating mastery and pleasure*: Using 0–10 scales, clients can rate the degree of mastery and the degree of pleasure they experienced in each activity during the day. Mastery and pleasure ratings can give depressed clients an insight into the activities that reduce their dysphoria.

3. *Hypothesis testing*: Hypothesis testing has both behavioural and cognitive components (Beck and Weishaar, 2005). Especially later in therapy, behavioural experiments may be designed to provide information that may contradict existing automatic thoughts, faulty predictions and underlying beliefs. A young man about to cancel a date because of the fear 'I won't know what to say' was encouraged to go on the date and treat not knowing what to say as an experimental hypothesis. The findings of this particular experiment disproved his hypothesis (Beck and Emery, 1985). In the earlier example Marjorie was engaging in a behavioural as well as a cognitive experiment to test her underlying belief that 'I must never allow myself to be vulnerable'.

4. *Rehearsing behaviour and role playing*: Behaviour rehearsal can be used to develop clients' skills for specific social and stressful situations. Demonstration and video feedback can be used as part of skills training. Behaviour rehearsals should have a number of trials and rehearse clients in a variety of responses. Also, clients can rehearse situations by using their imaginations.

5. *Assigning graded tasks*: Often clients fail at tasks because they try to do too much too soon. Therapists and clients can develop hierarchies of feared or difficult situations. Then clients can perform less threatening ones before moving on to more threatening activities.

6. *Using diversion techniques*: Clients may be encouraged to engage in activities that divert them from their strong negative emotions and thinking. Such activities include work, play, socializing and doing something physical.

7. *Assigning homework*: Homework forms an important part of cognitive therapy. Its purpose is both to shorten the time spent in therapy as well as facilitate the development of cognitive and behavioural skills for use after counselling. Homework assignments include self-monitoring, activities designed to reality-test automatic thoughts and underlying beliefs, implementing procedures for dealing with specific situations, and activities for developing cognitive skills such as identifying cognitive distortions, rational responding and refashioning beliefs.

Case material

Beck and colleagues (Beck, 2005: 115–31; Beck et al., 1979b: 225–43) present an initial interview with a depressed 40-year-old female clinical psychologist client who had recently been left by her boyfriend. The interview transcript is broken down into five parts: questioning to elicit vital information, broadening the client's perspective, 'alternative therapy', obtaining more accurate data, and closure. Beck and Young (1985: 206–44) illustrate in the case example of a depressed young female client how cognitive therapists elicit and evaluate maladaptive thoughts and assumptions throughout treatment. Beck and Weishaar (2005) illustrate in the case example of a 21-year-old highly anxious male college student both behavioural and cognitive interventions for attaining therapeutic goals. Throughout his book *Love is Never Enough*, Beck (1988) provides numerous vignettes of the use of cognitive interventions in relationship therapy.

Other sources of case material include Scott and colleagues' edited *Cognitive Therapy in Clinical Practice: An Illustrative Casebook* (1989); Freeman and Dattilio's edited *Comprehensive Casebook of Cognitive Therapy* (1992); Greenberger and Padesky's *Mind Over Mood* (1995); and Judith Beck's *Cognitive Therapy: Basics and Beyond* (1995), which uses a single case throughout to illustrate how to employ various cognitive therapy interventions.

Further developments

Cognitive therapy has been used with all ages, from children to the elderly. Beck reports that several controlled studies have shown it to be at least as effective as antidepressant medication in treating elderly depressed clients. Cognitive therapy has been used for group work with families. Some newer applications of cognitive therapy include working with clients with schizophrenia, post-traumatic stress disorders, substance abuse problems, hypertension and dissociative disorders as well as with clients who have committed sexual offences, such as exhibitionism and incest. Schema-focused approaches to personality disorders have been an important development in cognitive therapy.

Padesky and Beck (2003) note that cognitive therapy has spread more rapidly in recent decades than rational emotive behaviour therapy. Cognitive therapy has been evaluated by thousands of studies that examine its conceptual models, treatment methods, protocols and outcomes. Treatment protocols, such as those for depression and panic disorder, have been in existence for some time. Generally, cognitive therapy does as well or better than other active therapies for these problems. Other problems for which cognitive therapy has proved effective include social phobia, generalized anxiety disorder, post-traumatic stress disorder and obsessive-compulsive disorder. Research also indicates that cognitive therapy leads to lower relapse rates than other active therapies.

There are over 10 training centres for cognitive therapy in the United States, including the Beck Institute for Cognitive Therapy and Research, directed by Beck's daughter, Dr Judith Beck. In addition, training in cognitive therapy is widely available elsewhere, including Britain and Australia. With the current emphasis on containing costs through managed care, cognitive therapy's short-term approach will be increasingly popular with both third-party payers and clients (Beck and Weishaar, 2005).

Review and personal questions

Review questions

1. What are schemas and modes and why are they important?
2. What are automatic thoughts and why are they important?
3. What are cognitive distortions and why are they important?
4. What are Beck's views on the following causes of cognitions and behaviour:

    (a) evolutionary causes;
    (b) genetic causes.

5. What is the nature and role of each of the following factors in helping people acquire cognitive vulnerability: childhood trauma; negative treatment in childhood; social learning; and inadequate experiences for learning coping skills?
6. What are some factors relevant to activating cognitive vulnerability?
7. What is the nature and role of each of the following factors in helping people maintain cognitive vulnerability: failure to turn off hypervalent modes; inability to reality-test dysfunctional interpretations; and resistances to change?
8. Critically discuss the goals of cognitive therapy.
9. Describe the nature of the therapist–client relationship in cognitive therapy.
10. Describe the process of cognitive therapy.
11. What are some of the main cognitive interventions used in cognitive therapy for:

    (a) eliciting and identifying automatic thoughts?
    (b) reality-testing and correcting automatic thoughts?
    (c) identifying and modifying underlying beliefs?

12. What are some of the main behavioural interventions used in cognitive therapy?

Personal questions

1. List any significant factors when you were growing up that may have contributed to your acquiring faulty ways of processing information.
2. Think of a specific problem in your life. Elicit and identify some of your automatic thoughts regarding it.
3. Identify characteristic cognitive distortions, if any, in the way you process information.
4. Identify an automatic thought in a problem area and challenge it by means of Socratic questioning.

5. In a problem area, identify a thought that lends itself to being reality-tested through changing your behaviour. Design and implement a behavioural experiment to reality-test your thought.
6. What relevance, if any, has the theory and practice of cognitive therapy for how you conduct therapy?
7. What relevance, if any, has the theory and practice of cognitive therapy for how your live?

Annotated bibliography

Beck, A.T., Rush, A.J., Shaw, B.F. and Emery, G. (1979b) *Cognitive Therapy of Depression.* New York: John Wiley.
This book presents Beck's cognitive model of depression. The bulk of the book is a clinical handbook devoted to practical aspects of treating depressed clients, for instance the therapeutic relationship, the application of both cognitive and behavioural interventions, and problems related to termination and relapse.

Beck, A.T. and Emery, G. (1985) *Anxiety Disorders and Phobias: A Cognitive Perspective.* New York: Basic Books.
Part 1 of the book, written by Beck, is entitled 'Theoretical and clinical aspects' and presents his cognitive model of anxiety. Part 2 of the book, written by Emery, is entitled 'Cognitive therapy: techniques and applications' and has chapters on the principles of cognitive therapy, techniques for cognitive restructuring, modifying imagery, affect, and behaviour, and on restructuring assumptions.

Beck, A.T. (1988) *Love is Never Enough: How Couples Can Overcome Misunderstandings, Resolve Conflicts, and Solve Relationship Problems Through Cognitive Therapy.* New York: Harper & Row.
This book describes the power of negative and biased thinking in couple relationships. Beck shows how partners can improve their relationship by identifying and modifying their maladaptive automatic thoughts and underlying beliefs.

Beck, A.T. and Weishaar, M.E. (2005) 'Cognitive therapy', in R.J. Corsini and D. Wedding (eds), *Current Psychotherapies* (7th edn). Belmont, CA: Thomson Brooks/ Cole. pp. 238–68.
An authoritative chapter reviewing the theory and practice of contemporary cognitive therapy.

Beck, J.S. (1995) *Cognitive Therapy: Basics and Beyond.* New York: Guilford.
Beck's daughter Judith wrote this manual for cognitive therapy. Starting with case conceptualization, she shows the reader how to identify and work with deeper-level cognitions, prepare for termination and anticipate problems.

Greenberger, D. and Padesky, C.A. (1995) *Mind Over Mood: Change How You Feel by Changing the Way You Think.* New York: Guilford.
Padesky, C.A. and Greenberger, D. (1995) *Clinician's Guide to Mind Over Mood.* New York: Guilford.
These companion volumes are designed as step-by-step guides to the techniques and strategies of cognitive therapy. The manual is designed as a self-help workbook and the

clinician's guide provides therapists with instructions on how to incorporate the workbook into individual and group psychotherapy.

Weishaar, M.E. (1993) *Aaron T. Beck*. London: Sage.
Weishaar has been both a student and collaborator of Beck's, so she writes with authority. The five chapters in the book cover: Beck's life, his theoretical contributions, his practical contributions, some criticisms and rebuttals, and Beck's overall influence.

References and further reading

Alford, B.A. and Beck, A.T. (1997) *The Integrative Power of Cognitive Therapy*. New York: Guilford.

Beck, A.T. (1963) 'Thinking and depression. 1. Idiosyncratic content and cognitive distortions', *Archives of General Psychiatry, 9*: 324–33.

Beck, A.T. (1964) 'Thinking and depression. 2. Theory and therapy', *Archives of General Psychiatry, 10*: 561–71.

Beck, A.T. (1976) *Cognitive Therapy and the Emotional Disorders*. New York: New American Library.

Beck, A.T. (1978) *Anxiety Checklist*. Philadelphia: Center for Cognitive Therapy.

Beck, A.T. (1988) *Love is Never Enough: How Couples Can Overcome Misunderstandings, Resolve Conflicts, and Solve Relationship Problems Through Cognitive Therapy*. New York: Harper & Row.

Beck, A.T. (1991) 'Cognitive therapy: a 30-year retrospective', *American Psychologist, 46*: 368–75.

Beck, A.T. (1999) *Prisoners of Hate: The Cognitive Basis of Anger, Hostility and Violence*. New York: HarperCollins.

Beck, A.T. (2005) 'Cognitive therapy: an interview with a depressed and suicidal patient', in D. Wedding and R.J. Corsini (eds), *Case Studies in Psychotherapy* (4th edn). Belmont, CA: Thomson Brooks/Cole. pp. 115–31.

Beck, A.T. and Emery, G. (1985) *Anxiety Disorders and Phobias: A Cognitive Perspective*. New York: Basic Books.

Beck, A.T. and Rush, A.J. (in press) 'Cognitive therapy', in H.I. Kaplan and B.J. Sadock (eds), *Comprehensive Textbook of Psychiatry* (Vol. VI). Baltimore, MD: Williams & Wilkins.

Beck, A.T. and Weishaar, M.E. (2005) 'Cognitive therapy', in R.J. Corsini and D. Wedding (eds), *Current Psychotherapies* (7th edn). Belmont, CA: Thomson Brooks/Cole. pp. 238–68.

Beck, A.T. and Young, J.E. (1985) 'Cognitive therapy of depression', in D. Barlow (ed.), *Clinical Handbook of Psychological Disorders: A Step-by-Step Treatment Manual*. New York: Guilford. pp. 206–44.

Beck, A.T. et al. (2003) *Cognitive Therapy of Personality Disorders* (2nd edn). New York: Plenum.

Beck, A.T., Kovacs, M. and Weissman, A. (1979a) 'Assessment of suicide intention: the Scale for Suicide Ideation', *Journal of Consulting and Clinical Psychology, 47*: 343–52.

Beck, A.T., Rush, A.J., Shaw, B.F. and Emery, G. (1979b) *Cognitive Therapy of Depression*. New York: John Wiley.

Beck, A.T., Ward, C.H., Mendelson, M., Mock, J.E. and Erbaugh, J.K. (1961) 'An inventory for measuring depression', *Archives of General Psychiatry, 4*: 561–71.

Beck, J.S. (1995) *Cognitive Therapy: Basics and Beyond*. New York: Guilford.

Beck, J.S and Beck, A.T. (2002) *Beck Youth Inventories of Emotional and Social Impairment*. San Antonio, TX: The Psychological Corporation.

Clark, D.M. and Beck, A.T. (1988) 'Cognitive approaches', in C.G. Last and M. Hersen (eds), *Handbook of Anxiety Disorders*. New York: Pergamon. pp. 362–85.

Clark, D.M. and Beck, A.T. (2002) *Clark–Beck Obsessive-Compulsive Inventory*. San Antonio, TX: The Psychological Corporation.

Clark, D.M., Beck, A.T. and Alford, B.A. (1999) *Scientific Foundations of Cognitive Theory and Therapy of Depression*. Philadelphia: John Wiley.

Freeman, A. and Dattilio, F.M. (eds) (1992) *Comprehensive Casebook of Cognitive Therapy*. New York: Plenum Press.

Greenberger, D. and Padesky, C.A. (1995) *Mind Over Mood: Change How You Feel by Changing the Way You Think*. New York: Guilford.

Kelly, G. (1955) *The Psychology of Personal Constructs*. New York: Norton.

Kendall, P.C., Hollon, S.T., Beck, A.T., Hammen, C.L. and Ingram, R.E. (1987). 'Issues and recommendations regarding use of the Beck Depression Inventory', *Cognitive Therapy and Research, 11*: 289–99.

Lazarus, R.S. (1966) *Psychological Stress and the Coping Process*. New York: McGraw-Hill.

Padesky, C.A. and Beck, A.T. (2003) 'Science and philosophy: comparison of cognitive therapy and rational emotive behavior therapy', *Journal of Cognitive Psychotherapy, 17*: 211–25.

Padesky, C.A. and Greenberger, D. (1995) *Clinician's Guide to Mind Over Mood*. New York: Guilford.

Scott, J., Williams, J.M.G. and Beck, A.T. (eds) (1989) *Cognitive Therapy in Clinical Practice: An Illustrative Casebook*. London: Routledge.

Weishaar, M.E. (1993) *Aaron T. Beck*. London: Sage.

Weissman, A. (1979) *The Dysfunctional Attitudes Scale*. Philadelphia: Center for Cognitive Therapy.

Beck on audio-cassette and videotape

Beck, A.T. (1977) *Demonstration of the Cognitive Therapy of Depression: Interview#1 (Patient with Family Problem)*. Audio and video available.

Beck, A.T. (1979) *Cognitive Therapy of Depression: Interview#1 (Patient with a Hopelessness Problem)*. Audio and video available.

Beck, A.T. (1985) *Cognitive Therapy of Anxiety and Panic Disorders: First Interview Techniques*. Audio and video available.

Beck, A.T. (1990) *Cognitive Therapy of an Avoidant Personality*. Two audio-cassette set.

Useful addresses

The Beck Institute
GSB Building, City Line and Belmont Avenues, Suite 700
Bala Cynwyd
PA 19004-1610
USA
Website: www.beckinstitute.org
Email: beckinst@gim.net

Introduction

Multimodal therapy is an approach developed by Arnold A. Lazarus, a clinical psychologist, in response to the constraints of traditional behaviour therapy. Lazarus's first book on multimodal therapy was entitled *Multimodal Behavior Therapy* (1976). However, he considered including the word behaviour in the title to be misleading, since it did not take into account working with other modalities, such as cognition and imagery. Consequently, he shortened the name to multimodal therapy.

Lazarus (2005a) observes that the multimodal orientation transcends the behavioural tradition by adding unique assessment procedures and by dealing in great depth and detail with sensory, imagery, cognitive and interpersonal factors and their interactive effects. Clients' needs are often better served if therapists work in multimodal rather than unimodal or bimodal fashions. Multimodal therapy rests heavily on multimodal assessment to choose the most appropriate techniques for particular clients with their unique psychological profiles and circumstances. Lazarus observes about the term multimodal therapy: 'It might have been better to call it "multimodal assessment and comprehensive psychotherapy" or something like that' (Dryden, 1991: 107).

Arnold A. Lazarus (1932–)

Arnold Lazarus was born in Johannesburg, South Africa on 27 January 1932, the youngest of four children. His father ran a small retail business. At time of birth his two sisters were 14 and 17 and his brother was eight. Lazarus grew up feeling that as the youngest family member 'I was typically ignored and my opinion was considered unimportant' (Dryden, 1991: 101). This contributed to his feeling shy, inadequate and hypersensitive. Lazarus was a 'skinny kid who was bullied a lot' (p. 1), and, consequently, spent much time on body-building activities. He exhibited an early interest in writing and, in his teens, had some stories published in local newspapers. Another youthful writing assignment was that of Associate Editor of a South African body-building magazine. When Lazarus was growing up, broadening experiences included: attending several high schools, spending time on a farm, working in a department store and selling houses.

Lazarus started university with a view to becoming a journalist and writer. However, on discovering that he could be a psychotherapist without going through a formal medical education, he became seriously interested in psychology and psychotherapy. In 1955 Lazarus received a BA with psychology and sociology majors, in 1956 a BA Honours in Psychology, in 1957 an MA in Experimental Psychology, and in 1960 a PhD in Clinical Psychology, all degrees conferred by the University of the Witwatersrand in Johannesburg. His PhD research on 'New group techniques in the treatment of phobic conditions' used group systematic desensitization. Joseph Wolpe was chairperson of his dissertation committee.

Lazarus's occupational history started with a part-time psychologist position in 1958–9 with the Mental Health Society in Johannesburg. From 1959 to 1963 and then from 1964 to 1966 he was in private practice as well as being a part-time lecturer at Witwatersrand Medical School. Albert Bandura, on the basis of seeing a write-up of Lazarus's PhD findings in the *Journal of Abnormal and Social Psychology* (Lazarus, 1961), invited him to Stanford University where, from 1963 to 1964, he was Visiting Assistant Professor in the Psychology Department. Uneasy with apartheid and the South African political situation, in 1966 Lazarus and his family returned to the United States, where in 1976 he became a naturalized American citizen.

From 1966 to 1967, Lazarus directed the Behavior Therapy Institute in Sausalito, California. From 1967 to 1970 he was a Professor of Psychology in the Department of Behavioral Science at Temple University Medical School, Philadelphia. Joseph Wolpe, his former supervisor, was also at Temple University but he and Lazarus had an acrimonious falling out when Wolpe perceived Lazarus's views on the broadening of behaviour therapy to include cognition and 'technical eclecticism' as heretical and threatening to what he was propounding. From 1970 to 1972, Lazarus was Visiting Professor and Director of Clinical Training at Yale University's Department of Psychology. In 1972 he moved to Rutgers University in New Jersey being from 1972 to 1974 a Professor in and Chairman of the Psychology Department, from 1974 to 1998, a Distinguished Professor in the Graduate School of Applied and Professional Psychology, and currently Distinguished Professor Emeritus of Clinical Psychology. In addition to his private practice, he now is Executive Director at the Lazarus Institute in Princeton, where his clinical psychologist son Clifford is the President and licensed clinical social worker daughter-in-law Donna manages the Adolescent Therapy Unit.

One of Lazarus's current interests is in examining the impact of licensing boards and ethics committees. This concern was spawned around 1993 when two of his colleagues were severely censured by state licensing boards for transcending minor boundaries. He also grew alarmed when some of his students helpfully went beyond the call of duty on behalf of some of their clients and were reprimanded by authoritarian supervisors for 'stepping outside accepted boundaries'. He has published several articles and coedited a book (Lazarus and Zur, 2002) on the benefits that can accrue when certain boundaries are transcended. He has been serving as an expert witness in court cases involving colleagues whom he feels have been unfairly rebuked.

Lazarus has held numerous consultant positions and editorial board appointments. His professional awards include: in 1982, the American Board of Professional Psychology's Distinguished Service to the Profession of Psychology Award; in 1992, the American Psychological Association's Division of Psychotherapy's Distinguished Psychologist Award; in 1996 he was the first recipient of the prestigious Annual Cummings PSYCHE Award for his innovative contributions to time-effective psychotherapy; and in 1999 he received two lifetime achievement awards, one from the California Psychological Association and the other from the Association for Advancement of Behavior Therapy.

Lazarus's early interest in writing has continued unabated. By 2005 he had authored or coauthored 18 books and over 350 journal articles and book chapters. His books include *Behaviour Therapy Techniques* (Wolpe and Lazarus, 1966), *Behavior Therapy and Beyond* (1971), *Clinical Behavior Therapy* (as editor and contributor (1972)), *Multimodal Behavior Therapy* (1976), *In the Mind's Eye: The Power of Imagery for Personal Enrichment* (1984), *Marital Myths Revisited* (2001), *Don't Believe It For a Minute!* (Lazarus et al., 1993), *The 60-Second Shrink: 101 Strategies for Staying Sane in a Crazy World* (Lazarus and Lazarus, 1997), *The Practice of Multimodal Therapy* (1981) and *Brief but Comprehensive Psychotherapy: The Multimodal Way* (1997).

Lazarus values his humanity and works in order to live. In 1956 he married Daphne, and in 1959 Linda was born, followed in 1961 by Clifford. His priorities are: first, wife and family, second, meaningful friendships and the pursuit of fun (plays, music, brisk walks etc.), and third, work. By work, he means intellectual stimulation, making a social contribution and surviving economically. Given another life he has a fantasy that he would like to direct and create movies like Steven Spielberg's. The question Lazarus always asks when someone dies is: 'Did this person have enough fun on this earth?' (Dryden, 1991: 14). If not, he feels that they have had wasted lives.

Regarding his professional work, Lazarus mentions three contributions: first, showing that behaviour therapy can be more humanistic; second, broadening behaviour therapy's horizons to include cognitions, thus developing cognitive-behavioural therapy; and third, developing 'an even broader and more systematic framework in my writings on multimodal methods' (p. 112). Lazarus is listed in the *Who's Who in America* and in the *Who's Who in the World*.

Theory

Basic concepts

Technical eclecticism

Eclecticism is not a unitary construct (Lazarus, 1989a). Instead there are many different kinds of eclecticism. Lazarus distinguishes unsystematic eclecticism –

where therapists require neither a coherent rationale nor empirical validation for the techniques they use – and systematic (technical) eclecticism – where therapists are guided by a preferred theory but also draw techniques from other orientations.

Lazarus also distinguishes theoretical eclecticism from technical eclecticism. Unlike their theoretically eclectic counterparts, technically eclectic therapists use procedures from different sources without necessarily subscribing to the theories or disciplines that spawned them (Lazarus, 2005a). Systematic technical eclectics neither choose techniques that 'feel right' nor hop from theory to theory. Lazarus writes: 'The hallmark of technical eclecticism is the use of prescriptive treatments based on empirical evidence and client need, rather than theoretical and personal predisposition' (1989a: 252). Technical eclectics mainly use cognitive-behavioural ideas and techniques. In addition, they may draw from Adlerian, Rogerian, Eriksonian, psychodrama, Gestalt, reality and transactional analysis schools, but without embracing any of these diverse theories. They regard as excess baggage the needless addition or multiplication of explanatory principles.

An important distinction exists between observations and theories. Theories are essentially speculations trying to account for various phenomena. Observations reflect clinical data without trying to offer explanations. Lazarus gives these examples: 'Adolescents tend to imitate the behavior of peers whom they respect', which is a statement based on observation, and 'They do so unconsciously due to inadequate parental introjects', a statement based on theory (Lazarus and Messer, 1991). Though acknowledging that clinical practice cannot be totally a-theoretical, his technically eclectic therapy is governed by many observations (not theories) from different sources.

Unlike technical eclecticism, theoretical integration attempts to synthesize different therapy techniques as well as the theories underlying change from different orientations. Lazarus sees technical eclecticism as a step towards eventual integrationism. However, he urges caution in proceeding with integrationism. There is the danger of superficially merging theoretical tenets that are intrinsically incompatible (Lazarus, 1997; Lazarus et al., 1992). Furthermore, therapists can become more intent on attaching theoretical labels to what they do than on precisely stating both what they do with each client and how they select what they do.

Thresholds

Physiologically, people react to a variety of arousing stimuli with differing and distinctive patterns of autonomic nervous system activity. Lazarus (1997, 2005a) uses the term 'threshold' to describe people's differing capacities to tolerate negative stimuli such as pain, frustration, stress, cold, noise and pollution. People whose autonomic nervous systems are stable, which usually indicates high thresholds to many events, have a different personality pattern and are likely to be less anxiety prone than those whose autonomic reactions are labile, which usually correlates with low thresholds.

Thresholds, with their large innate component, can limit the effectiveness of psychological interventions. Lazarus gives the example of the limitations of hypnosis and other psychological techniques on a person with extremely low pain tolerance. While their pain tolerance may be raised, their innate threshold to overreact to pain stimuli nevertheless remains.

The seven modalities: BASIC ID

The concept of modalities is the bedrock of comprehensive multimodal assessment and treatment. Human personality can be divided into seven discrete, yet interacting, modalities or dimensions. Lazarus writes: 'These modalities exist in a state of reciprocal transaction and flux, connected by complex chains of behavior and other psychophysiological processes' (1992: 236). Box 14.1 presents the seven modalities, each illustrated by its description in the Structural Profile, a multimodal self-assessment questionnaire (Lazarus, 1997: 141). The acronym BASIC ID is formed by using the first letter of each modality. This provides a useful shorthand descriptor of the seven modalities. In addition, the acronym serves as an *aide memoire*.

Box 14.1   The seven BASIC ID modalities

1. *Behaviour*: Some people may be described as 'doers': they are action oriented, like to keep busy, get things done and take on various projects. How much of a doer are you?
2. *Affect*: Some people are very emotional and may or may not express it. How emotional are you? How deeply do you feel things? How passionate are you?
3. *Sensation*: Some people attach a lot of value to sensory experiences, such as sex, food, music, art and other 'sensory delights'. Others are very much aware of minor aches, pains and discomforts. How 'tuned in to' your sensations are you?
4. *Imagery*: How much fantasy or daydreaming do you engage in? This is separate from thinking or planning. This is 'thinking in pictures', visualizing real or imagined experiences, letting your mind roam. How much are you into imagery?
5. *Cognition*: Some people are very analytical, like to plan things and reason things through. How much of a 'thinker' and 'planner' are you?
6. *Interpersonal*: How important are other people to you? This is your self-rating as a social being. How important are close friendships to you, the tendency to gravitate towards people, the desire for intimacy? The opposite of this is being a 'loner'.
7. *Drugs/biology*: Are you healthy and health-conscious? Do you avoid bad habits like smoking, too much alcohol, drinking a lot of coffee, overeating and so on? Do you exercise regularly, get enough sleep, avoid junk foods and generally take care of your body?

Lazarus acknowledges people's behaviour is specific to situations and to other people. Nevertheless, people have tendencies, usually evident in the first decade of their lives, to favour some BASIC ID modalities over others. People's BASIC ID tendencies determine the tone and quality of how they function. For instance, to call someone an 'imagery reactor' means that their most highly valued and predominant modality is visual. Though they may not do so all the time, they are inclined to respond to and organize the world in terms of mental images. On the other hand, 'cognitive reactors' respond to the world from their intellects. In terms of brain research, the right hemisphere is probably dominant for imagery reactors and the left the hemisphere for cognitive reactors. Sensory reactors may be subdivided according to the predominance of each of the five basic senses. Lazarus observes: 'To "know" or to "understand" another person is to have full access to his or her BASIC I.D. Self-knowledge implies an awareness of the content of one's own BASIC I.D. as well as insight into the interactive effects therein' (Lazarus, 1989b: 16–17).

Thresholds and preferred modalities interact. For example, the person with low pain tolerance, high frustration tolerance, high activity and vivid imagery is very different from a person with low frustration tolerance, moderate activity, highly analytical (cognition) and capable of only forming fleeting images (Lazarus, 2005a).

Acquisition

Lazarus has never developed a full theoretical statement of his own regarding how people acquire and maintain their BASIC ID modalities and their personality strengths and weaknesses. Instead he prefers to be more of an empiricist and leave the theorizing to others. Nevertheless, he endeavours to understand other theorists' frameworks and principles to see which are the best scientifically proven ideas upon which he can draw. Lazarus (2005a) has studiously avoided theoretical integration and stresses that multimodal therapy is not a conglomeration of psychoanalysis, behaviour therapy and many other systems.

People's personalities stem from their genetic endowment, physical environment and social learning history. Multimodal therapy is not a-theoretical: instead its technically eclectic stance operates within a consistent *social cognitive learning theory* (Bandura, 1986). However, when dealing with dyadic and family, and other complex interactions, Lazarus adds explanatory concepts from communication and systems theory (Kwee and Lazarus, 1986).

Seven key constructs shape and maintain human personality:

1. associations and relations among events;
2. modelling and imitation;
3. non-conscious processes;

4. defensive reactions;
5. private events;
6. meta-communications; and
7. thresholds (Lazarus, 1992, 1997).

Associations and relations among events

Association, in the form of events occurring simultaneously or in close succession, is important in all learning processes. Much human behaviour is the result of classical and operant conditioning. For instance, many aversions appear to originate from *classical conditioning*. Lazarus (2005a) provides the example of the client who had experienced post-operative nausea a few years previously and been in a hospital bed next to a man who kept playing a cassette of Beethoven's *Moonlight Sonata*. Later the client became sick to his stomach any time he heard that piece of music.

Operant conditioning, where the probability of behaviour recurring is mediated by its consequences, is another major social learning process. For instance, a depressed woman can reinforce her depression by locking herself up in her bedroom and avoiding rewarding social contacts (Kwee and Lazarus, 1986). Another example is that of a woman who states: 'I now realize that my headaches were in large part due to the fact that the only time my husband showed me any real caring was when I was in pain' (Lazarus, 2005a).

Modelling and imitation

Modelling and vicarious processes are also important in learning. People learn from observing and imitating what others do. Furthermore, they learn from perceiving the positive and negative consequences of others' behaviour.

Non-conscious processes

Much learning is neither conscious nor deliberate. Non-conscious processes are not to be confused with the Freudian notion of the unconscious. What Lazarus means by non-conscious processes is that 'people have different levels and degrees of awareness, and that unrecognized – subliminal – stimuli can influence one's thoughts, feelings, and behaviors' (1992: 235). Frequent demonstrations have illustrated that, during altered states of consciousness, people have access to memories and skills that are unavailable to conscious recall.

Defensive reactions

Through their social learning experiences people may acquire a variety of unnecessary defensive reactions. Defensive reactions are avoidance responses attenuating pain, discomfort, anxiety, depression and guilt (Lazarus, 1997). Such reactions entail people lessening their awareness, denying or distorting their perceptions and mislabelling their feelings. Included among defensive reactions are: denial; overintellectualization and rationalization; projection, wrongly attributing one's feelings to others; and displacement, for instance of aggression towards other people, animals or things.

Private events

People filter and can override their conditioning and modelling because of their intervening thoughts about these stimuli. They do not respond to the real environment, but to their *perceived* environment. Factors influencing their perceptions include: idiosyncratic use of language, selective attention, problem-solving competencies, goals, performance standards, attributions, self-efficacy, expectancies, and values, attitudes and beliefs. Such thoughts determine which stimuli are noticed, how they are perceived and valued and how long they are remembered.

Misinformation and missing information are two of the major means through which people's private thoughts lead to emotional problems and disorders (Dryden, 1991). With *misinformation*, people have learned incorrect assumptions and beliefs about life and living. One area of misinformation encompasses the perfectionist beliefs held in western society, for instance that lifelong happiness results from fame and fortune. Other areas of misinformation include: the inability of people to realize that their lives are mainly controlled by their own thoughts and perceptions rather than by external events; the belief that it is good to ventilate anger; the belief in the importance of pleasing others; and the idea that it is better to play safe by leading a life where there are no risks. Marital misinformation includes the myths that 'Romantic love makes a good marriage' and 'If you feel guilty, confess' (Lazarus, 2001).

With misinformation, people have acquired erroneous ideas. With *missing information*, people do possess the information to enact basic skills required for successful living. Social skills provide an important area of missing information about such matters as eye contact and how to converse. In addition, many people lack information on how to handle job interviews and present themselves favourably.

Lazarus regards as terrifying the amount of ignorance pervading the world. Even events such as international terrorism and drug smuggling can be 'tied into extreme misinformation and missing information that people have about the sort of values and skills that could make for a happier world' (Dryden, 1991: 15).

Meta-communication

Humans can both communicate and communicate about their communications, otherwise known as meta-communication. People can step back and examine the content and processes of their own relationships and patterns of communication. For example, in couples therapy partners can either skilfully or unskilfully explore and discuss the processes of their relationship, including identifying unhelpful communication patterns. The ability to meta-communicate characterizes all high-quality relationships between friends, relatives and lovers.

Thresholds

For a review of Lazarus's ideas on thresholds, the reader is referred back to the relevant section earlier in this chapter.

Maintenance

People's personalities are not only acquired but also maintained through the interaction of genetic endowment, social learning and environmental influences. For example, people's genetic endowment persists in the form of different thresholds and favoured BASIC ID modalities. Social learning influences the maintenance of personality in a number of ways. People learn maladaptive habits or conditioned emotional reactions 'through various associations and unfortunate connections of events' (Dryden, 1991: 9). Such habits may be simple or complex and persist in interfering with their happiness. In addition, through conditioning and modelling, they learn not only behaviours, but perceptions of self-efficacy, performance standards and goals that they maintain for good or ill. In addition, people's environments can continue to offer reinforcements and models that contribute to maintaining their thoughts, feelings and behaviours.

Non-conscious processes influence maintenance of personality. People may remain unaware of what they have learned and keep learning from others. Consequently, such thoughts, feelings and behaviours are less easy to change. Once learned, defensive reactions act as habits that block people from full awareness of how they and others behave. Defensive reactions make it harder for people to work on their problems since they lack insight both into their defensive reactions and into their negative consequences. Consequently, defensive reactions are both part of and serve to maintain unhelpful aspects of people's BASIC IDs.

Lazarus (2005a) assigns a pivotal role to misinformation and missing information in maintaining behaviour and in causing people to become therapy clients. Gaps in people's repertoires, because they were never given necessary information and essential coping processes, render them ill-equipped to deal with societal demands. In addition, people can communicate about their communication in ways that maintain rather than solve problems, for instance by blaming one another.

The following are other factors, interacting with those already mentioned, that can contribute to people maintaining dysfunctional thoughts, feelings and behaviours (Dryden, 1991):

* *Conflicting or ambivalent feelings or reactions*: People can possess approach–approach or avoidance–avoidance conflicts resulting in extreme indecisiveness. Their prior learning experiences have contributed to their

indecision and inertia. Their indecisiveness may be both self-maintaining and also contribute to their inability to change aspects of how they function.

- *Interpersonal inquietude*: Many people remain upset because of undue dependencies, excessive hates and misplaced loves. Lazarus sees such interpersonal inquietude stemming from skills deficits and from unrealistic demands that people sometimes impose upon each other.
- *Poor self-acceptance*: People maintain negative feelings about themselves because they do not understand the difference between accepting their totality as human beings and functionally evaluating specific shortcomings and personal limitations. Self-acceptance means 'Don't put your ego on the line, accept yourself, your totality, even though there might be lots of little "i's" as part of the big "I", that are less than exemplary' (Dryden, 1991: 13). For instance, people can make mistakes and possess skills weaknesses without feeling totally crushed as persons.

Therapy

The practice of multimodal therapy possesses six distinctive features:

'1. The specific and comprehensive attention given to the entire BASIC ID
2. The use of Second-Order BASIC ID assessments
3. The use of Modality Profiles
4. The use of Structural Profiles
5. Tracking the modality firing order
6. Deliberate bridging procedures'. (Lazarus, 1992: 250)

Though not in the order listed above, this section reviews how each of these distinctive features forms part of multimodal therapy.

Therapeutic goals

Long-range hedonism is a guiding philosophy (Dryden, 1991). Though Lazarus does not define fun, a major goal for most humans is to have fun while alive. However, people need to attain a good balance between long-range and short-range hedonism.

Though individuals differ in their predominant modalities, the BASIC ID suggests illustrative sub-goals for effective functioning:

- *Behaviour*: Taking effective actions in pursuit of realistic goals;
- *Affect*: Acknowledging, clarifying and recognizing feelings; coping with negative feelings and enhancing positive ones;
- *Sensation*: Being in touch with and enjoying one's senses;

- *Imagery*: Being in touch with one's imagination; using coping images;
- *Cognition*: Possessing sufficiently accurate and complete information; thinking realistically;
- *Interpersonal*: Possessing good relating skills, for instance assertion and conversational skills; capacity for healthy interdependency;
- *Drugs/biology*: Taking good care of one's body and physical health; eating and drinking in moderation.

People can have weaknesses in one or more of the above modalities and still be happy. Humans are fallible, with a biological penchant sometimes to be self-defeating. However, people can feel self-acceptance and accept their fallibility, at the same time as attempting to be less fallible.

Multimodal therapy goals are tailored to particular clients and take into account their 'goals, coping behaviors, situational contexts, affective reactions, "resistances", and basic beliefs' (Lazarus, 1992: 237). Rigidity is to be avoided in all aspects of therapy, including assessment and goal setting. In some instances, clients' main problems are obvious and a thorough assessment of all seven BASIC ID modalities is unnecessary.

In most cases, multimodal therapy rests on a thorough assessment of the BASIC ID that leads to constructing a Modality Profile listing salient problems and recommended treatments within each modality. Outcome goals, namely overcoming or coping with the problem, are implicit for each problem listed by modality in the profile. For instance, depression is one of the problems listed in the Affect section of a client's Modality Profile. An outcome goal for this problem relates to a lessening of the client's depressed feelings, preferably in some measurable way. Inasmuch as Modality Profiles also list recommended interventions, decision and process goals are implicit in them. A therapist decision-making goal is to select the most effective treatments of choice for each problem. Could the therapist have selected better treatments of choice for the client's depression problem than the recommended interventions of coping imagery and increasing rewarding activities? Once chosen, to what extent does each intervention, on its own or in combination, contribute to the problem or outcome goal of lessening the client's depression?

Process of therapy

Multimodal therapy may be conducted in either complete or brief forms. The average duration of a complete course of multimodal therapy is approximately 50 hour-long sessions (weekly sessions for about a year). Lazarus (2005a) observes that fewer than 30 per cent of the clients seen at the various Multimodal Therapy Institutes seem to require or are willing to participate in 50 hours of therapy. The majority favour brief therapy consisting of about one to 15 hour-long sessions, which may take place either over a short period of time or extend over many months (Lazarus, 1997). Lazarus contends that by using the multimodal framework, therapy can be both brief and comprehensive.

Initial sessions

Initial sessions follow no rigid format. Therapists may meet with individuals, couples or families. They may begin with small talk and collecting basic information, for instance address and phone number, before embarking on a more detailed enquiry. Two main questions relating to clients' presenting complaints are: 'What has led to the current situation?' and 'Who or what is maintaining it?' (Lazarus, 1992, 2005a). In addition, therapists look for signs of psychosis, organic problems and depression. From the start, therapists are attuned to noting information about which modalities of the BASIC ID their clients' complaints apply to. In addition, they try to assess clients' expectations about therapy and the most appropriate kind of relationship style to adopt. Furthermore, they look for clients' strengths and positive attributes. Quite often in initial interviews therapists use specific interventions, for instance cognitive disputation. At the end of the initial interview, therapists give most adult clients the 15-page *Multimodal Life History Inventory* (Lazarus, 1997; Lazarus and Lazarus, 1991). This inventory asks numerous questions about antecedent events and maintaining factors with the answers being divided into BASIC ID categories.

An important multimodal therapy principle is 'Know your own limitations and other clinicians' strengths' (Dryden, 1991: 30). Referrals should be made where other therapists have skills that the therapist does not possess or more appropriate personal styles for particular clients. Lazarus does not consider himself particularly good at working with seriously disturbed people, for instance schizophrenics, substance abusers and antisocial personality disorders. He seeks out more expert or gifted people for such clients. Often referrals to other therapists are best made before bonding with the original therapist occurs. Lazarus also refers clients to self-help groups, such as Alcoholics Anonymous, Self Management and Recovery Training (SMART), Overeaters Anonymous, and Parents without Partners.

The Modality Profile

Lazarus writes: 'the mainstay of multimodal assessment centers on Modality Profiles and Structural Profiles' (1992: 246). A Modality Profile is a BASIC ID chart listing problems and interventions within each modality. Lazarus only draws up such profiles when therapy is not going quickly enough and unforeseen problems arise. Around the start of the third session, therapists have usually gleaned enough information from interviews and the *Life History Inventory* to spend 15 to 20 minutes drafting a preliminary Modality Profile for the client. Sometimes clients are asked to draft their own Modality Profiles separately from their therapists and then the two compare notes. Multimodal therapists treat their clients' Modality Profiles as sets of hypotheses. Modality Profiles are shared and discussed with clients.

Table 14.1   Example of a Modality Profile

Modality	Problem	Intervention
Behaviour	Procrastination; Tends to pout or withdraw when frustrated; Volatile and explosive.	Contingency contracting; Modelling and role playing of assertiveness skills. Relaxation and communication training.
Affect	Anxiety. Depression.	Breathing and deep muscle relaxation; stress inoculation training. Coping imagery; increase rewarding activities.
Sensation	Tension (esp. in jaws and neck); Lower-back pain.	Relaxation training. Orthopaedic exercises.
Imagery	Lonely images; Images of failure.	Picturing various coping responses.
Cognition	Perfectionism; Negative scanning; Dichotomous thinking. Self-downing.	Cognitive restructuring.
Interpersonal relationships	Passive–aggressive; Unassertive; Has few friends.	Social skills and assertiveness training.
Drugs/biology	Insufficient exercise; Overweight.	Healthy lifestyle programme.

Table 14.1 provides an example of a Modality Profile for a 37-year-old man in therapy for generalized anxiety (Lazarus, 1992: 242).

The Structural Profile

The Structural Profile comes towards the end of the *Multimodal Life History Inventory*. Here clients are asked to rate themselves across each of the BASIC ID modalities on a seven-point scale with 1 being the lowest and 7 being the highest. The descriptions for each modality were provided earlier in this chapter when introducing the seven BASIC ID modalities. The Structural Profile provides useful additional information to both therapist and client about how the client interacts with the world. It can be easily depicted on a bar graph.

In addition to the seven questions that form part of the *Multimodal Life History Inventory*, Lazarus (1989b, 1997) has developed a 35-item standardized instrument called the *Structural Profile Inventory* (SPI). In 1995 an *Expanded Structural Profile* was developed by Lazarus's son Clifford (Lazarus, 1997: 145–8).

The SPI has proved very useful in couples therapy. The profiles pinpoint reasons for misunderstanding and can lead to fruitful discussions of what to do about them. Sometimes the profiles may indicate that divorce therapy is a more realistic prospect than marital therapy. For instance, where one partner values affective expression and interpersonal intimacy and is low on behaviour and cognition and the other partner has the opposite profile.

Tracking

Clients have fairly reliable patterns or orderings of modalities in how they generate negative affect, though on occasion these patterns may vary. Tracking refers to the careful assessment of the 'firing order', the ordering of the chain reaction of the different modalities. For instance, one client may generate negative emotions through dwelling first on sensations (S) (e.g. heart palpitations) that 'fire' cognitions (C) (e.g. 'I may get very ill or die') that 'fire' aversive images (I) (e.g. pictures of catastrophic disease) that 'fire' maladaptive behaviour (B) (e.g. extreme withdrawal) (Lazarus, 2005a). Another client, instead of the SCIB firing order outlined above may display a CISB pattern (cognitive-imagery-sensation-behaviour).

One purpose of tracking is to provide clients with insight into the precise processes by which they generate negative affect so that they can intervene appropriately. Another purpose is to assist therapists in selecting and prioritizing treatment interventions. Box 14.2 provides an example of a female client tracking her firing order and then the therapist planning treatment accordingly (Lazarus, 2005a). Had the client a different firing order, the therapist would have trained her in a different sequence and encouraged her to use this different sequence in real life.

Box 14.2   Example of tracking

Tracking the firing order
An agoraphobic woman tracked in herself a CISA firing order:

- an illustrative cognition (C) was 'What if I pass out?';
- followed by mental images (I) of herself hyperventilating and fainting;
- which fired sensations (S) of light-headedness and sweaty palms;
- which fired feelings (A) of panic and anxiety.

Treatment based on the client's firing order
Following the client's firing order, her therapist:

- first provided her with self-instructional training (Meichenbaum, 1977) to counteract her self-defeating cognitions;

(Continued)

Box 14.2   (Continued)

- next, the therapist taught her coping imagery in which she vividly imagined herself remaining calm and controlled in feared situations (such as shopping in a supermarket); and
- taught her, in the sensory modality, slow abdominal breathing and differential muscle relaxation.

The client was instructed to practise her training in real life. When shopping in a supermarket, she was to follow the sequence of:

- using positive self-instructions (C);
- then adding coping imagery (I);
- using abdominal breathing while deliberately relaxing muscles not in use at the time (S).

Second-order BASIC ID assessments

When impasses occur in treating clients, therapists may perform second-order BASIC ID assessments. Such assessments allow a more detailed review of behaviours, affective responses, sensory reactions, images, cognitions, interpersonal factions, and drugs and biological factors in relation to the area in which change is proving difficult. For instance, unassertive behaviours may persist, despite role playing, behaviour rehearsal, modelling and other relevant training. When, as part of her second-order assessment, one client was asked for her BASIC ID associations to the concept of assertiveness, her answers were as follows: behaviour – attacking; affect – angry; sensation – tension; imagery – bombs bursting; cognition – get even; interpersonal – hurting; and drugs/biologicals – high blood pressure (Lazarus, 2005a). Although the therapist had attempted to convey to her the difference between assertion and aggression, the second-order BASIC ID showed that she still regarded assertive responses as tantamount to vicious attacks. Box 14.3 provides another example of a second-order BASIC ID profile (Lazarus, 1997: 58–9).

Box 14.3   Example of a second-order BASIC ID profile

The client
The client had an established alcohol addiction, and one of the items on his Modality Profile was 'Urges to Use Alcohol or Cravings'.

His second-order BASIC ID profile
When asked about the impact of these urges or cravings across the BASIC ID, the following profile emerged:

Box 14.3   (Continued)

- *Behaviour*   Clenches jaw;
                   Starts pacing or wringing hands.
- *Affect*   Anxiety;
                   Depression.
- *Sensation*   Muscle tension;
                   Dry mouth.
- *Imagery*   Visualizes drinking alcohol;
                   Imagines smell and taste of drink;
                   Pictures sense of intoxication.
- *Cognition*   Thoughts of unfairness;
                   Belief that craving will never subside;
                   Idea that intake can be controlled;
                   Various other rationalizations.
- *Interpersonal* Withdraws from social interaction or
                   lashes out irritably at others.
- *Drugs/biology* Smokes a cigarette or has a cup of coffee.

Possible strategies
The most obvious strategies based on this profile include:

1. more attention to deep muscle relaxation;
2. successful images of turning away from alcohol; and
3. cognitive disputation.

Selection of interventions

Multimodal therapy 'is an open system in which the principle of technical eclecticism encourages the constant introduction of new techniques and the refinement or elimination of existing ones, but never in a random or shotgun manner' (Lazarus, 2005a: 366). A fundamental premise of the multimodal approach is that clients are usually troubled by a multitude of specific problems that should be dealt with by a multitude of specific treatments. How do multimodal therapists select treatment interventions? Table 14.1 provided, as part of a Modality Profile, the techniques selected for a man in therapy for generalized anxiety. Multimodal therapists need to be aware of and skilled in a wide repertoire of techniques or interventions. If unaware of or unskilled in certain interventions they are unlikely to help clients with certain conditions. The first or main requirement for selecting interventions is the extent to which there are research data to support them. Empirical data exist for documenting treatments of choice across a variety of conditions including bulimia nervosa, compulsive rituals, social skill deficits, bipolar depression, schizophrenic delusions, focal phobias, tics and habit disorders, pain management, hyperventilation, panic disorders, autism, enuresis, vaginisimus and other sexual dysfunctions, and a variety of stress-related disorder ... (Lazarus et al., 1992)

However, probably some 'grey areas' will always exist. Practising therapists should familiarize themselves with the research outcome literature.

Multimodal therapists take a number of other factors into account in selecting and prioritizing interventions. Such factors include clients' priorities, firing orders and the desirability of early success experiences. Careful consideration is given to answers to the following three items on page 4 of the *Multimodal Life History Inventory*: 'In a few words, what do you think therapy is about?', 'How long do you think your therapy should last?' and 'What personal qualities do you think the ideal therapist should possess?' (Lazarus, 1992: 242–3). For instance, clients thinking the ideal therapist is an active listener may take unkindly to active-directive, task-oriented therapists.

Multimodal therapists start 'with the most obvious and logical procedures' (Kwee and Lazarus, 1986: 335). Once selected, therapists still need to accommodate their chosen interventions to the unique characteristics of each client in order to promote adherence and compliance. While the initial selection of interventions may be relatively straightforward, their implementation 'requires clinical experience, acumen, and artistry' (p. 337). If the initially selected interventions do not work, Lazarus may draw on other well-researched interventions. Sometimes he goes beyond well-researched interventions to try other interventions that may help specific clients: for example the technique of shrinking the feared object down to size from neurolinguistic programming (NLP) or using the conceptualization of Parent, Adult and Child from Transactional Analysis (Dryden, 1991). In addition, second-order BASIC ID assessments may be conducted to look for significant factors that may have been overlooked in initial assessment procedures.

Progress evaluations

Ongoing evaluations of progress are integral to multimodal therapy. Since Modality Profiles are commonly drawn up, therapists can evaluate progress for each problem within each of the seven BASIC ID dimensions. Such information is relevant both during therapy and for making termination-of-therapy decisions. Lazarus (2005a) provides the following example how a multimodal therapist specified a client's gains and achievements:

Behaviour: Less withdrawn; less compulsive; more outspoken.
Affect: More warm, less hostile; less depressed.
Sensation: Enjoys more pleasures; less tense, more relaxed.

Imagery: Fewer nightmares; better self-image.
Cognition: Less self-downing; more positive self-statements.
Interpersonal: Goes out on dates; expresses wishes and desires.
Drugs/biology: Stopped smoking; eats well; exercises regularly.

The therapeutic relationship

The therapeutic relationship can be divided into relationship behaviours that are universal and those that differ for specific clients. One universal relationship behaviour is the attempt to develop a collaborative alliance whenever possible. Multimodal therapists endeavour to work together with clients. A second relationship universal is never to attack a client's sense of dignity as a person, though their maladaptive behaviours may be assailed.

' "Relationships of choice" are no less important than "techniques of choice" for effective psychotherapy' (Lazarus, 1993: 404). For most clients the purpose of the therapeutic relationship is to provide 'the soil that enables the techniques to take root' (Dryden, 1991: 17). Unlike Rogers who would offer the same kind of 'carefully cultivated warmth, genuineness and empathy to all his clients' (p. 18), Lazarus tries not only to match the nature of the relationship to the client, but also to the clients' observed needs at different times in therapy. For some clients, good listening is sufficient. However, many clients require therapists to select and use specific techniques to help them develop coping skills for problems identified in their Modality Profiles. Thus, therapists need to offer relationships that go beyond good listening.

Lazarus (1993, 1997) emphasizes flexibility and versatility and uses the metaphor of the 'authentic chameleon' to indicate that multimodal therapists vary their relationship styles to fit with clients' expectations, personalities, problems and goals. He describes four different, yet overlapping, ways of varying relationships with clients.

1. *The relationship continuum*: Multimodal therapists view helping relationships on a continuum from 'a very close-knit, dependent bonding at the one end, to a rather formal, businesslike involvement at the other' (Kwee and Lazarus, 1986: 333). Throughout therapy, the relationship is used flexibly to fit each client's expectancies and preferred modalities. For instance, some people do not respond well to therapist warmth and empathy and like a more business-like approach.

2. *Matching therapist styles*: Therapist styles that Lazarus seeks to match to individual clients include: 'whether and when to be cold, warm, or tepid; when and whether not to be confrontational; when and whether to be earthy, chummy, casual and informal rather than "professional"; when to self-disclose or remain enigmatic; when to be soft-nosed, gentle

and tender, and when to come on like a tough army sergeant; and how to adjust my levels of supportiveness and directiveness' (Lazarus, 1993: 405).

3. *Supportivness and directiveness dimensions*: During therapy, multimodal therapists continually ask themselves how supportive and how directive they need be with their clients. Four possibilities are: high direction–high support, low direction–low support, low direction–high support and high direction–high support. Effective therapists switch among and between all four modes 'in the chameleon sense' (Dryden, 1991: 19). Lazarus works mostly in the high direction–high support mode, since he sees therapy as an educational process in which the therapist's main role is that of a clinical teacher. Furthermore, clients change most rapidly when ready for high direction and high support.

4. *Relationships differing with selected techniques*: Lazarus uses techniques that draw upon the work of Freud, Rogers, Perls, Ellis, Adler, Haley and the behaviourists, among others. As part of tailoring his interventions to the needs of each client, he also flexibly utilizes the kind of relationship implicit in these techniques (Lazarus, 1989b). For instance, he may use Rogerian reflection, Gestalt psychodrama and imagery techniques, or behavioural assertiveness training, and accordingly adjust the kind of relationship he offers.

The two *client* variables that most influence Lazarus's relationship style are his perceptions of their readiness for change and of their reactance level. Ongoing therapy interactions play a dominant part in selecting relationship of choice. For instance, Lazarus adopted an extremely gentle stance in which he was almost whispering to a very timid and shy young woman who expressed strong reactions about her dealings with 'loud, pushy, or obnoxious people' (1993: 406). The outcome was that the client, who had poor relationships with her two previous therapists, cooperated well with him.

Bridging

Bridging is a rapport enhancement technique that illustrates the flexibility of the multimodal therapy relationship. When bridging, therapists deliberately tune into the clients' preferred modalities before gently helping them cross bridges into other modalities that may prove more productive (Lazarus, 1992, 1997, 2005a). Clients are more likely to feel understood by therapists who first respond within their preferred representational system. Other ways of describing bridging are that therapists first 'talk their clients' language' or 'start from where they are' before moving into less preferred modalities. An advantage of doing this is that clients then become less resistant to working in these other modalities. Box 14.4 provides an example of bridging (Lazarus, 1992: 247–9).

Box 14.4   Example of bridging

The multimodal therapist is interested in understanding an initial emotional reaction.

Original interaction

Therapist: 'How did you feel about your father's decision to leave home?'
Client: 'My father tended to put his needs first, and neither my mother nor I were factored into the equation'.

Staying in the cognitive modality
Rather than pressure the client into the affective modality the therapist might first join with the client in the cognitive modality.

Bridging into the sensory modality
Then, after about five minutes, the therapist could bridge into a modality that was less threatening than the affective modality, for instance the sensory modality with a question like:

Therapist: 'By the way, can you tune into some sensations anywhere in your body?'

Bridging into the affective modality
Then, after discussing sensations, the therapist could bridge into the affective modality with a question such as:

Therapist: 'I really wonder how you feel about the things your father has done?'

By now the client should be much less defensive about revealing feelings.

Therapeutic interventions

The following are principal multimodal interventions or techniques for each BASIC ID dimension (Kwee and Lazarus, 1986; Lazarus, 1989b, 2005a). Frequently, these interventions are used in combination. Interventions should be used sparingly according to the assessed needs of individual clients.

Behaviour

- *Behaviour rehearsal*: Therapists, who start by playing the other person, repeatedly rehearse clients in how to behave in specific situations. Dialogues are either cassette- or video-recorded and played back. When ready, clients enact their skills in the actual situations.
- *Modelling*: Therapists provide role models for specific behaviours clients are encouraged to imitate. Therapists may model behaviours in real-life settings: for instance, assertively returning faulty goods to a shop.

- *Non-reinforcement*: By not attending to specific client behaviours, therapists and others in clients' social environments can facilitate their extinction.
- *Positive reinforcement*: To strengthen specific client behaviours, therapists can dispense social reinforcers such as praise, recognition and encouragement. With children and adolescents therapists may use tangible reinforcers, such as food and money. Therapists may also use tokens that may be exchanged for tangible rewards.
- *Recording and self-monitoring*: Therapists encourage clients to engage in the systematic recording, charting and/or counting of targeted behaviours.
- *Stimulus control*: The absence or presence of certain stimuli is related to the frequency of behaviours. For example, people trying to lose weight can keep snacks and desserts out of their homes. Students trying to increase study behaviours can arrange their desks without distracting stimuli and only sit at them when studying.
- *Systematic exposure*: Therapists encourage clients to expose themselves step-by-step to their feared situations. Many additional techniques, for instance *goal rehearsal or coping imagery*, may be used to overcome avoidances in conjunction with systematic exposure.

Affect

- *Anger expression*: Anger expression means assisting clients to own and express their anger. It is not an end in itself and clients may require *behaviour rehearsal* in how to express anger assertively. Techniques to get clients in touch with angry feelings include coaxing them to say louder and louder 'I am angry' and getting them to pummel and kick foam rubber cushions, pillows and inflatable objects.
- *Anxiety-management training*: First therapists teach clients general *relaxation training* and *goal-rehearsal or coping imagery*. Then they teach clients to generate anxiety-evoking cognitions and imagery and immediately after to relax and dwell on calm sensations, serene images, dispute irrational ideas, and concentrate on optimistic and relaxing thoughts.
- *Feeling identification*: Labelling feelings accurately is one area of feeling identification: for instance, clients may say they are 'depressed' when their symptoms are more those of 'anxiety'. The main area of feeling identification is on exploring the client's affective domain to help them identify significant feelings that might be unclear or misdirected.
- *The empty chair*: The client faces an empty chair and imagines it occupied by a significant other. The client starts a dialogue with this other person and then switches chairs back and forth to conduct both parts of the dialogue. Therapists may offer prompts about what to say, for instance, 'Ask her to tell you exactly how she would have wanted you to respond'. As well as assisting clients to own and express feelings, the empty chair helps them appreciate others' viewpoints.

Sensation

- *Biofeedback*: There are biofeedback devices that can help clients to monitor and modify physiological functions like muscular tension, heart rate, brain wave activity, galvanic skin response and skin temperature. For example, for a client suffering from painful tension in the jaw, the therapist can attach electrodes to the jaw muscles that are wired to a machine that provides tonal feedback (the more tension the louder the sound) according to the degree of muscular tension. Clients can learn to maintain a low decibel level or eliminate the tone altogether.
- *Focusing*: Therapists encourage clients in contemplative and relaxed states to tune into their spontaneous thoughts and feelings until one major felt bodily expression emerges. After several minutes of intense focusing, clients are asked to extract something new from their sensations, images and emotions.
- *Hypnosis*: Therapists can usefully learn several methods for inducing trances to maximize their chances of success with individual clients. Hypnotic-induction techniques mostly involve sensory fixation (for example, focusing on a spot on the ceiling) and monotonous repetitions, such as 'calm and relaxed'.
- *Meditation*: Therapists can teach clients meditation, for instance sitting down, gradually closing their eyes, and inwardly repeating a 'mantra' such as the word 'in' on inhaling and the word 'out' on exhaling. As thoughts float in and out of awareness, the meditator continues to think the words 'in' and 'out'. Often two daily 20-minute sessions are advocated. However, some clients gain most from mini-meditations of two- or three-minute sessions several times daily.
- *Relaxation training*: Clients can learn total relaxation and/or differential relaxation. Total relaxation is another term for progressive muscular relaxation involving alternate tensing and letting go of each major muscle area. Differential relaxation entails learning to relax those muscles not in use when performing various tasks. For instance, a person tensing their jaw, shoulders and neck and holding their breath when sitting and writing can deliberately relax the tense muscles and breathe abdominally in a slow and rhythmic fashion.
- *Sensate focus training*: Usually prescribed for sexually dysfunctional couples, sensate focus refers to sensual rather than to sexual pleasuring. The pleasuring partner is forbidden to touch the genitals or female breasts and no pressures for sexual performance are permitted. Instead the pleasuring partner massages, touches and stimulates a part of the body that the recipient enjoys having stimulated. Afterwards, partners can reverse roles.
- *Threshold training*: Threshold training is a common technique for the treatment of premature or rapid ejaculation. The female manually stimulates the man's penis. When he feels a preorgasmic sensation he says 'stop' and/or

removes her hand until the sensation abates. This procedure is repeated. Later more advanced variations can be added: for instance manual stimulation using a lubricant, and effecting vaginal entry and withdrawing on feeling a preorgasmic urge. Within a few weeks, many males can delay ejaculation for long periods.

Imagery

- *Anti-future shock imagery*: This intervention helps prepare clients for changes likely to happen in the coming months or years: for instance, becoming a parent, being promoted, or moving to a new location. Clients are encouraged to visualize themselves coping with these changes.
- *Associated imagery*: When clients experience unwanted emotions for which they are unable to account, therapists can ask them to focus immediately on any image that comes to mind and see it as vividly as possible. New images that emerge are to be visualized as clearly as possible. If no new images emerge, the original image is to be examined as if through a zoom lens, with this process often eliciting other images for tracking. Frequently clients report significant insights from using this technique.
- *Aversive imagery*: Clients can learn to associate unpleasant images with behaviour that is unwanted, yet self-reinforcing (for example, alcoholism, sexual deviations, overeating). For instance, clients on diets can be trained to imagine that someone has vomited over the rich food they wish to eat.
- *Goal rehearsal or coping imagery*: Clients are trained to break down the steps involved in difficult upcoming events. For each step, they visualize themselves faltering, but coping. For instance, a woman with an aversion to hospitals had the goal of visiting and supporting a sick friend. She imagined herself coping with the difficulties involved in the hospital visit and her sense of achievement for helping her friend.
- *Positive imagery*: Positive imagery entails visualizing a pleasant scene, real or imagined, past, present or future. Beneficial effects of positive imagery include: reducing tension, inhibiting anxiety and enhancing enjoyment.
- *The step-up technique*: Clients unduly anxious about upcoming events, for instance a public speech, are asked to picture the worst thing imaginable and then imagine themselves coping with the situation and surviving the most negative outcomes. Some clients require *self-instructional training* along with the step-up technique.
- *Time projection (forward or backward)*: Time projection or 'time tripping' can be used to help clients relive and work through past events. In addition, clients can imagine both what might happen in the future, for instance depressed clients picturing themselves engaging in more and more rewarding activities, and how the present might look from the vantage point of the future, for instance picturing an event after a few months and realizing the temporary nature of some current problem.

Cognition

- *Bibliotherapy*: A well-chosen self-help book 'can be worth more than a dozen sessions' (Lazarus, 1989b: 243). Books should be thoroughly read, even summarized in notebooks, and readings discussed during sessions.
- *Correcting misconceptions*: Therapists can provide clients with factual information to correct misconceptions about society, other people and themselves. Sexual misconceptions are common. Therapists should learn the relevant facts and realities. Bibliotherapy can form an important component of correcting misconceptions.
- *Ellis's A-B-C-D-E paradigm*: Therapists can teach clients Ellis's A (activating event), B (beliefs), C (consequences), D (disputing) and E (effects) paradigm. Clients can learn to identify their irrational beliefs (B) about activating events (A) that lead to negative consequences (C). Disputing these irrational beliefs (D) can result in the effect (E) of the diminution or elimination of negative consequences.
- *Problem solving*: Clients can learn to apply the rudiments of scientific methodology to problems. Problem solving involves generating plausible hypotheses that can be strengthened or weakened by gathering relevant information. Decisions are made on the basis of facts and probability rather than by mysticism or chance.
- *Self-instructional training*: Therapists can train clients to replace negative self-statements with positive, task-oriented statements that facilitate coping. For instance, clients anxious about a forthcoming event could instruct themselves to: develop a plan; handle the situation one step at a time; if anxious to pause and take a few deep breaths; remind themselves that they only have to keep fear manageable rather than eliminate it; focus on what they need to do; acknowledge the link between controlling self-talk and controlling fear; and recognize that it gets easier each time they use their self-instructions.
- *Thought blocking*: Thought blocking is a technique to combat obsessive and intrusive thoughts. Clients can be taught to sub-vocally scream 'STOP!' over and over again. A variation of thought-blocking is for clients to flick their wrists with a rubber band when they scream 'STOP!'. Some clients find it helps to picture huge neon signs flashing the letters 'STOP' on and off.

Interpersonal

- *Communication training*: Therapists can train clients in how to send and receive communications. Sending skills include eye contact, body posture, voice projection and the use of simple concrete terms. Receiving skills include active listening and rewarding senders for communicating. Role playing and *behaviour rehearsal* are especially useful in communication training.
- *Contingency contracting*: Clients agree to make rewards or negative consequences (usually self-imposed) contingent upon increasing, decreasing or maintaining a specific behaviour.

- *Friendship training*: In friendship training, therapists identify and train clients in how to interact in prosocial and affectionate ways. Skills that therapists emphasize include empathy, showing caring and concern, self-disclosing, positive reinforcement and give-and-take. Clients are taught to avoid competitiveness and self-aggrandizement.
- *Graded sexual approaches*: Partners are advised to engage in sensual and sexual activities only so long as pleasurable feelings predominate. They terminate such activities when anxious feelings erupt. With each encounter anxieties can recede and greater sexual arousal and intimacy become possible.
- *Paradoxical strategies*: Symptom prescription, for instance therapists telling compulsive clients to increase their checking and ritualistic behaviours, is a common paradoxical strategy. Clients may decrease their unwanted behaviours if their therapists prescribe that they exaggerate symptoms. Another common paradoxical strategy is that of forbidding a desired response. An example is that of therapists forbidding men with erectile difficulties to have intercourse until they get specific permission. Clients whose desired responses are forbidden may be more likely to enact them, for instance by engaging in sexual intercourse.
- *Social skills and assertiveness training*: Four specific assertive response patterns or abilities that therapists can train clients in are: saying 'no'; asking for favours and making requests; expressing positive and negative feelings; and initiating, continuing and terminating conversations. *Behaviour rehearsal* and *modelling* are two major techniques employed in social skills and assertiveness training.

Drugs/biology

Multimodal therapists encourage clients take responsibility for their health and to develop good habits of eating nutritionally, exercising and engaging in recreational activities. Therapists refer clients to physicians where they suspect organic problems or consider biological interventions, such as anti-depressant medication, indicated.

Strategies for saving time

In therapy, especially brief therapy, it is important that therapists do not waste their clients' and their own time. In brief therapy it is most important to select clearly defined goals quickly and to move into specific problem-solving interventions as soon as possible. Sometimes the application of an intervention may come well before assessment has been completed.

Clients can be educated as to the benefits of brief therapy. Furthermore, therapists can use time between sessions to good effect by thinking about clients' progress and, where necessary, revising their game plans. In addition, therapists can use phones, faxes, letters and emails to amend homework assignments or make sympathetic enquiries.

Brief therapy requires an educational stance and should avoid conversational therapy. Lazarus observes: 'Passive and reflective therapists are anathema to the process of brief and effective psychotherapy' (1997: 67). He disabuses clients of the widespread overvaluation of insight and the need to focus heavily on the past. Multimodal therapists as educators may use bibliography and prime clients as to the importance of practising homework assignments. Furthermore, Lazarus is not afraid to prompt clients with ideas, strategies and solutions rather than wait for these to emerge from clients themselves.

Case material

Case studies presented by Lazarus include his work with George, a 32-year-old agoraphobic patient who had previously been treated without success by a number of therapists (Lazarus, 1989b, 2005b). Another example of Lazarus's work is that with Al and Lisa, the former presenting with inhibited sexual desire (Lazarus, 1997). Lazarus spent two initial conjoint sessions, eight individual sessions with Al, six individual sessions with Lisa, and then three final conjoint sessions in improving this couple's emotional and sexual relationship. A further case study is Lazarus's (2005a) work over eight months with a 33-year-old woman, married to a successful company president, who was afraid of becoming pregnant, insecure and unassertive. Additional case material is contained in a chapter providing an example of the multimodal assessment and treatment of a case of panic, anxiety and social phobia, and a marital therapy case compounded by depression (Lazarus et al., 1991). In 1985 *A Casebook of Multimodal Therapy* edited by Lazarus was published. This book describes 14 different case studies in a variety of settings and situations.

Further developments

Multimodal therapy, with its BASIC ID assessment and interventions, has been applied in many areas in addition to individual personal therapy. Multimodal therapy has been used in marital work and in group work. In addition, multimodal therapy has provided a framework for career counselling and for Employee Assistance Program (EAP) counselling. Other areas of application of multimodal principles include working with children in classroom settings, developing gifted adolescents, parent training, working with inpatients in mental hospital, and counselling and therapy education. Thus multimodal therapy, at the same time as espousing breadth in how therapists assess and treat clients, has broad applicability to a wide range of areas.

Since 1972, training in multimodal therapy has been a formal aspect of the clinical psychology doctoral programme at Rutgers University in the United States. There are a few major multimodal therapy institutes in the United States as well as some smaller centres. In Britain, training in multimodal therapy is available at the Centre for Stress Management in London. Multimodal therapy is also taught and practised in other countries in Europe: for instance, in the Netherlands under the auspices of Dr M.G.T. Kwee, several therapists are using the approach. Books, articles and chapters on multimodal therapy have been written or translated into German, Italian, Portuguese, Spanish and Dutch. Multimodal therapy is also taught in South America. For example, in Argentina, Dr Roberto Kertesz and his colleagues have practised multimodal therapy, offered training seminars and translated many of Lazarus's books into Spanish (Lazarus, 1997). Thus, the influence of multimodal therapy spreads well beyond the United States.

Review and personal questions

Review questions

1. Why does Lazarus call his approach multimodal?
2. What does the term technical eclecticism mean?
3. What seven key constructs does Lazarus use to explain how human personality is shaped and maintained?
4. To what extent does multimodal therapy have a theoretical base? Why is Lazarus afraid of his approach being too closely tied to any theory?
5. What are the goals of multimodal therapy?
6. What is the role of assessment in multimodal therapy and how do therapists go about it?
7. Critically discuss the role of the therapist–client relationship in multimodal therapy?
8. What does Lazarus mean by bridging and tracking? Provide examples.
9. How do multimodal therapists select interventions?
10. What are some principal multimodal interventions for changing

    (a) behaviour;
    (b) affect;
    (c) sensation;
    (d) imagery;
    (e) cognition;
    (f) the interpersonal modality;
    (g) the drugs/biology modality?

11. How do multimodal therapists evaluate clients' progress?

Personal questions

1. Identify a specific problem area in your life. To what extent do each of Lazarus's seven key factors for explaining how human personality is shaped and maintained contribute to your acquiring and maintaining your problem?
2. Develop your Structural Profile by rating yourself, by using a seven-point scale, on each of the BASIC ID modalities?
3. Develop a Modality Profile for yourself.
4. Select and implement interventions to help you with one of your problems.
5. What relevance, if any, has the theory and practice of multimodal therapy for how you conduct therapy?
6. What relevance, if any, has the theory and practice of multimodal therapy for how you live?

Annotated bibliography

Lazarus, A.A. (1997) *Brief but Comprehensive Psychotherapy: The Multimodal Way*. New York: Springer.
Based on the central message 'Don't waste time', this book succinctly sets out the main rationale and distinctive assessment and therapy techniques employed in brief *and* comprehensive multimodal therapy. Elements of effective brevity are identified and case examples are provided from individual and couples therapy.

Lazarus, A.A. (1989b) *The Practice of Multimodal Therapy: Systematic, Comprehensive and Effective Psychotherapy* (rev. edn). Baltimore, MA: Johns Hopkins University Press.
This book is exactly the same as the 1981 version apart from a 1989 epilogue and the addition of the 35-item Structural Profile Inventory as Appendix 4. The book includes chapters on multimodal therapy's basic rationale, its basic concepts for practice, the initial interview, multimodal assessment–therapy connections, relationship factors and the selection of techniques. In addition, there are chapters on multimodal marriage therapy, multimodal sex therapy, and multimodal therapy in special situations, for instance working with children. In addition to the Structural Profile Index appendix, the book has appendices containing a glossary of 37 principal techniques, the Multimodal Life History Questionnaire, and the Marital Satisfaction Questionnaire.

Lazarus, A.A. (2005a) 'Multimodal therapy', in R.J. Corsini and D. Wedding (eds), *Current Psychotherapies* (7th edn). Belmont, CA: Thomson Brooks/Cole. pp. 337–71.
This chapter includes material on multimodal therapy's basic concepts, history and current status, theory of personality, theory of psychotherapy, process and mechanisms of therapy, applications and evaluation. A case example is provided.

Lazarus, A.A. (1992) 'Multimodal therapy: technical eclecticism with minimal integration', in J.C. Norcross and M.R. Goldfried (eds), *Handbook of Psychotherapy Integration*. New York: Basic Books. pp. 231–63.

This chapter presents Lazarus's ideas on systematic (technical) eclecticism and the risks of integration. Lazarus describes the distinctive features of the multimodal approach and how it differs from other eclectic approaches. Research findings are reviewed and suggestions made for clinical training and desirable future directions for psychotherapy.

Lazarus, A.A. (1984) *In the Mind's Eye: The Power of Imagery for Personal Enrichment*. New York: Guilford.
This is a well-written book of imagery techniques that therapists can use with clients and people can use for self-help. The book is divided into four parts: the power of imagery; using imagery to build confidence and skill; using imagery to overcome problems; and some additional imagery exercises.

References and further reading

Bandura, A. (1986) *Social Foundations of Thought and Action: A Social Cognitive Theory*. Englewood Cliffs, NJ: Prentice-Hall.

Dryden, W. (1991) *A Dialogue with Arnold Lazarus: 'It Depends'*. Milton Keynes: Open University Press.

Kwee, M.G.T. and Lazarus, A.A. (1986) 'Multimodal therapy: the cognitive-behavioural tradition and beyond', in W. Dryden and W. Golden (eds), *Cognitive-Behavioural Approaches to Psychotherapy*. London: Harper & Row. pp. 320–55.

Lazarus, A.A. (1961) 'Group therapy for phobic disorders by systematic desensitization', *Journal of Abnormal and Social Psychology, 63*: 505–10.

Lazarus, A.A. (1971) *Behavior Therapy and Beyond*. New York: McGraw-Hill.

Lazarus, A.A. (ed.) (1972) *Clinical Behavior Therapy*. New York: Brunner/Mazel.

Lazarus, A.A. (1976) *Multimodal Behavior Therapy*. New York: Springer.

Lazarus, A.A. (1981) *The Practice of Multimodal Therapy*. New York: McGraw-Hill.

Lazarus, A.A. (1984) *In the Mind's Eye: The Power of Imagery for Personal Enrichment*. New York: Guilford.

Lazarus, A.A. (ed.) (1985) *Casebook of Multimodal Therapy*. New York: Guilford.

Lazarus, A.A. (1989a) 'Why I am an eclectic (not an integrationist)', *British Journal of Guidance and Counselling, 17*: 248–58.

Lazarus, A.A. (1989b) *The Practice of Multimodal Therapy: Systematic, Comprehensive and Effective Psychotherapy* (rev. edn). Baltimore, MD: Johns Hopkins University Press.

Lazarus, A.A. (1992) 'Multimodal therapy: technical eclecticism with minimal integration', in J.C. Norcross and M.R. Goldfried (eds), *Handbook of Psychotherapy Integration*. New York: Basic Books. pp. 231–63.

Lazarus, A.A. (1993) 'Tailoring the therapeutic relationship, or being an authentic chameleon' *Psychotherapy, 30*: 404–7.

Lazarus, A.A. (1997) *Brief but Comprehensive Psychotherapy: The Multimodal Way*. New York: Springer.

Lazarus, A.A. (2001) *Marital Myths Revisited: A Fresh Look at Two Dozen Mistaken Beliefs About Marriage*. Atascadero, CA: Impact Publishers.

Lazarus, A.A. (2003) 'Multimodal behavior therapy', in W. O'Donohue, J.E. Fisher and S.C. Hayes (eds), *Cognitive Behavior Therapy*. Hoboken, NJ: Wiley. pp. 261–5.

Lazarus, A.A. (2004) Private communication to the author, 27 September.

Lazarus, A.A. (2005a) 'Multimodal therapy', in R.J. Corsini and D. Wedding (eds), *Current Psychotherapies* (7th edn). Belmont, CA: Thomson Brooks/Cole. pp. 337–71.

Lazarus, A.A. (2005b) 'The case of George', in D. Wedding and R.J. Corsini (eds), *Case Studies in Psychotherapy* (4th edn). Belmont, CA: Thomson Brooks/Cole. pp. 177–87.

Lazarus, A.A. and Lazarus, C.N. (1991) *Multimodal Life History Inventory.* Champaign, IL: Research Press.

Lazarus, A.A. and Lazarus, C.N. (1997) *The 60-Second Shrink: 101 Strategies for Staying Sane in a Crazy World.* San Luis Obispo, CA: Impact Publishers.

Lazarus, A.A. and Messer, S.B. (1991) 'Does chaos prevail? An exchange on technical eclecticism and assimilative integration', *Journal of Psychotherapy Integration, 1*: 143–58.

Lazarus, A.A. and Zur, O. (2002) *Dual Relationships and Psychotherapy.* New York: Springer.

Lazarus, A.A., Beutler, L.E. and Norcross, J.C. (1992) 'The future of technical eclecticism', *Psychotherapy, 29*: 11–20.

Lazarus, A.A., Hasson, C. and Glat, M. (1991) 'Multimodal therapy', in K.N. Anchor (ed.), *Handbook of Medical Psychotherapy.* Toronto: Hogrefe & Huber. pp. 123–40.

Lazarus, A.A., Lazarus, C.N. and Fay, A. (1993) *Don't Believe it for a Minute!* San Luis Obispo, CA: Impact Publishers.

Meichenbaum, D.H. (1977) *Cognitive-Behavior Modification.* New York: Plenum.

Wolpe, J. and Lazarus, A.A. (1966) *Behaviour Therapy Techniques.* Oxford: Pergamon Press.

Lazarus on cassette and videotape

Lazarus, A.A. (1976) *Learning to Relax.* New York: Institute for Rational Living.

Lazarus, A.A. (1982) *Personal Enrichment through Imagery* (three cassettes plus workbook). New York: BMA Audio Cassette Publications.

Lazarus, A.A. (1984a) *Mental Imagery: Your Hidden Potential.* Washington, DC: American Psychological Association (Psychology Today).

Lazarus, A.A. (1984b) *Mental Imagery: Techniques and Exercises.* Washington, DC: American Psychological Association (Psychology Today).

Videotapes of Lazarus doing Multimodal Therapy have been published by the American Psychological Association and by Allyn & Bacon.

multicultural therapy
15

Introduction

Corey writes: 'Multicultural specialists have asserted that theories of counseling and psychotherapy represent different worldviews, each with its own values, biases and assumptions about human behavior' (2005: 42). Over the past 30 years or so, there has been growing interest in diversity-sensitive counselling and therapy. The differences on which this burgeoning literature focuses include culture, race, gender, sexual and affectionate orientation, disability, religion, socioeconomic status, and mixtures of these, among others (Weinrach and Thomas, 1998). In the following two chapters, I provide introductory reviews of two dimensions of diversity that affect all therapists and clients, namely culture and gender.

Sue and Sue write: 'Because none of us is immune from inheriting the images/stereotypes of the larger society, we can assume that most therapists are prisoners of their own cultural conditioning. As a result, they possess stereotypes and preconceived notions that may unwittingly be imposed on their culturally different clients' (2003: 42). Critics of existing counselling and therapy theories assert that their Euro-American cultural bias means that western-oriented therapists may be failing their actual and potential cultural minority-group client populations in a number of significant ways (Sue and Sue, 2003; Sue et al., 1996). Counselling and therapy services are underutilized by minority groups because of issues like mistrust, perceived irrelevance and cultural insensitivity. Assessment may insufficiently take into account differences in how behaviours are perceived in different cultures. In addition, therapists may fail to understand and address the chronic stresses attached to being in a cultural minority group and the emotional disruption of migration to a different culture. Once therapy begins, apart from obvious language difficulties, therapists may experience difficulty comprehending the communication patterns and personal and social contexts of their clients' problems. If clients have not discontinued already, therapists may establish goals and intervene on the basis of mainstream cultural assumptions that run counter to the cultural norms and personal meanings of their clients. Furthermore, therapists may focus too much on dealing with individuals rather than dealing with individuals in the context of their families and their social networks. In addition the helping professions insufficiently attend to the need for institutional and social change to counteract the oppression of minority groups.

The terminology of culture

Many of the terms associated with culture possess different shadings of meaning according to who does the defining. The following discussion of some key terms and concepts relevant to cultural issues in therapy is illustrative rather than prescriptive. Some of these terms and concepts will be elaborated as the chapter progresses.

- *Culture*: Spindler, who taught the author a course in cultural anthropology at Stanford University, defines culture as 'a patterned system of tradition-derived norms influencing behavior' (1963: 7). He goes on to observe that cultural norms are in a constant state of flux. Another definition of culture is that it refers to 'an integrated pattern of human behavior that includes thoughts, communications, actions, customs, beliefs, values, and institutions of a racial, ethnic, religious or social group' (Cross et al., 1989: iv). A colloquial definition of culture is 'the way we do things here'.
- *Enculturation*: Enculturation refers to the transmission of cultural norms within a given culture. Another way of viewing enculturation is as the socialization process in which younger members learn cultural rules from their elders. Nowadays, there are many different avenues for cultural transmission, for instance the media and the internet.
- *Acculturation*: Acculturation refers to the behavioural and psychological changes that occur in individuals as a result of their interaction with a different culture. For example, all migrants to Britain and Australia undergo acculturation. However, in both countries, migrants acculturate at varying rates and attain different levels of assimilation to the mainstream culture.
- *Culture shock*: Culture shock, of varying levels of severity, is a fairly common reaction to the stresses of adapting to a new culture. Its symptoms can include anxiety, a sense of loss, confusion of roles, feelings of helplessness and a desire for a more familiar and predictable environment. If marked, culture shock can engender pathological symptoms, such as depression and psychological and physical withdrawal.
- *Cultural change*: Cultures are not static. Change can come from within and without, or a mixture of the two. For instance, in Britain and Australia there are traditional mainstream cultures adhered to mainly by the older generation as well as emergent cultures being created predominantly by the younger generation. Intermarrying between different ethnic groups is another stimulus for cultural change coming from within a country.

In addition, cultural change can come from without: for example, in Britain the influence of other European cultures has increased with entry into the Common Market and more business, educational and holiday travel to and from other European countries. Similarly, Australian culture changed with the post-Second World War influx of southern European migrants and the post-Vietnam War influx of Southeast Asian migrants. Furthermore the world is increasingly a 'global village' with cultural changes mediated by technological advances such as cable TV and the internet. Hermans and Kempen observe: 'In an increasingly interconnected world society, the conception of independent, coherent and stable cultures becomes increasingly irrelevant' (1998: 1111). Some changes due to globalization may lead to a blurring of cultural distinctions and some lessening of distinctive cultural identities.

- *Multiculturalism*: The central value of multiculturalism is that of cultural pluralism and acknowledging that nations like Britain, Australia and America are cultural mosaics rather than cultural melting pots (Sue et al., 1998). Multiculturalism can be contrasted with monoculturalism where high value is attached only to the patterns of behaviour of the dominant or mainstream culture.

- *Cultural cohesion*: Cultural cohesion or social cohesiveness refers to the extent to which the norms of a culture or nation help it to stick together. In Britain, Australia and the United States many of the problems of cultural minorities are those of equality of access to opportunities within the mainstream culture rather than the fact that a mainstream culture exists. In such culturally diverse countries, a balance needs to be struck between multiculturalism and cultural cohesion. If taken to extremes, in a highly culturally diverse country like Australia, multiculturalism could lead to each ethnic group following its own agenda and so coming into conflict with other ethnic groups. Northern Ireland provides a good example of inadequate cohesion, with its two main cultural groups insufficiently finding common ground.

- *Race*: Race refers to human subgroups possessing distinctive physical characteristics that distinguish them from other human subgroups. Such physical characteristics include skin colour, head form, facial features, and amount, colour and texture of body hair. Racial groups include Caucasian, Aboriginal, African, Asian, Polynesian or various combinations of mixed race.

- *Ethnic minority*: A neutral definition of ethnic minorities is that they are groups differentiated from the main population of a country by racial origin and/or cultural background. Another definition of a minority, be it ethnic or otherwise, is that it is a group of people who, because of physical or cultural characteristics, are singled out from others in the society in which they live for differential and unequal treatment, and who therefore regard themselves as objects of collective discrimination.

Culture and demography

Some indication of the importance of culture to contemporary counselling can be found in the demographic statistics of various countries. Demography is the study of population sizes, movements and trends, including those concerning ethnic minorities. In Britain, in 1999–2000, Caucasians formed 93.3 per cent of the total population of 56.9 million people. The overall ethnic minority population, comprising both those born abroad and those born in the UK, was estimated to have been 6.7 per cent or about 1 in 15 of the total population, up from 5.8 per cent or about 1 in 18 in 1995–6. In 1999–2000, the four largest ethnic minority groups were Indian, 1.7 per cent, Pakistani, 1.2 per cent, Black-Caribbean, 0.9 per cent, and Black African, 0.7 per cent (Tyrrell, 2001). The above figures disguise the full extent of cultural differences in Britain, for instance between the Welsh, Irish, Scots and English as well as between and within the more racially distinguished ethnic groupings.

Australia is one of the most multicultural and, increasingly, multiracial countries in the world. In 2000, about 23 per cent or nearly a quarter of the population of just over 19 million was born overseas. In June 1997, of the overseas born, the two largest groupings were European, 55.8 per cent, and Asian, 22.7 per cent (Department of Foreign Affairs and Trade, 2000). There is a shift in migration patterns with, in 1995–6, nearly 40 per cent of settler arrivals being Asian-born: 18.8 per cent from Northeast Asia; 13.3 per cent from Southeast Asia; and 7.8 per cent from Southern Asia (Department of Immigration and Multicultural Affairs, 1997). Because they have settled in Australia over a shorter period of time than other immigrants, the Asian-born population is largely concentrated in the 20–44 age bracket (Weston et al., 2001). In the 1996 Australian census, 352,970 people identified themselves as of Aboriginal and Torres Strait Islander descent.

Like Australia, the United States is undergoing a marked change in its racial/ethnic population distribution. The 2000 census found that the US population was over 281.4 million, of whom 11.1 per cent were born abroad. The Black and Hispanic populations were each about 13 per cent of the total population, the Asian population was just over 4 per cent, and the American Indian and Alaskan Native population was 1.5 per cent. Nearly 98 per cent of Americans answered that they came from only one race, with whites forming three-quarters of the population (US Census Bureau, 2003). Demographic projections indicate that non-whites will outnumber whites sometime between the years 2030 and 2050 (Sue et al., 1998). The rapid demographic shift stems from two major trends: immigration and differential birthrates. The largest groups of immigrants are Asian and Latin American. White American birthrates at 1.7 per mother are less than those of non-whites, for instance African-American at 2.4 per mother, Mexican-American at 2.9, Vietnamese at 3.4, Laotian at 4.6 and Cambodian at 7.4 (Sue and Sue, 2003).

Theory

Culture and full humanness

An important issue in thinking about cultures is the extent to which they are conducive to developing the full humanness of their individual members (Maslow, 1971). The idea that all cultures are equally benign in promoting the human potential of their members is both false and naïve: for example, think of the demeaning position of women when the Taleban ruled Afghanistan. Maslow was cautiously optimistic about the biological nature of human beings. However, he thought that positive aspects of human nature, such as altruistic concern for others, were frequently weak, needed a benign culture for their appearance, and could be inhibited or shattered by bad cultural conditions.

There is a reciprocal interaction between the development or lack of development of individuals and the cultures or societies to which they belong. Maslow considered that 'Individual and social interests under healthy social conditions are synergic and not antagonistic' (1970: 85). A criticism of the multicultural literature is that it has been insufficiently rigorous in addressing how cultures differ in being encouraging, benign, inhibiting or antagonistic to developing both the basic life skills and the higher potentials of their members. All cultures are not equally worthy of respect in all of their aspects.

Culture and values

One of the main dimensions of a culture is that of values or the underlying principles that guide how people live their lives. However, there is no exact relationship between how people think they ought to behave, their values and their actual behaviour.

Universal values

Schwartz (1992; Schwartz and Bilsky, 1990) is a prominent researcher in the area of values. He classified values into 10 types: power, achievement, hedonism, stimulation, self-direction, universalism, benevolence, tradition, conformity and security. Based on information from 20 countries in six continents, Schwartz (1992) confirmed that each of the 10 values was found in at least 90 per cent of the countries he surveyed, suggesting that his value types are near universal.

Cultural dimensions

One of the major cross-cultural research endeavours in recent years was the collection of data on work-related attitudes in 50 countries and three regions by the Dutch psychologist Hofstede (1980, 1983). Hofstede identified four cultural dimensions or factors in those countries and regions (see Box 15.1).

Box 15.1   Hofstede's four cultural dimensions

- *Power distance* refers to social inequality and the amount of authority one person has over others;
- *Uncertainty avoidance* relates to how a culture deals with conflict, especially the creation of beliefs and institutions to deal with disagreements and aggression;
- *Individualism versus collectivism* – individualistic cultures are those in which people only care for themselves and their close relations. In collectivistic cultures, people belong to ingroups or collectives that care for them in return for loyalty;
- *Masculinity–femininity* refers to two opposite sets of cultural values. In masculine cultures, the dominant values are success and money. In feminine cultures, the dominant values evolve around caring for others and quality of life.

Australia was one of the countries Hofstede studied. Of the four dimensions, Australia, relative to other countries, scored very high on individualism, mid-range on uncertainty avoidance and masculinity–femininity, and relatively low on power distance. Southeast Asian countries like Hong Kong, Malaysia and Singapore scored high to very high on power distance, high on uncertainty avoidance and collectivism, and mid-range on masculinity–femininity.

Asian values

In Britain, the two main ethnic minorities stem from Southern Asia: namely, Indians and Pakistanis. In Australia, the two main migrant groups are Northeast Asian and Southeast Asian. Though here I present two overlapping versions of Asian values, in reality there are numerous differences between Asian countries and within the populations of each country.

Laungani (1999a) suggests that there are four interrelated core values of factors that distinguish western from eastern cultures. In particular, he focuses on the differences between British and Indian cultures. Laungani stresses that the two concepts underlying each of the factors summarized in Box 15.2 should be regarded as extending along a continuum rather than as dichotomous. Note that the one factor which overlaps with Hofstede's four dimensions is that of *Individualism – Communalism (Collectivism)*, which is perhaps the most frequently cited value differentiating western from eastern cultures.

Box 15.2   Laungani's four core values or factors distinguishing western (British) from eastern (Indian) cultures

Individualism – Communalism (Collectivism)
Individualism emphasizes self-control, personal responsibility, self-achievement, individuals achieving an identity, and nuclear families.

(Continued)

Box 15.2   (Continued)

Communalism (Collectivism) emphasizes dependence on elders and other family members, collective responsibility, collective achievement, family and caste-related identity ascribed at birth, and extended families.

Cognitivism – Emotionalism
Cognitivism emphasizes rationality and logic, keeping feelings and emotions in check, work and activity, and relationships based on shared interests.
Emotionalism emphasizes feelings and intuition, expressing emotions openly, relationships as extremely important, and relationships being caste- and family-based.

Free Will – Determinism
Free will emphasizes freedom of choice, being proactive, success or failure largely due to effort, self-blame or guilt as a residual consequence of failure, and the possibility of failure leading to blaming the victim.
Determinism emphasizes limited freedom of choice, being reactive, despite success being important it is related to one's karma, no guilt is attached to failure, and no blame is attached to the victim.

Materialism – Spiritualism
Materialism emphasizes the world as 'real' and physical, rejection of contradictory explanations of phenomena, reality is external to the individual and it is perceived through the scientific enterprise.
Spiritualism emphasizes the world as illusory, the coexistence of contradictory phenomena, reality being internal to the individual and being perceived through contemplation and inner reflection.

Ho (1992) lists seven values held in common by Asian cultures that may be operating among Asian-Americans, who are predominantly from Southeast and Northeast Asia. These values, which overlap with Laungani's eastern (Indian) values, are also likely to be held by Southeast Asian and Northeast Asian migrants to Australia. Following is a summary of Ho's seven Asian values.

1. *Filial piety,* or a high degree of respect for parents;
2. *Shame,* or loss of face used as a method of reinforcing proper behaviour;
3. *Self-control,* requiring modesty in behaviour, humbleness in expectations, and hesitation, even when individuals highly desire an object;
4. *Assumption of the middle position,* or the Asian emphasis on consensus as a process that fosters the individual's sense of belonging and togetherness;
5. *Awareness of the social milieu,* involving an awareness and sensitivity to others' opinions and feelings and being prepared to subordinate one's feelings in the interests of solidarity;
6. *Fatalism,* a belief system that accepts events as predetermined;
7. *Inconspicuousness,* based on the fear of attracting attention.

One of the issues of any migrant group is the extent to which the values of the parents who originally migrated are held by their children and grand-children. Laungani provides some research evidence indicating that main-tenance of parental values is the case among British-born Indian school children. However, a greater degree of assimilation into mainstream British culture is likely as the generations become further removed from their original migrant ancestors.

Often, conflicts arise *between* migrants, who value their cultures of origin, and their children, who are under considerable pressure to adapt to their host cultures. These conflicts are heightened because the children of migrants often perceive young people in western cultures as being more independent and free than those in eastern cultures. Conflicts inevitably also take place *within* the hearts and souls of migrants and their children, all of whom, in varying degrees and in differing ways, experience the pulls and pushes of being caught between two cultures.

Theoretical assumptions of Asian therapies

In the above discussion on values, it is apparent that assumptions underlying Asian approaches to therapy will differ from those underlying western approaches. It is possible to divide people's developmental status into pre-conventional, conventional and postconventional stages of growth. Walsh (2000) considers that, while capable of addressing lower levels, Asian psycho-therapies aim primarily at postconventional growth and the transpersonal domains, which are the special interest of Asia.

The concepts of mind and of mental development are central to under-standing Asian therapies, whose starting point is that people's usual state of mind is underdeveloped. Because this state of affairs is so widespread, it often goes unnoticed. People suffer from a case of mistaken identity in that their true nature is something far more remarkable that the self-concept of 'ego' that they mistakenly assume to be their true selves. Psychological suffering is the result of insufficient mental development. It is possible to train and develop the mind both to reduce conventional self-created suffer-ing and to develop supra-normal capacities such as heightened concentra-tion and compassion. Meditation and yoga are included among effective ways of training the mind to function at higher levels and to access a vastly greater unconscious system than that offered by Freudian psychology (Walsh, 2000).

Cultural identity development

Cultural identity development theory is based on the assumption that indi-viduals in cultural, racial and other minority groups possess varying levels of consciousness or awareness about their membership both of their minority group and of the wider society. In addition, cultural identity development theory is relevant to mainstream or majority groups in relation to themselves, minority groups and the wider culture.

Helms (1995) presents two racial identity models for the United States, one for members of the white majority culture and another for people of colour. She assumes that whites and coloured people have to work through issues of racism in different ways: for example, many, though not all, whites may start by assuming entitlement to the privileges society offers and many non-whites may perceive their position as one of being oppressed and excluded from equal opportunity. For Helms, the most highly developed white people attain an 'autonomy status', involving an informed and positive commitment to racial equality and the capacity to give up the privileges of racism. The most highly developed coloured people attain the 'integrative awareness status' involving a capacity to value their own collective identities as well as the ability to empathize and collaborate with members of other oppressed groups.

A five-stage model of cultural identity development focused on minority rather than majority groups is presented by Cheatham and his colleagues (1997). In this model people start by being 'asleep' in that they have little awareness of themselves as cultural beings and progress to attaining a level of consciousness in which they both possess a knowledgeable pride about their culture and recognize positive dimensions of the mainstream culture. Cheatham and his colleagues' model is summarized in Box 15.3. The model can be extended to deal with the consciousness-raising of other minority groups such as women, gays and lesbians.

Box 15.3   A model of cultural identity development

Stage 1: Naïvety
Individuals have little awareness of themselves as cultural beings: for example, children do not distinguish skin colour as an important feature.

Stage 2: Encounter
Individuals encounter experiences in their environments that clearly demonstrate that their earlier naïve views were inadequate.

Stage 3: Naming
Naming involves identifying one's cultural or minority group and the nature of oppression against it, for instance, Afro-Caribbean-British, Indian-British or Vietnamese-Australian and racism; gays and lesbians and homophobia; women and sexism.

Box 15.3   (Continued)

Stage 4: Reflection on self as a cultural being
Individuals develop a keener awareness of themselves as Afro-Caribbean-British, Indian-British or Vietnamese-Australian. Individuals may turn inwards towards their own cultures and away from the majority culture. The developmental task is establishing a definite cultural consciousness.

Stage 5: Multi-perspective internalization
Individuals develop pride in their cultures, yet accept worthwhile dimensions of the predominant culture. They can use important dimensions of all stages of development.

Therapists and trainees can assess their own level of cultural identity development and, where necessary, take steps to improve their level of awareness of themselves as cultural beings. Therapists need also be aware of their clients' level of cultural identity and, where appropriate, use this knowledge to assist them in attaining higher levels of cultural consciousness. However, therapists need to be careful not to impose cultural agendas on those clients whose concerns lie elsewhere, for instance passing an upcoming test.

A theory of multicultural counselling and therapy

Sue et al. (1996) consider current theories of counselling and therapy too ethnocentric and mono-cultural and lacking conceptual frameworks that incorporate culture as a core concept in the therapeutic relationship. They propose a metatheory or theory about theories that they call Multicultural Counselling and Therapy (MCT). This metatheory is intended to offer a framework for understanding the numerous helping approaches that have been developed in both western and non-western cultures.

MCT consists of six propositions, each of which has corollaries. The first proposition is that MCT is a metatheory. The second proposition stresses that therapist and client identities are embedded in many levels of experience and contexts, for example, individual family and culture, and that the totality of these experiences must be the focus on treatment. The third proposition emphasizes the importance of the development of therapist and client cultural identity, including attitudes about dominant–subordinate relationships among culturally different groups. The fourth proposition is that MCT theory is likely to be enhanced when therapists define goals and use modalities consistent with the life experiences and cultural values of their clients. The fifth proposition stresses the importance of multiple helping roles, often involving larger social units, developed by culturally different groups. The final proposition emphasizes that the liberation of consciousness is a basic MCT goal. For example, to develop in clients a critical consciousness, therapists, who draw on both western and non-western systems of helping, may often teach clients about the underlying cultural dimensions of their present concerns.

Therapy

Therapeutic goals

There are many different client groups for whom cultural considerations are important: for example, indigenous people, such as Australian Aborigines and Torres Strait Islanders; first-generation migrants, with many different reasons for seeking out a life in a new country; descendants of migrants at varying levels of assimilation to the mainstream culture; and members of the mainstream culture, among others. Following are some goals, which may overlap, for working with clients in whose problems issues of culture play a significant role:

- *Support*: Migrants require culture-sensitive support when they first arrive in their new home countries. Think of the cumulative stresses involved in moving to a new culture including a change of home, parting from loved ones and previous support networks, language difficulties, climate change, change in physical environment (for instance the countryside and buildings look different), homesickness, loneliness, financial worries, concerns about children's education, and, for many migrants, racist incidents.
- *Dealing with post-traumatic stress*: Many migrants are refugees and some suffer from post-traumatic stress disorders. Reasons for their traumatization include being war victims, witnessing violence and living through missile attacks, torture, starvation, imprisonment, internment and rape. Such migrants may suffer persistent re-experiencing of traumatic events, hyperarousal, numbing of affect, or oscillate between hyperarousal and numbing of affect. Traumatized migrants, with their families and support networks, require special culture-sensitive post-traumatic stress disorder therapy.
- *Assisting acculturation and assimilation*: The multicultural literature is often overly negative about the virtues of mainstream cultures such as those in Britain, Australia and America. In addition, much the literature seems to insufficiently address the need for cultural cohesion as well as for cultural diversity. Most migrants move because the perceived benefits of their new countries far outweigh those of their former ones. Migration can be a time of great opportunity. However, it is also a time of considerable challenges. Migrants require practical help with such matters as housing, health, education and employment. Furthermore, all

migrants bring psychological strengths and deficiencies to their transitions to a new culture. Some may require culturally sensitive psychological assistance so as not to activate self-defeating patterns for dealing with change and stress, for instance withdrawal, being unwilling to alter old ways of behaving, and aggressively disparaging their new countries.

- *Assisting clients to handle cross-cultural relationships*: Difficulties in cross-cultural relationships can take many forms. Therapists can assist existing members of host countries and first-generation migrants to develop skills for accepting difference, reaching out to one another, and for building bridges rather than barriers between cultures. Therapist may also need skills in assisting migrants and their children to deal with issues of intergenerational conflict, for instance choice of boyfriends/girlfriends. In a country like Australia, where cross-cultural relationships are common, therapeutic goals can also include helping partners in intimate relationships to understand and accommodate to one another's cultural differences.

- *Consciousness-raising and liberation*: For those clients who suffer from discrimination and oppression on account of culture and race, therapeutic goals can and should address issues of cultural identity development. Some readers may also wish to review Box 15.3. Ethnic minority clients can be assisted to take pride in their cultures, liberate themselves from internalized negative stereotypes, and join the broader struggle against external oppression on account of culture and race. Consciousness-raising and liberation can also be important therapeutic goals for mainstream culture clients, who require assistance in relinquishing negative aspects of their enculturation, such as a false sense of cultural and racial superiority. Some mainstream culture clients may then also participate in the fight for cultural and racial equality.

- *Avoiding further marginalization*: Therapists need to be aware that, if they pursue cultural agendas clumsily, they can do more harm than good. Where appropriate, therapists can and should help ethnic minority group clients be assertive about attaining their human rights. However, there is a danger that therapists collude when some minority clients further marginalize themselves by unfairly 'demonizing' their host cultures, making their lives out to be worse than they are, and playing the psychological game of 'Ain't it awful', at the same time as doing little positive to change their situations. When dealing with issues of acculturation and change, people of all cultures and races can be inflexible and self-defeating.

- *Attaining higher levels of development*: The goals of some culturally different clients may be more oriented towards growth rather than adaptation to a mainstream culture. What constitutes higher levels of development can vary according to culture and to the therapeutic approach employed. For instance, eastern cultures stress heightened concentration, mental purification, kindness, compassion, sympathetic joy in one another's accomplishments, equanimity, wisdom and selfless service (Walsh, 2000).

- *The good society*: A broader goal of multicultural counselling and therapy is to develop formal and informal norms within societies that are synergistic rather than antagonistic to developing the full human potential of all members. This goal requires therapists to play social engineering and change agent roles, especially in regard to combating institutions and organizations that are instruments of cultural and racial oppression.

Therapeutic approaches

As may be seen from the above list of goals, there are many different considerations in selecting therapeutic approaches for problems that contain a significant cultural component. The issue of culturally relevant counselling and therapy can be addressed in at least three different ways: first, by making existing Euro-American therapies more culture-sensitive; second, by therapists developing multicultural counselling and therapy competencies; and third, by engaging in non-western approaches to counselling and therapy.

Making existing Euro-American therapies more culture-sensitive

To what extent can cultural issues be addressed by modifying the theory and practice of existing western counselling and therapy approaches so that they become more culture-sensitive? The following discussion addresses some issues in applying person-centred and cognitive-behaviour therapies to minority-group and mainstream-culture clients.

With mainstream-culture clients, person-centred therapists can use Rogerian empathy to assist them to experience and explore their cultural and racial concerns. However, this will only happen in those instances where clients have sufficient awareness and interest to work on such issues. The person-centred concept of empathy can be expanded to include cultural empathy (Ridley and Lingle, 1996). Person-centred therapists who see themselves and their clients as cultural beings can encourage non-western clients to share their experiences by such methods as listening carefully for and responding to culturally relevant cues rather than not attending to them and also by openly acknowledging that they are from a different culture and then asking their client's assistance in understanding the cultural context of their concerns. When clients reveal experiences, therapists can consciously try to understand the cultural implications of clients' communications. Furthermore, when therapists respond they can be tentative in checking out the extent of their cultural understanding.

There are barriers to western therapists being perceived as empathic by ethnic minority clients (Laungani, 1999b; Sue and Sue, 2003). For example, Asian clients want to perceive their therapists as expert and expect more direction from them. Furthermore, Asian clients may be reluctant to talk about their problems outside of their families. Communication may be made even more difficult because clients and therapists may not understand the meanings and nuances of one another's spoken and non-verbal communication. In addition, there is a distinct possibility that the western therapist does not understand the Asian client's cultural worldview, including the importance attached to family relationships, and may project parts of her/his own worldview on to the client. These difficulties can be addressed to some extent, if person-centred therapists, or any other therapists for that matter, are trained to understand the cultures and communication styles of one or more specific cultural groups from whom many of their clients come. However, really getting to grips with the mind-set of any foreign culture is much easier said than done. Ideally, learning about another culture in depth requires learning the relevant language and spending much time immersed in that culture.

The cognitive-behaviour therapies provide another example of how it is possible to extend existing Euro-American therapeutic approaches to become more culture-sensitive. Such therapies can be used to help both mainstream clients and minority group clients to think more rationally and realistically regarding culture and race. However, there is a paucity of literature regarding how to do this and where the cross-cultural difficulties lie.

Regarding rational emotive behaviour therapy, Ellis (1998) includes racial prejudice in his list of prejudice-related irrationalities. In REBT, clients' cultural and racial irrational beliefs and prejudices can be detected, disputed and, where appropriate, restated in preferential and rational terms. Similarly, in cognitive therapy, questioning by skilled therapists can assist clients to identify their underlying cultural and racial automatic thoughts, explore how realistic they are, and formulate more realistic thoughts and perceptions for the future. Regarding multimodal therapy, Palmer (2000) claims that this is sufficiently flexible to use with most ethnic minority clients suffering from stress.

Multicultural counselling and therapy competencies

An American approach to issues of culture and race in counselling and therapy has been to develop a statement of multicultural counselling competencies for culturally skilled counsellors and therapists (Sue et al., 1998). This statement is the work of a committee of the American Psychological Association's Division of Counseling Psychology (since 2003, Society of Counseling Psychology). The committee saw multicultural counselling competencies as having three main dimensions: awareness of own assumptions, values and biases; understanding the worldview of the culturally different client; and developing appropriate strategies and techniques. Each dimension is divided into beliefs and attitudes, knowledge and skills. The United States has a long history of serious, and often brutal, racial oppression that provided one of the main contexts in which this statement was compiled. One of the statement's major assumptions was that of widespread and systematic cultural and racial oppression.

Awareness of own assumptions, values and biases

The beliefs held by culturally skilled counsellors and therapists include being sensitive to their own cultural heritage, being comfortable with the differences of clients from other cultures and races, and recognizing the limitations of their competence and expertise. Counsellors and therapists should know about their cultural and racial heritage and how this affects the therapeutic process, understand how oppression, racism and discrimination may affect them personally and in their work, and know about the impact of how they communicate on culturally different clients. Skills include seeking out relevant educational and training experiences, actively understanding oneself as a cultural and racial being, and seeking a non-racial identity.

Understanding the worldview of the culturally different client

Beliefs and attitudes for culturally skilled counsellors and therapists include being aware of their negative emotional reactions and of the stereotypes and preconceived notions that they may hold towards culturally and racially different groups. Therapists should know about the cultural experiences, cultural heritage and historical backgrounds of any particular group with whom they work, acknowledge how culture and race can affect help-seeking behaviour, know how culture and race can influence assessment and the selection and implementation of therapeutic interventions, and know about the oppressive political and environmental influences impinging on the lives of ethnic and racial minorities. Skills include keeping up to date on research findings relevant to the psychological wellbeing of various ethnic and racial groups as well as being actively involved with minorities outside work settings to gain deeper insight into their perspectives.

Developing appropriate intervention strategies and techniques

Culturally skilled counsellors' and therapists' attitudes and beliefs include respecting clients' religious and spiritual beliefs about physical and mental functioning, respecting indigenous helping practices, and valuing bilingualism. Their knowledge base includes understanding how the culture-bound, class-bound and monolingual characteristics of counselling clash with the cultural values of various minority groups, being aware of institutional barriers to minority groups using helping services, knowing about the potential for bias in assessment instruments, and understanding minority group family structures, hierarchies, and community characteristics and resources. Skills include the ability to send and receive verbal and non-verbal communication accurately, interacting in the language requested by clients or making appropriate referrals, tailoring the therapeutic relationship and interventions to the clients' stage of cultural and racial identity development, and engaging in a variety of helping roles, beyond being a therapist. Box 15.4 identifies some of these additional helping roles (Atkinson et al., 1993; Sue and Sue, 2003; Sue et al., 1996).

Box 15.4   Additional roles for multicultural counsellors and therapists

1. *Adviser*: Advising clients how to solve or prevent problems and providing relevant information;
2. *Advocate*: Representing and speaking up for clients' best interests to other individuals, groups or organizations;
3. *Facilitator of indigenous support systems*: Knowing about and appropriately involving support systems, such as the client's extended family and community elders;
4. *Facilitator of indigenous healing systems*: Either referring clients to healers or, if sufficiently knowledgeable and skilled, actually using the indigenous healing methods;
5. *Consultant*: Working collegially with clients to impact or change a third party, including organizational change;
6. *Change agent*: Initiating and implementing action-oriented approaches to changing social environments that may be oppressing clients.

The statement of multicultural competencies is ambitious and has much to recommend it. However, possible reservations include the following. The statement assumes a high degree of cultural and racial oppression by the white mainstream culture, which may not be true in all instances. For example, some of the strongest supporters of minority group rights are white people. Furthermore, many white people are tolerant of and some are very positive about cultural differences, as witnessed by the growing number of cultural and racial intermarriages in countries like Australia and America (Kerwin and Ponterotto, 1995). In addition, cultural and racial biases are not the sole preserve of white people, and this fact should be more openly acknowledged and addressed. Another reservation is that the potential for modifying existing Euro-American counselling and therapy may be underestimated. Last, as migrants become more assimilated into their host cultures and as globalization increases the common ground among cultures, the need for a multicultural approach may become less pressing.

Despite these reservations, in countries like Britain, Australia and America, both obvious and less obvious oppression of cultural and racial minorities definitely exists. All therapists, regardless of their culture and race, need to address their own level of cultural identity development and their ability to offer culturally sensitive services to all clients, be they from minority groups or from the mainstream culture.

Non-western approaches to counselling and therapy

Non-western therapies come from many cultures: for instance, Asian and African. Such therapies may be the treatment of choice not only for some ethnic minority-group clients, but also for some mainstream-culture clients. Sue and Sue (2003) suggest that therapists should also be willing to consult with traditional healers or make use of their services.

Laungani writes of psychotherapy in the east:

> Although Western models of therapy continue to be used among the small Westernized clientele to be found mainly in large metropolitan cities, the therapists in Eastern cultures have almost reinvented their ancient indigenous approaches, which range from Astrology and Palmistry, Ayurvedic and Homeopathic treatment, religious therapy pilgrimages, shamanism and exorcism, to yogic exercises and meditation. (2004a: 205)

He stresses that these approaches are in keeping with the fundamental value systems of eastern thinking, including communalism, determinism, emotionalism and spiritualism. The philosophy of individualism, so prominent in western thinking, holds little sway in eastern thinking.

In Asia, there is a long tradition of training the mind to foster interdependence, minimize suffering and create happiness. The main teaching of Buddhism, which is a system of psychology as well as a religion, can be summarized in the Buddha's statement: 'Refrain from evil, do good and purify the mind'. Here I use meditation and Naikan therapy to illustrate some Asian approaches to therapy.

Meditation

Meditation tends to be central to Asian therapeutic approaches. It falls into two main categories: mindfulness of breathing or breath meditation and awareness or insight meditation. All meditation approaches require practice, with perseverance increasing the likelihood of better results. Meditation can be significantly enhanced by attending retreats in which clients engage in continuous meditation practice for days or weeks.

Breathing meditation consists of relaxed concentration on the flow of your breathing, on the in-breaths and on the out-breaths. Breathing meditation may be performed sitting, standing, walking or reclining. Buddhist insight meditations include calmly becoming aware of the impermanence of whatever experiences and sensations arise and meditations that cultivate the four divine abodes of mind: loving kindness, compassion, sympathy and equanimity (Thitavanno, 1995, 2002).

Walsh (2000) observes that meditation can lead to a wide variety of insights and experiences over time. For instance, many clients gain insight into their customary lack of mental control or 'monkey minds'. Meditators come to recognize that everything in their mind is in a state of constant change and that the notion of an unchanging self, or even a self for that matter, is an illusory construction. With this insight egocentricity may be lessened and compassionate identification with others may increase. In advanced states of meditation, supranormal capacities emerge such as heightened concentration, perceptual sensitivity and profound peace.

Naikan therapy

Naikan therapy is a Japanese approach adapted from a more intensive Buddhist meditation practice (Reynolds, 1990). It is aimed at assisting clients to find meaning in their lives, recognize human interdependence, feel and show gratitude, and repair relationships. Naikan therapy assumes that narrowly focusing on oneself creates suffering both for oneself and others.

Clients are encouraged to establish a calm meditative state and then to reflect specifically on three things:

- what another person or other people have done for them;
- how much gratitude is due to them; and
- the difficulties they have caused others and how little they have demonstrated gratitude.

Naikan therapy can elicit various thoughts and feelings, for instance guilt and unworthiness. However, many clients also get in touch with kinder and more generous feelings towards their caregivers. Clients may realize that, despite their weaknesses and failings, they were looked after and helped. Furthermore, they may start feeling very grateful to people in their pasts and want to make amends for their own inadequacies towards them.

Conclusion

At present, the mainstream cultures of Britain, Australia and America are insufficiently conducive to developing the full human potential of their members, and this is especially true for those in cultural, racial and other minority groups. The development of culture-sensitive counselling and therapy should not be restricted to any one of the three broad approaches mentioned above. Existing Euro-American therapies require further development to deal with the cultural issues pertaining to both minority and mainstream groups. All counsellors and therapists need to develop a set of core multicultural competencies as well as competencies specific to the main ethnic minority and racial groups with which they interact. Much more work is needed in defining, researching and providing good training materials that illustrate these core and culture-specific therapeutic competencies. In addition, greater attention needs to be paid to raising western therapists' awareness of non-western therapies. Furthermore, more research needs to be conducted into the effectiveness of these therapies, either on their own or in combination with western therapies, with clients from a range of cultures. East, West, North and South can learn therapeutic insights and skills from one another to the benefit of all.

Review and personal questions

Review questions

1. What is the meaning of each of the following terms:

    (a) culture;
    (b) enculturation;
    (c) acculturation;
    (d) culture shock;
    (e) cultural change;
    (f) multiculturalism;
    (g) cultural cohesion;
    (h) race;
    (i) ethnic minority?

2. Describe and evaluate each of the following:

    (a) Schwartz's universal value types;
    (b) Hofstede's four cultural dimensions;
    (c) Laungani's and Ho's views of Asian values;

3. Critically discuss Cheatham et al.'s views of cultural identity development.
4. Critically discuss the goals for culture-sensitive therapy presented in the chapter.
5. What are some ways of making existing Euro-American therapies more culture-sensitive?
6. What are multicultural counselling and therapy competencies? What is your reaction to Sue et al.'s statement of competencies?
7. What are some non-western approaches to counselling and therapy?

Personal questions

1. How would you describe:

    (a) the culture of your ancestral background;
    (b) if an ethnic-minority group member, the distinguishing features of your culture;
    (c) for all readers, the distinctive features of the mainstream culture in which you live?

2. To what extent do you consider the values you hold are universal and to what extent do you consider they are specific to your culture? Give reasons for your answer.

3. Describe instances, if any, in which you have been:

    (a) the recipient of cultural and/or racial oppression;
    (b) the purveyor of cultural and/or racial oppression;

4. What is your level of cultural identity development? Provide reasons for your answer.
5. To what extent and how can the main counselling and therapy approach you use be adapted for culturally different clients?
6. How can you make yourself a more culturally sensitive counsellor or therapist both now and in the future?

Annotated bibliography

Palmer, S. and Laungani, P. (eds) (1999) *Counselling in a Multicultural Society*. London: Sage. This multi-authored British book contains eight chapters on such topics as the challenges of counselling in a multiracial society; culture and identity; racial issues; models of counselling and therapy for a multi-ethnic society; counselling needs of ethnic minorities; client-centred or culture-centred counselling; and the search for effective counselling across cultures.

D'Ardenne, P. and Mahtani, A. (1999) *Transcultural Counselling in Action* (2nd edn). London: Sage.
This book is written by two clinical psychologists, one with a white-English and the other with an Indian background, working in London's East End. The book introduces the concept of transcultural counselling and then reviews practical issues concerned with clients and counsellors; starting the counselling process; sharing a common language; the therapeutic relationship; change and growth; and ending counselling. The book is illustrated by four case studies with clients with Bangladeshi, English, French and Nigerian cultural backgrounds.

Sue, D.W. and Sue, D. (2003) *Counseling the Culturally Diverse: Theory and Practice* (4th edn). New York: John Wiley.
This book is focused on the United States and consists of seven parts: 1. the conceptual dimensions of multicultural counselling/therapy; 2. the political dimensions of mental health practice; 3. the practice of multicultural counselling/therapy; 4. worldviews in multicultural counselling/therapy; 5. counselling and therapy with racial/ethnic minority populations; 6. counselling other culturally diverse populations; and 7. organizations and institutions as clients.

Sue, D.W., Carter, R.T., Casas, J.M., Fouad, N.A., Ivey, A.E., Jensen, M., LaFromboise, T., Manese, J.E., Ponterotto, J.G. and Vazquez-Nutall, E. (1998) *Multicultural Counseling Competencies: Individual and Organizational Development*. London: Sage.
This American book introduces the concepts of multiculturalism and ethnocentric monoculturalism and then presents the multicultural counselling competencies. Chapters follow on understanding the Euro-American worldview and on understanding racial/ethnic minority worldviews. Much of the remainder of the book focuses on multicultural organizational development, with the final chapter looking at issues of personal, professional and organizational multicultural competence.

Walsh, R. (2000) 'Asian psychotherapies', in R.J. Corsini and D. Wedding (eds), *Current Psychotherapies* (6th edn). Itasca, IL: Peacock. pp. 407–44.
This chapter examines the assumptions underlying Asian therapies, compares Asian with western therapies, provides a theory of personality from an Asian perspective, reviews Asian views of psychopathology and psychological health, and then describes different therapeutic approaches. The chapter includes a case example.

References and further reading

Atkinson, D.R., Thompson, C.E. and Grant, S.K. (1993) 'A three dimensional model for counseling racial/ethnic minorities', *The Counseling Psychologist, 21*: 257–77.
Cheatham, H., Ivey, A.E., Ivey, M.B., Pedersen, P., Rigazio-DiGillio, S., Simek-Morgan, L. and Sue, D.W. (1997) 'Multicultural counselling and therapy: 1. Metatheory – taking theory into practice; 2. Integrative practice', in A.E. Ivey, M.B. Ivey and L. Simek-Downing (eds), *Counseling and Psychotherapy: A Multicultural Perspective* (4th edn). Boston: Allyn & Bacon. pp. 133–205.
Corey, G. (2005) *Theory and Practice of Counseling & Psychotherapy* (7th edn). Belmont, CA: Thomson Brooks/Cole.
Cross, T.L., Bazron, B.J., Dennis, K.W. and Isaacs, M.R. (1989) *Towards a Culturally Competent System of Care.* Washington, DC: Child and Adolescent Service System Technical Assistance Center.
D'Ardenne, P. and Mahtani, A. (1999) *Transcultural Counselling in Action* (2nd edn). London: Sage.
Department of Foreign Affairs and Trade (2000) *Australia in Brief 2000.* Canberra: Department of Foreign Affairs and Trade.
Department of Immigration and Multicultural Affairs (1997) *Australia's Population Trends and Prospects 1996.* Canberra: Department of Immigration and Multicultural Affairs.
Ellis, A. (1998) 'The biological basis of human irrationality', in A. Ellis and S. Blau (eds), *The Albert Ellis Reader.* Secaucus, NJ: Citadel. pp. 271–91.
Helms, J.E. (1995) 'An update of Helms's white and people of color racial identity models', in J.G. Ponterotto, J.M. Casas, L.A. Sizuki and C.M. Alexander (eds), *Handbook of Multicultural Counseling.* Thousand Oaks, CA: Sage. pp. 181–98.
Hermans, H.J.M. and Kempen, H.J.G. (1998) 'Moving cultures: the perilous problems of cultural dichotomies in a globalizing society', *American Psychologist, 53*: 1111–20.
Ho, M.K. (1992) *Minority Children and Adolescents in Therapy.* Newbury Park, CA: Sage.
Hofstede, G. (1980) *Culture's Consequences: International Differences in Work-Related Values.* London: Sage.
Hofstede, G. (1983) 'Dimensions of national culture in fifty cultures and three regions', in J.B. Deregowski, S. Dziurawiec and R.C. Annis (eds), *Expiscations in Cross-Cultural Psychology.* Lisse: Swets & Zeitlinger. pp. 335–55.
Kerwin, C. and Ponterotto, J.G. (1995) 'Biracial identity development: theory and research', in J.G. Ponterotto, J.M. Casas, L.A. Sizuki and C.M. Alexander (eds), *Handbook of Multicultural Counseling.* Thousand Oaks, CA: Sage. pp. 199–217.
Laungani, P. (1999a) 'Culture and identity: implications for counselling', in S. Palmer and P. Laungani (eds), *Counselling in a Multicultural Society.* London: Sage. pp. 35–70.
Laungani, P. (1999b) 'Client centred or culture centred counselling', in S. Palmer and P. Laungani (eds), *Counselling in a Multicultural Society.* London: Sage. pp. 133–52.
Laungani, P. (2004a) 'Counselling and therapy in a multi-cultural setting', *Counselling Psychology Quarterly, 17*: 195–207.

Laungani, P. (2004b) *Asian Perspectives in Counselling and Psychotherapy*. London: Routledge.

Maslow, A.H. (1970) *Motivation and Personality* (2nd edn). New York: Harper & Row.

Maslow, A.H. (1971) *The Farther Reaches of Human Nature*. Harmondsworth: Penguin.

Palmer, S. (2000) 'Developing an individual therapeutic programme suitable for use by counselling psychologists in a multicultural society: a multimodal perspective', *Counselling Psychology Review, 15*: 32–50.

Palmer, S. and Laungani, O. (eds) (1999) *Counselling in a Multicultural Society*. London: Sage.

Reynolds, D. (1990) 'Morita and Naikan therapies – similarities', *Journal of Morita Therapy, 1*: 159–63.

Ridley, C.R. and Lingle, D.W. (1996) 'Cultural empathy in multicultural counseling: a multidimensional process', in P.B. Pedersen, J.G. Draguns, W.J. Lonner and J.E. Trimble (eds), *Counseling Across Cultures* (4th edn). Thousand Oaks, CA: Sage.

Schwartz, S.H. (1992) 'Universals in the content and structure of values: theoretical advances and empirical tests in 20 countries', in M. Zanna (ed.), *Advances in Experimental Social Psychology*. New York: Academic Press. pp. 1–65.

Schwartz, S.H. and Bilsky, W. (1990) 'Toward a theory of the universal content and structure of human values: extensions and cross-cultural replications', *Journal of Personality and Social Psychology, 53*: 550–62.

Spindler, G.D. (1963) *Education and Culture: Anthropological Approaches*. New York: Holt, Rinehart & Winston.

Sue, D.W. and Sue, D. (2003) *Counseling the Culturally Diverse: Theory and Practice* (4th edn). New York: John Wiley.

Sue, D.W., Carter, R.T., Casas, J.M., Fouad, N.A., Ivey, A.E., Jensen, M., LaFromboise, T., Manese, J.E., Ponterotto, J.G. and Vazquez-Nutall, E. (1998) *Multicultural Counseling Competencies: Individual and Organizational Development*. London: Sage.

Sue, D.W., Ivey, A.E. and Pedersen, P.B. (1996) *A Theory of Multicultural Counseling & Therapy*. Pacific Grove, CA: Brooks/Cole.

Thitavanno, P. (1995) *Mind Development*. Bangkok: Mahamakut Buddhist University.

Thitavanno, P. (2002) *A Buddhist Way of Mental Training* (2nd edn). Bangkok: Chuan Printing Press.

Tyrrell, K. (ed.) (2001) *Annual Abstract of Statistics: 2001 Edition United Kingdom*. London: HMSO.

US Census Bureau (2003) *Census 2000 Briefs*. Available at: www.census.gov.

Walsh, R. (2000) 'Asian psychotherapies', in R.J. Corsini and D. Wedding (eds), *Current Psychotherapies* (6th edn). Itasca, IL: Peacock. pp. 407–44.

Weinrach, S.G. and Thomas, K.R. (1998) 'Diversity-sensitive counseling today: a postmodern clash of values', *Journal of Counseling and Development, 76*: 115–22.

Weston, R., Qu, L. and Soriano, G. (2001) *Ageing yet Diverse: The Changing Shape of Australia's Population. Australian Family Briefing No. 10*. Melbourne: Australian Institute of Family Studies.

gender-role therapy 16

Introduction

Many therapeutic approaches seem based on the assumption of unisex therapists and clients. This chapter aims to provide a brief and basic introduction to some gender issues connected to the theory and practice of counselling and therapy. Of necessity, it is a tour of some of the main points rather than a detailed analysis of any of them.

Gender issues have been around since time immemorial. However, in the last third of the 20th and the beginning of the 21st century the rise of feminism and the growth of the men's movement have accelerated the debate over male and female roles. Gender issues permeate therapy: for example, in the gender-related assumptions that therapists and clients bring to their personal lives and to therapy. Nevertheless, the fact remains that all the main theorists whose work is presented in this book are men and all were educated before the last third of the 20th century.

This chapter is closely related to the previous one, since cultural issues and gender issues overlap. One of the main functions of enculturation is to transmit gender roles from one generation to another. However, to some extent, peer groups may be taking over from parents in performing this central aspect of enculturation (Maccoby, 1990).

Cultures have both similarities and differences in the roles they assign to men and women. Furthermore, as Hofstede's (1980, 1983) work shows, cultures vary in subscribing to masculine and feminine values. In addition, the acculturation of migrants can be much more difficult if there are large gender-role differences between previous and new cultures. For instance, in their cultures of origin men may have mediated between the home and the outside world, whereas in their new cultures women may work outside the home and also be the main breadwinners (Eleftheriadou, 1999).

Gender can also be an important aspect of cultural change and conflict, with the changes in women's roles affecting men and vice versa. Many British, Australian and American women strongly feel that they, like ethnic and racial minorities, are oppressed by white, male-dominated mainstream cultures. Cultural change can also influence how people learn gender roles: for example, with the movement from agrarian economies stemming from the industrial revolution, many men have spent less time with their families and local communities to the possible psychological impoverishment of all concerned. Consequently boys in western cultures may have less opportunity than previously to learn from their fathers and other mentors how to be confident and at ease in being male (Biddulph, 2003).

The terminology of gender

Like the terms associated with culture, many of the terms associated with gender possess different shadings of meaning according to who is doing the defining. Below is an introduction to some key terms:

- *Sex*: In this context sex refers to the biological differences between males and females such as differences in genitals, reproductive functioning, bone structure and size.
- *Gender*: Gender refers to the cultural and social classification of characteristics, attitudes, values and behaviours as appropriate for either females or males.
- *Gender role*: The role that a person adopts or that is ascribed to her/him on the dimensions of 'femininity' and 'masculinity'. The concept of gender role incorporates the power relations between men and women.
- *Gender-role identity*: The term gender-role identity relates to how a person views herself or himself on the dimensions of 'femininity' and 'masculinity'.
- *Gender-role socialization*: The processes of enculturation whereby children and adults acquire, internalize and maintain the characteristics, attitudes, values and behaviours associated with femininity, masculinity or a mixture of both.
- *Gender-role conflict*: Gender-role conflict can be both within a person, in relation to others, or a mixture of both. The most common form of gender-role conflict within a person is where the gender role the individual either adopts or wishes to adopt is at variance with the gender role prescribed by their culture or reference group. Gender-role conflicts between people relate to differences in perceptions regarding appropriate gender roles: for example, different ideas between partners in dual-career couples.
- *Sexism*: Sexism refers to external oppression on account of a person's biological sex. In turn, sexism can become internalized self-oppression. *Individual sexism* relates to any thoughts, feelings and actions that assume the superiority of one sex over the other. *Institutional or organizational sexism* relates to political, institutional and organizational structures that discriminate against, oppress and devalue a person on the grounds of sex. *Heterosexism* extends sexism to focus on individuals and organizations that assume the superiority of heterosexual thoughts, feelings and actions over homosexual or bisexual thoughts, feelings and actions.

Theory

Biology and gender

Do gender-role differences reflect nature rather than nurture? Underlying the issue of gender roles is the extent to which the sexes are biologically similar. From the viewpoint of evolutionary psychology men and women should share the same characteristics in those situations where they have faced the same or similar adaptive problems. However, men and women would evolve different characteristics in situations where their adaptive demands substantially diverge (Buss, 1995; Darwin, 1871). For example, from the viewpoint of the male, sexual selection involves successfully outcompeting members of one's own sex to gain access to more numerous or more desirable mates. From a female viewpoint sexual selection might involve identifying males willing and able to supply resources and protection through pregnancy and lactation.

Evolutionary psychology emphasizes the interaction between the biological and the social rather than assuming that biological characteristics between the sexes are immutable. For example, the primary difference in the trend towards small changes in cognitive abilities between the sexes is in the area of spatial ability, which is important to being a skilled hunter. However, as men evolve in societies that do not require hunting as a survival skill, this sex difference could gradually diminish.

Moir and Jessell review research indicating that from birth males and females are different. The main behavioural difference is the natural, innate aggression of men. These authors present evidence that the sexes are different because their brains are different and observe: 'To maintain that they are the same in aptitude, skill or behaviour is to build a society based on a biological and scientific lie' (1989: 5). Moir and Jessell report men as being better than women in skills requiring spatial ability. Both aggression and spatial ability skills are characteristics that may originate in male roles at earlier stages of evolution.

There are at least three possibilities for how the nature–nurture controversy can be positively resolved. One possibility is that 'masculinity' and 'femininity' become outmoded concepts because further research indicates that the two sexes are biologically highly similar. Another possibility is that additional research supports Moir and Jessell's assertion that there are important biological sex differences and that men and women then manage to use each other's strengths for everyone's benefit. Still a third possibility is that, over time, men and women evolve, possibly hastened by appropriate nurturing, so that biological sex differences no longer figure so prominently.

Masculinity, femininity, androgyny and gender schemas

In western societies, certain psychological characteristics have traditionally been viewed as being either feminine, masculine or neutral. The American researcher Sandra Bem (1974) developed the *Bem Sex-Role Inventory* (BSRI) with the purpose of being able to characterize a person as masculine, feminine or androgynous. Final items were on the basis of being more socially desirable in American society for one sex than for the other. Illustrative Masculine items were: aggressive, ambitious, analytical, assertive, competitive, dominant, independent, individualistic, self-reliant and willing to take risks. Illustrative Feminine items were: affectionate, compassionate, eager to soothe hurt feelings, gentle, loves children, sensitive to the needs of others, sympathetic, understanding and warm. Illustrative Neutral items were: adaptable, conscientious, conventional, reliable and truthful. In addition to Masculinity and Femininity scores, the BSRI provides an Androgyny score.

The androgynous sex role represented an equal endorsement of both masculine and feminine attributes. Other ways to define androgyny include either striking a balance between masculine and feminine characteristics or the ability to choose from among the most desirable masculine and feminine characteristics. In her summary of the research on androgyny and sex types, Cook observed 'The evidence delineating the types is not as compelling as many proponents of the typology would like ... Most differences between the categories are simply of degree, usually with modest differences in absolute size' (1987: 483). Another consideration relating to sex types, including androgyny, is that they are heavily influenced by cultural norms regarding what constitutes masculinity, femininity and androgyny (Ravinder, 1987).

Traditional gender-role or sex-role typing can cause considerable problems for both men and women. In western societies this may be particularly the case for women. Cook (1987) refers to 'the masculine supremacy effect' in American society, with masculine characteristics being more highly valued than feminine ones. However, a higher valuation of certain feminine characteristics, for instance understanding and compassion, is likely to be a feature of genuinely healthy cultures.

Bem (1981, 1993) extended her discussion of sex types to develop gender-schema theory. Perception is a process in which individuals make constructions of incoming information. A gender schema is a cognitive structure consisting of a network of associations that organize and guide and individuals' sex-linked perceptions. Sex typing derives, in part, from 'a generalized readiness to process information on the basis of sex-linked information that constitute the gender schema' (1981: 354). Society should become a-schematic and stop projecting gender into situations irrelevant to genuine biological differences. If this were to happen, human behaviours and personality attributes would cease to have gender.

Women and gender roles

Feminism

Feminism has a long history as the advocacy of women's rights on the grounds of equality between the sexes. Betty Frieden (1963) provided an impetus to the modern women's movement with the seminal book *The Feminine Mystique*, chronicling the apathy and frustration of many post-Second World War American wives trapped in comfortable domestic concentration camps. Frieden advocated a new life plan for women that would allow them to use their intelligence, enjoy adult company and undertake serious careers.

Greer asserts that liberation rather than equality is the goal for feminists. She writes: 'If we accept that men are not free, and that masculinity is as partial account of maleness as femininity is of femaleness, then equality must be seen as a poor substitute for liberation' (1999: 395). Liberation entails women defining their own values and proudly asserting genuine life-affirming female, as contrasted with feminine, differences from males. Though not heavily stressed by Greer, women's liberation also entails challenging men to assert life-affirming male differences from females.

The unequal distribution of power is a central issue in feminist thinking. While Freud thought that females envied males because they possessed penises, the neo-Freudian analyst Karen Horney considered their envy as being about men's greater power and status in society (Chaplin, 1999).

Over time, the nature of feminist therapy has become more diverse. Enns (1993, 2004; Enns and Sinacore, 2001) has identified eight somewhat overlapping philosophies of feminism that cause practitioners to interpret feminist therapy in different ways. Each of these philosophies has a different view on the sources of oppression and what is needed to bring about substantial social transformation (Herlihy and Corey, 2005).

- *Liberal feminists* see women deserving equality because they have the same abilities as men. Major goals of therapy are individual personal empowerment and equality;
- *Cultural feminists* believe in feminizing the culture so that it becomes more nurturing, intuitive, cooperative and relational. A major goal of therapy is the infusion of these feminine values into the culture;
- *Radical feminists* focus on the oppression of women due to patriarchy. Major goals include transforming gender relationships and societal institutions and increasing women's sexual and procreative self-determination;
- *Socialist feminists* consider that solutions to society's problems must take into account class, race and economics. Their major therapeutic goal is to transform social relationships and institutions;

- *Postmodern feminists* address the issue of what constitutes reality and propose multiple truths as opposed to a single truth. They deconstruct polarities such as masculine–feminine and analyse how such constructs are created;
- *Women of colour* feminists assert that they not only have to deal with gender discrimination, but also with oppression on account of ethnicity, race and class. They consider that feminist theory should pay attention to access to power and privilege and they emphasize activism;
- *Lesbian feminists* sometimes feel that heterosexual feminists do not understand their situation. Lesbian therapists want feminist theory to include an analysis of multiple identities and their relationship to oppression. They also want recognition of the diversity that exists among lesbians;
- *Global-international feminists* take a worldwide perspective and assume that women in different parts of the world live under unique systems of oppression. They challenge western feminists to understand how racism, sexism, class and economics affect women in different countries.

Despite the fact that there are so many different aspects to feminism, it is still possible to identify a feminist therapist. A feminist therapist believes that gender is central to the practice of therapy and that individual empowerment using feminist therapeutic methods and societal change are crucial goals. Feminist therapists emphasize the commonalities between women while recognizing their different life experiences. However, a large number of women who actively favour women's equality and liberation may not apply the label feminist to themselves. Some of these women even go so far as to hate the word feminism because to them it connotes anger, militancy and lesbianism (Tavris, 1989).

Oppression of women

Central to the thinking of many feminists is the idea that men have used their positions of power and influence to oppress women both inside and outside the home. Taylor provides a modified version of this position when she states: 'So while there is a recognition that men have been the victims of a sexist culture and its rigid patterns of socialization, it is still men who hold the balance of power and receive a disproportionate share of social rewards and privileges' (1996: 208). Men are on the inside and women on the outside.

Sue and Sue (2003) see mainstream white male culture as inherently biased against racial ethnic minorities, women, gays/lesbians and other culturally different groups. They delineate five components of oppression against such minority groups, which I have adapted to focus on the oppression of women. Oppression against women is also prominent in minority groups, so the components of oppression tend to hold good for them too.

1. *Belief in the superiority of men*: Men may possess conscious and unconscious feelings of superiority and consequently of entitlement to better treatment;

2. *Belief in the inferiority of women*: Women can be devalued because their capacities, including their sexuality, are viewed as inferior to those of men;

3. *Power to impose standards*: Men have the power to impose their standards on women. Early examples of this oppression involved excluding women from property and voting rights. Because of their generally having more control over financial resources, men are in a powerful position to impose their standards in the home. Threatened or actual use of greater physical strength can also be used as instruments of control and subjugation of women at home;

4. *Manifestation in institutions*: Chains of command in organizations and institutions favour men over women. Educational and training opportunities favour boys and men over girls and women;

5. *The invisible veil*: Since all people are the products of their cultural conditioning, including their gender-role conditioning, their values and beliefs can operate as an invisible veil outside of conscious awareness. Thus even well-intentioned individuals may experience difficulty in acknowledging that some of their thoughts, feelings and actions are sexist. Unconsciously and unintentionally, they may collude in perpetuating sexist biases and discrimination. Furthermore, the victims of oppression may fail to see that they have internalized the standards of the mainstream culture and so become the agents of their own oppression.

A final point is that at the heart of feminism are two different, and possibly contradictory, explanations for the past and current oppression of women. One explanation is that oppression results from men's greater power: 'Men did and are doing it to us'. Yet feminists also explain that the best way to gain more equality is through women banding together and being more assertive and socially active: 'We women have the power to bring about change'. One way to reconcile these explanations is to accept that not only men's greater power but also women's prior and possibly present insufficient social action to combat that power maintained, and may still be maintaining, women's oppression.

Women's experience and issues

A major criticism of existing counselling and therapy approaches is that they insufficiently address women's experience and issues. The women's movement stresses the importance of women understanding and valuing their own experience. It also stresses the importance of men understanding the extent and ways in which women's experiencing of life is different than theirs. A common theme in the literature on women and gender roles is that women's self-esteem tends to be lower than that of men.

One way of looking at women's experience is in terms of the interaction of the social, the political and the personal. Here concepts like patriarchy, oppression and social action are important. Another way to look at women's experience is in terms of the particular challenges throughout the life span inherent in being a woman: for example, premenstrual tension, infertility and miscarriage, giving birth, postnatal depression, mothering, menopause and frequently outliving a spouse. Still a further way to look at women's experience is in terms of problems that beset women in varying degrees: for example, domestic violence, sexual harassment, sexual abuse, relentless pressure to be beautiful, anorexia, bulimia, rape, abortion, single parenting, attitudes that constrain career choice, workplace discrimination, and depression and exhaustion resulting from carrying a disproportionate share of work/family responsibilities (Greer, 1999).

Women's identity development

Some models of women's identity development exist that are comparable to models of cultural identity development discussed in the previous chapter. Such models take into account and are stimulated by the oppression and subjugation that many women experience and feel. These models trace the development of women's consciousness or awareness from going along with the prevailing gender-role norms to becoming autonomous and socially active. Box 16.1 presents a summary of the five-stage model developed by McNamara and Rickard (1998).

Box 16.1   A model of feminist identity development

Stage 1: Passive acceptance
Passive acceptance of traditional gender roles, men considered superior to women, and prejudice and discrimination denied.

Stage 2: Revelation
Sexist events occur that cannot be ignored, an awakening to prejudice and discrimination, anger, dichotomous thinking in that all men are seen as oppressive and all women as positive.

Stage 3: Embeddness–Emanation
Close emotional and supportive relations formed with other women, sharing of emotions, solidifying of feminist identity, less absolutistic thinking regarding men.

Stage 4: Synthesis
A positive feminist identity is fully developed, less absolutistic thinking about sexism as the cause of all problems, ability to take an independent feminist stance.

Stage 5: Active commitment
Interest in turning attention to making societal changes.

Cheatham and his colleagues (1997) have also presented a five-stage model of women's identity development using the same five stages that they used in their model of cultural identity development: naïvety, encounter, naming, reflection on self as a cultural (in this case gender) being, and multi-perspective internalization. Stage models of feminist and of women's identity development are hypotheses that reflect the cultural, historical and political situations at the time of their development. Such models are open to question, for instance radical feminists are uncomfortable with the notion of synthesis in the McNamara and Rickard model.

Men and gender roles

The men's movement

For relationships between the sexes to take place on the basis of genuine equality, both women and men need to change. Partly in response to feminism, there has been a growing men's movement in western countries. For example, there are thousands of men's groups in the United States (Biddulph, 2003) as well as numerous men's groups in Australia and Britain. In important respects, the men's movement is complementary to rather than in opposition to the women's movement. Both seek equality between the sexes and liberation for persons, whatever their sex, to develop their full humanity without the limitations of rigid gender-role prescriptions.

The men's movement has been slower in gaining strength than the women's movement and appears more fragmented. Men's issues have not had prominent advocates as articulate as Betty Frieden and Germaine Greer. Furthermore, the men's movement lags behind the women's movement in publishing books and research articles. However, some women, such as Gloria Steinem, definitely want a men's movement (Biddulph, 2003).

Increasingly the men's movement's emphasis is less about feminizing men and more about developing a positive image of maleness and of men's inner life and experiences. Men who are confident and in touch with their feelings are able to be more flexible in how they deal with others at home and at work rather than live out phony stereotypes of how men should be that fail to meet others' and their own needs.

The overall trend in western societies is still to bring men up for the traditional male roles of providers and protectors and, as such, to encourage aggression, competitiveness, self-reliance and not showing vulnerability. Often men are brought up thinking that it is 'sissy' to show weakness, cry, be artistic and want close relationships with other males. Biddulph (2003) considers that men are a mess, with their three main enemies being isolation, compulsive competition and life-long emotional timidity.

Another factor in the rise of the men's movement has been anger at the extent to which some feminist writers have successfully portrayed women as victims and men as persecutors. Furthermore, some such advocates appear insensitive to the damage this overgeneralized negativity causes to boys' and men's self-esteem and to achieving mutually respectful men–women relationships. In addition, those feminist writers who sweepingly portray men as oppressors may insufficiently acknowledge the responsibility of women in their own oppression and women's contribution to socializing both boys and girls into oppressive sex-role stereotypes.

Sometimes there is insufficient recognition in the feminist literature of the pressures and sacrifices many men undergo to provide for their families. Most men are not in positions of great power at work and have to get along as subordinates, sometimes with considerable humiliation and long, dull hours, to do as best as they can to support their families. In addition, in areas like domestic violence, men as well as women can be the victims (see, for example, Tavris, 1989). However, the outcomes of male violence can be more severe due to their relatively greater strength and, especially in America, their tendencies to use guns and knives. Furthermore, in Australia, Britain and America the criminal statistics are heavily weighted towards male violence.

Men can also be angry or cynical about feminists who seem to 'want it both ways': retaining women's existing privileges at the same time as gaining access to those of men. In addition, men are angered by the phenomenon of 'men bashing' that occurs in many areas in ways that would probably be considered unacceptable if applied to women (Biddulph, 2003; Tavris, 1989). For instance, in advertising men are often portrayed as jerks in men–women relationships. Anti-male greeting cards are popular and, in Australia, calendars and diaries of the 'All Men Are Bastards' variety have sold well. Another example of men-bashing is that of 'Post-it' notes, with captions such as 'There are only two things wrong with men. Everything they say and everything they do'.

Men's gender-role conflict

Given the limitations of men's enculturation, many men find that they do not fit the mould. O'Neill and his colleagues (1986) have developed a *Gender Role Conflict Scale* (GRCS) that identifies four gender-role conflict patterns of factors for American men. Box 16.2 briefly describes each of the GRCS's four factors.

Box 16.2   Factors measured by the *Gender Role Conflict Scale* (GRCS)

- *Success, power and competition*: This factor represents an emphasis on over-achievement, control, strength, needing to move up the career ladder and being perceived as a 'winner';

(Continued)

Box 16.2　(Continued)

- *Restrictive emotionality*: Here men are frightened of the feminine part of themselves and by feelings that seem womanly. They experience difficulty with their own emotional self-disclosure as well as discomfort with the emotional expressiveness of others;
- *Restrictive affectionate behaviour between men*: This is an index of the degree to which men keep other men at a distance by restricting expressions of caring, being wary of friendly male overtures, and protecting themselves from feelings of anxiety or shame about feelings of attraction towards other men that might be interpreted by themselves or others as a gay orientation;
- *Conflict between work and family relations*: This factor measures the level of distress experienced by men due to the impinging of work or study on personal and family life.

The underlying idea behind the GRCS is that the process of male socialization creates conflict, stress and anxiety for men when they deviate from masculine ideals. For example, Good and his colleagues (1996) used the GRCS to examine the relation between masculine-role conflict and psychological stress in a sample of university counselling centre clients. Their findings supported earlier studies conducted with non-clinical samples of gender-role conflict being associated with higher levels of depression and interpersonal sensitivity. In addition, high scores on masculine-role conflict significantly predicted paranoia, psychoticism and obsessive-compulsivity. In another study that compared non-clinical samples of college-aged and middle-aged men, middle- aged men were less conflicted about success, power and competition, but were more conflicted between work and family responsibilities (Cournoyer and Mahalik, 1995). Such studies could be extended to take into account differences in culture and occupation, such as differences between business executives and blue-collar workers.

The work on men's gender-role conflict highlights the fact that males as well as females can feel trapped by their gender-role socialization. Furthermore, these studies illustrate that wanting to deviate from traditional masculine roles often comes at a psychological price. The role-conflict research suggests that there is a place for models of men's as well of women's identity development in regard to gender roles. Currently numerous men remain at low levels of awareness about the effects of gender conditioning on their psychological wellbeing.

Men's experience and issues

Though largely formulated by men, perhaps existing counselling and therapy approaches are insufficiently sensitive to men's as well as women's experience and issues. A case can also be made for the institutional oppression of men as well as of women. For example, in times of war, men rather than women are called up to the horrors of combat and the possibility of serious injury, if not death. Another example is that some men consider that women are favoured when it comes to taking paid leave for childcare and in divorce court decisions about child custody. Regarding life-span problems, men do not have the kind of problems that women do, for instance going through the menopause. However, men's life expectancy is on average five years lower than women's. For instance, 'American men have twice as many vehicle accidents, twice as many deaths from heart attacks, three times as many deaths from injuries, twice the deaths from liver disease. In fact, men exceed women in all thirteen leading causes of death' (Biddulph, 2003: 7). Furthermore, boys and men commit suicide five times more frequently than girls and women.

There are psychological problems that beset boys and men: for example, behavioural problems in school, hurt stemming from absent or neglectful fathers – sometimes called 'father hunger' – work-related stress, alcoholism, being physically violent, pressure to initiate relationships with the opposite sex, pressure to perform sexually (men cannot fake erections), difficulty showing tender feelings and vulnerability, insufficient preparation for fatherhood, insufficient intimacy with same-sex friends, pressure to be financially successful, loss of identity through unemployment, and loss of daily contact with children after a relationship break-up.

Furthermore, many men are challenged to adjust to the changes brought about in their partners by the women's movement. Women easily outnumber men as clients in therapy (Good et al., 1989). This imbalance indicates that another problem for men may be their greater unwillingness to admit and seek psychological assistance when experiencing difficulties themselves and creating difficulties for others.

Therapy

Therapeutic goals

Where gender-role issues are involved, it is possible to state therapeutic goals for both sexes and for each sex. These general goals include helping individual clients use their strengths and potential, make appropriate choices, remedy poor skills, and develop positive and flexible self-concepts. In addition, therapeutic goals relating to gender roles can often involve both male and female partners: for example, learning to deal with demand/withdraw interaction patterns in marital conflict (Christensen and Heavy, 1993) and handling the numerous issues confronting dual-career couples in a time of rapid technological and economic change (Fallon, 1997; Serlin, 1989).

Therapeutic goals for women

Worell and Remer (2003) state that the ultimate goal of feminist therapy is to create the kind of society where sexism, along with other kinds of discrimination, is no longer a reality. They consider that many of women's symptoms can be seen as coping or survival strategies rather than as evidence of pathology. Consequently, the goals of feminist therapy are helping them to acquire better strategies, an approach that avoids 'blaming the victim' for her problems.

Chaplin observes that women and others at the bottom of hierarchies usually have considerable experience of being put down and losing self-esteem. She continues: 'Feminist counselling aims instead to empower people and develop more self-confidence and control over their lives' (1999: 8). Herlihy and Corey (2005) emphasize self-acceptance, self-confidence, joy and authenticity as fruits of empowerment from feminist therapy.

Two studies of feminist therapy throw some light on the goals of feminist therapy in practice. Maracek and Kravetz (1999) studied 25 experienced feminist therapists in the American state of Wisconsin. They report that most feminist therapists, when asked 'What does it mean to you to say that your therapy is feminist?', did not mention resocialization, raised consciousness or political and social change. Instead respondents focused on the processes of feminist therapy and, in particular, on how the therapist enacts the therapeutic relationship.

Chester (1994) surveyed 140 Australians who considered themselves to be both feminists and counsellors, though just over 14 per cent did not consider themselves feminist counsellors as such. Participants were asked to choose from a list of 26 characteristics, which ones they considered essential for feminist counsellors. Table 16.1 presents characteristics that the participants chose as essential. Underneath I have translated these characteristics into goals for feminist counselling, the most essential goals being women valuing themselves on their own terms and becoming free of sex-role stereotypes.

Statements of therapeutic goals that take women's sex and gender issues into account can focus both on women's life-span issues and on problems that are much more commonly faced by women and men. For example, gender-aware and feminist therapists can counsel mid-life women to cope with the menopause constructively (Huffman and Myers, 1999). In addition, suitably trained and qualified therapists can help women address issues such as insufficient assertion, eating disorders, domestic violence and sexual harassment.

Therapeutic goals for men

Since considerably fewer men than women come for therapy, one broader goal may be to increase the number of men prepared to address their gender role and other problems in therapy. Men, like women, need to free themselves from limiting gender-role stereotypes and develop more of their unique potential. Consequently, another therapeutic goal is, where appropriate, to make men aware of the extent to which their thoughts, feelings and behaviours

Table 16.1   Characteristics of Australian feminist counsellors translated into goals for feminist counselling

Essential feminist counsellor characteristics	%
Encourages women to value themselves on their own terms	92
Encourages clients to free herself from sex-role stereotypes	83
Encourages female clients to increase their sense of commonality with other women	68
Encourages female clients to work for social change	44
Encourages androgyny	17

Goals for feminist counselling
Valuing herself on her own terms
Freeing herself from sex-role stereotypes
Increased sense of commonality with other women
Working for social change
Androgynous functioning

have been and continue to be heavily determined by their past and current gender-role socialization.

Therapeutic goals for men can include addressing at least three of the issues identified in the issues identified in the *Gender Role Conflict Scale*: excessive need for success, power and competition, restrictive emotionality and restrictive affectionate behaviour between men. Though coping with the fourth GRCS factor – conflict between work and family relationships – is a legitimate therapeutic goal, this problem is shared by both sexes: there has been a long-term trend towards women's increased participation in the paid workforce, often accompanied by longer hours. Other therapeutic goals for men clients include stopping being physically violent both inside and outside of the home, dealing with work-related stress, overcoming tendencies to treat women as sexual objects, and developing better healthcare skills.

Since women are redefining their gender roles faster than men, many men are then put in positions of exploring, understanding and altering their own gender roles. Positive maleness, combining tenderness and toughness and treating women with respect and as equals, is a desirable outcome from this change process. Men as well as women can take pride as they struggle to achieve inner strength and beauty. Boys and men are likely to be more constructive and caring if assisted to become confident in their manhood rather seeking to prove themselves all the time by pretending to be what they are not.

Therapeutic approaches

The above discussion indicates that there are many goals for gender-aware counselling and therapy. Here I present four overlapping approaches to women's and men's gender issues and problems: making existing therapies more gender-sensitive, developing gender-relevant counselling and therapy competencies, feminist therapy and men's therapy.

Making existing therapies more gender-sensitive

Undoubtedly the rise of feminism and of the men's movement has already had an effect in influencing many therapists of both sexes to perform therapy with a greater focus on healing psychological distress stemming from restrictive gender-role socialization and sexism. Of the two psychodynamic approaches presented in this book, Jung's analytical therapy emphasizes the importance of the feminine much more than Freud's psychoanalysis. Jung (1982) acknowledged the importance of the mother archetype, which appears in numerous aspects. Furthermore, Jung saw people as psychologically bisexual, with men possessing an anima (the personification of the feminine nature in their unconscious) and women possessing an animus (the personification of the masculine nature in their unconscious). Thus Jungian psychology provides a base on which to explore gender-role issues at varying levels of consciousness (Schaverin, 1999).

Humanistic counselling and therapy approaches can also be used and adapted to deal with gender-role issues. Clients in person-centred therapy can experience and explore issues connected with prior gender-role socialization, and current gender-role issues and conflicts in an emotional climate of safety and trust. Gestalt therapists can use interventions like awareness experiments, the use of the empty chair, and dream analysis to focus on clients' gender-role learnings and behaviours that block excitement and authentic living. Furthermore, in transactional analysis, therapists can assist clients to explore script directives about gender-role behaviours and to gain freedom of choice in regard to abandoning damaging ones.

The cognitive-behavioural approaches too lend themselves to focusing on gender-role issues. For instance, in rational emotive behaviour therapy, gender-related irrational beliefs can be detected, disputed and either discarded or restated more rationally. In cognitive therapy, therapists and clients can identify and question the reality of gender-related automatic thoughts that confuse fact with inference. Afterwards, where necessary, therapists can work with clients to replace previous sexist and self-oppressing automatic thoughts with conscious and realistic ones.

Gender-relevant counselling and therapy competencies

In the previous chapter, I presented a statement of multicultural counselling and therapy competencies (Sue et al., 1998). This statement can be adapted for gender-relevant counselling and therapy competencies which consist of three main dimensions: awareness of own assumptions, values and biases; understanding the worldview of the sex-different client; and developing appropriate strategies and techniques. Each dimension is divided into beliefs and attitudes, knowledge, and skills. The basic presumption in stating these competencies is that all therapists need to address their own levels of gender identity development and their ability to offer gender-sensitive services.

- *Awareness of own assumptions, values and biases*: The beliefs held by gender-skilled therapists include being sensitive to their own gender heritage, being comfortable with the differences that exist between them and clients of the other sex, and recognizing the limitations of their competence and expertise. Therapists should know about their gender heritage and how this affects the therapeutic process, understand how sexist oppression and discrimination may affect them personally and in their work, and know about the impact of how they communicate on clients of the other sex. Skills include seeking out relevant educational and training experiences on gender-related factors in psychological wellness, actively understanding oneself as a gender being and seeking an autonomous and appropriately flexible gender identity.
- *Understanding the worldview of the sex-different client*: Beliefs and attitudes for gender-skilled therapists include being aware of their negative emotional reactions and of the stereotypes and preconceived notions that they may hold towards clients of the other sex. Therapists should know about the gender-related experiences, heritage and historical backgrounds of any particular group of men or women with whom they work, acknowledge how gender can affect help-seeking behaviour, know how gender can influence assessment and the selection and implementation of therapeutic interventions, and know about the oppressive political and environmental influences impinging on the lives of women and men. Skills include keeping up to date on research findings relevant to the psychological wellbeing of women and men as well as being actively involved with minority and other relevant groups outside work settings to gain deeper insight into their gender perspectives.
- *Developing appropriate intervention strategies and techniques*: Therapists' skills include the ability to send and receive verbal and non-verbal communication accurately, making appropriate referrals to either same-sex or other-sex therapists, tailoring the therapeutic relationship and interventions to take into account the gender-related dimensions of clients' problems, and engaging in a variety of helping roles, beyond being a therapist, for example, adviser, advocate, consultant and change agent.

Feminist therapy

Feminist therapists challenge sexism in diagnostic categories and propose alternatives that reflect women's experiences (Herlihy and Corey, 2005). Feminist therapists can subscribe to many different theoretical orientations (Chaplin, 1999; Chester, 1994). Feminist therapy can be described by the values or principles that have emerged from the joining of feminism with therapy. Box 16.3 describes five such central principles underlying feminist therapy (Ballou, 1996; Cheatham et al., 1997).

Box 16.3   Five central principles of feminist therapy

1. *Egalitarian relationships*: Feminist therapists are extremely sensitive to issues of power and its distribution. They emphasize sharing power with clients and believe that hierarchical forms of power distribution are inappropriate. Self-disclosure of one's own experiences as a woman can be an important part of the therapeutic process.
2. *Pluralism*: Feminist theory acknowledges and values difference, including complex and multiple-level diversities. Respect for others, including their differences, is a basic tenet of feminist therapy.
3. *Working against oppression*: Feminist therapists work against all forms of oppression: for instance, on the basis of sex, affectional/sexual orientation, race, culture, religious belief, life-style choice and physical disability.
4. *External emphasis*: External factors, such as social/political/economic structures are crucial to shaping the views of women, how they see themselves and how others see them. Women as individuals are shaped by and interact with political, environmental, institutional and cultural factors.
5. *Valuing women's experiences*: Relying on the actual experiences of women for descriptions of 'reality'. Grounding knowledge claimed about women on the actual women's experience. Valuing highly the experience of women rather than ignoring or discounting it and assuming men's experience to be normative.

What are some specific interventions in dealing with women clients? In gender-role analysis, a feminist therapist explores the impact of past gender-role expectations on the client, and together therapist and client use this information to make decisions about future gender-role behaviours (Herlihy and Corey, 2005). Feminist therapists can also make clients aware of the power difference between men and women in society and help them to recognize the different kinds of power that they either possess or to which they have access. For instance, women can learn to appreciate themselves as they are and not rely on men for their sense of worth. Bibliographies of autobiographies, self-help books, counselling and psychology textbooks and other non-fiction books may each be used at appropriate times to learn about gender-role stereotypes and the effects of gender inequality. Other feminist therapy interventions include women's groups and suggesting to clients that they participate in social action, for instance providing community education about gender issues or participating in rape crisis centres.

Assertiveness training, gender-role analysis and consciousness-raising may be particularly appropriate for the needs of women. Chester (1994) asked her feminist counsellor sample whether they used any techniques or interventions related to their feminism. Ninety-one per cent of the respondents replied in the affirmative. The most commonly cited interventions were challenging sex-role stereotypes and challenging patriarchal norms (each around 15 per cent), assertiveness training, strategies to encourage a sense of empowerment, and self-disclosure (each around 12 per cent). Needless to say, many women clients bring to therapy specific issues, such as procrastination, for which gender-related interventions can be, but not always are, irrelevant.

An issue in feminist therapy is whether and how to confront clients with issues of sexism. It may be important for therapists to assess and take into account the level of gender identity development of clients. In addition, therapists need to help women clients anticipate and deal with the consequences of changing their gender roles. One danger of bringing up issues of sexism too soon is that clients' resist the explanation and do not see its relevance. The opposite is also possible in that clients simplistically latch on to a sexist oppression analysis of their situations, get extremely angry with their partners, and prematurely leave them rather than attempt to work through their relationship issues.

Many feminist therapists develop their own approaches to working with clients. For example, the British therapist Jocelyn Chaplin (1999) has developed a 'cognitive feminism' approach. Chaplin distinguishes between the masculine control model, in which opposites, such as mind–'masculine'–strong and body–'feminine'–vulnerable, are split hierarchically into superior and inferior constructs and the feminine rhythm model. In the rhythm model there is flow and balancing between extremes, for instance alternating between joy and sorrow throughout a day. Each client needs to find her own unique rhythms and balance between her 'active' and 'resting' sides, her 'private' and 'public' sides, and her 'self-expression' and 'caring for others' sides.

Therapy starts with a trust-building mothering stage. Depending on the client, in varying degrees the therapist acts as a container, non-judgmental presence, and provides a space for emotionally letting go. The second stage involves focusing on specific issues, identifying themes and separating out the opposites: for instance the head must rule the heart. The third stage explores the past to understand where the opposites and inner hierarchies came from. The next stage involves dissolving the inner hierarchies, facing ambivalence and accepting opposites. Then therapy progresses to the last stage where clients make decisions and behave differently in the world. During this stage, assertiveness training helps many women express themselves more effectively, for instance by asking clearly for a change.

Men's therapy

I include a section on men's therapy to highlight the need for more work on therapeutic approaches to men's problems and issues. Many boys and men are suffering psychologically and need assistance to become confident and positive males. Virtually all of negative behaviours towards women chronicled by Greer (1999) are symptomatic of men's psychological wounds and insufficient personal development rather than of their innate badness. Unfortunately, the behaviours of some wounded men, for instance aggression and violence, do little to generate sympathy for their underlying suffering and low self-esteem.

There needs to be a greater development of men's therapy to complement – and definitely not to compete against – responsible feminist therapy. In many books on counselling and therapy (see, for example, Sue and Sue, 2003; Sue et al., 1996; Woolfe and Dryden, 1996), there is more attention paid to women's issues than to men's issues. Much of the existing literature on men's issues focuses on changing negative aspects of men's behaviour, such as curbing domestic violence and sexual abuse. There is a dearth of counselling and therapy books and articles advocating positive maleness and how to achieve it (see Biddulph, 2003). However, the American Psychological Association's recently inaugurated journal *Psychology of Men and Masculinity* may go some way to redressing this deficiency.

Just as the men's movement can be seen as the missing half of the women's movement, men's therapy can be seen as the missing half of feminist therapy. Men's therapy can be conducted both on an individual basis, in men's groups and as part of working with couples and families. In addition, sometimes both men's and women's issues are addressed in mixed-sex groups. The goals for men's therapy are like those of feminist therapy: valuing himself on his own terms, gaining freedom from sex-role stereotypes, an increased sense of commonality with other men, and working for social change. With some adaptation, the five central principles of feminist therapy – egalitarian relationships, pluralism, working against oppression, external emphasis, and valuing the experience of one's own sex (see Box 16.3) – are highly relevant for men's therapy too. Many therapists need to become more skilled at working with the specific issues facing boys and men. Then they can help these clients to celebrate, liberate and develop the better parts of their male humanity.

Conclusion

Though a promising start has been made in developing a counselling and therapy literature that takes gender-role issues and their treatment into account, much still remains to be done. There are risks as well as benefits in focusing on gender-role issues. The benefits include a lessening of sexist oppression, a greater chance for people to develop their full human potential rather than lead lives constricted by gender-role stereotypes, and greater attention paid to developing interventions for the specific problems that beset each sex.

There are also risks in changing the current balance of gender roles. For example, 'the masculine supremacy effect' in which masculine values are more honoured in market-driven western cultures, may lead women to feel under pressure to relinquish some of their feminine virtues, for instance compassion, as they compete in a workforce dominated by masculine values. In addition, gender-role liberation can play into people's selfishness in already highly individualistic western cultures. Both men and women may sacrifice communal values, and possibly the welfare of children too, in the interests of their own individual development.

For the most part, existing counselling and therapy approaches have insufficiently addressed gender-role socialization and the therapeutic problems and issues arising from it. Feminist therapy is the main example of an attempt to redress this neglect. There is still considerable scope for originating new counselling and therapy approaches, as well as for modifying existing ones, to promote equality between the sexes and to liberate girls, women, boys and men to become more fully human.

Review and personal questions

Review questions

1. What do each of the following terms mean:
    (a) gender role;
    (b) gender-role identity;
    (c) gender-role socialization;
    (d) gender-role conflict;
    (e) sexism?

2. What is feminism and what are some of the ways in which women are oppressed?
3. What is the men's movement and why is it important?
4. Describe some therapeutic goals that apply

    (a) to both sexes;
    (b) to women more than men;
    (c) to men more than women.

5. What are some ways of making existing counselling and therapy approaches more applicable to gender-role issues?
6. Describe and critically discuss the idea of gender-relevant counselling and therapy competencies.
7. Describe and critically discuss feminist therapy.
8. What role, if any, do you see for men's therapy?

Personal questions

1. How would you describe:

    (a)   the process of your gender-role socialization;
    (b)   the influence of your culture on your gender-role socialization?

2. To what extent do you consider that your attitudes, values and behaviours to be masculine, feminine or androgynous?

3. Describe instances, if any, in which you have been

    (a)   the victim of sexism;
    (b)   the purveyor of sexism.

4. To what extent and in what ways do you possess psychological problems involving gender-role issues?

5. Assuming that you possess some psychological problems involving gender-role issues, either what are you doing or what do you intend doing about them?

6. How can you make yourself a more gender-sensitive counsellor or therapist both now and in future?

Annotated bibliography

Chaplin, J. (1999) *Feminist Counselling in Action* (2nd edn). London: Sage.
This book presents a multi-stage rhythm model of feminist therapy already briefly described in this chapter. Chaplin illustrates each stage of the process with three case studies.

Biddulph, S. (2003) *The Secret Life of Men: A Practical Guide to Helping Men Discover Health, Happiness, and Deeper Personal Relationships.* New York: Marlowe.
This book emphasizes having a positive view of maleness, the desirability of fathers and sons understanding one another's experience, and the importance of caring and involved fathers and male mentors in the raising of boys. The book also addresses topics such as making school good for boys, sex, relating to women, friendship between men, spirituality and men's groups.

Herlihy, B. and Corey, G. (2005) 'Feminist therapy', in G. Corey, *Theory and Practice of Counseling & Psychotherapy* (7th edn). Belmont, CA: Thomson Brooks/Cole. pp. 338–81.
This textbook chapter provides a history of feminist therapy and reviews some of the key concepts and principles of feminist psychology. It then describes the process of feminist therapy, with sections on therapeutic goals, therapist's function and role, client's experience in therapy, and relationship between therapist and client. This is followed by a discussion of the role of assessment and diagnosis and then a review of feminist therapy techniques and strategies, including gender-role analysis, gender-role intervention and power analysis and intervention. In addition, feminist therapy is discussed from a multicultural perspective and there is a feminist therapy case study.

Seu, I.B. and Heenan, M.C. (eds) (1999) *Feminism & Psychotherapy: Reflections on Contemporary Theories and Practices.* London: Sage.
This book discusses the theory and practice of contemporary feminist therapies. Chapters include those on feminism and narrative therapy, object relations therapy, Jungian therapy, Chaplin's rhythm model, and systemic therapy. Other chapters discuss psychotherapy in relation to sexually abused clients, clients with eating disorders, and working-class women. The book concludes with a chapter on questions, answers and absences in feminist therapy.

Greer, G. (1999) *The Whole Woman.* London: Anchor.
Greer eloquently argues that women throughout the world are still at risk and that, despite gains made by feminism, their lives are becoming more difficult. She provides a comprehensive, irreverent, amusing, earthy and thoroughly one-sided tour of contemporary women's issues in 35 self-contained 'chapterkins' divided into four main areas: body, mind, love and power. Feminist therapy is not one of the topics Greer covers.

Moir, A. and Jessel, D. (1989) *Brain Sex: The Real Difference Between Men & Women.* London: Mandarin.
Based on the research of many scientists around the world, this book claims that men and women are different because their brains are different. The 12 chapter headings are: the differences, the birth of difference, sex in the brain, childhood differences, the brains come of age, the ability gap, hearts and minds, like minds, the marriage of two minds, why mothers are not fathers, minds at work, and bias at work.

References and further reading

Ballou, M. (1996) 'MCT theory and women', in D.W. Sue, A.E. Ivey and P.B. Pedersen (eds), *A Theory of Multicultural Counseling and Therapy.* Pacific Grove, CA: Brooks/Cole. pp. 236–46.
Bem, S.L. (1974) 'The measurement of psychological androgyny', *Journal of Consulting and Clinical Psychology, 42:* 155–62.
Bem, S.L. (1981) 'Gender schema theory: a cognitive account of sex typing', *Psychological Review, 88:* 354–64.
Bem, S.L. (1993) *The Lenses of Gender.* New Haven, CT: Yale University Press.
Biddulph, S. (2003) *The Secret Life of Men: A Practical Guide to Helping Men Discover Health, Happiness, and Deeper Personal Relationships.* New York: Marlowe.
Buss, D.M. (1995) 'Psychological sex differences: origins through sexual selection', *American Psychologist, 50:* 164–8.
Chaplin, J. (1999) *Feminist Counselling in Action* (2nd edn). London: Sage.
Cheatham, H., Ivey, A.E., Ivey, M.B., Pedersen, P., Rigazio-DiGillio, S., Simek-Morgan, L. and Sue, D.W. (1997) 'Multicultural counselling and therapy: 1 Metatheory – taking theory into practice; 2 Integrative practice', in A.E. Ivey, M.B. Ivey and L. Simek-Downing, *Counseling and Psychotherapy: A Multicultural Perspective* (4th edn). Boston: Allyn & Bacon. pp. 133–205.
Chester, A. (1994) *Feminist Counselling in Australia.* Unpublished MA thesis, University of Melbourne.
Christensen, A. and Heavy, C.L. (1993) 'Gender differences in marital conflict: the demand/withdraw interaction pattern', in S. Oskamp and M. Constanzo (eds), *Gender Issues in Contemporary Society.* Newbury Park, CA: Sage. pp. 113–41.

Cook, E.P. (1985) 'A framework for sex role counseling', *Journal of Counseling and Development*, 64: 253–8.

Cook, E.P. (1987) 'Psychological androgyny: a review of the research', *The Counseling Psychologist*, 15: 471–513.

Cournoyer, R.J. and Mahalik, J.R. (1995) 'Cross-sectional study of gender role conflict examining college-aged and middle-aged men', *Journal of Counseling Psychology*, 42: 11–19.

Darwin, C. (1871) *The Descent of Man and Selection in Relation to Sex*. London: Murray.

Eleftheriadou, Z. (1999) 'Assessing the counselling needs of ethnic minorities in Britain', in S. Palmer and P. Laungani (eds), *Counselling in a Multicultural Society*. London: Sage. pp. 113–32.

Enns, C.Z. (1993) 'Twenty years of feminist counseling and therapy: from naming biases to implementing multifaceted practice', *The Counseling Psychologist*, 21: 3–87.

Enns, C.Z. (2004) *Feminist Theories and Feminist Psychotherapies: Origins, Themes, and Diversity* (2nd edn). New York: Haworth.

Enns, C.Z. and Sinacore, A.L. (2001) 'Feminist theories', in J. Worell (ed.), *Encyclopedia of Gender* (Vol. 1). San Diego: Academic Press. pp. 469–80.

Fallon, B. (1997) 'The balance between paid work and home responsibilities: personal problem or corporate concern', *Australian Psychologist*, 32: 1–9.

Frieden, B. (1963) *The Feminine Mystique*. London: Penguin Books.

Good, G.E., Dell, D.M. and Mintz, L.B. (1989) 'Male role and gender role conflict: relations to help seeking in men', *Journal of Counseling Psychology*, 36: 295–300.

Good, G.E., Robertson, J.M., Fitzgerald, L.F., Stevens, M. and Bartels, K. (1996) 'The relation between masculine role conflict and psychological distress in male university counseling center clients', *Journal of Counseling and Development*, 75: 44–9.

Greer, G. (1999) *The Whole Woman*. London: Anchor.

Herlihy, B. and Corey, G. (2005) 'Feminist therapy', in G. Corey, *Theory and Practice of Counseling & Psychotherapy* (7th edn). Belmont, CA: Thomson Brooks/Cole. pp. 338–81.

Hofstede, G. (1980) *Culture's Consequences: International Differences in Work-Related Values*. London: Sage.

Hofstede, G. (1983) 'Dimensions of national culture in fifty cultures and three regions', in J.B. Deregowski, S. Dziurawiec and R.C. Annis (eds), *Expications in Cross-Cultural Psychology*. Lisse: Swets & Zeitlinger. pp. 335–55.

Huffman, S.B. and Myers, J.E. (1999) 'Counseling women in midlife: an integrative approach to menopause', *Journal of Counseling and Development*, 77: 258–66.

Jung, C.G. (1982) *Aspects of the Feminine*. London: Routledge.

Maccoby, E. (1990) 'Gender and relationships: a developmental account', *American Psychologist*, 45: 513–20.

Maracek, J. and Kravetz, D. (1999) 'Power and agency in feminist therapy', in I.B. Seu and M.C. Heenan (eds), *Feminism & Psychotherapy: Reflections on Contemporary Theories and Practices*. London: Sage. pp. 13–29.

McNamara, K. and Rickard, K.M. (1998) 'Feminist identity development: implications for feminist therapy with women', in D.R. Atkinson and G. Hackett (eds), *Counseling Diverse Populations*. Boston: McGraw-Hill. pp. 271–82.

Moir, A. and Jessel, D. (1989) *Brain Sex: The Real Difference Between Men & Women*. London: Mandarin.

O'Neill, J.M., Helms, B.J., Gable, R.K., David, L. and Wrightsman, L.S. (1986) 'Gender Role Conflict Scale: college men's fear of femininity', *Sex Roles*, 14: 335–50.

Ravinder, S. (1987) 'Androgyny: is it really a product of educated, middle class western societies?', *Journal of Cross-Cultural Psychology*, 18: 208–20.

Schaverin, J. (1999) 'Jung, the transference and the psychological feminine', in I.B. Seu and M.C. Heenan (eds), *Feminism & Psychotherapy: Reflections on Contemporary Theories and Practices*. London: Sage. pp. 172–88.

Serlin, B. (1989) 'Counseling dual-career couples', *Journal of Career Planning and Employment,* *50*: 80–6.

Seu, I.B. and Heenan, M.C. (eds) (1999) *Feminism & Psychotherapy: Reflections on Contemporary Theories and Practices.* London: Sage.

Sue, D.W. and Sue, D.W. (2003) *Counseling the Culturally Diverse: Theory and Practice* (4th edn). New York: John Wiley.

Sue, D.W., Carter, R.T., Casas, J.M., Fouad, N.A., Ivey, A.E., Jensen, M., LaFromboise, T., Manese, J.E., Ponterotto, J.G. and Vazquez-Nutall, E. (1998) *Multicultural Counseling Competencies: Individual and Organizational Development.* London: Sage.

Sue, D.W., Ivey, A.E. and Pedersen, P.B. (eds) (1996) *A Theory of Multicultural Counseling and Therapy.* Pacific Grove: Brooks/Cole.

Tavris, C. (1989) *Anger: The Misunderstood Emotion* (rev. edn). New York: Simon & Schuster.

Taylor, M. (1996) 'The feminist paradigm', in R. Woolfe and W. Dryden (eds), *Handbook of Counselling Psychology.* London: Sage. pp. 201–39.

Watkins, S.A., Rueda, M. and Rodriguez, M. (1999) *Introducing Feminism.* Duxford: Icon Books.

Woolfe, R. and Dryden, W. (1996) *Handbook of Counselling Psychology.* London: Sage.

Worell, J. and Remer, R. (2003) *Feminist Perspectives in Therapy: Empowering Diverse Women.* New York: John Wiley.

Introduction

You have now had a chance to read about the many counselling and therapy approaches presented in this book. Undoubtedly, you have already started drawing your own conclusions about the usefulness of the different approaches and how comfortable you would be implementing each of them. In this chapter I want to broaden your perspectives about evaluating the quality of counselling and therapy approaches by reviewing eight key issues.

While there is much to be said for learning about the different theoretical positions separately, in practice most counsellors and therapists use interventions that stem from more than one theoretical position. They find that operating out of one position is too restrictive to help them to understand the range of clients and client problems that they see. Clients who vary according to how responsive they are to different explanations and interventions can also pressure therapists to work more broadly. Consequently in this chapter I also examine issues of eclecticism and of integrating counselling and therapy approaches.

Eight key evaluation issues

Issue 1: What is the relationship between theorists' personal histories and their therapeutic approaches?

In Chapter 1 I mentioned that, without exception, all the theorists whose work is described in this book encountered periods of significant psychological suffering in their lives. Furthermore, theorists' suffering motivated them to create therapeutic approaches that would help themselves as well as others. Being highly motivated to develop therapeutic approaches that they could use themselves has both advantages and disadvantages. In evaluating the theory and practice of the different originators, relevant questions are: 'How much of their own problems were or are the theorists projecting onto clients at large?' and 'Is the approach that worked or works for any particular theorist necessarily that which is best for all clients?' The same sorts of questions can be asked of those studying counselling and therapy approaches. For example, when evaluating the different theoretical approaches, how much are your own needs and problems restricting your ability to be objective?

Issue 2: What is the influence of the theorists' historical and cultural contexts on their therapeutic approaches?

Undoubtedly theorists are influenced by the historical and cultural contexts in which they live. When evaluating therapeutic approaches, relevant questions here include how much the problems affecting clients change over time and how much across cultures. For instance, the current breakdown of respect for authority may mean that many young people, unlike Rogers, are facing problems of too little rather than too much structure. In addition, the materialism and rampant consumerism of western societies may be exacerbating people's tendencies to greed and consequent feelings of depression and alienation when their attempts to buy happiness fail. In the 21st century, the increasing pace of technological change may also create new sets of problems, which current therapeutic approaches may be insufficiently equipped to address, stemming from changes in how people work and communicate.

As illustrated in the chapter on cultural perspectives, culture influences the creation of theory. To what extent and how are each of the therapeutic approaches presented in this book limited because their Euro-American originators either were or still are wearing cultural blinkers?

Issue 3: What is the influence of all the major theorists being men?

In *The Female Eunuch*, Germaine Greer (1971) observed that Freud was the father of psychoanalysis and that it had no mother. Though many women have also been prominent in developing therapeutic approaches, all of the major theorists presented in this book are men. In addition, none of the theoretical approaches presented in *Current Psychotherapies* (Corsini and Wedding, 2005), probably the most authoritative American therapy textbook, were mainly developed by women.

A number of interesting questions are raised by the predominance of men in developing major therapeutic approaches such as 'Do some theories contain male bias?' As mentioned in the previous chapter, Freud's notion of penis envy is uncongenial to many women who envy men their power rather than their penises. Furthermore, if women had been more prominent in theorizing, 'Might we have seen the emergence of different and more humane therapeutic approaches?' In addition, given equal mental ability between the sexes and women's greater interest than men in relationships, 'Why have women not made more of a contribution to originating major counselling and therapy approaches?'

Issue 4: What is the nature of human nature?

Maslow (1971) raised the issue of whether psychology has been based too much on a 'bad animal' rather than a 'good animal' underlying view of human nature. Both Freud, and to a lesser extent Jung, were rather pessimistic about human nature and emphasized the darker individual and collective unconscious forces lying beneath the veneer of civilization. If anything, the psychodynamic theories stress curbing negative instincts and impulses rather than cultivating positive ones.

Traditional behaviourists view people's behaviour as the result of evolutionary drives, for instance for sex, food and shelter, and conditioning. Their mechanistic view of human nature is scarcely flattering to humans. The cognitive-behaviourists allow for personal agency. Nevertheless, if anything, theorists like Ellis, with his focus on biological tendencies to irrationality, and Beck, with his underlying maladaptive schemas, have focused more on the negative than on the positive aspects of human nature. Of the theorists in this book, Rogers is perhaps the main one to take predominantly a good animal view of human nature. For Rogers, the actualizing tendency in humans is positive and it only becomes negative to the extent that it is blocked and frustrated by environmental forces.

A fundamental question in evaluating theories is the extent to which they are realistic about humans' underlying animal nature. Neither neutrality nor cautious optimism involves the need to deny humans huge potential for destructive and aggressive behaviours, but they just balance it by also noting humans' huge potential to think, feel, act and communicate constructively. Thus therapy can become a matter of releasing and cultivating higher human potentials as well as of containing and overcoming destructive tendencies.

Issue 5: To what extent does the approach address subnormal, normal and supranormal functioning?

When evaluating the different therapeutic approaches, consider the populations for which their originators intended them. You may remember that Jung thought his analytical therapy more suitable for patients searching for meaning in the afternoon of their lives than those requiring help with conventional adaptation in the morning of their lives.

It is possible to look at human functioning in three broad categories – subnormal, normal and supranormal – with, at any given moment, individuals being placed somewhere along this continuum. Subnormal functioning is that where individuals are psychologically distressed and have problems that are more severe than the normal run of the population. Such clients might suffer from the mental disorders that are listed in the American Psychiatric Association's *Diagnostic and Statistical Manual of Mental Disorders* (2000). Normal functioning is that where people are capable of conventional adaptation to the societies in which they live. Such individuals may still experience problems for which counselling and therapy are appropriate: for instance, relationship problems, stress problems and study problems.

Some clients who are functioning well may want to function even better. Supranormal functioning refers to going above, beyond or transcending normal human functioning. Psychotherapy has its origins more in dealing with the problems of the subnormal and normal that in trying to assist well-functioning people to develop their full human potential. There has yet to be a major therapeutic approach developed by professionals, such as counselling psychologists or counsellors, who predominantly deal with normal client populations, let alone superior functioning ones.

Some theorists in this book, for instance Rogers and Ellis, have paid attention to defining full human functioning. Nevertheless, none of the approaches presented sufficiently addresses helping clients to be compassionate, engage in selfless service and synergistically foster the interests and ideals both of themselves and of humankind. A possible criticism of western psychotherapy is that it errs too much in the direction of being self-centred therapy. The Austrian psychiatrist, Alfred Adler (1933/1998), with his emphasis on social interest and community feeling, stands out as an advocate of the need to show more concern for others and for the human species.

Issue 6: To what extent does the therapeutic approach foster self-therapy for afterwards?

Sooner or later all clients are going to part from their therapists. Though a full course of psychoanalysis or of analytical therapy may last for years, that option is for the few. Nowadays there is great pressure from those paying for therapeutic services, for example governments and insurance companies, to encourage short-term managed care. Furthermore, most private clients have limited resources, which makes paying for long-term therapy either difficult or impossible. Even though some clients genuinely require longer-term contact, increasingly most counselling and therapy is short-term, say from one to 10 sessions or medium-term, say from 11 to 25 sessions. Important questions then become: 'What are the ingredients of effective time-limited therapy?'; 'How can therapeutic gains best be maintained afterwards?'; and 'To what extent is the therapy a training in self-therapy?'

In Chapter 1 I mentioned that one of the functions of theories was to provide languages both for the therapeutic conversation and so that clients can converse with themselves. Choosing from the theories presented here, Freud's psychoanalysis, Jung's analytical therapy, Rogerian person-centred therapy and Perlsian gestalt therapy appear not to give high priority to sharing the language in which the therapy is conceptualized with clients. For instance, Rogerian therapists do not share concepts like actualizing tendency, conditions of worth and organismic valuing process with their clients. Though clients in each of these four approaches may end therapy able to lead their lives more skilfully, the skills of so doing tend not to be clearly articulated during therapy. Clients may learn self-therapy skills, but this is more a by-product of the therapy rather than an integral part of it. For example, person-centred therapists assist clients to listen to their feelings and 'inner voices' and in doing so clients can learn to do this better on their own. However, person-centred therapists do not teach these skills directly to clients.

In the cognitive-behavioural school the therapist's role is more that of an educator than in either the psychodynamic or the humanistic schools. As part of the therapeutic process the language of the approach gets shared with clients. For instance, in rational emotive behaviour therapy, clients learn to detect, analyse in ABC terms, dispute and restate irrational beliefs both during therapy sessions and when completing homework assignments. In inelegant REBT, this sharing of language may be only in relation to specific symptoms, but in elegant REBT, this sharing can lead to disputing irrational beliefs becoming a way of life.

In cognitive therapy, clients learn that they need to test the reality of their thinking and are taught how to do this. By sharing a common language with clients and educating them in cognitive and, sometimes, in behavioural skills as well, these cognitive-behavioural approaches may be more clearly helping clients to become better at self-therapy than those approaches leaving relevant skills to be indirectly acquired and maintained. Perhaps adherents of other than cognitive-behavioural approaches might further develop their theory and practice, without losing the essence, so that clients can learn more about how to conduct self-therapy for afterwards.

Issue 7: What is the role of research in evaluating therapeutic approaches?

Though counselling and therapy approaches may have different goals, nevertheless a pertinent question in evaluating any approach is always going to be 'Where is the research evidence for its effectiveness?' Dictionary definitions of research tend to use adjectives like 'careful' and 'systematic' and nouns like 'study', 'enquiry' and 'investigation'. In Chapter 1 I stated that a function of counselling and therapy theories was to provide research hypotheses. Good theory provides good research hypotheses, poor theory provides poor ones.

Research can have a role in laying the scientific base for a therapeutic approach. However, here my emphasis is on the role of research in evaluating the practice of therapeutic approaches. A pertinent question is 'What therapy, conducted by which therapists, is appropriate for which clients, with which problems, under what circumstances?' Conducting research into therapeutic approaches can be difficult since there are so many considerations to take into account.

Research variables

Below are suggestions of variables, albeit sometimes interrelated, that can be explored when researching therapeutic approaches:

- *Therapist variables*: These include age, sex, race, culture, professional training, relevant background and experience, and emotional wellbeing;
- *Client variables*: These include age, sex, race, culture, nature of problem or problems, prior history of therapy, severity of disturbance, degree of family and environmental support, and whether any and what medication is involved;
- *Process variables*: These consist of specific details concerning the content and management of therapy. Such variables include frequency and duration of sessions, what interventions were used and how, and how between-session time was used;
- *Outcome variables*: These are criteria for measuring what changes occurred at the end of therapy and the degree to which they were maintained. Sources of outcome information include tests and measures, and therapist, client and third-party observations.

Research methods

Methods for evaluating counselling and therapy approaches fall into two main categories: qualitative and quantitative. Qualitative approaches to researching therapeutic approaches include detailed case descriptions and open-ended interviews. Quantitative approaches emphasize the systematic collection and analysis of quantitative information. Both quantitative and qualitative research methods can be used in evaluating therapeutic approaches – they are not mutually exclusive.

In quantitative research, client change can be estimated by comparing information obtained at different times: for example, at the start of therapy, when it ends, and after one or more stipulated follow-up periods. Often quantitative information is in the form of answers to standardized questionnaires measuring variables such as anxiety or depression. Another important source of quantitative information can be recording the frequency and duration of specific thoughts and behaviours.

Quantitative research designs fall into two main categories: comparison-group designs and single-case designs. In a simple comparison-group design, those receiving treatment would form a treatment group and those not receiving treatment would form a control group. Comparison-group designs can be more elaborate: for example, as well as a control group, there could be two or three experimental groups each being varied in some clearly defined way.

Increasingly single-case designs are being used in counselling and therapy research. Kazdin writes: 'Single case experiments permit inferences to be drawn about intervention effects by using the patient as his or her own control. The impact of treatment is examined in relation to the patient's dysfunction over time' (1986: 39). He states that there are four main characteristics of single-case designs: clear specification of goals; use of repeated observations; the delineation of time periods in which different conditions (baseline, treatment) apply; and relatively stable data – the more variable the data, the more difficult it is to draw conclusions about intervention effects.

Empirically supported treatments

Especially in the United States, research into therapeutic approaches is being used to establish empirically supported treatments (ESTs). In 1993, the Society of Clinical Psychology (Division 12) of the American Psychological Association established a Task Force to identify treatments with scientifically proven effectiveness for particular mental disorders. This Task Force has identified a number of effective, or probably effective, psychological treatments for disorders including depression, eating disorders, marital discord, panic disorder with and without agoraphobia, post-traumatic stress disorder, social phobia, and smoking cessation (Barlow et al., 1999).

A number of observations are relevant about empirically supported treatments. Where such treatments exist, there is a professional and ethical obligation on the part of therapists to find out about them. Furthermore, unless they have good reasons for not doing so in terms of particular clients' circumstances, therapists must seriously consider either implementing the treatments themselves or referring clients to those competent to do so. Currently, there is a research–practice gap in which therapists underutilize evidence-based treatments emanating from the findings of their research-oriented colleagues (McLeod, 2000). One reason for this gap is that some therapists require further training before they can properly implement the protocols for specific empirically supported treatments. Another reason is that the presentation of therapy research findings tends not to be user-friendly to practitioners. Relatively few empirically supported or evidence-based treatments come from outside the area of cognitive-behaviour therapy (Lazarus, 1997).

Limitations of research

Clearly research studies have an important role to play in evaluating therapeutic approaches. Furthermore, all therapists should be reflective practitioners willing to honestly evaluate their own therapeutic processes and outcomes.

However, good researchers like good practitioners should acknowledge the limitations as well as the strengths of their endeavours. Even in those areas where empirically supported treatments exist, there may be still better ways of treating clients. Skilled researchers not only find out what they know, they often obtain a sharper insight into what remains to be discovered. The concerns of many clients do not fall into circumscribed problem areas, and the unavoidable messiness of much of therapeutic practice does not easily lend itself to narrow research studies. In addition, currently some important issues, such as how to encourage supranormal functioning, obtain scant research attention.

Issue 8: How adequately is the theory of each therapeutic approach stated?

In Chapter 1 I mentioned that counselling and therapy theories may be viewed as possessing four main dimensions if they are to be stated adequately:

1. a statement of the *basic concepts* or assumptions underlying the theory;
2. an explanation of the *acquisition* of helpful and unhelpful behaviour;
3. an explanation of the *maintenance* of helpful and unhelpful behaviour; and
4. an explanation of how to help clients *change* their behaviour and *consolidate* their gains when therapy ends.

Box 17.1 provides the reader with a basic checklist of questions to ask when assessing how adequately a therapeutic approach's theory is stated.

Box 17.1   A checklist for assessing a therapeutic approach's theoretical statement

Model of human development
1. What are the basic concepts of the theory and how adequate are they?
2. How well does the theory say how helpful and unhelpful thoughts, feelings, physical reactions and communications/actions are acquired?
3. How well does the theory say how helpful and unhelpful thoughts, feelings, physical reactions and communications/actions are maintained?

Model of therapy
1. How clear and adequate are the approach's therapeutic goals?
2. How clearly articulated and adequate is the approach's process of therapy?
3. What is the nature of the therapeutic relationship and what are its strengths and weaknesses?

(Continued)

Box 17.1   (Continued)

4. What interventions are used in the approach and what are their strengths and limitations?
5. To what extent are cultural and gender considerations adequately taken into account in the approach's theory and practice?
6. How consistent is the approach's model of human development with its model of therapeutic practice?
7. What is the research evidence for the effectiveness of the approach with different kinds of clients?

Readers can use the checklist in Box 17.1 to identify gaps in how thoroughly theories are stated. For example, a theoretical statement may be more thorough in assessing how behaviour is maintained than how it was acquired in the first place, or vice versa.

Another way to use the checklist is to evaluate how well the theoretical statement answers each question. For example, one way to answer the question about the basic concepts of the theoretical statement is in terms of how adequately they lay the building blocks for the therapeutic approach. Freud's concepts of levels of consciousness and the tripartite structure of the mental apparatus provide a good foundation for the remainder of his theory and practice.

Another way of reviewing an approach's basic concepts involves assessing its assumptions about human nature. I find that some theoretical statements contain an overly negative view of human nature. Furthermore, I would like to see a clearer statement about the concept of mind and a clearer acknowledgment of the importance of mental development and discipline throughout life in the basic concepts of all theoretical approaches, even rational emotive behaviour therapy and cognitive therapy. Above, I have provided you with a few ideas on how to answer the first question on the checklist. When answering all questions on the checklist, remember to have the courage to think for yourself and to think critically.

Eclecticism

The word eclectic means deriving items from various sources, whereas meanings of integrated include made up of parts, whole, complete (Thompson, 1995). Here, I stipulate a definition of integration to mean a complete and coherent theoretical position that is made up of parts. Since such a complete and coherent integrated position has not really been attempted to date, the present discussion will focus on eclecticism, though I return to the issue of integration later.

To say that a therapist is eclectic is a relatively meaningless statement, since there are literally hundreds of theoretical positions that she or he could be using. One way of looking at eclecticism is in the ways in which therapists select the positions out of which they operate. Therapists differ in the ways that they make such choices. For instance, therapists can work eclectically in analytic ways by combining features based on the ideas of Freud, Jung and Melanie Klein. Alternatively, therapists can work eclectically in humanistic ways by combining features of person-centred therapy and gestalt therapy. In addition, therapists can work eclectically in cognitive-behavioural ways by combining features of traditional behaviour therapy with rational emotive behaviour therapy and/or cognitive therapy. Other alternatives are to work in ways that combine psychoanalytic, humanistic and cognitive-behavioural approaches. In addition, multicultural and gender-related approaches can be incorporated into how therapists work.

The reasons why therapists practise eclectically vary and this influences how they practise. One reason is that therapists practise the positions that they are initially exposed to and/or initially find attractive. They may be taught more than one position from the start. Thus, without necessarily admitting it, they are trained to practise eclectically. Then, as therapists work with clients, they may be prompted to learn more about other approaches. For example, someone exposed to and attracted to any approach may find shortcomings in it in practice and seek to supplement it when working with particular clients. The range of clients' problems varies and theoretical positions may seem better for some than for other problems. Furthermore, the range of clients' personalities and backgrounds differs and therapists may feel the need to take this into account when selecting how to intervene.

Related to eclecticism is the issue of how disciplined are the decisions with which the therapist practises it. Arguably, much of the eclecticism practised by therapists is relatively undisciplined. In varying degrees, it is unsystematic eclecticism (Lazarus and Beutler, 1993). Interventions are adopted without being soundly thought through because of the whim of therapists. Increasingly, it is probable that therapists will have to justify more of their therapeutic decisions to funding bodies. This does not mean that they cannot still be eclectic. In fact, sometimes, it may lead to an increase in eclecticism in that the interventions that work for different problems may be derived from different theoretical positions. Lazarus (2005) describes as 'technical eclecticism' the drawing of interventions from different sources without necessarily subscribing to the disciplines that spawned them. The meaning of the term technical eclecticism can be broadened to denote not only specific therapeutic procedures, but also relationship stances (Lazarus et al., 1992).

Wherever possible, Lazarus's technically eclectic therapists use treatments based on empirical evidence and client need. Their theoretical leanings are to draw interventions mainly based on social and cognitive learning theory, but they can borrow interventions from other schools, without embracing any of their theories. As research evidence accumulates for various kinds of problems, it is probable that increasing numbers of therapists will be using a technically eclectic framework. Eventually, enough may be understood about the causes of various problems and the most suitable interventions for them that there can be more of a move towards an integrative rather than a technically eclectic approach.

Even technical eclecticism has its limitations. There are still problems that are hard to define in such a way that therapy on them can be researched. For instance, although Yalom is noted as a psychotherapy researcher, his and May's existential psychotherapy lacks a research base because of the highly individualized nature of the issues addressed in it. As people become wealthier, the number with existential concerns is likely to increase. In addition, clients sometimes have combinations of problems that make it difficult, if not impossible, to use the research literature for specific problems with them.

Eclecticism in counselling and therapy will continue to be developed. In future, the nature of clients' problems may vary and the ways of doing therapy with clients may change. For instance, the internet may be used much more than at present, with face-to-face interactions possible even when therapist and client are in different locations. It is probable that, as time goes by, some existing counselling and therapy approaches will increasingly be viewed as no longer useful. However, undoubtedly some existing approaches can be improved and it is also possible that useful new approaches will be created. In addition, improved and new ways will be found for dealing with multicultural and gender issues, which tend to evolve over time. Wherever possible, empirical support should be gathered to guide the development of counselling and therapy. Value decisions will also need to be made and re-examined as to what are desirable therapeutic goals and methods of achieving them.

Integration

To date therapists have worked eclectically rather than in an integrated fashion. Using interventions from more than one theoretical position falls far short of integrating the theoretical positions intellectually. For instance, person-centred therapy does not distinguish to whom and at what stage of therapy the core conditions are offered by therapists. Furthermore, person-centred's theoretical base offers a rationale for approaching therapy this way. Therefore when therapists claim to use a person-centred relationship as part of other therapeutic approaches, for instance in conjunction with cognitive therapy, they are not using it in the way advocated by Rogers. Thus there can be no real integration between person-centred therapy and cognitive therapy on the level of either theory or practice. However, such difficulties do not mean that developing an integrated theoretical position is impossible, but that great care needs to be taken over the task.

Reasons for integration

Present approaches to counselling and therapy may be said to have started with Freud around the turn of the 19th into the 20th century. Much progress has been made since then, but there is still much more to achieve. The world is still a much less happy place than it could be, even in the wealthiest countries.

In future, one or more theoretical positions may be developed which are genuinely integrative in that they are complete positions made up of parts that are coherent and based on the same assumptions. The scope of the integrated theoretical position will span across much of the ground covered somewhat separately by today's theoretical positions. For instance, such a therapeutic position will have concepts that cover unconscious and conscious functioning – thinking, feeling and communicating/acting – and take into account multicultural and sex differences. It will also take into account how thinking and behaving are acquired, maintained and changed as well as pay attention to feelings and physical reactions. Furthermore, it will pay attention to subnormal, normal and supranormal levels of functioning.

There are many reasons for developing one or more integrated theoretical positions. Eventually, world leaders may become fed up with trying to deal with the world's problems by political means, when the problems are basically psychological. Developing a realistic and workable view of the nature of human functioning may become viewed as a task to be undertaken on a world level. If so, funds may become available to develop one or more truly integrated positions about what is basic to humans and how best to bring up, live together and deal with problems that occur.

No existing theoretical position covers the range of human development and of clients' problems. Thus the issue of breadth is inadequately dealt with to date – this is one of the main reasons why eclecticism has flourished. An integrated theoretical position would recognize the commonality of humanity. It would take into account the latest research findings of what can be attributed to nature and to nurture. Its main task would be to identify what is central to being fully human and how best to bring this about both developmentally and therapeutically. In addition, it would recognize differences caused by particular factors such as upbringing, culture, race, social class and gender expectations.

At the moment counselling and therapy deal mainly with people with problems of some degree of severity. However, all people have problems and the need to attain higher levels of functioning is universal. Along with the increase in material wealth, there is the expectation and possibility for people to be happier and more fulfilled than they are presently. A truly integrated theoretical position will take into account the needs of different kinds of people: how to help those with specific problems: how to educate all people, and how to assist people to attain their full potential. In addition, an integrated theoretical position can allow the possibility for people to be different, whether by nature, nurture or by choice.

It is likely that there will be many educational and therapeutic interventions needed to achieve the higher levels suggested by those who fashion an integrated view of human functioning. These interventions will focus on bringing whole nations to higher levels of functioning as well as on the needs of groups, families and individuals. Possibly, psychological education will become both better and more widespread. Counselling and psychotherapy will definitely be needed for the more disturbed elements of the population and psychological coaching may even be used more than presently by ordinary people wanting to attain higher levels of functioning. As technology advances, one can only speculate about the range of ways that counselling and therapy will be offered.

Reasons slowing integration

The development of one or more integrated approaches to counselling and psychotherapy is unlikely to take place soon. While there might be an increase in approaches like Lazarus's technical eclecticism as more and better research gets done, this falls far short of genuine integration. One of the main barriers is the pride and status of the regulating agencies of the present approaches to psychotherapy. In differing degrees, they control entry into whether or not one can become a psychotherapist. In addition, much of psychotherapy training takes place in academic institutions and, there, the positions and promotion of staff members depend on their doing relatively narrow research. Another barrier is going to be the hidden theoretical biases, cultural biases, racism, sexism, nationalism and other prejudices that people are likely to bring to the task of developing an integrated theoretical position.

An issue is the degree to which developing one or more integrated theoretical positions can be based on existing concepts and research. If a sound integrative model of the main aspects of human development throughout the lifespan can be arrived at, it may become easier to reach agreement on what might be appropriate ways to deal with the problems people face in living successfully.

To date, there appears no institution or group of people willing to fund or to undertake the huge task of developing an integrated model of human functioning and a corresponding integrated model of counselling and psychotherapy. Even, if at some stage in the future, funds do become available, those conducting the task are likely to come to it with blinkers from their cultural upbringing and their previous academic and therapeutic training and experience. Developing an integrated model of counselling and psychotherapy is likely to be a long reiterative process of testing and refining ideas and practice. Such a model or models will need to take into account how people with different problems and backgrounds can be helped towards functioning not only better, but ultimately at really high levels.

Review and personal questions

Review questions

1. What do you consider the influence of each of the following factors on the development of the counselling and therapy approaches presented in this book:

    (a) the theorists' personal histories;
    (b) the theorists' historical and cultural contexts; and
    (c) the fact that all the theorists were or are men?

2. Taken as a group, do you consider the theorists are too negative or positive in their views about human nature? Provide reasons for your answer.
3. Critically discuss the role of research in evaluating therapeutic approaches.
4. Apply the checklist for assessing the adequacy of a therapeutic approaches' theoretical statement (see Box 17.1) to at least one of the counselling and therapy approaches presented in this book.
5. What are some reasons why therapists can justify practising eclectically?
6. What do you think about the assertion that a genuinely integrative theoretical position has yet to be attempted? Provide reasons for your answer.

Personal questions

1. What counselling and therapy approaches covered in this book appeal to you and why?
2. If you favour practising therapy eclectically, how might you do so?

References and further reading

Adler, A. (1933/1998) *Social Interest: Adler's Key to the Meaning of Life*. Oxford: Oneworld.
American Psychiatric Association (APA) (2000) *Diagnostic and Statistical Manual of Mental Disorders* (DSM-1V-TR). Washington, DC: APA.
Barlow, D.H., Levitt, J. and Bufka, L.F. (1999) 'The dissemination of empirically supported treatments: a view to the future', *Behaviour Research and Therapy*, 37: 147–62.
Corsini, R.J. and Wedding, D. (eds) (2005) *Current Psychotherapies* (7th edn). Belmont, CA: Thomson Brooks/Cole.
Greer, G. (1971) *The Female Eunuch*. London: Paladin.

Kazdin, A.E. (1986) 'Research designs and methodology', in S.L. Garfield and A.E. Bergin (eds), *Handbook of Psychotherapy and Behavior Change* (3rd edn). New York: Wiley. pp. 23–68.

Lazarus, A.A. (1997) *Brief but Comprehensive Psychotherapy: The Multimodal Way*. New York: Springer.

Lazarus, A.A. (2005) 'Multimodal therapy', in R.J. Corsini and D. Wedding (eds), *Current Psychotherapies* (7th edn). Belmont, CA: Thomson Brooks/Cole. pp. 337–71.

Lazarus, A.A. and Beutler, L.E. (1993) 'On technical eclecticism', *Journal of Counseling and Development, 71*: 381–5.

Lazarus, A.A., Beutler, L.E. and Norcross, J.C. (1992) 'The future of technical eclecticism', *Psychotherapy, 29*: 11–20.

Maslow, A.H. (1971) *The Farther Reaches of Human Nature*. Harmondsworth: Pelican.

McLeod, J. (2000) 'Research issues in counselling and psychotherapy', in S. Palmer (ed.), *Introduction to Counselling and Psychotherapy: The Essential Guide*. London: Sage. pp. 331–40.

Thompson, D. (ed.) (1995) *The Concise Oxford Dictionary of Current English*. Oxford: Clarendon Press.

glossary

Abbreviations
AT, Jung's analytical therapy; BT, behaviour therapy; CT, cognitive therapy; ET, existential therapy, GT, gestalt therapy; LT, logotherapy; MMT, multimodal therapy: PA, Freud's psychoanalysis; PCT, person-centred therapy; REBT, rational emotive behaviour therapy; RT, reality therapy; TA, transactional analysis.

ABCDE theory (REBT) A theoretical model for understanding psychological distress and change in which A = Adversities or activating events in a person's life; B = Beliefs, both rational and irrational; C = Consequences, both emotional and behavioural; D = Disputing irrational beliefs; and E = Effects and/or effective philosophy of life.

Active imagination (AT) is a technique devised by Jung to help people get in touch with unconscious material. Clients begin by concentrating on a starting point. Then they allow their unconscious to produce a series of images, which may make a complete story.

Activity scheduling (CT) Activity scheduling involves planning and timetabling specific activities with clients. A principle of activity scheduling is to state what activity the client agrees to engage in rather than how much they will accomplish.

Actualizing tendency (PCT) is an active process representing the inherent tendency of the organism to develop its capacities in the direction of maintaining, enhancing and reproducing itself.

Adult (TA) An ego state oriented towards objective, autonomous data processing and probability estimating.

Anima and the animus (AT) The anima is the personification of the feminine nature in a man's unconscious, whereas the animus is the personification of the masculine nature in a woman's unconscious.

Archetypes (AT) are 'primordial images' and 'primordial thoughts' rather than the representations of the images or thoughts themselves. Archetypes provide instinctive patterns for mental activity.

Assertive training (BT) involves training clients in the appropriate verbal and non-verbal behaviours for expressing both negative and positive thoughts and feelings. Contemporary assertive training often focuses on thinking assertively as well as on behaviour.

Automatic thoughts (CT) are less accessible to awareness than voluntary thoughts, but not so deeply buried as beliefs and schemas. Automatic thoughts are part of people's internal monologue – what and how they talk to themselves. They can take the form of words, images, or both, occur very rapidly, and are usually at the fringe of awareness.

Autonomy (TA) refers to the capacity for non-script behaviour that is reversible, with no particular time schedule, developed later in life, and not under parental influence.

Awareness technique (GT) is a concentration technique in which clients are asked to become aware of their body language, their breathing, their voice quality and their emotions as much as of any pressing thoughts.

BASIC ID (MMT) Human personality can be divided into seven discrete, yet interacting, modalities or dimensions: behaviour, affect, sensation, imagery, cognition, interpersonal and drugs/biology.

Basic needs (RT) Choice theory sees humans as driven by five basic needs that are genetic in origin: survival, love and belonging, power, freedom and fun.

Behavioural assessment (BT), sometimes known as a functional analysis, allows therapists to identify the context, antecedents and consequences of the responses they wish to treat. When conducted after initial sessions, behavioural assessment aims to assist both in evaluating treatment effectiveness and in deciding whether to continue, discontinue and alter treatment.

Being (ET) Being as a participle of a verb and implies that someone is in the process of becoming something. When used as a noun being can mean potential.

Bridging (MMT) A rapport-enhancement technique in which therapists deliberately tune into the clients' preferred modalities before gently helping them cross bridges into other modalities that may prove more productive.

Child (TA) The Child or archaeopsychic ego state is a set of feelings, thoughts, attitudes and behaviour patterns which are archaic relics of an individual's childhood. The Child ego state is exhibited in two major forms: the adapted

Child, which follows parental directives, and the natural Child, which is autonomous.

Choice theory (RT) or internal control psychology explains that, for all practical purposes, humans choose everything they do, including the misery they feel.

Choice theory language (RT) Language that assumes personal responsibility for one's total behaviour, for instance using active verbs like 'depressing', and allows others' freedom of choice to assume responsibility for their total behaviour.

Classical conditioning (BT), also known as respondent conditioning, is a form of learning whereby existing responses are attached to new stimuli by pairing these stimuli with those that naturally elicit the response.

Cognitive-behaviour therapy A term describing therapies that extend behaviour therapy to have a major focus on changing covert thoughts as well as overt behaviours: examples include cognitive therapy, rational emotive behaviour therapy and multimodal therapy.

Cognitive distortions (CT) are information processing errors that both characterize and maintain psychological distress: for instance, arbitrary inference, selective abstraction, overgeneralization and dichotomous thinking.

Cognitive vulnerability (CT) refers to humans' cognitive frailty. Because of their schemas, each person has a set of unique vulnerabilities and sensitivities that predispose them to psychological distress.

Collaborative empiricism (CT) Therapists and clients collaborate together in the scientific endeavour of examining the evidence to confirm or negate the client's cognitions, all of which are viewed as testable hypotheses.

Collective unconscious (AT) At its deepest levels the unconscious is a vast collective and universal historical storehouse whose contents belong to mankind in general. The contents of the collective unconscious have never been in consciousness, but owe their existence to heredity.

Complexes (AT) are an important feature of the personal unconscious and are accumulations of associations, sometimes of a traumatic nature, that possess strong emotional content: for example, the mother complex.

Conditions of worth (PCT) The internalization or introjection of others' evaluations, which do not truly reflect the person's actualizing tendency but may serve to impede it.

Congruence (PCT) Consistency between the thoughts and feelings the therapist experiences and her or his professional demeanour. Not putting on a professional façade.

Contact boundary (GT) is the boundary between organism and environment where all feelings, thoughts and actions take place. Contacting the environment represents forming a gestalt, whereas withdrawal is either closing a gestalt completely or mobilizing resources to make closure possible.

Counselling A relationship in which counsellors assist clients to understand themselves and their problems better. Then, where appropriate, counsellors use various interventions to assist clients to feel, think, communicate and act more effectively. The term counselling is often used interchangeably with psychotherapy. Since there are many different theoretical orientations, it may be more accurate to speak of counselling approaches than counselling.

Death anxiety (ET), the fear of ceasing to be, can be both conscious and unconscious. It is the fundamental source of anxiety, whether it be neurotic, normal or existential. Strong death anxiety is likely to be repressed.

Decision (TA) A childhood commitment to a certain form of behaviour, which later forms the basis of character.

Defence mechanisms (PA) are infantilisims that operate unconsciously to protect the ego and may impede realistic behaviour long after they have outlived their usefulness. Examples include repression, reaction formation, projection, fixation and regression.

Dereflection (LT) Dereflection aims to counteract hyperreflection, or excessive attention by assisting clients to ignore their symptoms: for example, a woman dereflects excessive self-observation regarding sexual performance by becoming more focused on her partner.

Disputing (REBT) involves challenging and questioning unsubstantiated hypotheses that clients hold about themselves, others and the world.

Dream analysis (AT) Dreams are utterances or statements from the unconscious and are comparable to texts that appear unintelligible, but the therapist has to discover how to read them. An understanding of myths and symbols is fundamental for analysing dreams.

Dreamwork (GT) Dreams are existential messages, not just unfinished situations, current problems or symptoms. There are four stages to dreamwork:

sharing the dream, retelling the dream in the present tense, talking to the different actors in the dream, and conducting a dialogue between different elements in the dream.

Eclecticism The practice of drawing from different counselling and therapy approaches in formulating client problems and implementing treatment interventions. A distinction can be made between theoretical eclecticism and practical or technical eclecticism.

Ego (PA) The ego or 'I' acts as an intermediary between the id and the external world and strives to bring the reality principle to bear upon the id in substitution for the pleasure principle.

Ego disturbance (REBT) arises from the demanding and irrational belief 'I *must* do well and win approval for all my performances' because it leads to people thinking and feeling that they are inadequate and undeserving when they do not do as well as they must.

Ego state (TA) A consistent pattern of feeling and experience directly related to a corresponding consistent pattern of behaviour.

Empathy (PCT) The therapist's capacity to comprehend accurately the client's inner world or internal frame of reference and to sensitively communicate back this understanding.

Excitement (GT) The energy people create, which coincides with the physiological function of excitation.

Existential (ET) The word existence is derived from the Latin word *existere*, literally meaning 'to stand out, to emerge'. Existential approaches to therapy are concerned with the science and processes of being.

Existential defence mechanisms (ET) In addition to conventional defence mechanisms, there are specific defences for each of the four ultimate concerns – death, freedom, isolation and meaninglessness – to defend people against these fundamental fears.

Existential frustration (LT) results when the will to meaning is frustrated. Apathy and boredom are the main characteristics of existential frustration.

Existential guilt (ET) Three forms of existential guilt are failure to live up to one's potential; distorting the reality of one's fellow humans; and 'separation guilt' in relation to nature as a whole.

Existential psychodynamics (ET) Existential conflicts and existential anxiety flow from people's inescapable confrontations with the givens of existence – death, freedom, isolation and meaninglessness.

Existential ultimate concerns (ET) Four existential ultimate concerns are death, freedom, isolation and meaninglessness. Each concern begets a different existential conflict.

Existential vacuum (LT) describes a state in which people complain of an inner void. They suffer from a sense of meaninglessness, emptiness and futility.

Experiments (CT) Beliefs are treated as testable hypotheses. Together therapists and clients set up cognitive and behavioural experiments that encourage clients to test the reality of their beliefs.

Experiments (GT) Therapists and clients develop experiments in which clients try out different ways of thinking and acting. Repeatedly clients are encouraged to 'Try this and see what you experience'.

Exposure (BT) In exposure, confrontation with the feared stimulus continues until the unwanted responses to the stimulus have been reduced.

External control psychology (RT) involves choosing to control and allow oneself to be controlled by others. Choosing to coerce, force, compel, punish, reward, boss, manipulate, motivate, criticize, blame, complain, nag, badger, rank, rate and withdraw.

Feminist therapy Approaches to counselling and therapy that address women's problems and issues in the context of constricting gender-role socialization and power imbalances in society. Feminist therapy emphasizes egalitarian therapist–client relationships, valuing women's experiences, liberating women from sex-role stereotypes, and working against oppression.

Flooding (BT) In contemporary flooding techniques, therapists arrange for clients to be exposed to relatively strong fear stimuli that, either real or imagined, are presented continuously.

Free association (PA) Clients must tell their analysts everything that occurs to them, even if it is disagreeable and even if it seems meaningless. The object of free association is to help lift repressions by making unconscious material conscious.

Frustration (GT) Providing situations in which clients experience being stuck in frustration and then frustrating their avoidances still further until they are willing to mobilize their own resources.

Game (TA) An ongoing series of complementary ulterior transactions progressing to a well-defined predictable outcome or payoff.

Gestalt (GT) means form or shape, and among the meanings of the German verb *gestalten* are to shape, to form, to fashion, to organize and to structure. Other terms for gestalt are pattern, configuration or organized whole.

Homeostasis (GT) Homeostasis or organismic self-regulation is the process by which the organism satisfies its needs by restoring balance when faced with a demand or need that upsets its equilibrium.

Id (PA) The id or 'it' contains everything that is inherited and fixed in the constitution. Filled with energy from the instincts, the id strives to bring about the satisfaction of instinctual needs on the basis of the pleasure principle.

Incongruence (PCT) A discrepancy between the self as perceived and the actual experience of the organism.

Individuation (AT) is the process by which the person becomes differentiated as a separate psychological individual, a separate whole as distinct from the collective psychology.

Inelegant and elegant change (REBT) Inelegant change largely consists of some kind of symptom removal. Elegant change goes further than developing an effective new philosophy that supports removal of specific symptoms to assisting clients to develop and implement an effective philosophy of life.

Instincts (PA) represent somatic or biological demands upon the mind, which are grouped into two basic instincts. *Eros* and the *destructive instinct*.

Integration Attempting to blend together theoretical concepts and/or practical interventions drawn from different therapeutic approaches into coherent and integrated wholes.

Interpretation (PA) involves offering constructions or explanations. Interpreting dreams represents an important – sometimes the most important – part of the analyst's work.

Introjections (GT) are experiences that are swallowed as a whole rather than being properly digested and assimilated. The outcome of introjection is that undesirable as well as desirable thoughts, feelings and behaviours get retained.

Irrational beliefs (REBT) are rigid, dogmatic, unhealthy, maladaptive beliefs that mostly get in the way of people's efforts to achieve their goals. Such beliefs are characterized by demands, musts and shoulds.

Logotherapy (LT) is an education for responsibility that seeks to unblock clients' will to meaning. It is the treatment of choice for persons suffering from noogenic or existential neurosis.

Low frustration tolerance (REBT) or discomfort disturbance arises from the grandiose belief that people think they are so special that conditions must be easy and satisfying for them.

Medical ministry (LT) A term for how logotherapists work with somatogenic cases where the somatic cause cannot be removed. Where possible, logotherapists assist the non-diseased part of clients in finding meaning in the attitude that they take towards their suffering.

Men's therapy An underdeveloped area of counselling and therapy focusing on men's problems and issues. Many feminist therapy goals and principles are applicable to men's therapy, which is sometimes considered feminist therapy's missing half.

Modality profile (MMT) A BASIC ID chart listing problems and interventions within each modality.

Modes (CT) are networks of cognitive, affective, motivational and behavioural schemas. Modes are fundamental to personality since they interpret and adapt to emerging and ongoing situations.

Multicultural therapy Approaches to counselling and therapy that take into account the cultures and worldviews of clients and therapists. Such approaches include making existing Euro-American therapies more culture-sensitive, developing multicultural counselling and therapy competencies, and using non-western therapeutic approaches.

Multimodal Life History Inventory (MMT) A 15-page inventory that asks numerous questions about antecedent events and maintaining factors with the answers being divided into BASIC ID categories.

Non-Being (ET) The opposite of being is non-being or nothingness. Death is the most obvious form of non-being. However, there are numerous other threats to being in the form of loss of potentiality through anxiety and conformity and through lack of clear self-awareness.

Noogenic neurosis (LT) refers to those cases where the existential vacuum leads to clinical symptomatology. Existential frustration plays a large part in noogenic neuroses.

Observational learning (BT) Learning behavioural and cognitive skills by observing models, including observing how the models' behaviours get reinforced.

Openness to experience (PCT) Allowing all significant sensory and visceral experiences to be perceived, the capacity for realistic perception without defensiveness.

Operant conditioning (BT) A way of learning in which the person or animal has to operate on the environment to produce a response. Responses are maintained, modified or extinguished by the likelihood of eliciting reinforcing consequences.

Organismic valuing process (PCT) refers to a person's continuous weighing of experience and the placing of values on that experience in terms of its ability to satisfy the actualizing tendency.

Paradoxical intention (LT) In paradoxical intention, clients are invited to intend precisely to that which they fear. Their excessive fear or hyperintention is replaced by a paradoxical wish: for instance, fear of perspiring is replaced by trying as hard as possible to perspire.

Parent (TA) The Parent or extereopsychic ego state is a set of feelings, thoughts, attitudes and behaviours which resemble those of parental figures. The Parent ego state may be seen in one of two forms: the controlling Parent and the nurturing Parent.

Participant modelling (BT) involves therapists repeatedly modelling feared activities, for instance handling snakes or dogs. Then joint performance with therapists may enable clients to start engaging in activities that would be too threatening to engage in on their own. Ultimately clients perform the feared activities on their own.

Persona (AT) A concept derived from the mask worn by actors in antiquity. At one level, the persona is the individual's system of adaptation or way of coping with the world. At a different level, the persona is not just an individual mask, but a mask of the collective psyche.

Personal unconscious (AT) The contents, which are definitely personal, fall into two main categories: material that lost its intensity either because it was forgotten or repressed; and material which never possessed sufficient intensity to reach consciousness but has somehow entered the psyche: for instance, some sense-impressions.

Preconscious (PA) The preconscious is latent and capable of becoming conscious, while the unconscious is repressed and is unlikely to become conscious without great difficulty.

Psychodynamics (PA) The concept of psychical or mental energy and its distribution among the id, ego and super-ego is central to psychoanalysis.

Psychotherapy Literally 'mind healing'. It is more accurate to speak of the psychotherapies since there are many different theoretical and practical approaches to psychotherapy.

Quality world (RT) A personal picture album consisting of detailed pictures of what an individual wants to satisfy her or his needs. The pictures in people's quality worlds fall into three categories: (a) the people they most want to be with; (b) the things they most want to own or experience; and (c) the ideas or systems of belief that govern much of their behaviour.

Rational beliefs (REBT) Healthy, productive and adaptive beliefs that are consistent with social reality, and are stated as preferences, desires and wants.

Rational coping statements (REBT) range from articulating simple words of encouragement to generating longer statements containing preferential thinking. This step often, but not necessarily, follows vigorous disputing.

Rational emotive imagery (REBT) In rational-emotive imagery (REI) clients: (a) vividly imagine an adversity; (b) once feeling unhealthily upset, hold on to the image for a minute or two; and (c) then tell themselves strongly and repetitively sensible rational beliefs or coping statements.

Reattribution techniques (CT) test automatic thoughts and underlying beliefs by considering alternative ways of assigning responsibility and cause.

Reciprocal inhibition (BT) encompasses all situations in which the elicitation of one response appears to bring about a decrement in the strength of evocation of a simultaneous response.

Reinforcement (BT) The presentation of a reward or the removal of an aversive stimulus following a response. Reinforcement always increases the future probability of the reinforced response. Schedules of reinforcement can be either intermittent or non-intermittent.

Relationships of choice (MMT) Not only matching the nature of therapeutic relationship to the client, but also to the clients' observed needs at different times in therapy.

Search for meaning (LT) The basic human need is a search for meaning rather than a search for the self. Identity is only achievable through being responsible for the fulfilment of meaning. Work, love, suffering, the past and the suprameaning are each sources of meaning.

Schemas (CT) are structures that consist of people's fundamental beliefs and assumptions. They are relatively stable cognitive patterns that influence, through their beliefs, how people select and synthesize incoming information.

Script (TA) A life plan based on a decision made in childhood, reinforced by the parents, justified by subsequent events, and culminating in a chosen alternative. The purpose of script analysis is to get clients out of their script and thus to behave autonomously.

Second-order BASIC ID assessments (MMT) When impasses occur in treating clients, second-order BASIC ID assessments allow a more detailed review of behaviours, affective responses, sensory reactions, images, cognitions, interpersonal factions, and drugs/biological factors in relation to the area in which change is proving difficult.

Self (AT) The self is the central archetype, the archetype of order. The self, that expresses the unity of personality as a whole, encompasses both conscious and unconscious components.

Self-actualizing (GT) is a process involving an effective balance of contact and withdrawal at the contact boundary and the ability to use energy or excitement to meet real rather than phony needs.

Self-actualizing (PCT) A process of living and of personal development, based on an individual's organismic valuing process, that genuinely reflects their unique actualizing tendency.

Self-concept (PCT) is the self as perceived and the values attached to these perceptions, or what a person refers to as 'I' or 'me'.

Self-transcendence (LT) The human capacity to reach out beyond the boundaries of oneself by either fulfilling a meaning or encountering another person lovingly.

Shadow (AT) The shadow archetype reflects the realm of human's animal ancestors and, as such, comprises the whole historical aspect of the unconscious. For the most part, the shadow consists of inferior traits of personality that individuals refuse to acknowledge.

Socratic dialogue (CT) A Socratic style of questioning assists clients to expand and evaluate how they think. Typical questions are: 'Where is the evidence?'; 'Where is the logic?'; 'Are there other ways of perceiving the situation?'; and 'What would be the worst thing that could happen?'.

Stimulus control (BT) entails either modifying in advance the stimuli or cues associated with maladaptive responses and/or establishing cues associated with adaptive responses.

Structural analysis (TA) consists of diagnosing and separating one feeling-thinking-and-behaviour pattern or ego state from another.

Structural profile (MMT) Clients rate themselves across each of the BASIC ID modalities on a seven-point scale with one being the lowest and seven being the highest.

Super-ego (PA) The super-ego is a residue formed within the ego in which parental influence is prolonged. Parental influence may be defined broadly to include cultural, racial and family influences.

Systematic desensitization (BT) involves three elements: (a) training in deep muscular relaxation; (b) the construction of hierarchies of anxiety-evoking stimuli; and (c) asking the client, when relaxed, to imagine items from the anxiety-evoking hierarchies.

Technical eclecticism (MMT) Technically eclectic therapists use procedures from different sources without necessarily subscribing to the theories or disciplines that spawned them.

Thresholds (MMT) People's differing capacities to tolerate negative stimuli such as pain, frustration, stress, cold, noise and pollution. Physiologically, people react to a variety of arousing stimuli with differing and distinctive patterns of autonomic nervous system activity.

Token economies (BT) Reinforcement programmes that use tokens as tangible conditioned reinforcers which may be exchanged for back-up reinforcers such as prizes, opportunities to engage in special activities, food or other purchases. An example is that of points for good classroom behaviour being exchangeable for prizes of differing value.

Total behaviour (RT) is always the sum of the following four components: acting, thinking, feeling and physiology. Acting and thinking are under voluntary control, while feeling and physiology can only be changed by altering acting and thinking.

Tracking (MMT) refers to the careful assessment of the 'firing order', the ordering of the chain reaction of the different modalities to assist therapists in selecting and prioritizing treatment interventions.

Transaction (TA) In transactional analysis a stroke or unit of recognition is viewed as the fundamental unit of social interaction. An exchange of strokes constitutes a transaction. Transactions take place between ego states. Transactions between ego states may be complementary, crossed and/or ulterior.

Transference (PA) Clients perceive their analysts as reincarnations of important figures from their childhoods and transfer onto them moderate to intense feelings and emotions appropriate to these earlier models.

Unconditional positive regard (PCT) consists of two dimensions: first, prizing and feeling positively towards clients and, second, non-judgmental acceptance of clients' experiencing and disclosures as their subjective reality.

Unconditional self-acceptance (REBT) Clients can always choose to accept themselves just because they are alive and human, whether or not they perform well or are approved of by others.

Unconscious (PA) The unconscious, or unconscious proper, consists of material that is inadmissible to consciousness through repression. The censorship on unconscious material coming into awareness is very strong indeed.

WDEP system (RT) Each letter represents a cluster of skills and techniques for assisting clients to make better choices in their lives: W, asking clients what they want; D, asking clients what they are doing and their overall direction; E, asking clients to conduct a searching self-evaluation; and P, asking clients to make plans to fulfil their needs more effectively.

Will to meaning (LT) The fundamental motivating drive since people are confronted with the need to detect and find meaning literally until their last breaths.

name index